THE BOOK OF INSIDE INFORMATION

MONEY • HEALTH • SUCCESS
MARRIAGE • EDUCATION • CAR
COLLECTING • FITNESS • HOME
TRAVEL • SHOPPING • TAXES
INVESTMENTS • RETIREMENT

BY THE EDITORS AND EXPERTS OF BOTTOM LINE/PERSONAL

BOARDROOM® BOOKS

330 West 42nd Street, New York, N.Y. 10036

**Library of Congress Cataloging in Publication Data
Main entry under title:**

The book of inside information.

    Includes index.
    1. Life skills—United States.   I. Bottom line
personal.
HQ2039.U6B66   1982   016.64'04   82-9408
ISBN 0-932648-50-9   AACR2

Printed in the United States of America

Contents

3 • TAX SHELTERS

4 • SAVING TAXES

8 • SUCCESS STRATEGIES

9 • MARRIAGE AND FAMILY LIFE

10 • HOME OWNERSHIP

11 • SHOPPING FOR YOUR MONEY'S WORTH

12 • COLLECTING FOR PLEASURE AND PROFIT

13 • YOU AND YOUR AUTOMOBILE

14 • TRAVEL

15 • HEALTH

16 • FITNESS AND EXERCISE

17 • EDUCATION

I

Everyday Money Management

Run Personal Finances Like a Business

Most executives neglect their personal finances because they are too busy with their jobs or businesses. That's a serious mistake. Stay alert for opportunities to save and profit:

Pension plans. Business owners and the self-employed can take full advantage of the special pension options open to them. If you are making $100,000 a year, you could easily put away $30,000 pre-tax into a defined benefit pension plan. Greater earnings may justify even larger contributions. Compounding tax-free dollars gives an enormous investment edge.

Let your children pay for their own education. Start planning now. Employ your children. If you have a business, go into an investment partnership with them or encourage them to start businesses of their own. Advantage: With the right combination of earned and investment income, a dependent child can receive up to $3,400 without paying income tax. This assumes $2,300 in wages from

working in your business and $1,100 from investments, including $100 of dividends that qualify for exclusion. Social Security tax on the child's earnings (which has to be paid unless your business is a sole proprietorship and your child is under 21) would be slightly over $320. Net income: $3,080. In the 50% bracket, you must make $6,160 to provide as much money.

Types of jobs children could do: Write checks or send out bills for your business, do simple maintenance and painting for investment real estate you own, etc. Key in on hobbies. One client's son started collecting coins when he was 11 years old. Ten years later, he had a multimillion-dollar gold-and-silver-coin business.

Set a spouse up in business. Most male executives don't realize the tax benefits they could get from encouraging their wives to start business. Some of the benefits:

• As long as the business shows a profit for two of the first five years, the IRS generally won't challenge the right to deduct losses in the other three years. These losses can be offset directly against the high-earner's high-tax-bracket income.

• If the wife's business travel plans coincide with those of her husband, she can travel with him, all fully deductible. (Of course, a business trip can also coincide with vacation travel. But be sure it's *predominantly* business travel.)

• There's a special deduction of 10% of the wife's earnings up to $30,000.

• Beginning in 1982, the wife can invest up to $2,000 of earned income in an individual retirement arrangement. Result: Full deduction of the amount invested, with all earnings tax-free.

• Three-generation financial planning. If your own net worth is growing healthily, you should consider asking your parents to transfer some of their wealth directly to your children. (Easiest way to skip a generation: Each grandparent gives each grandchild $10,000 a year in tax-free gifts.)

Supporting elderly parents. Inflation is making elderly parents more and more dependent on their adult children. If you are self-employed, consider employing your parent in the business. Opportunities: Write the monthly checks. Manage a piece of real estate. Investigate any investment you are considering.

Special concern: If your parent is under 70 and receives Social Security benefits, he or she will lose $1 of Social Security for every dollar earned over $6,960 a year for 1984 and $7,320 a year for 1985. One way around this: Set up a Subchapter S corporation with the parents as stockholders. The dividends paid out of the Sub S corporation do not diminish Social Security payments. Of course, once the parent reaches 70, no earnings affect Social Security payments.

Executive corporation. This can be a major advantage for a corporate executive with an independent job function and the clout to negotiate a major tax-saving arrangement with his employer. Best candidates: Marketing or sales executives. The tactic: Set up your own corporation with a long-term consulting arrangement with the employer. The reward: Tax benefits and opportunities are maximum.

Source: Terrance M. Gill a financial planner head of the Professionals' Financial Group, 1303 W. Freeway. Fort Worth, TX 76102.

Family Financial Review

The same skills required to run a company are also needed for truly effective household management. The technique: Apply business skills. Hold periodic reviews of family finances; keep family members informed about changes in financial status. Checklist for review:

Balance sheet. Updating it will show changes in the family's net worth (the difference between assets and liabilities) since the last review.

Income. Salaries, business profits, stock dividends, capital gains, etc. Categorize these as either regular or nonrecurring income.

Debts. Personal, automobile, life insurance policy and other loans, as well as installment purchases and charge account balances. Make sure the wife has her own credit line.

Current budget. This spending guide helps assure achievement of short- and long-term goals. While it must be realistic, it shouldn't be so restrictive as to create family tensions.

Contingency budgets. Revise, if necessary, the budgets that would apply if either wage earner died.

Home. Determine the current market value of the house and the principal balance on the mortgage. The difference is your equity, all or part of which would be available if the house were sold or refinanced. Does the fire insurance reflect inflated value? Using life insurance to pay off a mortgage is a useful estate-planning element. Generally, husband and wife should own a house jointly.

Life insurance. A review of assets, resources, and the revised contingency budgets will show whether present coverage should be increased or decreased. It may or may not be wise for each spouse to own the policies on the other's life. Since interspousal gifts and bequests are 100% deductible beginning in 1982, consult your estate planner to find out what is best for your family.

Social Security and pensions. Check for changes in retirement and death benefits. If an employment-related pension is vested, find out its current value. If applicable, check for potential death benefits from the Veterans Administration and from unions, professional association, or fraternal memberships. Update data on your Individual Retirement Account (IRA) and/or self-employment (Keogh) pension plan.

Health insurance. If existing coverage (obtained through employment or otherwise) is inadequate, consider supplementing it with a major-medical policy that will pay $1 million (or more) above other benefits.

Other insurance. Have your auto, homeowner's, fine arts, jewelry and other property and liability policies been increased to keep up with inflation? Rather than raising individual liability policies, consider buying a low-cost umbrella policy to cover claims against you of $1 million (or more) above your present coverages.

Banks. Make a list of checking accounts, regular and time-deposit savings accounts, and the contents of your safe-deposit box. Do both spouses have access to that box? At death, a person's assets, for tax and probate purposes, are frozen. To make certain that the survivor has funds with which to operate, each spouse should have a bank account in his or her own name. Do not store wills, life insurance policies, and other documents that would be required shortly after death in a safe-deposit box, which normally would be sealed by the bank at the owner's death. (Note: Boxes in a corporate name are not sealed.)

Securities. List all your stocks, bonds, commodity-futures contracts, Treasury notes, and other securities, showing where they are stored and whether they are individually or jointly owned. For tax purposes, keep careful records of dates and prices of all purchases and sales. Names of the investment brokers also should be noted.

Other investments. Follow the securities-review pattern in dealing with investments in real estate (other than your home), gems, precious metals, art objects, etc.

Charitable contributions. Reappraise the list of recipients and the sizes of gifts. Would a widowed spouse, or an estate, be liable for pledges or commitments made while the spouse was alive?

Family business. If a husband or wife is sole proprietor or a principal in a partnership or private corporation, there should be a plan that goes into effect when death occurs. That plan, perhaps funded by life insurance, would provide for payment to the surviving spouse for the deceased spouse's share of the business. In the case of a sole proprietorship, the insurance proceeds would allow time to liquidate or sell the business (perhaps to employees).

Wills. They must be revised to reflect any changes in family circumstances, both economic and personal. This should be a joint effort, with each spouse fully aware of the contents of the other's will. They should also be reviewed whenever the tax law changes, as it does so often.

Source: Sal Nuccio, president, Nuccio Organization Ltd., financial consultants, 60 Algonquin Rd., Yonkers, NY 10710, and author of *The New York Times Guide to Personal Finance*.

Businesslike Management of Family Spending

Don't confuse family financial control with a penny-pinching budget. The purpose of control is to look ahead, to use many dollars that might be wasted.

Adapt two corporate tools: A cost-accounting system and a balance sheet.

Cost accounting controls spending by establishing yearly budgets. Base the budgets on past spending patterns and anticipated changes in costs, procedures, goals, and other factors. Purpose: Better financial planning. Don't track each expenditure down to the last penny. Look back only to get a better perspective on the future.

Main guide: A projected 12-month budget. Recommendations:

Every month, compare actual expenses with the planned amount.

Note deviations.

Change your spending pattern or your program.

Implementing budget control requires

cooperation of all family members. Steps to take:

Set realistic short-and long-term objectives. Estimate the sums you have set to aside regularly to achieve your goals.

Estimate income for the year. Include savings' interest, stock dividends, pensions, and money from all other sources. When income is irregular, as may be the case for sales and professional people, estimate a yearly minimum. Divide the total into equal parts over selected budget periods (weekly, semimonthly, or monthly).

Spread fixed expenses. Total the year's periodic bills (taxes, rent or mortgage payments, utilities and heating fuel, insurance, association or union dues, installment loans and purchases, tuition, etc.). Divide that sum by the number of budget periods. Purpose: To eliminate the diversion of needed cash and last-minute scrambles to pay large bills that should have been anticipated.

Estimate flexible expenses. Prime ones are clothing, furniture, equipment, charities, medical care, gifts, and entertainment. Include an emergency fund to make up for wrong guesses on costs. Spread the total evenly over the budget periods.

Estimate regular living expenses. Among these are personal allowances, food, household supplies and help, laundry, dry cleaning, automobile maintenance and other transportation, newspapers and magazines, postage, and entertainment. To make a reliable estimate, record actual expenses for several weeks or longer.

Plan to pay old bills. Include loans from friends or relatives, as well as installment debts. They should be spread, where possible, over future budget periods. Pay them as quickly as feasible to maintain good credit, good family and social relations.

Prepare a tentative budget. Match total expense (about the same for each budget period) against income.

How to use the program: Treat a surplus of income over expenses as a saving toward meeting future goals. If the surplus is tiny, or if it is a deficit, trim expenses. It may be necessary to temporarily increase income by seeking extra work. Each family member should help develop cost-cutting or income-producing ideas. Children may take on chores that had been done by hired help. Even some fixed expenses can be trimmed temporarily.

Bottom line: Once you establish a cost-accounting system, keep it flexible to allow for changes in financial status, family size, attitudes, or interests.

The balance sheet shows net worth, the value of all assets less liabilities. Purpose: Year-to-year comparisons of balance sheets mark your family's economic progress.

A satisfactory rate of growth is not necessarily enough. Make certain that the growth in specific assets applicable to your overall goals is adequate to achieve them.

Time saver: Banks generally use balance-sheet forms to measure the financial substance of potential borrowers. Your local bank may be willing to give you a few blank forms for your personal use.

Source: Sal Nuccio, president, Nuccio Organization Ltd., financial consultants, 60 Algonquin Rd., Yonkers, NY 10710, and author of *The New York Times Guide to Personal Finance.*

A Better Measure of inflation

The Consumer Price Index (CPI) is *not* an accurate barometer of changes in the cost of living. Reason: It counts items that people don't buy every day. Examples: A new home or car.

Better measure: The Personal Consumption Expenditures Index (PCE). This figure reflects real living costs more fairly and usually does not rise as quickly as the CPI. It's one of the factors used in computing the Gross National Product (GNP), and it is released monthly by the U.S. Department of Commerce. It is published in *The New York Times* and *The Wall Street Journal,* as well as other leading newspapers.

Suggestion: If someone asks you to sign a contract with a built-in inflation adjustment (for example, your landlord on a lease renewal), insist that it be tied to the PCE rather than the CPI.

The Lure of Easy Bankruptcy

True tale: A husband-and-wife team of practicing psychiatrists, with joint income of $78,000, accumulate personal debts totaling $22,000 plus a $33,000 mortgage on their comfortable suburban New York home. They're not in arrears, nor even over their heads. They simply want more discretionary spending power.

Solution: They file for bankruptcy, and reduce their debt load to less than 10 cents on the dollar, repayable on an extended painless schedule. Notes an officer of one of their finance companies: They could have sold the house or refinanced the mortgage, and paid off all their bills in full. But why should they?

Traditionally, personal bankruptcy has been a life-wrenching last resort for people so deeply in debt, and so harried by creditors, that no other option seemed viable. The typical profile: Low-income, undereducated laborers or clerical workers. Very young or over 65. Rootless non-homeowners.

The profile today: People with good jobs. Quite often two-income families. Household incomes as high as six figures. Declaring bankruptcy not from dire necessity, but merely to rid themselves of debts that cramp their lifestyle.

Most common:

Recent college graduates, who file bankruptcy to avoid paying back government-guaranteed student loans. Rationale: Society owed them the education.

Older, keep-up-with-Joneses types. From suburban executives to Park Avenue professionals, they're unwilling to live within their means.

Making it easier:

Passage of the Federal Bankruptcy Act of 1978. This significantly liberalized personal filing procedures in the name of consumer rights:

• Chapter 7 makes no reference to the debtor's income. It permits debtors to clear the slate by turning over all their assets *except those specifically exempted* to creditors, Among the exemptions: Up to $7,500 equity in the debtor's house ($15,000 if both spouses file); $4,000 in accrued dividends; $1,200 in automobile equity; $500 in jewelry; $200 per category of household items (clothing, books, etc.) and more.

• Chapter 13 requires that debtors show only a regular income to handle a reasonable three-year pay-back plan. Court definition of reasonable: As little as 1% to 10% of the total debts, even where 50% or more could easily be managed.

Payoff: Either way, the law does not require a bankrupt to show financial hardship. The debtor merely claims bankruptcy, eliminates most outstanding debt, and keeps most tangible assets. Even the stigma is gone, because the law forbids use of the term bankrupt when legally describing a "debtor."

The economic recession. The Federal Reserve Board's credit controls that were imposed early in 1980 tightened the screws on many people with debts.

Federal Trade Commission approval of the right of lawyers to advertise their services. This opened the eyes of debtors to the opportunities.

Result: Lawyers are aggressively promoting this new way out of debt. Focus: California, Florida, New York.

Two things lawyers don't mention in their ads: (1) Lawyers always get paid up front, even before filing the papers; some even accept credit cards. (2) The bankruptcy goes on the client's credit record for up to 10 years, meaning the slate is not clean. Clients cannot even seek to square matters with past creditors. Reason: Reaffirmation of debts, once they have been wiped out, is prohibited, unless the offer is court-approved. (Chances for that are slim).

Sending Cash in An Emergency

Western Union (WU) will handle the transaction by telephone and charge it to a MasterCard or VISA card. The service is better domestically than overseas. Maximum amount: $1,000. Advantage: If the recipient has no identification, WU will ask an identifying question (such as mother's maiden name) before completing the transaction.

American Express can send up to $1,000 in cash or traveler's checks anywhere in the world overnight. A personal check will be accepted if the sender has an American Express card. Otherwise, cash or a certified check only.

Wire transfers can be made by banks, but they don't like to do it for small amounts. Major drawback: It can take as long as three days for the money to become available. Best use: Backup for American Express or Western Union if large amounts of cash are needed.

Postal Service money orders and certified or cashier's checks can also be used. Drawbacks: Delivery is unpredictable unless the Express Mail premium is paid; it's limited to the U.S.

Reminder: Never send a personal check. Few out-of-town banks will cash one. If they do, they will hold the funds until the check clears, often a week or more.

If You Lose Your Wallet

Close your current checking and savings accounts. Open new ones.

Report the loss of credit cards to the issuing companies. You then can't be held responsible for any unauthorized charges.

Apply for a new driver's license. You can usually get a temporary one while you wait.

Call the Social Security office for a new card. It takes three weeks if you know your number.

Getting Favored Treatment at Your Bank

Banks have a good deal of leeway in dealing with their customers. You can:

Pay interest on a loan below the going rate.

Get costs waived for services such as obtaining cashier's or traveler's checks.

Ask the bank to have someone there call you if your checking account is ever overdrawn so that you can avoid writing checks that might bounce.

To get favored treatment:

Show loyalty by doing your banking at one place. Include: Savings and checking accounts, safe-deposit boxes, loans, etc.

Repay loans on time.

Establish a personal relationship with bank employees.

Bring in business for the bank.

Ask for favors. The bank is often prepared to do things that you ask for.

How to Fight Computer Errors

If you disagree with a computer, be prepared to document your side. Often, human beings still have more credibility than machines. One case: Mrs. Judd's monthly bank statement showed two withdrawals totaling $800 that she had never made. When she complained, the bank said someone had used Mrs. Judd's bank identification card and secret code number to make withdrawals from a computerized cash machine.

Mrs. Judd went to Small Claims Court with a letter from her boss saying she had been at work when the withdrawals were supposedly made. She testified that she had never lent her card to anyone nor told anyone her secret code. In rebuttal, the bank's branch manager, armed with a computer printout, described the system and its security measures. He said only someone who used her card and number could make the withdrawals.

The winner: Mrs. Judd. Courts often hear conflicting versions of the same event. In this case, the judge felt Mrs. Judd was a believable witness. He was not prepared to discount her testimony just because of the "adverse 'testimoney' of a machine."

Judd v. Citibank, 184 N.Y.L.J., No. 118, p. 15.

Safeguards for Safe-Deposit Boxes

Valuables stored in bank safe-deposit boxes are not automatically protected against loss through burglary, flood, or fire. To be compensated for missing valuables, depositors must initiate lawsuits against the bank. The chances of winning are very, very slim.

Safeguards:

Buy insurance for the contents of the boxes even though reimbursement levels are low. And most negotiable items, such as securities, bank notes, gold, coins, and cash, are not covered.

Alternative: Store stocks and bonds at the brokerage house where they were purchased. These firms have a legal and financial responsibility to guard securities stored with them.

Another option: Open a custody account with a bank. The bank holds securities and other assets in its vault. It collects and credits all dividends, but does not manage the assets. The bank will replace any asset in the vault that is lost, stolen, or harmed. Charges are generally based on the size of the account and the composition of the holdings.

How Check-Clearing Time Is Changing

Although the time it takes banks to process checks is generally shrinking, high volume is causing bottlenecks in some areas. Example: Denver banks are processing checks in about two-thirds the time it took them in 1974. But in Milwaukee, checks take an average of nearly a day longer to clear than they did a few years ago.

Cities where out-of-town checks clear in an average of less than 2.5 days: Atlanta; Chicago; Dallas; Denver; Houston; Kansas City; Louisville; Minneapolis; New York; Philadelphia; Pittsburgh; St. Louis.

Cities where checks take longer than three days to clear: El Paso, TX; Helena, MT; Los Angeles; Milwaukee; Nashville; Newark, NJ;

New Orleans; Omaha; Portland, OR; San Francisco; Seattle.

Source: Phoenix-Hecht, Inc., a cash-management analysis and consulting firm, 30 W. Monroe St., Chicago 60603.

Shopping for the Right NOW Account

NOW accounts (interest-paying checking accounts) are legal throughout the U.S. Warning: Not all NOW accounts are the same. Shop for one suited to you. Some of the differences:

Minimum balance required for NOW accounts varies from no minimum to $1,000 at a savings and loan and $3,000 at commercial banks. How the balance is computed: (1) Average monthly balance must be above the minimum. (2) Daily balance must be above the minimum. (3) Some institutions count money kept in other accounts toward the minimum.

Penalties for going under the minimum: Range from zero interest paid to a flat service charge and/or a fee for each check.

Interest may be paid on the average daily balance or on the lowest balance over a certain period. Interest can be compounded either quarterly or daily. To check: Ask for the annual rate.

Possibility: Those in upper tax brackets may be wise to forego taxable NOW accounts and negotiate for free bank services and a lower interest rate on loans. Alternative: Check how NOW accounts stack up in a given period against money-market funds with check-writing privileges.

Postdating Checks

Postdated checks, frequently demanded of delinquent installment plan debtors by finance companies or collection agencies, sometimes are deposited immediately. No one owns up to this tricky business, except to blame it on a clerical error and to stress that the

7

payee is not legally at fault. The check may clear the bank because: (1) Checks in batches tend not to be date-scrutinized. (2) The account somehow contains sufficient funds when it's presented. However, your post-dated check may be paid while other checks bounce.

When a Check Bounces

Writing a bad check can cost you several dollars for a service charge at the bank, and writing many of them can hurt your credit rating. There's no confusion on these points, but there are some misconceptions about other aspects of bad checks.

Is it illegal to write a check for which there are insufficient funds?

Not necessarily. There usually must be evidence of intent to defraud before authorities will prosecute.

Will banks ever honor a bad check?

Occasionally, as a gesture to long-time customers whose business they don't want to lose. Or, they will make up the difference and charge you interest on the "loan."

Can a check bounce even though there are sufficient funds in the account?

Yes, because the funds may be in the form of deposited checks that have not yet cleared at their own banks. A check drawn on a California bank, for instance, may take as long as 10 days to clear after it is deposited in a New York bank.

Who is responsible for the loss?

The person or company that accepted the check. Banks are not responsible. They are basically agents rendering services to customers.

When the Bank Can't Bounce a Check

The bank may have to honor a check if it takes too long to bounce it. Uniform Commercial Code requires that the bank take some action by midnight of the business day after it receives the check. But the bank gets more time if there's an emergency beyond its control; for example, computer breakdown.

Cashing a Letter

Letters or telegrams may serve as checks. Requirements: The letter must be addressed to a bank. And it must state that a specific amount is to be paid on demand either to the bearer of the letter or to the order of a named person. Point: If any one of these requirements is not met, the letter will not be valid as a check. Of course, the bank will make its usual effort to verify that the "check" is valid. *United Milk Prods. Co.* V. *Lawndale Nat'l, Bank,* 392 F. 2d 876, 5 UCC Rep. 143.

Checks Marked 'Payment in Full'

If there's no dispute as to the amount, a check tendered for less than the amount due and marked "payment in full" (or the like) may be cashed without prejudicing the right to recover the balance.

If there's a bona fide dispute as to the amount owing, the creditor must be wary. Alternatives: Reject the check and demand full payment. Or: Accept the check but run the risk that payment will be deemed to have settled the disputed claim for the lesser amount. It's easy enough for a debtor who wants to pay less than the amount for which he's billed to create a dispute on the basis of quantitative or qualitative deficiencies in the goods or services supplied.

Stamp the check with a statement to the effect that "Check is accepted without prejudice and with full reservation of all rights under Section 1-207 of the Uniform Commercial Code." The effectiveness of this technique is untested in the courts, but it may help protect a creditor's rights and provide leverage in a settlement.

When a Note Is Too Old to Collect

The statute of limitations on a demand note begins to run on the date the note is due. Point: If the limitation period runs out under local law, the holder of the note cannot collect. Example: A note was payable 30 days after demand for payment was made on or after September 20, 1967. The statute of limitations provided for by local law was six years so the holder of the note could not collect on it in 1974.

Checking Out Checks

Spotting bad checks. About 90% of cleared bad checks are numbered 101 to 150, indicating a new account.

Spotting forged checks. Legitimate checks have at least one perforated edge. Most forgeries are cutouts. Another difference: Hold a suspicious check up to the light. If the print is shiny, the check is a forgery.

When a check is too old to cash. Checks dated more than six months ago are usually not cashable, no matter how much money the issuer has in the bank. (Exception: U.S. Treasury checks are valid indefinitely.)

If the amounts differ. If the amount written on a check in words is different from the amount written in numbers, the bank will pay the sum shown *in words*.

Undated checks. When you receive a check with the date missing, it's legal to fill in a date reasonably close to when it was mailed. Invalid: To predate or postdate it by several weeks. Such action might constitute a criminal act.

Stopping a certified check. Normally, this check cannot be the subject of a stop-payment order. Exception: If the bank is informed by the person who wrote the check that fraud was involved in the transaction, the bank may stop payment. But it does not have to.*

*Lincoln Secs. v. Morgan Guarantee Trust Co., 8 UCC Rep. 215.

How to Spot a Fake ID

Best identification: Photograph, physical description, and signature. Other safeguards:

Repeat some information from the ID card back to the holder, but make a small mistake in repetition. Example: Is your address 733 Lake Dr.? (743 is the real number). Imposters are often unfamiliar with details.

Don't accept IDs that have the name of the state or issuing agency typed in instead of printed. Also, a typographical error is almost always a sign of a fake.

Check wear patterns on old cards. A genuine card will be worn mostly around the edges from handling. Some forgers artificially age cards, which gives a uniform look of wear all over the card.

Look for raised edges around photographs, which is a sign that a substitution has been made.

Feel for flaws in laminated cards, another sign of tampering.

Compare the typewriter face on various parts of the card. Reject it if there is a mismatch.

Check the holder's signature against the one on the ID.

Beware: Birth certificates are poor IDs because they fail to describe the adult using them. Better: A driver's license, passport, or credit card (that can be checked to see if stolen).

Source: *The National Notary Magazine.*

Forged Checks: Who's Liable?

Examine canceled checks immediately when they are returned from the bank. Reason: A bank is normally liable if it honors a forged check, but it is not liable if it pays out on repeated forgeries that a customer should have discovered. Example: An employee embezzled money by making out stolen company checks to himself. Held: The bank was liable on only the first forged check. Reason: If the company owners had regularly examined their returned checks, they would have discovered the first forgery and prevented the later ones from occurring.

Terry v. Puget Sound Nat'l Bank, 492 P2d 534, 10 UCC Rep. 173.

Bank Credit Cards Are Not All Alike

Should you keep the bank credit card you have now, or apply for ones that offer greater advantages? One VISA card or MasterCard could be very different from another VISA card or MasterCard. What counts is the bank issuing it.

The MasterCard and VISA organizations do not issue credit cards themselves. They provide a clearing system for charges and payments on the cards and license banks to use the VISA or MasterCard name. It is the issuing bank that determines the interest rates and fees.

A bank's name on a credit card does not necessarily mean that it is the bank actually issuing the card. Issuance of credit cards is a high-risk, low-profit business. Seldom does a small bank issue its own.

Generally, a small bank will act as an agent for an issuing bank. The agent bank puts its name on the card, but it is the issuing bank that actually extends any credit.

Aside from costs, this can be important if the cardholder encounters an error. The correction might have to be agreed upon, not by a friendly local banker, but by an unknown, larger institution, perhaps in a different state.

VISA, for example, has about 1,400 issuing banks in the U.S. and about 10,500 agent banks.

Choosing which card to take is becoming more difficult, because some of the nation's largest banks have begun active solicitation of customers throughout the U.S. Individuals must be especially careful about accepting any offer that might come in the mail.

A recently discovered quirk in the federal law allows federally chartered out-of-state banks to ignore state usury laws that limit the amount of interest or fees that the issuing bank may charge on its credit cards. In Arkansas, for example, state usury laws prevent local banks from charging more than 10% interest on credit card balances. But a federally chartered out-of-state bank, in lending to Arkansas residents, may charge whatever its home state allows even within individual states, the terms on credit cards can vary widely.

Aside from the actual rates and fees, individuals must carefully check the fine print of their contracts. Most banks, for example, do not charge interest on balances stemming from purchases until the customer is billed for such purchases. If the bill on which the charges first appear is paid in full by the stated due date, there is no interest charge to the holder. But some banks, those in Texas, for example, begin charging interest as soon as they receive the charge slip and make payment to the merchant. Thus, interest begins accumulating even before the cardholder receives the bill. These interest charges continue until the bank receives payment from the customer.

Source: Robert A. Bennette, banking correspondent, *The New York Times*.

Credit Card Cautions

Debit card risk. If lost or stolen, unauthorized use of your bank-automation card leaves you liable for the first $50, even if the loss is reported before use. It's up to $500 if you delay reporting it until after someone has tapped your account for a teller-machine withdrawal. Point: That makes the convenience of a debit card potentially ten times costlier than a credit card, which limits your liability to $50 tops and charges you nothing if a loss is reported in time to flag it before use.

Don't disclose the account number of your check-cashing identification or electronic funds transfer (EFT) card, even when reporting it lost or stolen. Why: Authorities don't need to know the number. But thieves posing as bank officers may try to get it in order to use it.

Check your credit card statement against your receipts. It's very easy for a dishonest storeowner to run off several slips when you present your card and submit them later for payment.

Be sure that it's your card that the store clerk returns. Accidental switches do happen. The number of switches is increasing. It's not costly, but it can be inconvenient, especially if you're traveling.

You are not automatically responsible for any of the credit card charges of family members, even if they're using family card. Example: An executive's son continued to use his father's credit card after he was told to return it. Under a Federal Trade Commission ruling, the father had only to inform the credit card issuer that the card was being used without permission. Having done so, the father would be responsible only for the next $50 charged.

Withholding Credit Card Payments

Disgruntled consumers may be able to withhold payments on a credit card they used to purchase goods or services that proved substandard. This is the result of a provision of the Fair Credit Billing Act, which enables the credit card companies to reclaim disputed amounts from merchants after credit card slips are signed.

Four conditions must be met for a consumer to be entitled to withhold credit card payments:

• The amount of the charge must be more than $50.

• The charge must be made within the customer's home state, or within 100 miles of the customer's home.

• The customer must first attempt to settle the dispute with the merchant directly.

• The customer must give the bank that issued the card written notice that the attempt to settle has failed.

How it works: When the bank receives the customer's notice, it credits the account with the amount of the charge. It then charges this amount back to the bank that serves the merchant. The bank then charges the merchant.

This provision of the law has been little publicized by the banks and credit card companies. Reason: They fear that if too many customers take advantage of this feature of the law merchants will begin to refuse credit cards.

Borrowing Money At 5% Interest

Loans at a 5% interest rate are still possible for people with whole life insurance policies that have accumulated some cash-surrender value. Reason: Policies issued prior to the mid-1970s allow borrowing against their cash-surrender value at an interest cost of 5%. If your policy is not that old, interest rates are higher, but still a bargain. Advantages: Interest payments on loans may be tax-deductible. The IRS disputes their deductibility, but so far has not won any cases. There is no fixed schedule for repaying the loan as long as interest is being paid. If it hasn't been repaid by the time the borrower dies, it's simply deducted from the proceeds.

Here's what to do: Check your policy's table of cash values to determine how much you can borrow. Contact your broker, agent, or insurance company to provide a form.

Important: The interest rate is contractually fixed when you take out the policy. You can borrow any amount up to the cash value. There are no negotiations. You cannot be turned down.

The insurance company has the contractual right to postpone the loan up to six months. However, at present, such delays are uncommon.

If you are insured by a mutual insurance company, you may have dividends available. Don't borrow on your cash value until you take out your dividends. They are tax-free rebates of the premiums you paid in the past.

Advantages of Owning a Debit Card

Debit cards, issued through banks by MasterCard and Visa, are often misunderstood. On the surface they can look like ripoffs. When you pay for a purchase with a debit card, the money is deducted from an account that you have at the bank or occasionally from a money-fund account at a brokerage firm. In other words, you're not getting a free loan of 25 or more days as you would with a bank credit card or convenience cards.

However, these cards have the other advantages of bank cards and are often linked to automatic teller and out-of-state check-cashing privileges.

Guideline: If you have a convenience or bank card and are in the habit of paying promptly with a check written on an interest-bearing checking account, it probably pays to continue one of those cards. But if you're lazy about paying and would have to pay from a noninterest-bearing checking account, a debit card can make sense because you won't forget to pay since the amount is taken automatically from your account.

At large stores, debit-card purchases are sometimes deducted electronically and immediately from your account. But at most other places, the transaction is handled much as a check would be, giving you a float of from three to 20 days. When that happens, the advantage of a debit card is immense: While other cards would merely give you the equivalent of an interest-free loan for the float period, a debit card lets you keep earning interest on the amount of the purchase until the transaction clears.

Source: Herbert Mueller, representative of the American Bankers Association and president of North Valley Bancorp, 292 Hempstead Dr., Redding, CA 96049-3517.

Low-Interest Loans For Homeowners

Homeowners with Federal National Mortgage Association mortgages may be able to obtain considerable amounts of cash by trading in their mortgages. How it works: They receive a new mortgage worth up to 90% of the home's current market value, at a rate almost always well below prevailing rates. Those whose homes have appreciated stand to receive significant amounts. To determine eligibility: Check with the mortgage holder.
Source: *Credit News*

Should You Take Out A Personal Loan?

If you're unsure about whether or not to take out a new personal loan, this basic calculation can be helpful.

1. Add all sources of income for a month.

2. Total all monthly living expenses and your savings requirements, mortgage, debt, and insurance payments.

3. Avoid a loan that requires monthly payments that are bigger than the balance left when you subtract expenditures from monthly income.

Best collateral for a bank loan: Cash value of life insurance policies, certificates of deposit, U.S. government securities (90% of value), stocks (70% of market value), mutual-fund shares (40% of market value).

Frequently Overlooked Loan Sources

Executives can borrow funds from their vested accounts in a qualified company retirement plan. The retirement account itself serves as security for the loan. Requirements: (1) The plan must specifically provide that such loans are available to all plan participants. (2) The loans must be genuine and bear a reasonable rate of interest. (3) Loans may not exceed the lesser of $50,000 or one-half accrued benefits. (4) Loans must be repaid within 5 years (except for loans to finance a personal residence).

Broker loans. Instead of selling stock, consider using it as collateral for a broker's loan. Since brokers borrow at wholesale from banks, you'll probably get money closer to the prime. And there are no compensating balances.

Certificate of deposit (CD) loan. You need money, but your CD isn't due yet. Instead of cashing it in, use it as collateral for a loan. The interest charge is usually 2 percentage points above the rate paid by the certificate. These 2 points, divided by a short period of time, don't amount to much.

Before You Cosign A Loan

Three out of four cosigners of finance company loans are eventually asked to pay up. There may also be late charges due to a friend's or relative's delinquency. Sometimes even court costs and legal fees. Besides having to pay off the original loan, cosigners may damage their own credit rating in the bargain.

Advice: Never cosign a loan unless you can pay it off if necessary. Try to get the lender to hold your obligation to the principal of the loan. Never pledge your own property to secure such a loan.

Request notification in writing of any missed payments. That way you are aware of the borrower's delinquency and can either make the payment yourself or prod the friend or relative before the loan is called for or there are penalties.

One-to-one loans. No matter how friendly a loan, it's a good idea to draw up a note stating terms and conditions. Be businesslike. Include a provision for reasonable interest. Good reason for formalizing the loan: The IRS. With documentation, you should be able to take a deduction on any loss. Unless the loan was directly connected with your business, it will be treated as a short-term capital loss.

How Credit Bureaus Work

Nationwide, there are 2,000 credit bureaus, which issue 150 million consumer credit reports annually. How they work: A credit bureau starts a file on you when you apply for your first credit card. It records your place of employment, income, and every purchase on credit or on the new credit card. Financial information passes in and out of the bureau. Lenders, such as banks, supply information on their account holders. When you want credit, the lender draws information from your credit file.

Important: You have a right to see your credit file, particularly if you have been denied credit because of its contents. Advice: Contact the credit bureau within 30 days after your credit application has been denied. The bureau *must* tell you the contents of your file at no cost to you. After 30 days the fee is $3 to $5.

For the location of your credit bureau, ask your bank which one it uses, or check the telephone directory.

Credit Application Tips

Never list a finance company where you have had a loan as a credit reference. Reason: Computers that most large lenders use to score applications will subtract points if a finance company appears on your credit history. Caution: Any loan that is still outstanding when you fill out a credit application must be listed. False or incomplete applications are the most common reason for denying discharge of a debt in bankruptcy.

Two people who live together, but who are not married, have the power to insist that their incomes be aggregated to determine their credit-worthiness for a joint-mortgage application. Reason: The Equal Credit Opportunity Act bars discrimination on the basis of marital status.

Markham v. Colonial Mortgage Service Co.,

Late Mortgage Payments

As long as you pay a mortgage payment within 15 days of the due date, it's unlikely that the bank will complain. Even bankers admit to juggling their finances this way, with no harm to their credit rating.

Know Your Installment Debt Limit

Rule of thumb: Installment debt should not exceed 10% of take-home pay. More than 20% debt indicates trouble ahead. Note: Do not include mortgage payments when calculating the amount of debt.

How Credit Unions Work

Credit unions are usually more lenient than other institutions about making loans to members, and they generally charge lower rates for those loans. Since credit unions are owned by their members, profits, if there are any, are distributed either through higher dividends (interest) or lower loan rates.

Credit unions are federally chartered by the National Credit Union Administration, and deposits are insured up to $100,000.

You can join a credit union if:

You work for a firm whose employees sponsor one.

You're a member of a sponsoring association (union, club, and so on).

You are a resident of a geographical area with a credit union charter.

If these options aren't available, you may want to start your own credit union. You may form a credit union under these circumstances:

You work for a firm with more than 200 employees. (Actually, for it to be economically viable, there should be many more members. However, the corporation may deposit up to $100,000.)

You belong to a club, union , or fraternal organization of a substantial size that wants to sponsor a credit union.

You live in a cohesive community. Recent laws have been changed to permit communities of over 25,000 people to obtain credit union charters. However, they must qualify as cohesive communities and cannot be even as large as small cities. For instance, New Haven CT with a population of over 120,000 would not qualify.

More information: Contact the National Credit Union Administration, Washington, DC 20456. (There are also five regional administrators: Austin, TX; Boston, MA; Harrisburg, PA; San Francisco, CA; and Atlanta, GA).

How Pawnshops Work

A pawnbroker makes loans on personal property left as collateral. The property can be redeemed when the loan plus interest is repaid.

Interest rates (regulated by state or local laws) may be from 5% to 6% a month. (The 3% limit in New York City has sharply reduced the number of pawnbrokers there.) Loans can usually be renewed but only if the interest for the original period is paid up.

What articles pawnbrokers will accept: Usually, items that are small or of modest value: Jewelry, musical instruments, clocks, typewriters, cameras, radios, silverware, etc. Brokers won't lend more money than they think they can get if the pledged item isn't redeemed and has to be sold.

When a pledge isn't redeemed: Brokers are usually required to notify pawners that the loan period has expired and to give them a final opportunity to redeem their pledge before the broker has the right to sell the item. In some jurisdictions, brokers may keep all the money received from the sale of unredeemed pledges. Under other codes, they may recover the cost of the loan made plus interest due, but must turn any excess over to the pawner.

Stolen property: In many states, brokers are legally obliged to file with police daily lists of items pledged. They must give the object's description, serial number, etc. This gives the police a chance to check the items against property reported stolen. If somebody buys a stolen item from a pawnbroker, it must be returned, and the broker must refund the purchase price to the customer.

Settling a Big Accident Claim

Should a severely injured victim of an accident take a $1 million lump-sum payment, or $200,000 in immediate cash plus $25,000 a year for life?

As large awards become more frequent, insurance companies are seeking less costly alternatives. One of the cheaper alternatives is the structured settlement: A package of up-front cash and monthly income. It is offered to an accident victim before the case goes to trial, if the insurer's lawyers believe it likely that the victim will win a large award.

Insurers save money: Structured settlements generally cost casualty underwriters 20% to 60% less than lump-sum settlements.

The package: The up-front cash may be used for medical bills, legal fees, a reserve fund, lost income, and specific needs (such as a specially designed house for a paraplegic). The scheduled income may be for a specific period or for life. It may be designed to increase or decrease on given future dates or at the occurrence of certain events. All aspects are negotiable.

Caution: This type of settlement can look attractive to the injured party (and advisers), but it may *not* be the wisest choice. Litigation can be protected, but if a plaintiff has a strong case the insurer strives to settle quickly. It is axiomatic that the longer the delay in such a case the larger the settlement. The structured settlement was designed as an expeditious, less costly pretrial settlement device. However, it would not be offered if the plaintiff had a weak case. In that instance, though the insurer would be likely to win in court, it might first offer a small settlement that would be less costly than litigation.

Insurance companies sell the settlement by:

Guaranteeing income for life.

Protecting minors and incompetents from inadequate or unscrupulous advisers and dishonest outsiders.

Matching benefits to the individual's needs, reducing the risk of financial mismanagement.

Getting plaintiff's lawyer paid immediately, or in installments over years.

Arguments against the idea:

The guaranteed income is vulnerable to erosion by inflation. Contrast: A $1 million lump-sum settlement is reduced by immediate expenses to $750,000. That sum could safely yield an annual income of $60,000 to $75,000, leaving the principal intact. Or: It could buy an annuity that provides a considerably greater lifetime income than the $25,000 settlement figure noted above.

The courts are empowered to protect minors and incompetents. With a large lump-sum settlement, the court could direct the purchase of an annuity or the establishment of a trust, limiting it to specific types of investments and appointing a reputable counselor as trustee. Either way, the accident victim has greater assurance of continued financial security than under the restriction of a structured settlement.

Accident victims who win lump-sum settlements have a better opportunity to set up an adequate estate program for their survivors.

Bottom line: If a structured settlement is accepted, it should be made inflation-proof by including an escalation clause, which could be tied to the cost of living index.

The Pros and Cons of Suing to Collect Small Claims

A suit for a small amount may be more trouble than it's worth.

The negatives:

Lawyers' fees.

Time lost in court, including postponements, perhaps several.

Once the case is won, the debtor may not be found.

The debtor may not have any money.

If the debtor does have money, it may cost more than it's worth to enforce the judgment and collect it.

Seizing property, garnishing wages are expensive, too.

Most judgments are never recovered, especially in large metropolitan areas.

The positives:

You may get paid when the suit is filed. Some people resist everything else, but the summons and the fear of the courtroom scares them into paying.

The debtor may not have money now, but he may come into money or property later, and the judgment can be collected, with interest.

The judgment can prove the debt uncollectible and thus tax deductible as a worthless bad debt.

Law on Collecting IOUs

If you have made a loan to a friend or colleague and received an IOU, don't disregard it when collection time falls due. Courts are sympathetic to the lender. An IOU is a promise to pay back money. Unless the borrower can prove otherwise, the courts will order payment. Of course, that procedure does not absolutely assure payment of the loan.

Verbal IOUs are binding in courts. However, it is best to have witnesses to such agreements. Written IOUs are necessary for enforcement if there is a promise to repay a debt in a period of time that exceeds a year. Example: A $5,000 loan is repaid in increments of $1,000 per year for five years. Written IOUs also are needed if the IOU is a promise to repay someone else's debt. Example: A relative, friend, or associate.

Source: Robert Green, attorney, Green, Sharpless & Greenstein, 1 Rockefeller Plaza, NY 10020.

Redeeming Damaged Paper Money

Paper currency will be redeemed by the U.S. Treasury at its face value if more than half of the original paper note is intact. Fragments of currency that are not clearly more than half of the original note can be exchanged at face value only if the treasurer of the U.S. is satisfied that the missing portions have been totally destroyed. The treasurer's judgment, based on such evidence of total destruction as he deems necessary is final.

Advice on handling mutilated paper currency:

Do not disturb the fragments any more than is absolutely necessary.

If it is brittle, or likely to fall apart, pack it carefully in cotton and box it, without disturbing fragments.

If the money was in a purse, box, or other container when damaged, it should be left there, if possible, to prevent loss of fragments or further deterioration.

If the money was in a roll when mutilated, do not attempt to unroll or straighten it out.

If coins, or any other metal, are mixed with the currency, remove them carefully. Do not send coins in the same package with fragile paper, as the coins can tear the paper.

In submitting mutilated currency, use registered mail service, with a return receipt requested. Send to Bureau of Government Operations, Division of Currency Claims, Room 132, Treasury Annex #1, DCS-BEPA, Washington, DC 20226.

Redeeming Damaged Stamps

If stamps were sold damaged (stuck together or backed with so little glue they won't stick), the Postal Service will replace them if the request for exchange is made promptly after purchase. If embossed stamped envelopes are mutilated, they may be exchanged for a new supply at their postage value. Postal cards, if unmutilated, may be exchanged for a new supply equivalent to 85% of their full value. Air-letter sheets, if unmutilated, are exchangeable for a new supply at 90% of their full value.

The Postal Service will not redeem: Stamps that are torn, stuck together, or otherwise damaged through usage. It will not redeem uncancelled stamps steamed or cut from unmailed envelopes. Postscript: The Postal Service never makes refunds in cash.

2
Investment Strategies

Who Wins and Who Loses in The Stock Market

Investment brokers' lore: They can tell whether a new client will be a winner or a loser within the first few minutes. Investors' mistake: Forgetting that the broker is essentially a salesperson working for a commission. (Often a loser makes more money for the broker.) Don't rely on a broker for financial and money-management advice.

Classic losing syndrome: An investor loses money in the stock market and swears never to get involved again. Then, after resisting the early publicity about the latest investment fad, the investor moves back into the market just before prices collapse. Worse: Investors who buy a glamour issue on margin after a substantial and fast advance. They get hit the hardest during the inevitable correction.

Investment advisory services and systems and inside information don't help much either. Facts:

Advisory services establish a reputation after making a few good investment pre-dictions or good calls on a specific kind of stock. But they have to keep making predictions, and soon end up with losses.

Technical analysis is as subject to chance as is dart throwing.

Only 65% to 70% of insider trades work out for insiders. Investors usually tend to overestimate the impact of the "insider news" on the stock's price. Or they miscalculate the effect.

Wall Street analysts are too slow. By the time their buy/sell recommendations make the rounds, all the action has been taken.

The sound way to become a winner:

Keep your neuroses under control. While you will never escape fears and doubts, don't allow your emotions to override your judgment.

Initiate your own investment decisions. Don't let someone talk you into buying or selling.

The average investor doesn't need to talk to his broker more than once a month.

Do your homework before entering the stock market. Most winners educate themselves and manage their own money. Read books and financial papers. Take basic investment courses. Learn investment jargon so that you can't be intimidated.

Break away from the fear-greed-guilt cycle that produces losers with the belief that gains are made by magic and fantasy. Learn to deal with reality.

Think about taxes as well as investment. All middle-income wage earners are now in high tax brackets. Tax consequences are an important part of success.

Picking stocks: If the fundamentals of the company sound good and are high quality, and if the price/earnings ratio is under 10, buy at the low end of the stock's trading range for the past two years.

Divide savings into four investment categories: (1) Ready cash to meet emergencies. (2) Income to help maintain your standard of living. (3) Growth to make capital grow and, at the least, keep pace with inflation. (4) Mad money to speculate on the long shot.

Distribute investments appropriately, if there's enough capital.

Source: Jerome Tuccille, author of *Mind Over Money*. William Morrow & Co., New York.

Rules for Picking Common Stocks

Try to buy the industry leader or, at the very least, a company that has an important position in its industry.

Look for an industry with a limited amount of competition.

Avoid an industry that is an essential part of the Gross National Product or the Consumer Price Index, such as autos or steel. Reason: Highly visible companies are easy targets for government pressure.

Stick to stocks that have price/earnings ratios lower than that of the Standard & Poor's 500 index.

The stock should yield at least 4½% to 5%.

The company should have a record of significant dividend increases.

The market price of the stock should be close to book value per share.

Both the industry and the company should have growth rates higher than the median of American business. One rule of thumb: Sales and earnings ought to have doubled over the past decade. If they haven't, you probably won't be able to keep ahead of inflation in the years ahead.

Stay away from companies that are too heavily in debt, especially in relation to industry-wide standards.

Look for companies where managers are owners, too. Nepotism can be a danger in such situations. More often, though, owner-management is a big plus. Owner-managers have a real incentive to keep the company growing as well as to boost the stock's value.

While you may not find a stock with all these characteristics, insist on at least these two: It should be in a growth industry with owner-management.

Source: Roy Papp, investment counselor, 5631 Echo Canyon Circle, Phoenix, AZ 85018.

Easy Profit for Small Stockholders

Some companies are willing to pay a premium of 10% to buy back small holdings (under 100 shares). It helps them cut the cost of servicing minor shareholders. There's no broker's fee for selling holdings directly to the company.

Ten Stock Market Traps

Getting caught up in the bargain-hunting game. The stock market is not a supermarket. If a stock is declining, despite what logically appears to be a very cheap price, there is a good reason for it. Professional traders may be aware of bad news about the company that is not generally known. Better strategy: Buy stocks that are acting better than the market as a whole. (Stocks that outperform the averages during rallies and declines.)

Being too quick to take profits while holding on to losers. Most investors buy a stock at, say, 20, and they sell it at 23 or 24. They may do this successfully a few times. The trap: Eventually they buy a loser and watch it plummet, wiping out all their previous profits. Preferable: Let your winners run. Cut your losses.

Averaging down. Most investors think that if a stock is a good buy at 20, it must be an even better buy at 15. Commonsense rule: If a stock acts poorly after you buy it, you probably made a poor decision. Admit your error, and move on to another situation. Even the smartest professional investors make mistakes. It's how you handle these mistakes that makes winners out of losers.

Buying stocks based on news headlines. Stocks go up in anticipation of favorable news. When the good news finally comes out, it may be too late to buy. The stock may be close to a top.

Holding a stock without a stop-loss order. The stop-loss gives you selling discipline. And it enables you to cut losses and hold on to gains. Where to place a stop-loss order: Just below the last meaningful low in the stock.

Buying a stock without a potential upside target in mind. Learn how to evaluate the risk/reward ratio of a stock. If you buy a stock at say, 20, and you see its downside support as 15 and its upside potential as 35, you have an attractive speculation. Rule: Always look for at least a three-to-one risk/reward ratio.

Trying to be fully invested all the time. There are certain times when it's better to be out of the market altogether. Example: 1973-74.

Buying a stock without looking at its chart pattern. First determine from the chart whether the major trend of the market is up. Then look for the strongest group in the market. Last, pick the stock that shows the best relative strength of the group. Key: Look for a stock that isn't too far above its support level. That way if you are wrong on timing, the stock might still find support only a little below where you bought it.

Trying to catch the exact low of a stock. It's nearly impossible to do consistently. Stocks frequently take a long time to bottom out. Thus, your capital may sit idly for some time before the stock breaks out of its base.

Being afraid to sell short. Simply forget the specter of unlimited losses in a short sale with a limited gain. You can avoid the prospect of enormous losses by shorting with a buy/stop-loss order.

Source: Stan Weinstein, investment counselor, publisher, *The Professional Tape Reader.*

Selecting an Investment Adviser

Key to the future: Pick the right investment adviser. It is the most important financial decision you will ever make. In this difficult era of capital preservation, the adviser can make or break you as well as be the key ingredient in your overall financial planning.

Recommendations: Mutual funds are the best way for small and medium-sized investors to play the stock market. The problem is that most funds don't practice market timing, and even the ones that claim they do aren't good at it. Some of the aggressive growth funds lost up to 80% of their value in the 1973-74 bear market.

Overall, you will do much better finding a really top-rated money manager with whom you can have a real dialogue about your investment objectives, tax situation, and feelings about risk and reward. Also, most small money-management firms with excellent records have a good sense about the major trends in the economy. Thus, you can also get a lot of useful advice concerning strategy for your own business.

The ideal investment firm for the individual is a small- to medium-sized one. Once a firm gets too big (say, $500 million of assets under management) its record deteriorates. Primarily, large firms can only track the 500 largest companies, thereby eliminating investment in some 3,000 others, many of which have exciting prospects. Avoid: Bank trust departments. Their bureaucracy and lower pay scales are serious hindrances to superior performance.

Be sure to look for the following: The firm did well in adversity. Don't judge it by only its good years. Find out about the bad ones.

The firm has continuity of management. If you do find a good investment record, be sure that the money manager responsible for it is still around. Equally important: The manager must still have actual portfolio responsibility. It's no good if the person performs an administrative function and leaves the decision-making to the staff.

The firm's managers have humility. The big talkers are either exaggerating or have run up a good record largely through luck.

There's no evidence of the burnout syndrome. After a while, many successful managers become too wealthy or too tired, and their incentive to keep making money for investors disappears.

Source: Michael Stolper, president, Stolper & Co., financial advisers, 770 B St., Suite 308, San Diego, CA 92101.

How a Professional Investor Handles His Own Money

While no professional investor ever wants to admit to investing in anything other than what he recommends to clients, there is one outstanding difference between investing personally and professionally: Patience. Although many investors claim they are buying for the long term, if the recommended stock doesn't move up within a few months, they want to know what's wrong and how long before it makes its move.

I use exactly the same technique of determining trends to make my own investments that I use for my clients' investments. Unlike most investors, however, I am not disappointed when a stock takes several years to show major strength.

Principle that should govern stock investing: Determine areas where there is substantial growth capability. Invest only in the companies having a good chance to benefit from those trends.

Example: In the 19th century, British investors realized that railroads were a key investment in the U.S. They knew little about each line and there was little in the way of balance sheet information. However, if they invested in several, at least one was bound to be an outstanding winner, and possibly every one of them held the prospect of sharing in that advance.

Don't buy cyclical stocks: I never buy a stock at the bottom of its cycle. If you buy stocks during down periods, you are a speculator, not an investor. You are speculating that you know the bottom of the business cycle for the company. Few people know that.

Avoid companies that can't grow. For example, General Motors was a good buy when it sold only two million cars a year and there was still a large market to penetrate. As it stands now, there is no growth ahead of it.

Don't try to spread risk. Once you have chosen your areas and stocks, don't bother trying to spread the risk with other stocks. It just dilutes effort.

Outside of the stock market: My primary feeling is that nonliquid investments are not very beneficial to my portfolio. Reason: it doesn't matter that a Rembrandt painting I may own is worth $3 million if it takes a long time to find a buyer.

Real estate: I hold no property except my own home. Naturally, it has appreciated, but I bought it to live in, not for investment.

Collectibles: I have a baseball memorabilia collection that has appreciated quite a bit, but that's due to luck. I collected baseball cards and programs when I was a preadolescent sports fan. I also have an art collection, but I have no idea whether my selections are worth more or less than the price at which I bought them. I buy art for pleasure, not investment.

Tax shelters: I like oil and gas drilling shelters best. I have several and strongly recommend sticking to the most conservative deals. The more conservative the tax shelter, the better chance you have to make money and also get some write-offs. Avoid: Shelters that have suspiciously high write-offs like five-to-one. I never buy the leftover ones that are marketed to desperate and often ignorant investors at year-end.

Bonds: as long as inflation continues, there's only one investment rationale for bonds—in the portfolios of elderly people who need income.

Source: Louis Ehrenkrantz, partner, Rosenkrantz, Ehrenkrantz, Lyon & Ross, Inc., 6 E. 43 St., New York 10017, and author of the *Investment and Technology Report.*

ABCs of Investment Clubs

They are most useful if you join to keep in touch with friends and colleagues, instead of joining strictly to make money. How one successful club operates:

Members, usually about eight, contribute about $50 per month. That gives the club a reasonable amount to invest. But not so much that it detracts from what is essentially a social club.

Meetings are held every two months (some meet monthly), alternating among members' homes. Dinner is served. Then, the members play cards. Half of the evening's winnings go into the club's investment fund.

At least once a year, each member is responsible for a report recommending a stock or industry group. If the recommendation is approved by a majority vote, it's acted on.

All other decisions are reached by majority vote, too.

Members contribute their respective skills. Examples: A CPA provides tax services, a broker explains annual reports.

Ideas discussed at the meetings can be used to develop an investment portfolio. (This can be very profitable. One club raked in $300,000 in six years.)

When Not to Trust a Stockbroker

Recognize excessive trading (churning). Divide the total cost of commissions and account costs for the past year by the average monthly equity (stocks and cash) in the account. The result is called a turnover rate. The Securities and Exchange Commission (SEC) considers a turnover rate of more than four excessive. A turnover rate of six is considered churning.

Keep your eyes open for excessive markups (greater than 5% above the market price of an investment vehicle). A market like this can mean the brokerage firm is buying the stock at the market price and then is reselling it at a higher price to customer accounts.

Basic ways to protect yourself:

Don't open a margin account unless you are prepared to take significant risks in playing the market. A margin account is inherently speculative and is thus the easiest target for churning.

Don't have more than one active account at the same time. Having two or more will probably negate claims that the accounts are being churned or that unsuitable investments are being made.

Make sure any discretionary account agreement is in writing.

Consider filing a complaint with the SEC. It can censure the broker and help the investor recoup losses.

Take the matter to arbitration. All the national exchanges are bound legally to settle broker/customer disputes in this fashion, if the customer chooses.

Warning: Avoid actual litigation unless there's big money involved. Legal costs in a securities case can run as much as $200 an hour and amount to $50,000 or more, since these cases often run on for years.

Obviously, it is extremely important to make sure that you get any sales agreement with a broker in writing.

When Not to Pay Stockbroker Commissions

It's not necessary to use a broker and pay a commission to make a gift of stock. And if a sale is negotiated privately, that can be completed without a broker, too.

How to transfer stock ownership to another person:

Enter the other person's name, address, and Social Security number on the back of the certificate.

Sign the back of the certificate and have the signature guaranteed by a commercial bank.

Send it by registered mail to the transfer agent, whose name is on the certificate.

Allow two to six weeks for the other person to receive the new certificate. There will be no charge, although in some states the seller, or donor, has to pay a small transfer tax. Good idea: Phone the bank first to find out its procedure and exact address of the stock transfer department.

Getting Extras From Your Stockbroker

If you are a good customer at your brokerage house, generating upwards of $5,000 in commissions, you may be able to negotiate for some perks. What to negotiate for:

A stock quotation terminal.

Cash in the form of commission rebates.

Discounts of as much as 20% off published rates on many types of trades. Shop around. Some firms are more liberal about this than others. Best areas: Where discount brokers advertise frequently and may steal away customers. Particularly: New York, Chicago, the Sun Belt.

An attractive interest rate on your margin account if it is worth at least $200,000. This may be as little as ½% above the broker call loan rate.

Breaks in the rate charged when you buy on margin.

Interest on idle cash from stock sales or dividends awaiting reinvestment in the same firm. This may be done automatically, or you may have to ask that the cash be parked in the broker's money-market fund.

Frequent statements on your account. One broker is willing to give a computer printout daily if your account is large enough.

Availability of special research reports and opportunities to meet with the firm's analysts.

Note: Although brokers have been reported to wine and dine special clients lavishly, and to shower free vacations and limousine service on them, good customers might obtain such perks from any consumer service. Caution: The perks can be taxable.

Mailing Stock Certificates To Brokers

Send stock certificates unsigned via registered mail. This way, they're non-negotiable. Then, under separate cover, mail the broker a stock-power form with your signature and the number of shares in the transaction, which authorizes the broker to sell the stock.

How to Choose A Discount Broker

Discount brokerage houses can save you 50% to 80% of the commissions charged by most firms. There are now close to 80 discount houses across the country. They service stocks, bonds, and options, and offer both cash and margin accounts.

How to find one: Through advertisements in financial publications and by word of mouth. Discounters seldom actively solicit accounts. While advertisements inform you about the rate structure, only word of mouth and trial and error will apprise you of other important elements.

Rate structures:

Small to medium trades: Approximately $2,000 to $20,000. Expect to get about 50% off from most discounters, although there are some who will give 70% off on small orders. Problem: Most discounters have a minimum commission of $25 to $35 per trade. Frequently, the ones with lower rates for small trades have a higher minimum charge. Purchases under $2,000 will not save much. You may be better off going with a non-cut-rate broker to take advantage of extra services like research. You will never get any investment advice from a discount broker.

Large trades: $20,000 to $75,000. Expect about 60% to 75% off.

Very large trades: Over $75,000. The saving should be 70% to 80%.

Ways to evaluate discounters:
• Is the person on the other end of the phone competent and able to understand what you want?
• Does the telephone get picked up during busy market periods?
• Are your trades executed correctly and within a reasonable period of time?
• Are your monthly statements and confirmations of transactions delivered promptly?

Protection: Brokerage houses must be protected for up to $100,000 worth of securities by the Securities Investor Protection Corporation, as specified by the government. Many (but not all) full-commission firms have an additional $400,000 in protection. If you plan a portfolio of more than $100,000 worth of securities, find a discounter who has the additional coverage, or split your account among several discounters.

Discount brokers' employees are usually on salary, so there's no pressure on you to make more trades. Basic attitude of the discounter: You call us, we don't call you.

Disadvantages: You can't buy commodities, set up a tax shelter, or get trading or investment advice.

Idea: Some investors use a discounter and a full-commission broker in tandem. They get research reports and recommendations from the full-service broker when they do some investing. They do the rest of their business with a discounter.

Source: J. Bud Feuchtwanger, president, Royal Investors Group, discount brokers, 120 Wall St., New York 10005.

When to Switch Stockbrokers

Get a new broker if:

The stockbroker doesn't return your calls within a half-day.

Bad news breaks for a stock you own and the broker does not phone.

You have a trading account with a high volume of daily activity, but the broker fails to phone you often when the market is choppy.

You have an active account, but the broker has not made a profit for you in six months.

You have a less active account, and the broker has not made a profit for you in one year.

You ask a question about a recent economic or political development, and the broker cannot relate it to your short- and long-term holdings.

Source: E. Lee Hennessee, assistant vice-president, Thomson McKinnon Securities, Inc., stockbrokers, 1 New York Plaza, New York 10004.

How to Be Your Own Securities Analyst

Any investor, even a small one, can do the kind of analysis of his own stocks that two of Wall Street's most sophisticated security analysts do for the nation's major institutional investors. Robert Olstein and Thornton O'glove sell their *Quality of Earnings Report* for fees running into five figures a year in security transaction commissions. They don't forecast the market or recommend buys, sells, or holds. They critique the financial statements of hundreds of major corporations, looking for problems. And they find them.

In an interview, Olstein and O'glove disclosed ways that individual investors can examine their own holdings in the same ways—if they'll just take the time.

When they have a question about a company, the first thing they do is call the company for an answer. Individual investors have an advantage over professionals here: Corporate executives are less wary of them, more likely to answer straight rather than evade or smooth-talk. Steps to take:

Look for financial statement peculiarities: Deviations from trends, inconsistencies, especially between stockholder reports (annual and quarterly) and filings with the Securities and Exchange Commission (SEC)—10Ks, 10Qs, proxy statements, prospectuses, etc.— that companies must provide.

Focus on big deviations between the financial report and the tax returns. No outsider, not even a shareholder, can see a tax return. But corporations must reconcile deviations between the two sets of books in their SEC 10K filings. They must explain the significant differences between tax costs in financial statements and what's actually paid to the IRS. Key items: Deferred taxes, differences between effective tax rates and statutory rates because of depletion allowances, investment tax credits, offshore tax credits, FSC benefits, etc. Example: Corporation's reported earnings went from 93 cents to $1, but 5 cents represented deferred taxes. Real earnings growth may have been only 2 cents—not 7 cents.

Inventory figures are crucial: Not only the turnover ratio changes, but also the mix of raw materials, work in progress, finished goods, etc. Look at these figures to see if there are buildups of finished goods, maybe signifying plans to cut production, or an increase in raw materials without increases in work in progress, meaning a production problem.

Accounts receivable: What's happening to allowance for doubtful accounts? Worry if the ratio to receivables is up or down. Could mean they are expecting trouble if it's up or manufacturing false earnings if it's down. Another key number worth figuring can be number of

days of sales in the receivables total, indicating level of activity compared with previous years.

Accounts payable: Are they stretching out payments? Why? Credit problems?

Sources and uses of funds statement: How is company's liquidity situation? Is it going to need new financing?

Income statement: Look at ratio of marketing costs, R&D costs, cost of goods sold, etc., compared with trends. Is it controlling its expenses at past rates or losing control? Did changes in trends penalize earnings? Increase them? Deviations in either direction are worth following up with calls to management (play the bumpkin; you may get better information).

How to Interpret Insider Trading

While automotive officials were making brave and uplifting speeches about industry prospects, they were selling off stock in their own companies. When insiders like auto executives won't leave their money where their mouths are, that's worth knowing about. How to interpret insider action:

Insider selling: This is not as reliable an indicator as insider buying. Reason: There are all kinds of personal reasons why an insider might sell shares. However, if there is consistent insider selling, and only selling, it may be an early warning sign of poor performance. Example: One California-based computer company's troubles didn't become apparent until some 18 months after considerable insider selling had been recorded.

Insider buying: It has a definite correlation to stock performance if it occurs in the open market rather than as a result of exercising options or warrants or as part of a profit sharing plan. (However, if insiders are exercising those options, it reflects some optimism about the company.)

Watch for: Three or more insiders buying

within a short period of time (several weeks). This often indicates that there are merger talks being conducted. However, it is not a confirmation of a takeover. Consistent inside purchasing by officers, directors, investment advisers and other affiliated groups means confidence in strong earnings potential and, therefore, a stock price that is higher.

Note on volume: Ignore small purchases or sales (100 to 200 shares), unless they happen on a very frequent, consistent basis.

Big block purchasers: The Securities and Exchange Commission (SEC) requires individuals or firms that acquire 5% or more of another company to state their purchase and purpose in a 13-D statement and record all additional purchases. Although 90% of the time the purchasers claim to be buying for investment purposes, it is frequently a first step toward a tender offer or merger. Even if a tender offer is not made, these investors usually do not buy into a company unless the underlying fundamentals warrant it.

To find out where insiders are placing their bets, you can follow their activities by using the SEC's *Official Summary* and newsletters such as *The Insider's Chronicle.* Both publish data three to six weeks after actual insiders' purchases or sales are made. (The filings themselves are made 10 days after the insider trade.)

Source: William Mehlman, editor, *The Insider's Chronicle.*

How to Evaluate High-Technology Stocks

High technology is the last frontier in American business. Although these stocks have declined sharply during bear markets, they have outperformed other stocks, rebounding more sharply in subsequent recoveries.

Smaller companies developing new technologies, or making a breakthrough on an old one, have three things going for them. These advantages:

Since they are small, the impact on their earnings from the new product or system can be significant.

They are generally free from government regulation because their earnings are often in a new field (except in the case of medicine, where the Food and Drug Administration reigns supreme).

If the company scores a significant breakthrough, it has a chance to dominate a growing market. That's an extremely profitable position even if the market served is relatively small.

Rules for the budding high-technology investor:

Invest in a technology company only if you perceive it as serving a current social need. Some technologies are ahead of their time and are initially rejected. Example: When cable TV was introduced in the 1960s, it attracted hordes of investors but few subscribers. Today, there is a definite subscriber demand and cable TV is a far more attractive investment.

The high-technology expertise of the proposed company must be a meaningful part of the firm's business. For instance, the largest contractor in electronic warfare is General Telephone and Electronics Corp. However, that technology accounts for a mere 1% of its earnings. But the number four in the field, Sanders Associates, gets most of its income from its electronic warfare technology. Point: Large firms don't always have the edge on high technology or research.

No matter how attractive a scientific breakthrough may seem, don't buy a company operating at a deficit. Business graveyards are loaded with firms that couldn't deliver because of their poor financial situation. Following this rule may force you to pay a little more for your stock, but it will eliminate a good deal of the risk.

Ignore the market indexes: Companies with technological superiority are not tied to a stock market environment over time.

Keep current on technological innovation. Read scientific papers, magazines and investment guides that deal with technology.

Source: Louis Ehrenkrantz, vice president, Rosenkrantz, Ehrenkrantz, Lyon and Ross, Inc., investment bankers, 6 E. 43 St., New York 10017, and author of *Growth Investing and Technology.*

Big Opportunities in Small Companies

Charles Allmon has been analyzing small, fast-growing companies for over two decades. What he looks for in a young, growing company:

Balance sheet. The current ratio (current assets matched to current liabilities) should be at least two to one. The company should have no long-term debt. Preferably: No short-term debt, either. The return on shareholders' equity should run at least 22% and, ideally, 30%.

Ideal: As few shares outstanding as possible. (This is where the real leverage comes in.) If a company has only 250,000 shares, a fast growing rate will have a real impact on the equity position. Try to stick with companies that have less than one million shares outstanding, and preferably less than 500,000 shares.

Income statement. Look for a company with very high profit margins. An after-tax profit margin that is over 10% is excellent. (By the same token, avoid those companies that have after-tax margins that are 1½% to 2% or less.)

Pay attention to the company's tax rate. Many investors buy the stock of a company with very high after-tax profit margins only to realize a year or so later that the tax rate was artificially low. Then, when the tax rate returns to normal, the margins shrink dramatically. Thus, if a company pays a full tax rate, give it more points in your rating system than a company with a low tax rate and a higher profit margin.

Management. This is the hardest to evaluate, but the most important. Prime management ingredient: Integrity. The best way to check on honesty is to get hold of the annual reports for the last five to ten years. Read the president's letter to the stockholders. How many of his predictions came true? Did he consistently make outlandish statements that never came to pass? Did everything that he forecast happen?

Try to find out what motivates the chief executive now. What might motivate him in five years? All too frequently, a company president suddenly decides to sell out, and the company loses its momentum.

Focus only on companies in which management holds a very large interest (50% to 70% of the stock). That way, you can be sure they will do everything in their power to get the stock up. That's your goal, too.

Geographical location. Concentrate on companies located in the Sun Belt, preferably in Texas. That part of the country is growing much faster than any other region. It has a pro-business economic and political environment. The Northeast, on the other hand, is losing population, and it is not so positive toward business. Also, after the 1982 elections, the southern and western states will elect half or more of the representatives to Congress, so the political influence of the Sun Belt will grow as well.

Best-situated industries. For the rest of the 1980s, concentrate on energy (North American oil and gas producers), communications (radio, TV, and cable TV), data processing and data communications, and food (convenience stores are booming due to the need to conserve gasoline).

When to sell. Many entrepreneurs don't have the ability to take their company beyond a certain annual sales level. The first major hurdle is $10 million in sales; the second is $50 million. Be sure to watch the company closely as its sales volume approaches these points. If the company gives signs of languishing there, it's probably time to sell.

Source: Charles Allmon, publisher, *Growth Stock Outlook.*

Spotting Low-Priced Stocks Ready to Bounce Back

The key to success in the stock market is knowing how to recognize value. Here is the successful approach of Robert Ravitz, director of research at the investment management firm David J. Greene & Co.

At the Greene operation, value has little to do with a good company versus a bad company. A top-quality large company selling at a high price/earnings multiple is less attractive than a lesser-quality company selling at a depressed price in terms of its past and future earning power, working capital, book value, and historical prices.

Here is where Greene's analysts look for value:

Stocks that have just made a new low for the last 12 months.

Companies that are likely to be liquidated. In the process of liquidation, shareholders may get paid considerably more than the stock is selling for now.

Unsuccessful merger candidates. If one buyer thinks a company's stock is a good value, it's possible that others may also come to the same conclusion.

Companies that have just reduced or eliminated their dividends. The stock is usually hit with a selling wave, which often creates a good buying opportunity.

Financially troubled companies in which another major company has a sizable ownership position. If the financial stake is large enough, you can be sure that the major company will do everything it can to turn the earnings around and get the stock price up so that its investment will work out.

Opportunities, also, in stocks, that are totally washed out—that is, situations where all the bad news is out. The stock usually has nowhere to go but up. How to be sure a stock is truly washed out:

Trading volume slows to practically nothing. If over-the-counter, few if any dealers making a market.

No Wall Street research analysts'are following the company any more.

No financial journalists, stock market newsletters, or advisory services discuss the company.

Selling of the stock by company's management and directors has stopped.

Signs of a turnabout:

The company plans to get rid of a losing division or business. If so, be sure to learn whether the company will be able to report a big jump in earnings once the losing operation is sold.

The company is selling off assets to improve its financial situation and/or reduce debt.

A new management comes on board with an established track record of success with turnaround situations.

Management begins buying the company's stock in the open market.

Also, be sure to follow 13d statements filed with the Securities and Exchange Commission (SEC). A company or individual owning 5% or more of a public company must report such holdings to the SEC. If any substantial company is acquiring a major position in a company, it's possible a tender offer at a much higher price is in the wind.

Source: Robert Ravitz, director of research, David J. Greene & Co., an investment management firm, 30 Wall St., New York 10005.

Venture Stocks: Investing in Start-Up Companies

They used to be called penny stocks. But now they are called venture stocks.

What venture stocks are: Stocks that go public at between 10 cents and $1 a share, giving investors a chance to invest in start-up, entrepreneurial companies. Since the entry price for these investments is so low, some of them rack up astonishing returns.

The factors that favor venture stocks right now:

• Tax laws have changed to encourage entrepreneurs.

• With its simplified registration form, the Securities and Exchange Commission has made it much easier and less costly for a young company to go public.

• Many venture-stock offerings involve oil and gas exploration companies. Since the U.S. has a long-term need to free itself from dependence on oil from the Organization of Petroleum Exporting Countries, venture capital and energy make good companions.

Rules for investing in any venture-stock situation:

Don't use limit orders. Venture stocks are just too volatile. Investors typically lose money by trying to get the stock at 2 cents less a share, or by selling it for 5 cents more. When you think it's time to sell or buy, do it at the market.

Use only 10% to 20% of your investment assets. (Don't speculate with funds needed to maintain liquidity.)

Understand that most gains will be short-term.

Sell half of a position if the stock doubles. And then sell the other half if it doubles again. Don't try for a long-term gain.

Don't buy in a strong market or sell in a weak one. Venture stocks are illiquid. You must consistently sell into strength and buy on weakness.

Deal with a quality firm and a knowledgeable stockbroker. There's little public information available on these issues. You must rely heavily on your broker.

What to look for in a venture stock:

People, people, and people. You want entrepreneurs who know how to survive and have a big stake in making the company succeed. Also important: Friends and relatives of the management should have money invested in the company. That puts even more pressure on the owners. As a general rule, owners should have many hard reasons that prevent them from simply walking away from the company.

Management's track record. Do they have the experience necessary to succeed?

The investment banker doing the underwriting. How have the firm's last five deals done? Last ten? Does the firm have regulatory or back-office problems?

What the funds from the public offering will be used for. Money should be used for basic needs of the company, not for overhead or salaries.

Source: J. Carlos Schidlowski, president, OTC Net, Inc., 1776 South Jackson, Denver. CO 80210.

Investing in New Issues

It's important to be selective when investing in new issues. What to look for:

The company should be an established factor in a popular and growing industry.

The managing underwriter of the public offering should be highly respected in the investment community. Big plus: The last few deals by the underwriter were successful and the stocks currently sell at a premium over the original offering price.

Stick to managements that have a proven track record. Read the offering circular closely to make sure that the company makes money now and has good prospects for growth.

The company should be raising money in the offering to expand the business. Generally speaking, avoid new issues intended chiefly to reduce debt or to cover general expenses.

Warning signal: Insiders plan to sell a lot of stock in the offering. Prospects for the future might not be that great if management gives every indication of bailing out.

Good signs:

• The managing underwriter takes warrants to buy shares at a price higher than the offering price. (No outsider knows the business' prospects better than an underwriter.)

• Major investment banking firms are in the underwriting syndicate.

• Well-known people are on the company's board of directors.

• Venture capitalists with a history of successful investments are involved with the company.

• The stock market environment is bullish. No matter how good the company, a lousy stock market or economic environment can wreak havoc on the best of public offerings.

When to sell: Some investors sell their stock shortly after the offering, if the profit is substantial. This strategy is not recommended. The real money is made over a long-term period. A new issue should be looked at as a five-to ten-year investment. If the buy decision is made with care, holding should offer the most rewarding prospects.

Source: Norman G. Fosback, editor, *New Issues* newsletter.

How to Invest in Utilities

Utility stocks, more than most issues, are purchased for reliable income by conservative investors who may require current income from investment holdings. Here are some guidelines that may help avoid unpleasant surprises.

Is the utility located in a state with favorable regulatory climate? Some states make it very difficult for utilities to pass along rising costs to consumers, some states are more permissive. The typical state will generally grant the utility approximately two-thirds of the rate increase requested. It will usually require approximately one year following such requests to provide the necessary authorization.

The utility should have ample earnings from which to pay interest on any bonds outstanding. Utility companies are generally heavy borrowers of capital for expansion. Should a cash flow bind develop, dividend payouts may have to be suspended, since bondholders hold first call on company assets. Earnings for the company should amount to at least 2.5 times the interest payments due on corporate notes; preferably more. In considering any stock for its dividends, make certain that earnings are ample to cover projected dividend payouts.

The price of the shares should be no lower than book value if the company has plans to issue more shares. Otherwise, shareholder equity will be diluted by such distribution.

The company shouldn't pay out too high a percentage of earnings in dividends. Approximately 65–70% is average payout. The lower a percentage of earnings in dividend payout, the more protected the dividend will be.

Check the balance sheet for excessive debt and for favorable asset-to-liability ratios.

Your broker should be able to provide the above information either by means of in-house research or through access to Standard & Poor's ratings of corporations and corporate debt.

Source: Prescott, Ball & Turben, 900 National City Bank Building, Cleveland.

Adding Foreign Stocks To Your Portfolio

Advantages of foreign stocks:

Spreading the risk. Some economic pressures that depress stocks in the U.S. boost them abroad.

Specific investment opportunities. Examples: South Africa is the only place to invest in certain minerals, as France is for wines and Japan for cameras.

Drawbacks:

Currency fluctuations are an additional risk and complicate already tricky buy-sell decisions.

Investors usually pay taxes to the country where the stock is traded (the average rate on dividends is 15%) and to the U.S. Foreign taxes can be recaptured at least in part (by filing IRS Form 1116) to claim a foreign tax credit. But the time lag in doing this delays an investor's realizing his profit for some time.

No other country regulates equities as tightly as the Securities and Exchange Commission (SEC) does here. Result: Deals considered fraudulent at home are common abroad. Accounting standards are lax in many countries, too. Dividends often fluctuate for no apparent reason.

Small investors only should consider foreign companies with growth and earnings potential in stable countries. Investors able to allocate a minimum of $250,000 to overseas stocks can hedge with blue chips in several countries.

How to invest: Some companies (Britain's Burmah Oil Co. Ltd., Japan's Canon, Inc.) are traded over the counter in the U.S. Others (Canada's Dome Petroleum Ltd., Japan's Sony Corp.) are on the New York or American stock exchanges. Larger brokers in the U.S. can handle transactions on most foreign exchanges.

Cost: Standard commission for better-known issues, minimal extra charges for others. (Customers with large portfolios should have to pay little or nothing extra for the service.)

Research on foreign equities is difficult because governments rarely require companies to publish the kind of data that the SEC mandates. However, annual reports are readable and informative in countries such as Japan, France, and Canada.

Source: Jerrold Mitchell, vice-president, international, Thorndike Doran Paine & Lewis, investment counselors, 28 State St., Boston 02109.

should only be considered by an investor with a high degree of confidence in the future outlook of the issuing company.

Source: Robert Ferris, Georgeson & Co., 100 Wall St., New York 10005.

Dividend Reinvestment Plans

Some 1,000 corporations now offer stockholders special inducements to reinvest dividends. An expert on investor relations and dividend investment plans, Robert Ferris of Georgeson & Co., advises on what an investor should know about such offers:

• Some companies offer a 5% price discount.

• Buying additional stock this way eliminates brokerage commissions. (A few plans have a small service charge.)

• Stockholder may be able to invest additional cash, saving more on commissions and price discounts.

• Provides discipline for those who would otherwise fritter away small amounts.

• New feature: Agent for the plan will hold original shares for safekeeping and send a regular statement to the stockholder.

• Tax treatment: Private ruling* by the IRS states that administrative service charges and brokerage fees subsidized by company reinvestment plans may be treated as additional dividend income to the investor.

• Reinvested dividends are still subject to income tax, except for the first $100. (If sufficient shares to produce $100 are put in a spouse's name, the exclusion is boosted to $200.)

• Tax break. Beginning in 1982, certain public utilities will be able to issue new stock that qualifies for a dividend reinvestment exclusion. Maximum exclusion: $750 for a single taxpayer, $1,500 on a joint return.

Important: Dividend reinvestment plans

*7830104, July 24, 1978, Rev. Ruling 79-42.

How Cash-Poor Executives Can Exercise Stock Options

Finding the cash to exercise a stock option is a common problem, even for high-salaried executives. One technique: The executive can exchange stock already owned for the new share options.

How it works: An executive wants to purchase 1,000 shares of the company stock. The option price is $20 a share when the market price is $40 a share. The executive already owns company stock for which he paid $10 a share. The executive exchanges 500 of the old shares at their market value of $40 each ($20,000) for the 1,000 new shares (also $20,000).

Result: The employee must treat the difference between the new shares' option price and their market value ($20,000) as compensation. Maximum tax: 50%. So the executive's net cash outlay is $10,000.

Comparison: An employee who purchases the new stock for cash has the same taxable gain. But $20,000 also has to be paid for the stock. Net cash outlay: $30,000. That's three times the cash that would have been necessary in a stock exchange.

The IRS has approved option stock exchanges. The law specifically permits use of corporate stock to pay for stock in the same corporation acquired on exercise of an incentive stock option. And the Securities and Exchange Commission has said that these exchanges may be undertaken by corporate insiders.

Source: Francis M. Gaffney, national director of tax services, Main Hurdman & Cranstoun, CPAs, 280 Park Ave., New York 10017.

How to Read a Stock Ticker

Most investors do not have the time to follow the ticker tape closely. But there are some tape-watching tactics used by professional stock traders that don't take minute-to-minute observations and can help predict short-term market swings.

Techniques to consider:
Watch the prices of the market leaders. They usually change direction ahead of the broad list. Timing: If the Dow is down for a day, but the market leaders close near their highs, anticipate an imminent upswing in the market.

Compare price changes in mutual funds at the end of each day with price changes in the Dow and other major market averages. If the Dow changes significantly either up or down, but mutual funds do not show an equivalent percentage change, the Dow is not reflecting the true state of the market that day.

Good customers can ask their brokers for the final tick each day. (Truest tick pattern can be obtained at around 3:55 p.m. New York time.) Goal: Find how many issues traded at the close on an uptick (closing price was higher than the preceding price) and how many traded on downticks (closing price was lower than the previous price). Unchanged trades count as of the previous price change.

Rules:
If the market closes with a strong plurality of upticks (+ 200 or so) or with a rapidly improving tick, the odds are strong that the market will open favorably the next day. If the market closes with a strong plurality of downticks, the odds favor a weak opening.

A shift, say from −200 to + 200 right at the close indicates a short-term change in market direction.

If a falling market is about to rise, ticks often change from negative to positive at around 10:30 a.m. If a rising market is about to fall, positive ticks will turn negative then.

Even a strongly rising market will usually pause for breath during the day. Expect some tick weakening at around noon and again at around 3:00 p.m. Investors should use these pauses to accumulate positions.

It rarely pays to buy into a late tape or when trading volume is running at the rate of 13 million shares per hour. Prices are often better a day or so later when the tape quiets down. Be particularly careful about buying or selling options into a late tape. The worst option executions take place at such times.

How to Use the Daily Stock Charts

Use the daily charts of major market averages published in *The Wall Street Journal* and many local newspapers to forecast stock market reversals. Major clue: A gap between the bar line of one day's trading and the next, an area where no trading took place.

The gap represents an area through which prices are likely to move on the next market dip or rise. If the most recent gap was formed during a market advance, there is a good chance the gap will be filled during a subsequent market decline. If a gap was formed during a recent market decline, it will probably be filled during a subsequent market advance.

If a gap occurs following an advance or decline that has already lasted for several days, and the market then pauses, expect an immediate market reversal back through the gap.

Gaps formed on the first day of a market reversal often signify a strong move.

The Five Best-Performing Stock Market Indicators

Sentiment index. The number of bearish investment services as monitored by *Investors Intelligence,* a stock-market advisory. Bullish sign: Almost 50% of the investment advisers are bullish. Fewer than 17.8% of the advisers are bearish. (The advisory consensus is usually wrong at significant turns in the market.)

Member trading. Bullish when members of the New York Stock Exchange (NYSE) swing from the sell to the buy side. Bearish when they swing to the sell side. This indicator has a bias toward the sell side as a general rule, so deviations are what are significant.

Funds' cash. Bullish when funds have more than 9.4% in cash. Bearish when cash is below 6.2%.

Swing direction. Swings of more than 5% on the Dow. Bullish when up. Bearish when down.

Advance-decline figures. Two week daily average of advances minus declines on the NYSE as a percentage of total issues traded. Bullish when over + 13.8%. Bearish when below – 18.2%.

Investment strategy: The study that analyzed these indicators suggests that long positions in the stock market are justified when at least four out of five of the above indicators are in a bullish mode. Hold positions until the majority of indicators turn bearish. Sell short only when four out of five are in a bearish mode.

Source: Merrill Analysis, Inc.

Spotting a Stock Market Decline Before It Starts

Strong market moves frequently end in one- or two-day reversal spikes. Those spikes often provide advance warning of significant market turning points. Here are signs that a market decline may be coming.

The market will rise sharply in the morning on very high volume, with volume running at close to 15 million shares during the first hour of trading.

From 10:30 a.m. (Eastern time) on, the market will make little or no progress despite heavy trading throughout the day.

By the end of the first day, almost all the morning's gains will have been lost, with the market closing clearly toward the downside. Occasionally, this process will be spread over a two-day period.

Steps to take: When you see the pattern, either sell immediately or await the retest of the highs that were reached during that first morning. Such a retest often takes place within a week or two, on much lower trading volume. This may prove to be the last opportunity to sell into strength.

The patterns seen during one-day reversals occasionally take place early in the intermediate advances, with the backoff representing a test of previous lows. If such action appears prior to significant market gains, do not sell. Rather, buy during any near-term weakness. The market will probably resume its rise. However, if such a trading pattern occurs following a period of several weeks or months of rising prices, the odds increase that a genuine one-day reversal is occurring. Then take protective action.

How Professional Stock Traders Limit Their Losses

To preserve capital, professional stock traders almost always use stop-loss points to restrict losses when they assume short stock positions. How to do it: Set a loss point at which you will close out your position.

Stop distance guidelines from the experts
(as % of stock price)

Price	Low Volatility	Average Volatility	Speculative Volatility
Over 100	5	5	5
40 to 100	5	5	6
20 to 40	5	5	8
10 to 20	5	6	10
5 to 10	5	7	12
Under 5	5	10	15

Source: *The J.C. Bradford Market Timing Letter.*

When to Sell a Stock

It's very difficult to know when to sell a stock. Very little research has been done on the subject, and advice from brokers is usually vague and confusing. Typical comments: "Let's watch it one more day." "Can't tell it now, but you should get out on the next rally." "It's not doing well right now, but it's sure to come back over the long haul." If the stock you've bought has gone up, the two conflicting cliches on Wall Street are:" Can't get hurt taking a profit," and "Let your profits run."

What to do instead: When it comes to evaluating an individual stock, you should look for one thing—failure. This sounds austere, but what to look for is very specific: A stock that tries to rally fails to make a new high.

How to identify failure: The stock must sell below the price level at which it had held in a previous "correction" (decline). If you were to look at this sequence visually, on a stock chart, you would see a series of lower highs and lower lows. That type of action establishes failure. It defines the stock's trend as down, not up.

Sell! Put aside all hopes that the stock will stabilize or rally wildly or that it will come back if you hold it long enough. The market is telling you, in no uncertain terms, that something is wrong. You don't have to know what or why. That information frequently doesn't come out until the stock has tumbled a very long distance down. You've made an objective decision. Stick with it.

When to decide to sell: When the stock market is closed. That way, each little gyration won't emotionally affect your decision.

After you've made an objective decision, use a protective stop order. How it works: Tell your broker to sell the stock automatically when it drops below a certain point.

You can use stop orders effectively even if the stock rises. Each time the price advances, cancel the old stop order and enter a new one. One arbitrary rule: Set the stop order price at 10% below the current market price.

More information: *When to Sell,* by Justin Mamis and Robert Mamis, Farrar, Straus & Giroux, New York.

How to Call Turns In the Market

The adventurers who call turns in the stock market for a living depend on a number of indicators to identify a major turn. Every serious investor, however, should make some regular assessment of when a major move is more or less likely. Reason: 80% of the issues traded go with the overall market trend.

Fundamental rule: Market moves usually exhaust themselves after traveling a maximum 25% up or down from the 40-week moving average of the Dow Jones industrial average, Standard & Poor's 500 index, and the New York Stock Exchange composite index.

To calculate the moving average (usually called the current mean by professionals):

• Average the closing numbers on the index for the past 40 weeks.

• Each week, add the current number on the index and drop the earliest week's number. Then recalculate the 40-week average.

To read the results: The further the current average is from the current mean, the greater the chance that the market will shift direction.

Individual investor strategy: Keep the basic situation in view. Factor in what the forecasters are saying. Relate that to fundamental economic factors, especially interest rates, that affect the stock market. Make a personal judgment about the market trend. Use temporary fluctuations in the trend to execute strategy. Investors anticipating a major rise should buy during temporary drops, and vice versa.

Source: Peter De Haas, portfolio strategist, L.F. Rothschild, Unterberg, Towbin, 55 Water St., New York 10041.

How Options Traders Make Money in Declining Market

Puts provide a way of selling stock short in hope for a market decline, without the risk of severe loss usually associated with short selling. How puts work: Suppose XYZ Corp. is selling at $50 and you can purchase a July-50 put on the options exchange for $350. The put entitles you to sell 100 shares of XYZ at 50 until the expiration of that option the following July.

If XYZ were to decline to, say 40, at or before the option, an option conveying the right to sell the shares at 50 would be worth $1,000 (the $10 difference times 100 shares). The profit would accrue immediately to the option holder, who could exercise the option on shares that he could purchase on the open market at 40. Since the option holder paid $350, his gain would be $650, or 186% on a stock that declined by 20%.

Of course, if XYZ rose or stood still through the life of the option, the option would expire. This would result in a 100% loss. However, the maximum risk to the short-seller using the put would be $350, which is the cost of the obligation.

Straddles: More flexibility. The availability of listed puts, used with call options, provides some interesting opportunities for mathematically oriented investors. Straddles (using puts and calls) can produce profit regardless of the direction of market movement, provided that the underlying common moves away from its starting price by a certain amount.

Example: Assume XYZ at 50 again, the listed put selling for $350 (3½) and the listed July call, which entitles the option holder to buy 100 shares at 50, also selling at 3½. Instead of purchasing the put alone, you purchase both. Here are the workouts at different prices of XYZ at the expiration of both options.

Price XYZ	Put Value	Gain (Loss)	Call Value	Gain (Loss)	Net
70	0	– 350	20	+ 1650	+ 1300
65	0	– 350	15	+ 1150	+ 800
60	0	– 350	10	+ 650	+ 300
55	0	– 350	5	+ 150	+ 200
50	0	– 350	0	– 350	– 700
45	5	+ 150	0	– 350	– 200
40	10	+ 650	0	– 350	+ 300
35	15	+ 1150	0	– 350	+ 800
30	20	+ 1650	0	– 350	+ 1300

The position shows a profit as long as XYZ moves beyond the 43 to 57 price range, a 14%

movement in either direction from the starting price of 50.

It's possible to profit on both sides of a straddle. Example: If XYZ first rises to 60 and then falls to 40, you might sell or exercise your call at a profit in the rise and then sell or exercise your put for an additional profit in the fall. However, in practice, one side or the other of a straddle is usually exercised, not both.

Straddles are best purchased after the market has rested with a trading range for some time and you expect a breakout but are uncertain of the direction. And, of course, you should purchase an option only when option premiums (the price of options) are running below normal.

Options: The Pitfalls

Grim warning from a recent Securities and Exchange Commission study: 90% of individual investors who trade stock options lose money.

Reason: An option (to purchase a stock at a certain price in three, six, or nine months) can double in value within minutes. Unless brokers are sitting in their office watching the tape minute-by-minute (or investors are able to monitor options that closely), there is a good likelihood investors will miss their chance to make money.

Guideline: Many investment firms suggest that individuals should not put more than 20% of their portfolios in options. Trap: Still, brokerage firms are eager to sell options because the broker's commission, as a percentage of the purchase price of the security, is much higher for options than for stocks.

How options are pushed by brokers: They often persuade stockholders to write options on the stocks they hold to get extra income. Trap: You are limiting your upside potential by writing an option on stock you think has good long-term value.

Example: If a stock sells at $60, and you write a call at $70 (to make a small profit of, say, $500), you have to be willing to let the stock go at $70. You may then miss a substantial upward move at some later date.

Lure of options: Many investors are attracted by the leverage. Reality: Leverage is worse than useless if investors don't have a profitable investment.

How to Buy Options at Cheaper Prices

Since the options market is less fluid than stocks, it's important to buy on weakness and sell on strength.

The best times to buy call options are often around 11:00 a.m., 1:00 p.m., and 3:15 p.m. Eastern time. Why it works: The market often pauses then, even on strong days. Worst hours: 10:30 a.m., 2:30 p.m., and near the close.

It rarely pays to buy any type of option near the close of a strong day. Reason: Impatient buyers usually bid prices up at that time in anticipation of continued strength the following day.

Selling options is usually easier during periods of market strength.

Close-term options (less than six weeks of remaining life) should be purchased only with definite risk capital. Reason: Option markets are more liquid and volatile for the near term than the far term.

When interest rates are declining, purchase options only in anticipation of an immediate upside move in the underlying common. Principle: Option premiums tend to rise and fall with interest rates.

The Pros and Cons Of Investing in Warrants

A warrant is similar to an option in that it represents the right to purchase shares of stock at a specified price, the exercise price.

However, while listed call options have a maximum life of nine months, most warrants last several years. Rights for perpetual warrants never expire.

How they work: Like stock options, warrants sell either above or below their exercise value.

Example of a premium-priced warrant: An oil company warrant, with a life of two years, sells at 10⅛. That's a premium of nearly $3 over its exercise price of 7¼. The price of the company's stock is currently 15¼. It could possibly double within two years. Therefore, some investors are willing to pay a premium to have the right to buy what could be a $30 stock at a much lower price.

Example of a discounted warrant: A mini-conglomerate company's warrants expire next May. They can be exercised at $90. However, the stock is priced at only $44 currently. So it is highly improbable it will ever be exercised. Therefore, the warrant is selling at a deep discount. 75 cents. It is essentially deemed worthless, unless the stock takes an incredible leap.

If the stock price remains the same: The warrant will go down in value as the expiration date nears. It becomes totally worthless, of course, after the expiration date.

Warrants tend to be very volatile: Whichever way the stock moves, the warrants move in the same direction, but proportionally faster.

Advantages of warrants: Greater leverage. You can control a larger number of shares of the stock with a significantly smaller amount of capital than if you bought shares outright. This is an additional reason for the premium placed on many warrants. Warrants also give you the opportunity to limit your losses. Since the price of the warrant is minimal, you don't have to commit as much cash. If the stock market plummets, the percentage loss on the warrants may be high, but the face value is low.

Disadvantages of warrants: There is a limited universe of warrants to choose from. Also, warrants are issued for the most part by companies with less than AAA ratings. Don't expect to build up a portfolio of blue-chip warrants.

Best buys in warrants: Companies with stock that has taken a sudden heavy plunge for unusual causes. The stock may be cheap for six months or a year, then surge back upon recovery. Key: Look at the stock's underlying book value. If the stock is selling well below book while other stocks in the same category are much higher, the stock price may correct itself, causing the warrant to rise even faster.

More information: *Value Line Options and Convertibles.*

Stock Market Forecasting Through Technical Analysis

What is technical analysis? A discipline that focuses on the action of the stock market, as opposed to the earnings and dividend outlook for individual stocks. Assumption: The knowledge and future expectations of all the market participants are already reflected in the price. Key goal of technical analysis: To monitor the major trends and try to identify a major reversal or end to the trend. Reason it works: Price levels reflect not what stocks are worth, but what people think they are worth.

The strengths of technical analysis: For one thing, it allows you to make money without inside information or the input of the top research analysts. The charts of the price action of a specific stock tell all. What's more, an individual can follow a wide range of stocks, industry groups, commodities, and foreign stock markets with the aid of technical analysis. To study the fundamentals of each one of those markets, you are limited to a few of them.

By looking at the price pattern, you also get somewhat of a feel for how big a price move might be. Fundamental analysis cannot do this for you. For example: The Dow Jones industrial average built a base below 1000 for 15 years. When it finally broke through, the resulting move was an extraordinarily large one, as expected.

Technical analysis can tell you at what point to buy and sell a stock. The key: Where the stock has found support or met resistance in the past.

The limitations of technical analysis: It is not a science, but an art. It doesn't lend itself to precise formulas. Indicators work most of the time, or some of the time, but certainly not all the time.

The most frequent mistake in technical analysis: Investors anticipate a buy or sell signal before it actually happens. They lose patience and objectivity. The way to avoid this is always to let the market do the talking.

Dow signs of a breakthrough beyond 1000:
• A substantial number of stocks (at least 250 to 300 of them) hit the new-high list.
• Volume runs in excess of 60 million shares a day.
• Interest rates clearly peak and head down.
• The action of the stocks on the Dow Jones industrial index is confirmed by strong moves in the utility and transportation averages.

Source: Martin J. Pring, consulting editor, *The Bank Credit Analyst,* and author of *Technical Analysis Explained,* McGraw-Hill Inc., New York.

Stock Splits: Myth and Reality

Stock splits, usually welcomed by investors, are not really in the investor's best interest at all. Reason: Stock splits nearly always raise the cost of investing. Sales commissions, listing fees, and state transfer taxes all increase.

Example: If you want to buy 200 shares of a $40 stock that recently split two for one, commissions and fees will be twice as much as what they would be to buy 100 shares of an $80 stock.

Corporations tend to misrepresent this consequence of stock splits. Since they must report higher costs in a proxy statement, many firms state that, after a stock split, fees may go up. Reality: They go up and only up.

Another misconception: People believe a stock that is split and selling for a lower price is more marketable. Reality: Any upward effect is very short-term. Split stocks often go down. For instance, in the eight months after IBM split four for one in 1979, the price went down about 40%.

How to Judge a Mutual Fund

Equity mutual funds are an alternative to individual stocks. They are an easy way to participate in the stock market. They enable the investor to diversify risk and obtain professional management.

Key question: How do you chose the right equity fund out of the hundreds available? How do you know what kind of risk you are taking?

To choose a fund:

Determine your goals. Decide if you are in for the short term (a year or two, because you would like to make a profit and buy a house) or for the longer term (awaiting retirement).

Use comparative fund listings (like those charted at the end of the *Wiesenberger Report*) to identify which funds have performed best over the past 20-, 15-, 10-, and 5-year periods. The charts make it simple to pick out the funds that have performed best.*

Research the performance of the best funds by comparing an individual fund's performance for the past years with the performance of the Dow Jones industrial average and the Standard & Poor's Index for those years. Example: If the Dow is up 20% and the fund is up 50%, the fund is likely to do well in an up market. (Its record should be fairly consistent and its management stable.) If the Dow in a number of years is down, and the fund is down much more, it usually means the fund is a high risk in a down market.

*Listings of mutual funds and their performance data are available from: Investment Company Institute, 1775 K St NW, Washington, DC 20006; Lipper Analytical Distributors, 74 Trinity Place, New York 10006; No-Load Mutual Fund Association, 655 Third Ave., New York 10017; Wiesenberger Investment Companies Services, 870 Fifth Ave., New York 10019.

To maximize dollars for the short term:

• Pick a high-risk speculative fund that tends to do extraordinarily well in an up market.

• Invest in more than one.

• To make more (and risk more), borrow money against your mutual fund shares to leverage your investment. This type of investing requires a good sense of market timing to determine when to take profits. While you may be able to make substantial profits on your leveraged investment, you are betting that the fund will appreciate more than interest rates. If the market starts falling, you will have to take a beating.

For a long-term investment in a mutual fund: Look at the record of funds that have done well in up markets and have conserved their capital in down markets. Use *Wiesenberger* to track individual years. Choose good performers that went down no more than the Dow in poor years.

Open-end versus closed-end funds: With an open-end fund you have a guaranty that the fund will buy back your shares at whatever market value they are worth. This gives you both liquidity and an element of security. In a closed-end fund, there are a finite number of shares traded on the open market. They may sell for less than their underlying asset value if there is little demand. There is more risk with a closed-end fund when it comes time to take your profit.

Load versus no-load: Load funds charge a sales commission up to 8½% when you purchase them. No-loads do not. Both charge management fees. No-loads are attracting most of the money these days. The record shows no performance difference between the two.

Management: Look for a fund with consistent management. A parent company that is financially strong can attract better managers and has the ability to keep them. Make sure the fund's manager is the same one who was with the fund last year and the year before, assuming the record is good.

Look at a fund with a family. It may be convenient to use a fund that has other types of funds in-house. Examples: Tax-free funds, bond funds, money-market funds. Reason: An investor doesn't know where the stock market, bond market, or money market will be five years from now. Although you can always switch funds on your own, it's more convenient to switch by just making a telephone call.

Look at the total net asset of the fund. It may be a factor in profitability. Smaller funds are likely to outperform large ones. Reason: If managers have a large amount of money to invest, they are not going to take a position in a small company even if it is a very attractive one. Why: Tracking it is too time consuming and will not be significant in the fund's earnings. Also, if a company turns sour, it's hard for a large fund to sell so much stock quickly without forcing down the price. Probable limit: $500 million in assets. Better: Less.

Watch the redemption rate of the funds. That's the rate at which people are withdrawing their money. Reason to keep alert: If a fund is having massive redemptions, its management is having problems. Worse: The fund now is being forced to liquidate positions for cash to meet redemptions, which complicates its problems.

Funds where there are huge fluctuations of assets may signal a problem. They may be flooded with money at times by pension-fund managers and overseas money managers who play the U.S. stock market through no-load mutual funds. Trap: When the mutual fund manager has to redeem these positions quickly, it will hurt the performance of the fund, and therefore your investment.

Source: Stanley Egener, executive vice-president Neuberger Berman Management Co., Inc., managers of nine mutual funds with $500 million in assets, 522 Fifth Ave., New York 10036.

Choosing a Money-Market Fund

Timing investments is more important in picking a money-market fund than choosing the best yield over a short period of time,

which is the rate usually advertised. Criteria: Best performance over the latest two years. Current average maturity of securities in fund's portfolios.

How to use the information: The average maturity of securities is used as an indicator of what will happen to interest rates in the near future. When maturities shorten: Interest rates may rise. When maturities lengthen: Interest rates may be about to fall.

Simple strategy for individual investors: Pick a fund with short maturities when interest rates are rising. Go into a fund with longer maturities when rates are going down. Reason: As interest rates fall, the assets in the money fund's portfolio appreciate, which means increased income for the fund when these assets are sold.

Safety of money funds: Many potential money-fund investors shun the funds because there is no Federal Deposit Insurance Corporation-type protection, as there is for bank deposits. Reality: There is little risk. No fund is allowed to have more than 5% of its assets in a single security. Massive multibankruptcies and defaults on government debts would have to precede a money-fund collapse.

Conservative strategy: Investors who feel nervous about funds invested in offshore certificates of deposit can stick with funds that invest in nothing but Treasury bills (T-bills) or in repurchase agreements from banks (so-called repos, which are backed by T-bills). Other funds pledge not to invest in anything foreign.

Check services and service charges. As a guideline to good service: Some funds invest your money the day your check arrives.

Minimum initial investment: None, to over $3,000. Subsequent deposits also may be limited: Over $100 or over $500. Key: You won't get the high yield on all your money if you can't put together the minimum amount quickly.

Checking privilege: Some charge for the service, others do not. The minimum check can be $250, or it can be $500 or more, depending on the fund. A lower minimum allows a family more flexibility.

Bottom line: A bigger annualized rate of return on your money is possible this year if you are willing to switch from one money fund into another, and back and forth to equity funds occasionally. (Some 80 to 100 funds offer convenient switch services.)

Fund size: It's unimportant. Frequently, the best performers are the leanest, because they're the fastest-moving.

Source: William E. Donoghue, publisher of *Donoghue's Moneyletter*, and *Donoghue's Money Fund Report*. Donoghue is also the author of the *Complete Money Market Guide*, Harper & Row, New York.

Buying Treasury Bills

People buying Treasury bills (T-bills) through their banks or brokerage houses pay a fee of $30 or more. It's possible to bypass the fee, however, and place the order yourself by submitting what's known as a noncompetitive tender. That means you are willing to pay the prevailing price set at the weekly government auction of T-bills every Monday.

To understand the bidding process, you need to know how T-bills are priced. That is, they are sold at less than face value, and at maturity they are redeemed at full face value. So while interest is being earned, there is no interest payment as such.

The interest rate earned by the purchaser usually is expressed in terms of the commonly used discount rate. This rate is based on the face value of the bill. It understates the investor's real return.

To make a valid comparison with coupon-bearing securities, such as corporate bonds, investors need to know the coupon-equivalent yield of the bill. This is the yield on the amount they actually invest.

Interest from T-bills, unlike the interest on bank savings certificates pegged to them, is exempt from state and local income taxes.

Investors who wish to bid on T-bills should submit their bids to one of the 12 regional Federal Reserve Banks around the country. The Banks have similar but not identical operating policies. Those described below apply to the Federal Reserve Bank of New York, so check with the Bank in your area to see if there are

any differences.

To be on the safe side, investors should mail their bids early enough to arrive at least one business day before the Monday auction. But people submitting bids in person can do so up until 1:30 p.m. on the day of the auction. The Wall Street office of the New York Fed—which serves residents of New York State, Connecticut's Fairfield County, and the 12 northern counties of New Jersey—is open for business between 9 a.m. and 3 p.m.

You must either fill out a tender form (provided by the Fed) or send a letter that indicates, among other things, whether you wish to reinvest your money when the T-bill matures.

Even though T-bills are sold at discount, you must pay the full $10,000 face value of the bill at the time you submit your bid. You may pay in cash, with a personal certified check, or with an official bank check drawn on a bank in the New York Federal Reserve District.

Any check must be made out payable to the "Federal Reserve Bank of New York." A check from a third party, payable to you and then endorsed by you over to the Bank, will not be accepted. Nor will a check drawn on a money-market mutual fund.

A few days after the auction, the New York Fed will mail you a discount check, representing the difference between the purchase price and the face value of the bill.

What you will receive: An ordinary receipt that links up to a book entry in a government ledger, attesting to ownership of a T-bill.

More information: Write for the free booklet *Basic Information on Treasury Bills*, Federal Reserve Bank of New York, 33 Liberty St. NY. 10045.

Treasury Bills as Leverage in Stock Trading

Margin-account investors can take a beating in a volatile market when interest rates are high. A better strategy: Invest in Treasury bills

(T-bills) or bonds. Then borrow against the bills (brokerage firms will lend up to 90 cents on the dollar of face value) for money to trade in the stock market.

Several advantages:

• Assured income on the T-bill, no matter what happens to the stocks. Thus, a hedge.

• T-bill income is not taxable on state and local returns. Bonus: The interest paid to brokers is fully deductible.

• T-bills offer instant liquidity.

• No margin calls. Timing of trades is totally your own decision.

• Like a passbook loan, it makes credit easier to get as money becomes tighter.

Think in terms of buying and selling securities on a short-term price basis. Use the guaranteed income from the T-bill to neutralize the effects of market volatility.

If you elect to hold a stock, the numbers begin to go against you if interest rates continue to climb during the holding period. This is because interest on the T-bill is fixed. To avoid this danger, establish an annual rate-of-return goal for every invested dollar. Whenever that goal is reached, take the profit. This gives you the option of sitting out the rest of the year if you don't like market conditions.

Bookkeeping bonus: Collateralizing a margin account with T-bills is not only the best but also the most convenient and economical way of taking advantage of high interest rates and, at the same time, keeping trading money available. Accounting is easy, since the account is debited with interest on a running basis. You see your margin charge every month and know what you can expect in interest at the end of every holding period.

Source: Peter De Haas, portfolio strategist, L.F. Rothschild Unterberg Towbin, 55 Water St., New York 10041

Bond-Buying Strategy

The classic bond-buying opportunity when interest rates drop: Investors can lock in high yields and defer interest income, too. One study calculates that 20-year, AAA-rated industrial bonds rose an average of 15.6% during five interest rate swings. These swings, from peak to trough, usually lasted for about one year.

Conservative strategy: AAA-rated corporates or Treasury issues.

Aggressive strategy: Lower-rated issues that swing more in price, providing greater tax deferral (and greater risk). However, even speculators avoid bonds rated lower than A when the depth of recession is not completely clear.

When to Avoid Bond Mutual Funds

Bond mutual funds, either corporate or municipal bond funds, are probably *not* a good deal unless the management fee charged by the fund is very low (½ % or less). They do provide diversification, but for most investors buying the bonds directly through a broker is cheaper. One-time sales commission on a purchase of $25,000 worth of bonds is about $125. Fund annual management fees can be as much as $250/year on same-sized purchase.

Exception: Money market funds provide more services and are worth the fees.

Source: *The Only Investment Guide You'll Ever Need,* by Andrew Tobias, Harcourt Brace Jovanovich, New York.

Profiting from Junk Bonds

Institutional investors generally ignore junk bonds, which is why prices are low. Reasons: (1) Pension-fund managers stay out because they're investing conservatively for people's retirement. (2) The volume of junk bonds is limited, and institutional investors with massive cash inflows to invest find that they distort the market and ruin profitability by making large purchases. (Small purchases aren't worth their effort.) (3) Institutional investors often abandon lower-paying junk bonds during periods of rising interest rates to take advantage of higher yields on more recent issues.

When to buy: The best time is when interest rates are peaking. As interest rates drop, low-yielding junk bonds become relatively more attractive and prices tend to rise quickly.

Who benefits from buying junk bonds: People with as little as $25,000 to invest as speculative capital.

Risks: Junk bonds derive their name from their poor rating, and the specter of default scares many people off. Should the recession become severe, the dangers are multiplied. But junk bonds are safer than they appear. The evidence:

(1) In the past 20 years, less than 3% of all junk bonds have defaulted.

(2) When default is imminent, senior creditors (banks, insurance companies, etc.) usually defer their claims or settle for much less to keep the company out of bankruptcy. Junior bondholders, in practice, almost always come out with full payment.

(3) Many junk bonds are issued by America's top corporations, which may experience hard times but aren't likely to go bankrupt.

Strategy for investing in junk bonds:

Diversify. Spread a $25,000 investment over five to ten issues.

Pick bonds where the discount is due to lower yield and not to the risk of insolvency.

Look for bonds trading at the lowest prices. (Note: Junk bonds are traded on the New York and American Bond exchanges. Remember to add a zero to quotes when figuring price.)

Avoid issues where the government might intervene. (Example: Railroads, airlines, municipals.) Stay away from the real estate investment trusts (REITS) because they are illiquid and hard to figure.

Rule of thumb: If the junk bond has a ten-year maturity, assume the price ought to rise by 10% a year. Sell the bond if the price rises by 20% one year and reinvest in something else—unless attractive interest rates make the bond worth holding longer. Buy more bonds

if the price falls, because the return on investment at maturity will be that much greater.

Important: Junk bonds are discounted because the company's rating isn't very good. Don't expect to hear good news about the company. Don't get cold feet and sell out if the price begins to fall.

A Quick Course on Convertible Bonds

Many savvy investors look to convertible bonds as an attractive alternative to common stock. Convertibles can be exchanged for common shares in lieu of repayment of the note signified by the bonds. They generally yield more than the underlying common and provide nearly as much upside potential as the common with less risk.

One drawback: Convertibles usually sell at a premium over the conversion value (the value of the common shares into which they may be converted) because of the higher yields.

What to look for: Situations do occur where the common provides the higher yield and/or where the bond is selling so far above par value that its yield has become relatively insignificant. As a result, the convertible bonds may be selling close to or even below their actual conversion value.

Investors familiar with convertible opportunities may be able to take advantage of such situations by following this procedure:

Before purchasing common stock, check to see if convertibles either at conversion value or below happen to be available.

If you purchase convertibles at conversion value, you will save on commissions. And if you buy below conversion value (rare, but sometimes possible), you will have purchased the underlying common at an effective discount: The differential between the bond's conversion value and actual price.

If the common provides a higher yield than the convertible bonds, have your broker submit the bonds for conversion (usually takes two to three weeks). You will then be holding the higher-yielding common, purchased at a discount. Warning: Don't submit the bonds for conversion until immediately after the next interest payout, unless the payout has just passed. Bondholders lose accrued interest upon conversion. Most bonds pay interest semiannually.

Buying advice: Don't place "market orders" for convertibles. Bond markets are thinner than stock markets, and you can be hurt by a wide spread between bid and asked prices. Place definite limit orders.

More information: KV Convertible Fact Finder, Kalb, Voohris & Co., New York; *Value Line Options & Convertibles.* 5 East 44 St., New York.

Investing in Tax-Free Municipal Bonds

Tax-free bonds have always been popular with people in the upper income brackets. But middle-income investors should study them as well. If your family income is over $45,000 a year and you are in the 50% bracket, tax-frees may be a good alternative to your savings account. The higher your bracket, the more appropriate municipal bonds are.

The purpose of tax-free bonds is to preserve capital, with a good after-tax income. Use them instead of huge savings accounts or heavy investment in money-market funds. They are not usually used as a way to build an estate. They are generally more appropriate for older investors who need income but are not yet retired. As people approach retirement, they can pick the maturity most appropriate (municipals can mature in anywhere from one to fifty years). When income falls into lower brackets after retirement, investors can switch to corporate bonds or stocks.

To judge the yield, calculate the return for your tax bracket. For instance, if you buy a tax-free bond at 9% and your bracket is 50%, you would have to get an 18% yield on another investment for it to be equivalent after taxes.

Ways to invest in tax-free bonds:

Unit Investment Trust: A portfolio (put together by professionals) of various tax-free elements to diversify risk and maximize yield. In many states with income tax, a Unit Investment Trust uses a portfolio that qualifies for double tax-free status, generally state and local bonds plus Puerto Rican issues. A Unit Investment Trust does not use a professional portfolio manager after the original assortment of bonds is put together. You can get monthly, semiannual, or annual interest payments or participate in a reinvestment plan. There is also a secondary market enabling you to sell your shares. (Unit Investment Trusts require a $1,000 minimum investment. There is no annual management fee.)

Managed bond fund: The fund is a diversification of bonds, like the Unit Investment Trust, but it is professionally managed throughout its lifetime. Its yields are expected to be somewhat higher. And there is a management fee.

Individual bond: It requires research to select the right one. The quality of municipals is rated by Moody's and Standard & Poor's independent rating services. If you are extremely concerned about the risk of bankruptcy, buy a bond that is insured against default by an insurance association. Another way: An AAA-rated low-risk issue. While 98% of all municipalities met their debt obligations during the Great Depression, it pays to buy something you won't lose sleep over.

General obligation versus revenue bond: A novice in tax-free investments would probably feel more secure with a general obligation bond. It is backed by the full faith and credit of the issuer. A revenue bond depends on the income of a specific facility. For instance, some bridge and road bonds may not have sufficient revenue from cars and trucks to pay interest.

Liquidity of municipals is fairly good. Tax-frees are usually bearer bonds and can easily be sold. However, if the market is down because interest rates have gone up, you may lose some of your capital if you sell before maturity. Therefore, avoid investing money that may be needed. Have a savings cushion as well as bonds.

Tax-swapping is a trading technique that allows you to take a tax loss when you trade one bond for another of equivalent return and quality, if your original bond is below cost. (In reality, you have lost nothing if you hold your next purchase to maturity.) This has traditionally been done by insurance companies and corporations aggressive in money management. Do it when you want to offset a capital gain on another investment.

Don't be passive about bond investment. You shouldn't be tied down to one of these bonds. Big tax swaps should be used to offset large capital gains.

Discounted tax-frees enable you to get not only the yield but also a capital gain when the bond matures. Important: Quality, price, yield, maturity.

Source: William E. Mercer, vice-president, Merrill Lynch Pierce Fenner & Smith, 1 Financial Plaza, Fort Lauderdale, FL 33394

When to Invest in Annuities

Annuity advantages:
• The principal invested is safe, comparable to a bank account.
• High interest rates.
• Interest earned is tax-deferred. Interest earned is not taxed until the annuity is cashed in or annuitized. Investors should weigh the advantages of annuities versus municipal bonds. The bonds are tax-exempt, not tax-deferred. But annuities are not subject to investment risk.

Disadvantages: Investors must pay a penalty for cashing in an annuity before a stipulated number of years has passed. Investors pay a 7% penalty for cashing in an annuity in the first year, a 1% penalty for cashing it in the sixth year and zero thereafter.

Who should investigate annuities:
• Individuals who are in a high tax bracket.
• Those willing to set aside funds for a number of years.
• Those who do not want investment risk.

• Those looking for a relatively high rate of return.

How annuities work: There are two ways to fund an annuity: (1) A single, lump-sum payment. (2) Systematic (e.g., monthly) payments. At maturity, the annuity must be cashed in or annuitized.

The interest rate is pegged each year by the insurer. In general, the yearly rate fluctuates with general interest rates. Some policies give the investor an option to withdraw his principal without penalty if at any time the interest rate drops below a certain level.

Payout after cashing in comes in several forms: in a lump sum, as a life annuity, or as a joint and survivor annuity. The latter can include guaranteed payment for a predetermined number of years: 10 years, 15 years, and so on.

Key: Investors pay tax on interest earned only as received.

Early withdrawal: Investors may withdraw their principal from an annuity without cashing it in, provided withdrawals are made before the annuity starting date. But there is a tax cost: Taxes are due on the difference between the cash surrender value and the amount of the withdrawal. A 5% penalty is imposed on the taxable part of the withdrawal if it occurs within 10 years of the investment.

Sample annuity investment: A 48-year-old executive invests $100,000 in an annuity yielding 11.5% annually. Assuming that the interest rate remains the same, the annuity's value after seven years is $214,000. At that point, the investor withdraws his principal, puts it to other uses, and lets the accrued interest alone compound. His tax cost at a 50% rate: $50,000 plus a $5,000 penalty. He will have $45,000 to reinvest.

Result: After another ten years, assuming an annual interest rate of 11.5%, the annuity is worth $338,000. Upon retirement at 65, the investor elects to receive an annuity for life with ten years guaranteed. (He will receive $35,000-$38,000 per year.) This annuity will be subject to an exclusion ratio for the amount of the original investment of $100,000.

Source: Paul E. Fierstein, CLU, benefits and compensation consultant, 9 E. 38 St., New York 10016.

Trading Commodities

The fundamental fact about commodities that all players must reckon with: Incredible volatility. The fluctuation *per day* averages about 1%. Multiplied by a leverage factor of 20, the trader can anticipate at least a 20% profit or loss *per day*. It's hard to have the stomach to cope with these losses or gains in a businesslike fashion. But anyone who actively trades tangibles (gold, diamonds, paintings, or antiques) is probably a good candidate for commodities.

Comparison to the stock market: The aggregate value in commodities is much larger than the stock market. And the dynamics are much greater. Result: Money is made and lost faster. And there are many more pitfalls.

In the stock market, you can lose money in bits and pieces. You don't realize a loss until you sell out your position. Capital invested in the commodities market is all at risk. You don't have to place a buy or sell order to win or lose. Money is credited to your account if your position is right. If it's wrong, the broker tells you how much you owe.

An old saying in the commodities market: You never make money from the market; the market only lends you money until it takes it back from you. It's probably true. And so is the estimate that 95% of the investors in commodities lose money. Although the commodity exchanges have arbitrary limits governing how much prices can rise and fall daily, investors can lose much more than they initially put up.

For beginners: Brokerage houses will let you put up as little as $50,000 for an individual commodities trading account. There are also managed group accounts for people who are ready to put at risk only $10,000-$20,000. Caution: A few of these groups have good records, but most are only a couple of years old. Results are not sufficient to evaluate them.

Making an emotional move is the most common way speculators get hurt. The market is so volatile and moves so fast that an investor is, in effect, constantly making a buy or sell decision. And the leverage is so great that a move of a few cents means a few thousand dollars.

Investors must: Expect to make wrong decisions that could cost a great deal of money. Set a time horizon once a decision is made, and stick to it.

General rule: With leverage so high, you may expect to win or lose 25% of capital on any day.

Problem: When you are making and losing such large sums you forget one of the basic principles of running a business: Recognize the real costs.

The average holding in commodities is only four or five days. A $60 commission every time you make a move can mean thousands of dollars in commissions a year that wipes out a good part of your gain.

The difference between the bid and asked prices for a commodity can run three times the commission cost. Result: When you get into a commodity you are frequently already down 20%.

Human frailties are likely to emerge in commodities trading. Reason: People get excited about making a lot of money, due to the volatility. Professionals recognize that the chief effect of volatility is to relieve the public of the maximum amount of money in the minimum amount of time.

The psychology of trading:

• Movements during the day play on the emotions. If you are wrong, you have to adopt a very unemotional attitude toward the loss. The worst thing to do: Keep calling your broker all day.

• Have the moral fiber to stay with your conviction. The average trader must increase the time horizon for holding a contract 15-fold before getting the chance to make a profit. Example: Instead of trading every three or four days, hold on to the contract for 50 days. That gives you a saving on commissions and the bid/asked penalties.

• Worst mistake of all: Doubling up after a gain or loss. When you do this just a small loss will wipe you out.

• Looking for bargains is a mistake in the commodities market. When prices drop, don't buy. It is better to short when things start to look cheap.

Strategy for outsiders: Don't convince

yourself that you can read the daily financial pages and get sufficient insight into commodities. You are trading against experts who know the number of freight-car loadings in Peru and the hourly temperatures in Russia. Whatever insight you have probably won't be superior to theirs.

Exception: If you are in a business where you are sensitive to certain trends (like the impact of a fall in sugar prices on the candy business), your understanding may be of value in a long-term time frame.

Personal knowledge gives you a realistic outlook that helps you invest in commodities. If this is the case: Consider at least a six-month horizon in which you want to move. Don't put up a minimum margin. Put up 15% instead of the required 5%. Plan on maintaining your position.

Fundamental impact of interest rates on commodities: When rates are high, everything else goes down. Investors lose sight of this, because when rates are high everything is usually booming. They forget that a disaster could just be around the corner. If you are long when interest rates are high, you will get wiped out.

Rule: Go against short-term trends and with long-term trends. Example: If soybeans have gone down 15% in a month and up 3% the last week, don't buy. Sell short!

Source: Victor Niederhoffer, chairman, Niederhoffer, Cross & Zeckhauser, Inc., a merger and acquisitions firm that specializes in selling companies in the $2 million to $25 million range, 49 W. 57 St., New York 10019.

Mistakes Commodity Speculators Make

Niederhoffer, Cross & Zeckhauser Commodities is an active trader of commodities for its own account. Its operation involves the use of microcomputers, which principals Victor Niederhoffer and Susan Cole have programmed to take account of the interrelated nature of commodity markets all over the world on a minute-by-minute basis. So far, Niederhoffer, Cross & Zeckhauser has

achieved great success in maintaining a highly profitable record. However, on the road to success, they made numerous mistakes that they feel every speculator should guard against. They are of three types:

Emotional errors:

Buying and selling on hope and fear, rather than on principle. Hope springs eternal for commodities traders since there is so much upside potential. Urge when you have a loss: Give it a little more time. Pure human emotion prods traders to wait "another half hour, until the price goes back up." When traders have a profit, they think: Take the money and run. Best: Have a plan and follow it.

Following the advice of a broker. They usually call when you have a profit, which they encourage you to take. It seems sage to say: You can never go broke taking a profit. But the truth is, you will always go broke taking small profits. Speculators can only really win in commodities by taking a very large profit. You must average the many small losses against a few large gains.

Having a bullish bias. In the commodities market, unlike the stock market, it is as easy to sell short as to buy long. Many traders got into the market when gold was rising, and they got stuck because they only knew how to go long and hold. On short positions the tendency is to close out too soon.

News-jerking—taking action because of a breaking news story. Example: Buying a metal because the prime interest rate has just been lowered. Key: The market is too smart and varied for people to make money by doing the obvious a few minutes before the herd.

Lacking perspective. One advantage average speculators do have over the instant traders is distance from the market. They are not influenced by hourly price gyrations. Once you start waking up in the morning wanting to know the closing price of gold in Hong Kong or the morning opening in London, you are on your way out. Reason: You wind up making trading decisions based on international rumors, which represent temporary factors. Example: Gold moved right back down when the Russians marched a few miles away from Poland, and just a few hours later the Socialist party won the election in France.

Capital management mistakes:

Taking a position so large it becomes impossible to offset if the market moves against you. You're locked in.

Pyramiding. Adding to positions going in your favor. You can be wiped out by a small move against you.

Having too much of your capital on one side of the market, either long or short.

Trading in markets that are illiquid relative to the size of your position. The risk: There are not enough floor brokers to bid against your positions. You are exposed to poor executions and are locked in.

Short-term perspectives:

Not having a specific buy and sell rule in mind when opening a position. Result: You hold on indefinitely.

Being overconcerned about commissions and spreads. They really represent a very small fraction of the potential return or uncertainty. A related mistake is to try to buy at the bid and sell at the offer.

Relying too much on opening and closing calls. These calls are only estimates based on transitory factors. They frequently fool the public and even experienced floor brokers.

Trading during inactive periods, before holidays, near the close on Fridays. Moves during these periods tend to be in the opposite direction from the next big price change and are designed to relieve the speculator of good positions.

Forgetting momentum. Trends in commodities reverse only for a day or two and tend to continue for extended periods. Don't stand in the way of a freight train.

Focusing on selling out at round numbers. The way floor traders manipulate stop orders (usually at round numbers) militates against being able to sell at round numbers.

Buying on the cheap. Never buy a commodity just because the price is low. The longs have lost all their capital at these lows, and it will be a long time before they have the courage to bull things up again.

Source: Victor Niederhoffer and Susan Cole, Niederhoffer, Cross & Zeckhauser, Inc., 49 W. 57 St., New York 10019.

Investing in Foreign Currencies

There are two ways to take advantage of the ups and downs of managed floating rates between currencies: Investing and speculating.

Investing: Your main concern should be to conserve your capital, not to make large gains. At any time that your dollars are weak you want to put them into a stronger currency. For several years, it made sense to put savings into German marks, Swiss francs, and Japanese yen.

This has changed however. While several years ago there were strong and weak currencies, the flight into the strong currencies is coming to an end. The philosophical reason: The strong currencies have become weaker. Currency valuation is based in part on inflation rates, and the inflation level is creeping up in Germany, Switzerland and Japan.

If you have savings: It may be better to have them in Swiss francs than in U.S. dollars at any time the Swiss bank pays you 5% interest or better on those francs. Allowing for inflation and currency depreciation, that could be the equivalent of getting 12% interest on a savings account in the U.S. Problem: Converting currency from dollars to francs may be costly, especially if it's done in Switzerland. Have the currency exchanged in New York, and expect to pay ½% to 1% of the entire amount for the currency translation.

If you can only get a 2% or 3% interest rate on a Swiss bank account, forgo the option. There is some inflation in Switzerland, and the low interest rate will wipe out any advantage the differential could give.

Speculating: It still offers a way to make large gains on currency fluctuations. Example: If you can anticipate that the British pound will decline in the near future by 3%, then you might think about selling the pound on margin on a forward basis. Then, a 3% decline on a 3% margin will mean a 100% profit on the actual amount put at risk. (If you are known to a bank, you may be able to get the currency forward without paying the margin. Or it might cost you 5% if you are not a regular customer.)

Even experts are frequently misled in foreign-currency dealings. So if you are a rank amateur, you may have a hard time juggling foreign inflation rates, interest rates, and balance of payments, the most important bases for the way a currency will turn.

Source: Guenter Reimann, editor-in-chief, *International Reports*

Investing in Gold and Silver Without Buying Bullion

Gold and silver certificates are available through Citibank, the Bank of Nova Scotia, and Bache Halsey Stuart Shields.

Advantages of certificates:

• Avoid sales tax, since the gold and silver are held outside your state, and you never take physical possession.

• Eliminate storage fees, insurance costs, and shopping for best price.

• Add no assaying fees when you sell the bullion.

Certificates are offered in dollar values instead of ounces. Example: Citibank requires a minimum initial purchase of $1,000. Subsequent purchases: $100. A buyer can purchase fractions of an ounce of gold or silver.

Cost: A 3% service charge for purchases below $50,000, and another 1% upon sale. Plus a ½% annual service charge. And certificates can be used as collateral for a loan.

Purchasers of large amounts of gold or silver may be better off with a commodities broker, whose commissions are negotiable.

How to Make Money in Real Estate

Best way to make money from real estate: Buy when times are so tough that insurance companies and banks are taking possession of properties they don't want and are trying to sell them off quickly. The best places to look are regions experiencing major economic dislocations.

Indications of a good deal: No new building is going on in the area. You can purchase an older office building and rent space for $9 per square foot while owners of new buildings must rent at $14 per square foot or more just to break even.

How to do it: Find a general partner who can locate and arrange the right deal and will help you manage the property.

Pool funds with a group of investors to meet the purchase price, if you don't have the sum to invest.

Avoid investing in an area too far from where you live. You should be able to visit the property and return home in one day. Proximity ensures that you will visit the property frequently, and keeps you in touch with demographic changes and economic conditions.

Get invited to meetings of the local property manager's association. (It will be easy.) They are held once a month to give managers a chance to talk over common problems. You will meet many promising general partners who can help you manage any property that you decide to buy.

Picking a general partner: The importance of finding a good general partner cannot be overemphasized. You may have to talk to hundreds of candidates before you finally pick one. The general partner should:

• Be able to buy a property at 25% under the market. To determine value expertly, the partner probably should be a member of the American Institute of Real Estate Appraisers.

• Be willing to screen as many as 100 deals before coming to you with the one that makes sense for you.

• Have a proven history of money-making deals.

• Know how to manage a property effectively. Best: A Certified Property Manager.

Sales commission limit: 1½%. Typically, sales commissions can run as high as 6% to 10%. (That can amount to more than individual limited partner's equity in the project.)

To run an independent check: Get references from the partner. Call up a bank or insurance company on the list of references. Ask how they would compare the pros and cons of your prospective partner with another manager whose name you pick out of the yellow pages. You will be amazed at how much you can learn when reference makes an actual comparison.

Look at some of the properties the partner manages. Spend some time with the partner. Is the person's style one that you feel comfortable with? When you ask questions, does the partner answer each one immediately? (That could be a bad sign.) Or does the person promise to check first and get back to you with a reply?

Structuring the deal: Be sure it's set up so that the general partner has plenty of incentive to work hard for you. Most general partners get quite a bit on the front end and only, say, 15% of the profits. That is the wrong way. Get the partner to invest at least 1% of the money put into the project. Give up a larger share of the profits. Recommended: 25%. This way, the general partner doesn't get paid before you do. Strategy: Pay a bonus of perhaps $25,000 if all targets are met after the first 12 months.

Turning a property around: It is not as hard as it seems, provided that you select basically good properties that have been neglected due to the former owner's cash-flow problems. With some spending on improvements and maintenance, you can boost tenant morale and attract new tenants.

First priority: Never entrust the management of a $3 million to $4 million property to a $555-a-month live-in manager. Offer the manager a profit motive to discover and find solutions to problems. Suggestion: Give the resident manager 25% of every new tenant's first month's rent in addition to salary and apartment.

Interview tenants yourself. You may discover that their dissatisfaction can be easily remedied. Example: One apartment owner wouldn't change the air-conditioner filters, which meant higher electrical bills for the tenants. Indicate to tenants that major changes are in the works. Example: An office building had 80% occupancy for a four-year period. When tenants were told that a major campaign to attract new tenants was soon to be launched and that the current tenants could have first pick of extra space, the occupancy rate shot up to 95%, solely from expansion by the existing tenants.

Plan on selling the building at a profit in a few years. Sell when occupancy is up from 80% to 100%, rents are up to market level from way below, and the building is throwing off a lot of cash flow.

Source: Robert J. Underwood, a real estate agent specializing in turnaround real estate investments, Underwood Financial Planning, 400 Century Park S. Bldg; Birmingham, AL 35226.

Screening Potential Real Estate Investment

Rules of thumb can be dangerous if relied on exclusively for real estate investments, but they do offer a quick and simple way to screen properties. Two rules: (1) Don't pay more than six to seven times the gross annual rent, or ten times the net operating income, unless the going rate in the area is consistently higher. (2) Operating expenses eat up from 50% to 70% of gross rentals in an apartment building (leaving 30% to 50% gross income), depending on geographic area. Major costs include vacancy and collection losses, repairs and maintenance, management fees, and heating oil, before deducting taxes and mortgage payments.

Caution: In-depth analysis of area and property, plus expert legal and real estate advice, is still a must before a final decision is made.

The Absentee Investor

A group of investors decided to buy a garden apartment 200 miles away from their primary residence. A month before the closing, a problem arose. Operating expenses suddenly went up. The developer had great difficulty collecting the increases from the tenants. As a result, the buyers decided not to invest. Reasoning: At that distance, they would have an even harder time than the current owner, a local developer, controlling expenses and collecting rents.

They made a sensible decision. Absentee landlords should not insulate themselves from problems. If they do, their problems magnify.

This does not mean that you should never invest outside your area. But if you do, be prepared for some aggravation. To protect yourself:

Retain an established and financially sound management company. But do not abdicate all your responsibilities. Insist on written reports, at least monthly. They describe the status of the project. Also: Carefully monitor the financial and operating statements.

Make periodic visits. There is no substitute for being on the scene. It is the best way to judge how well or how poorly your investment is doing, and why. If there is bad news, the sooner you learn about it, the better.

Consider an experienced real estate operator who lives near the project as a partner. It is not the same as being there yourself, but it is better to have a surrogate who has a stake in the success of your project than someone who is working for a fee.

Protection when investing at a distance: Purchase passive real estate (a project that is not management-intensive). Example: Management is usually more important to the operation of rental apartments than to a neighborhood shopping center. The best investment is probably a retail store net-leased to a high-credit company. The tenant in this kind of transaction pays a fixed but guaranteed minimum rent. It is responsible for maintenance and repairs. It pays all operating expenses. Your upside potential is limited since the rent is fixed for the term of the lease. Possibility: The tenant may pay additional rent based on the volume of sales in the store.

Source: Robert L. Nessen, chairman, March-Eton Corp., a real estate investing and consulting firm, 81 Middle St., Concord, MA 01742 and author of *The Real Estate Book*, Little, Brown & Co., Boston.

How Real Estate Sellers Trick Buyers

The urge to invest in real estate exposes buyers to sharp practices by sellers.

Most common distortion: Claims of high-paying tenants. Example: The rent roll of a commercial building shows that nine tenants pay $6 to $8 per square foot and three pay $12. Essential: Find out who the high-paying tenants are. One may be the building owner, and the others may be affiliated with the seller.

Any fudging of current and future income can cost an investor tens of thousands of dollars. Example: In a small building, the seller reports that 10 tenants each pay $400 a month ($48,000 a year). If buildings in the area sell for six times gross, the market price would be $228,000. But suppose the owner had prepared to sell the building by raising the rents from $350 to $400 a month. Impact: That increase in the rent roll cost the buyer $36,000 (the difference between six times $48,000 in annual rents and six times $42,000).

Even worse: The impact on future rent increase. Very likely: If the rents in the building were close to market before the increase, the owner may well have offered tenants a free month's rent or a delayed increase. A delayed increase means: The buyer will not realize as much income as forecast. A free month's rent means: The actual increase in rents was only $17 an apartment, not $50. If the new owner tries to jump rents well above that, tenants may move.

Other claims that buyers must investigate:

Low operating expenses. Sellers may be operating the building themselves to avoid a management fee. If buyers cannot take care of the building personally, this fee must be added to real operating expenses. And if sellers do not factor it in, the bank will when it calculates the maximum supportable mortgage.

Reasonable property tax. If the building has not been assessed for several years, the buyer may have a substantial tax bite on the next assessment. Another trap: The seller has made an addition to the building that has not yet been recorded with the tax assessor. Precaution: Ask the local assessment office for a tax card or listing sheet. It will show the building's assessment and when it was assessed. If it was assessed a year and half ago and there has been no significant addition to the building, reassessment may not hurt the buyer. But if it has not been assessed for eight years, there could be a significant tax boost.

While checking the tax card or listing sheet, check the owner's property description against the one listed. If the owner says that 20,000 square feet are being sold, but the tax card says 15,000 square feet, there has been some addition to the structure that has not been recorded and, therefore, has not been assessed. Or, there may be an assessment error that, when corrected, will raise costs.

Low insurance premiums. Is coverage in line with the structure's current value? What does the policy cover? Ask to see the policy. Ask an insurance adviser: If coverage is insufficient, how much more will proper coverage cost?

Energy efficient. Verify the owner's claim with the local utility to determine actual energy costs. Also: Check with regulatory commissions to see whether utility companies are scheduled to increase their tariffs.

A real buy. Check the income statement with those of comparable buildings in the area. Helpful: The annual income and expense analysis by geographical area and building type of the Institute of Real Estate Management.*

*430 N. Michigan Ave., Chicago 60611.
Source: Thomas L. O'Dea, O'Dea & Co., Inc., investment real estate consultants, 285 Stratford Rd., Winston-Salem, NC 27103, and senior editor of *Rental House and Condo Investor.*

Traps for the Real Estate Investor

Steer clear of existing shopping center and apartment house complexes. The cash flow thrown off by these deals is small in relation to the purchase price. There's little risk in such an investment. Accordingly, you will have to pay a premium to buy into one.

Be skeptical of any deal that sounds too good. The better the deal sounds, the riskier it probably is.

Don't get involved in government-sponsored or guaranteed projects. The government puts a cap on the amount of profits you can make. In a highly inflationary environment, you don't want to have your profits controlled.

Before you invest in apartment houses, make sure they have paved parking lots, pitched roofs (flat roofs leak), an exterior more than 50% nonwood, and floors made from lightweight concrete.

Information to get from the developer before you invest:

The developer must be strong financially. The biggest risk is noncompletion of a project due to financial problems of the developer. The developer should have liquid net worth two to three times the amount of equity capital to be invested in the project.

The most sophisticated real estate lenders in the country now should be involved in the front-end financing. That indicates the deal has credibility. The most sophisticated lenders in the country are Aetna, Travelers, Connecticut Mutual, and Connecticut General. If any of them participate in a project, it probably makes economic sense.

The developer should personally guarantee the deal, as well as provide an assurance in writing that the project will be completed.

Limited-partnership real estate investments: They are a good way to invest small amounts of money in real estate. But you must be careful. Guidelines:

• Be sure that the brokerage house underwriting the deal and offering it to you is participating in the investment. If the firm doesn't have enough faith to put its own money behind the project, you certainly shouldn't do so either.

• The law firm involved in the offering should be top quality. Take a look at the actual operating document. Ask your lawyer whether it's professionally prepared.

• Get an opinion from the law firm on the tax benefits of the deal. Many limited-partnership tax write-offs do not hold up in an IRS audit. Also, confirm the extent of your liability. Frequently, the exposure is not as limited as investors are led to believe.

Subdivision Lots: Investor Beware

Buying land as an investment or future (retirement or vacation) homesite can be a mistake. Some installment buyers have been stuck with heavy hidden costs. And they haven't gotten title even after the land was paid off. What you need to know:

About the development: Have your lawyer check the Federal Property Report required of all big developers selling interstate. Make sure at least 25% of the development has been set aside for open space. Also: Find out in advance who pays to install water, sewerage and drainage systems, paved roads, electricity, and for garbage collection.

About the lot: There is no substitute for a personal inspection, especially for proximity to roads and shopping centers. Is the property prone to flooding or landslides? Is the slope too steep? Check the average resale value in the area (it is often less than original purchase price).

About the contract: Be sure you have the right to build upon or improve the lot before it's fully paid. What are the payments used for? Check for hidden financing charges. Are challenges to the ownership of the lot likely? Important: Make sure the contract is recorded in your name by the county clerk or that the title is placed in escrow for you.

If you get a bad deal, you can cancel within seven days of signing the contract. If a large developer selling interstate does not provide a Federal Property Report, you can claim a full refund for two years. Recommended: If it looks like a loss, wait until you have a sizable capital gains profit elsewhere before taking the write-off.

Source: *The Insider's Guide to Owning Land in Subdivisions,* by Patricia A. Simko, INFORM, New York.

Investing in Raw Land

Buying undeveloped land is risky, since it can drop in value or, at best, lag well behind the inflation rate: Added burdens: There's no tax advantage. That's because land cannot be depreciated. And there's usually no income.

But a parcel of land that is in the path of urban growth can increase enormously in value. Moreover, buying raw land is uncomplicated, and it requires no upkeep.

Best sites: Determine from local planning and zoning records where roads will be built and where housing or commercial developments are spreading.

Caution: Avoid physical barriers to growth (such as mountains, a lake) or a large parcel of land held by a single owner. Problem: Owners of large holdings may disguise them by deeding them in small parcels to paper, shell, or dummy owners.

Look for: Acreage that has a special feature (such as great view) or is strategically located. Avoid: One of 100 identical tracts. Availability keeps prices low.

Also desirable: Land that can be subdivided (check the zoning code); a tract that can be leased for some interim use to generate income. Examples: Trailer park, campsite, tree farm, parking lot.

Before buying : Have a civil engineer check the site for usability. Look out for: Land that drains poorly (or is the natural drainage repository for adjacent areas). A flooding history, even if only once every century. Acreage that has been used as dump, even if years ago.

Source: Thomas L. O'Dea, O'Dea and Co., Inc., investment real estate consultants, 285 Stratford Rd., Winston Salem, NC 27103

Speculating in Rural Land

Rural land is not the bargain investment it was a few years ago. But there are still plenty of lots that are well below suburban price levels.

Decent land with water, situated within 300 miles of a metropolitan center, ranges from $2,000 to $5,000 an acre. Note: Land that is priced below the local market value should be suspect.

When buying land for speculation:

Keep the land classified as agricultural, if possible. The tax rates are lower.

Buy substantially improved country property, since the most profit comes from it. Why: The buildings on usable farms rise in value as rapidly as the land (perhaps even faster). Also, tax depreciation is available on income-producing assets, such as buildings and equipment.

Basic rules:

Make sure the zoning of the land matches your plans for its use. You may want the site as a place to park your camper, but the zoning laws may forbid that.

Determine the water rights before signing the contract. Water that is visible on the land may not belong to the landholder.

Have any lot surveyed. Fences don't always indicate legal boundaries. Make sure your land has the right of way to public roadway.

Investigate how much it will cost for the local public utility companies to run electric, telephone, or natural-gas lines to your site. Caution: Power lines are expensive (as much as $10,000 to land half a mile from the power source).

Source: *Profits from Country Property,* by J.H. Koch, McGraw-Hill, Inc., New York.

Buying Real Estate at Public Sales of Seized Property

Buying property sold for delinquent taxes can be a bargain. But often it only looks like a bargain. Beware of these traps, says real estate consultant Douglas M. Temple:

Back taxes can exceed potential value.

Zoning restrictions may prevent development for profit.

Previous owner may retain right under state law to reclaim property by paying tax and penalties after it's bought. Result: Unclear title, which makes property hard to resell.

Deteriorating neighborhoods should be avoided unless the plans for redevelopment are certain.

Property should be investigated with utmost discretion to avoid alerting competitive bidders. Strategy: Don't have property appraised. Ask instead about similar property nearby.

Best deal: Vacant land (taxed at low rate) in an undeveloped area targeted for build-up.

Property lists: Sales are announced in advance but not necessarily in general newspapers. Contact city or country tax collector for details, information on special mailing lists.

The Art of Real Estate Negotiation

There are only three areas of commerce (antiques, used cars, and real estate) in which prices and terms are all set by negotiation. Fixed labels and prices in these three categories don't mean a thing.

Real estate is the most complex of these items. Numerous factors come into play: financial, legal, and the fact that each piece of real estate is unique.

The person who negotiates for property must approach the deal with a positive self-concept. Along with his financial offer, he is presenting his image. He must know how his personality affects others. Example: Someone who comes across as a wise guy, even if he's making a generous offer, increases his chances of being turned down. He is perceived as someone who is trying to put something over on the seller.

Understand the other side. It is essential to see what the deal looks like from the other person's point of view. Find out what he's like. Talk to people who have done business with him.

Do your homework. Know what the property is worth to you before you begin to talk about the price. Know all the possibilities of financing and the peculiarities of the property involved. That way you will have realistic expectations of what can be negotiated. It is better to have a satisfactory deal that will close than an outstanding one that will fall through.

Determine the property's value by its usefulness to you, not its investment value based on the inflation rate. Cash intended for real estate investment might be used more profitably in other ways. Inflation may not affect a particular building because of its location or other reasons. Example: A building can decrease in value if a road is changed.

Seek advice from your lawyer, consultant, accountant, and other advisers before you try to negotiate price and terms. If you try to make changes after negotiations, the deal is likely to fall through.

It usually pays to ask: What is your best offer? If you've done your homework, you'll know if the buyer or seller is putting you on. And if it's too much of a bargain, be cautious. You can never underpay for a bad deal.

Source: Murray Niedergang, Esq., partner in Blum, Haimoff, Gersen, Lipson, Slavin & Szabad, 270 Madison Ave., New York 10016.

Bargains in Distressed Real Estate

Distressed real estate is creating some attractive deals. Why: The owners or backers need cash in a hurry. Specifically: Developers who are overextended, properties with tax troubles or foreclosed mortgages, houses or businesses in rundown areas.

To locate distressed real estate properties:

Check the legal notices in the newspapers for foreclosures, bankruptcies, and tax delinquencies.

Peruse the records at the municipal clerk's office. The records, which are open to the public to examine, list those properties with legal action pending.

Watch the real estate section of the newspaper for co-op or house-for-sale ads that show up again week after week. If the property isn't moving, the sellers will probably listen to an offer that they may have not even considered previously.

Be alert for houses placed on the market for quick sale. Examples: Contractors having trouble with unsold houses. Recently divorced couples who are desperate to get rid of the house. How to proceed: Contact real estate agents, lawyers, and accountants. They usually have clients who are eager to sell property as quickly as possible.

Strategies for Raising Rents

Time rent increases to coincide with improvements to the building.

Explain the need for the increase to tenants. Use pie charts and other visuals. Note: It's not necessary to discuss taxes or other advantages of real estate investment.

Keep rents up to current market levels by closely monitoring what competitors are receiving. Important: When tenant turnover is almost negligible even though the market is tight, and tenants rarely complain about an increase, the rent hikes may be consistently too low.

Pay close attention to tenant reactions, especially any that are unexpected. They can be used as guidelines to plan and carry out the next increase more effectively.

To put through a higher-than-average increase: Consider granting tenants a one-month rent holiday for the first month of the new lease. This softens the blow for the first year, but puts a more profitable rent structure in place for subsequent leases and accustoms tenants to paying the higher rate.

Source: William Finlayson, vice-president, Bleznak Organization, 51015 N. Park Dr., Pennsauken, NJ 08109. quoted in *Real Estate Investing Letter.*

3

Tax Shelters

Determining the Profit Potential of a Tax Shelter

Look at a tax shelter first as a straight business investment for after-tax yield and only second as an opportunity for a tax saving. The decision to invest in a shelter is no different from other investment decisions. The basic criterion: Is the potential yield commensurate with the risk involved?

To determine profit potential: Measure the potential after-tax return against the after-tax cost. This allows comparison of the cost of the tax-shelter investment with other alternatives, such as stocks and bonds acquired with after-tax dollars. Be sure to take into account how long it will take to get the yield from after-tax dollars. A three-to-one return ($3 of cash received for each $1 invested) looks better than two-to-one at first. But it's not any better if it takes several years longer to realize the full profit.

The cardinal rule the IRS uses in allowing tax shelters: There must be evidence of intent to make a profit. If a shelter is based on deductions of interest and capital cost recovery, with only a remote possibility of the receipt of revenues, it stands a greater risk of being disallowed.

Example: A shelter that marks up a $10 product to $100, gets a 10% investment tax credit to make back the $10 initial contribution, then takes accelerated capital cost recovery on the rest, is unlikely to be approved.

Choose carefully the lawyer or accountant who will evaluate the deal for you.

An unfamiliar lawyer or accountant who brings a deal to an investor's attention at a social gathering may simply be representing the promoters.

It also can be unwise to rely on one's own lawyer or accountant in evaluating a deal. They are prejudiced another way. If the deal goes bust, they could lose a client. Result: They have very little incentive to recommend anything so risky.

Other lawyers and accountants have their own deals. These should generally be shunned, because the fees are often excessive.

Four basic questions for evaluating a tax-shelter program:

• Is the program sufficiently diversified to protect the investor against loss of his investment?

• What are the sharing arrangements and front-end fees? A general partner's share of revenues should be reasonably related to the services he renders to the program. Fees, commissions, and other front-end-loaded charges should be reasonable.

• Is there a discussion of the partner's previous activities in the offering documents? If not, be suspicious.

• Does the program provide for additional assessments? Investors must be told the maximum amount of additional capital that the general partner can assess for unexpected expenses, when the assessment can be made, the tax consequences of meeting the assessment and, finally, the penalty for failure.

Source: Myron Neugeboren, CPA, tax attorney, partner in charge of tax shelters, L.F. Rothschild, Unterberg, Towbin, investment bankers, 55 Water St., New York 10041.

Appraising Tax Shelters

Be leery of real estate deals that buy property from other programs managed by the same operator. The risk for substantial cost overruns is greater if a partnership buys an incomplete real estate project or develops its own projects.

In equipment-leasing deals, interest and capital cost recovery charges often decline after a few years to a level *lower* than the rental income. Result: An accounting profit on which added taxes must be paid. Another consideration: Most or all of the gains from the sale of equipment are taxed as ordinary income and not as a capital gain.

In farm shelters, be aware that nut, citrus and fruit groves, and grape vineyards take several years to develop. Profitability depends on the weather and volatile farm prices. Caretaking costs increase as plants grow older.

Cattle tax shelters are risky because the subscriber may invest in a year when cyclical beef prices are relatively low. *Better idea:* Spread cattle investments over several years to minimize the risk.

Generally, the track record of an oil or gas operator is a less reliable indicator than the track record of a real estate operator. Success runs in cycles. Oil and gas operators hit dry holes as well as productive ones, but they can all have bad years.

Tax-Shelter Fallacies

The most common misconceptions about tax shelters:

Misconception: Tax shelters save taxes. Fact: Most shelters only defer taxes.

Misconception: Tax shelters are good investments. Fact: Most are not. And there is good reason to be wary of any deal promoted primarily for its tax features. Criteria for a good shelter: A sound investment, with tax advantages as a bonus.

Misconception: The IRS is trying to stamp out tax shelters. Fact: The IRS is attacking deals that have no economic purpose other than the avoidance of taxes. But the government actually fosters many tax shelters. Examples: Qualified retirement plans, municipal bonds, savings bonds, investment credits, accelerated cost recovery, capital gains.

Misconception: Tax shelters are for just about everyone now. Fact: Most tax shelters don't make sense until a taxpayer reaches the 50% tax bracket. All shelters require careful tax planning and expert advice.

Source: Edward Mendlowitz, partner, Siegel & Mendlowitz, CPAs, 310 Madison Ave., New York 10017.

Four Tax Shelters That Can Still Pay Off

Despite declared war by the IRS on tax shelters, attractive sheltered investment opportunities remain. The key: Familiarity with the re-defined limits.

Most important: All sheltered investments are now governed by the IRS's "at risk" rule. Investors can deduct a loss only if it's less than the amount invested from their own funds or from borrowed funds for which they are personally liable.

Another barrier: Investors may deduct interest paid on investment borrowing only if it's less than their net investment income, plus an annual allowance of $10,000.

Oil and gas shelter benefits: Intangible drilling and development costs, which normally amount to 70% to 90% of the total invested. Some tangible costs may qualify for the 10% investment tax credit.

If the venture is successful 15% of the gross income is tax-free to small producers through the depletion allowance.

Profit from selling equity in an oil or gas well is normally taxed as a capital gain, except for partial recapture of the intangible deduction.

Warning: Taxpayers could lose some of the benefits from these shelters because they are considered tax preference items.* And the 20% alternative minimum tax may apply to the deduction for intangible drilling costs and the percentage depletion allowance.

Timber investment benefits: Deductible care and maintenance; profits from selling timber or cutting rights are taxed as long-term capital gains.

Racehorses are a good shelter investment because most expenses are deductible as soon as they are paid, and expenses usually precede income. However, the IRS may reject deductions under its "hobby loss" rule if profits are not realized in at least two of the seven years of investment.

Equipment leasing remains an excellent sheltered investment because it usually permits an investor to make substantial deductions in the early years. Since 1976, however, noncorporate lessors cannot claim investment tax credits on equipment they have purchased to lease. Tighter laws have also re-stricted the buying of equipment with borrowed money, leasing it out, and then depreciating it rapidly.

Trap: One of the old favorite tax shelters, motion pictures, is no longer attractive in most cases. Reason: The cost of film production must be capitalized and written off over the film's anticipated income life. Although large deductions may come in the first few years, IRS's "at risk" rule means that nonrecourse debt can no longer be used to generate a loss.

Source: *Alternative Investment Opportunities,* published by Seidman and Seidman, CPAs, 15 Columbus Circle, New York 10019.

When to Turn Down a Tax Shelter

The farther away from home the investment is, the worse it usually is. When a California oil and gas deal is being sold in New York, begin wondering why it's being marketed so far away. There are an awful lot of wealthy people in between. Why won't those who are closer to the deal touch it?

The smaller the minimum unit of investment, the worse the investment. With a really good situation, it's easy to raise $100,000 to $200,000 per investor. These are sophisticated investors who know what they're doing and have experts around looking for deals and reviewing them, too. As the unit comes down, it's promoted to less and less sophisticated individuals, people who are less willing to pay someone to look over the deal.

Another negative feature of small-unit offerings: Large percentage taken by promoters in finders' fees, management fees, general partners' compensation, etc.

---

*Certain kinds of income (including accelerated depreciation on real property, depletion allowances, etc.) are subject to a 20% alternative minimum tax.

General rule: A deal with a $50,000 minimum investment is probably more than twice as good as one with a $25,000 minimum.

The better the anticipated tax deduction, the worse the deal. For really solid investments, it shouldn't be necessary to promise five-to-one write-offs (deducting as expenses a sum of five times the actual cash investment). People go into the deal confident they will make a lot of money on it. Tax deductions are just icing on the cake—not the substance.

Warning: Any deductions taken in excess of cash contributions as a liability come back to the taxpayer or his heirs sometime. A tax-shelter deal is nothing more than a postponement of tax liability—and that liability may turn up just when it is needed least. For people who get the bulk of their income as salary, most tax shelters aren't worth the risk.

The better the promised economics, the worse the deal. If someone comes to you promising to quadruple your money in a short period of time, you've got to ask why he isn't begging or borrowing all the money he can to put in the deal himself. For deals like that, wealthy people would be standing in line at the door, and smaller investors wouldn't be able to benefit from the opportunity.

The IRS has set up a special task force to attack shelters and a comprehensive IRS manual alerts agents on what to look for.

Many tax shelters have overused their tax advantages, exposing them to extinction. Example: If at least 90% of the ordinary taxable income of a real estate investment trust is distributed annually to the shareholders, only the remaining undistributed income is taxed. Result: Many real estate investment trusts (REITs) escape tax completely by distributing all such income, leaving nothing for reinvestment and growth.

Tax Shelter Traps

Many otherwise smart executives throw their money away on shaky tax shelters. Steven D. Oppenheim, partner in the accounting firm Oppenheim, Appel, Dixon & Co., comments on the basic questions potential investors should ask.

Liquidity: Investments that compromise liquidity are especially dangerous for investors during a recession. Most tax-shelter investments are essentially illiquid because they give the investor tax breaks up front and pay back only after a few years, if at all.

A potential investor would be very wise to assume that he is going to lose all his deductions and all his money on a deal. If such a loss would threaten the investor's overall liquidity, he should not go into the venture, no matter how attractive the tax benefits may appear to be.

Hidden risks: If there is leverage in the shelter deal, the investor stands the risk of being sued for more than the amount of his investment. The only exception is real estate shelters, where nonrecourse loans can be used to limit the investor's exposure.

Additional risks:

• Investors often cannot find a buyer for their unit of a shelter if they need to sell in a hurry.

• In many cases, the partnership agreement specifies that units cannot be sold, assigned, or transferred to someone else. The buyer is stuck with it.

• Some deals give operators the right to raise additional funds from other subscribers, diluting the original subscribers' equity. High interest rates are drying up mortgage money quickly. A question to consider: Are real estate tax shelters more attractive because operators already have their mortgage money? Or are they less attractive because the potential unavailability of mortgage money undermines the economics of the investment?

The effect the windfall profits tax may have on small oil producers is still unknown. This increases the already substantial risks in oil and gas shelter. Beginning in 1985, there is an exemption of 3 barrels a day for qualified royalty owners. Before that it was 2 barrels.

Source: Steven D. Oppenheim, partner, Oppenheim, Appel, Dixon & Co., an accounting firm, 1 New York Plaza, New York 10004

Mistakes in Tax-Shelter Investing

The lure of losses can lead to trouble with the IRS. Trap: One of every four partnerships that shows losses of over $25,000 is audited by the IRS.

For the IRS to consider a deal legitimate, tax credits and depreciation must be in line with the fair market value. Big tax losses occur only when the price of the assets or tax risks are too high.

Beware of the offbeat deal. For example, uranium mines in Australia will attract the attention of the IRS. An unfavorable ruling means the complete loss of the shelter. Worse, if the deal is a fraud, the total capital investment is lost.

Giving away a shelter will not avoid recapture (taxation of losses already taken on the sale or disposition). The only sure way to escape recapture is death. Taxes are levied on the recaptured portion any time an asset is given away.

Vital point: Under the "at risk" tax rules, losses are limited to the actual amount of cash invested. The few exceptions have complex conditions that must be studied.

The only no-risk shelter is a cash contribution to charity.

Source: Robert Stanger, publisher, *The Stanger Report.*

Traps in Safe Tax Shelters

Investors may be shortchanging themselves when examining a tax shelter. They ought to consider the potential write-off after investigating the real investment potential of the tax shelter's business. A write-off is only one factor among the many necessary ones to determine eventual yield to the investor. Example: An investor in the 50% tax bracket puts $10,000 into an oil and gas drilling limited partnership. Because of the immediate deduction opportunities, the investor gets an 80% write-off. Result: The $10,000 investment costs $6,000. The sting: But then the drilling partnership strikes nothing but dry holes. Bottom line: The investor is out $6,000.

Point: If the investor had paid taxes on the original $10,000, and not bothered trying to shelter that sum, there would have been $5,000 left plus the interest earned during the period the partnership was drilling dry holes.

Investors can also get stung if a tax shelter has no nontax economic purpose. How: If the IRS rules that a tax shelter has been devised specifically to create write-offs, and not as a bona-fide investment, it can bill the investor for his tax savings plus new interest and possible penalties. Example: An investor in the 50% bracket puts $10,000 into a leveraged real estate deal. Point: Real estate deals are the only kind of sheltered investment that offers an investor a tax saving greater than the amount of capital put at risk. The tax write-off on the real estate deal is $20,000. Result: Because of the savings, the $10,000 investment appears to cost the investor nothing. The sting: But then the real estate deal realizes zero return, and the IRS rules that it was bogus.

Bottom line: the investor has to come up with the $5,000 tax originally owed the IRS on that $10,000, at a time when he may be hard-pressed to turn up the cash. By investing in the bogus shelter because of the attractive-sounding write-off promised, the investor closed himself out of the opportunity of going into an investment with a real, if more modest, return.

Key to identifying bad tax shelters: Analyze the general partners of each deal the same way investors analyze a company whose stocks or bonds they consider purchasing. What this means:

- Make sure to find out how much capital is available to the general partners.
- Look at the general partners' actual investment in the deal.
- Make certain the general partners have valid experience in the business the tax shelter is engaging in.
- Find out if the general partners' profits come out of earnings or out of the initial investment of the limited partners. (The deal is

suspicious if $2 to $3 out of every $10 goes to the general partners up front.)

Source: Myron Neugeboren, CPA, tax attorney, and partner in charge of tax shelters at L.F. Rothschild, Unterberg, Towbin, investment bankers, 55 Water St., New York 10041.

You May Make More From a Tax Shelter By Giving it Away

The benefits of a tax shelter may be maximized by giving it away at an opportune moment. Recipient of gift: Another family member in a lower tax bracket, typically a child. Result: Income taxes can be cut significantly. There are estate planning advantages as well.

How the typical shelter works: The early years bring large deductions, which result from accelerated depreciation or deductible up-front expenses. The deductions are valuable because the shelter owner is in an upper tax bracket. Ultimately, however, the shelter investment is intended to bring in a real profit (when an oil well starts producing profitably). At that point, the investor's tax bracket works against him. Reason: The income derived from the shelter is investment income that is taxable at rates up to 50%. By giving the shelter away to a low-bracket family member just before the heavy income starts to come in, the family unit can derive large tax savings.

Example: An oil well has already generated $15,000 in tax losses and is now expected to produce $30,000 in income. The typical shelter investor might be required to pay 50% of that amount in income taxes. But if the shelter is given to a child in the 12% tax bracket, the tax would be $7292 at most. Cash saving: $7708. (Computations are for 1982.)

Estate planning advantages can be attained by giving a tax shelter away. The objective of estate planning is to transfer real wealth to the next generation at the minimum tax cost. By giving a shelter to a child, the value of the income that is derived from the shelter is prevented from passing through the original investor's estate. The value of that income will escape the estate taxes that would have applied if it had been retained by the investor and included in the estate. Point: Estate tax rates effectively start at 32%, and rise to 65% for 1982. When estate tax savings are added to the income tax savings, it is clear that the gift of tax shelter can result in large tax benefits.

Problems that are likely to arise when giving a shelter away:

Gift taxes. The gift of a tax shelter is subject to taxation under the same rules as any other gift. But if the transfer is handled correctly, gift tax liability can be minimized or even avoided entirely. Objective: To give away the shelter when it has a low market value. Reason: An individual may make a gift with a value of up to $10,000 tax-free. For a married couple the limit is $20,000. Therefore, if a married investor gives away a shelter when it is valued at less than $20,000, gift taxes can be avoided completely.

Point: The market value of a tax shelter is likely to vary during its life cycle. In the early years, when it is producing large losses, it may have little value. In later years, when it is producing a steady stream of income, it may have a high value. There is often a point in the life of a shelter investment when most of the tax losses have been generated, but the full value of future earnings cannot be readily ascertained. Examples:

• An oil deal when most of the drilling has been completed, but the full size of any newly discovered oil reserves has not been finally determined.

• A real estate deal when most of the costs of construction have been incurred, but income-generating leases have not been finalized. That moment is the time to transfer the shelter investment to the lower-bracket family member.

Problem: It may not be possible to reduce the market value of the shelter to less than $20,000 before giving it away. Alternatives: Give away a $20,000 portion of the investment each year. Or give away the full investment, but take back a note in the amount by which the market value of the investment exceeds $20,000. Cancel $20,000 worth of the note each year.

Debt. When liabilities attached to an asset or investment are given away with the investment, the donor may receive taxable income. Reason: The donor is relieved of the obligation to pay off the liability. If the size of the liability exceeds the investor's basis in the property that is given away the difference may be a taxable gain.*

One solution: When an investor has borrowed personally to finance a tax shelter, the debt can be repaid before the shelter is given away. Another loan can be secured immediately after the gift is made. Problem: This tactic will not work when the debt was incurred by a partnership, or when the transferred assets secure a loan. But even in these cases, the specific circumstances may enable a smart tax adviser to devise a way to minimize the adverse impact that the existence of debt may have on the deal. And even if the transfer of liabilities does result in some income to the donor, that person may well come out ahead when the current cost of the deal is weighed against future income and estate tax savings.

The transfer of a sophisticated shelter may affect the investor's tax bill in unexpected ways. Such a deal should be thoroughly examined by a tax specialist before it is made.

*Basis equals the original cost of the asset, possibly reduced by tax-free distribution.
Source: Robert Stanger, publisher, *The Stanger Report.*

Oil and Gas Shelters: Whom Are They Good For?

Oil and gas drilling deals are so attractive to high-bracket taxpayers that limited partnerships now raise $50 million in as little as three or four weeks. Reason: Investors expect a potentially high return on investment in addition to tax write-offs.

Best candidates for a public deal are investors in the 50% tax bracket, with a relatively liquid net worth of at least $100,000 (excluding home, furnishings, and automobiles).

Best candidates for a privately offered deal are investors with reportable income of at least $150,000, and relatively liquid net worth of at least $250,000 (excluding home, furnishings, and automobiles).

Caution: The tax advantages of oil and gas drilling deals have changed because of lower tax rates, and the elimination of the difference between earned and unearned income. The tax deduction is now worth less, and the income worth more.

Result: Oil and gas drilling deals will have to be chosen more on their investment merits and less on their tax-shelter advantages.

Strategy for oil and gas deals:

Restrict interest to programs in which general partners have a good drilling record. (Minimum acceptable results are a two-to-one gross return on gross investment.)

Use a broker with knowledge in oil and gas tax shelters.

Diversify a minimum investment of $20,000 over two or three programs.

Source: Laurence B. Rossbach Jr., vice-president, Drexel Burnham Lambert, Inc., 60 Broad St., New York 10004.

• **Tax-shelter investors** must now report the registration number of any tax shelter from which they claim any benefit, by filing Form 8271 with their tax returns. A $50 penalty will result if the form is not mailed. The IRS wishes to emphasize the fact that its issuance of a registration number to a shelter in no way indicates that the shelter has been either approved or disapproved as an investment.

• **Tax-shelter interest.** The new tax law increases the rate of interest charged on tax underpayments resulting from tax-shelter cases. The new interest rate is 120% of the rate charged in normal, non-shelter cases. When the normal IRS interest rate is 13% for example, the new rate applying in shelter cases is 15.6%.

Oil and Gas Ventures

Tax reforms did not nullify the advantages of investing in tax shelters: They just changed the rules of the game.

The day of the small investment generating gigantic tax losses for high-income investors is now gone. There are fewer kinds of sheltered investments that make economic sense. But there are a handful that have been entirely legitimized by tax reforms, and they offer a possible combination of tax advantages and satisfactory return on investment.

Of the three most common kinds of sheltered investments—real estate, equipment leases, oil and gas drilling ventures—oil and gas ventures look especially promising now. Even though windfall profits legislation has reduced after tax earnings of oil production 15%, the economics of domestic oil and gas drilling work to the investor's advantage.

Result: Investors buying into a limited partnership that gets one productive well in eight wells drilled can probably expect 2 to 2½ times their original investment in cash distributions in 10 or 12 years, plus a write-off in first year of 70% to 90% of their investment. and the odds of striking oil and gas in the U.S. are just what they were 20 years ago.

The downside risk:

As the field gets crowded, finding ventures with low administrative and operating costs, and a minimum of middlemen, gets harder.

The IRS says it plans to audit 25% of those individual returns that declare an interest in a limited partnership and show a loss of $25,000 or more.

Source: Robert Stanger, editor, *The Stanger Report.*

What to look for:

A general partner who's a true oil expert. If the head person is in a distant city, check out the field operator. Look for past success.

Precise locations for the drilling field and a lease assigned specifically to the partnership. Drilling near or between producing wells is a good bet. When there's no site listed, the partners are waiting to see how much money can be raised before they decide where to drill.

A geologist's report, including what formations will be drilled, the probability of success, and estimates of how much oil and gas is in each well. Also: How fast the reserves can be drawn out.

Specific breakdowns on how profits are to be split. The landowner generally gets 12%, the lease seller 5%. Avoid any drilling deal that leaves less than 70% to 80% for the investors.

Profit distributions that give the general partner a smaller share until the investors have recovered their capital. Make sure he gets a share only of the production profits, not the investment dollars.

What happens if the well is a dry hole? Good shelters specify that the unused money is either returned or used to drill replacement wells. Caution: An unscrupulous partner can make a bundle by drilling failures and pocketing the difference.

A guarantee that the partner has access or an actual hookup to a major gas pipeline. Oil can be trucked out, but natural gas can't.

Cost overrun assessments in the 10% to 25% range. Beware of deals requiring open-ended payments or penalties for not investing further.

Source: Lawrence B. Rossbach, Drexel Burnham Lambert Inc., 60 Broad St., New York 10004 writing in *Medical Economics.*

How to Read An Oil Company's Prospectus

Reading an oil company's prospectus is an imposing task, but hidden in those 100-plus pages are some very critical points.

Real Estate Tax Shelters: The Long View

Real estate tax shelters can provide significant benefits. But once your money is invested, there is very little flexibility. It is not unusual for a real estate partnership to last 10 to 12 years. And once you are in, there is no easy way to get out. That is the reason it is so important to take a long view before you invest.

Leveraged write-offs: In a real estate deal, it is possible to deduct more than you either invest or obligate yourself to pay. In effect, you can deduct expenses paid with borrowed money even though you are not personally liable for the loans. Contrast: With most investments, your tax deductions cannot go beyond the amount you have at risk. Your amount at risk consists of cash you put up and debts for which you are personally liable to someone who is not part of the venture.

At one time, it was possible to put $10,000 into a real estate deal and end up with $100,000 worth of deductions. But lenders are no longer willing to finance projects with only 10% down. Many require investors to put up 50% of the cash. Result: There are few deals available today that provide solid write-offs much greater than 1½ times your initial investment.

Caution: Some publicly offered shelters appear to promise write-offs that are three or four times as large as the initial investment. Problem: Many of these deductions involve "soft" costs—expenses that wouldn't be there if it weren't a "tax shelter." And some of these cannot be deducted at the outset. Example: Promotional expenses connected with sales of tax shelter units. These are properly treated as capital expenditures rather than current deductions. Sometimes, promoters are paid large "advance management fees" that actually turn out to be promotional payments.

IRS targets: On occasion, promoters will acquire a property for, say, $2 million and then turn around and sell it to a tax shelter partnership they have organized for something like $5 million. In some of these cases, the IRS is contending that the partnership price is artificially inflated. Result: Partnership deductions are reduced substantially. And there is a potential over-valuation penalty of up to 30%.

Another common practice the IRS is attacking involves "wraparound" financing. Example: Promoters acquire property subject to an 8% mortgage. They then sell it to the partnership with a 14% mortgage. The IRS now argues that the 6% "spread" in a deal like this is really a capital expense (another promotional fee in disguise) rather than an interest payment.

Deductions and cash flow: Most deals provide paper losses for the first 7 to 10 years. For example, you might put in $10,000 a year for the first five years. In return, your deductions might be as high as $20,000 the first year, dropping down to $800 by the ninth year, and totaling about $75,000 for the entire period (on an investment of $50,000). At that point, the project will usually start to show a paper profit. Actual cash flow is likely to be minimal.

At the point where taxable income begins to be generated, the project is likely to be sold. This is when those previous excess deductions catch up with the investor. And investors may find themselves with a tax liability that exceeds their share of the sales proceeds. That ultimate liability should be taken into account at the outset, before the investment is made.

Tax shelter investors should also assess carefully their employment and income prospects. Reasons: Investors who are close to retirement may end up with a shelter for income they will no longer be earning. On the other hand, people who invest early in their careers may be unwittingly deferring income to a period when their earnings (and tax bracket) are substantially higher. That's a costly error.

Bottom line: Your tax adviser can help you work out the long-term consequences of buying into a real estate shelter. Until then, you can't be sure that the projected initial write-offs are worth the price.

Source: Edward Mendlowitz, partner, Siegel & Mendlowitz, CPAs, 310 Madison Ave., New York 10017.

Real Estate Syndication Tax Shelters

Real estate syndications usually take the form of limited partnerships in which a number of investors are brought together by a general partner to own a piece of property for joint profit. The property may be commercial, residential, industrial, or have a special purpose.

Syndications have become a popular form of tax deferral. Investors are able to shelter other income through the large mortgage interest payments and depreciation charges on the property.

Likely bonus: As real estate values skyrocketed in the late 1970s, syndications also brought investors generous capital gains when the properties were sold. While there is no assurance that syndicated properties acquired at today's inflated prices will increase in value, the long-term trend in real estate remains essentially upward.

If you are in the 50% bracket, want a tax shelter, and think the real estate market still has room for appreciation, the next decision is whether a private or public syndication best suits your needs. Caution: Recent increases in property values have increased investor interest in these offerings. More ''marginal'' deals (from an economic and tax viewpoint) are now available as supply is rushed to meet demand.

Requirements:

For a public syndication: $2,500 to $5,000 to invest, a minimum net worth of $50,000 in addition to the equity in your home, and income that is taxable at least in the 40% bracket.

For a private syndication: $50,000 (sometimes over a period of years), a net worth of $250,000 besides the equity in your home and income taxable in the 50% bracket.

One significant difference between public and private deals is as follows: Since Regulation T of the Federal Reserve Board doesn't allow the extension of credit on an initial public offering of a security (as in the case of public syndications), your investment is made upon subscription. In a private offering, capital contributions can be made in installments. They are exempt from Regulation T.

The following chart shows the benefit of phasing in your capital contribution over several years (assuming the same property was acquired by the public or private fund).

Rough Comparison of Tax Benefits

	PUBLIC		PRIVATE	
	Invest-ment	Tax Loss	Invest-ment	Tax Loss
First year	$1,000	$250 (25%)	$250	$250 (100%)
Second year		$150 (15%)	$250	$167 (67%)
Third year		$120 (12%)	$250	$125 (50%)
Fourth year		$100 (10%)	$250	$100 (40%)

Private syndications are generally more tax sensitive than public deals. For example, they may be more aggressive about depreciating the property over a shorter time frame than public ones.

Disclosure: Public offerings must be registered with the Securities and Exchange Commission (SEC). Private placements are exempt from SEC scrutiny. This doesn't necessarily mean there is less disclosure in private deals. It depends on the sponsor offering the deal. If you are considering a private deal, have a lawyer and/or accountant look over the prospectus before you make any decision.

Most important things to look for in the prospectus:

Management (experience, depth of staff, financial strength).

What the proceeds will be used for. How much is earmarked for actual property investment, and how much for admission, prior debt service, etc.

Prior performance of general partners. Their track record for previous partnerships should be in the prospectus. What fees are paid to the general partners? Are profits distributed to the investors first?

Tax factors: Some deals will be tilted more toward tax benefits than others. Sale-leaseback deals, for instance, can be structured for either income or tax deferral. Partnerships that buy new buildings, or ones under construction, emphasize tax shelter. Axiom: There is no real estate deal that can maximize all elements (tax shelter, cash flow, equity buildup, and capital appreciation). Make sure the deal's benefits fit your goals.

Property being purchased. Private syndications usually buy only one property and specify it in the prospectus. In public syndication the properties are specified fully, but frequently the blind-pool technique is used. This permits the property to be found and acquired after the investors' money has been collected. Assessing the risk: Since the public syndication buys several properties, you are diversifying and therefore spreading your risk.

Bottom line guidelines: Check out the location of the property; try to see the actual property. Judge it on the basis of this question: Is this a piece of property that is worthwhile to own and use? When a buyer comes along after your tax benefits are used up, the desirability of that building will be the primary factor in getting the appreciation you want.

Source: Stephen Blank, vice-president, Kidder Peabody Realty Corporation, 10 Hanover Square, New York 10005.

Do-It-Yourself Real Estate Tax Shelters

Steve Burn has syndicated numerous real estate tax-shelter deals, but he says intelligent investors don't need the services of a syndicator. They can do better on their own. Investing through syndicators costs 20% to 40% more than investing directly, he points out. Where the money goes: (1) Syndicator's fees. (2) Syndicator's attorney for drafting memorandum documentation. (3) Big commissions for salesmen. Caution: Syndicators often pay commissions to lawyers and accountants for the investors they bring into a deal.

Another strong reason for doing it yourself: Too many syndicators are competent promoters but poor real estate operators. Some lose interest in a deal once it's sold and devote most of their time to new syndications. Should a property fail, the syndicator won't be hurt because he has gotten most of his profit up front.

How to do it yourself: Form a group of seven or more people, each with $100,000 or more to invest. If possible, at least two of the group members should be savvy in real estate. They should be paid for their professional services.

How to find good properties: Work through an accountant, lawyer, or real estate professional who has wide-ranging contacts. Those active in the business hear about the most attractive properties first. Syndicators use these same experts.

A typical deal: A $700,000 investment, which can usually be made through staged payments, provided there are accompanying letters of credit. Each person usually puts some money down and makes four equal annual payments thereafter.

Leverage: At least $5 of purchase price for every $1 of cash invested. There is a risk: Too much leverage, unless there are nonforeclosure covenants in the deal, can sometimes mean that a temporary loss of income or unusually high repair bills will create a cash-flow shortage that could result in foreclosure (if the investors are unwilling or unable to personally fund the deficiency).

Expected return: $2 to $2.5 million in direct income and tax savings on a $700,000 investment over 10 years.

To avoid personal liability, the individuals can delegate a general partner. The risks of running into trouble through a limited partnership are remote. And, contrary to popular opinion, there is no great risk in being a general partner. Mortgages don't normally require personal guarantees except when new construction is involved. It is wise, however, to make sure one has more than adequate liability coverage. Disadvantage of designating a general partner: Loss of control over the deal.

What to look for in a tax-shelter deal:

Good cash return that will escalate with inflation.

Opportunity for resale or refinancing with potential for substantial gain.

Paper losses up front that will shield income. Examples: (1) Depreciation of a property that in reality is appreciating. (2) Deducting expenses up front that normally would be paid out over a number of years, such as covenants not to foreclose and qualifying guaranteed payments to partners and others. A competent real estate expert is creative at finding substantial write-offs.

Properties that can be profitably held for 10 years or longer.

Substantial investment tax credits. A good real estate expert should be able to help in this area.

The IRS is scrutinizing tax shelter deals closely. It is seeking to disallow claimed losses. It generally checks partnership returns with losses as low as $25,000. Warning: The examination of a tax-shelter partnership return can result in a personal audit. The IRS often audits the entire personal returns of those who invest in tax shelters.

Source: Steve Burn, 1234 Summer St., Stamford, CT 06905.

Investing in Research And Development Tax Shelters

Not many people understand R&D tax shelters because of the complexity of the tax benefits they provide. The benefits:
•Deductions taken against ordinary income.
• Tax credits.
• Long-term capital gains upon receipt of royalties.

The attractiveness of certain R&D investments has increased with the enactment of additional energy-related credits. Examples: Plants that convert geothermal heat to electricity and that make biomass and cogeneration equipment. Reason: In addition to the standard 10% investment tax credit, Congress has enacted energy credits up to a maximum of 15%, providing a total maximum credit of up to 25%.

How R&D deals often originate: They are offered by major corporations that don't want to tie up capital in R&D because it is charged directly against current earnings. By creating an R&D partnership, they can maintain their current earnings and still control the product when it is developed.

Trap: An R&D deal with a prearranged plan to return the finished product to the corporation, sometimes by paying the investor in company stock. The IRS may view this as a stock offering and disallow the deductions. You can avoid the trap by having a nonforfeitable proprietary interest in the asset in development.

Percentage ownership deals offered by companies as a way of raising sufficient cash to carry through a product's development are often fraught with problems. Example: A company finds it can fund $80 million of a $100-million project and so offers a 20% share of the project to a tax shelter partnership. But the tax shelter rarely shows any economic value under such an arrangement.

Danger in R&D shelters: Underestimating the cost of developing the project. Make sure there are provisions that limit the investor's commitment, in case of cost overruns or product modifications. Keep in mind a hard-nosed financial fact: The last dollar in usually demands the best deal. Don't get caught in a position where the original tax shelter investors have to give away the store to raise enough cash to complete the project.

Guidelines in choosing an R&D shelter:
Expertise of the general partner or partners.
Attempted accomplishment. Is it a new wonder drug (high risk)? Or is it development of equipment that depends on proven technologies (lower risk)?
Risk/reward. With municipal bonds paying tax-free double-digit returns, a minimum acceptable projected return on a tax shelter is about 30% pre-tax. For higher risk deals: 60% pre-tax.

Source: Myron Neugeboren head of tax shelters, L.F. Rothschild, Unterberg, Towbin, 55 Water St., New York 10041.

Sheltered Investments in Subsidized Housing

Limited partnerships in subsidized housing projects for the poor and elderly can bring executives in the 50% tax bracket about $60,000 in net tax savings over 15 to 20 years; even more if the project is sold or refinanced.

This yield is significantly better than the return on most other tax shelters. Reason: Real estate was exempted from recent tax reforms, which ruled out deductions on investments greater than the capital put at risk: Actually subsidized housing projects sometimes generate tax deductions three to four times the capital put at risk.

Cost to buy in: On average, $40,000 to $60,000 over five years.

How it works:

A developer gets approval from the Department of Housing and Urban Development (HUD) to put up a subsidized project.

The developer sells his project to a syndicator or syndicates it himself.

Through a broker, the syndicator makes limited partnerships available. To qualify, an investor must show that he has sufficient funds and is in a high enough tax bracket to benefit from the deal's tax write-off.

Once the project is completed, under some government programs, HUD will guarantee a portion of the rent for a specific time. Method: HUD guarantees payments necessary to make up the difference between a sliding-scale percentage of an eligible tenant's income and the fair market rent for up to 40 years.

Before buying in:

Check out the track record of the development team.

Realize that this type of investment is illiquid; you must remain in a high tax bracket in order to realize the desired benefits.

Source: Harriet Fried, real estate investment analyst, Oppenheimer Properties, Inc., 1 New York Plaza, New York 10004.

Investing in a Sailboat as a Tax Shelter

The sailing enthusiast who can't justify the expense of a yacht is the right prospect to in-

vestigate sailboat tax shelters. Charter companies now advertise them as leaseback programs or management programs since the Securities and Exchange Commission sued one firm for offering them as a shelter when the firm was not registered as a broker/dealer.

How programs work: You purchase a fully equipped yacht to charter. A management company takes care of it. Since the boat is a business asset, it can be depreciated and earn the 10% investment tax credit. Deductions for interest payments on the boat loan and business expenses lend the deal a tax-shelter quality.

Limit: To qualify for full tax benefits you may use the boat no more than 14 days a year in most cases. Exception: If the boat is rented 150 days or more, you can use it for 10% of the number of days it is rented. Further limit: Most of your deductions are tied to a fractional formula if you use the boat even one day a year. Under this formula your deductions are cut for each day the boat is not rented. The amount of the cut depends on the number of personal-use days.

Peak season charter rates: Up to $3,000 a week for a fully staffed luxury yacht. Each charter firm offers its own fleet of charter yachts. They are usually large, well appointed vessels fit for Caribbean cruising. Most accommodate several couples to hold down costs to customers.

Benefits: these programs reduce ownership costs substantially. They sometimes produce a small profit. And they provide the prestige of yacht ownership.

Caution: Do not mistake these deals for investments. Boats are not an inflation hedge.

Judge the value of the boat you purchase by comparing it with the price of the same boat at your local yacht broker. It should be the same. Reason: The charter firm makes a brokerage commission, too, which should be sufficient profit. Check yachting magazines and newspapers' classified sections for used yachts for the type you want, to see how prices compare.

Sorting out the deals:

Leaseback programs guarantee fixed income from the charter business annually. Example: 8% of the purchase price annually. If it is chartered more often, the management firm keeps the additional profit. Problems: If the amount of profit guaranteed is too low, you could have trouble demonstrating to the IRS that the deal is a genuine business for profit. Check with your tax counselor.

Caution: If the leasing firm goes bankrupt, you might lose your investment tax credit unless you find another charterer to take the boat immediately.

Management programs mean more risk for the boat owner. Income depends on how often the yacht is chartered, especially during the peak season. The fee for each charter is split, since the management firm gets fees to cover advertising, maintenance, cleaning, and other details.

Owner expenses: Bank payments, maintenance fees, and insurance.

When choosing a chartering management firm look for one that:

• Is convenient to get to, where sailing is attractive.

• Puts a lot of money into advertising and promotion.

• Has an understandable and prompt accounting system.

• Runs a sound, cost-effective maintenance program.

• Charges rates that are competitive with local charter outfits.

• Offers a break on insurance.

Source: Robert J. Romberger, president, Cruising Center Charters, 541 Thames St., Newport, RI 02840.

Tax Shelter Registration

Most tax shelters now have to register with the Internal Revenue Service. Registered shelters must provide their investors with the registration number, and investors must show that number on their tax returns. Registration does not imply any kind of approval by the Internal Revenue Service, but rather serves as a warning to investors that the shelter is under IRS surveillance.

4

Saving Taxes

Fine Points of Tax Law

• Some financial institutions offer merchandise to customers who induce others to make deposits. The value of the merchandise depends upon the size of the induced deposit. The fair market value of the gift merchandise is includible in the recipient's gross income. (Now institutions file an information return with the IRS when the fair market value is $600 or more.)

• A solvent taxpayer freed of a debt by a lender must report this windfall as income. *Malmstedt et al. v. Comm'r., T. C Memo. 1976-392, reconsidered on remand, 4/20/79.*

• Interest paid on back taxes is deductible. So when you make a partial payment of back taxes, tell the IRS how to allocate it between principal and interest. If you don't, the IRS will apply the amount toward principal. Result: No deduction, but smaller interest payments in the future. Recommended: Weigh the value of any deduction against the cost of larger payments in the future.

• An individual reimbursed by his company for the business use of his car at a rate greater than the standard 20 ½ cents per mile must include the excess as income. He can then deduct the excess as a business expense, if he has substantiation that will satisfy the IRS. *IRS Letter Rulings 8003119 and 8004052, 10/29/79 and 10/30/79.*

• Gain on a house sale may not be taxable if the sale proceeds are used to purchase a yacht. But both the house and the yacht must qualify as the taxpayer's principal residence. *IRS Letter Ruling 8015017, 1/18/80.*

• Recording serial number of stocks might help reduce capital gains tax liability. It proves to the IRS when, and for how much, the stock was purchased. If the share's price went up, sales of those shares that cost the most produce the lowest capital gain. But if the taxpayer can't prove which shares he's selling, the IRS computes the gain on a straight first-in, first-out basis. *Kluger Associates, Inc., et al. v. Comm'r., 2d Cir., 3/17/80.*

• Silver lining to an unhappy land investment: IRS considers land a long-term capital investment. Buyers can write off losses in full against short-term capital gains and 50% of their losses, up to $3,000 per year, against their regular income. If you bought an undeveloped lot from a shady land-sales company, it may pay to finish paying it off, sell at any loss, and take the tax deductions.

• An employee who relocates because of a

job transfer loses the right to deduct moving expenses if he doesn't stick it out in the new location for at least 39 weeks.

• If your employer reimburses or pays your moving expenses, take allowable tax deductions and report the reimbursement as additional income.

• Moving expenses paid by landlord. Landlords seeking to persuade tenants to move often agree to pay part of all of the tenants' moving costs. Tax trap: The landlord's payment is fully includible in the taxpayer's income. But the expenses reimbursed are not deductible. Reason: the move isn't connected to a change in employment. This is one of the conditions to be met before moving expenses can be deducted. Impact: A tenant in the 50% tax bracket needs a $4,000 reimbursement to get enough after taxes to cover $2,000 of non-deductible moving expenses.

IRS Letter Ruling 8104100.

• If the doctor orders you to take a vacation, and says it's medically necessary, it may be deductible. One case: Doctor wouldn't permit the executive to go to Europe unless he took his wife along, since she was specially trained to deal with his heart illness. The wife's travel expenses were allowed as a medical deduction.

• Your last dollar of income could add $20 to your tax. That's because the tax tables use brackets, rather than exact calculation.

• If the check you mail to IRS should bounce, you can sometimes avoid interest and late-payment charges. Just be sure to send in a new check within 10 days after the IRS notifies you that the original check was not honored. Enclose a detailed explanation of the circumstances beyond your control that caused the check to bounce. If the circumstances were not beyond your control, you are stuck with the extra charges.

Internal Revenue Manual, P-2-8; P-2-16.

• IRS usually will not try to collect back taxes by levying against current Social Security benefits, veteran's benefits, GI Bill awards, and similar payments, even though it has the authority to do so. Exception: Flagrant or aggravated cases of neglect or refusal to pay.

Internal Revenue Manual, P-5-30.

• IRS can search your safe-deposit box: (1) If you refuse to pay taxes due. (2) If the auditor thinks you are hiding assets. The IRS can force open the box if you won't supply the key.

• If an IRS agent calls: find out if the person is a Revenue Agent or a Special Agent. (The agents are required to identify themselves.) Exercise extreme caution if it's a Special Agent. They are assigned to suspected fraud cases. Call your lawyer at once.

• If a parent buys a car for a dependent child, but keeps it in the parent's name, the sales tax, any uninsured casualty losses, and interest payments on the car are all tax-deductible. If the child cosigns the loan, interest is deductible as long as the car qualifies as part of the parent's support of the child.

• Proof that a car was used for business purposes: Keep a simple log in a 3- × 5-inch notebook, listing the date, beginning and ending mileage, and purpose of each tax-deductible trip. You may not take any deductions for business use of a car unless you keep such a log. Separate pages for business, medical, charitable, and moving-expense mileage simplify preparation of the tax return.

• Deductible costs of business driving include payments to injured pedestrians. A recent decision: Accidents by drivers are inseparable incidents of driving a car. Costs incurred as a result of such an incident are just as much a part of overall business expenses as the cost of fuel and maintenance.

Dancer et al. v. Comm'r., 73 T.C. No. 88, 3/13/80.

• Bigger deduction for sales tax: Keep a record of the amount of money paid for items on which sales tax is charged. Those who keep records usually get a higher deduction than the IRS tables allow.

• Casualty losses. Damage or loss of home or personal property entitle you to a casualty deduction, but not to the amount of the replacement cost. You can only claim the lower of either (1) the actual cost or (2) the fair market value immediately preceding the loss. In either case, you can only deduct that part of your loss that exceeds 10% of your adjusted gross income and the first $100 of each loss is not deductible.

Gay et al. v. Comm'r., T.C. Memo 1980-19, 1/23/80.

• You can't be audited twice by the same IRS agent. Exceptions: (1) A three-year gap or longer between the periods under investigation. (2) An intervening audit by a different IRS agent. (3) Cases that are part of the IRS's Coordinated Examination Program.
Internal Revenue Manual, P-4-5.

• IRS audits can be postponed if an immediate examination would adversely affect your business or personal activities. If you need a particular attorney, accountant, or employee to help with the audit, a postponement will be allowed to minimize impact on that person's business or personal activities. Under ordinary circumstances, postponements are for up to 60 days. A request for a longer extension must be approved by an IRS group manager.
Internal Revenue Manual, P-4-11.

• Investment advice currently is deductible. But the cost of acquiring an investment (a broker's commission, for example) is not. Recommended: Have the person who advises you and handles your investment transactions itemize the bill for services. Recent case: A valuable deduction for investment advice was lost when the taxpayer could not prove how much of a one-shot investment fee was allocable to advice.
Honodel, 76 T.C. No. 26.

• Casualty losses are deductible even when caused by the taxpayer's carelessness. But they are not deductible if caused by *gross* or *willful* negligence. The difference: Damage to a car is deductible even when caused by the owner's poor driving. But the damage is not deductible when caused by drunken driving.
IRS Publication 547 (1979).

• Legal costs incurred in an action to secure title to a piece of real property are not a deductible expense. They are capital costs, which must be added to the taxpayer's basis in the property.
Estate of Santiago Franco v. Comm'r., T.C. Memo 1980-340.

• Bankruptcy proceedings release an individual's wages for a levy by the IRS. One case: A taxpayer declared bankruptcy on May 14. So the IRS released a levy on her wages on May 15. But on May 16 her employer sent to the IRS wages she earned between May 5 and May 11. The taxpayer got her wages back. Reason:

Under state law, she wasn't entitled to receive her wages until payday, which was May 16. And that was after she filed the bankruptcy petition.
In re Florian Robert Babiarz, No. CHP 13 80 20591 (W.D. N.Y., 8/26/80).

• Long-distance phone calls made to a psychological counselor are a deductible medical expense.
Letter Ruling 8034087.

• A per diem living expense allowance paid to an employee who traveled around the country in an executive training program did not have to be reported in his income. Such an allowance is not reportable if it is received while traveling away from home. Key: The employee kept his tax home in the city where he originally lived by maintaining an apartment and bank account there, and paying local taxes.
Revenue Ruling 80-212.

• A settlement agreement between a taxpayer and an IRS appeals offices is not binding until it is reviewed and approved by a superior IRS officer with final settlement authority. One case: A taxpayer signed a settlement agreement and considered his case closed. Later, the IRS sued him for more taxes. Ruling: The taxpayer was liable. Trap: The IRS agent who agreed to the original settlement never submitted it for approval.
Michael J. Gardner, 75 T.C. No. 41.

• Closely held corporation's shareholders can benefit from the occasional sale of small amounts of stock to family members. Reason: Valuation of stock of a closely held corporation is among the most difficult income and estate tax problems. But value can be readily ascertained if there has been a recent trade of stock for fair market value. Sales to family members will suffice because even close relatives have to look out for their own interests. But the sales must be genuine.
Sirloin Stockade v. Comm'r., T.C. Memo 1980-303, 8/11/80.

• Medical expenses are not deductible when covered by insurance, whether or not a claim is filed. One case: A taxpayer incurred medical expenses that were covered by insurance. But he didn't file a claim because of the extensive paperwork involved. Held: The ex-

penses were not deductible. Reason: Even though the insurance did not pay for the expenses, it would have if the taxpayer had filed a claim.
Letter Ruling 8102010.

• Casualty losses are not deductible when there is a reasonable chance that they may be recovered through a lawsuit. But they may be deducted when the chance of recovery is very slight. One case: A taxpayer suffered uninsured losses in a house fire, which he felt was caused by a defective television set. He deducted the loss on his return. He also brought suit against the television set's maker. The IRS disallowed the deduction because of the possibility that the loss would be recovered through the lawsuit. Court's ruling: The loss was deductible. Reason: Even the taxpayer's own lawyer thought there was little chance of winning the suit.
William Johnson, Jr. v. Comm'r., T.C. Memo 1981-55.

• Trips to shareholder meetings are generally not deductible. But the trip may be deducted if it is directly related to the management of the shareholder's investment. One case: A shareholder traveled to a meeting to try to prevent the issuance of new shares that would have diluted his interest in the company. So the travel costs, including meals and lodging, were deductible.
Letter Ruling 8042071.

• New siding was deductible by a homeowner as a medical expense. Facts: The homeowner was allergic to mold, and the shingles on the old siding had grown moldy. So the old shingles were replaced with clapboard. Deduction: Cost of the siding minus any increase in the value of the home attributable to it. A doctor's recommendation helps.
Letter Ruling 8112069.

• A retired salesman was denied a business expense deduction for traveling to maintain contact with people he might do business with if he ever decided to come out of retirement. Point: You can be out of business and still deduct business expenses if you have concrete plans to go back into business and serve your old customers. But a vague hope isn't good enough. Suggestion: Sit down and prepare a written business plan, and show what you have done to implement the plan.
Mac Buckner, T.C. Memo 1981-165.

• The owner of a two-family house in a deteriorating neighborhood left an apartment vacant for five years while she searched in vain for "decent, desirable," working tenants. Result: Depreciation and maintenance expenses on the vacant apartment were not deductible. Reason: Her standards were so unrealistic that the court decided she wasn't really in the rental business anymore, so her expenses were not deductible.
Louise Hudson, T.C. Memo 1981-175.

• When a business is sold, the sales agreement should allocate a portion of the purchase price to each of its assets. Reason: Specific values are needed to compute such tax items as the investment credit and deductions for depreciation. Specific values are also needed for possible recapture of tax liability when the assets are sold. Danger: If values aren't assigned in the sales agreement, the IRS usually assigns its own.

Common Tax Return Mistakes

Medical expenses:
• Forgetting to deduct the premium charged for Supplementary Medicare (Part B).
• Failing to check auto insurance policies and dependent's student-fee charges at college. Often, there is a separate charge for medical coverage that can be deducted.
• Overlooking taxi or bus fares to and from the doctor's office.
• Not deducting parking fees and tolls in addition to the 9 cents per mile that can be deducted when you use your own car for medical travel.
• Not including trips to the drugstore, optician, or other health facility in medical travel.
Interest expenses:
• Not listing the finance charge you incur when you pay insurance premiums in installments.

• In the case of buying or selling a home, forgetting to deduct interest—and real estate tax—proration.

• Forgetting to deduct penalties you've paid on premature saving withdrawals.

• Overlooking the mortgage prepayment penalty assessed against you.

• Neglecting to add up and deduct the total credit card finance charges for the year.

Charitable Deductions

• Neglecting to calculate charitable mileage for you and your spouse for church, school, scouting, and other volunteer activities. Deduction for charitable mileage is set at 12¢ a mile, beginning in 1985.

• Not deducting the charitable percentage of *National Geographic, Smithsonian,* and similar organization dues in excess of value of subscription received.

• Not including the excess of payments for Christmas cards and other items purchased from charities over value received.

• Forgetting to document and deduct out-of-pocket expenses incurred on behalf of charitable activities—such as Scout leaders' uniforms, donated purchases.

• Not listing excess cost of attending charitable benefits or of purchasing property from a charity (for example, public television auction) over value received.

Sales tax:

• Itemizing sales tax on expenditures you have receipts for (to determine if more of a deduction can be claimed than the IRS tables allow) without including items you don't normally get a receipt for. Example: Lunches at work ($5 a day @ 250 workdays = $1,250 × 8% sales tax = $100).

Using the tables the IRS supplies for figuring the sales tax deduction without reading all the accompanying instructions and footnotes.

Example: The tables are keyed to your family's adjusted gross income (AGI, line 32 on your tax return). But in using the tables, you can add nontaxable income that is not included in your AGI, such as Social Security benefits, unemployment compensation, excluded dividend payments (line 9b) on the return), and the nontaxed portion of your capital gains (line 22 on Schedule D).

Example: The tables themselves reflect only state sales tax amounts. The footnotes tell you how much to add to reflect local taxes. New York City residents, for example, can increase the figure in the table by 107%. Massachusetts residents can add on the sales tax for any single item of clothing that costs $175 or more.

Investment expenses:

• Not claiming stock transfer taxes as an itemized deduction on Schedule A. Most people simply include it in the cost basis of their stock because it is included in the net figure on the confirmation slips they get from their broker. This deduction is worth up to 2½ times as much if you treat it as an itemized deduction.

• Not counting newspapers or other publications that you buy to keep track of investment information.

• Not deducting the fee for a safe deposit box holding your stocks, bonds, and other income producing assets.

• Not claiming a deduction for investment counseling fees.

• Overlooking the cost of alarm systems and home safes that are used primarily to protect investments, such as art or coin collections.

Interest and Dividend income:

• Not checking to make sure the dividend income you are reporting is fully taxable. Some part of it may be a nontaxable distribution. Example: The dividend from a regulated utility, such as Pennsylvania Power.

• Forgetting to elect to report annually interest earned on Series E bonds owned by *children* to take advantage of their low tax bracket.

Source: Randy Bruce Blaustein, J.D., tax manager, Siegel & Mendlowitz, CPAs, 310 Madison Ave., New York 10017.

Understanding the Capital Gains Tax

Examine all investments from a tax point of view before year-end to make sure that profits aren't lost through a lack of sophistication about taxes. Point: Long-term capital gains bestow tax benefits. But numerous tax traps result from the way capital gains and capital losses interact.

What to do: Examine all investment transactions that will be completed by the end of the year. Sort them out as:

- Net long-term capital gain.
- Net long-term capital loss.
- Net short-term capital gain.
- Net short-term capital loss.

Basic: To qualify as long-term, a gain or loss must result from the disposition of a capital asset held for more than six months.

How gains and losses are taxed:

Long-term capital gains. Individuals get to deduct 60% of the gain from income. The remaining 40% is taxed at normal rates. Example: If an individual is in the 50% tax bracket, the effective tax on a long-term capital gain will be 20% (50% × 40%). Corporations can choose to be taxed either at the normal corporate tax rate or at an alternative rate of 28%, whichever is lower.

Short-term capital gains. Taxed as ordinary income to both individuals and corporations.

Capital losses for individuals. Deductible, but only to the amount of $3,000 per year. And long-term capital losses are deductible only at a rate of 50 cents on the dollar. Result: It takes $6,000 in long-term capital losses to get a $3,000 deduction. Carryover feature: Losses generating deductions in excess of $3,000 can be carried over to later years.

Capital losses for corporations. Not deductible in the year they occur. Carryover: Such losses can be carried back three years or forward five years to offset capital gains.

Tax-Wise Timing of Capital Gains and Losses

The first step in planning year-end tax moves in your investment portfolio: Decide what you would do if you were not con-

cerned with taxes. Then you can weigh the tax benefits of various strategies against your overall investment goals. A bad investment decision with mitigating tax consequences is still a bad investment decision.

The basic rules:

It's better not to realize short-term losses in the same year that you realize long-term gains. On long-term assets,* only 40% of any gain is included in your taxable income. If you have an overall loss on short-term assets, it must be used to wipe out any long-term capital gains income you may have. After that, any remaining loss can be applied against up to $3,000 of non-capital gains income. Since only 40 cents of every long-term capital gain dollar is taxed, you're better off taking short-term losses in a year when they will be applied against fully taxed income from other sources.

Take long-term losses in a year when you have short-term gains, if possible. One dollar of long-term loss wipes out one dollar of short-term gain, which would otherwise be fully taxed. Trap to avoid: If there is no short-term gain to apply it against, a dollar of long-term loss wipes out only 50 cents of taxable income.

Do not take long-term losses and long-term gains in the same year. When they occur in the same year, they must be offset against each other. A long-term loss dollar that's applied against a long-term gain dollar reduces taxable income by 40 cents. If that same long-term loss dollar is applied against non-capital gains income, it reduces taxable income by 50 cents.

Example: Let's assume that you own two blocks of stock bought at the beginning of last year. One block has gone up in value by $2,500. The other block of stock has gone down $2,500. If you sell both blocks this year, they cancel each other out. If you take the loss now and defer the gain to next year, you cut this year's taxable income by $1,250 (50% of the loss). And next year's taxable income is increased by only $1,000 (40% of the gain).

Don't forget the limit on deducting capital losses. After you apply capital losses against

---

*Assets held for more than six months.

capital gains, the losses that remain can only be used to offset up to $3,000 worth of other income. Any leftover loss is carried forward to future years until it's used up.

How to postpone gains and losses:

Suppose you have a paper gain or loss that you don't want to realize this year because you'll run afoul of one of the basic tax-saving rules. You don't have to risk your gain or worry that your loss will increase. A short sale against the box nails your profit down immediately, while postponing the tax. To execute the play: Your broker sells borrowed stock on your behalf.

Example: You have 100 shares of Acme Industries, which you bought two years ago at $10, and that you believe has now peaked at $50. But you don't want long-term gain this year. Your broker sells 1000 borrowed shares of Acme on your behalf. This locks in your profit at $50 a share. In January, you turn over your 100 shares to replace the ones your broker borrowed.

The IRS says you do not have a gain on this transaction until you replace the shares that were borrowed. Result: Gain is taxable next year.

Caution: Even though this rule postpones the time when a gain is recognized, you can't use it to convert a short-term gain into a long-term one. A special rule prevents that.

Use the same technique to put off recognizing a loss. A short sale against the box right now protects you against future price declines. And by waiting until next year to replace the borrowed shares, you delay reporting the loss.

Caution: Don't use this technique for stock bought within the last six months.

Reason: Unless you replace the borrowed stock within six months of the date your own shares were acquired, the loss will be long term instead of short term. In most cases, a long-term loss is only half as valuable for your tax purposes.

Puts postpone, too. You can achieve pretty much the same effect by writing an option to sell your stock at a fixed price on an agreed-upon date in the future. This put is treated like a short sale for tax purposes.

Ask your broker which tactic is most likely to cost less in your particular set of circumstances.

Watch out for wash sales. If you're selling stock now in order to realize a loss this year, make sure you have not bought other shares of the same stock within 30 days before the sale date. Don't buy more shares of the same stock for at least 30 days after the sale. Reason: The transaction will be treated as a wash sale and the loss will be disallowed. This rule only applies to sales at a loss. Remember that you sell stock at a gain, your gain is taxable even if you repurchase the same shares the following day.

Save Taxes through 'Wash Sale' Of Securities

Taxes can sometimes be reduced by selling and repurchasing the same security.

Example: A taxpayer has short-term gains for the year. He also owns securities that have declined in value.

Wash sale technique: The taxpayer should sell the securities to get a capital loss. That offsets the gain. Then he repurchases the same securities.

Result: Taxable gain to the taxpayer is eliminated but the investment portfolio remains unchanged.

Note: The same securities can not be repurchased within 30 days of their sale, or the loss will be disallowed. But they can be repurchased after 30 days. And similar securities can be bought immediately.

Opposite problem: A taxpayer has a long-term capital loss for the year. He also owns securities that have gone up in value. Wash sale: Sell the securities for a profit without incurring tax because of the offsetting loss. Then immediately repurchase the same securities. (The 30-day rule does not apply to profitable sales.) Result: The taxpayer's cost basis in the securities is increased. Future profits that may result from their ultimate disposition will be reduced.

Net effect: Current long-term capital losses are used dollar for dollar to reduce future capital income.

Smart Timing of Income and Deductions

It's often possible, within limits, to choose when you will receive certain kinds of income, when you will take certain kinds of losses, and when you will make expenditures that qualify you for a tax deduction or a tax credit.

The general goal: To even out taxable income from one year to the next. Reason: Income that's bunched into high-earning years will generally be taxed at higher rates.

Watch out for the alternate minimum tax (AMT). The rule is just the opposite for an AMT year: If you face that tax instead of the regular tax, you will want to accelerate income into your AMT year. Reason: Maximum AMT is 20%.

If you are very confident of earning a high return on investments, then you might find it worthwhile to postpone income and accelerate deductions this year, even though you expect to be in a higher tax bracket next year. Calculation: Putting off paying tax means greater current cash flow to generate further income. Essential: Projected return must offset taxation at a higher rate next year.

If you qualify for four-year income averaging (or if you are close to qualifying), it may pay to bunch income somewhat in order to make the most of the special advantage income averaging gives you. But this is tricky, and it requires complex calculations. Have your tax adviser check it out.

Reminder: In order to do the income averaging computation, you will need copies of your returns for the three previous years. If you don't have copies in your own files, check with your tax adviser. If they are not available from your adviser, you can get back copies, for a fee, by filing Form 4506 with the IRS Service Center where your returns were filed.

Timing income is a matter of controlling when income is received. Cash-basis taxpayers (the category that covers most individuals) count income in the year it's received, not the year it's earned. Ways to take control of timing:

Bonuses and year-end commissions can be postponed if you make an agreement with your employer that entitles the company to hold off payment until next year. Caution: You have to do this before the bonus becomes payable. Asking your boss after that date to hold the check until next year doesn't make it taxable next year.

If you are self-employed, you can delay mailing December bills to clients and customers to lessen taxable income in December and beef it up in January.

If you own income property, consider declaring a Christmas rent "holiday." Advise tenants whose rent checks are normally due during the last two weeks in December that they can delay payment until, say, January 10, to ease the strain of holiday cash flow. Make it clear, though, that this is only a one-time deal and that January rent payments will be back on the normal schedule.

Timing deductions. A cash-basis taxpayer usually deducts expenses in the year they are paid. But prepaying certain kinds of expenses does not yield a current deduction. (Details are explained below.) What's more, current deductions don't always reduce your taxable income because of the way the Zero Bracket Amount (ZBA) works.

How the ZBA affects deductions: Many people don't realize that a few years back, Congress got rid of the old "standard deduction" and replaced it with the ZBA, which is built into the tax table. If you are single or the head of a household, the ZBA is $2,390. It's $3,540 if you are married, filing jointly, and $1,770 if you are married, filing separately. You can deduct only the portion of your itemized deductions that exceeds your ZBA.

If your itemized deductions this year will be less than your ZBA, postpone as many deductible expenditures as possible into next year and prepay deductible expenses next year that would ordinarily be paid the year after. Payoff: Instead of just missing the ZBA every year, you can beat it every other year.

One way to accelerate deductions. A deductible item charged to a credit card this year is deductible this year, even if the bill is paid next year.

Medical expenses. Prepayment usually does not work because you can't deduct a medical expense until it is incurred. But delaying payment until next year is smart if this year's expenses are not likely to go beyond 5% of adjusted gross income. (Anything below 5% is not deductible.)

Timing tax payments. Take advantage of any leeway in paying deductible taxes. If you prepay next year's real estate tax, for example, you can deduct it now. Alternative timing: It may be cost-effective to put off a tax payment that's due this year, even if you incur a small penalty, if the deduction will be more valuable next year.

If you are required to pay estimated state income tax: Don't wait until January to make the fourth-quarter payment. This is a very important move to make if you have had unusually high income this year. Don't be afraid to err on the side of overpayment. Reason: The payment is fully deductible this year. Any overpayment will be refunded and taxed as income at next year's lower rate. Caution: Don't overinflate an estimated state tax payment. The IRS could call it a sham and disallow the tax deduction.

If a federal income tax audit left you owing money to the IRS: Prepare an amended state return for the year in question and pay the additional tax before the year is out. Benefits: Reduces the interest due on the state income tax deficiency. Nails down a federal income tax deduction for this year.

Bear in mind: Most states now have information-sharing agreements with IRS. It's virtually certain that your state tax agency will get a copy of the IRS audit report and that you will be assessed additional state income tax eventually.

Big ticket purchases: If you are going to be buying a car, a boat, a mobile home, or building materials for a new house at some point in the near future, time your purchase for the year when you are likely to need deductions. Reason: The sales tax on these items is deductible over and above the standard sales tax deduction that the IRS allows you on the basis of your income and the size of your family.

Interest. In general, interest payments are only deductible for the period the interest payment covers. If you prepay January interest on a mortgage or other loan, you can't claim the deduction until next year. Major exception: Points on a loan to purchase or improve your principal residence are fully deductible in the year you pay them. (Points on any other kind of loan are deducted pro rata over the life of the loan.)

Charitable contributions. Generally deductible in the year they are made. Limitation: The ceiling on how much you can deduct in any one year may be either 20%, 30%, or 50% of your adjusted gross income. It varies, depending on what you are donating (cash or various types of property) and what type of organization you are donating it to. Check with your tax adviser before making an unusually large donation. There are also new proof rules that apply to large donations.

Bad debts and worthless stock. These are deductible in the year they become worthless. It's up to you to establish when that takes place. What to do to establish a loss: If, say, you are holding an old IOU from someone who has left town, visit a lawyer and find out whether there's any chance of collecting. If the lawyer says it's impractical to bring suit, ask the lawyer for a letter confirming that fact.

Dependents. If you have been supporting an adult relative who is not working, you may be able to claim a dependency exemption ($1,040). Key: You must provide more than half the support, and the dependent must have less than $1,040 of gross income.

Social Security payments are not income for purposes of the $1,040 test. But if, say, your mother spends too much of her own money on herself, you might fail the 50% support test. What to do right now:

Figure out how much you have sent her so far this year and how much she has spent on her own support.

It may pay to send a little extra money in December and have her bank part of her Social Security check.

If she earns some income from part-time work, consider asking her to take a vacation in December if the earnings would otherwise disqualify your dependency exemption.

Plan now for next year. Suppose your mother (or other dependent) now derives two-thirds of her support from savings and Social Security and one-third from you. Work it out so that you increase next year's payments to cover more than half of her support. Have her put more of her Social Security check into the bank or draw out less of her savings. The following year, you can reduce your contributions to make up for the extra payments next year. The extra savings from next year can make up the difference. Result: On a two-year basis, your cash contribution for support is about the same. But you get a $1,040 dependency exemption every other year.

Added break: If you are single and living alone, a dependent parent makes you eligible for head of household rates, which are considerably lower than the rates paid as a single taxpayer. Your parent does not have to live with you for you to qualify as a head of household.

Pay medical expenses for a potential dependent as part of your contribution to support. If you pay a $500 dental bill on your mother's behalf, that $500 is counted in determining whether you have provided more than half of her support. If you meet the 50% support test, you can also deduct the payment as a medical expense, which may help lift those expenses up over the 5% of gross income point and allow them to be deducted. You get this deduction even if you lose the dependency exemption because your parent's income is too high.

Tax-saving gifts. The annual gift-tax exclusion: $10,000 per recipient, or $20,000 per recipient if you and your spouse elect to be treated as joint donors. This exclusion does not carry over from year to year. If you don't use each year's exclusion, it's lost.

Large gifts: If you're giving away property that's worth more than the annual exclusion, have your lawyer draw up a deed of gift covering a part interest in the property. Using this technique, you and your spouse could make a tax-free gift of $60,000 over a three-year period to an individual. If you're making a gift to a couple (your son and daughter-in-law, perhaps), you can make a tax-free transfer worth $60,000 in the 13 months between December of one year and January of the second following year.

Tax Traps When Starting A New Business

Individuals are often surprised to find out that expenses incurred in deciding whether or not to enter a new business are not deductible.

Companies that are considering a new business venture can deduct the expenses one way or another, either by amortizing start-up costs over a five-year period or, if the venture doesn't work out, writing it off in one year. It's different for individuals. If they haven't advanced beyond the investigatory stage then, at best, they can perhaps get deductions for some financial or legal advice related to their personal taxes. The IRS reasons that allowing investigatory deductions might encourage people to write off personal expenses (trips, materials, etc.) as business deductions.

Bottom line: If you are considering going into a new business, it's better to actually do it (on a small scale) than to spend many nondeductible dollars on feasibility studies and financial and legal advice. These are deductible once you are in business, not before.

The same applies to the costs of incorporating. If a business idea under investigation requires spending, say, $10,000, it would be well worth investing $500 to $1,000 to incorporate a business first.

To carry this philosophy a step further, if you do decide to go into a business, prolong as many start-up costs as possible until after you actually are in business. Then they become deductible.

Source: Edward Mendlowitz, senior tax partner, Siegel & Mendlowitz, CPAS, 310 Madison Ave., New York 10016, and author of *Successful Tax Planning,* Boardroom Books, Millburn, NJ.

The Corporate Owner's Salary

The head of a closely held corporation must be careful in setting his own salary. Problem: Determining what salary will keep personal and corporate tax liabilities to a minimum.

Dangers: Salary payments considered unreasonably large by the IRS will be deemed dividends paid from profits. They will be subject to double taxation, first as corporate income, then as personal income. Counterpoint: If too little salary is taken, the corporation may accumulate excessive earnings and face an accumulated earnings tax penalty.

In favor of a low salary: The company may be able to afford greater fringe benefits (for example, insurance), which are deductible to the firm and excluded from the individual's income. Also, retention of earnings will increase the value of the firm and maximize the capital gain available if it's sold or liquidated.

How to show a salary is reasonable: Compare it with the salaries of individuals performing similar duties for other firms. The Bureau of Labor Statistics is an excellent source of compensation figures. One way to justify an unusually high salary: The owner shows that he took a correspondingly low salary in earlier years to help the firm get established.

How to avoid trouble with the IRS:

• Don't be greedy. A salary that impinges on cash flow will be questioned by the IRS.

• Separate salaries from stock. If salaries are paid in proportion to stockholdings, the IRS may call them dividend distributions instead. Helpful: Have all working shareholders receive raises at the same time other employees do.

• Avoid bonuses. A bonus paid out at the end of a good year might be considered a distribution of profits (taxable to the company and to the recipient).

• Pay dividends regularly. When the IRS doesn't find declared dividends, it looks for hidden ones.

The specific tax effects of various distribution schemes must be worked out on a trial-and-error basis. Consider the different investment opportunities available to corporations and individuals, as well as the differences between the corporate and personal tax rates.

Useful: A repayment agreement. This calls for the employee to repay the firm any amount of his salary that might later be deemed excessive. The repayment is deductible by the employee. Caution: Repayment agreements can be dangerous, and must be carefully considered and drafted by an expert. Example: The repayment of a large amount of salary could result in a firm's having to pay taxes on excessive accumulated earnings.

Tax Status of 25 Fringes And Perks

Company payment or reimbursement of medical and disability insurance. Tax status: Tax-free to executive. Deductible by corporation.

Medical examinations. Tax status: Tax-free to executive. Deductible by corporation.

Company payment or reimbursement of medical-dental expenses for executive and family. Tax status: Deductible by company. Tax-free to executive only if the same benefits are provided for other employees.

Company gym. Tax status: Tax-free to executive. Deductible by company.

Group term life insurance. Tax status: Tax-free to executive up to $50,000 coverage; excess taxable on favored basis. Fully deductible by corporation. Plan must not discriminate against ordinary employees.

Split-dollar life insurance. Tax status: Taxable to executive on basis of "cost" of one-year term, less part of premium paid by executive. Company gets no deduction for premiums paid but gets them back tax-free eventually out of proceeds.

Interest-free and low-interest loans. Interest bargain taxable to executive and deductible by him to extent allowable. Interest bargain taxed to company.

Business and professional clubs. Tax status: Tax-free to executive. Deductible by company.

Country clubs, social, athletic, or sporting clubs. Tax status: Tax-free to executive and deductible by company only if primarily and directly used for business.

Luncheon clubs. Tax status: Tax-free to executive and deductible by company if conducive to business.

Meals furnished on company premises, including executive dining room. Tax status: Tax-free to executive and deductible by company if for company's convenience.

Supper money. Tax status: Tax-free to executive. Deductible by company.

Lodging on company premises. Tax status: Tax-free to executive only if a condition of employment. Deductible by company.

Travel away from home. Tax status: Tax-free to executive and deductible by company if reasonable and necessary for business.

Travel expenses of wife. Tax status: Taxable to executive unless wife's presence has a bona fide business purpose. Deductible by company if ordinary and necessary.

Local travel, parking fees, tolls, etc. Tax status: Tax-free to executive and deductible by company if business-related, excluding commutation.

Entertainment. Tax status: Business meals, employee recreation and social activities, business conventions generally are tax-free to executive and deductible by company if they are "ordinary and necessary." Other entertainment expenses are tax-free to the executive and deductible by company only if directly related to or associated with business.

Logging required. No deduction for any of the above items unless a contemporary record of business use exists.

Legal services. Tax status: Tax-free to executive and deductible by company if provided under qualified plan.

Financial counseling. Tax status: Taxable to executive, but deductible by him to extent attributable to tax or investment advice or preparation of tax returns. Deductible by company.

Education and training to improve existing job skills. Tax status: Tax-free to executive. Deductible by firm. Plan must not discriminate, and yearly benefits can't exceed $5,000.

Company car, airplane, or boat. Tax status: Tax-free to executive to extent of business use and minimal personal use.

Chauffeur. Tax status: Same as company vehicle.

Mixed use property. New limits apply to credits and deductions for business use of mixed use property—property suitable for both business and personal use. Logging is necessary to prove business use.

Death benefit. Tax status: Tax-free to executive's beneficiary up to $5,000. Deductible by corporation.

Moving expenses. Tax status: Tax-free to executive and deductible by company subject to special limitations.

Officer and director liability insurance. Tax status: Generally not taxable to executive. Deductible by company.

Tax Savings for Commuters

Executives whose offices are located in states with high income taxes, but who work at home, can lower their tax payments by splitting their state tax liability, if their home state tax rate is lower.

Principle: An executive who can prove he does only a percentage of his job in his office (located in a high-tax state) only has to pay income tax to that state on the percentage of his salary he earns in his office.

Case: A resident of New Jersey worked in New York as the publisher of specialty magazines about firearms, home improvements, dogs, and horses. His job included testing new products, which required access to storage facilities, a firing range, and stables—all of which were at his home. Since New Jersey's taxes are lower than New York's, he allocated his state income tax accordingly.

New York contested this allocation, arguing that the testing facilities "could have been set up somewhere in New York," and were located in New Jersey merely for the publisher's convenience.

Ruling: Publisher's allocation was justified. The argument that the testing facilities could have been set up in New York was irrelevant. *

Commuting expense might be deductible if the job is far from home but temporary, so that it doesn't make sense to relocate permanently. One taxpayer recently won by showing that he thought the job would be temporary, even though it lasted for three years.

If a person works at least two jobs in the same day, the cost of traveling from first job to second job is deductible as a business expense. (Still can't deduct travel from home to first job or from second job back home.)

*Myron Fass v. State Tax Commission, 3/15/79; 17-447.

Transferring Shares in The Family Business

When you transfer shares in a family business to your kids, you *must* do it right. Otherwise, the IRS will treat you as the continuing owner. A recent IRS court victory illustrates some do's and don'ts:

Do appoint a guardian or custodian if the children are minors. Your spouse is okay. But the guardian must exercise genuine control.

Don't act as your child's proxy at shareholder meetings.

Don't accumulate funds in the corporation without specific plans showing how the money is to be used and what corporate purpose is to be served.

Do pay dividends that are reasonable in relation to the company's earnings.

Don't go too far in reassuring major suppliers or key customers that you will continue to be involved in managing the company. A letter saying that the whole thing was done for tax purposes could be used against you.

Do make sure that any loan you get from the company is adequately secured, bears reasonable interest, and in all other ways meets standards that an arm's-length lender would impose.

Deducting the Cost of an Office at Home

Taking a home-office deduction will increase the chance of your return being audited. The IRS doesn't have to go over the return with a fine-tooth comb to pull out the office deductions, either, since taxpayers are asked directly on Schedule C whether or not they deducted "expenses for an office in their home."

What's allowed: The office space must be regularly and exclusively used as the taxpayer's principal place of business or for meeting patients, customers, and others in business. A new decision expanded the definition of "principal" business.

Sample case: A dermatologist was employed full time by a hospital. He also owned six condominium units, which he rented to others. He managed these units entirely himself, using one of the two bedrooms in his own condominium exclusively as an office. The room contained the usual office equipment (books, desk, files, telephone answering device, calculator), but no TV or couch. No guests stayed in the room at any time. Even the closet was used only for storing tools, cleaning materials, extra lamps, and other items for managing the rental properties. The IRS claimed that (1) The taxpayer's rental activities did not qualify as a "business." (2) Even if they did, the taxpayer's "principal" place of business was the hospital where he was employed, not his office at home.

Wrong on both counts, said the tax court. Renting even a single piece of property has been held to be a business, if done for the production of income. And the IRS was mistaken in trying to add the income from all the dermatologist's "businesses" to determine if the rental units were the "principal" source of his income. Managing the units was, in itself, a "principal" business worthy of a deduction for expenses.

Residential exemptions. There has also been a great deal of speculation about the fate of the up to $125,000 lifetime exclusion on capital gains (for taxpayers 55 years old and older) from the sale of a residence, where part of the residence is used for business purposes. Would having even a small part of a residence as an office (or a room rented to a boarder) kill the exclusion? No, said a recent ruling. But the up to $125,000 exclusion is reduced in proportion to the amount of "business" conducted at the taxpayer's residence.

Example: A home bought 12 years ago for $70,000 is now sold for $120,000. But 35% of the residence's space has been used for a business, so only 65% of the $50,000 difference, or $32,500, is exempt from capital gains taxes.

Caution: Taxpayers can lose both ways if they are not careful. The IRS may be able to claim that an activity does not meet the requirements for a home-office deduction, but that the activity is enough of a business to reduce the exclusion.

Complying with "exclusive use" restrictions: There's no clear ruling, but a work area probably does not have to be totally walled off to qualify for an exemption. A low partition might be enough.

Also qualifying: Workers who do most of their work at a client's location (salespeople, artists showing the portfolios, and others), but who are self-employed or have no office provided by their employer. An office at an employer's business can void the deduction even if it is not used.

Expenses that can be deducted if the taxpayer qualifies: Books, magazine subscriptions, phone charges, filing cabinets, and other equipment of the business (depreciated each year). Also: A portion of the utility costs; maintenance of the entire structure; rewiring of the entire structure. Not qualified: Maintenance or remodeling of a portion of the structure, such as a kitchen or living room, that has no bearing on the home's business use.

Professional tax help is needed for home-office matters. Where expenses for business use of a home are deducted depends on each taxpayer. Employees not reimbursed by the employer treat the deduction as follows:

Expenses to be deducted are not entered on line 24 of Form 1040 (as an employee business expense). They belong on line 22 of Schedule A.

Salespeople normally deduct the home office on Form 2106 as an unreimbursed business expense.

Self-employed taxpayers place deductions on Schedule C. If space is used to generate rental income, use Schedule E instead.

Source: Sidney Kess, tax partner, Main Hurdman & Cranstoun, 280 Park Ave., New York 10017, and adjunct professor at New York Law School.

Tax Tip for the Self-Employed

Self-employed people are likely to have their returns audited if they take the standard deduction instead of itemizing personal non-business deductions, especially if their business shows a high gross and a low net. The IRS will suspect that personal deductions have been charged to the business.

Deduct Travel to Check on Investments

Investors can deduct expenses of travel, including foreign travel, to check on investments in real estate or business.

Keep careful records, though. Expect IRS to be skeptical. A diary should clearly show how much of the trip was spent inspecting properties and how much was personal and recreational.

Important: IRS can challenge any transaction that doesn't have a serious business purpose, but appears to be only an effort to avoid taxes. Frivolous investments in faraway places will be challenged, and trips to look for investments are not deductible.

Trips Mixing Business and Pleasure

The tax rules governing travel deductions are very complicated. The rules for allocating personal and business costs on a trip are subject to interpretation. Also: The rules vary, depending on whether the trip is domestic or foreign.

Basic point: Travel costs are deductible if they are "ordinary and necessary" for conducting business. Depending on the industry and on the company, that can leave room for fancy suites and travel with your spouse. But beware: The IRS can do more than disallow a deduction for travel expenses. It can clamp a 5% penalty on the entire tax owed for the year if it finds an "intentional disregard" for the rules.

Necessary proof. There will be no deduction allowed for business travel unless supported by a contemporaneous record showing dates, costs, and business purpose.

Domestic travel: Enjoying some rest and relaxation on a business trip is fine, says the IRS. Expenses attributable to the "non-business" aspects of the journey—extra days of hotel expenses and extra meals—are not deductible. But the cost of travel itself, from home to the "away-from-home" location, is entirely deductible if the business portion of the journey takes more time than the pleasure.

The reverse is also true: The taxpayer pays for all the travel if personal matters take even a day more than the business ones. The only deduction then: Meals, lodging, and necessary incidentals for the business matters, but meals can't be deducted unless lodging is, too.

There's no deduction ever for meals on one-day trips—even if it's a trip from New York to Chicago in the morning and back at midnight.

Foreign trips: The IRS is generally more liberal in allowing deductions for foreign business travel. But the rules are more complicated than for domestic trips. Example: The IRS will allow deductions for expenses if the trip lasts a week or less. Or if the vacation days total less than one-fourth of the days spent abroad. Journeys that exceed those limits cannot be deducted at all. But, if the limits are not exceeded, travelers can deduct on-the-site expenses attributable to business, along with a portion of the transportation to the site and home again.

Figuring transport costs: First, add the cost of tickets, limos, meals, and lodging en route. Secondly, multiply the total by the number of business days on the trip. Finally, divide by the total number of days. Result: The portion that is deductible.

Length of trip: Don't count the departure day if doing so would result in an "eight-day" trip. In other words, a Saturday-to-Saturday trip is only "seven" days as far as the IRS is concerned. But do count the departure day if the trip is longer. Example: A Saturday-to-the-following-Sunday trip should be considered nine days, as are days in which: (1) A majority of the business hours are devoted to business. (2) Business was scheduled, but circumstances beyond the traveler's control made it impossible. (3) Business reasons dictated that the traveler's presence was required, but only for a small part of a day.

In addition: Legal holidays or weekend days that fall between business days may be considered business days if the traveler is trying to conduct affairs "with reasonable dispatch."

A big loophole: Even if more than 25% of the trip is devoted to pleasure, and even if the trip lasts more than a week, a deduction is still possible, if: (1) The traveler shows that he or she did not have "substantial control" over the trip arrangements. (Mere control over travel time is not "substantial control.") (2) The traveler made the trip on behalf of an employer under some expense-allowance reimbursement plan (and owns or controls 10% or less of the company stock). (3) The traveler shows hard evidence that business reasons alone dictated the need for the trip.

Conventions: Travel to domestic meetings and conventions is treated for tax purposes just like any other "ordinary and necessary" business expense. Conventions in Puerto Rico, however, are considered "domestic." But other types of business travel there are considered "foreign."

The IRS has placed heavier restrictions on

foreign "convention travel." If the convention takes place outside North America, the traveler must prove that it was as reasonable to hold the convention abroad as to hold it in North America.

More information: *Executive's Guide to Travel and Entertainment Expenses*, Arthur Andersen & Co., Chicago.

Deducting a Spouse's Convention Tab

One of the most difficult expenses to justify as deductible is the convention tab of executives' spouses.

A Tax Court decision shows that this is indeed possible.

Case: A bank required its employees who went to annual conventions of the industry to take their wives as registered participants. At these conventions, executives fraternized with key personnel of other banks with whom they regularly discussed such mutual problems as loans, investments, and leveraged lease transactions. Wives entertained and socialized with other bankers and their spouses.

The IRS sought to disallow wives' expenses on the ground that what the wives did wasn't necessary to business activities. But, ruled the court, the conventions were working sessions and not vacations for the executives or their spouses. The employer had found the presence of spouses was so useful in fostering good working relations with other companies that executives had to bring their wives.

An expenditure qualifies as a necessary expense when it is appropriate and helpful to the taxpayer's business, and such was the case here.

Warning: Note that here we are dealing with a customary industry practice. Also: (1) The executives were obliged to bring their spouses. (2) None of the executives involved was a major stockholder in the corporation. (3) There were both individual and group activities on the program. (Be sure to keep a copy of the printed program for the Revenue Agent.)

Bank of Stockton, T.C. Memo 1977-24, 1/31/77.

A Private Plane as a Deductible Expense

A private plane used partly for business purposes can yield substantial tax benefits: Investment tax credits, depreciation write-offs, and deductions for operating expenses. All are keyed to the percentage of time the plane is flown for business purposes. Deciding what is and what is not considered to be business flying can be crucial.

Taxpayer victory: Kenneth L. Knudtson flies all over the country visiting auto-wrecking yards. In his business, rebuilding windshield-wiper motors, the major problem is maintaining an adequate supply of old motors. When Knudtson bought a Beechcraft Bonanza plane in 1975, he didn't have an instrument rating. To get it, he flew 53.6 training hours. The IRS called this nonbusiness flying and tried to cut Knudtson's tax write-offs accordingly, but the Tax Court disagreed with the IRS.

Key: Acquiring an instrument rating was "appropriate and helpful" to Knudtson's business. Weather conditions would often ground him without it. So it was proper to treat the training flights as business use, decided the Tax Court.

Kenneth L. Knudtson, T.C. Memo 1980-45.

Keeping an Expense-Account Diary

Proper documentation for your expense account is essential for a tax deduction. Deduction will be denied without it.

Best bet: Keep a diary of expenses to supplement your receipts, vouchers, and cancelled checks. Keep this up to date.

What to include: The amount spent, where, on whom, and for what business purposes. Make the entries daily. Tax laws demand a timely recording of expenses. Shortcuts: Daily costs of meals can be lumped as one entry. So can taxi fares and phone calls.

What to keep: Receipts for any expenditures under $25, even when not formally required.

Example: A receipt for $13 worth of cocktails. These detailed tallies are appreciated by your accountant and the IRS. Also, be sure to retain all bills for lodging when traveling on business.

Substantiating Lost Expense Records

The taxpayer bears the burden of proof when records are lost or destroyed and must be reconstructed. For travel and entertainment expenses, this task is not easy. The IRS does not have to allow a cent that can't be supported by records indicating how much was spent, when, where, upon whom, and for what business purpose.

If records are lost, reconstructing them from external evidence is permitted only if the taxpayer can establish that at one time he did possess adequate records and that the present absence of records is due to a fire, flood, or some other disaster beyond the taxpayer's control. Sample case: The taxpayer could show complete records for one month. That was enough to indicate that the data missing for other months probably conformed to IRS requirements.

Not all excuses are considered valid. After one taxpayer's business and personal records had been destroyed by his wife, a court observed: Marital difficulties and their consequences, no matter how seemingly independent of [the taxpayer's will], do not sufficiently resemble floods or fires to be considered a casualty.

Other excuses that are not allowed by the IRS: Records lost during a move, misplaced in storage, or misfiled. A corporate executive who destroyed his files when he retired lost his deduction. And so did the heirs who threw away a decedent's "old junk," which included his travel and entertainment expense record.

Particularly unfortunate (and far from rare) is the loss of a taxpayer's records by the IRS during an audit. Such a loss, declared the court in one case, would surely constitute a circumstance beyond the taxpayer's control. But the IRS still required substantiation of everything the records had shown.

What to do:

• Make photocopies of all travel and entertainment records. Don't give the IRS any unduplicated papers. When material is taken from files for an audit or a review by corporate personnel, make certain it gets back where it belongs as soon as possible. An "out card" is no substitute for documents, names, and explanations.

• Be wary of a displaced or dead-ended employee who could destroy essential records.

When a company is liquidated: Request a "prompt assessment" by the IRS so that an audit is more likely to take place before records are lost. Don't send records into difficult-to-reach dead storage until it is certain they won't have to be retrieved. Do not destroy documents or back-up data until a tax adviser has checked the statute of limitations.

Deducting for Home Entertainment

The cost of a business party at home is tax deductible even if business isn't conducted directly. But keep excellent records. Even though entertaining for goodwill is allowed, the IRS is suspicious when it's done at home. Records required:

• Receipts for food, drink, flowers, bartender, waiters, and all similar expenses.

• Complete list of everyone who attended, with their business relationships specified.

• Statement of the purpose of the party.

Better still: Dictate a memo at the office the day after a party, stating what business ideas were generated by the party. File the information in the office and keep it up to date.

Caution: If the IRS isn't satisfied with some of the records, the whole deduction may be disallowed.

Club Membership and Entertainment as a Deductible Expense

Any recreational club—tennis, golf, etc.—can qualify as a tax deduction if it's also used for business meetings.

Membership dues. The IRS uses a days test to determine whether membership dues are tax deductible.

• The test: The number of days the club was used for business is compared with the number of days it was used entirely for recreation. If you used it for business more than half the time, that percentage of the dues is tax deductible. However, if you don't meet that over-50% requirement, then none of the dues are deductible.

Expenses. Keep a diary, indicating business discussions at the club and money spent on those meetings. Regardless of what percentage of club time is devoted to business, you can deduct bar tabs, restaurant bills, and guest fees for entertaining business associates, if business is discussed.

If the club requires you to sign vouchers for expenses: Add to the voucher the subject of the business discussion and the guest's name and business connections. If you pay cash, keep a diary. If the expense is more than $25.00, be sure to get a receipt.

Planning pays. By November, do an analysis of how many times you've used the club during the year. Apply the IRS days test. If you have used it for recreation all summer and can't pass, fill up your November and December calendar with business guests.

Strategy: If you need a hefty tax deduction in the current year, join a club in late November and use it for business colleagues only until year-end. Result: The entire dues fee is tax deductible for that year. Caution: If the dues cover more than one year or are suspiciously high (say, $5,000, and you only brought three guests), the IRS may deem a deduction unwarranted.

Source: Randy Bruce Blaustein, J.D., tax manager, Siegel and Mendlowitz, CPAS, 310 Madison Ave., New York 10017.

Deducting Your Live-In Maid as a Business Expense

It's illegal to hire a live-in domestic and put her on your company's payroll. However, you could deduct the part of her salary which is a related business expense. Example: if the maid makes $125 per week, and you do at-home business entertaining once a week, you could claim $25 of her weekly salary as a business deduction. That portion of her Social Security taxes would also be deductible.

Tax-Deductible Tuition

Education expenses to improve or maintain professional skills can be deducted from your taxes only after you have met minimum requirements for your profession, and only if the courses do not qualify you for some new profession. But if you are already licensed in one state, you can deduct expenses for a course that prepares you for license or practice exams in another state.
Letter Ruling 8046040.

When to Incorporate for Personal Tax Purposes

Forming a corporation for personal tax considerations is a device generally used by professionals and independent businesspeople. It may also be an opportunity for: Employees with substantial outside income, salespeople who work on commissions, and real estate brokers and managers in companies that allow it. (It can be especially valuable if the company does not have a profit-sharing or pension plan.)

Tax advantages: Incorporation vastly increases the deduction you can take for contributions to a pension or profit-sharing plan.

The law permits employees to deduct no more than $2,000 a year for an Individual Retirement Account (IRA).

By contrast: An incorporated individual is entitled to deduct up to 25% of the annual salary he gets from his corporation under a defined contribution plan. Or he can deduct an even greater portion of the salary from his corporation under a defined benefit plan (an arrangement where you get a predetermined percentage of your salary when you retire).

Purchase of group life insurance through a personal corporation has three tax advantages: (1) The corporation can deduct the cost of premiums. (2) Premiums on coverage up the $50,000 aren't includible in an employee's income. (3) Insurance proceeds won't be taxed to the beneficiary.

You can spread income over a number of years, saving it for low-income periods and reducing taxes. If the corporation's tax rate is significantly lower than your personal tax rate (the first $25,000 of corporate income is taxed at only 15% in 1983 and later), you can profit by leaving earnings in the corporation until you find yourself in a lower tax bracket. Caution: The corporate tax rate escalates to 46%. Corporate earnings will be taxed twice—first to the corporation, then to you. The effective tax rate is the cumulative rate. Warning: If the corporation accumulates over $150,000 in earnings, it may become liable for extra taxes.

You can determine your own fiscal tax year. This is an advantage in the year you start the corporation. For instance, you begin business as a corporation in January on a June 30 fiscal-year basis, thereby pushing the greater part of the first year's earnings into the next fiscal year, the full 12 months that will begin July 1.

Disadvantages of incorporating:

• It costs a minimum of about $450 for legal and filing fees to start and isn't deductible in the year you pay it. It must be amortized over five years.

• Whether your firm makes or loses money, you have to pay an annual franchise fee to the state (and sometimes city) where the corporation is registered.

• Even if you are already an employee of another company, you have to pay quarterly Social Security taxes and other payroll taxes on yourself. Thus, you must also cover yourself for some unemployment insurance, even though your employer is already doing so.

• In the event of an income-tax audit, your corporation has fewer rights to withhold information, since corporations are not privileged with Fifth Amendment rights.

More advice: Such a corporation should be formed by a lawyer who specializes in taxes and/or pensions. Otherwise, you may not make the most of potential deductions. Avoid: S corporation status. Reason: Earnings of an S corporation are included in your personal income for tax purposes, which is what you want to avoid.

Source: Sidney O. Raucher, an attorney who designs pension and profit-sharing plans, 122 E. 42 St., New York 10168.

Tax Credits You Can Take on Your Personal Return

Since every dollar of tax credits saves a full dollar in taxes—a dollar of deductions saves only about 49 cents for a taxpayer in the 49% bracket—it is worth knowing that a number of tax credits are available to individuals as well as to corporations. In some cases it takes a rare and unusual set of circumstances for an individual to qualify, but those who meet the tests should not fail to take advantage of the credits that are available, including the following:

Political contributions tax credit: Uncle Sam bears half the cost of political contributions up to $100 for a couple and up to $50 for a single individual. Half of contributions up to those limits may be taken each year as a tax credit.

Tax credit for child care or dependent care: A tax credit originally intended to help working women has now been broadened considerably and may be useful to high-bracket families as well as others. The credit is available if the family hires a sitter, nurse, or companion to take care of a family member who cannot be left alone (it could be a child, an aged parent, or a mentally or physically handicapped person), provided the care is needed in order to enable the taxpayer to go out to work to earn income.

And there's a special provision allowing the credit to be taken if one spouse works and the other goes to school full time. Thus, a high-bracket husband may earn the credit if a sitter is hired to make it possible for the wife to attend college.

The credit is 20% of amounts actually paid for dependent care, except that the credit may not exceed $480 (20% of $2,400) if there is one dependent at home, or $960 (20% of $4,800) if there are two or more, for 1982 and later. The credit may be taken if the sitter or nurse is a relative of the taxpayer except for dependents and children under 19. Also, a higher credit percentage (up to 30%) is available for couples with adjusted gross income of $10,000 to $30,000, on a phase-out basis.

Residential energy credit: Homeowners or tenants may take a tax credit of 15% of amounts up to $2,000 spent for storm windows and doors, additional insulation, and expenditures for certain other equipment intended to reduce energy consumption in the home. The maximum credit (15% of $2,000) is $300, and it can be taken only once, not every year. This credit applies to homes completed by April 20, 1977 only, for improvements after that date and before January 1, 1986.

Taxpayers may take a larger credit for expenditures for windmills, solar collectors, or other equipment to produce energy from solar, wind, or geothermal sources. This one-time credit is 40% of the first $10,000 of eligible expenditures. The maximum credit is $4,000 on $10,000 of expenditures. (Note: solar swimming pool heaters are not eligible.)

The larger credit applies to old and new homes as to renewable energy source expenditures completed not later than January 1, 1986. Co-op and condominium owners are also eligible for the credits on their pro rata share of expenditures on the building.

Credits for individuals on investment and purchase: An individual who invests money personally or as a member of a partnership is eligible for any or all of the business tax credits. One that often is overlooked is the investment tax credit on a car that is purchased personally but used partly for business. Business use must be at least 50%. The credit is prorated according to the proportion of total mileage that is for business. (If the business proportion drops after the year of purchase, all or part of the credit will be recaptured and will have to be paid back.)

Other non-business credits: A tax credit for the elderly. Expenditures for rehabilitation of certified historic structures can be amortized over five years.

Source: *Successful Tax Planning,* by Edward Mendlowitz, Boardroom Books, New York.

Tax Options You Can Choose From

The tax law isn't as cut-and-dried as people think. It presents taxpayers with a number of options and lets them choose the path that leads to the lowest tax. Which of these options can you use to your advantage?

Year-end stock sales. If you sold stock at a gain through a broker in the last few trading days of the year, your gain will be treated as an installment sale, taxable in the year of payment, unless you choose to have it recognized in the year of sale. You have until the due date of your tax return to decide.

Two reasons to report the gain early: (1) You have losses that can offset the gain. (2) You expect your income to be much higher next year, and the gain to be taxed in a higher bracket. Note: This election can be made on a stock-by-stock basis.

Meals on the road. If you traveled out of town on business last year, you can take advantage of a new IRS allowance for meals. You can deduct a flat rate of $14 a day for meal costs, without having to prove the amount you actually spent. The meal allowance drops to $9 a day if the trip lasts for 30 days or more in one general area. Downside: An election to use the flat rate must apply to all your away-from-home business meals during the year. You can't take the flat rate for one business trip and your actual meal expenses for another.

Filing Status. Married couples have the choice of filing a joint return or separate returns. Most couples are better off filing a joint return. When both spouses work, there's an incentive to file a joint return—the couple can deduct up to 10% of the first $30,000 of the lower-earning spouse's qualified earned income.

Nevertheless, filing separate returns can sometimes save taxes:

• Deductions for casualty losses must be reduced by 10% of adjusted gross income (AGI). On a joint return, a couple's combined AGI is reduced even if only one spouse suffered the loss. If separate returns are filed, the loss is reduced by only 10% of that spouse's income. Example:

A husband has AGI of $70,000 . . . his wife, $20,000. The wife's jewelry, worth $25,000, is stolen. On a joint return, the loss must be reduced by $9,000 (10% of combined AGI), but on a separate return, by only $2,000 (10% of the wife's income).

• The same considerations apply if one spouse, but not the other, has heavy medical expenses, since you can deduct only expenses in excess of 5% of adjusted gross income.

Caution: The only way to know whether it's better to file jointly or separately is to figure the tax both ways. Remember to take into account loss of the two-earner working couple's deduction and the child-care credit when you're figuring the tax under separate returns.

Other options: If you're married but living apart from your spouse and have a child living with you, or a dependent, you may be entitled to file as an unmarried head of household (at favorable tax rates) rather than as a married person filing separately. Or you could file a joint return with your spouse, if that works out better.

Selling your home. If you are age 55 and you sell your principal residence, you can elect to exclude up to $125,000 of gain from taxable income. Sale of a residence owned jointly by a married couple will qualify for the exclusion if either spouse is at least 55 and a joint return is filed.

This is a once-in-a-lifetime exclusion. If you elect to use it now, neither you nor your spouse can ever use it again. And it can't be split up. Say you sell your home at a $75,000 profit. You can't exclude the $75,000 now and reserve the $50,000 balance in case you sell another home later.

If you buy a new principal residence within two years before or after selling the one you have, you can defer all or part of the gain (depending on the cost of the new residence) without touching your $125,000 exclusion. If you can defer the entire gain, there's no sense using up the $125,000 exclusion now. Save it for later. But if you're going to be hit with a tax, you have to weigh the amount of any present tax against the possibility of a later sale of the new residence.

Source: Philip B. Kimmel, partner, Hertz, Herson & Co., New York City.

Shifting Income to Low-Bracket Kin

Tax sheltering should start at home. For many high-income families, the key way to cut taxes is to shift income to children or to other relations who are taxed in lower brackets.

With proper planning, this technique can shrink and sometimes eliminate tax on part of the high-earner's income.

The key ways to shift income:

Short-term trusts are the most popular tactic.

Gift-leasebacks. These are gaining acceptance, although they are more vulnerable to IRS attack than the more traditional techniques.

High-interest borrowing. A few taxpayers have used this successfully. But it is an aggressive tactic (vis-a-vis IRS), to be used with caution.

Short-term trust: This is also known as a Clifford trust. It is the classic income-shifting technique. How it works: Transfer either cash or income-producing property to a trust, with your child as beneficiary. If the trust is set up to last at least 10 years and a day, the income is taxed either to the trust or to the child, depending on when the income is required to be distributed. In either event, the tax will normally be less than you would pay.

Caution: Small details can trip you up. Don't try to do this without a lawyer who has experience in estate planning and is familiar with local laws. Major pitfalls:

State law may cause the trust to be disqualified. Example: If the trust earns capital gains, you (as the grantor) are usually liable for tax on the gain. New York law may require the trustee to pay the grantor enough of the gain to cover the tax. And unless the grantor waives this right when the trust is set up, the IRS can argue that there is a possibility the trust will terminate, at least in part, before 10 years are up. That could make all of the trust's income taxable to you.

A transfer in trust may be subject to gift tax if the value of the income interest exceeds the donor's annual gift tax exclusion ($10,000 per recipient). The value of the income interest is determined by IRS tables. Under current tables (effective for transfers after November 30, 1983) you can transfer about $16,000 into a 10-year trust ($32,500 for a married couple) without exceeding the $10,000 annual gift tax exclusion. Beyond that you must pay gift tax or use up part of the lifetime gift and estate tax credit. Caution: Any other gifts you make during the year to the same child (birthday or Christmas presents, for example) also count toward the annual exclusion and reduce the amount you can transfer tax-free to the trust. And there is no gift tax exclusion if the trust is not required to distribute all of its income each year.

The $32,500 limit for a husband and wife is an annual limit. You can beat the limit by setting up a separate 10-year trust each year for a number of years. Fund each trust with assets worth $32,500 and have each trust run for at least 10 years. Drawbacks to multiple trusts:

• A separate document must be drawn up for each trust.

• Each trust must have its own identification number and file its own tax return. You'll have to pay accounting fees for each trust.

• The $32,500 limit you put in each trust is an awkward amount of money to manage. The trustee won't be able to make investments that require a $100,000 minimum deposit.

Note: Under the 1984 Tax Act, certain multiple trusts can be treated as one trust for income tax purposes.

You can avoid the drawbacks of multiple trusts by setting up one trust that runs longer than 10 years . . . and by making contributions in the year you set the trust up . . . and in subsequent years. The trust must still have more than 10 years to run after the last contribution has been made. Examples:

• Have one trust that runs for 10 years and 10 months. You and your spouse can make one ($31,072) contribution when you set up the trust, say in April 1985, and another ($32,395) contribution in January 1986. Total investment: $63,467.

• Or, set up one trust that lasts 15 years and a month. Make contributions in each of six years. Amounts you can contribute to a 15-year-plus trust without fear of a gift tax . . .

	one parent	husband and wife
Year 1	$13,137	$ 26,274
Year 2	13,575	27,150
Year 3	14,077	28,154
Year 4	14,676	29,352
Year 5	15,396	30,792
Year 6	16,274	32,548
Total investment	$87,135	$174,270

Problems with longer running trusts: Your money is tied up for longer than 10 years. If your child is too old when you set up a 15-year Clifford trust, it may run into his or her earning years and increase the tax bite. Best: Set up a long-running Clifford trust when your child is very young.

Gift-leasebacks: This technique is used

most often by parents who are in business for themselves, particularly as professionals. How it works: The parent gives business property (such as office furnishings, equipment, or even an office building) to the child. The child then leases the property back to the parent, who pays rent and deducts it as a business expense. Note: You don't have to be self-employed to use this technique. The IRS has attacked gift-leaseback arrangements, but recent court decisions have upheld such deals when they are set up to have "economic reality." To meet this test:

• Be sure the lease payments are about what you would have to pay if you were not dealing with a related party. And make sure the lease has no other features (such as a very favorable purchase option) that would not appear in a deal negotiated at arm's length.

• If the deal is handled through a trust, be sure to have an independent trustee. This could be an in-law or a business colleague. Ideal: A bank or trust company. Unfortunately, they often won't handle trusts below a certain size, or will insist on relatively high fees. A bank that has substantial dealings with your business may be willing to accommodate you.

IRS will not attack a gift-leaseback if the lessor is a third party (other than a partnership or an S corporation). So you should consider incorporating your business at the time you give its physical assets to your children. Then the children (or their independent trustee) can enter a lease with your corporation.

Aside from IRS hostility, there are some other traps in a gift-leaseback that make careful planning a must:

• Investment credit recapture if a parent transfers property on which an investment credit was claimed. The amount of this credit is keyed to the useful life of the property. If the property is disposed of before the end of the useful life (as claimed), the credit is recomputed on the basis of the actual holding period. Any excess credit taken is then paid back to the IRS. To avoid this problem: It may be best to give or lend money to the trust, which, in turn, purchases the business property new.

If the lease is drafted right, the investment credit can then be passed through to the parent-lessee.

• There may be an unanticipated gain when the gift is made. This often happens when a parent transfers property that has not been fully paid for. The child (or trustee) agrees to take over the payments. This is technically a part-sale, part-gift. If the parent's tax basis is lower than the debt that is taken over, the difference is a taxable gain. (The tax basis can easily be lower than the outstanding debt on property subject to depreciation.)

High-interest borrowing: Basic technique: Borrow money from a low-bracket family member, and pay as high an interest rate as possible. Deduct the interest. The lender treats it as income. Example: Suppose your father is sick and his medical expenses are high enough to wipe out all his taxable income. Unless you provide half of his support, any medical expenses you pay on your father's behalf cannot be deducted on your return. But if your father were to lend you $5,000 on a demand note bearing interest at, say 45%, you could pay and deduct $2,250 per year. If you are in the 50% bracket, your after-tax cost for that $2,250 is $1,125. And your father will probably pay no tax at all.

Pitfalls: There have been only a few court decisions on whether a taxpayer can deduct extra-high interest payments to a related party. And although the taxpayers have won, the precedents don't seem strong enough to guarantee smooth sailing ahead. Moreover, interest payments are not tax deductible if they violate local usury laws or if the debt they are connected with is not bona fide. Further problem: An interest rate substantially beyond what you'd pay a stranger may be treated, in part, as a taxable gift.

Bottom line: Before adopting any of these methods, sit down with a competent tax adviser. You need to know the dollar impact, the state tax effect, and the local tax effect, and the nontax legal consequences before you make any move.

Source: Jonathan G. Blattmachr, partner, Millbank, Tweed, Hadley & McCloy.

Buying Relatives' Deductible Losses

If you are a high-bracket taxpayer and have a relative with little or no taxable income, consider taking advantage of a tax law provision that allows you, in effect, to acquire your immediate relatives' deductible losses.

How it works: If a member of your immediate family sells property to you at a loss, that loss can't be deducted. But, when you turn around and sell that property, you don't have to pay tax on any gain unless the gain is more than your family member's loss. Even then, only the portion of the gain that exceeds the previous loss is taxable.

Example: John White's mother is very ill. She has some income from dividends and a modest pension. But her deductible medical expenses are so high that her taxable income is zero. Her portfolio includes 100 shares of Consolidated Conglomerate that she bought at $35 a share. Current price is $11. If Mrs. White sells on the open market, the $2,400 loss won't save a penny in taxes. If John buys the stock, he can hold on to it until the price recovers. And even though he bought the shares at $11, he won't have a taxable gain until the stock hits $35 again.

Added twist: John can give his mother a note for the purchase price of the stock with a reasonable interest rate for today's market. The money can help defray Mrs. White's medical costs, while John gets an interest deduction.

Who can do it: This special rule applies on any transaction between you and your parents, grandparents, children, grandchildren, siblings, or any corporation in which you own more than 50% (by value) of the shares.

Paper Work for an Income-Shifting Gift

A gift made to reduce family taxes won't be fully effective unless the person receiving the gift also receives certain key information. The purpose: To make sure the recipient can treat the gift in a way that minimizes personal taxes.

Practical suggestion: Give each donee a statement prepared by your tax adviser. It should contain the following data:
- Date of the gift.
- Date you acquired property. (If you got it as a gift originally, establish when it was acquired by the person who gave it to you.)
- Your tax basis in the gift property. Usually, basis is identical with cost. But it may be more complicated than that is you have claimed depreciation on the property, if you got it as a gift, if, as in the case of a house, you have added to it, or if you inherited it.
- Fair market value of the property on the date the gift was made. (Include the source of the estimate.)
- The amount of gift tax you paid, if any.
- The portion of that gift tax that is based on appreciation of the property's value while you owned it.

Source: Sidney Kess, tax partner, Main Hurdman & Cranstoun, CPAs, 280 Park Ave., New York 10017.

A Child With Income Can Still Be Your Dependent

As long as a child is in school, parents can generally claim him as a dependent if they contribute *more than* 50% of his total support. Under IRS rules, support includes food, lodging, clothing, medical and dental bills or insurance premiums, tuition, charitable donations, transportation, and recreation.

Parents contribution to support can include: (1) Reasonable value of food and lodging furnished at home. (2) Value of the room maintained year-round for the child's use when home. IRS has ruled that purchase of a car and a daughter's wedding expenses qualify as support. The child's own income has to be included in calculation only if it's actually used for support.

Paying Your Child a Tax-Deductible Allowance

Paying your children to work in your business is a good way of providing tax-deductible allowances. A child with no other income can earn up to $3,300 tax free. Added bonus: If your business is unincorporated, your children's wages are exempt from Social Security and unemployment taxes until they turn 21.

Caution: Keep very good records of the type of work they do and the hours they put in. The mere fact that you pay wages to your children won't trigger an audit. Their pay is lumped in with wages of other employees on your return. But if you are audited for some other reason, the IRS is likely to question this expense. Be prepared to show the pay was reasonable.

Avoid Being Taxed On Income from 'In Trust' Accounts

Interest on bank accounts "in trust" for your children will usually be taxable to you. Reason: Under state law, these accounts, often referred to as Totten trusts, are considered revocable. That means you have the right to take the money out and use if for your own purposes any time.

Suggestions: If you want the interest treated as your child's income, make an irrevocable gift of the funds to the account. Most states provide a simple procedure for doing this under the Uniform Gift to Minors Act. Your bank officer knows how to set this up.

Important: The gift has to be irrevocable. But it doesn't have to be forever. You can set up a so-called Clifford trust so that the funds on deposit come back to you after 10 years. Your child gets to keep the interest that accumulates during this period. You don't have to pay tax on it.

Sidestep Tax Trouble on Family Property Sales

If you sell property on installments to a family member, have your tax adviser help you draw up a memorandum outlining the reasons for the sale. Do this when the sale takes place, in order to avoid problems that may crop up later one.

Here is why: Too many taxpayers were taking advantage of a loophole. Most common scheme: A man would sell property on installments to his wife. The wife would then sell the property to someone outside the family for cash. Price: About what she bought the property for. Result: No profit to pay tax on. The family, as a unit, collected the full cash price for the property. But the tax on the profit was deferred.

The new rules, which apply to family installment sales made after May 4, 1980, result in a loss of the tax-deferral benefits, in most cases, if the second family member sells the property for cash within two years. If the property is marketable sercurities, or if the family buyer enters into a transaction (such as a put, call, or short sale) that cushions the risk of falling prices, then the deferred tax benefits can be lost even if the subsequent cash sale is made after two years.

But the new rules don't always apply. You won't be subject to them if you can prove that the sale within the family wasn't done principally to avoid taxes. The burden of proof, however, is on you.

Example: The father has a heart attack. He decides to sell the family business to his daughter, who has been helping him run it. The deal is set up so that she can pay for the business out of future profits. A year later, Conglomeration Inc. offers to buy her out.

The way around: The original deal should be documented with doctors' reports and a business plan showing how the daughter expected to make the payment. Include any other evidence that shows why the sale took place at the time it did and demonstrates that the daughter did not intend, at the time she bought the business, to turn right around and sell it. Then there is a solid basis for arguing that the sale to Conglomeration Inc. should not trigger all of the father's tax at once. Therefore, the daughter can feel free to make the deal that is best for her.

Taxes and an Aged Relative

Many taxpayers contribute to the support of parents or other aged relatives. Common case: A taxpayer helps support his mother in her own home. The mother also receives $2,000 per year by renting out one of the rooms in the house to a boarder. Expenses applicable to the renter total $1,500, so her net income from the transaction is $500 annually.

Problem: The child can't claim his mother as a dependent, because she has a gross income of $1,040 or more. The lower net is irrelevant to the IRS. What to do: Have the mother deed the house to the child so she can qualify for a deduction as a dependent on the child's tax return. That's a $520 saving if the son is in the 50% tax bracket.

There are larger benefits if the child is single. Having a dependent qualifies him to file as a "head of household" and to pay taxes at a rate more favorable than those for single individuals. (The rate still isn't as favorable as that for a married person filing a joint return with a spouse.)

Another way to save: A relative 65 years old or older can receive as much as $4,570 per year with no federal tax liability (the $1,040 personal exemption, plus another exemption for being at least 65, plus the zero-bracket flat deduction of $2,390 and tax-free dividend income of $100). Problem: Giving that $4,570; to a relative requires an individual in the 50% bracket to earn twice that amount, or $9,140.

To give the $4,570 with pre-tax rather than post-tax dollars, have your tax expert (accountant or lawyer) set up a Clifford Trust for your relative to run for 10 years and a day, or until the relative's death, whichever comes first.

The trust will tie up some assets, of course, but they will come back eventually. How much? At today's interest rates, about $50,000 in cash to pull in $4,570. The trust can be in other income-producing forms.

Parent Supported by More Than One Child

When several taxpayers contribute to support a dependent there is an exemption to be claimed—even if no one contributed more than the mandatory 50%. Example: Several siblings help maintain an aged parent, but no one pays more than half the total.

What to do: Everyone paying more than 10% reaches agreement about which one will get the deduction. Nonclaimants each fill out Form 2120, Multiple Support Declaration, indicating they are not claiming this deduction. The forms are then filed by the taxpayer who does get the exemption. You can't prorate the deduction, but you can rotate it among the providers year by year.

Double deduction for dependent parents. Even if only one parent is actually being supported, a taxpayer can take two deductions (one for each parent). This is permissible because the IRS considers parents one unit when supported by children. To get the deductions, you must provide more than half of the combined support of this unit.

Divorce and the IRS

Two basic tax principles to keep in mind: First, alimony payments over many years are tax deductible. However, no other payments are deductible. (Possible exceptions: Child's medical bills, for the parent who pays them.) Second, if the husband deducts the alimony, the wife must declare it as income. Child support, lump-sum payments, wife's legal fees, premiums on life insurance policies owned by the husband—all these are non-deductible by the spouse paying them. And they need not be reported as income by the spouse who receives the payments.

In the still-common case among executives, in which the husband has a large taxable income and the nonworking wife has little or none, it probably makes sense to make all the payments alimony. The result is to shift income from the husband's high bracket to the wife's lower bracket. It's essential to prepare carefully several alternative plans, varying the mix among alimony and other types of payments.

Usually the parents can decide between them who will claim the children as dependents. Thus, the father probably can claim them even if they live with the mother. Of course, only one can claim them.

A parent having a child living with him or her may be able to file as (a tax-favored) head of household by claiming that child as a qualifying individual.

Conceivably, both parents might have head-of-household status. This could happen if the younger children stayed with mother but an older child—away at college full time—stayed with father when home on vacation.

Child support normally stops when the children become independent. Alimony often goes on until the wife remarries.

If it's agreed that the husband will pay for the wife's divorce lawyer, estimate fee and add this amount to the alimony that has been negotiated. Then get a deduction for that amount. (It's income to the wife.)

Tax Traps for Divorced Couples

• A husband was penalized by the IRS for voluntarily increasing monthly payments to his ex-wife without getting something in re- turn. The case: Under the terms of the separa- tion agreement, he agreed to pay a stipulated monthly amount to his ex-wife until her death or remarriage, in return for her relinquishing all her support rights. A year after the divorce, the husband increased his monthly payments because he was making more money. The wife's part of the bargain remained the same. IRS ruling: He must pay a gift tax each time he makes the supplementary payment. *Revenue Ruling 79-118.*

• Alimony tax trap: Husbands giving mon- ey to their separated wives before a separation agreement is put in writing will not be able to deduct that money as alimony. Case: Follow- ing their separation, but prior to divorce, a husband gave $500 a month to his wife. A year later, they were divorced, and he was required under the decree to pay her $500 a month. The court ruled that he could not deduct the payments made to her prior to the divorce. Reason: Deductible alimony refers to pay- ments made pursuant to a court decree, or a written separation agreement. *Alexander v. Commissioner, T. C. Memo 1979-244.*

Tax Impact When Marriage is Annulled

The IRS position is that annulment means the marriage never existed. Hence, the IRS re- quires anulled couples who had filed joint tax returns to refile up to three years back as un- married persons, even if one of the former spouses had no separate income to declare. **Source:** *The Professional Report.*

When Homeowner Marries Homeowner

Two adults, each owning a home, get mar- ried. Their plan is to sell one house and live in the other. Problem: Loss of tax-free capital gain on one residence.

Homeowners over 55 are allowed to sell a house without paying any tax on the capital gain up to $125,000. But this tax break can be used only once in a lifetime. And if it is used once by a married couple, it cannot be used again by either spouse.

The only way to have two tax-free sales is for them to sell both houses before getting married (if they are both over 55). If they get married first and then sell one house, they forfeit the chance for a tax-free sale of the other.

Tax Advantages for Two-Income Families

Husbands and wives who each have sizeable personal wealth or income should handle their financial affairs differently than do other couples. Prime areas:

Life insurance. It's probably a good idea for spouses to give their life insurance policies to each other. That removes life insurance proceeds from the taxable estate. Each should pay premiums on the policy on the other spouse's life. There is a full gift tax deduction for gifts between spouses after 1981, so gifts can be made at any time, regardless of cash value. Term life, including group term policies paid for by the employer, are suitable for interspousal gifts.

Policies should not be willed to each other, unless the parties intend to put the insurance proceeds into the estate. A further complication arises if one spouse dies, willing the policy on the other's life to a trust for children, but making the surviving spouse the trustee. In this situation, some courts have held that the spouse, as trustee, has incidents of ownership in the policy on his (or her) own life. Thus, proceeds are included in the estate of the surviving spouse. Careful planning is necessary here to make sure the estates of both spouses get full advantage of the estate tax credit. State and local income tax: The couple would probably file those returns separately. Most states use the same tax rates for single and married people. Filing separately produces a lower total tax, since one income isn't piled on top of the other to reach the higher brackets.

Federal income tax: In most cases, joint federal returns should be filed. Federal rates for married couples filing jointly are the lowest available. The rates for married couples filing separately are the highest—even higher than those for single taxpayers.

Beginning in 1982, there is a special deduction for married couples if both spouses work. The deduction: 10% of up to $30,000 of the lesser-earning spouse's earned income, or a maximum deduction of $3,000.

However, in certain situations there could be a saving by filing separate returns. Make calculations both ways to see which is better under these circumstances:

• One has large medical deductions and the other doesn't. The nondeductible part of medical bills (equal to 5% of adjusted gross income) will be less if the couple file separately.

• One has municipal bonds and the other has interest deductions for money borrowed to carry investments. On a joint return, the interest deductions might be disallowed.

• One has realized capital gains and the other losses. The tax advantage of long-term gains is lost if they are offset by losses. And the tax advantage of losses (using them to offset ordinary income) is lost if they are offset by gains.

Unmarried Couple Living Together

Living together for financial reasons is all right for tax purposes. You can claim a dependency exemption for a household member whose annual income is less than $1,000, unless the relationship violates a state law. Case: A single woman with a job shared her home with a single man who had no income. The IRS sought to disallow the exemption because state law said that an unmarried couple living in open and notorious adultery committed a misdemeanor. "But today," asked the court, "can it be said that merely living together is open, gross lewdness or lascivious behavior?" The exemption was permitted.

In Re Shackleford v. United States, D.C., W.E. Mo., 2/28/80.

Making the Most of Your Medical Deductions

The IRS and court decisions have expanded the definition of medical costs that can be deducted from personal income taxes. Plan ahead to take advantage of as many medical expenses as possible.

Basics. Medical deductions can be taken for the costs of diagnosis, the treatment or prevention of a disease, or for affecting any structure or function of the body. Limitation: Treatment must be specific and not just for general health improvement.

Example: The IRS successfully denied taxpayers deductions for the cost of weight-control and stop-smoking classes that were designed to improve general health, not to treat a specific ailment or disease. On the other hand, a person with a health problem specifically related to being overweight might be allowed the deduction.

If an employer tells an overweight employee to lose weight or leave, and the boss has previously enforced such a rule, the plump employee can deduct the cost of a weight-loss program, because money spent to help keep a taxpayer's job is deductible. The IRS says it will allow a deduction if two physicians prescribe a weight-reduction program for the treatment of hypertension, obesity, or hearing problems. The same could go for a person whose doctor certifies that a stop to cigarette smoking is necessary for a specific medical reason (such as emphysema).

The same logic applies to home improvements. The cost of a swimming pool might be deductible if it is specifically necessary for a person who has polio, as would the cost of an elevator for a heart patient.

Caution: Only the actual cost (over the increase in value to the property) is deductible. The IRS makes taxpayers subtract from the cost of an improvement the amount that the feature adds to the value of the residence.

Example: If a swimming pool costs $10,000, but adds $4,000 to the value of the property, only $6,000 would be tax-deductible. To determine the value, have the property appraised before and after the improvement. (The appraisal fee is deductible.)

Medical or business? Because medical costs are deductible only after they exceed 5% of a taxpayer's adjusted gross income, it is tempting to declare them as business expenses. Trap: The IRS rarely allows those business deductions. But there is a sizable gray area. A professional singer was once not allowed to deduct the cost of throat treatments as a business expense, but an IRS agent did allow a deduction for a dancer who found it necessary for her career to have silicone breast implants.

Medically unproven treatment is generally deductible since the IRS has taken the position that it cannot make judgments in the medical field. Example: Laetrile treatments are deductible if the taxpayer receives them legally. Disallowed: A deduction for the cost of a food processor for a special diet consisting of vegetables. Or a special vitamin-enriched diet, even though the taxpayer is diabetic.

Deductions for nondependents are sometimes possible. How it works: The daughter of a highly paid executive ran up medical bills of more than $5,000. She married later that year and filed a joint return with her husband. Nevertheless, her father was allowed to deduct the cost of treatment on his return for the year, even though the daughter didn't qualify as a dependent.

Education. The IRS draws a hard line on deductibility of special schooling for children with medical problems. Not deductible: The cost of attending a school with smaller classes, even for a child with hearing or sight problems. To be eligible to make such a claim, the school would have to offer special programs for children with specific disabilities. Approved by the IRS: a deduction for the full cost of sending a child to a boarding school equipped to handle deaf children with emotional problems. Denied by the IRS: A deduction for extra costs, including travel, that was claimed by a parent who sent his deaf child to a distant public school that was better equipped than the local public school to handle such students.

Other deductible costs: Birth-control pills, and medical devices, vasectomies, legal abortions.

Source: Sidney Kess, tax partner, Main Hurdman & Cranstoun, CPAs, 280 Park Ave., New York 10017.

Unusual Medical Deductions

Payments have been held to be deductible when made to:
- An untrained companion hired to look after an invalid's needs.
- An acupuncturist, even though the state medical association did not recognize acupuncture as a form of medicine.
- A Christian Science practitioner, even though the payer wasn't seeking medical help.
- Social Security, for taxes on the wages paid to a private nurse.

In addition, deductions have been allowed for the cost of:
- Whiskey prescribed by a physician to relieve pain.
- A wig prescribed by a psychiatrist for a patient upset by hair loss.
- A face-lift, even when not recommended by a doctor.
- Extra costs for salt-free or other special food prescribed by a doctor.
- A stereo for a person confined to the house by multiple sclerosis.
- Hand controls for the car of a handicapped person.
- A guide dog for a blind person.
- A car telephone for a person who may require instantaneous medical help.
- Transportation to and from an Alcoholics Anonymous center.
- Lip-reading instructions for a person hard of hearing.

- The extra cost of braille editions of books for a blind person.
- A reader to assist a blind businessperson at the job.
- Insurance on contact lenses for a person who requires them.
- Extra electricity costs for medically necessary equipment, such as a whirlpool or central air conditioning.
- Travel expenses made necessary by illness. Example: The fare to the Mayo Clinic. Also deductible: Travel expenses for a nurse to accompany the patient or even for a spouse who performs medical services. Lodging expenses are also deductible to obtain outpatient treatment at a distant location.
- The portion of a housekeeper's salary that goes toward the medical care of a sick resident.

Setting the Value of Donated Goods

Expect some skepticism on the part of the IRS when contributing old clothes, books, artwork, furniture, pianos, even yachts, to charity. Some ways to stave off IRS disapproval:

Make a very detailed itemized list of donations. Include every piece of clothing, furniture, etc. and its cost when it was new. Get an itemized receipt from the charity. Don't ask the charity for a valuation. Example: Six cartons of hardbound books, three cartons of clothing, two lamps, an antique flowerpot. Attach both lists to your tax form.

Take the original price (including sales tax) of each item when new and calculate 25% of that figure. This is the fair value of what the goods are worth on the market right now. Naturally, this does not apply to items that have appreciated, such as antiques.

Determining the value of your donation may be easier if the charity has a thrift shop where the items are sold. Some charities also have valuation boards. Use them only if it appears they will be higher than your own estimate. The IRS will look more favorably on the charity's estimated value than on the donor's estimate.

In case of an audit, expect the IRS to disagree with your valuation, whether you set it or the charity did. *The burden of proof falls on you.* However, whether you valued the item at 25% of its original price or 10% of it, the IRS will try to reduce it. Therefore, try for the high number.

Audit tactic: The IRS auditor will try to use the Salvation Army's valuation of the price of your clothes and furniture. Check the date on the auditor's list. It is frequently two years old and completely unreliable. Challenge it.

For credibility with the IRS on the original cost of goods, bring your credit card and receipts from the current year to show that you shop at expensive retailers. This shows that the value of your donation is higher than that of the person who shops at J.C. Penney.

Best donation game plan: Give appreciated assets (real estate, stocks, antiques, paintings, and collectibles of any sort). Reason: If you sold them, you would get the wholesale price in most cases and have to pay a capital gains tax on the profit. It may be more profitable to give them away, since you don't have to pay the capital gains tax and you get to deduct the full retail price.

Example: You bought a painting for $500 ten years ago, and it could be sold for $10,000 retail today. If you donated the work, you would hope to get a deduction of the full $10,000, which might be more profitable after taxes than the sale. Note: Be prepared to defend the valuation against an IRS challenge.

Proof requirements. For a property gift of $5,000 ($10,000 for stock), you must obtain a written appraisal, and attach a summary of the appraisal, signed by the appraiser and including his tax identifying number, to your tax return.

Not deductible: Giving blood.

Unallowable: Don't get involved in schemes where you buy a gem or artwork wholesale, hold it for a year, then give it to a museum at an appraised retail value. The IRS has ruled this practice is no longer allowable.

Expect an audit if your donations are dis-proportionate to your income. Example: You made $35,000 and donated $9,000. However, if you made $150,000 and donated $9,000 it might not arouse suspicion. Another signal to the IRS: Giving disproportionate amounts of property compared to the amount of cash you donate to the charity. Example: You donate $5,000 in goods and $300 in cash. The relationship would be more acceptable to the IRS if there were a $2,000 cash contribution and $3,000 in goods. Chances of an audit decrease if you make sure to attach documentation.

Source: Edward Mendlowitz, partner, Siegel & Mendlowitz CPAS, 310 Madison Ave., New York 10017.

Charitable Contributions That Are Not Deductible

Contributions to foreign organizations or domestic charitable groups that are not formally set up to qualify.

Cost of babysitters, even if they are needed when you perform a volunteer service. That's the IRS position. But a taxpayer once won on this issue when he took it to the small case division of the U.S. Tax Court.

Donations to colleges that will benefit a particular individual. Example: Making a big contribution to a medical school so it will accept a relative.

The cost of tickets to charitable events. Only the excess (the amount over the normal cost of the event) is deductible.

Donations to organizations not deemed charitable by the IRS. Example: Groups that devote much of their time to lobbying, even if the lobby is for a social cause such as better health care or improvement of the environment. Exception: Although veterans' groups lobby, they generally qualify for tax-deductible donations.

Donations in lieu of court-ordered fines and gifts to civic leaders.

The value of free or low-rent use of property by a charity.

Donations of cash in excess of 50% of the taxpayer's adjusted gross income, stock in excess of 30% of income (but the excess amount can be carried forward), and donations of appreciated property to private foundations of over 20% of income. Caution: Some states scale down these limits even further.

Recommended: The IRS publishes two brochures that help explain these areas of deductions. They are *Valuation of Donated Property,* IRS Pub. 561, and *Cumulative Listing of Exempt Organizations,* IRS Pub. 78, quarterly. Both are available from the Government Printing Office, Washington, DC 20402.

Source: Sidney Kess, tax partner, Main Hurdman & Cranstoun, CPAS, 280 Park Ave., New York 10017.

Taking Deductions for Money Spent on Hobbies

Many activities individuals engage in may be looked upon as hobbies but also may have some profit potential. It's clear that if they do produce income it will be possible to deduct the ordinary and necessary expenses incurred. But unless the activity is profit-making, or is being conducted with the intention of making profit in the eyes of the IRS, deductions in excess of income won't be allowed.

The Internal Revenue Code creates a presumption in favor of the taxpayer. This places the burden of rebutting the presumption on the IRS.

IRS regulations list factors that are normally taken into account in determining whether the activity under consideration is a business:

Keeping complete books of account.

Expertise of the taxpayer and his advisers in the activity.

Time spent on the activity by the taxpayer or his employees.

Expectation that the assets may appreciate in value.

Taxpayer's past success in similar activities.

Occasional substantial profit, where investment or losses are relatively small.

Absence of substantial income or capital from other sources.

On the other hand, factors indicating a non-profit motive are:

Losses continuing beyond the period usually necessary to bring the activity to profitable status.

Substantial income from other sources.

Substantial tax benefits.

Significant personal pleasure.

Here's a list of activities with an indication of IRS treatment:

Activity	Treatment
Farm	For profit*
Breeding cattle	For profit*
Horses (breeding, show)	For profit**
Racehorses	Uncertain
Dogs (breeding, show)	Uncertain
Experiments by employed chemist	May be for profit

* If profitable in 2 of 5 years.
**If profitable in 2 of 7 years.

In order to apply the rules to a particular activity, professional tax guidance is important. In many cases it will be possible to conduct a hobby or activity that provides personal enjoyment in a way that will make the government a partner to the extent of sharing any losses incurred.

New Taxes Under Other Names May Not Be Deductible

With the fear of taxpayer revolts, some cities are increasing revenues by imposing new taxes but calling them something else. Example: To pay for a new water system, one city hit taxpayers with a "front door benefit charge," covering the cost of building the new water system, plus interest on money borrowed for construction, plus the cost of maintaining the new system.

The problem: "Local benefits taxes" are not deductible on IRS returns. Reason: The revenues raised to pay for new water lines or curbs or other local improvements increase the value of taxpayers' property. Exception: Local benefits taxes assessed to pay for more than physical improvements. In the case of the city's "front door benefits charge," the portion of that local tax covering interest payments and maintenance costs was deductible on IRS returns.

What taxpayers should do: Insist that cities furnish them with a breakdown of exactly how all local benefits tax revenues are used. Rev. Ruling 79-201.

When Legitimate Interest Payments Are Not Deductible

Trap: If you pay interest to someone with money that same person has lent you, the IRS position is that you are simply putting off paying the interest. Result: The payments are not currently deductible. There's no deduction until you start making payments with outside funds.

Getting Your Money's Worth from Your Tax Accountant

Clients who meet their tax advisers well prepared usually get more for their money. If an hourly fee is charged, the rate (if the adviser is a top-notch one) should be much too high to justify having your adviser sort and organize your records. Do these tasks yourself. If you pay a flat fee, time spent on essentially clerical chores eats into time that should be spent assessing your tax situation and looking for ways to cut taxes.

What to prepare beforehand:

A list of all earnings. Include: Salary, dividends, interest, net income or loss figures from partnerships as well as from Subchapter S corporations and tax shelters.

The amounts and dates of any estimated tax payments (federal or state).

Copies of your tax returns for the last four years if you are meeting with a new adviser for the first time.

A list of any securities you have sold, showing date of purchase, date of sale, cost, and proceeds. Stock transfer taxes and commissions on each transaction should be shown. Best: Confirmation slips received from the broker for each transaction, which contain all these data. Also, copies of your monthly brokerage statements.

A compilation of items you know you can deduct. Examples: Medical expenses, interest, taxes, contributions, and business expenses.

A record of income, expense, and loss items about which you are not sure.

Escrow or closing papers on any real estate you have purchased. If you have sold real estate, bring closing papers from the original purchase as well as from the sale. If you no longer have closing papers from the original purchase, request copies from the title company or attorney that handled the transaction. Also: List any amounts you spent on improvements.

Easy ways to keep records:

File/envelope system. Establish a separate file folder or envelope for each category of income and expense. Set up an additional one for items you are not sure about and another one for items you think are nontaxable or nondeductible. At the end of the year, simply add up the items in each file or envelope.

Checkbook system. Maintain a separate checking account for tax-deductible expenses. At the end of the year, sort through and total the checks in each category. Some firms will do this for you by computer. All you do is mark each check with a code number (from a list the firm will supply) and mail the checks in. Cost: $75 to $100 a year, tax deductible.

Source: Randy Bruce Blaustein, J.D., tax manager, Siegel & Mendlowitz, CPAs, 310 Madison Ave., New York 10017.

IRS Pressure on Accountants

Accountants are asking clients to verify in writing that the data supplied for preparation of tax returns is accurate. Reason: The growing IRS crackdown on preparers of inaccurate (or fraudulent) returns. Negligence can cost an accountant $100 per improper return and may subject the accountant and his clients to closer IRS scrutiny. Mistakes the IRS judges are "willful," however, can set preparers back $500. Accountants are questioning clients much more closely about their financial activities in an extra effort to head off IRS trouble. More significant: Accountants will not be taking the same strong position in handling clients' tax problems in the absence of appropriate substantiation.

Source: Martin Helpern, Laventhol & Horwath, 919 Third Ave., New York 10022.

Filing Estimated Income Taxes

Many more people have to file estimated tax returns now. Reason: High interest rates on bonds and money-market funds have sharply increased personal tax liabilities. To date, estimated taxes have been filed primarily by professionals, independent contractors, and other self-employed workers. Now, more executives are finding that their ordinary withholding fails to meet government requirements to "pay as you go."

If you owed the government additional taxes last year, you should probably be filing estimated tax returns this year (Form 1040ES). Or employees may ask their firm to increase withholding from paychecks if this is feasible.

There are two ways to avoid penalties for not paying the entire estimated taxes quarterly:

• If your current tax liability exceeds last year's liability, you are only required to prepay taxes equal to last year's liability. Example: if you made $20,000 last year and made $100,000 this year, you pay quarterly taxes as if you were making $20,000 and postpone the rest until year-end.

• If your payments equal 80% of the tax due on the quarter you pay. Benefit: Deferring large chunks of income until the last quarter will also defer tax payments.

Be careful when using these exceptions. You must be exact about your payments. For instance: You owed $10,000 last year and will owe twice that this year. Don't carelessly pay in a few dollars less than $10,000. (The penalty will be levied on the entire amount owed.)

Warning: These prepayment exceptions only defer a portion of your tax payments to the end of the year. Meanwhile, be sure to have enough money to pay the IRS what you will owe at year-end.

Suggestion: Invest what you defer in tax-free bonds. Best strategy: A tax-free bond fund that has a mix of short-term securities, which may prevent it from having wild swings of value if interest rates fluctuate.

Problem: If your income taxes are lower than last year's, it may be difficult to make a safe estimate based on the previous year. You don't want to duplicate the previous year's estimated payments if last year was exceptionally profitable. Watch your books carefully to see if you can use one of the exceptions.

Dates for filing estimated taxes: April 15, June 15, September 15, January 15. There are no extensions. Penalty for late payments: 13% per year, simple interest. IRS adjusts the rate twice a year to conform it to the prime. Penalty is charged from the day payment is due and is not tax deductible.

Source: Arthur Spiro, CPA, partner in Brout & Co., 380 Madison Ave., New York 10017.

If You Haven't Been Filing Tax Returns

Nonfilers ought to know:

You are not alone. Some accountants, lawyers, doctors and heads of major corporations have not filed either. Every tax professional knows that failure to file returns is among the more common human frailties.

Not having filed a previous return should not deter anyone from filing this year. Many people fear that if they file currently, they will draw attention to themselves. Then the previous year's delinquency will show up. Fact: The simple filing of a return for the current year does not trigger a routine check to see if the previous year's returns have been filed.

Many nonfilers actually owe little or nothing in back taxes. Example: The owner of a business that was going under went to a lawyer to investigate bankruptcy. The lawyer urged his client, who had not filed tax returns for the previous four years, to take care of his tax problems at the same time. As it turned out, the unprofitable business had generated substantial net operating losses, wiping out virtually all personal income tax liability.

The best thing for nonfilers to do is to gather their records together, organize them as best they can, and see an accountant, attorney, or other tax professional. Point: The fact that these individuals have let one or more years slide doing taxes on their own suggest that they would be better off working with someone to ensure that the job gets finished. Further benefits: Professionals may spot technical items, such as net operating losses or capital loss carryovers, that nonfilers are not familiar with and that could reduce both tax liability and any penalties.

Caution: Most people are better off not going to an IRS office for assistance in filing delinquent returns. The IRS does not have any formal policy of providing amnesty for people who voluntarily file delinquent returns. But as a practical matter, individuals are much less likely to be treated harshly if they file past-due returns without receiving an IRS reminder. And chances are even better if they do not draw attention to themselves by walking into an IRS office. Worst prospect: Nonfilers could end up talking to a member of the Criminal Investigation Division without knowing it. Even though they are not, at that point, the target of a criminal investigation, they may be questioned without being made aware of their rights. Best tactic: Mail each delinquent return in separately.

Generally, the IRS will not seek criminal penalties unless returns have been skipped for three years or more. Reason: The IRS must prove the omission was willful. Even if several years have been skipped, other factors affect the decision: If tax liability is small, prosecution is less likely. If the nonfiler belongs to a target occupational group (doctors, lawyers, accountants, and owners of cash-heavy businesses) the risk is higher.

Lost and incomplete records:

Request missing W-2s from employers. If an employer has gone out of business, it is best to reconstruct both the earnings and the tax withheld, and to file IRS Form 4852 in place of the missing W-2. Suggestion: Estimate what the weekly or monthly salary was and how many exemptions were claimed. A tax professional then can use withholding charts to estimate how much tax was taken out.

Reconstruct deductible expenses. Some tax advisers may suggest attaching a statement to the return indicating that estimates were used, to preclude any later fraud charges.

Past-due returns are more likely to be audited. Be prepared to prove all the figures on the return or to show how they were estimated. Reduce the risk by filing each return separately. But don't forgo legitimate deductions or simply claim the Zero Bracket

Amount (the old standard deduction). Reason: Late-filing penalties are 5% of the tax due each month it's overdue, with a maximum of 25% overall. Each deduction that reduces tax liability reduces the penalty as well.

The statute of limitations does not *begin* to run until a return is filed if there is tax due on a return. If a refund is due: The return must be filed within two years of the original due date, or the refund is forfeited. But even if it is too late to get a refund, a return should be filed to start the statute of limitations running, in case the IRS later tries to claim additional tax is due.

Bottom line: Those who have missed filing old returns should file now. The longer they wait, the harder it gets and the greater the risk of developing or reinforcing a potentially disastrous pattern of nonfiling.

Source: Randy Bruce Blaustein, J.D., tax manager, Siegel & Mendlowitz, CPAS, 310 Madison Ave., New York 10017.

Correcting Mistakes You Made on Old Tax Returns

Each year, millions of Americans pay too much tax. Even if your tax return was prepared by a professional, the complexity of the tax law makes it all too easy to overlook deductions, credits, and alternative computation methods that might have saved you money. That is why it is important to know when and how to file an amended return to take advantage of tax-saving opportunities you may have missed.

Most people think that filing an amended return automatically leads to an audit. Fact: Each amended income tax return is scanned or screened by the IRS. But a return will not usually be audited unless there is something that does not fit within normal IRS guidelines. In most cases, the IRS simply processes your refund claim and pays interest to boot. Note: Of course, the IRS will then tax you on that interest for the year it is paid.

Tax rule: The IRS has up to three years from

the time a tax return was due to go back and audit it, or two years from the time you actually paid your taxes, whichever is later.

A two-way street: You have the same time limit. Example: 1984 returns due April 15, 1985. You have until April 15, 1988, to make amendments.

Forms to use: An amended return is filed on Form 1040X. In addition, if the change you are making affects one of the backup schedules, such as Schedule A for itemized deductions, you need a copy of that schedule as it appeared in the year you are amending. Prior year's forms and schedules are available from the IRS. Most tax professionals also keep an inventory of forms. In a pinch (for example, the time for amending is about to expire), look at the form as it appeared on your original return and make your own "reasonable facsimile." Reason: If you file your amended return too late, the IRS generally will not waive the deadline just because other forms were unavailable.

Other changes: If you amend your federal tax return, you probably should think about amending your state and local returns as well. The local authorities will find out about the change from the IRS anyway. But they won't issue a refund unless you ask for it.

Amended returns that won't normally get you audited:

Income averaging: Probably the most commonly overlooked tax break. It can only help, not hurt. If you missed it, by all means, file one. You will need the taxable income figures for the three years preceding the year you are amending. This is the safest type of amended return.

Joint returns: If you have already filed jointly, you cannot, after the return's due date, choose to amend and file separately. However, if you filed separately, you can change your mind and switch to a joint return.

Short to long form: Many people think that if they don't have enough itemized deductions to beat the standard deduction (which is now called the zero bracket amount, or ZBA), there is no point in filing a long form. Fact: There are all sorts of other tax breaks that can only be filed on a long form. Examples: Moving expenses, residential energy credits, alimony.

Caution: Simply switching to the long form won't raise the red flag. But some of the items just mentioned could make the IRS a bit suspicious, particularly alimony or child-care credits. For these items, it is a good idea to attach an explanation with your amended return.

Interest on Treasury bills (T-bills): When you buy a T-bill, you pay the full face amount of the bill. Within a week to 10 days, the Treasury sends a check for the interest. But, technically, that interest is not taxable in the year you get that check from the Treasury. The tax is not due until the year the T-bill matures.

Club dues: You are allowed a business-expense deduction for a portion of the dues you pay to athletic or sporting clubs. Key: More than half of your club activities must have been business related. Back in 1979, this deduction was repealed. But Congress changed the law again and restored the deduction retroactively. So you may be entitled to refunds.

There are many other examples of safe items for amended returns. For example, you may have:

Understated your sales tax deduction.

Failed to deduct certain job-hunting expenses.

Overlooked a claim for a flat mileage allowance for driving in connection with charitable work and for medical transportation. If you are not sure how routine a particular change might be, talk to your tax adviser.

Red-flag items: There are, of course, a number of items that are likely to make the IRS red flag your return. Prime problems:

Job-related transportation costs. (The IRS is on the alert for commuting expenses, which are nondeductible.)

Entertainment expenses.

Other employee business expenses.

Partnership losses.

Vacation-home rental expenses.

Large charitable contributions (particularly if you have donated property worth $200 or more).

Losses from commodity transactions.

Mandatory contributions to your employer's pension plan. (A number of IRS employees tried, without success, to file amended returns and deduct such contributions a few years back.)

Office-at-home expense.

Shorter useful life for rental property.

What to do: If you file an amended return with a red-flag item on it, be aware that your original return will be scrutinized. That doesn't necessarily mean other items on your original return will be audited. But, it can happen. If there is something on the original return that would be hard to document, you must weigh that risk before you file an amendment.

Source: Paul N. Strassels, a former IRS tax-law specialist, publisher of the *Washington Money Letter,* and coauthor of *All You Need to Know About the IRS*, Random House, New York.

Missing the Tax Deadline Without Penalty

If you are not quite ready to file your income tax on April 15, there is a way to get a reprieve.

What to do: File IRS Form 4868. This automatically extends the due date to August 15. You don't have to give a reason or explain the delay. But you do have to:

Estimate the total tax you will be liable for.

Subtract any amount you have already paid (through withholding or estimated tax payments).

Send in the difference along with your extension request.

If your estimate is inaccurate and there is still some tax due when you actually file:

You have to pay interest at the rate of 1% a month.

If you miss by more than 10%: The IRS imposes a failure-to-pay penalty of ½% for each month or part of a month, starting from April 15. Unlike the 1% interest, the ½% penalty is nondeductible for 1981.

If you are very far off: You run the risk that the IRS will disregard your filing extension and hit you with a failure-to-file penalty (5% for each month or fraction of a month, running from April 15). Maximum penalty: 25%.

If you are still not ready by August 15: Request a further extension by filing Form 2688 or by sending a letter to the IRS service center in your region. In this case, you must state:

The type of return, the tax year involved and the reason for the delay.

Whether your returns for the previous three years were on time. If not, why they were late.

Whether you were liable for estimated tax payments and, if so, whether each payment was made on time.

Another escape hatch: Being outside of the U.S. on April 15. This automatically gives you until June 15 to file your return and to pay any tax due. You do not have to file any request for this extension. When you file your return, you attach a statement explaining that you were out of the country on the regular filing date. Since this rule extends your normal filing date to June 15, you can get an automatic filing extension to August 15. File Form 4868 and pay the estimated balance due.

Note: Puerto Rico is considered part of the U.S. for purposes of this rule. People who live near the Mexican or Canadian borders might be tempted to spend a day or two over the border around mid-April. Caution: The IRS could argue that your trip was a sham if it had no other purpose than to extend the filing date and defer your tax payment.

State and local rules vary on extensions. In some states, filing a federal extension request automatically extends the filing date for your state return. Others require that you file an extension request on a separate state form. The state filing request may or may not be automatic. Check the rules for your jurisdiction.

If You Can't Pay

Contrary to popular belief, the IRS is usually lenient to those who are genuinely unable to pay personal or corporate income taxes, pro- vided they cooperate with the IRS in working out a payment schedule.

Guidelines for income taxes: Never fail to file an income tax return because the company (or individual) does not have the funds to cover the tax due. That's a crime. Instead, file by the date due, but do *not* include a check for the amount owed.

What next: The IRS will send a bill. Respond to it immediately. Write to the address indicated on the bill and include a copy of the IRS notice. The notice is coded to speed the disposition of the case. In the letter, suggest working out a payment schedule. No detailed explanation is necessary.

It's important not to delay the response, even by a few days. The IRS's mailing sequence is computer-controlled. If the system doesn't hear from the taxpayer promptly, it triggers further action.

Next: The IRS will contact the taxpayer to work out a payment schedule that can be comfortably afforded. What a typical schedule might call for:

• The IRS won't force an individual to refinance a home or sell a car. And it won't force a company to liquidate working assets. But it will force a taxpayer to pay over any assets that are readily convertible into cash, and it will try to get the taxpayer to borrow on other assets (including a second mortgage on a home).

• The entire amount will be paid off in fixed monthly payments.

• Interest is due on the payments (but that's deductible). A nondeductible penalty will also be charged.

• The IRS will reassess the taxpayer's financial position periodically (once or twice a year). If it improves, the IRS will ask for a speeded-up payment schedule.

Don't worry if the letter to the IRS doesn't draw a quick response. But if there's no response in three months, give them a call to determine the disposition of the case.

Warning: Never ignore a letter from the IRS. Otherwise, they'll assume the worst and could move to seize visible assets.

Source: Edward Mendlowitz, tax partner, Siegel & Mendlowitz, CPAS, 310 Madison Ave., New York 10017.

What the IRS Is Watching on Your Tax Return

Sidney Kess, a lawyer, CPA, and a partner in Main Hurdman and Cranstoun, advises thousands of tax lawyers and accountants around the country. He recently surveyed a number of tax practitioners and asked them which parts of personal income tax returns were most often challenged by IRS. Key items:

Expensive cars used in business. The IRS is disallowing depreciation of the full cost of a Mercedes, Rolls, or Seville. There must be an allowance for estimated salvage value at the end of the car's useful life.

Bank deposits. Agents seeking unreported income examine bank statements and ask for the source of all of the deposits.

Dividend income. Agents compare form 1099 data (sent by company to IRS) with dividends shown on the return. Agents pay special attention if dividends drop sharply from one year to the next. IRS will question the return if it does not show that the stock has been sold.

Medical deductions. The IRS is questioning whether part of the medical expense was reimbursed by insurance or by the company directly. If so, the deduction must be reduced accordingly. If the reimbursement comes in a later year, it should be reported as income for that year (less trouble than filing an amended return for the earlier year).

Medical deductions for drugs. The only drugs now deductible are those prescribed by a physician and insulin.

Change of address. This may flag the return for examination if no capital gain is reported on the sale of the former home. (Or, alternatively, a statement that the capital gain is being deferred because a replacement home was purchased.)

Sale of home. Agents may check whether depreciation was deducted in past years, when part of the home was used for office or business purposes. If so, the part of the gain equal to depreciation taken may be taxed.

Travel and entertainment. These deductions are being scrutinized more carefully than ever.

Scholarships and fellowships. Students who receive a scholarship and must perform services (example: graduate students who teach some classes) must report a portion of their income. (Since scholarships are nontaxable, students sometimes fail to report any income at all.)

Separated and divorced parents. Agent will check whether both are claiming exemptions for children (only one is allowed to). And if one spouse claims a deduction for alimony paid, the other must report exactly the same amount of alimony received, which is taxable income. Agent also may ask to see the separation agreement, since alimony is deductible only if it's required to be paid.

Source: Sidney Kess, partner, Main Hurdman and Cranstoun, 280 Park Ave., New York 10017.

Avoiding a Tax Audit

Is it possible to have a reasonably aggressive income tax return, producing a low tax bill and, at the same time, a return that will have a relatively low audit potential? Answer: A resounding YES.

Before getting into the actual moves available to you, let's set the stage:

Each return filed with the IRS is checked for mathematical accuracy. The IRS checks for over a dozen simple errors. Examples: Forgetting the 5% limitation on medical deductions, using an incorrect tax rate schedule or claiming a partial rather than full dependency exemption.

Each personal return is processed. And refunds are mailed out where appropriate. Only then are returns graded for audit potential by IRS computers. Each area of each return is graded. A comparison is made against the norms to see how your return lines up against others in similar circumstances. The closer to the averages, the lower your audit exposure.

There is no way to guarantee that your return will never be audited. There is always a certain risk factor.

The averages are well known to tax professionals. Openly and honestly assess your real audit exposure with them. The closer to the averages, the lesser your risk of having to defend your return to an IRS auditor. But don't forgo deductions and credits to which you are entitled just because they may result in increasing your audit potential. Also: Do not assume you can take deductions and credits you are not entitled to because you find yourself below average. Example: It's about average to make a charitable contribution of 2% of the adjusted gross income. But you cannot deduct $600 just because your wages are $30,000. However, if you donated $1,600 worth of money and property, deduct it even though you may be above normal for your income range.

Learn the averages. It gives you another advantage. You may have overlooked deductions and credits. If you are well below average, you should ask yourself and a tax professional why.

The IRS is outnumbered. They can audit only about 2% of the returns. Even for individuals in the highest income brackets, the risk of facing an IRS auditor is one in ten. So the odds are nine-to-one that your return will get through IRS processing without any problem.

There are different kinds of audits. If the mathematical review finds an error on your return, you may get a letter from the IRS service center. Although that's one form of an audit, it's usually not a problem. Other kinds of audits:

• Office: Checks one or two points on the return.
• Field: Much more extensive.
• Taxpayer Compliance Measurement Program (TCMP): Can go into every detail of your return and financial records. About 50,000 out of 90 million-plus individual returns are scheduled for a TCMP audit, based on a random computerized sampling. If your return is fingered, you can't avoid it.

Simplest tactics to reduce your audit exposure:

File your return between April 1 and April 15. IRS's official position: It doesn't make any difference when a return is filed. Off the record: Some IRS insiders feel that the later you file, the less likelihood of an audit. Even if the official IRS statement is correct, you lose nothing by filing then.

Avoid tax protest returns at all costs. The IRS will go after a tax protester for as little as $25 to make an example of the person.

Lower the risk of audit in tax planning: Stay away from tricky or novel tax shelters. The IRS is using more personnel currently to shut down abusive tax-shelter investment schemes. That means fewer auditors are available to check on non-tax-shelter returns. If you are investing to cut taxes, and are looking to make a decent return on your investment in later years, you should have little difficulty with the IRS. But if you are involved with less than forthright promoters, you will have problems.

The IRS checks returns that show:
• Large charitable deductions of property (more than $5,000).
• Schedule D losses from investments.
• Schedule E losses due to partnership investments.
• Schedule F losses on hobby farms.

You can be a fairly good judge of whether or not your tax-shelter investments will cause the IRS computer to blink.

Avoid problem preparers. Find someone whose overall philosophy is similar to yours. Example: If you are conservative, find a preparer who leans that way, too. Stick with firms that people you know have dealt with. Inquire about the preparer's past dealings with the IRS. If your preparer has been identified by the IRS under its problem preparer program, count on an audit. That's one more reason why a highly reputable firm can help to reduce your audit exposure.

No escape: As in the past, the higher your income, the greater your risk of being audited. But the IRS has changed its criteria for deciding who has a high income. The change focuses attention on a small group of taxpayers and eases the pressure on most of us.

Background: Returns used to be grouped according to adjusted gross income (AGI). This figure included wages, interest, dividends, and other income, less investment and business losses. Impact: You might have $75,000 in wages, dividends, and so forth. Your neighbor might have the same income minus a $30,000 paper loss from an oil and gas venture ($10,000 in a deal with three-to-one write-offs). Result: You would have been in the $75,000-a-year category, facing a higher risk of audit than your neighbor, who would have been lumped in with those making $45,000.

Now, the IRS will classify returns based on total positive income (TPI). That means, for audit selection, the computer will pick up positive figures and ignore losses. Outcome: Your neighbor is more likely to be audited than he was in the past. In fact, he is in the same selection category as you. But his return is more likely to be chosen because his tax-shelter investment puts him into a target group.

The Odds of Getting Audited

Individual (based on adjusted gross income)	% audited
Under $10,000, standard	0.67
Under $10,000, itemized	2.90
$10,000 to $50,000	2.63
$50,000 and over	10.40

Business income	
Under $10,000	3.28
$10,000 to $30,000	2.03
$30,000 and over	6.68

Fiduciary	0.69

Corporation (based on assets)	
Under $100,000	3.83
$100,000 to $1,000,000	9.26
$1,000,000 to $10,000,000	26.97
$10,000,000 to $100,000,000	42.14
$100,000,000 and over	78.52

Gift tax	3.33

Source: *IRS Annual Report.*

Audit Advice from a Top Tax Accountant

The prospect of an IRS audit of a company return instills fear into the heart of almost any executive. But when properly planned for, audit dangers can be minimized.

The chance of an audit depends on the size of the company. The greater the corporation's assets, the greater the probability of an audit.

Audits are more likely still if the company: Shows low profits relative to industry averages. Pays salaries or claims deductions that are out of line with its reported income

IRS agents involved in audits: Revenue Officers usually do nothing more than ask the company to produce income, payroll, and excise tax returns. Revenue officers do *not* conduct full-fledged audits.

Internal Revenue Agents (the most common type of IRS representative) may conduct narrow or in-depth audits of corporate and personal returns.

Special Agents conduct criminal investigations. Consult a tax adviser *immediately* when a special agent identifies himself.

Types of audits: By mail. Not true audits. They usually result when the IRS finds minor errors on the return. Examples: Arithmetical mistakes or improperly claimed deductions. The IRS tries to resolve the problem through an exchange of letters.

Office audits. The IRS asks the taxpayer to appear at an IRS office to discuss the return. Most audits are of this type. Point: These audits usually concern only a few items on the return. An IRS letter to the taxpayer will specify which items are at issue. Recommended: Bring all records relevant to the specified items. Do not bring any other records. If the agent asks questions about any item not specified in the IRS letter, *do not answer.* Explain that relevant records must be consulted first.

Field audits. These are more general examinations of taxpayer records. They usually take place at the taxpayer's place of business and may last for several days.

Facing an audit: The most important thing to do is prepare. Meet with the tax adviser to evaluate the situation. Ask: What is the IRS interested in? What records do we have to depend on? Then, devise a strategy for handling IRS questions. Point: If a large amount of money is at stake, or complicated points of law are involved, the tax adviser should meet the agent with the taxpayer. If given a power-of-attorney, the adviser can meet the agent without the taxpayer.

How to act during an audit: With professionalism. If records are comprehensive and well organized, the auditor may conclude that it is unprofitable (from the IRS's point of view) to continue. Sloppy records and haphazard documentation encourage the IRS to believe that a fishing trip could turn up something.

Essential: Do not display any hostility you might feel toward the tax authorities or the government. If the auditors are personally antagonized, they are in a position to cause the taxpayer a great deal of trouble.

To prevent audit trouble: Assume that there will be an audit every year. Consult with a tax adviser at the beginning of the year to devise strategies and keep records as though an audit were sure to follow. Usual result: Less chance of facing a real audit. And should an audit occur, the trouble will be minimized.

Source: Irving Blackman, partner, Blackman, Kallick & Co., CPAS, 180 N. LaSalle St., Chicago 60601.

Audit Advice from a Former IRS Agent

If an IRS representative visits you, don't answer any of his questions or discuss anything with him. Politely, but immediately, refer him to your tax attorney or accountant.

Don't meet with the IRS auditor at all if you can help it. When tricky questions are asked, your attorney can say: I'm not sure I know the answer to that. I'll have to talk with my client and get back to you. That will be an honest statement, and it will give you time to prepare a response. There is also some possibility that the auditor may forget to ask these questions again.

Avoid having the IRS auditor at your place of business. Although his rule book tells him to conduct the audit at your office, you may avoid it by offering to give him a tour of your office. Tell him that it will disturb your staff or cause other business interferences (when this is true). Ask him to do his work at your attorney's office.

Reason: If you have your wife or relatives on the company payroll and they are not present, the IRS agent may claim that the salary you pay them is unallowable. If you try to create the impression that they do work when they don't, the agent may question them and discover that they know nothing at all about the business.

In addition, disgruntled employees may tell the IRS agent something you would rather not have revealed.

Have friends and neighbors been questioned by the IRS? If they have, try to find out what they've told the IRS agent about your lifestyle and spending habits.

The crux of a successful tax audit is knowing when you should stop giving the tax auditor any more records. Strategy: Give the IRS agent the information asked for in an organized manner. Although it may seem smart to give him cartons full of odds and ends, it could work against you. He may discover cancelled checks and invoices you really don't want him to see.

Advise your accountant or attorney not to give the IRS representative anything more when he starts copying down everything in sight, such as invoices, cancelled checks, sales records. It usually means he suspects fraud.

Stop giving the IRS records by exercising your Fifth Amendment privilege against self-incrimination and refusing its requests for more records.

If the audit lasts too long, it's another sign to prepare for legal tactics by hiring an attorney knowledgeable in IRS work. The auditor may be fishing around in an attempt to justify the amount of time spent. For businesses with assets of under $5 million, the audit should not last more than two days.

Source: Randy Bruce Blaustein, J.D., tax manager, Siegel and Mendlowitz, CPAS, 310 Madison Ave., New York 10017.

Tax Fraud: Who Gets Caught

Executives, lawyers, doctors, and other high-income professionals are accused of tax fraud more often than the general population. Charges stem from IRS challenges that there was willful or intentional failure to file, understatement of income, or claiming of fraudulent deductions. About one out of every five charges brought by the IRS in one recent year involved a professional or business executive. The average claim for back taxes is nearly $70,000.

	Investigations	Convictions
Total	8,901	1,476
Of which:		
Business owners	2,059	328
Other executives	485	94
Company officers	438	94
Attorneys	299	46
Dentists & doctors	199	33
Non-CPA accountants	164	40
CPAS	89	13

Less than 20% of IRS fraud investigations end in convictions. Other cases are dropped, Justice Department refuses to prosecute, or they end with acquittal or dismissal.

Penalties for Tax Evasion

Reckless handling of a tax return is a risky gamble. Reasons:

If any part of an underpayment is due to negligence, a 5% penalty can be added to the entire unpaid amount. But if the IRS charges that any part of an underpayment is fraud, a 50% penalty is added to the entire unpaid amount. Note: Fraud is defined as the willful evasion of taxes known to be due.

When fraud is involved, there is no statute of limitations. So the IRS may reexamine any return the taxpayer ever filed.

The IRS discovery of a single mishandled item can turn a cursory review of the return into a line-by-line examination. Worse: The IRS may decide to reexamine prior years' returns not closed by the statute of limitations.

Any underpayment of tax that is discovered must be paid with 12% interest.

A penalty of 0.5% of the unpaid tax is added each month, up to a total of 25% of the underpayment.

Late filing of a return results in a penalty of 5% of the tax owed. An additional 5% penalty is imposed for each month that the return remains unfiled, up to a total of 25%.

How IRS Informants Are Paid

Informants get cash awards based on the value of the information they furnish. Here are the IRS guidelines for making awards:

If the information was specific enough to get the investigation started and it led to a recovery, the informant gets 10% of the first $75,000, 5% of the next $25,000, and 1% of the remainder.

If the information triggered the investigation and was helpful, though not specific, in determining liability, the award is 5% of the first $75,000, 2.5% of the next $25,000, and 0.5% of the rest.

For information that triggered an investigation but did not help to establish liability, the award is 1% of the first $75,000 recovered and 0.5% of the rest.

Maximum award in any case: $50,000. Note: These awards are taxable.

When it Pays to Take a Tax Case to Court

Most taxpayers are afraid of going to court against the IRS. They picture a costly fight against high-powered government lawyers in

113

front of a judge who, in tax court, might well be an ex-IRS employee. But it can pay for a taxpayer to take a case to court, even when the law is probably in favor of the IRS. Reason: It provides an opportunity to compromise the case.

When a taxpayer goes to court the case is removed from the jurisdiction of the IRS district office, which started the investigation. It's then in the hands of the regional counsel. The difference: Agents in the district office are primarily concerned with the letter of the law, but the regional counsel's staff is more concerned with disposing of cases.

Point: It costs the IRS time and money to litigate a case, just as it costs a taxpayer. If there's no special reason to contest a case (to emphasize a stand the IRS is taking on a particular issue), the regional counsel may offer a settlement just to save the trouble of going to court. If the offer is only 10% of an amount that the district office disallowed completely, the taxpayer may come out ahead.

The costs: A $60 filing fee will place a case in tax court and bring it to the attention of the regional counsel. The taxpayer might have to retain a lawyer. The further the case is pressed, the greater will be the attorney's fees.

Types of cases the IRS is most likely to settle: Disputes over facts rather than interpretations of the law. Cases in areas where recent court decisions have been against the IRS. And cases where the IRS might have insufficient evidence, even when the law is on its side. Point: You might not learn how weak the IRS's case is until the pretrial conference.

Type of case the IRS is least likely to settle: Disputes in areas of the law that are still developing. Reason: Even if the disputed amount is small and the cost of litigation is high, the IRS might press the case to set a precedent that other taxpayers will have to follow.

Shopping for a court: The object is to bring the case to the court most likely to be sympathetic to the taxpayer. The four choices:

• U.S. Tax Court. Great expertise in handling complicated tax issues. But no jury trials. Major advantage: Disputed tax is not paid until after the trial, or until the case is settled.

• Tax Court's small tax case division. Hears cases when the disputed amount is under $10,000. Procedures are simplified and no attorney is necessary. No appeal, though.

• District Court. Only place where a jury trial is available. The judge might be more sympathetic since he won't be a tax specialist. Drawback: Any disputed tax has to be paid in advance of the trial. If the taxpayer wins or compromises, he gets a refund (plus interest).

• Claims Court. Here, too, the tax has to be paid in advance. Major advantage: The Claims Court doesn't have to follow the same precedents as do the Tax Court and District Court. Strategy: If the other courts appear unfavorable, try this one.

The place a case is filed: Every bit as important as the court it is filed in. The U.S. is divided geographically into 11 judicial circuits, each with its own Court of Appeals. District and Tax Court decisions in each circuit must follow the precedents of that circuit's Court of Appeals. Significance: The Courts of Appeals of different circuits do not have to agree with each other. And if one circuit's Court of Appeals has not ruled on an issue, the lower courts of the same circuit may disagree among themselves. Strategy: A little research into just which court might see a taxpayer's case most favorably can bring big rewards.

Source: Edward Mendlowitz, partner, Siegel & Mendlowitz, CPAS, 310 Madison Ave., New York 10017.

Tax Dispute Tactics

When the IRS questions an item on a tax return, the taxpayer's main concern often is to keep the examination from spreading.

One approach is to not fight the district office over the questioned item. Let the IRS assess a deficiency and send a 90-day letter. This letter gives the taxpayer 90 days to pay the tax or bring the case to court. Point: The IRS must give notice of all the items it is disallowing. Typically, it will cover only items that the IRS has already discussed. (If the IRS had questions about other items, it would have discussed them too.) Result: The IRS becomes locked into a position, and generally will not raise any new issues.

Caution: This tactic does not guarantee that an investigation is dead-ended. The IRS can always disallow other items by following other procedures. But that's very unlikely. Reason: It costs the IRS time and money to reopen a case in this manner. If it doesn't have a special reason to do so, it won't.

Tax Court Scorecard

Trial courts	For taxpayer %	For IRS %	Split decision %
U.S. Tax Court (1,051 cases)	11	51	38
District Courts (344 cases)	26	63	11
Claims Court (47 cases)	26	64	11
Appeals courts			
Court of Appeals (186 cases)	15	76	9
U.S. Supreme Court	33	67	0

Source: Annual report of the Commissioner of the IRS.

When Not to Fight the IRS

When a deduction is disallowed on a recent return, don't argue that it was allowed in prior years. Trap: It could result in the disallowance of the same item in all the years not closed by the statute of limitations. Reason: The IRS is not bound by its past mistakes. Worse: Your argument could result in a general examination of all your returns for past open years.
Sickel v. Comm'r., T.C. Memo 1980-278, 7/29/80.

You can't sue the government for damages resulting from bad tax advice given negligently by the IRS' own agents. Reason: The Federal Tort Claims Act, under which citizens derive their general right to sue the government for negligence, does not extend to tax cases.
Charles E. Applegate v. U.S., Civil Action No. 79-0056(L), W.D. Va., 7/1/80.

How the IRS Can Mislead You

Every year, the IRS advertises that it will "help" taxpayers prepare their forms. Case history: A taxpayer with a net operating loss was confused about the carryback adjustment and went to his local IRS office for advice. When the resultant tax return was audited, a tax deficiency was issued because the adjustment was incorrect. Taxpayer went to court. Tax Court ruling: It may seem unfair, but erroneous advice by the IRS is not binding on the Commissioner of Internal Revenue. Imposition of the tax assessment was allowed to stand.

A letter from IRS not to trust: Insist that tax counsel check any formal notification from the government that releases you or your company from an obligation. A letter terminating a case may not be the final word.

5

Retirement Planning

Arithmetic to Do Before You Retire

How to size up your financial situation:

1. List your assets. Include income-producing assets (stocks, bonds, other annuity-generating insurance policies, real estate, company profit-sharing plans), plus non-income-producing assets (paid-up life insurance, furniture, and household goods) and assets that require expenditures for maintenance (houses, cars, etc.). Estimate total dollar value, factoring in appreciation.

2. Figure out post-retirement income. Add up income from assets, pensions, and Social Security.

3. Calculate post-retirement expenses, then deduct costs stemming from work (commuting, clothes). Next add on the cost of benefits (health insurance) which will no longer be covered by an employer. Estimate an annual dollar figure. Factor in inflation rate.

4. If post-retirement expenses outstrip post-retirement income, develop a plan for li-

quidating assets. Rule of thumb: The percentage of total capital which a retired person may spend annually begins at 5% at age 65, and increases by 1% every five years, until reaching 10% at age 80.

Bottom line: Only those whose post-retirement expenses still outstrip total income at this point will have to cut back. Generally, a retired person needs 75% of his pre-retirement, after-tax income to maintain his present standard of living.

Improving Your Chances For Successful Retirement

Only 2% of all U.S. families will be able to match their current standard of living when they retire. Problem: Inflation and taxation are eroding savings and investment income.

Many people arrive at a brokerage firm or financial-planning office saying they just want to make money. That isn't sufficient. As the value of pension plans and investments falls off, the opportunities to make up the loss in other areas is much more limited than most people perceive. Essentials:

It is more important than ever to calculate the tax consequences of an investment. For instance, most people are satisfied if they invest in a stock and their investment goes up 30%. However, they haven't assessed the real return.

Example: A $10 stock goes up to $13 within six months. After adding on the commission for buying and selling, plus any taxes (assuming that state and federal taxes take up to 60% if it isn't a capital gain), you'll be left with only a 12% return ($1.20 on $10).

Focus on investments that will enable you to take advantage of the capital gains tax. The principal of debt instruments (bonds, savings bonds, Treasury bills, etc.) erodes with inflation. These become negative investments when you adjust for taxes and inflation.

Alternative: Try buying short-maturity bonds at a discount on full margin. This lets you convert the interest payments into a capital gain since they can be postponed to the bond's maturity. You can only do this with bonds issued before July 18, 1984. Bonds issued on or after that date will produce ordinary income at maturity, not capital gains.

Example: Buy a low-face-value bond currently selling at $900. Put up $300 and borrow $600. Pay interest on the $600, which is tax deductible over time, and to the extent interest is earned. In two years, when your bond matures, you will have a $100 capital gain, plus the interest. The real growth in recent years has been in things.

A good tax shelter is debt, since you can deduct the interest. If you have a home or your business has property, consider remortgaging it. Those assets may be tying up opportunity money. You may be able to invest it in your business, a tax-free annuity, or more real estate.

Use your own business knowledge if you are going to invest in the stock market. Many investors treat the stock market as a slot machine. It's a total gamble. They don't relate the market to the economy or to their own business. It's important to invest in what you understand and know about.

Example: If you are in the auto repair business, you should know what's going on in auto parts, tires, oil companies, etc.

You can no longer sit on investments for years. The time frame of swings in the economy, and therefore the stock market, is getting ridiculously swift. Corporations can't even make five-year plans these days without external conditions making them obsolete before the five years are up. Don't expect to buy a stock and hold on to it for five or ten years. Reevaluate your investments often.

Keep your eye on Washington. Understand what the probabilities are for government intervention in certain industries.

Be disciplined about your life-style and investments. The 2% of people who will be able to maintain their life-style don't fall prey to jazzy titles without high salaries. They don't try to keep up with the neighbors or think that they can easily afford to pay the government too. They can't. Tax planning is now an essential investing element.

How Company Retirement Plans Work

Retirement plans fall into two broad categories—"qualified" and "nonqualified." A qualified plan is simply one that meets the stringent requirements of Section 401 of the Internal Revenue Code and qualifies for highly favorable tax benefits. Nonqualified plans do not receive such benefits but are significantly easier to set up and administer. A typical nonqualified plan would be a deferred compensation arrangement in which a company agrees to pay an employee at some future date (usually after retirement) for services he is currently performing.

Suppose you are a corporate officer, 60 years old, and in a 38% personal tax bracket. Your firm wants to give you a raise of $4,000 per year until you retire at age 65. The firm now pays taxes at a 20% average rate.

If you accept the raise now, you pay personal tax on it at your present rate (38% × $4,000) and take home just $2,480 per year [($4,000) – (38% × $4,000) = $2,480]. This raise has an after-tax cost to the company of $3,200 [$4,000 – (20% × $4,000) = $3,200]. Over the five years until you retire, you take home only $12,400. The after-tax cost of your raise to the company is $16,000 over those five years (5 × $3,200).

But if you take the raise as deferred compensation, payable after retirement when you will probably be in a lower tax bracket—say 20%—you receive the $4,000 per year at the lower tax rate (20% × $4,000 = $800 tax), which is $3,200 take-home. The corporation, which we will assume has expanded over the five years so that it now pays at a 46% tax rate, has an after-tax cost of [$4,000 – (46% × $4,000)] = only $2,160 per year for your raise. Over five retirement years, you take home $720 more per year, a five-year tax saving of $3,600. Similarly, the company pays (5 × $2,160) = $10,800 after-tax over the five years, a tax saving for the company of $5,200.

A nonqualified deferred compensation plan is subject to the following guidelines established by the IRS. The tax court reasons that, if these rules are followed, the tax on the income may be deferred because the employee doesn't actually get his hands on the extra money until he is in fact retired. Rules for deferred compensation plans:

The deferred compensation arrangement must be established before the employee actually earns the income.

The employee must be on a cash basis.

The agreement may not be unconditionally funded by placing the deferred payment in an escrow or a similar type of account. The employee can have the company's promise of payment, but the compensation may not be secured in any way.

The employee may not demand the compensation before the date agreed upon.

The amount of compensation must be reasonable. If either current or deferred compensation is deemed unreasonable, it will not be deductible to the employer.

Usually, the employee agrees to the following in a deferred compensation agreement:

The employee may not receive any part of the deferred pay until he reaches the established retirement age or becomes disabled. His heirs may receive the compensation if he dies.

The employee may not join the competition or engage in competitive activity.

The employee must remain in the employer's service for an established period of time in order to receive the deferred pay.

The employee will, as an outside contractor, be available for consultation if needed after retirement. (Note: It must be clear that the employee is acting as an independent contractor when he does consulting work for the company. There should not be confusion about his relationship to the company.)

Advantages of deferred compensation:

No legal restrictions exist on who or how many employees can take advantage of deferred compensation plans. The plan may cover any number of employees.

The employee makes a substantial tax saving by deferring part of his salary into lower tax years.

The employer may realize a substantial tax saving if he anticipates a higher tax rate in later years.

The employer may have access to the deferred funds during the time of deferment.

The arrangement is easy to set up.

Disadvantages of deferred compensation:

There is no guarantee that the company will be able to pay the deferred compensation when the employee is ready to retire.

Since IRS regulations forbid unconditional funding via an escrow account, it may be a good idea to have the company purchase a high cash value life insurance policy on the employee with the employer as beneficiary. When it comes time for the employee to retire, the policy is cashed in and the monies are available for the deferred payment.

The employee doesn't get the use of the deferred monies until the agreed-upon date.

As we have seen, in a nonqualified compensation deferment plan the employee, and often the corporation as well, winds up paying a reduced tax on the compensation. Furthermore, the nonqualified plan is free from the more stringent IRS requirements for qualified plans.

Qualified plans, on the other hand, have these advantages:

Current tax deduction. Pretax corporate money goes into the plan as a deductible contribution.

Tax-free accumulations. Income from investments in the plan may accumulate and be reinvested tax free.

Deferred tax on benefits. Benefits are not taxed until actually received. Even if the entire amount due an individual is paid out in a lump sum, the distribution receives preferential tax treatment under a special ten-year averaging method.

Distribution of employer securities. Under certain circumstances, employer securities credited to an individual's account may be distributed, but tax is not due on any appreciation until the securities are actually sold.

Stockholders. In no way are stockholders prohibited from participating in a qualified plan as long as they are also employees of the company.

Pension *vs.* profit sharing:

Many people are confused by the differences between the two major types of qualified plans—pension and profit sharing. Under a pension plan, the company has a fixed obligation to continue to contribute a certain amount of money each year toward the plan, rain or shine. With profit sharing, there is no such fixed commitment—contributions are contingent on profits and can be skipped or reduced in a bad year. Usually, a formula is established that defines the way in which the employer's profit sharing contributions will be made. For example, it might be 15% of pretax profit over the first $10,000 in profit. But the retirement benefit under profit sharing will vary according to the amount of contributions and the fund's accumulated earnings.

Generally, profit sharing plans tend to be more attractive to smaller or recently formed businesses with unstable year-to-year profits. On the other hand, pension plans are generally more attractive to older management and employees who want the security of a fixed contribution by the company to the plan each year. A little-known fact about profit-sharing plans: Retirement benefits do not necessarily have to be provided for the plan to qualify for the tax break. Other benefits, such as house mortgage financing, tuition assistance, and emergency loans, can be substituted. Hence, profit sharing tends to be more attractive to younger individuals.

Comparison of Qualified Profit Sharing vs. Pension Plans

	Profit Sharing	Pension
Orientation	Favors younger employees.	Favors older employees.
Benefits	Retirement benefits need not be provided. Other benefits, such as accident and health, may be provided.	Retirement benefits must be provided. Other benefits limited to disability coverage.
Contribution	At discretion of management and based only on profits. Cannot exceed 15% of total payroll.	Fixed obligation which must be made in both profit and loss years.
Forfeiture	May be allocated to remaining participants of plan.	Used to decrease employer's cost.
Distribution	After as few as two years.	Only on retirement, death, disability, or termination of employment.

Requirements to qualify:

To obtain IRS approval and the tax benefits, the main requirement is that a qualified plan be permanent and not discriminate in favor of a particular employee group, such as top management.

It is generally possible, however, to design the plan so that long-term employees (including management) indirectly receive preferential treatment. For example, some plans stipulate rigorous ''vesting'' provisions. Any employee who leaves in the first five years of employment forfeits all contributions to the plan. (These funds then accrue to the remaining members in the plan.) After five years there is 50% vesting, with additional 10% increments each year, resulting in full vesting only after ten years of continuous employment. But watch this: Special rules apply to closely held businesses that require much faster vesting for non-owner employees.

Furthermore, there is no requirement with qualified plans that all employees receive the same amount of benefits. Allocation of contributions among participants can vary according to (1) years of service, (2) age, and/or (3) compensation. A payout formula based on a combination of compensation and years of service generally works out best for long-term employees and management.

Other requirements for qualified plans:

Who must be included. Qualified profit sharing plans and pension plans must cover 70% of all employees who work more than 1,000 hours in 12 months. Also, an owner of two separate businesses may not establish a plan for one business that discriminates against his employees in the other.

Voluntary contributions. In a profit sharing plan, a participant may pay extra money voluntarily into his retirement account. This is in addition to the amount paid in by the employer. There is, however, a limit to the amount of voluntary contributions, and such contributions are not deductible to the participant. However, once in the account, they do escape tax on their compounded earnings. (New "Cash Option" plans permit a tax deduction for voluntary contributions by reducing the amount declared on the W-2 form.)

Benefit limitation. The limit on the amount a retired employee may receive each year under a pension plan is the average compensation received over his three consecutive highest paid years. The benefit limitation on the profit sharing plan is limited by the restrictions on the amount that may be paid into or credited to his account.

Benefit taxation. Retirement benefits are taxed as ordinary income if they are disbursed as annuity payments. Of course, the ordinary income tax rate is usually significantly less as a retiree. A lump-sum payment of the benefit—be it at retirement time or when the plan is terminated—is taxable as long-term capital gain if attributable to contributions and earnings made before 1974. Payments attributable to earnings after 1973 are treated as ordinary income subject to a special ten-year averaging stipulation, which results in a substantial saving in taxes.

What if a participant dies before retirement age? Then the beneficiary of the employee may exclude $5,000 from income tax as an employee death benefit.

Allowable investments. In most cases, funds contributed to a retirement plan may be invested in any of the following instruments: Bonds, savings accounts, real estate, life insurance contracts, stock, or mutual funds. However, there is a diversification requirement in regard to such investments.

Rollover. Rollover or "portability" is the term applied to the tax-free transfer of accumulated retirement benefits from one company to another or to an Individual Retirement Plan. Usually, an employee who terminates his employment is taxed on the vested interest he withdraws when he leaves. But if he transfers the amount taken out into his new employer's retirement program within 60 days, or to his own Individual Retirement Account, he is not taxed on his accumulated retirement benefits.

There are two other common forms of retirement plans, a stock bonus plan and a "defined contribution" plan. Under a stock bonus plan, a company contributes its own stock to the retirement plan instead of cash. In virtually all other respects it is the same as a profit sharing plan.

A defined contribution plan resembles a pension plan in that the employer must contribute a fixed amount annually to the retirement fund. However, the employee is not promised a specific amount of retirement compensation. Rather, when he retires, a pension annuity will be purchased with the money that has been allocated to his retirement account.

Source: *The Complete Guide to Running a Business,* by John R. Klug, Boardroom Books, New York.

Bigger Pensions In Closely Held Corporations

A provision in ERISA (the pension law) makes it possible for a small, closely held corporation to provide its older insiders, in a relatively short time, with pension benefits substantially larger than their compensation—and with the cost fully deductible by the corporation.

Example: A Mr. Smith, having elected early retirement from a major corporation, starts up his own consulting corporation. He brings his wife into the business as an assistant and has two part-time employees to help her with various chores. He puts his wife on the books for $6,000 a year, although she's worth more. Even though he considers increasing her pay, he has prudent misgivings, because her earnings will only add to the taxable income on their joint return.

Taking advantage of ERISA, Smith sets up a defined-benefit pension plan (where benefit payout is fixed) for his corporation. Under the so-called de minimis provision of ERISA, he can set his wife's defined benefit upon retirement at $10,000 a year—$4,000 more than her annual salary. She's able to escape the benefit limit of 100% of her annual salary (or the average of the three highest-paid years up to $50,000 a year), because her salary is under $10,000.

To establish the $10,000 benefit, he must show actually what it would cost to provide her with a straight-life annuity of $10,000 a year at age 65. That's easy. All he has to do is ask a life insurance company how much such a policy could cost. Answer: $140,000 lump sum. Thus, if she is 55 and you assume 8% annual interest, compounded, it works out that he must put away $10,000 a year for 10 years—or a total of $100,000.

What we've done is provide her with a benefit worth $140,000, with $100,000 in tax-deductible dollars.

Another plus: If those dollars had been paid to Mrs. Smith as straight compensation (assuming that Mr. and Mrs. Smith filed joint returns and were in the 50% tax bracket), she would have paid out $50,000 in taxes over the 10 years of employment by the corporation. And that means she'd end up with only $50,000 after 10 years of working—plus any interest.

But by having Mrs. Smith elect a lump-sum distribution of the $140,000 in the pension fund at age 65, tax computed under the special 10-year averaging formula of ERISA would be $32,100, leaving her with $107,900.

Don't fail to investigate annuities. The savings from them could be sizable in the right situation.

Pension Rights When Companies Merge

Management is not required to continue the retirement plan of an acquired company. It may be terminated immediately after the merger or purchase. Assured rights: Each participant in the discontinued pension plan must receive a distribution of benefits that is not less than he would have received if the plan had been terminated before the merger.

Company Insurance For Retired Executives

Many executives who think they have adequate life insurance through company policies do not. By the time they find out—often at retirement—the cost of doing anything about insurance coverage can be prohibitive. There is a way for the company to pay for a key executive's life insurance at a substantial savings in premium costs.

Most executives lose their group life insurance coverage when they retire and find that the cost of individual coverage — if available — is exorbitant. Solution: A post-retirement life reserve plan which enables a company to make tax-deductible life insurance premium payments during the executive's working years so that when he retires he has a fully-paid-up policy with benefits he can count on.

How it works: In addition to its regular group term insurance, the company buys a post-retirement life reserve policy for an executive. The money paid for this policy each year goes to fund a tax-free trust that earns interest. The policy is converted to fully paid upon retirement. If the executive dies or leaves the company before retirement, all the money plus interest is returned to the trust to be used to pay insurance premiums on the others still in the firm.

Example: A company wants to insure the life of a 45-year-old executive for $100,000. It pays $650 a year for group term insurance and, in addition, puts aside $2,000 a year to build up a reserve for his post-retirement years. At age 55, the group term insurance premiums have risen to $1,500 a year, but the reserve premiums are still $2,000 annually.

If the executive dies at 55: His family receives $100,000 under the group term policy. The entire $20,000 (plus interest) that has built up in the reserve trust in the 10 years is returned to the trust (reducing the company's future cost).

If the executive lives to 65 and beyond: The trust (which now has $40,000 plus interest in it) supersedes the group term policy. The executive has $100,000 in insurance for the rest of his life. No future payments are required.

Taxes. In addition to getting a $100,000 policy for $40,000 (instead of $90,000), the company takes a deduction for these premium payments. Result: The policy costs $20,000 in after-tax income. If the owner of a corporation in a 50% tax bracket took that $20,000 as personal income, he would have received only $10,000. The IRS has approved some post-retirement life reserve plans, but it is still cautious. Until there's a more definitive ruling, most insurance companies are selling these plans selectively.

Estate planning. The post-retirement life reserve policy can be used to make sure the executive's family has enough liquid assets to pay estate taxes. (No tax if spouse receives the money.) The insurance is also a good way to make a gift to beneficiaries. For the $40,000 pre-tax cost of the post-retirement life reserve policy, the holder makes a $100,000 tax-free bequest.

Closely held companies. Any corporation can set up a post-retirement life reserve, but it's most advantageous for the owner of a closely held corporation or members of a professional corporation (such as commonly formed by accountants, lawyers, and doctors). However, the new law permits payment of tax over 14 years. Principals in a closely held company can also structure the plan so it benefits them more than others.

Setting up a plan. Benefits can be determined by length of service or by compensation level. Caution: All plans within a company must be consistent. Thus, if a chief executive and a vice president have been with the company for 20 years and the benefits are determined solely on length of service, both are entitled to the same benefits. A company can lose its tax deduction and face potential penalties if the plan favors an individual.

Idea for founders: Chances are the company founder has been there longer than anyone else. Structure the benefits based on length of service only. But, if there are many long-time employees, consider basing the benefits on salary only, because his is likely to be the highest.

Companies that should not use the post-retirement reserve: Those doing only marginally well. It's dangerous to be committed to the additional long-term expense of funding such a benefit.

Recommended: Have an expert organize the plan as a 501(r)(q) Trust and get IRS approval.

Important: The $50,000 limit on the amount of tax-free insurance an employee can receive is not necessarily a good reason to limit coverage to that amount. Reason: The saving on group rates usually more than offsets taxes the employee must pay on premiums for the additional coverage.

Source: Leon Sicular, CLU, 350 Fifth Ave., New York 10001.

What You Should Know About Social Security and Keogh Plans

To take full advantage of Social Security and Keogh Plan options, you must keep up with changes in the laws and tax regulations.

Social Security. In 1984, for the first time, Social Security benefits will be taxable. If your adjusted gross income, plus one-half your Social Security benefits, plus tax-exempt interest, exceeds $25,000 (for individuals) or $32,000 (for joint returns), one-half the excess is taxable. Maximum taxable amount: One-half your Social Security benefits.

Social Security taxes: The 1985 rate for employees is 7%, the effective rate for the self-employed is 11.8%. The amount of earnings subject to tax rises from $37,800 to $39,600.

Keogh Plans for the Self-Employed. From 1984 on, these plans will be subject to the same rules as corporate plans. One minor change: Allowable contributions rise from 15% of earnings (maximum, $15,000) to 25% of earnings (maximum, $30,000). But the 25% figure is misleading. You can't contribute 25% of total earnings—only 25% of total earnings minus the amount contributed to the Keogh. This reduces the effective contribution limit to 20%.

Example: You're self-employed and earn $100,000 in 1984. You can contribute $20,000. The contribution reduces your earnings base to $80,000. Twenty-five percent of $80,000 is $20,000. If you contribute more, you reduce your earnings below $80,000, and your contribution exceeds the legal limit.

Self-employed persons nearing retirement age (say, over age 50) can make larger contributions by setting up a "defined benefit" plan, guaranteeing a specific income at retirement age. Maximum: $90,000 or 100% of average annual compensation. Drawbacks: These plans are expensive to set up and administer. And annual contributions would be extremely large for persons with comparatively few working years left.

For self-employed persons with employees, there are complications. For one thing, total earnings must be reduced by contributions for employees, as well as your own contribution. Other laws with tighter restrictions may apply, including the new "top-heavy" rules.

A plan is "top-heavy" if more than 60% of benefits go to "key employees" (officers, over-5% owners, certain highly paid employees). Top-heavy plans must contain special provisions, including faster vesting and minimum benefits for non-key employees. Even plans that are not top-heavy must include the provisions—to take effect if the plan ever does become top-heavy.

Plans must be amended, if necessary, to comply with these rules by the end of 1984. Otherwise they lose "qualified" status, and all pension contributions are taxable.

The rules apply to Keogh Plans as well as to corporate plans. If you have a Keogh, don't waste time trying to figure out if it's top-heavy or needs amendment. The rules are too technical. Take your plan straight to your lawyer or financial adviser and let him make any necessary changes.

Self-employed persons can now name any trustee they choose, not just banks or financial institutions. You can name yourself, even if you have no employees and are both trustee and sole beneficiary of the account.

You'll probably still want to name a financial institution, because it's simpler. But be cautious. Comparison shop. If you decide to change trustees later, you don't want to be stuck with a trust agreement that limits your rights or imposes fees or penalties.

Source: Michael F. Klein, partner, Price Waterhouse & Co., New York City.

Company Retirement Plan Plus Your Own Keogh

Any executive with a second source of employment income should not overlook the possible opportunity to make tax-deductible personal retirement contributions. Keogh plans are allowed on some second incomes as well as for the self-employed.

The rules and deadlines for making contributions that are deductible against income:

Self-employed persons, including owners of businesses that are sole proprietorships, can establish Keogh plans. The plan must also cover employees and make contributions for them on same formula used for owner. Up to 25% of net self-employment income (minus the amount contributed to the Keogh) can be set aside and deducted. Year's contribution can't be more than $30,000 for each individual.

Working partners are also eligible for contributions to Keogh plans set up by the partnership, not by the individuals. And the plan must also cover employees on the same formula as the partners.

Outside self-employment income: Outside consulting, selling, free lance writing, or other work qualifies. *Maximum contribution:* 25% of total earnings less Keogh contribution (limit: $30,000).

Executives who receive directors' fees are eligible for Keogh plans on the fee income. That's true even if the fees they receive are for sitting on the board of their own company. Directors' fee must be paid separately, though, and with no withholding or Social Security taken out.

Keogh plans are for employment income only. They can't be used for interest, dividends or other investment income. And owner-officers can use them only for compensation, not for dividends.

Investment alternatives. Law permits the money to be invested in four ways:

1. Banks and savings and loan associations. Usual way is to buy certificates. But it's also possible to set up a trust account and have the bank invest in other things (for a fee). Most brokerage firms now offer self-directed Keogh accounts in which the individual can decide how the money is invested.

2. Mutual funds.

3. Annuity or endowment contracts. If the contract includes life insurance, the portion paid for that coverage is not tax deductible.

4. U.S. Government Retirement Bonds.

Keogh money can be switched from one investment to another without penalty. And, of course, there's no tax on the earnings until the money is taken out after retirement.

A Keogh plan must be set up before the end of the year in order to take tax deductions for that year. But the deadline for actually making contributions to a Keogh is the day the tax return is due. (That is, April 15 of the following year, or later if there is an extension.)

Source: Michael F. Klein, CPA, partner, Price Waterhouse & Co., 153 East 53 St., New York 10022.

Smart Move For Keogh/IRA

If more than a few hundred dollars in interest has accumulated in an Individual Retirement Account (IRA) or a Keogh account set up when interest rates were lower, look into rolling over the interest into one of the high-interest accounts now offered by the bank. There's no penalty for the rollover of accrued interest into better-paying accounts. The principal, however, cannot be withdrawn or switched without a penalty.

IRA Pitfalls

An individual can't contribute more than $2,000 for any one tax year. Exception: You can contribute up to $2,250 if your spouse is not employed and you contribute at least $250 to a spousal IRA.

Trap: To be deductible, your contribution must be made by April 15. Extensions are no longer allowed.

If you contribute too much during the year, you must remove the excess amount (plus earnings) by the time your tax is due. Otherwise, you'll be hit with a nondeductible 6% penalty each year until the excess is withdrawn.

You can't contribute in the year you reach age 70½ or thereafter. But: You can continue contributing up to $2,000 to the spousal account of a nonworking spouse under that age.

125

Important: Trustees' fees do not count as part of your contribution. Furthermore, they're deductible on Schedule A, if you itemize your deductions.

Contributions must be in cash only, not stocks, bonds or other property. And, if you sell anything to raise the $2,000, you must pay tax on any capital gain. Tip: Sell stocks that have declined in value. You can fund the IRA and also get a capital loss on the sale. Furthermore, if you desire, your IRA can repurchase the stocks immediately. The wash sale rules shouldn't apply, as you and your IRA are separate legal entities.

Any withdrawals made before you reach age 59½ will be hit with a nondeductible 10% penalty, in addition to the regular tax on the withdrawal. If you withdraw $1,000 for example, the money becomes part of your ordinary taxable income and in addition, you must pay a penalty of $100. There are two exceptions:
- You become permanently and totally disabled, or
- A transfer of a person's interest in an IRA to a former spouse under a valid divorce decree.

You can't borrow from your IRA, or pledge it as security for a loan. Any such transaction is considered a taxable withdrawal that is subject to penalty if you're under 59½.

You must begin making withdrawals no later than the year in which you reach age 70½. The minimum withdrawl for each year is determined by the life-expectancy tables. And there's a whopping 50% penalty on any amount that should have been withdrawn but wasn't

You can transfer (roll over) all or part of any IRA into another IRA. For this purpose, you can make a tax-free withdrawal for up to 60 days. But if you haven't made the transfer by that time, the withdrawal becomes final, taxable and subject to penalty.

If you receive a lump-sum pension distribution (for instance, if you leave your job), you can avoid taxation by rolling over all or part of it into an IRA. The rollover must be made within 60 days of receiving the distribution, or the right is lost.

This type of rollover is permitted at any age.

Of course, if you're over 70½, you'll have to start making withdrawals immediately.

Source: John S. Kearney, tax manager, Coopers & Lybrand, 1251 Ave. of the Americas, New York 10020.

Social Security: It's Worth More Than You Think

In the foreseeable future, probably no single piece of legislation will affect you, your employees, or your company more than the Social Security Act. Yet many businessmen are unaware of the basic provisions of this law and how it can influence their personal and business planning.

Scope of the law: The Social Security law actually covers 12 major programs, but the benefits of most concern to the executive are these four:
- Retirement benefits.
- Survivor benefits.
- Disability benefits.
- Lump-sum payment at death.

Retirement and survivor, benefits: The following table summarizes the retirement and survivor benefits available to the executive and his family.

Social Security Benefits Summary

	Status	Percent of Basic Benefits
Executive	Age 65 or over	100 %
	Age 62	80 %
Spouse	Age 65 or over or age 62 with child under 18, student under 22, or disabled child	50 %*
	Age 62, no children at home	37½ %
Widow	Age 65 or over	100 %**
	Age 60	71½ %
	Age 50 and disabled	50 %
Child	Under age 18 or disabled child at any age if disability began before age 22	50% if wage earner alive / 75% if wage earner deceased

*Subject to family maximum
**of spouse's benefit

Survivors' benefits are an especially valuable insurance benefit for young families. If the head of the family dies or becomes disabled before age 65, the spouse and children under 18 will each receive a monthly benefit. The amount of current life insurance you now have under Social Security depends on your age. If you and your wife are both 35, for example, with two young children, it can be worth about one-half million dollars.

For an executive who retires at age 65 in 1990, the "basic benefits" are estimated to be $1,071.66 per month. In other words, you and your wife could expect to receive $1071.66 per month plus her 50% if she is age 65, totalling $1,607.49 per month. And the 1972 revision to the basic act stipulates that all benefits are to be corrected for inflation.

There is another Social Security benefit which should interest an executive. If you become blind or expect to be disabled for 12 months or more, you will receive your basic benefits at any age.

Eligibility: The rules that must be met to be considered "fully insured" under Social Security are complex, but almost every executive, whether self-employed or working for an employer, should be fully qualified.

Watch these gaps: While Social Security provides a base for you and your family's personal security, there are important gaps that you should consider. One concerns widow's benefits. If you should die, your spouse will get benefits only if she is over 60 or caring for a child under 18. Hence, you should consider an insurance program to meet this shortcoming. Also, if you become a widower with dependent children, it could cause a substantial financial burden. More and more executives are considering life insurance on their spouses to meet this need. Another problem area is disability benefits; the government's definition of disability is exceedingly strict and it is often difficult to collect. Consider a private program to at least supplement Social Security benefits.

Source: *The Complete Guide to Running a Business,* by John R. Klug, Boardroom Books, New York.

Social Security Errors

Check every three years on the earnings credited to your account. Send a preaddressed Request for Statement of Earnings postcard (Form SSA-7004-PC), available from any local Social Security Administration office. Why: Your retirement, disability, or death benefits will be based largely on the total wages credited to your Social Security number, and you have a three-year deadline for correcting errors. The authorities admit a 6% error factor. Stunner: $69 billion of workers' income was not properly credited in *one* recent year.

Applying for Your Social Security

If you want your Social Security income payments to start promptly, apply for them three months in advance of when you are actually entitled to receive them. It takes some time for applications to be processed.

Applying later will delay your receipt of the first payments, but won't cost you any money in the long run. You will get all that is due you.

How to 'Cash In' A Business With Minimum Tax Bite

Practical way to transfer a business to the principal's children (or other family members) with a minimum of tax liability: (1) Arrange to transfer some stock to family. (2) Later, have the corporation buy the rest of principal's share. (3) Instead of paying him a lump sum of cash, have the money paid as a lifetime annuity. In that way, the money is distributed in fixed, annual installments. The advantages:

The business is removed from the owner's estate immediately, without the imposition of gift or inheritance taxes.

The owner gets a lifetime income, which can meet retirement needs just as well as a lump-sum payment.

The estate isn't swollen with cash or notes that would be received in a lump-sum redemption. The annuity lasts only during the principal's lifetime.

Business isn't saddled with a traumatic outflow of working capital. The annuity is paid out of profits and is spaced evenly over the lifetime of the former owner of the business.

How to do it: Calculate the fair market value of the shares. Then use IRS actuarial tables to translate the value of those holdings into a monthly lifetime annuity plus interest.

Taxes are paid only on the income that's received each year, not on the cash value of the annuity in the year received. For tax purposes, the annuity payments are divided into three layers: (1) Return of capital (not taxed). (2) Profit on the sale of stock (capital gains tax). (3) Interest on the unpaid balance (taxed as ordinary income).

When the Founder Of a Family Business Won't Let Go

Only about 30% of the country's family businesses survive into the second generation. The problems usually originate with the company's founder. He may be:

Too busy with the company to plan for retirement.

Lacking confidence in his offspring.

Unable to see continuity of ownership as a goal.

Other reasons are often psychological. Some owners can't accept their own mortality. One aged boss, for instance, left instructions to his survivors that began: If I die . . .

Owners of family businesses usually like to give orders. Many have no other interest in life outside of their business.

Recommended: Family-business owners should look at retirement as a challenging goal and make plans well in advance to leave the business. Important: Don't keep an office at the company after retirement.

Source: Randall Poe of the Conference Board, writing in *Across the Board.*

When the Company's Founder Retires

Mistake: When the founder-entrepreneur approaches retirement, he often begins searching for someone to replace himself.

Trap: Few such people can be replaced. Prime reason: Their value during their last years with the company is often the continuity they bring to its operations.

Main reason: The special combination of talents that helped the founder-entrepreneur succeed can rarely be duplicated.

The better way for owners who do not want to sell out is to select a successor team of four people:

Chief executive officer. Point: This is the position for a first-generation family member who wants to stay in the business. (Don't expect second-generation family members to fill the shoes of their elders.)

Production head. In many entrepreneurial companies, there will already be a production lieutenant who is a contemporary of the founder-entrepreneur. Back him up with a younger successor. Allow at least three to four months for the new person to learn the job.

Marketing head. Typically, someone in the company already serves as a liaison between the founder and the outside marketing and advertising consultants retained over the years. This arrangement should be dissolved and a professionally trained marketing vice-president brought on staff. Allow seven or eight months, or one entire season, for the new person to learn the job.

Financial head. Founder-entrepreneurs usually rely heavily on outside accountants, not only to audit their books and handle their taxes, but also to function as controller.

Point: When the founder-entrepreneur is near retirement, plans should be made for an in-house controller to be hired and for the outside CPA to assume a reduced role.

Reason: The management team will need an expert to participate in the group decisions previously made by the founder-entrepreneur. Allow six to seven months for the controller to learn the details of his job.

Source: Edward Mendlowitz, chief tax partner, Siegel & Mendlowitz, CPAs, 310 Madison Ave., New York 10017.

Tax Boon For Retiring Executives

Retiring key executives often make arrangements to work for their former company on some informal basis. Problem: Every dollar the executive earns above $6,600 (in 1983) cuts into Social Security benefits.

Practical new way around that: Use a stand-by consulting agreement. Advantage: Amounts received in exchange for an agreement to be available to do consulting work do not count towards the $6,600 limit. So if the individual is available to do work, but doesn't actually do any, the person won't lose any benefits. Note: Any payments received for a period in which the executive does work will count towards the limit.

Source: Steven F. Holub, national director of tax services, Laventhol & Horwath, 8630 Fenton St., Silver Spring, MD 20910.

Tax Precautions When Retiring to Another State

Moving from one state to another can open a tax trap.

Goal: To make sure you, or your heirs when you die, are not taxed in more than one state, which can easily happen.

Specific aim: Establish a domicile in the low-tax or no-tax state. Make the arrangement so airtight that questions won't arise about its being a tax dodge.

Aids in clearly establishing the preferred domicile:

Sell your current home and buy one in the new state. Then establish a physical presence. This may be an extreme step. Alternatively, transfer your current home to one of your children so that it will be available to you on visits.

Get a certificate of domicile. It is issued by the local county clerk upon request.

Get a driver's license and car registration from your new state. Return your old plates to the motor vehicle bureau in the old state with a letter indicating your change of domicile.

Close your checking and savings accounts in the old state. Open new accounts in your new state. Rent a new safe-deposit box, too, or at least don't keep the old one.

Close investment accounts with your brokers in the old state and open accounts in the new state.

Notify tax authorities in the old state of your change of domicile. File a final state income tax in the old state. File state and federal income tax returns in the new state.

Notify the Social Security Administration of your change of address. This is particularly important if you are actually receiving Social Security checks.

Notify insurance companies, credit card companies, and the like of your permanent change of address.

Register and vote in the first available election in the new state, and in subsequent ones, too.

Join local groups and organizations in the new state.

Establish relations with a local doctor and dentist in the new state. Have your records sent to them.

Have a local lawyer in the new state draw up a new will for you using local residents as witnesses. Remember that state law governs wills; your old one may no longer be valid.

In Case You Are Incapacitated

The simplest step: Delegate power of attorney to someone with financial expertise to handle your business and financial affairs. Drawbacks: The power ends in some states if you become legally incompetent. It ends in all states when you die. You are personally liable for any acts the proxy commits in your name. Some third parties may be reluctant to deal with the proxy for fear he may be exceeding his mandate.

Set up a standby trust triggered by a specific event. Example: An illness. The trust ends when the disability ceases. Advantage: Avoids probate.

Declare yourself trustee of all or part of your property. If you become incapacitated, a substitute trustee automatically steps in. This type of trust also avoids probate. Drawbacks: The trust can be overridden in some cases. If you own shares in an S corporation, an improperly drafted trust could end the company's favored tax status.

Avoid a judicial guardianship. It's complex and expensive because the courts require a periodic accounting from the trustee.

Retirement Income From a Reverse Mortgage

This new mortgage arrangement allows older homeowners to supplement retirement income by drawing on the equity in their homes.

How it works: The homeowner, who must be at least 60, can borrow up to 70% of the home's market value. Typically, the borrower receives part of the proceeds at once, with the remainder paid out in monthly installments over the life of the loan (five years). Interest may be payable currently, while the principal is due at the end. If the borrower dies before the five years are up, his estate has one year to pay back the loan. If the borrower survives, the loan may be refinanced. Major drawback: Refinancing may prove difficult if the house hasn't maintained its value, or if credit markets continue to be squeezed.

Retirement Planning For Inflationary Times

With high inflation rates, the purchasing power of a dollar can be sliced in half in less than 10 years. Ways out: After retirement, find a job that matches your personal strengths and interests. Example: A retired insurance executive works for an auction house cataloging objects of art. Trick: He loves visiting museums as a hobby. Thus, he turns his leisure-time activity into rewarding work.

Parlay your house sale into an annuity. How: After the age of 55, your first $125,000 profit from a house sale is tax-free. Buy a smaller home and invest the profit in a steady interest-bearing security.

Alternative: Refinance your home and invest the money in rental property. Why: Good tax breaks; deductions for depreciation, operating costs, and interest on the mortgage. Bonus: You can increase rents to keep pace with inflation.

Source: *Strategies for the Second Half of Life,* by Peter Weaver, Franklin Watts, Inc., New York.

6

Estate Planning

How Much Life Insurance You Need

First step: Determine what the surviving members' short- and long-term economic needs are likely to be. Then, estimate the amount of these needs covered by available resources (savings, home equity, existing insurance, pension benefits, veterans' benefits, and Social Security). Buy only enough life insurance to make up the deficit between needs and available resources.

How to determine needs:

Immediate cash for death-related expenses. For uninsured medical costs, funeral expenses, debts, taxes, and estate-settlement fees (including the lawyer's bill). Minimum amount of cash: $4,000.

Readjustment fund. Takes economic pressure off the family, allowing them to make important decisions without haste. Optimum size: Six to 12 months of the lost net income of a working parent, or the one-year cost of replacing the family services of a nonworking parent.

Mortgage fund. Mortgage canceling life insurance gives survivors relatively low-cost housing (that is, they pay only taxes and upkeep). If they decide to sell the house, insurance relieves the pressure to sell too quickly at a distress price.

Family income. Make two budgets and periodically review them. One budget applies if the father's income is lost. The other applies either to replace a working mother's lost income or the cost of replacing her services at home.

Emergency fund. For an unexpected crisis, such as a major illness. Amount: About $2,000 (adjust for the size and health of the family).

Widow's income. Drops in proportion to her decreasing financial responsibility to the children. After the children are on their own, she may not need extra income if she remarries or takes a job. Otherwise, she would need extra income if she does not remarry or work; or Social Security benefits stop when her youngest child turns 18 and will not resume until she reaches 60.

Special funds. To cover the cost of the children's college educations, and so on.

131

Some guidelines:

Comparison shop for price and quality of insurance coverage.

Fill short-term needs, such as mortgage protection or supplemental income during the children's early years, with the lowest-cost term insurance available. Fill long-term needs with the least expensive whole-life insurance.

Know your life-insurance needs before talking to insurance agents. Don't get pressured into the wrong purchase.

Useful rule of thumb:

After the death of its principal income-producer, a family requires 75% of its former after-tax income to maintain its standard of living, according to a Citibank report. It must, according to that report, have at least 60% to get along at all.

Here is the amount of life insurance (in terms of annual earnings multiples) needed to provide this income at different ages (taking into account Social Security benefits and assuming the insurance proceeds were invested to produce an after-inflation return of 5% a year, with the entire principal consumed over survivor's life expectancy).

Present Age	Your Present Earnings				
	$15M	$23.5M	$30M	$40M	$65M
25 years					
75%	4.5	6.5	7.5	7.5	7.5
60%	3.0	4.5	5.0	5.0	5.5
35 years					
75%	6.5	8.0	8.0	8.0	7.5
60%	4.5	5.5	6.0	6.0	6.0
45 years					
75%	8.0	8.5	8.5	8.0	7.5
60%	6.0	6.5	6.5	6.0	6.0
55 years					
75%	7.0	7.5	7.0	7.0	6.5
60%	5.5	5.5	5.5	5.5	5.0

While the chart shows insurance needs, it would be more useful to say that it shows capital requirements. Those requirements can be met by life insurance or through savings and investments, employee benefits, or inheritance. Thus, to the extent that the independent capital resources are built up, insurance needs diminish.

Example: An individual, aged 55, with earnings of $40,000 and a net worth of $240,000,

instead of requiring insurance in the face amount of $280,000, could get by with $40,000 in life insurance coverage and still meet the seven-time-earnings multiple indicated by the chart.

Understanding Term Insurance

Term insurance is usually the least expensive form of insurance to get for a maximum of five years.

The choices:

Yearly renewable term. The rates start low and rise annually as your age (which increases the risk) goes up. Choose this policy if you're in a short-term venture (a construction project or a short-term contract).

Five- and ten-year term insurance. Appropriate for a person starting a high-risk or highly leveraged business when the bank may insist that the entrepreneur's life be covered by a large policy for a specified period of time. The premium is averaged out on an annual basis over the life of the policy.

Yearly renewable term policy with a reversion to lower premiums on evidence of insurability. This is a recent development. At a specified time (usually after four or five years), if you pass a medical exam, the premiums can be reduced by perhaps 35% of what they might have been. Example: If your insurance premium starts at $1,000 a year and climbs $200 annually, you must pass an exam during the fifth year to get the premium lowered to $1,300. Potential problem: Bad health at the time of the examination will negate the possibility of lowering the premium.

Avoid term insurance even for the short haul if you are almost 70 years old. Since the risk at that age is so high, the point at which term and straight-premium rate would cross would be attained within five years. At that point, a permanent (or straight) life policy is best.

If you need life insurance for more than five

years, permanent insurance is usually best.

Reason: The total acquisition price usually evens out over a period of 10 years. If the buyer is relatively young, say in his thirties, the cash value of the policy may increase at a greater rate than the premium after the third year. The straight-life policy holder may borrow on the cash value at a tax-deductible, low rate of interest.

Alternative: Some creative insurance agents combine the two types of insurance coverage, thus lowering premium costs and ensuring cash value at a specific time.

Source: Leon Sicular, president, Leon H. Sicular Associates, 350 Fifth Ave., New York 10001.

Single Payment Life Insurance

This form of insurance is worth considering for the executive who wants a mixture of life insurance, investment opportunity, and tax savings.

What it offers:

Complete safety of capital.

Liquidity. Get money back without penalty after one year.

Moderate income.

Income tax shelter.

Possible estate tax shelter.

Life insurance protection that increases over the years.

Single premium life insurance is a whole life policy paid for by one lump sum premium at the time the policy is taken out. Many companies offer such policies up to age 75, but the insured must pass a physical examination.

Cash values, death benefits, and dividends increase over the years. Example:

$10,000 Single Premium Policy for 54-Year-Old Man

Year	Annual Tax-Free Dividend	Cash Value	Death Benefit
2	$395	$ 9,875	$13,580
5	425	10,630	13,690
10	481	12,033	14,250

Tax advantage: Dividends and increases in cash value are completely free from income and capital gains taxes. Exception: If dividends are collected in cash, they'll be taxed after about 19 years, because accumulated dividends will then equal the original premium paid.

Borrowing against the policy: The IRS will not permit interest payment deduction if the individual borrows to make the lump-sum payment on this tax-advantaged insurance investment.

The cash value of the policy is good collateral, however. The policyholder can borrow against a policy and then deduct the interest payments on his income tax return. If the policy is given away to the beneficiary, that person can borrow against it. (But the original purchaser can't.)

Estate tax: When a policy is given to a beneficiary, the insurance proceeds will be free from estate tax. However, the policy is then considered a taxable gift (except if given to a spouse) that uses up part of the combined lifetime gift-estate tax exemption under the current tax law.

Disadvantages: Income and cash value buildup are lower with single payment life than with other investments that don't provide insurance protection.

Split-Dollar Insurance: More Protection At Less Cost

Adequate life insurance is a concern of every executive. But during heavy spending years when an executive most needs insurance, he has the least money available to buy it. Furthermore, insurance premiums are not deductible to the individual and, hence, have to be paid with after-tax dollars. This is where "split-dollar" comes to the rescue. It provides a way for a corporation to assist executives with their personal insurance programs by

133

Split-Dollar Plan
$100,000 Ordinary Life Policy — Annual Premium $2,350

Year	Dividend	Net Premium (Annual Premium Less Dividend)	Cash Value	Increase in Cash Value (Employer Pays)	Net Premium Less Employer's Contribution (Employee Pays)	Employee's Death Benefit
1	$ 185	$ 2,165	$ 225	$ 225	$1,940	$99,775
2	250	2,100	2,050	1,825	275	97,950
3	315	2,035	3,900	1,850	185	96,100
4	385	1,965	5,775	1,875	90	94,225
5	445	1,905	7,680	1,905	0	93,320
1-20	$12,600	$36,200	$37,000	$33,300	$2,490	$63,000 (end of 20th year)

"splitting" the premiums with them. Additionally, it is one of the few compensation benefits that can be awarded on a discriminating basis to selected individuals.

Split-dollar in practice: Every permanent life insurance policy (as opposed to the term variety) has two aspects: The cash value and the death benefit. With split-dollar, the corporation pays that portion of each annual premium that represents the increase in cash value of the policy. The favored executive pays the remainder of the premium. With respect to the death benefit, two beneficiaries are designated— the corporation for an amount equal to the cash value of the policy at the time of death and the executive's beneficiary for the remainder.

A look at the numbers: Let's look at the numbers for a typical plan (summarized in the table). Consider the case of a $100,000 split-dollar policy on a 36-year-old executive. The first year, the policy has a cash value of $225, which the employer pays, and the executive pays the remaining premium of $1,940. (To make it easier, many companies advance executives the amount of their portion of the first year's premium which is then repaid out of future salary.) The second year, the executive's payment drops to $275, and the company pays $1,825. By the fifth year, the cash value increases as much as the premium, so the company pays the entire premium thereafter for the life of the policy.

Death benefit: At all times, the death benefit stands at $100,000 and eventually goes to the two beneficiaries — the company for an amount equal to the cash value (ranging from $225 in the first year to $37,000 by the twentieth) and the executive's widow or family for the remainder.

In other words, with split-dollar, the executive receives far more insurance than he could normally afford if he bought it himself, and the employer is absolutely sure of getting back whatever was spent on the policy, whether the executive lives, dies, quits, or retires.

Source: *The Complete Guide to Running a Business,* by John R. Klug, Boardroom Books, New York.

Minimum Deposit Insurance: Premiums Become Tax Deductions

Adequate life insurance can be expensive, and the premiums are not tax deductible. As a result, many businesspeople, especially those in their early years, feel that they can afford only term insurance, although they know its protection is temporary. It's surprising how few businesspeople realize that they can purchase whole life insurance at less cost than term insurance.

Financing life insurance: Interest on house or car payments is tax deductible. If policyholders borrow to pay life insurance premiums, that interest is also deductible, leading to the innovative practice of borrowing against the cash value of whole life insurance to pay the premiums. After the third or fourth year, the cash value normally grows by more than the premium each year, so the policy can effectively become self-financing. When certain rules are followed, the result is a triple benefit for the policyholder:

• The expense of carrying the policy can effectively become tax deductible.

• All proceeds still pass to beneficiaries free of income tax.

• Whole life protection can usually be obtained at a cash outlay below that of an equivalent amount of term insurance.

Minimum deposit practice: The table on the next page illustrates how a $100,000 minimum deposit policy could work out for a person 35 years old.

The tax laws (Section 264 of the Internal Revenue Code) state that a deduction for interest payments to finance life insurance is allowable as long as at least four full premiums are paid in the first seven years of the policy's life ("minimum deposit"). All other premiums may be borrowed from the insurance company.

Therefore, for the first four years, the full premium is paid (Column 5). In the fifth and subsequent years, the amount of the net annual premium is borrowed from the cash value of the policy (Column 6), and a tax deduction is taken for interest payments (Columns 8–9). Over a 20-year period the net cash outlay would total $19,690 as shown in Column 10.

However, to obtain the true net cost so that it may be compared with an equivalent amount of term insurance, the residual cash value must be deducted because term insurance normally has no cash value.

As shown, the net cost is $409 per year, which works out to $4.60 per $1,000 of in-force coverage. The result is permanent protection at a price less than that of an equivalent amount of term insurance.

As funds are borrowed against the cash value of the policy to pay the annual premium, the death benefit (Column 11) is reduced by an equal amount. To retain full coverage, many minimum deposit plans allow for application of part of the annual dividends to pay for one-year term insurance equal to the amount borrowed. This is referred to as the "fifth dividend option." Each year, as the policy loan increases and death benefits decline, the term insurance guarantees that the death benefits to beneficiaries (after deducting the amount of the loan) will equal the full face value of the policy.

How to "raid" the cash value: As noted above, IRS regulations state that at any time during the first seven years of a policy, no more than the amount of three net annual premiums may be borrowed. Since the cash value grows faster than the annual premium after the first year, a residual cash value builds up (Column 7), which cannot be borrowed without jeopardizing the tax status of the previous loans. However, beginning in the eighth year, the full cash value not yet taken out ($5,740 for the above example) may be borrowed without upsetting the interest deduction. Since most people feel that they can obtain a greater return on funds than the 5% to 8% it costs to "raid" the policy, they normally withdraw all available cash value and make up the reduction in death benefits with additional one-year renewable term insurance.

Integration of minimum deposit with an existing estate plan: The minimum deposit concept can be applied to any existing whole life policy. Check with a competent insurance adviser for assistance.

Also note that on a new policy the sequence of premium payments does not have to be the same as that described above. In summary, minimum deposit offers the following significant advantages:

Whole life protection can be obtained at a net cost (after taxes) below that of term insurance.

The loan plan may be discontinued at any time, and the original premium rate will still be guaranteed for life, even though the individual may for one reason or another no longer be insurable.

Minimum Deposit Plan
$100,000 Ordinary Life Policy — Annual Premium $2,300

	(1)	(2)	(3)	(4)	(5)	(6)	(7)	(8)	(9)	(10)	(11)
			Premiums		How Paid		Cash Value	Interest		Outlay	In-Force Insurance
	Year	Annual Premium	Annual Dividend	Net Annual Premium	Premium Paid	Premium Borrowed (total loans)	Cash Value (after loans)	Annual Interest (8%)	Value of Interest Deduction (40% tax rate)	Net Cash Outlay (Cols. 5 + 8 − 9)	Death Benefit ($100,000 − Col. 6)
	1	$2,300	$ —	$ 2,300	$2,300	$ —	$ 500	—	—	$ 2,300	$100,000
	2	2,300	115	2,185	2,185	—	2,900	—	—	2,185	100,000
	3	2,300	165	2,135	2,135	—	4,900	—	—	2,125	100,000
	4	2,300	240	2,060	2,060	—	6,900	—	—	2,060	100,000
	5	2,300	315	1,985	—	1,985	5,900	—	—	—	98,015
	6	2,300	385	1,915	—	3,900	5,625	$ 153	$ 61	92	96,100
	7	2,300	450	1,850	—	5,750	5,730	312	125	187	94,250
	8	2,300	520	1,780	—	7,530	5,740	460	184	2176	92,470
	•										
	•										
	•										
	20	2,300	1,050	1,250	—	25,100	11,500	1,915	766	1,149	74,900
	Total			$33,780	$8,680	$25,100	$11,500	$18,350	$7,340	$19,690	$ 74,900

Calculation of $19,690   (Total net cash outlay from Column 10)
Net Cost of   − 11,500   (Residual cash value from Column 7)
Insurance $ 8,190

= $409/year = $4.60/$1,000 of in-force insurance

Life Insurance Pegged To the Inflation Rate

In recognition of inflation, insurance companies now sell policies with death benefits that rise with the Consumer Price Index.

Disadvantage: The companies set ceilings in periods of high inflation. Also: The holder is obliged to pay for increased coverage to keep the inflation-adjustment feature of the policy.

Result: These policies are currently an expensive way to buy protection.

Other ways: *Adjustable life insurance.* The purchaser determines the amount of insurance needed and the affordable premium. Then the purchaser matches the two by varying the period of coverage. The shorter the term, the lower the premium. *Policies with fluctuating premiums.* These are whole-life insurance policies with premiums that decline when prices rise. How it works: The death benefit remains the same. But the insurers shift the premium up and down, depending on interest rates, mortality experience, and administrative costs. Bonus: The companies place ceilings on how much they can charge. Example: A 15% increase maximum, over the life of the policy.

Life Insurance For Two-Income Families

Business partners, two-income families, and owners of closely held corporations have usually relied on whole life insurance policies to insure against each others' deaths. Several new types of insurance policies may offer even cheaper alternatives.

Next-death plans. With these policies, two or more individuals can be covered with permanent, cash-value life insurance that pays death benefits on the first participant to die and then, sequentially, on the others covered.

Premiums are based on the actuarially weighted average age of the participants. Premium savings are generally 15% to 55% compared to the cost of separate whole-life policies covering each person individually. When a participant dies, premiums are recalculated and new policies automatically issued.

The per-person cost decreases as the number of participants increases. Point: Consider including your spouses and children, but keep in mind that by doing so you may buy more insurance than you need.

The predominant next-death coverage is marketed by First Colony Life Insurance Co. of Lynchburg, VA, and its subsidiary, American Mayflower Life Insurance Co. of New York.

Multiple life. In this plan, a term policy covers two or more lives and provides either a fixed amount of protection or a decreasing amount. The first variety, known as level-term coverage, is similar to next-death plans, but it is based on a five-year renewable term policy.

Since participants will be older upon each renewal, premiums increase each five years. If two or more members die in a common disaster, benefits will be paid on both. However, if all the members die, total benefits will be paid as though all but one had died.

Advantage: The premium saving over comparable separate term policies is about 15%, depending on average age of the participants.

For a specific purpose, where less coverage is needed as years pass, companies offer decreasing-term multiple life. Under this variation, insurance can be bought for 10-, 20-, or 30-year periods. The amount of protection decreases annually until 80% of the insured period has elapsed. From then on, the coverage is 20% of the original.

Analysis: Consider more than just premiums themselves in choosing a policy. In many cases, the type of partnership arrangement will determine coverage. To back a debt or to protect children's dependent years, a decreasing-term policy may be best. A family, however, would also have lifelong needs. Tax implications and cash-flow objectives may also be deciding factors.

Reminder: Because these less costly insurance plans mean smaller commissions to the agent, many tend to ignore them. If they're not interested in talking about them, persist.

Source: Sal Nuccio, president, the Nuccio Organization, Ltd., a financial consulting firm, 60 Algonquin Rd., Yonkers, NY 10710, and author of *The New York Times Guide to Personal Finance.*

Preparing for Your Insurance Physical

Control the situation. Presenting yourself in the best possible way is neither deceptive, illegal, nor questionable. It also can save time, money, and frustration.

Recommendations:

Have the testing done at your convenience. Do it when you feel best. Early mornings are good since most people are relaxed then. It does not take much time out from a busy workday, and it's easier to fast then if blood tests are required.

If you have to be tested in the afternoon, avoid caffeine and don't eat heavily during the day. If you must have coffee, make it decaffeinated.

Limit your intake of salt for several days before the physical. Avoid alcohol for at least 24 hours. Both can raise your blood pressure.

If you're a nonsmoker, make sure the examining physician knows it. Reason: Premiums are lower for nonsmokers who meet a specific height and weight standard. (If you do smoke, go "cold turkey" for two hours or more before the exam.)

See your personal doctor before the exam to make sure there'll be no surprises. If there is any sensitive medical or physical information in your records, ask your doctor exactly what you should tell the insurance company. Reminder: Health questions asked at the examination could be confusing or embarrassing. Get a copy of these questions beforehand and prepare your answers.

If you take any medication regularly, stick to

the regimen. The insurance company will know about it anyway. Maintaining the treatment correctly will keep all test results in line.

If you feel tired or ill before the physical, cancel it. Don't worry about delaying the process. The most important thing is to feel relaxed and healthy when you take the exam.

Source: Benjamin Lipson, Benjamin Lipson Insurance Agency, 100 Federal St., Boston 01220.

Life Insurance if You Can't pass a Physical

Can't pass the life insurance physical? Don't give up—there may be a way.

Find an agent who knows his way with insurance companies. Their standards vary on overweight, blood pressure, smoking, other medical conditions. Example: Six-foot middle-aged man weighing 270—many companies would add a big surcharge premium for his age. But one company will insure him with no surcharge at all.

The agent's job is to find the exceptional company, know how to present the application in the most favorable light. Few agents do this well. You've got to insist the agent shop for you.

If an individual policy isn't available (or only at very high cost), group policies can be found in clubs, fraternal orders, religious orders, volunteer firemen. It may pay to join a club just for the group insurance. The saving on premium is usually more than the dues.

Source: Frank J. Crisona, attorney and principal of the Crisona Agency, P.O. Box 130, Carle Place, NY 11514.

How to Fight A Bad Insurance Rating

The discovery that an insurance company is charging you extra for an individual health or life insurance policy can be infuriating. It's especially so when you are not told why. Some 10% of all life and health insurance applicants wind up with these extra charges (rating, in insurance jargon) for physical or moral reasons.

You know you are rated when:

The premium charge is higher than your agent originally quoted.

Your policy arrives with the word *rating* printed discreetly on the first page. (For health insurance policies, this may say Rating—two years or Rating—five years, after which time you can request a review.)

The usual reasons for a rating:

Your application listed a health problem.

A medical examination revealed some health problem.

The company received a physician's statement in which a problematic history was disclosed.

An information-gathering service (most companies use Equifax) found evidence to suggest a lifestyle problem such as drug or alcohol abuse or criminal activity. Homosexuality is considered a problem, too.

The Medical Information Bureau, which compiles all previous insurance applications and claims, alerted the company to the existence of a medical situation.

What to do about changing the rating: When you signed your insurance application, you gave the insurance company permission to undertake a thorough investigation of your past medical, psychiatric, and social history. To challenge the rating: You must refute the existing underwriting records. The nature of the negative information will not be volunteered. Make a written request. In addition, have your insurance agent contact the proper person at the company. The more facts, the better.

Medical problems: The most effective refutation is a presentation of detailed reports from doctors. Next: Use your insurance agent to influence the company. Example:

You were 30 pounds overweight when you first applied for insurance, but have now lost that weight. While reexaminations are unusual, if the agent testifies for you, the company might reconsider.

Trap: The insurance company may have received information from a doctor that the physician requests be kept from you. Example:

Your psychiatrist claims you have suicidal tendencies, but would rather not risk its becoming a self-fulfilling prophecy. You may feel like Kafka's victim in *The Trial,* but you won't get that information. However, it's the reason for the rating.

Moral ratings: These are even harder to fight. Generally, you will not be told the source of a bad reference. You will just get a statement such as: Sources told us you come back from lunch drunk every day. Such sources may be vindictive or themselves mentally unbalanced.

While you will not have an opportunity to answer these charges, the Fair Credit Reporting Act does give you the right to make the insurance company and its sources recheck their facts, which should not take more than two to three weeks.

If the charge is proved wrong: They will probably correct their files. If it's a matter of opinion, have your own response placed along with the allegations in your file. Ask the company to talk with other sources. Give them personal references.

Battling an insurance company requires patience and dedication. However, if you make enough noise, and with good reason, your chances are good for eventually erasing a costly insurance rating.

Source: Leonard B. Stern, president, Leonard B. Stern & Co., an insurance brokerage and consulting firm, 65 E. 55 St., New York 10022.

Payout of Life Insurance Proceeds

Lump sum or monthly income? Life insurance proceeds taken in cash can be invested to provide current income while preserving principal. Alternative: Have the proceeds of one or more of the policies paid in monthly installments.

Reminder: All installment plans pay periodically from both principal and accumulated interest (usually well below the going money-market rate).

Best Use Of Life Insurance Dividends

The dividends paid on participating life insurance policies aren't taxable. They are actually a return of part of the previously paid premiums (though insurance policies rarely spell out the method by which these dividends are figured out). What to do with the dividends depends on the insured's situation.

Chief things to consider: Do I need more insurance? Do I need insurance to provide estate liquidity? Can I put the money to better use outside insurance? The options:

Take cash. Obviously the first choice if the insured needs the cash or can invest it well. Reduce premiums. Dividend dollars applied to reduce premiums reduce them dollar for dollar. It takes more than a dollar in taxable income to pay a dollar in premiums. (Two dollars for the person in the 50% tax bracket.)

Accumulate interest. Dividends can be left with the insurer to accumulate interest at a guaranteed rate. May be used to increase retirement benefits guaranteed under a policy's retirement options. The earned interest and the dividends may be includible in the estate of the insured unless steps are taken to exclude them.

Example: An individual buys a $50,000 ordinary life participating policy at age 40. Annual premium: $1,400. Accumulated dividends after 10 years: $2,800. At that time the policy and accumulated dividends are transferred to his spouse. She uses dividends on additional $10,000 insurance coverage. When the eighth premium falls due, the accumulated dividends on both policies should be sufficient to pay it and all additional future premiums.

No gift tax is due on the transfer of policy to the spouse (because of the 1981 law).

Paid-up additions: Using dividends to buy additional paid-up insurance is a particularly valuable option, where the insured's health is impaired and he is uninsurable. No medical examination is required.

Buy term insurance. Part of the dividend can be used to buy one-year term insurance, usually equal to the amount of increase in the cash value of the policy. This practice keeps the amount of pure insurance level.

Tax Advantage of Irrevocable Life Insurance Trusts

The new estate tax unlimited marital deduction provides a special incentive to consider the tax and planning advantages of irrevocable life insurance trusts.

Why a trust? If you still have ownership rights in an insurance policy when you die, the proceeds will be included in your taxable estate. This is true even though the proceeds pass outside your will to the policy's designated beneficiary.

You could have your spouse own the policy, or you could leave the proceeds to your spouse and take advantage of the unlimited marital deduction. That keeps the proceeds out of your estate. But in either case the proceeds would be in your spouse's estate. Your goal: To remove the proceeds from both estates.

If you do leave your entire estate outright to your spouse, bear in mind that your spouse will be taxed on the income from it. Use of a carefully drafted trust will allow the trustee to be flexible in distributing income based on the relative needs and tax brackets of your beneficiaries. This will save taxes to the overall family unit.

How this trust works: You give the policy and all control over it to a trust that you can't change or terminate. On your death, the proceeds of the policy are paid to the trust, and invested. Your family has the right to the trust's income for life. At some time in the future, your children or other beneficiaries you've named share the remainder.

Caution: If the trust isn't set up to be totally irrevocable, there won't be any estate tax savings. The entire proceeds will be included in your taxable estate.

Gift tax liability: When you transfer the policy to the trust, you make a gift that may be subject to gift tax. But if the policy is essentially "naked," that is, if it has little or no cash surrender value, your gift tax on the transfer will be negligible. If the policy *does* have a large cash surrender value, you can reduce the size of your taxable gift by borrowing against the policy before you give it over to the trust.

Best policies to give: Those with the greatest dollar spread between their present value and their date-of-death value. Term policies and ordinary life policies with maximum loans are prime candidates. Or policies you can't do anything at all with while you're alive, but which have very high payout values. Example: Employer-paid group term.

Worst policies to give: Those with cash surrender values close to their face values. Reason: You may pay gift tax on the transfer. And the value won't increase much between the time you make the gift and the time you die. So the estate tax savings won't be very great.

When you pay the premiums each year, you are again making a taxable gift. The new annual $10,000 per-donee gift tax exclusion doesn't apply to most life insurance trusts. Reason: Future interests don't qualify for this exclusion. And most life insurance trusts defer enjoyment until the future. Solution: Set up the trust so that it provides what's known as a *Crummey* power.

How a Crummey power works: You reserve the right to make annual contributions to the trust. You give your beneficiaries the right to take out their share of the additions for a limited period of time, say 90 days. If the beneficiaries don't exercise their right within the time limit, they lose it. Impact: Your annual contributions to the trust can now qualify as tax-free gifts. And the beneficiaries have a strong incentive not to exercise their power, since that would leave the trustee without funds to pay the premium, which would cause the policy to lapse. Caution: In practice, your contributions may be limited to $5,000 per trust because of interaction with other federal statutes that have not been changed to conform to the increased gift tax exclusion.

Drawbacks of a trust: You lose complete control over the policy. You can't borrow against it once you've given it to the trust. If you decide you've made a mistake, your only recourse is to stop making additions to the trust. The trustees may then be forced to let the policy lapse.

Source: David S. Rhine, CPA, a tax manager with Seidman & Seidman, 15 Columbus Circle, New York 10023.

When Someone Close Is Very Ill

It may seem callous to even think about taxes when a loved one faces a life-threatening illness. But if tax planning is ignored at that point, assets carefully accumulated over a lifetime may be squandered unnecessarily. For many facing a final illness, dealing with these matters provides a life-oriented focus that helps them to combat depression and achieve a sense of completion in seeing that their affairs are well ordered. Some things to consider:

Gifts by the patient. In many cases, estate taxes can be saved by making gifts to family members and other intended beneficiaries. An unlimited amount may be transferred tax-free provided no one person receives more than $10,000. The maximum tax-free gift per recipient can increase to $20,000 if the patient's spouse is still alive and consents to treat each gift as having been jointly made.

Under the old law, gifts made within three years of death were figured back into the taxable estate. The '81 tax act repealed this "con-templation-of-death" rule in most cases. One major exception: The old rule still applies to gifts of life insurance.

Gifts to the patient. This tactic may be useful when the patient doesn't have enough property to take full advantage of the estate tax exemption ($325,000 in 1984, $600,000 by 1987). Reason: Property that passes through a decedent's estate gets what's known as a stepped-up basis. That is, the person who inherits it is treated for income tax purposes as though he bought it and paid what it was worth on the date of death. (Or what it was worth six months after the date of death if the executor chooses this alternate date to set the value of the taxable estate.)

Example: Mr. Jones, a cancer patient, has $150,000 worth of assets. His wife has a large estate, including $75,000 worth of stock that has a tax basis of $10,000. That means there's $65,000 worth of taxable gain built into the stock. She gives the stock to her husband. (There's no tax on gifts between spouses.) Mr. Jones leaves the stock to the children. The children inherit the stock with the basis stepped up to $75,000. So if they turn right around and sell it for $75,000, there's no taxable gain. With these shares, Mr. Jones' estate is still only $225,000—under the exempt amount. So the stepped up basis is achieved without paying estate tax. And the property is taken out of Mrs. Jones' estate where it might be taxed.

In most cases, it doesn't pay to use this tactic with property that will be bequeathed back to a spouse who gave it to the patient. Reason: Unless the gift was made more than a year before the date of death, stepped-up basis will be denied. But when the patient is expected to survive for substantially more than a year, this tactic can be quite useful.

Example: Mr. Smith owns a $150,000 rental property with a $25,000 tax basis. Mrs. Smith has a disease that will be fatal within two to five years. She has few assets of her own. So Mr. Smith gives her the building and inherits it back from her a few years later with the basis stepped up to $150,000. This substantially increases his depreciation deductions if he keeps the building and eliminates any taxable gain if he sells it.

Loss property. In general there is a tax disadvantage in inheriting property that is worth less than its original cost. Reason: Its tax basis is stepped down to its date-of-death value and the potential loss deduction is forfeited. If the patient has substantial income it might pay to sell the property and deduct the losses. But it doesn't pay to generate losses that are more than $3,000 in excess of the patient's capital gains. Reason: These excess losses can't be deducted currently, and there's likely to be no future years' income on which to deduct them. Alternative: Sell the loss property at its current value to a close family member. Result: The patient's loss on the sale is nondeductible, because the purchaser is a family member. But any future gains the family member realizes will be nontaxable to the extent of the previously disallowed loss.

Charitable gifts. In some cases, bequests to charitable organizations should be made before death. Benefit: Current income tax deductions. But it's important not to give too much away. This tactic may generate more deductions than the patient can use.

Flower bonds. Certain series of U.S. Treasury bonds can be purchased on the open market for substantially less than their full face value, because they pay very low interest. But if a decedent owns these so-called "flower bonds" on the date of death, they can be credited against the estate tax at their full face value.

Timing: Flower bonds should be bought when death is clearly imminent. There's little point in holding them for substantial periods before death because they yield very little income. On the other hand, it does no good for the estate to purchase them after death because they won't be applied against the estate tax. In some cases, flower bonds have been bought on behalf of a patient in a coma by a relative or trustee who holds a power of attorney. The IRS has attacked these purchases. But the courts have, so far, sided with the taxpayer.

A power of attorney should be prepared early on. If it's properly drafted, it can cover flower bond purchases and authority for a wide variety of other actions that can preserve the patient's assets and allow for flexible planning.

Income tax planning. A number of income tax moves should be considered. Examples:

Income timing. If the patient is in a low tax bracket, it may pay to accelerate income. The key here is to compare the patient's tax bracket with the bracket his estate is likely to be in. In some cases it will pay to accelerate income to make full use of deductions that would otherwise yield little or no tax benefit. Medical deductions, in particular, may be very high.

Choosing gift property. In making gifts to save estate taxes, it does not pay from an income tax standpoint to give away property that has gone up in value. Reason: The tax basis of gift property is not stepped up. So the recipient will have a potential income tax liability built into the gift. This potential is eliminated if the property is kept in the estate and passes by inheritance. For similar reasons, the patient should not give away business property that has been subject to depreciation. (There's a built-in tax liability for recapture of the depreciation deductions. This is eliminated if the property passes through the estate.) Also, copyrights on work the patient has created shouldn't be given away. Reason: If the copyright is received as a gift and later sold, the gain is fully taxed as ordinary income. If it's inherited and then later sold, it's treated as long-term capital gain (60% nontaxable).

Other moves. (1) For owners of stock in an S corporation it may pay to accelerate distribution of income particularly if the ill shareholder has previously taxed income that wasn't distributed.

(2) Where death is expected but not "clearly imminent," a private annuity may be a useful way of disposing of property. Reason: IRS regs will key the required annuity payments to a healthy person's life expectancy.

(3) If the patient owns an unincorporated business or an interest in a partnership, it may pay to incorporate, particularly if the business has substantial accounts receivable or inventory that has gone up in value. Reason: Incorporation can secure capital gains treatment for these assets if the business is later sold.

An experienced estate planner can help you

explore all aspects of these moves and other possibilities.

Source: G. William Clapp, a tax partner in the accounting firm of Deloitte, Haskins & Sells, One World Trade Center, New York 10048.

Tax Avoidance: A Small Part of Estate Planning

Most Americans don't have a will. And they probably have no clear idea what will happen to their property when they die.

State laws vary, but the provisions of most are very similar when someone dies without leaving a will.

The general rules: A surviving spouse is always entitled to a substantial part of the estate, sometimes all of it. If there are also surviving children, the spouse's share is usually one half or one third, depending on state law and on the number of children.

If there are no children or grandchildren, the spouse often takes the entire estate. Some states, however, give a share to parents or brothers and sisters. The spouse usually takes a specified amount plus a fraction of the balance.

It doesn't matter if the parties have been separated. Only a legal dissolution of the marriage (by divorce or annulment) will cut off the spouse's right to inherit.

Subject to the rights of the spouse, descendants usually have first claim on the estate. Each child takes an equal share, and the children of deceased children take the share their parent would have received. If all children are deceased, the grandchildren inherit. If great-grandchildren enter the picture, the same rules apply.

The rules on adopted children vary from state to state. The trend is to treat them exactly the same as non-adopted children. Illegitimate children inherit from their mother. But the laws on inheriting from the father vary widely.

Ancestors: In practice, this means parents.

In rare cases, a grandparent may survive though both parents are dead. If the deceased left any descendants, parents generally take nothing. If a spouse survives, but no descendants, parents take a share in some states. If there are no surviving descendants or spouse, the surviving parent or parents usually take the entire estate. Some states divide it among parents, brothers and sisters.

If there is no surviving spouse, descendant or ancestor, the estate goes to those persons with the closest degree of blood relationship to the deceased. Some states bar remote relatives by limiting inheritance to a specified degree of relationship.

If there is no relative who can inherit, and no will, the property goes to the state.

One misconception: Lack of a will won't keep your estate out of the courts. Even holding property jointly won't necessarily do that. Most assets such as stocks, bonds, and savings accounts above a certain amount cannot be transferred without court administration.

Administration: The court will appoint an administrator, usually one of the heirs. The administrator normally has to post a bond, with the cost paid by the estate. If there's more than one heir, any unresolvable disputes among them (including who is to be administrator) must be settled by the court. Such family quarrels can be highly destructive, especially if the estate includes a going business or any other assets that require management.

Once appointed, the duties of an administrator are the same as those of an executor: To collect and manage the assets and to distribute them to the proper persons.

If any of the heirs are minors, the court must appoint a guardian or trustee of the property. The trustee's job is to conserve the inheritance until the minor grows up. Income from the property can be used for the child's benefit or saved, but the principal can't be touched without a court order. This can mean a great deal of trouble and expense if money is needed to cover items such as educational costs or medical bills for the minor.

Avoid problems. A simple will (without trusts) drawn up by a competent attorney should cost no more than $150, depending on local custom. It can avoid many of the possible costs and problems of administration, as well as making sure that your estate goes to persons you really want to have it.

Are You Sure Your Will Is Valid?

Even if you have made a written will, it may not be accepted as a valid one by the court for any of several reasons:

Handwritten. The statutes of many states hold that handwritten (sometimes called "holographic") wills are invalid, unless they conform to specific requirements.

Do-it-yourself. Many standard will forms obtainable from stationery stores or books do not conform to the letter of the law, and are easily contested and often declared invalid.

Out-of-state. Your will is administered according to the laws of your domicile. If you have moved, be sure your will conforms to the laws of your new state.

Improperly witnessed. Strict requirements are stipulated for witnesses in many states.

Marriage, divorce, and children. In most states, marriage, divorce, and the birth of children cause automatic revocation or alteration of part or all of a will.

Modification of a will: After it has been properly prepared and executed, it is not necessary to redraft the basic will to make changes or updates. Changes are made in a separate document, or codicil, appended to the will. However, the codicil must be executed with the same formality as the will. Under no circumstances should you simply cross out certain clauses in the will and insert changes.

Probate and priority of claim: No will is legal until the proper court or official declares that it meets all statutory requirements. This act is known as the decree of probate.

Once the will has been admitted to probate, several claims have priority before any distribution can be made under the terms of the will. While the exact order varies by state,

they follow this general pattern:
1. Funeral expenses.
2. Administration. Fees due the court, attorneys, and others for administering the estate.
3. Allowance to provide for the needs of the decedent's family while the will is being administered.
4. U.S. Government. Any taxes and other claims due.
5. Expenses pertaining to last illness.
6. State, county, and local governments.
7. Wages due others.
8. Claims secured by liens.
9. All other debts.

Source: *The Complete Guide to Running a Business*, by John R. Klug, Boardroom Books, New York.

Points Often Neglected In Drawing up Wills

• Does the will take full advantage of the marital deduction, which allows a tax exemption of up to the full amount of the gross estate?

• How are death taxes to be allocated among beneficiaries?

• Have all insurance arrangements been considered in the will?

• Have safeguards been provided to ensure minimum double taxation of the estate—once at the death of each spouse?

• Have proper provisions been made to establish who legally died first in the event of apparent simultaneous death of both spouses?

• Should the executor of the estate have the power to run or dispose of your business?

Limits on How You Can Leave Your Money

Any will or estate plan must take into account the legal limits that govern the allocation of inherited property. The principal ones:

Under the varying state laws, a widow has the right to a minimum portion of her late husband's estate as dowry. A particular state's law may specify, for example, 35%. If the widow is left a smaller amount, she can sue. Comparable rights to surviving husbands are called curtesy. In a few states, minor children are allowed specified percentages of a parent's estate.

An individual may have left property to persons who actually die before he does. Or a beneficiary may refuse to accept a bequest for personal or financial reasons. Unless the decedent makes provision for contingent or successor beneficiaries, the property will go to the remainderman (the person named to get what is left after all specific bequests have been honored). This could leave the remainderman with far more than had been intended.

The IRS can make a prior claim against an estate. If the deceased owed back taxes, the IRS can attach the cash-surrender value of any insurance policies on the decedent's life that he owned, or in which he had a significant incident of ownership.

Sharply Lower Taxes On Estates

By 1987 only three-tenths of 1% of all estates will be taxable. But few of the changes in the tax law took effect before January 1, 1982. And it will be six years before they are fully effective.

Highlights of the 1981 law as it pertains to federal estate tax:

• Gift and estate taxes are eliminated on all qualifying gifts and bequests between spouses. Impact: In and after 1982, a surviving spouse will be able to inherit an estate of any size tax-free.

• Phased-in increase in the size of estates that can be passed to heirs tax-free, from the present $175,625 to $600,000 in 1987, as follows:

Year of Death	Exempt from Tax	Year of Death	Exempt from Tax
1982	$225,000	1985	$400,000
1983	275,000	1986	500,000
1984	325,000	1987	600,000

• Increase to $10,000 (from $3,000) in the amount of tax-free gifts an individual can give to any one person in a single year. (Raised to $20,000 from $6,000 if a spouse joins in on the gift.)

• Reduction of the top estate tax rate to 50% (from 70%) in four steps:

Year of Death	Top Tax Rate	Year of Death	Top Tax Rate
1982	65%	1985	55%
1983	60%	1986	55%
1984	55%	1987	50%

• If newly liberalized requirements are met, a break is available for business property left to family members: A portion of the value that property would have if it were used for some purpose other than the family business can be ignored in setting the value of the taxable estate. The new law raises the amount that can be disregarded from $500,000 to $750,000 (in two steps).

• Rules that allow estates of certain business owners to spread estate tax payments over a period of years have been simplified and liberalized.

Planning priorities:

• Wills drafted to take maximum advantage of prior estate tax law may not get the best possible treatment under the new law. The long phase-in period for the changes makes a long-term estate plan essential. Important: All wills containing marital deduction clauses must be reviewed now.

• The increased annual gift tax exclusion opens up new possibilities for lifetime gifts, either outright or in trust. Consideration: Reduction in estate taxes may make lifetime giving less desirable.

• Trusts set up for tax-planning purposes under the old law should be reviewed.

• Insurance policies taken out to pay estate taxes may now be superfluous, since so many more estates will be tax-exempt.

Bottom line: With careful planning, it

should be possible to transfer large estates with no estate tax impact and also to make substantial gifts without paying gift tax.

Source: Sanford J. Schlesinger, a partner in the law firm Goldschmidt, Fredericks & Oshatz, 655 Madison Ave., New York 10021.

Appreciated Property Should Not Be Sold Late in Life

Earned income is taxed, investment income is taxed, estates are taxed, long-term and short-term capital gains are taxed. It often seems that everything is taxed, that there is no escape from the tax collector.

But there is one escape, and an important one. Increases in the value of property (that is, unrealized capital gains) will be free from capital gains tax if the property is bequeathed to heirs rather than sold.*

Suppose a stock investment or a piece of real estate was bought many years ago for $5,000 and is now worth $55,000. If the original purchaser sells it, he must report and pay taxes on a long-term capital gain of $50,000. If he gives it away and the recipient of the gift sells it, the same $50,000 capital gain is taxed, because the recipient assumes the donor's "cost" basis of $5,000.

But if the original purchaser dies and leaves it to heirs, they do not assume the $5,000 cost basis. Rather, the heirs' cost basis is stepped up to the value at the time of death. If they sell the asset for the same $55,000, they do not report any capital gain. If they sell it for $65,000, they report and pay taxes on a $10,000 capital gain.

When property has increased markedly in value and the owners are advanced in years, they should probably avoid selling it and realizing a taxable capital gain. Within a few years it may pass to heirs with a stepped-up

*That is, it will never be subject to capital gains tax. The asset will be part of the estate and subject to estate tax. But if it is sold before death, the proceeds (or what is left after capital gains tax) are subject to estate tax.

cost basis, and appreciation before death will never be taxed.

If it is absolutely necessary to dispose of the asset before death, every effort should be made to work out a nontaxable exchange for other property. Or, if it is a residence, to purchase a replacement residence within the time limit or to use the once-in-a-lifetime tax-free home sale provision.

Note: The stepped-up basis for heirs has been a major factor enabling families to build wealth over a number of generations. In 1976, Congress moved toward ending stepped-up basis by providing that appreciation after 1976 would be taxed to the heirs when they sold the property. However, in 1978 the effective date of this provision was postponed and in 1979 the provision was repealed entirely. Of course, it may come up again in future years.

Source: *Successful Tax Planning,* by Edward Mendlowitz, Boardroom Books, New York.

Leaving Bequests In Percentages Instead of Dollars

A will customarily makes bequests in the form of specific dollar amounts, such as "To my beloved daughter Mabel, if she survives me, the sum of $25,000." But this standard practice makes two assumptions that may be out of line: (1) That the dollar value of the estate to be distributed is known with some reasonable degree of accuracy. (2) That there will be enough wealth available to implement the designated dollar bequests.

Making such assumptions, especially in times of serious economic uncertainties, can be problematic. For one thing, specific dollar bequests are no guarantee that the decedent's estate will be distributed in accordance with his wishes—although this is the principal objective of estate planning.

The solution: Make your bequests in the form of percentages of your estate rather than predetermined dollar amounts. Then, if inflation or assets of unsuspectedly high value make the estate worth more than you had anticipated, the originally conceived allocations of your dollar worth will be self-adjusting. On the other hand, if the estate should prove to be smaller than you had anticipated, the beneficiaries you had named continue to be the recipients of your bounty, but bequests will automatically be scaled down in terms of what is available at that time.

The percentages you select should take into account certain minimum provisions required by state law. Check with counsel to learn the minimum percentages the state requires you to leave to a widow, widower, or child.

Source: *Encyclopedia of Estate Planning,* by Robert S. Holzman, Boardroom Books, New York.

Caution When Will Includes Real Estate

Real estate should be described in your will by its proper legal description, not just by its street address. Failure to include it can result in costly litigation after your death.

Example: A mother left her "home known as No. 94 Cleveland Drive" to her daughter. Tax records showed that the mother actually owned two adjacent lots at that address. The house was on one, a tennis court on the other. Result: The daughter had to prove in court that both lots were considered part of the family home, and that her mother intended her to inherit both.

Estate of Schnell, 185 N.Y.L.J. 70, p. 19.

If Beneficiary Can't Be Located

It is common practice in a will to provide that a gift won't take effect unless the beneficiary outlives the person making the will.

Example: You would like to leave a Ming vase to your niece. But if your niece isn't around to enjoy it, you would rather have the vase go to a local museum than to your niece's heirs. So the gift is made "on condition that my niece survive me, but if she fails to survive me, then to X museum."

A related problem that is often overlooked when wills are drafted involves missing heirs. Nowadays, people move around frequently and often lose touch. Failure to provide for that possibility can have frustrating results.

Recent case: A Florida resident left half of her estate to her son and the other half to her three stepchildren. When the will was probated, the stepchildren couldn't be found. Ten years later, they still couldn't be located. As a result, half of the woman's estate went to the State of Florida. Her son argued that he should have a prior claim on the remainder of his mother's property. The judge agreed that that would have been a fairer outcome. But it wasn't what the Florida statute called for.

Suggestion: Your will should provide that if any beneficiary can't be located within the forfeiture period prescribed by the state where the will is probated, the gift will lapse and either go back into the residue of your estate or go to an alternative beneficiary.

Estate of Russell, 387 So. 2d 487.

Providing for Care of Ailing Testator in Will

Many families use a promise of a bequest to provide for lifetime care of a testator.

But a carelessly worded bequest of a flat sum to a nurse or caretaker doesn't provide any incentive to give the testator good care.

Solution: Create a written contract with the caretaker with the specific terms repeated in the will. Provisions:

Fair salary plus room and board for as long as required.

Annual or semiannual bonus, depending on quality of care.

147

Increase in the amount of the bequest for each year that testator remains alive.

Tax consequences: The bequest may be considered a debt owed by the estate for compensation to the caretaker and thus not subject to estate tax.

Discourage Heirs From Contesting a Will

One way to avoid squabbling over the estate: Include in the will a no-contest clause. Any beneficiary who challenges the will forfeits the inheritance. It's not foolproof, though. This provision cannot disinherit anyone entitled by state law to a certain share. And it wouldn't stop a challenge from somebody who was disinherited entirely.

Making A Secret Bequest

Sometimes a bequest (to a friend or a black-sheep relative) will upset family members. Thus, the estate owner wants to keep the bequest secret. But the will must be probated in court, making all bequests public knowledge.

How to keep the secret: Take out a life insurance policy. Proceeds will be paid immediately on death without waiting for probate, and there will be no public announcement. (The executor will know about it and it will be subject to estate tax unless the policy is given to the person, too.) The insurance company will probably require that the first beneficiary named be a family member. Get around the provision by changing the beneficiary after the policy has been issued.

Or, set up a trust now and provide instructions in the trust document and a letter to the trustee. These papers remain private. The will discloses only how much money goes to the trust, not what the trust does with it.

Source: Mintz, Girgan & Hanlon, insurance brokers, Grand Union Plaza, North Arlington, NJ 07032.

Settlements Outside The Will

Not all of your property and personal matters can be settled within the will. Here are some other arrangements you should consider:

Contract benefits. Ample life insurance is a good way to tide the family over until your estate is settled. The payments are made to the beneficiary named in the contract, apart from any will. However, the total value of the benefits may be treated as part of the taxable estate. Remember that the security of a paid-up life insurance policy does not obviate the real necessity for a well-drawn will.

Joint tenancy. Securities, real estate, and bank accounts that are jointly owned can bypass probate and go directly to the survivor. But you cannot avoid federal and state estate taxes by the use of joint tenancy—and at the death of the survivor, this property can be taxed again. Moreover, while you can easily change a will, some joint tenancy holdings create a legal title which cannot be changed without the consent of the other party.

Last instructions. If you have specific wishes regarding your funeral and interment, it is wise to leave a memo (a letter of last instructions) with a trusted friend or relative describing the funeral arrangements you desire. It should also give the location of the will, other important papers, ready cash, and valuables.

Source: *The Complete Guide to Running a Business,* by John R. Klug, Boardroom Books, New York.

What You Need Besides a Will

Make up (and periodically update) an inventory of important personal documents and names. Be sure your family knows its location. The inventory should include:

Location of your will.

Name and address of your attorney.

Name and address of the accountant who

prepares your tax return.

Name and address of your banker.

Name and address of your life and general insurance brokers.

Location of your policies.

Location of your safe deposit box and its number. Where is the key?

List of real estate you own and whereabouts of relevant papers.

If you are active in real estate, name and address of your broker.

Names of creditors (with amounts).

Names and addresses of those who owe you money (with amounts).

A list of credit cards with numbers.

A list of charge accounts with numbers and company addresses.

The location of stocks and bonds.

Name and address of your stockbroker.

Location of ownership certificates for autos, boats, motor homes, etc.

Location of your birth certificate.

Your Social Security number and your spouse's.

Location of your military discharge papers.

Location of your marriage certificate.

Source: *Ideas & Trends,* Israeloff, Trattner & Co. P.C., CPAs 11 Sunrise Plaza, Valley Stream, NY 11581.

Plan for Your Funeral

Funerals generally rate only below the cost of a home, car, and education in a family's finances. Those who don't want a fancy funeral should plan now. *Best bet:* Join a memorial society, which is an information center run by a reputable undertaker that lists alternatives to big-money funerals. *Cost:* $25 to join. For a list of memorial societies, send a stamped self-addressed envelope to: Continental Association of Memorial Societies, 1828 L St., NW, Washington, DC 20036. Another solution: Will your body to a medical school. Contact one for the necessary papers. Then leave instructions to loved ones to hold a memorial service instead of a funeral.

Where to Put a Will For Safekeeping

The question of where to keep a will isn't as easy as it sounds. It should be in a safe, private place. But it must also be available to the executor immediately upon the death of the testator. The answer generally depends partly on state law.

Some ideas:

If the bank is the estate executor, the natural choice is the bank vault. (If testator changes his mind and executes a new will naming another executor, remember to remove the will to another place.)

A safe-deposit box is not a good place if no one else has access to it without a court order. Best: Authorize executor's access in advance, if local law permits entry by two or more people and the death of one does not affect entry right of the other. Use a separate box for the will only, if the testator doesn't want the executor to see other private documents.

Your attorney's safe is a good choice only if it is fireproof and burglar resistant. The law firm's safe-deposit box in a bank vault is a better choice.

Whatever place is chosen, keep another copy of the will elsewhere. Make sure it is identical to the original but clearly marked "copy". It should not be signed. Too risky that it will be thought to be the original. If the will is then changed, it could cause confusion and challenges.

Source: *You & Your Will* by Paul P. Ashley, McGraw-Hill, New York.

The Marital Deduction

The new marital deduction is the first significant estate-tax change for well-off couples. Highlights:

Dollar limits are removed. Starting on January 1, 1982, married individuals can leave an unlimited amount of wealth to the survivor free of federal estate tax. The new law removes the old dollar limits on the marital deduction ($250,000 or half the estate, whichever was greater).

Transitional rule: Many current wills have formula clauses designed to capture the "maximum" marital deduction. To protect individuals who did not intend to leave the survivor more than half the estate, the new law has a transitional rule. Impact: The 100% marital deduction will not apply to wills executed before September 13, 1981, that have formula maximum marital deduction clauses. Individuals who want to take advantage of the new unlimited deduction must have their wills amended. So consult your lawyer.

New interests qualify. Two new kinds of property interests for spouses now qualify for the marital deduction. (1) Qualified Terminable Interest Property (Q-TIP) and (2) a spouse's interest as a life-income recipient of certain charitable trusts.

Q-TIPS: A cute name for an important new tax break. An individual can now leave his spouse a life income from property, dictate how the property will be disposed of after the spouse's death, and still get the marital deduction. Under the old law, a life-income interest for a surviving spouse did not qualify for marital deduction unless the survivor had control over final disposition of the property. Example of a Q-TIP: A trust pays income each year to the surviving spouse with the property going to the children when the survivor dies. All income from the property must be payable to the survivor at least annually. No one else can receive trust assets during the spouse's lifetime. The executor must elect to have the property qualify for the deduction.

Problems Caused by Husband-and-Wife Wills

• A husband might want to leave a big chunk of property to his wife when he dies, but he may fear that she will make no provision to bequeath any of this property to his relatives or friends. She may feel the same way about leaving property to him. One solution to this dilemma is to have the spouses make mutual wills, in which each party agrees to leave inherited property to the survivor, who after death will leave specified property to designated relatives or friends of both parties.

State law is important here to determine whether the property passing to her under her husband's will was really contractually subject to a condition. In one decision on this frequent issue, the court held that under New York law, a state resident is bound by such a restriction and hence the property earmarked for the children upon her death didn't qualify for the marital deduction because she didn't receive this property outright and without strings. *

Indicated action: Check with tax counsel for the precedent in your state.

* *David A. Siegel Estate,* 67 T.C., No. 50, 1/12/77.

• When a husband and wife name each other as primary beneficiaries in their wills, a good lawyer includes a common-disaster clause. This spells out how the property is to be disposed of if the spouses die together, or at almost the same time.

Unfortunately, some lawyers forget to provide for another problem, one that is more likely to occur. That is, the first spouse dies and then later, without making a new will, the second spouse dies. Problem: The primary bequest cannot be followed, since it names the spouse who died earlier. The alternate disposition (the common-disaster clause) applies only when the couple dies together. Result: The will contains no clear directions for disposing of the estate.

When this happens, it can mean heavy litigation costs for the estate and for the potential beneficiaries, with little assurance that things will turn out the way the deceased would have wanted. Two cases of this type were decided by the same court on the same day.

• Mr. and Mrs. Reiser made a joint will, naming each other as beneficiaries. In the event of a common disaster, they asked to have their estate parceled out among three individuals. Mr. Reiser died first. His wife died six months later. All of the couple's property was in Mrs. Reiser's estate. Since her husband had passed away, and since there was not a common disaster, there was no named beneficiary. If the estate were distributed as though no will existed, everything would have gone to one of the three people named in the common-disaster clause. But the judge, looking at all the circumstances, was convinced that Mr. and Mrs. Reiser wanted all three alternate beneficiaries to have a share if the couple could not leave their property to each other. Outcome: He divided the estate as though the common disaster clause applied.*

* *Estates of Otto Reiser and Ann Reiser,* 185 N.Y.L.J., No. 15, P.11.

• Mr. and Mrs. Wolsky had also named each other as beneficiaries. Their common-disaster clause called for dividing half the estate among a set of beneficiaries designated by Mr. Wolsky, with the remainder going to a group Mrs. Wolsky had designated. Mrs. Wolsky died in 1973. When her husband died seven years later, he had not made a new will. With Mrs. Wolsky unavailable to inherit, the court considered applying the common-disaster clause. But the judge found little reason to believe that Mr. Wolsky would want half his estate to go to a group of relatives his wife had designated many years earlier. Result: With no other evidence of Mr. Wolsky's wishes to rely on, the court ordered his estate administered as though he had not left a will.*

Bottom line: Be explicit about what you want done with your estate if you outlive your spouse. A periodic review is always a good idea.

* *Estate of Felix Martin Wolsky,* 185 N.Y.L.J., No. 15, p. 11.

Four Kinds of Joint Ownership

1. Joint tenancy. Each of the parties has an undivided interest in the entire property, so that if one owner dies, the survivor or survivors own the property. Each party reports the income from his portion of the property.

2. Tenancy in common. Each person owns a specified portion of the property. On his death, his interest goes to his estate rather than to the surviving co-owner(s).

3. Tenancy by the entirety. This form of ownership applies only to legally married couples, and in some states it applies only to real estate. Each spouse has an undivided interest in the entire property, and on the death of one spouse, the survivor doesn't succeed to the decedent's right and title because she already had it. One-half of the value of the property goes to the estate of the first to die regardless of which spouse furnished the consideration for the property. Upon sale of the property by the couple, gain or loss is divided between the spouses.

4. Community property. In eight states that have enacted community property laws, each spouse is deemed to own one-half of the property acquired by the other spouse after the marriage took place or after they moved into the state.

Source: *Encyclopedia of Estate Planning,* by Robert S. Holzman, Boardroom Books, New York.

Checklist: When a Trust Can Be Useful

Trusts are, of course, used in a number of ways. Some of their chief purposes:

To remove property from the grantor's gross estate.

To reduce income taxes during years of greatest productivity (and highest income tax brackets) without depriving the grantor of the benefit of the property after retirement, or in later years when income might be lower.

To save property taxes on many forms of tangible or intangible property transferred to the trust.

To save custodial, insurance, management, and conservation expenses on property transferred to the trust.

To protect an inexperienced beneficiary from his own lack of financial sophistication.

To make money available for the use of dependents without having the principal subject to the dependent's creditors (the so-called "spendthrift" trust). State laws vary as to whether such trusts will be recognized. And they cannot protect the beneficiary against claims made by the federal government for unpaid taxes.

To provide periodic income for a charitable organization after the grantor's death, in line with his previous customary donations.

To continue operating the grantor's business after his death, something the executor might be unwilling or unqualified to do. The trustees might include certain key employees, the firm's accountant, and other knowledgeable persons.

To set up funds for the lifetime support of a dependent. Property might be placed in an irrevocable trust for the benefit of aged dependents, handicapped children, etc., and thus escape being thrown into the gross estate.

To set aside funds for purposes that might not be met unless specific arrangements were made. One woman set up a $10,000 trust fund in her will to provide $100 a month for the care and feeding of her cat.

To establish how designated trustees will function and how beneficiaries will respond with a modest fraction of the money and property that will ultimately be transferred—if problems arise, the grantor has time to make other arrangements.

Source: *The Complete Book of Estate Planning,* by Robert S. Holzman, Boardroom Books, New York.

of distribution of funds is the primary motivation behind a sprinkling trust, whereas primary motivation for other types of trusts may be avoidance of litigation, tax minimization, efficient management of funds, or reduction of administrative costs and court costs or a number of other reasons.

There are two common methods for structuring a sprinkling trust. They are known as the fixed share and single fund methods. Although each has advantages and disadvantages, keep in mind the system you might use to provide for your children's needs if you were paying for them directly out of your wallet at the present time.

Fixed share: Under this method each child covered by the sprinkling trust is allotted a fixed share of the principal. The child's needs are then paid for by sprinklings from his own individual share of the income and principal of the trust. When the trust reaches its termination, the child receives whatever is left of his allotment.

Single fund: The single fund approach provides that all the principal and income from the trust be kept in a single fund and that sprinklings be taken from the fund as needed to meet the different needs of the children. Therefore, if one child falls ill and another decides to go to graduate school, the extra expenses for each child are met by the whole of the trust fund instead of just by the children's individual share. When the single trust fund is terminated, the remaining assets are distributed (usually) evenly among the children. Generally, the single fund method for a sprinkling trust is considered to be most flexible in meeting the needs of the children.

Flexible Bequests for Heirs' Changing Needs

A sprinkling trust is a trust established for your children or grandchildren that is flexible enough to "sprinkle" funds out to them in proportion to their varying needs. Flexibility

Parent's Foresight Can Save Taxes For Two Generations

If the estate will be over $800,000 (in 1985) it could be a mistake to leave everything to the widow, even if it reduces or eliminates the es-

estate tax.

Reason: That's only for the first estate tax. It's also important to plan for the second estate tax which comes when the widow dies.

New York attorney Marvin W. Weinstein, who specializes in taxes and estate planning, suggests using dual trusts in some cases, with one qualified and the other not qualified for the marital deduction. Important when the objective is to provide liberally for the surviving spouse, but reduce estate taxes on transfers to the next generation.

A marital trust is eligible for the marital deduction from the estate tax, but it has the disadvantage that the assets will be taxed in the wife's estate when she dies.

By contrast, a nonmarital trust isn't eligible for the marital deduction from the estate tax. The assets are moved to the next generation without being taxed in the widow's estate when she dies. A typical nonmarital trust would be one in which the widow gets all of the income as long as she lives, but on her death the principal passes to the children.

The two types of trust differ in the degree of control of the assets that the widow has. And there are legal/technical requirements that a good trust lawyer should handle.

These procedures are unnecessary if the estate is less than $400,000 (in 1985) because there's no significant estate tax below that.

erty which is to produce the beneficiary's income is never his; therefore, neither he nor his creditors can squander it.

How it works: A trust is set up and furnished with income-producing assets. The trustee, a bank or other independent fiduciary, is given discretion as to when, under what circumstances, and in what amounts to pay out the income. Provision may be made that if the trustee isn't satisfied that the beneficiary will be using the money for what the trust agreement and correlative instructions have defined as normal living expenses and pleasures, no money will be paid out at that time. If the trust instrument provides that income is to be paid out for support, the heir may go to court to argue that he is not getting enough to meet that test, especially if he is still of the age where his parents are legally obliged to support him. If the arrangement was created by will and the parents are dead, their obligation of support is nebulous, and in any case, most spendthrift trusts are created for persons of legal age.

When a spendthrift trust won't work: Counsel should check the state law to determine whether spendthrift trusts will be recognized in that jurisdiction in the face of creditors' claims. Some states regard spendthrift trusts as a fraud against the creditors. Usually a gambling debt is not regarded as a valid and enforceable claim under state law.

Source: *Encyclopedia of Estate Planning,* by Robert S. Holzman, Boardroom Books, New York.

Preventing Heirs From Squandering Money You Leave

You wish to provide for your son for his lifetime, but you want him to be the actual beneficiary. If you have reason to suspect that he will run up huge debts or otherwise waste his inheritance, you can set up a spendthrift trust for an heir. Courts have held that the grantor of property to a trust has the right to protect the beneficiary against his own voluntary improvidence or financial misfortune. The prop-

Advantages of Avoiding Probate

Probate is the legal process by which the authenticity of a will is proven to the satisfaction of a state court designated for this purpose. If there is no valid will, approval will be given to the disposition of the estate's assets under the state's intestacy law. When a will is probated, it is publicly recorded.

Estate planning legitimately may seek to keep as much of the estate as possible out of probate. Among the reasons:

As previously stated, a will is publicly recorded. But if an individual is more concerned about the confidentiality of his affairs than about the public's right to know, he could, in complete privacy, transfer the desired property to an irrevocable trust, the assets to go to his secret beneficiary upon his death without the knowledge of anyone except the trustee. And the trustee could be an impersonal bank.

Fees paid to executors and to estate lawyers are usually a percentage of the value of assets passing through their hands. Any assets kept out of probate because they are not part of the decedent's property when he dies won't be part of the basis for administration charges by the professionals.

Time: Since the probating of a will is a legal and judicial process, it can be very time-consuming. If a person places assets in trust for the benefit of a named party or parties, for distribution immediately upon his death, the beneficiaries can receive their entitlements quickly.

Liabilities: Under very real circumstances, an executor can be held personally liable for federal estate taxes if he distributes assets to beneficiaries without leaving enough resources to pay these taxes. A timid executor (and that includes experienced attorneys who know all too well how expensive this personal liability can be) often stubbornly refuses to distribute anything to the will's beneficiaries until he has made his peace with the IRS. That could take years. The use of a trust will keep these assets out of the hands of an overcautious executor whose own misgivings are of more importance to him than are the needs of beneficiaries.

Challenges: Beneficiaries (or nonbeneficiaries) under a will may challenge distributions which are spelled out there. There may be family squabbles about who should get what. But when property has been held in joint ownership with right of survival, this prearranged disposition scheme takes place automatically when death occurs. The assets are not part of the estate which the executor submits for probate.

Insurance: Insurance proceeds are often counted on to meet the immediate needs of beneficiaries while the rest of the estate is being administered. But if the policy is made payable to the executor in his or her official capacity, or to the estate, the insurance payout will have to pass through probate. Making the policy payable directly to the beneficiaries avoids this problem.

Source: Dr. Robert S. Holzman, author of *The Encyclopedia of Estate Planning*, Boardroom Books, New York.

Naming the Right Executor

It's a touching gesture to name a spouse or grown child an executor. And they'll also get to keep the estate's administration fee (which can run to 4% or more of the gross estate). The fee would otherwise go to an outsider.

True, the relative (most often the widow) may not have any specialized knowledge of estate administration matters, but so what? An experienced lawyer and accountant can be hired to see things through. You might even supply a few recommended professionals to help when the time comes.

Life—and death—aren't that simple, however. Point: The executor is personally responsible for estate-tax liabilities and late filings, as well as for making sure that the estate is distributed in accord with the will. He or she is not relieved of this responsibility by delegating to a lawyer the task of "doing whatever is necessary."

Exception: In a very few cases, courts have waived personal penalties when an executor with no business or tax experience, and with scant formal education, had relied upon a seasoned lawyer to take care of the matter. Warning: The great weight of court authority is to the contrary.

An executor also may have to pick up the bill personally if he or she distributes estate assets to beneficiaries so that there isn't enough left to pay federal taxes. That would happen if there was any reason to suspect that the IRS would still be owed money.

Example: An IRS agent warns the executor that the value of shares in a closely held corporation as shown on the federal estate tax return probably will be jacked up.

The executor may also be held personally responsible for unpaid taxes if the IRS had not put him on notice that more taxes might be payable.

One case: An executor spoke to an officer of the bank where the decedent had conducted his business. She was informed that the decedent hadn't paid any federal tax on his considerable earnings for years. This should have alerted her to the fact that estate assets couldn't all be distributed to heirs without leaving enough for what Uncle Sam would demand. The IRS was paid out of her own funds.

Another liability: An heir can hold the executor personally responsible for the amount the heir may have lost through mismanagement of the estate's assets.

Other problems for a spouse:

A spouse, in particular, may be too emotionally upset to do a competent job as executor. That has happened even when the spouse was an attorney with vast estate-tax experience.

A spouse or other really close relative is also at a disadvantage in gathering all of the estate assets as required by law. Relatives and friends may insist that money or property which the decedent had lent to them really had been intended as gifts, with an alleged "understanding" that the advance would be forgotten when the decedent died. A widow would have the unpleasant task of trying to collect from her husband's relatives—or of having to sue them. A common occurrence in such cases: The widow instead fails to report assets of that type on the estate-tax return, then gets caught by the IRS.

Another danger: An executor might regard her husband's will and its property dispositions as sacrosanct, to be honored at all costs —including the cost to herself.

Example: State laws generally allow a widow a certain percentage of her husband's estate, such as 35%, as dower rights. If he leaves her a lesser amount, she can "take against the will" and get this 35% at the expense of other beneficiaries. But, to preserve family sensitivities, the executor might refuse to tamper with her husband's instructions and hence would be shortchanging herself.

The saving on administrative fees is not large enough to make that the basis for selecting a family member. An individual is not subject to federal tax on what he or she inherits.. But if the widow is executor, the IRS may claim that part of what she inherited actually had been intended to be payment for administering the estate, and she will be assessed income tax on it.

The other side: Consider the potential expense and other consequences of being an executor. That should help to shape your response if a relative or friend flatters you by inviting you to serve as his executor. Even if they offer you a fee, it may not be worth it.

IRS Rules for Executors

The IRS does not limit itself to a demand for money from an estate. A good deal of informational material is needed for the protection of the government, the estate, and the executor personally.

Notice of fiduciary relationship:

Form 56, notice of fiduciary relationship, should be filed by the executor or administrator with the IRS to provide notification that he does what he is doing as a fiduciary, not as an individual.

If the notice is not filed, the executor may not receive from the IRS any notice of tax assessments against the estate or the decedent. This could lead to penalties, interest, and lawsuits. By filing this form, the executor establishes that he is not binding himself personally by his acts.

Once the executor gives notice to the IRS of his fiduciary powers, he is expected to exercise them.

Ordinarily, the IRS will release an executor when the estate pays the amount of tax in accordance with the Service's notification. Form L-118 is used by the IRS for this purpose.

Executors may use this same form, together with proof of payment, to establish that their personal liability for the estate tax has been satisfied.

Estate's income tax:

The executor must file federal income-tax returns for the estate when due, and pay the tax determined, up to the date of discharge from his duties.

Executors do not meet the required standard of care merely by employing an attorney or accountant to represent them. They must assume at least the minimum responsibility of seeing to it that the professional party they engage acts with diligence.

Alternate valuation dates for estate assets:

Ordinarily, assets are valued as of the date of the decedent's death. But the executor may elect to have the assets valued as of the date six months after death. This valuable privilege is only available where asset values have dropped since the day the decedent died. The election can be made only by checking a box provided for this purpose on a federal estate-tax return that is filed on time. The election cannot be revoked after the last day set for the filing of the return.

When the estate-tax return must be filed:

The federal estate-tax return, Form 706, must be filed on gross estates of $400,000 (in 1985) or more within nine months after death.

If an executor believes that he will not be able to file the return on time, he should send to the IRS a Form 4768, "Application for Extension of Time to File U.S. Estate Tax Return and/or Pay Estate Tax."

Unless it can be shown that failure to file a return was due to reasonable cause, there is a penalty of 0.5% per month, up to a maximum of 25%. The penalty for such negligence, such as ignorance or carelessness, is 5% of the amount of the tax. Nonfiling that is the result of a willful attempt to evade tax known to be due constitutes fraud, and there is a 50% penalty plus various criminal penalties.

When the estate tax must be paid:

The federal estate tax must be paid when the return is filed.

Special extensions for closely held business property. A 14-year period for payment of that part of the estate tax attributable to the decedent's interest in a closely held business is allowed if the value of that interest in the decedent's estate exceeds 35% of the value of the adjusted gross estate.

Request for prompt assessment:

Ordinarily, the IRS has three years after the filing of an income tax return in which to assess any additional tax that is determined to be due from a taxpayer, including an estate. But an executor may request a more prompt assessment of tax. The effect of this is to reduce the time for making the assessment or to begin proceedings to collect the tax, from three years to 18 months from the date the request for prompt assessment was made.

This permits earlier final distribution of the assets to the beneficiaries. The request must be made in writing, and it must be filed separately from any other document or letter.

Closing agreement:

Even after an estate-tax return has been audited by the IRS, the results can be changed upon a showing of the proper facts, either by the Service or by the executor, until the statute of limitations expires (three years after the return is filed). An executor may well feel that he does not want to distribute estate assets until he knows that there will be no further taxes to pay. A closing agreement, signed by both the executor and the IRS, on either Form 866 or Form 906, makes this possible.

Source: *The Complete Book of Estate Planning,* by Robert S. Holzman, Boardroom Books, New York.

Power of Appointment

People frequently want to provide for beneficiaries in light of circumstances that may develop when the grantors are no longer here to make decisions, choices, and allocations of their wealth. One way to accomplish this: The power of appointment. The individual delegates the authority to bestow his assets or the income from them to somebody familiar with, and sympathetic to, his goals and desires.

The chief use of a power of appointment is to entrust another person, the holder of the power, with decisions the decedent was not yet able to make at the time of death. For example: When the testator is uncertain what his spouse's need for funds will be; when there are several children with unpredictable financial needs; when friends and associates might be in desperate but temporary need of financial assistance; when the size of the estate is dependent on the performance of business or investments. There is no tax penalty, other than the usual gift or estate taxes, for the creator of a power of appointment. But the estate of the holder of the power could then be severely taxed. The reason: A decedent's estate is taxed on the value of all property that he was in a position to divert to his own use at the time of his death. If the holder does not take property that he could take, his estate is taxed nonetheless.

Source: *The Complete Book of Estate Planning,* by Robert S. Holzman, Boardroom Books, New York.

Avoid Tax on Debts Cancelled in Will

Suppose your son owes you $10,000. Your will provides for cancellation of that debt upon your death. Tax result: Even though your estate does not collect it, the value of that debt is considered an asset of the estate that is subject to federal estate tax.

Better way: When the debt is first established, spell out that the payment obligation will cease at your death. Result: When you die, there is no repayment right for your estate to succeed to and there is no asset to be taxed.*

Caution: The transaction establishing the debt should reflect the cancellation feature. Example: Your son is buying some stock from you. The stock is worth $100,000. If he gives you a note with a cancellation-at-death clause, the purchase price should probably be higher than $100,000. Otherwise, the IRS can argue that your son got more than he paid for and

treat the transaction as partly a sale as well as partly a taxable gift.

Estate of Moss, 74 T.C. No. 91.

Tax Precaution for Heirs

Ask the executor for a written statement of the property's tax basis (the market value of the property as assessed for federal estate-tax purposes). Reasons: Knowledge of the basis is necessary to (1) compute gain or loss when the property is disposed of (gain equals sale price minus basis), (2) determine the deduction available if the property is stolen or damaged in a fire or other casualty, and (3) compute any depreciation that may be allowable.

When Not to Accept Your Share of Inheritance

It can make sense to refuse an inheritance. Example: If a wealthy heir accepts the inheritance, it may well diminish the amount that goes to other family members.

The inheritance can be disclaimed by notifying the executor within nine months of date of death. The heir who disclaims the bequest must be very careful not to accept or use any of the property before the disclaimer.

Estate Tax Briefs

• Jointly held property passing to a surviving spouse is treated as though each spouse owned half. Old law: Presumed the spouse who died owned the entire property unless the survivor paid some or all of the cost and could prove it. The change helps some couples by cutting estate taxes. But it hurts others by reducing income tax breaks on inherited property. Suggestion: Couples should meet with tax advisers to review how they hold title to property.

• When a legitimate gift isn't. A bedridden homeowner gives a four-fifths interest in her house to her children. She kept a one-fifth interest herself. Until her death, she lived in one bedroom of the house, cared for by one of her daughters. Estate tax result: Despite the gift, the entire value of the house was taxable in her estate. Rationale: Though she transferred the property, she retained possession and enjoyment of it for the rest of her life. Hence the property was part of her taxable estate. Though she did not retain a formal right to the house, the court assumed that there was a family arrangement amounting to the same thing.

Estate of Callahan, T.C. Memo 1981-357.

• Another estate tax break. Monthly government benefits checks payable to the widows and divorced wives of deceased Social Security recipients are not includible in the deceased spouse's taxable estate. Rationale: Unlike annuity payments from a company retirement plan, widows' Social Security benefits arise, not from any employment contract the decedent made, but from the federal government's taxing authority.

Revenue Ruling 81-182, IRB 1981-28, p. 6.

• If you overpay estate taxes with flower bonds, your refund is limited to the fair market value of the bonds. You don't get back the full face value. But the interest you receive is the statutory IRS interest on overpayments, not the interest rate the bond itself bears (which may be as low as 3%).

Girard Trust Bank, 47 AFTR 2d 148, 449.

• A child support agreement required the father to maintain insurance on his own life for the benefit of the child. The insurance policy was placed in a trust that the father controlled. IRS ruling: When he died, the insurance proceeds were includible in his gross estate. But the estate was entitled to an estate tax deduction for amounts that it was legally required to pay to the child.

IRS Letter ruling 8128005.

• Unqualified heir. Estates of owners of closely held businesses can qualify for a special break that reduces the taxable value of business property if certain conditions are met. Catch: The business property must pass at the owner's death to a qualified heir. Recent ruling: A child who lived as a member of the decedent's family for 22 years, but whom the decedent never legally adopted, wasn't a qualified heir.

Revenue Ruling 81-179, IRB 1981-27, p. 13.

• Qualified heir. Another recent ruling: The widowed son-in-law of the owner was considered a member of the family for the purpose of computing this special tax break. It was not necessary that the decedent's lineal descendent (his daughter) survive in order for the spouse to qualify as a member of the family.

Revenue Ruling 81-236, IRB 1981-41, p. 9.

7

Business Management

Characteristics of A Good Manager

Contrary to conventional wisdom, all the best top managers don't spend their days making broad policy decisions or creating long-range corporate strategies. Many are savvy opportunists who successfully muddle through problems as they arise.

Characteristics:

Top managers develop a company-wide network of information to use at all levels. That keeps them involved in operations without having subordinates filter the information to them.

Their time and energy are focused on important concerns. Activities are limited to matters that need their special talents. One way: They train subordinates to bring them certain matters for decisions. Point: They know how to keep fully informed without getting totally involved.

They know how hard they can push. Their support and opposition is clearly identified within the company. They transmit proposals through key individuals (not from the top) in the organization. Reason: Good organizations tolerate only so many proposals from on high.

Direction is transmitted without being openly committed to specific objectives. Reason: Changing business conditions require constant revision of company strategy. The more explicit the announced strategy, the harder it is to get the organization to change. Example: The company president, who knows he must drastically reposition the company's principal business, won't disclose the new strategy to his managers. Reason: The shock will overwhelm them and give the opposition the chance to organize against the new strategy.

A talent for compromising and accepting modest progress towards goals. Successful managers are both persistent and optimistic. Typical attitude: There must be some useful parts of the plan.

Related characteristics: A wide range of interests and curiosity. They are not necessarily intellectual or creative. They envision new combinations and opportunities for restructuring. Most important: They can see relationships between different plans and proposals

159

that no one else has been aware of previously.

Source: H.E. Wrapp, professor, Graduate School of Business at Harvard University, writing in the *Harvard Business Review on Human Relations,* Harper and & Row, New York.

Developing Your Own Management Style

There are as many management styles as there are managers. Trick: Find one that is personally comfortable and most appropriate to the situation. Discard those that do not fit.

Each new position offers an opportunity to redefine a personal managing style, often with a totally new group of subordinates.

If the operation's previous manager had a style different from yours, see what there was in that style that you might want to adapt.

Questions to help identify your best management style:

Are you prepared to be a manager? Do you prefer to do every task personally?

Are you a problem seeker or a problem solver? (Some people find problems in every opportunity.)

How much status, prestige, and power do you have? How much do you need?

Do you like a lot of managerial distance or a little? Clue: Does it bother you to have subordinates who are close in salary?

Do you apply sophisticated supervisory techniques?

Is your reputation based on ability with people or production? Are you known as a hatchet man? A fire fighter? A problem avoider?

Don't automatically assume that others see you as you see yourself. If you have been with a firm for any length of time, you already have a reputation and a style. But that doesn't mean you can't gradually change it. A style that worked for one job may not fit in a new position.

Recommended: Open channels of communication with new subordinates. Listen. Find out what their expectations are. Give people a chance to contribute suggestions as to how departments can work together better. Obtain an agreement on job standards. Develop team working commitments. Demonstrate real interest in subordinates. Be sincere in dealings with people. Work toward objectives that have been cleared by top management. Communicate them to subordinates.

Source: *"Supervision Can Be Easy!"* by David K. Lindo, AMACOM, New York.

What it Takes to Succeed As a Chief Executive Officer

Commitment: To the company, the shareholders, the bottom line.

Leadership: Strength and discipline necessary to take command in an unstructured environment and direct it.

Problem-solving: Ability to reduce a complex problem to manageable pieces.

Self-confidence: A quiet, consistent assurance that can pinpoint weaknesses and strength and accentuate the latter.

Dedication: The job's demands must be the chief executive officer's prime motivator, or he won't be able to make the necessary sacrifices.

Consistency: Not just occasional effectiveness or charisma, but personal discipline that precludes any slacking off.

Good health: Improves the ability to cope with tension and risks.

Willingness, even eagerness, to go out on a limb: Otherwise competitors who take risks will get an edge.

Respect: For others as people. Uses power responsibly and fairly.

Perceptive human relations: Ability and willingness to recognize the talents of others and appraise them periodically.

Sense of humor and willingness to admit a mistake.

Source: *Industry Week.*

Questions to Ask Before Accepting a Directorship

Does the company have any serious operating, legal, or financial problems?

Are any of its activities socially or ethically questionable?

Is there serious squabbling among the directors?

Does an outside director have a real voice in decisions?

What level of commitment does the company expect from an outside director?

If there are major problems in two areas, reject the offer.

Don't join a board where directors aren't protected by liability insurance paid for the company.

Source: Robert W. Lear, former chairman of the F & M Schaefer Corp., writing in *The Corportate Director.*

How to Be A Better Boss

The basics of managing are very different from just knowing how to give orders.

The core of being a manager is understanding the total activity you are seeking to make work. Concentrate more on the interconnections and the relationships than on the parts.

To assign time priorities to yourself and to others, form a mental picture of how each step relates to the others.

Something that must be ordered well in advance must be given attention over items with shorter leads.

When a key person falls ill or a machinery breakdown occurs, knowing the interconnections enables the manager to think through the consequences quickly to decide what action is most critical.

Overall efficiency depends on parts fitting together: What A does makes B's work go well. The manager must concentrate attention on the boundaries of jobs (not so much their insides), with the goal of making the whole work smoothly. The overall results will be satisfactory only if the parts are integrated.

Key: Focus on the system and keep it going. Identify where the flow between tasks is rough or not working. Get it going again by intervention.

Expect the unexpected: Poor managers always report that they failed because someone "unexpectedly" let them down or some unexpected problem occurred. Effective managers keep checking so that when a time or resource problem begins to emerge, they are prepared to fix it or to work around it.

Keep alert to recurring problems. Such problems mean a change is necessary. Poor managers never have time to rethink and restructure their organization. They are too busy putting out fires. A vicious circle: Failing to take the time and energy to manage a change in regular tasks means you will never have the free time to innovate and make a mark as an effective manager.

Delegating for performance: The oldest catchword in management is delegation. It's also the truest. Many executives like doing things themselves rather than persuading, training, or criticizing recalcitrant subordinates. Penalties: Little time for true managerial work and poorly trained employees.

But delegating means much more. New employees require patient breaking-in so that the manager won't be disappointed in their performance and take over the job. First stage: Frequent checking and feedback. Tell subordinates what they have done well (as encouragement) and what they have done badly (as discipline). Reduce the frequency of checking when you're confident of the subordinate's performance.

Coping with stress:

Successful managers must be able to withstand the psychological stresses that go with administrative work. The unsuccessful get upset when mistakes are made, promised completion dates are missed, or when employees appear to do irrational things. Taking the initiative with problem people or departments is effective only when the manager is in control of himself, when he is neither enraged nor sulking.

Reminder: There will always be more to do than time to do it. The good manager must be able to avoid becoming anxious and jumpy because each day ends with unfinished business.

Limits: It's nice to have the authority to fulfill your responsibility. . .but don't be surprised if you don't. You almost always will be dependent on someone or something you don't directly control. It's your job to learn how to persuade and negotiate with those outside your control. Successful managers make up for inadequate authority with personal skill, enthusiasm, energy, and employee's loyalty to them.

Rules and fault finding: Setting rules saves time and helps facilitate work because people know what is expected of them and can measure their usefulness. But rules never cover all problems. And they often must be bent. Poor managers constantly seek to find a rule to cover a problem. Good managers concentrate on solving the problem. The ineffective manager looks for someone to blame (what rule has been violated), while his more successful colleague is already coping effectively with the emergency.

Source: Dr. Leonard R. Sayles, Professor of Management, Columbia University Graduate School of Business, New York 10027.

A Quick Course In Problem Solving

Look at the problem from all sides. The aim is to grasp complexities and remember them. This fixes your mind on the total picture. It keeps you from prematurely fastening on just one aspect and trying to solve only that one.

Don't jump to conclusions. The first few solutions may not be the best. Keep trying.

Change the order of the components in the problem. A rearrangement of the parts frequently provides unsuspected insights.

Develop a second solution after the first is reached. At this point, the mind is no longer dominated by pressures to reach a solution. It becomes problem-oriented and usually produces a better solution.

Ask others for criticism. Evaluate it with an open mind. Meanwhile, regard your own ideas critically. Reason: You get a constructive attitude when you focus on the weak points in your own solution and the strong points in other's ideas.

When at an impasse, switch from words to pictures or numbers. Change thinking from abstract to concrete or vice versa. This frequently helps.

Take a break when really stuck, since there's no point in keeping your mind churning.

Discuss the problem with others. The history of thought is filled with brilliant ideas that followed communication with others.

Source: *Chemtech.*

How to Give Orders

Giving orders is an uncomfortable task for many managers. Recommended: Use a three-step process called DAD (Describe, Ask, Direct).

Describe the situation objectively in terms of company needs. Example: "Mary, this report for tomorrow's board meeting needs to be retyped today."

Ask for clarification or suggestions. Example: "How can we fit this into your schedule?" Frequently, the subordinate's suggestion will be exactly what you had in mind all along.

Direct, issuing the order in a clear, declarative sentence. Example: "I need the report tomorrow morning."

When giving orders: Avoid fidgeting: disqualifying prefaces ("This may sound silly, but. . ."); and tag questions ("Don't you think. . .?") since they leave room for doubt. Helpful: Eye contact and a warm tone.

Source: *Turning Around: The Behavioral Approach to Managing People,* by Beverly A. Potter, AMACOM, New York.

Learning How to Say No

The inability to say "no" causes many people to be uncomfortable and makes them less effective in dealing with others (in business and their personal lives). Solution: (1) Instead of giving in on small things, assert yourself gently. Simply say, "I prefer not to" or "I'd rather do it this way . . ." (2) Give a good reason for not going along with another person's request. Examples: It's inconvenient; it conflicts with other plans; etc. (instead of saying yes and feeling imposed upon). (3) When you know you'll be put on the spot, figure out in advance what you really want to do, then meet your own needs. Remember: It's more important to please yourself than others, as long as you do it tactfully.

How to Use Authority Effectively

How effectively do you use your authority? Key questions: Do people look to you for orders? Are your orders carried out as intended? Guidelines for issuing directives:

1. Know what has to be done before telling someone else what to do. Don't worry about all the details. Make sure you know exactly what objectives are to be achieved.

2. If you have decided upon the approach, tell the subordinate what method to use. When you correct a subordinate after the fact for failing to use the right method, it means that you gave the order poorly.

3. Fit the order to the intelligence, knowledge, and experience of the subordinate. A simple suggestion is enough for some employees. Others require clear commands.

4. Don't overload an order with details. Keep directives precise and accurate.

5. Make sure the order is understood. Have the subordinate repeat it back to you. (Example: Read it back to me, Dave, so we know we're on the same wavelength.) Be prepared to repeat and clarify.

6. Put complicated orders in writing. It improves the logic and coherence of the directive.

7. Give orders in a calm, lucid manner. Anger, impatience, or sarcasm only distract and confuse.

8. Don't give too many orders at once. An overwhelmed subordinate is justifiably confused.

9. Make sure present orders don't conflict with previous ones. They shouldn't violate lines of authority, either. When there are exceptions, let the subordinate know you are aware of them—and that you take full responsibility.

10. Assure the subordinate that you won't interfere, but that you will monitor progress through reports or other checks. Thus, you pass along authority to do the job but retain responsibility.

Source: Don Fuller, Don Fuller Associates, Olmsted Falls, in *Machine Design.*

The Art of Making Decisions

Don't brood over the possible consequences. Imagine the worst effect your decision could cause. If you take this thinking to absurd lengths, it will place your fears in their proper perspective.

Don't negate your gut reactions. They could be telling you something.

Don't postpone. If you can't make up your mind, set a date for a resolution. By removing the immediate pressure, you will be more relaxed to judge the options.

Broaden the array of choices. Example: You can't decide whether or not to spend the money for an Alaskan vacation. Consider other vacation spots and their costs. Then you will have a better idea of how much the Alaskan trip means to you and be able to make a decision that pleases you.

Let two friends literally pull a decision from you. Stand between the two friends. Have

163

each tug at an arm while trying to talk you into deciding his way. When your body begins to lean toward one side, it is telling you what to do. Sometimes you will remain suspended between the rival tugs. That means neither option is suitable to you.

Remember: There is seldom a right choice in decision-making. You simply make up your mind to do something, and then accept the consequences of your decision.

Secrets of Becoming A Better Listener

Becoming a better listener is not easy. Simple techniques that help:

Relax yourself and the speaker. Give your full attention to what's being said. Stop everything else you're doing. Maintain eye contact.

Don't let the speaker's tone of voice or manner turn you off. Nervousness or misplaced emotions often cloud the message the speaker is trying to get across.

Prepare beforehand for the conversation. How: Take a few minutes to read or consult information pertinent to the discussion. That also helps you to quickly evaluate the speaker and the subject.

Allow for unusual circumstance (extreme pressure or disturbing interruptions). Judge only what the speaker says given the conditions he is faced with.

Avoid getting sidetracked. Listen very closely to points you disagree with. (Poor listeners shut out or distort them.)

Mentally collect the main points of the conversation. Occasionally, ask for clarification of one of the speaker's statements. Reason: It shows your interest and helps the speaker better organize his thoughts.

Restate what you've heard at the end of the talk to avoid misunderstandings. Emphasize important issues brought up in the discussion.

Source: *Communicating at the Top,* by George de Mare, John Wiley & Sons, New York.

Helping a Secretary to Help You

Train her to sort your mail while you are away. She can distribute assignments and information. She can answer some correspondence herself. Caution: Set clear guidelines about what work she can delegate.

Establish a procedure so that if your dictation (or instruction) time with her is interrupted, she will return to her desk and do other work, unless you signal her to stay.

Schedule a meeting with her once a day to establish priorities for work.

Share your time-management goals with her. Have her make an activity sampling of your day or keep a time diary.

Let her do some of your information-gathering. She can, for example, check project progress, ascertain problems in meeting deadlines, and report them to you.

Encourage her to read and think about your memos instead of just typing them. She can help you become more specific in your written communications.

Encourage her to look for improvements in procedures, schedules, etc. Have her write them in detail and set aside dates for putting them into effect. Let her know that unless you tell her otherwise, she can go ahead.

Help her write her job description to show all the work that she actually does. Too often, secretaries are paid on the basis of typing, filling, and dictation, when they are actually working most of the time as administrative assistants.

Source: Norman Kobert, Norman Kobert & Associates, 1611 S. Ocean Dr., Ft. Lauderdale, FL 33316.

Running a Business Meeting

Discuss only pertinent matters.

Don't recap for latecomers. Let them catch up.

Keep invitees to a minimum. A recent study found five to be the most effective number. Groups of 13 or more become a conference, geared for discussion rather than decision-making.

Don't allow any breaks.

Use a tape recorder and let all participants know their comments are being taped.

Set a personal limit on the amount of time spent in meetings per day. Don't go to the ones in which you have little to contribute.

Before calling a meeting ask: Do I really need all of these people participating?

Develop policies about when to have meetings and when not to. Ninty percent of meeting time is spent on relatively unimportant matters.

Look for meeting substitutes. Example: A well written report can take the place of many meetings.

Source: *Supervision Can Be Easy*, by David Lindo, AMACOM, New York.

Other suggestions:

Ask questions that induce a free flow of opinion and draw out information. Avoid questions that elicit simple yes or no answers, which require no thinking. Ask:

Who, what, where, when, why questions, which make a simple answer impossible.

Questions that don't lead or restrict respondents. Bad leading question: Why do you think this solution is good? It inhibits an honest response. Better question: What do you think of this solution? Rule of thumb: Direct "why" questions can be threatening. Better form: What are your reasons?

Questions that contain only one point.

Short questions. Long ones induce rambling answers.

Probing questions. They keep people talking and revealing more and more of what is on their minds. Methods: Nod and smile, or use short neutral interjections or questions. Other methods: Ask for clarification or more information or repeat some of the speaker's words. Most important element: Listen neutrally, without offering opinions, and speak only occasionally.

Dealing with objections and disagreements. Listen to objections carefully. Too quick an answer suggests it hasn't been given full consideration. Next: Formulate the best possible answer, then translate it into a tactful question. Example: Would you like to join us to tell others how you feel?

Reminder: Don't fight back when participants pose objections or obstacles. Turning answers into questions and allowing the participants to discover the answer is a far more effective way of inducing interest and agreement.

Source: Paul Mills and Bernard Roberts, partners in Mills Roberts Associates, 25 W. 45 St., New York 10036, speech experts specializing in training of executives.

Running a Civic Meeting

Keep the purpose of the meeting in mind. Budget time accordingly.

Insist that all proposals for action be formulated as motions. Point: Diffuse thoughts couched in the form of "kicking an idea around" are common to many civic meetings. They are a principal source of frustration and wasted time.

Refer all complicated business to subcommittees for recommended action, before allowing that business to be considered by the group as a whole.

Follow a standard parliamentary agenda as much as possible. Sequence to be observed: Minutes of previous meeting. Main items of business. Reports from officers and standing committees. Items postponed from previous meetings. New business, as a means of shaping future agendas.

Problem: Office business meetings and their civic counterparts differ in action and follow-up. Civic groups are notoriously poor on both points. Solution: A civic-group leader must specifically list all action to be taken following a meeting and then promptly delegate reponsibility for executing that action to specific individuals. Critical: Keep at those individuals to carry out the action by the next meeting.

How to Chair A Committee

Be aware of every member's interests, hopes, and suggestions for the committee. How: Meet privately beforehand with each person. Payoff: No unpleasant surprises during the session.

Handle housekeeping details efficiently. Be sure agendas and supplies are distributed on time. Welcome members at the door to relax them.

Don't let talkative members dominate and quiet ones fade into woodwork. Suggestion: Privately urge quiet people to speak up. Or get permission to pass on their views.

Remain neutral. Avoid: Granting individual favors or advancing narrow causes. Point: Chairpersons are judged by how their committee performs as a whole, not by personal contributions they might make.

Stress the blending of divergent opinions into a consensus. Be wary of advancing too many opinions from the chair.

Check the final report with the full committee before submitting it. Reason: To make sure it accurately represents the group's findings.

Source: Dr. John E. Tropman, professor of social work, writing in *Directors and Boards*.

Secrets of Successful Negotiators

• Getting an edge in a bargaining session:

Try to keep the negotiations on company premises.

If the adversary refuses, pick a neutral site in a light, pleasant, colorful room, with all the necessary creature comforts.

Arrange the seating carefully. The best place is at the head of the table with back to the window and facing the door. This puts the glare in the adversary's face and allows you to see who's entering the room.

Source: *What To Say . . . How To Say It*, by N.H. Mager, William Morrow and Co., Inc., New York.

• How to make concessions without coming off the loser:

Get the other party to put all his demands on the table first (and keep yours to yourself). Don't be baited into item-by-item negotiations and concessions until you know all his demands.

Never be the first to make a major concession. When your opponent makes one, don't assume you have to make one of equal importance.

Get something in return for each concession you make.

Conserve your concessions—give a little at a time, make your opponent work for whatever he gets.

• How to handle a "final offer": First, listen very carefully to your counterpart across the negotiating table for hedges and face-savers to determine just how "final" the offer really is. Then, choose among any of these reactions:

In your reply, interpret the offer in the way that is most favorable to you.

Give the other party a face-saving way to retreat from his position.

Get angry if it suits your purpose.

Tell your opponent what he stands to lose by a deadlock.

Change the subject.

Introduce new alternatives and possible solutions.

• How to say no without ruffling feathers: Pin the blame for the negative answer on somebody (or something) else. That "something else" could be a superior, company policy, government regulation, manufacturing standard, etc.—but not yourself. Lack of authority can prove a powerful negotiating tool.

• Tactic when session bogs down:

Walking out abruptly can clear the air and often leads to a strategic gain. How to do it: Announce that the talks aren't progressing, suggest a break, and walk out before your opposite number can reply. Results: This dissipates the tension of the stalemate and can also make the other person think (and begin to consider whose inflexibility prompted the walkout). Important: Be ready with a fresh idea when you get back to the table.

Signs That Negotiators Are Ready to Make a Deal

It's valuable to know as early as possible that the other side is preparing to settle negotiations. It allows strong points to be pressed home and helps avoid overkill. Clues to look for:

The discussion shifts focus from the points of contention to the areas of agreement.

The two sides are significantly closer together.

The opposition starts to talk about final arrangements.

A personal social invitation is made. At this point, agreement is almost always just a formality.

Other side starts to make notes. Important: Follow through at once, even if nothing but a napkin or envelope is at hand to write on.

Caution: Don't handle the signing of the formal agreement through the mail. Both parties should sign it together. This adds importance to the event and helps cement the ties that were formed during the final stage of negotiation.

Source: *Negotiate Your Way to Success,* D.D. Seltz and A.J. Modica, Farnsworth Publishing Co., Rockville Center, NY.

How to Prepare A Speech

Decide exactly and precisely what your subject is. Then logically think through your subject. List the ideas and conclusions to stress. Become thoroughly familiar with the important books, speeches, and other literature on the subject.

Prepare an outline of the speech: Introduction, main body (usually divided up into two to four sections), and conclusion.

Start by writing the speech. Be complete.

Prepare a brief introduction. Various ways in which you can introduce your speech: (1) Attack the topic head-on by simply announcing it. (2) Begin with a human interest story, an illustration, or a funny anecdote relevant to the topic. (3) Startle the audience by beginning with an exciting question or an arousing statement. (4) Use a quote or an idea from somebody else. (5) Explain in factual terms why the topic is important to your audience.

The main body of the speech should make it apparent to your audience that you have a thorough knowledge of the topic. Back up your points with facts, numbers, examples. If you want to convince your audience of the wisdom of your views on the topic, begin with material that agrees with those views. Don't argue. Just explain your points. Those points should be clearly defined either at the beginning or the end of the speech, or as they develop within the speech, or any combination of those three.

Conclude: Briefly go over the points you've made. Use a quote. Strive for a big climax. You can compliment the audience. Or end by being encouraging and optimistic, or by detailing a particularly dramatic story, an historical anecdote, or a joke. You can also recommend that your audience take some action. Another ending would be to suggest that they change their views to yours.

Type the last line of each page on the top of the next page.

Don't have speech typed in all capital letters. Word recognition is easier when normal upper- and lower-case letters are used.

Have speech typed triple-space.

Don't hyphenate words.

When gesturing, keep a finger (or pencil) on the line being read (so place won't be lost). Gesture with other hand.

Don't staple speech manuscript. Allow completed pages or large cards to be casually (and noiselessly) slid off to side.

Memorize important points. Then eyes can lift from text to look directly at audience when these points are being made. Memorize both opening and closing lines.

Use slant-top lectern so manuscript can be read by dropping eyes only slightly—but not your head.

167

Write words "slow down" in large letters at top of each page. That compensates for general tendency to speak too rapidly.

Speaker who writes on blackboard or easel pad as a visual aid should keep it on his left (when he's facing the audience) if he's right handed. This prevents him from turning his back on audience or blocking what's written.

When your remarks are scheduled for the end of a program, have two versions ready, a long and a short one.

Tape-record your speeches. Tension could be tightening your vocal cords, causing your pitch to rise. Relaxation can cure that.

How to Hold An Audience

Make eye contact with the audience. Sweep your gaze over the audience, spanning the whole group. But don't jump from individual to individual.

Don't worry about your hands. Putting them in your pockets does not aid in relaxing. Hold them behind your back if you don't need them to illustrate a point. Don't gesture awkwardly. The audience isn't worrying about your hands, and neither should you.

Lean closer to the audience when sharing a personal or intimate thought. Stand straight or move slightly back to be more formal.

Before answering a question, stop and think. Frame the principal thought of your answer before starting to speak. Use anecdotes and actual personal experiences.

Start talks with something that grabs the audience. Ask a question. Or tell a joke, but only if it is relevant to the topic and leads directly to the main thought.

Source: *How to Think on Your Feet and Say What you Mean—Effectively*, Communi-Vu, New York.

Other tips:

Remember that your audience is interested first in people, then in things, finally in ideas.

Only rarely is it possible to change deep-seated attitudes or beliefs. Aim no higher than getting the listeners to question their attitudes. Avoid: Alienating an audience by pressing points too hard.

The most successful speeches state conclusions and call for action.

When you have to speak extemporaneously, develop a theme early and stick to it.

Use silence to underline a point.

End a speech with a short, emotional, conviction-filled summary of the main points.

Source: Michael Klezaras Jr., director of research and planning, Roger Ailes & Associates, Inc., communication consultants, 230 Central Park South, New York 10019.

How Speakers Can Duck Questions

Ask another question.

Change the subject.

Point out that someone else is better qualified to answer.

Answer with a generalization.

State that the question is irrelevant.

Stand behind the protection that the answer is "personal, privileged, or classified."

Suggest several alternative answers, without choosing a "right" one.

Say the question can't be answered specifically.

Comment on the subject of the question with enthusiasm but no answer.

Tell a joke or compliment the questioner, instead of answering.

Source: *What to Say. . . How to Say It* by N.H. Mager, William Morrow and Co., Inc., New York.

Improving Your Business English

Verbosity wastes time and diminishes comprehension. Check your reports and memos, for these common business phrases, and substitute the shorter version for the more wordy one.

Enclosed please find—Here's.

According to our records—We find.

At an early date/At your earliest convenience—Soon/Now.

In the event of—If.

In the amount of—For

In accordance with—By/Under.

Inasmuch as—Since/Because.

In our opinion—We believe.

It is obvious—We believe.

It is obvious that/It goes without saying—Clearly/Obviously.

Finalized our decision—Decided.

For the purpose of—For.

Reflects a balance of—Shows.

With regard to—Re:.

With the result that—So that.

Sounding Better On the Phone

The telephone transmits lower frequency sounds with more fidelity than higher frequencies. Point: Keep your voice low and speech slow.

Posture affects the way you sound. If the chin is pressed against the chest, or the head is bent back (which happens when slouching), the throat is tense and strained. And the voice sounds that way, too.

Cradling the telephone between the head and shoulder produces a sloppy, tough sound at the other end.

Style:

Answer the phone with a rising inflection. It sounds warm and responsive.

Say the other person's name (or "you") slowly to emphasize closeness.

Don't slur R's and L's. "Buyah" and "awright" sound slovenly. "Buyer" and "all right" sound precise.

Source: Paul Mills and Bernard Robert, Mills Roberts Associates, Inc., 25 W. 45 St., New York 10036, speech consultants to radio and TV performers and executive and sales personnel.

To Write as Clearly As You Think

Concentrate on simplifying sentence structure in business writing. It's the easiest way to say what is meant and to make sure the message gets across. Remember three basic rules:

• Keep sentences short. They should be no more than 17 to 20 words.

• Vary the length of sentences. The 17 to 20 word rule is the average. When sentences drone on at unvarying lengths, the reader's attention begins to wander.

• Vary the punctuation. Include plenty of commas, as well as a sprinkling of semicolons, to go with the necessary periods. Reason: Clarity of communication. Well-placed punctuation is a road map, leading the reader comfortably and accurately through the message.

Source: "Sentence Control: Solving an Old Problem," by Paul Richards, independent writing consultant, writing in *Supervisory Management*.

Another good approach: A four-question review of any written communication.

Who is the audience? Not just the addressee, but everyone else who may read it.

What's the value of the message to the audience? Not its purpose to the writer, but what it will do for the readers.

What's the point of the message? Is it made clear in the first sentence or two?

Can the gist of it be gathered by skimming the title and heading, if it's a long piece? Do those guides make the audience want to learn the details?

Source: *Communicating for Leadership*, John Wiley & Sons Inc., New York.

Writing a Good Sales Letter

Think the message through beforehand.

Use an attention-grabbing sentence or phrase in the first few lines.

Clarify the subject within the first few sentences.

Personalize the message with terms and examples the recipient can apply to his own situation and experience.

Anticipate the most likely questions and objections. Handle them in the body of the communication without waiting to be asked.

Repeat the key points in the closing to help fix them in the recipient's mind.

Source: *Managing a Sales Team,* Lebhar-Friedman Books, New York.

How to Stay Well Informed

There is no easy route to becoming informed about the world. It takes real work, and it is harder than it used to be.

One reason: The idea of objectivity, honored in principle, is practiced less by journalists today. This is the legacy of the advocacy journalism of the 1960s.

The main point: Reading from many sources offers a much better view of what the issues and arguments are and a much better possibility of telling when a particular story is biased. Become aware of the political bent of various news outlets and organs of opinion. Keep that in mind when reading or listening to the news from the media.

Required reading:

The New York Times and *The Wall Street Journal* editorial pages, at a minimum. The *Times* is indispensable for the news, and the editorials should also be read. Reason: *The New York Times* editorial page is a reliable guide to established, mainstream liberal opinion on any issue. (Knowing what various groups are thinking is an important factor in knowing what's going on.) *The Wall Street Journal* has the best editorial page in the country (possibly in the world). It's generally supposed to represent the neoconservative viewpoint, except on economic issues, where it is usually strictly free market (old-style conservative).

Much less important: Newspapers like *The*

Washington Post. It's good for people who live in Washington, but otherwise not a necessary source of information. It does offer a few good columnists not available in New York papers, notably George Will, one of the most important columnists in America, and Joseph Kraft. *The New York Daily News* is worth reading for local news and a few columnists, mainly James Buchanan (very conservative in view).

Weeklies: One of the few worth reading is *The New Republic,* despite being a mixed and unpredictable bag. It is much more reliable and diversified than the *The Nation,* which pursues a rigidly radical-left line.

News magazines: Both *Time* and *Newsweek* have to be taken with a grain of salt because both can be quite slanted, but they're worth looking at for their coverage.

The important monthly and quarterly magazines are *Commentary, The Public Interest,* and *Encounter* (British).

Look at selectively: *The National Review.* Concentrate on the front matter—unsigned articles and columns by Brian Crozier and William F. Buckley Jr. By-lined articles are rarely useful and are sloppily edited.

Only occasionally worth reading: *The Atlantic Monthly.* The trouble is extreme unevenness and unreliability of material.

Television news: A poor bet. Reason: Television reporting is terrifically overheated and so warps the perspective on news. It makes some trivial things more important than they are and doesn't give proper importance to some issues simply because they don't lend themselves to visual coverage and the excited, breathless format that TV news cultivates.

Big exception: The MacNeil—Lehrer report. Objective, fair coverage.

Radio news: National Public Radio's A.M. and P.M. programs, *Morning Edition* and *All Things Considered.* Simply the best news and feature coverage in broadcasting. Uses domestic and foreign journalists.

Personalized sources of information, such as conversations with friends, are usually a poor substitute for reading. More likely result: An exchange of misinformation rather than the broadening of one's information base.

The goal: Becoming informed does not mean approaching the news with a totally neutral, open mind. Everyone needs, and should work to develop, a point of view with which to interpret the world. Without a perspective, the news of the world becomes incomprehensible.

Speedreading: Fact vs. Fiction

Speedreading is a simple set of skills, not a miracle. What to be wary of:

Any system that guarantees increased reading speed. (The respected International Reading Association is on record against "Speed" reading, and its members are not allowed to guarantee that a student will ever read at any particular level.) The most deceptive thing about guarantee: It gives a false sense of confidence to the individual with low verbal skills. If you don't start out with basic skills, you will not learn them in speedreading.

Anyone who suggests that you can read 900 or 1,000 words a minute. Impossible, except when reading very easy material. Average reading speed is around 250 to 300 words per minute. Some reading specialists claim 600 to 800 is maximum for good reading comprehension. When reading speed is blown out of proportion, look elsewhere for your lessons.

How reading can be speeded up:

Preview material. Skim for key words and phrases. Then decide which memos, reports, surveys, business and professional journals you should keep to read.

Organize. Quickly decide what to delegate to someone else, what to file, and what to throw in the wastebasket. Many executives discard as much as half the material that comes across their desks after taking a quick look at it.

Read flexibly. Most experts believe learning to read flexibly is the real key to speedreading. A fast look is valuable when you need to get through repetitious material that doesn't require you to take in every word. It is also helpful when you're trying to locate a specific fact or phrase. Adjust to a slower reading tempo when the information is unfamiliar.

Constant use. It's necessary to keep good reading habits sharp.

Keeping Your Mind Young

The mind, like a muscle, can either be agile or allowed to grow flabby with disuse. Atrophy often results from one-track concern with work, family, and social responsibilities. Symptoms:

Habitually prefacing statments with phrases like: "As I always say."

Eagerly saying something you have said a thousand times before.

Feeling resentment when someone introduces an unfamiliar topic into a conversation.

Solution: Read at least one lively, well-written book a month about a subject completely unrelated to your field. Also helpful: A good thought-provoking movie, a hike through the woods, museum visit, attending a good concert.

Improving Your Memory

• Repeat the name of someone you have just met. Say: Nice to meet you. Then repeat the person's full name. If the name is complicated, ask the person to spell it.

Make up a rhyme that incorporates something about the person. Example: Al Ferrago from Chicago.

Concoct a ridiculous mental image concerning the name. The wilder the image, the more likely that you won't forget it. Example: You have met someone named Don Bacon. Imagine him arising at dawn to fry bacon.

Make acronyms from the first letters of keys words in a list or speech you want to remember. Example: The word *homes* contains the first letters of the names of the Great Lakes.

Source: *Memory Made Easy.* by Robert Montgomery, AMACOM, New York.

• Select only important things to remember. Relegate the unimportant to lists and files.

• Quit telling yourself that you have a bad memory. Test yourself regularly to see if you can recall the names of the people in a meeting or what's on schedule for tomorrow.

• Organize facts into patterns. Make logical and rhythmical associations. Example: To remember 173, say one-hundred and seventy-three to yourself instead of one, seven, three. Or relate 173 to something else, such as thinking that it's two less than 175.

• Use all your senses. When meeting someone, associate the name with appearance, voice or the smell of their after-shave or perfume. Relate these sensations to someone you already know.

• Use repetition. It's no secret that it works with names, but it is also effective for other things.

Source: *Time Talk*

Improving Your Concentration

Don't waste time willing yourself to concentrate better. Instead: Sharpen your concentration with a better work ritual. Specifically, develop a work ritual that:

Takes you from the first few minutes of concentration through the distractions that habitually sidetrack you, to the point where you are settled down and producing.

Anticipates interruptions. Eliminate them, especially the less obvious ones. Examples: If you habitually get thirsty, have your favorite beverage on your desk. Or if you run short of supplies, stock up.

Practice stopping your mind from wandering. Point: Your mind usually wanders because you are worried about how the project you are working on will turn out. To overcome this:

Focus on the separate pieces of the project, without worrying about the end results.

Work a set period of time each day to get into rhythm.

Write down the worst that can happen if the project aborts. Reason: Once you have faced the worst, you will be free to concentrate on doing your best.

Remember where you have concentrated best in the past. Then, try to recreate that work environment.

Why You Can't Get Enough Done

If you start your business day by reading the memos and mail that piled up on your desk, that's your first mistake. Then, if you put them down until you're ready to deal with them, that's mistake number two. If you do this because your phone just rang, that's mistake number three.

Advice:

Very few people with work to be done will deliberately waste time. But many use time unwisely. Example: People who do their best work first thing in the morning should reserve this "prime time" for the most demanding task of the day. Let the mail wait. Let the phone calls wait. Don't give them your best shot.

When scheduling your day, schedule the interruptions, too. Set aside specific times when you can be reached on routine matters. If calls come in at other hours, have your secretary say you'll call them back. (Even VIPs will accept this if you establish a reputation for returning calls when promised.)

Set deadlines for what you want to do. Make them known to the people around you. This not only keeps people away, it strengthens your motivation to get things done.

To get through daily correspondence faster: (1) Handle each piece of paper only once. Do what needs to be done—checking, forwarding, phoning, and replying—immediately. (2) If your reply is brief, write it on the incoming letter or memo. File a copy. (3) Don't write when you can phone. Use the written word primarily to remind, confirm, or clarify.

Don't keep records of information easily obtained elsewhere. To avoid unnecessary filing, never ask, "Is it possible we'll ever need this?" The real question: "What would happen if we needed it and it wasn't there?" The answer in most cases is that it wouldn't matter.

Instead of having a meeting, set up a conference call. You can do it locally as well as long distance at surprisingly low rates.

If you must have a meeting: Agenda should include specific questions to be decided, not just a list of topics. At the meeting, reach a decision on each item or assign responsibility for action. At the close, state once again the decisions reached, assignments made. Confirm in writing the next day.

Best use of mid-day time: Work during noon hour when interruptions are rare, because most others have gone to lunch. Go out to eat at 1 p.m. or later.

Which tasks to perform first: Don't make the usual list based on what's needed fastest and what can wait. That often relegates the really important things to the last place. Instead, list your projects in order of how much you will benefit from getting them done. Select the top two or three and concentrate on accomplishing them. Don't feel guilty about slighting the others. By your own definition, they count less.

Why the best of us procrastinate: When we put off something important, it's usually because of nagging fears that we won't do it right. To handle these little anxieties, ask yourself, "What's the worst thing that could happen if I goof?" Often it will simply be embarrassment.

If a task looks too hard or too big: Break it down into small manageable "instant" things to do. The first one is to list—in writing—all the simple steps involved. Without such a list, you may never get started at all.

Most effective time-saving technique ever developed: Frequent use of the word no. Learn to decline, tactfully but firmly, every request that doesn't contribute to accomplishment of your goals for the day.

The real reason for not taking work home: It gives you an excuse for not getting things done in the office.

The two worst time traps: Keeping your door open and answering your own phone.

Source: Edwin C. Bliss, expert in time management and author of *Getting Things Done*, Charles Scribner's Sons, New York.

Time Savers

Use a time reminder device to limit length of conversations. (Often "politically" desirable to look annoyed when it goes off.)

Set some appointments at odd times instead of on the hour or half hour. Meeting at 2:50 or 3:20 makes others more prompt and puts across the message of careful time management.

Accumulate quick easy, yes/no type work in a special "children's hour" folder. Set aside odd periods to work on it (while waiting for a meeting to start, while waiting in airport, while riding on commuter train).

To find your coat fast on a crowded rack, tuck one sleeve over a hanger bar. To spot your car quickly in a crowded parking lot, mark antenna with brightly colored tape.

How to Spend Less Time On the Phone

When calling a long-winded party, time call for just before he goes out to lunch or leaves for the day. Gives him a reason to keep call short without offending him.

When asking somone to call back later, suggest best time to call. Avoids repeated interruptions at inconvenient moments.

Never hold the phone waiting for someone

who's on another line. Request an immediate callback instead.

Make phone calls before 9 a.m. or after 3 p.m. At other hours, too many people are in meetings.

Don't return all calls the minute you get back to the office. Spot the crucial ones. Half the rest will be from people who've already solved their problems; the rest will be back to you soon enough.

List six elements in your life that need better organization. How to do it: Mentally run through a typical day. Note problems. Example: Read or skim the magazines and reports cluttering up the table and desk at home.

Rank each of the six problems on the list on a scale of one-to-ten (one being the most serious).

Tackle the problem. Good idea: If you can't find the time to think out and solve the problem, make a date with yourself in your appointment calendar.

Source: Stephanie Winston, *Getting Organized*, Warner Books, New York.

When Perfectionism Is a Waste of Time

Rid yourself of time-consuming habits and add hours of productive time to each work week.

Recommended:

Eschew perfection. Stop having routine memos and letters retyped because of minor typographical errors. Exception: Any important correspondence.

Dictate letters, memos, and reports only once, then let them fly. Let your secretary draft a reply to correspondence. But first tell the secretary what you want the letter to say.

Don't confuse neatness with efficiency. Straightening up is often just an excuse for putting off a job. Organized clutter makes many jobs easier.

Be dispensable. Delegate tasks, pass on projects, and share your work load with others. Usual result: You'll be pleased at how most of your co-workers respond.

Source: *Execu-Time.*

Getting Organized

Buy a small pocket notebook in which you can write down all reminders. It will serve as a master list, replacing those small slips of paper and other memoranda of things to do that clutter your pockets and desk.

Setting Up a Sideline Business

Business executives (especially the aggressive or entrepreneurial types) are often attracted to sideline businesses. The businesses serve as legitimate investments or tax shelters, and, more often, they spur the pursuit of a special interest.

A sideline can be an expensive craving, though. Start-up costs inevitably multiply. And the first-year mortality rate for small businesses is 33%. Bottom line: Use the same judgment in starting a sideline business as you would to build a successful career:

Be sure you have enough money. Start-up money alone is not enough. You also need a cushion to absorb losses when there's an emergency, a sales downturn, or an operational problem. Rule of thumb: Work up a detailed one-month operating budget and multiply it by four. That amount plus basic investment and cash flow should pull you through the low points.

Know more than the basics about the sideline business. Find out about prices, sources of supply, quality, popular tastes, inventory, how to market, legal pitfalls, cash-flow cycles, and day-to-day operating expenses. Remember, you won't have the support staff you're used to. You'll have to deal directly with suppliers, employees, sales personnel, customers, and others. Hire the very best people you can afford, people who have strengths to match your weaknesses.

Do solid planning. If you don't run your job on hunches and guesses, why run your sideline that way? Have you truly identified your market? Can the market really use your product or service? Are you in the right location? Are you getting the best supplies for your money? Should you advertise?

Identify sources of money. Most banks like to see liquidity equal to 50% of the investment plus additional equity. The bank may also take a chattel mortgage on your equipment. The Small Business Administration (SBA) will support some higher-risk loans. But first you have to be turned down by all your local banks. The SBA also offers practical help through groups like Service Corps of Retired Executives and Procurement Automated Service Systems.

Understand the tax consequences. You can deduct losses only if you can satisfy the IRS that your sideline is a profit-making venture rather than a hobby. Income from a hobby is taxable, but losses are not. Also, on an enterprise designed to make a profit, you're entitled to deduct business losses. The IRS has several standards for measuring your motives. If you show a profit in two or more years out of five, it's presumed to be a profit-making business. But even failing that, the IRS may let you deduct losses. They'll judge how businesslike an approach you have, the expertise you and your staff bring to the business, time and effort expended, expectation of growth, success, or failure in other similar ventures, and elements of personal pleasure.

Becoming a Consultant

There are between 35,000 and 50,000 consultants in the U.S. The number is growing by more than 10% a year. Over 70% of them have 10 or fewer employees. Half are one-person operations. Most of the new consultants are people who have decided to go on their own, to do jobs they have been doing for corporations.

Investment is mainly in time. Set-up costs can be as little as a few hundred dollars (for brochures, answering service, telephone, used furniture, office supplies) for someone operating out of his home. They can range to several thousand dollars if high-price office space is thrown in.

How to become a consultant:

Keep your contacts. People you worked with earlier may be your first clients.

Use your corporate background as a selling point. It will give you credibility with potential clients.

Keep in mind you must sell your services. You must convince the client that his company has a problem. Then convince him that you can solve it.

Don't spend more money than is necessary. You don't need an impressive office.

If you take a partner, make sure he's one who brings clients with him.

Your rates should reflect the price of consultants in your area.

Clinching A Finder's Fee

If you put together a business deal or arrange for a merger, an acquisition, or a financing, getting the agreed-upon commission for your service may not be easy. Many people will not pay a finder's fee for the simple act of bringing parties together. They might prefer compensation based on time charges and out-of pocket expenses.

Problem: Once a deal has been consummated, both sides minimize the importance of the broker (or finder). They easily convince themselves that the finder was unnecessary and doesn't deserve a payment. Point: Clients are more clearheaded about the value of the finder going into the deal the coming out of it.

Best posture: The finder should analyze the upside potential in the deal and be cool about the downside risks. Next: Decide which party fits into the profile with the greatest upside potential.

Basic rule: You cannot serve as an agent for both sides of a deal. Exceptions:

The fact is disclosed to both parties.

Both parties are willing to sign an agreement to that effect.

Reason: If you try to enforce separate agreements drawn up without the knowledge of both, the deal will not stand up in court. Why: It is duplicitous to pay someone for a service for which they are already receiving a payment from someone else. Example: A manufacturer cannot pay a shoe buyer at a retail store a secret commission. After all, the buyer is being paid by the store to perform the function of choosing shoes. Any time one is paid by both sides without knowledge of both, there is a conflict of interest.

The law in New York and some other states (check your own state) provides that finders' fees, to be enforceable, must be in writing and signed by the party to be charged.

The party who pays is not always the party who engages the finder. Example: Real estate is an anomaly. The broker is retained by the buyer. But the fee is an obligation of the seller. The agent turns out to be the seller's *de facto* agent, although he is the buyer's *de jure* agent.

Key: The person who undertakes to act as a finder must identify who will pay the finder's fee. The agreement must cover:

The amount of money to be paid. This is frequently decided by some formula, such as a straight percentage of the sales price of the money raised.

The time of payment and other conditions. If you put the parties together and the deal goes through, should you be paid at the closing or over a period of time? In cash or in stock, at your option or at the option of your client? Why: People frequently refuse to sign when they see the figures.

The Warburg Rule: The most popular finder's fee formula is the 5-4-3-2-1 rule of the old merchant banking family of Sigmund Warburg (now part of Warburg Paribas Becker).

That rule fixed the finder's fee at 5% for a $1 million deal, 4% for $2 million, and so on. Beyond $5 million, the fee is negotiated down to less than 1%.

Although this rule is widely acknowledged, it is frequently ignored in practice. In many cases, finder's fees for small deals run as much as 10% for a $2 million or $3 million deal.

Contracts themselves need not be written by a lawyer. Just write a sensible agreement that says:

I hereby engage _____ as an agent to find this company an acquisition or financing for a project. We are willing to pay _____ contingent on the consummation of the deal. This is a commitment letter.

Recommended for finders: Be choosy about whom you present with an interesting deal. People do not want to go into deals that have been peddled around too much.

Source: Robert P. Beshar, an attorney practicing at 63 Wall St., New York 10005.

Going into Competition With Your Employer

If you do not have a contract that prohibits you from going into competition with your current employer, there is no problem in doing so after you quit or get fired, providing you don't use trade secrets or other confidential information.

However, if you take time off during work hours or in other ways break the basis of the sound employer-employee relationship, you could find yourself on the losing side of a lawsuit if you make your former boss bitter enough.

Here are some rules to follow to ensure a clean break: Spend your own time getting to know the market and looking for financing and office space for your new business. If these things must be done during work hours, send your spouse or trusted friend or relative to investigate. Remember, you must resign before you actually begin to compete.

Avoid:

Using your employer's telephone for your business.

Saying to colleagues: We are the team that makes this corporation really function. Why don't we leave and do it ourselves?

Telling customers your employer is bad, and you will do a better job for them when you're on your own.

Destroying customer lists or other records.

If you have a covenant in your employment contract not to compete, it may not be enforceable anyway. A few years ago, the highest court in New York State decided: Unless your services are unique and extraordinary, (for example, the services of doctors, lawyers, entertainers), a covenant not to compete will be enforced only to prevent misappropriation of confidential information.

Most states have a strong policy against enforcing broad noncompete covenants, especially when they appear to deprive you of your livelihood, are too broad in geographic area, or cover too long a period of time.

Courts will be most sympathetic if you leave your job involuntarily. They are only a bit less sympathetic if you leave on your own.

If you have signed a noncompete covenant and you think you want to compete, see a lawyer first. It's better to pay for legal advice than risk a lawsuit.

Problem: Even though the former employer can't enforce the noncompete clause, he may prevent you from getting another job. Your prospective employer may fear he will be sued. This can be very troublesome even if the former employer can't win.

Use Accrued Pension To Start Your Own Business

Employee Getum has "had it" working for his present boss. He wants out now, he has $100,000 coming from his employer's quali-

fied plan, and he is entitled to and qualifies for lump-sum treatment. Getum finds out the tax bite on the $100,000, if distributed this year, would be $35,000; he needs $50,000 to finance his new business. What to do?

The steps would be as follows:

1. Getum forms a new corporation, Go-Getum Co.

2. Go-Getum Co. adopts a qualified profit-sharing plan.

3. The distribution—the full $100,000—from Getum's former employer's qualified plan is rolled over to the new Go-Getum plan.

4. The new plan would have a provision to allow loans to be made to participants in an amount not to exceed 50% of the participant's vested interest, or $50,000.

5. The new profit-sharing plan would loan $50,000 to Getum to be repaid over five years at 11% interest per annum.

Obviously, the documentation from the new plan itself, the plan administrator's minutes describing and approving the loan, and the note payable by Getum to the profit-sharing trust must be impeccable in every detail.

Source: Irving L. Blackman, CPA, is a senior partner with Blackman, Kallick and Company, Ltd, Chicago, IL

Do You Really Want To Be an Entrepreneur?

Almost all of us play an entrepreneurial role at some time in our lives. (Most common: During courtship, when one has to sell oneself.)

Being a true entrepreneur, however, has a much deeper dimension. It's usually misunderstood.

Misconception: An entrepreneur is head of a small business. Fact: Our studies show that size and entrepreneurship share almost no spiritual kinship. The small-business person tends to be other-directed. He is sensitive to what the marketplace wants and operates accordingly.

The entrepreneur, on the other hand, is inner-directed. He has a great sense of personal mission. And he has unique need to achieve. Typically, he either wants to do something different or to do something conventional in a new way. Usually he seeks to make some statement through doing it. Entrepreneurs aren't in business for the fun of it, though that's what is commonly supposed. Nor are they in business primarily to make a lot money.

Misconception: Entrepreneurs need to demonstrate to the world that their new ideas have validity. The market place is a vehicle. Making money is vindication. Dollars are votes. Note: The late anthropologist, Margaret Mead, saw herself as an entrepreneur in the sense that she was selling her ideas to the world.

Misconception: Entrepreneurs are willing to take more risks than the rest of us. Certainly they realize that they will have to take some risks attempting to get a new idea across. But our research shows that entrepreneurs are not high-risk gamblers. They always opt for a moderate, rather than a high risk. Typical business-school graduates, on the other hand, think of reducing risk to an absolute minimum. They seek to find a workable pattern and they run it at full steam. The entrepreneur notoriously loses interest when an idea has launched and is running along smoothly.

A true definition of an entrepreneur comes closer to: A poet, visionary, or packager of change. Pollsters find that no more than 3% to 5% of the population really desires change. (Fortunately, however, behind them comes another 20% who are emulators or followers of a good new idea.)

Historically, entrepreneurs flourish about one-third of the way through an era of social change. What happens is that change is in the wind and the entrepreneur's sensitive antennae pick that up and want to harness and run with it. In today's postindustrial society, for example, most entrepreneurs are concerned with the extension of human potential and the whole area of information storage, retrieval, and transmission.

Typically, the entrepreneur enters from a negative stance. That is, he doesn't like the status quo or can't make it work for him. This provides impetus to go all out to establish something better. (A medical analogy: While a bright surgeon might strive to develop a new operation or perfect a surgical technique, an entrepreneurial doctor might turn to a whole new discipline, such as holistic medicine.)

Entrepreneurs often come from the periphery of a town or from a group that is somewhat removed from the society around them, even from the so-called "counterculture."

While entrepreneurs hear a different drummer, what distinguishes them from mere dreamers (of whom there are many) is the unique ability to both visualize and actualize or carry out an idea.

Entrepreneurs have an inextinguishable sense not only of what they want to do but of how they do it. They don't by any means all succeed. The best ones learn from their mistakes, pick themselves up, and keep forging ahead toward their goal. One thing they must learn: The marketplace, but more particularly the financial world, has its own rules. Entrepreneurs who can follow the well established codes of conduct and sustain their vision are the successful ones.

On a personal level, entrepreneurs (like politicians) derive satisfaction for most of their emotional needs from their work. Being so self-driven to accomplish their mission, they are often difficult to live with. Further, they are intolerant of anyone who does not share their vision. For an employee to steal from their fledgling operation, for example, is unthinkable and pardonable. By contrast, the average business head expects a certain amount of "shrinkage."

Small-business people individually may have some entrepreneurial traits. But as a group they are more likely to be actualizers, i.e., people who make things work. Case: Franchisees, who can take someone else's good new idea and get it going on a local level. Though these managers or actualizers may prosper, even build on or improve an entrepreneur's idea, few of them could have conceived the original vision.

Source: Robert Schwartz, director, the School for Entrepreneurs, Tarrytown Conference Center, Tarrytown, NY 10591.

Traps for First-Time Entrepreneurs

Like building a home for the first time, setting up one's first business can create many frustrations.

The most prevalent mistakes:

Being too dependent on others. This is particularly true of 40-year-old executive successes who leave the corporate umbrella with a little capital (say, $100,000) and grand dreams. Reason: They expect to have all the services and resources they had at their disposal at the corporation. Reality: They must do most things themselves. Every step of the plan will probably take longer.

Picking the wrong banker for the first loan. A bank can be a first-time entrepreneur's best source of venture capital. However, many first-timers turn to their neighborhood banker. Problem: Branch managers have no decision-making capacity. If cash flow isn't as good as projected, they may get nervous. What entrepreneurs need: A lending officer at the bank's downtown headquarters to assure the entrepreneurs that they will get cooperation if there is a positive long-term outlook despite periodic cash-flow problems.

Neglecting to write a business plan. Most entrepreneurs like to take action, not to write a business plan. Many prefer to farm the plan out or to hire a consultant to do it. The trap: If they let someone else do it, they are most likely giving up the guts of their business. Entrepreneurs are usually natural salespeople. They are the best at generating excitement about their business for bankers and venture capitalists, who say they want numbers but actually may be sold by an entrepreneur's enthusiasm. Solution: Read a book (preferably several) about business plans and get advice from an accountant. Have the accountant review the plan.

What goes into a business plan? A statement about your background and why you feel qualified to start your business. Attach your resume.

A brief decription of your proposed business. Include:

Legal form of the business.

Detailed background of the principals and their areas of expertise.

Nature of the business. Examples: The products or service it offers, where it's located, and what its primary and secondary markets are.

Demand for the product or service (based on your detailed market research and marketing plan).

How much business the firm has done already, or what orders it has on the books to date.

A statement about how your business is financed, including your personal financial statement. Describe how much you want to borrow and how much you will be investing from your personal savings, if any. Be clear about how the rate of return is measured. Indicate how the money will be used and how you can repay a loan based on various rates of return. Idea: You might want to use a computer package that makes those calculations and provides a model.

Summarize the business. Describe why you think it will be a success, and how you plan to operate and manage it. Point: Here's an opportunity to sell potential lenders, investors, key customers.

Other mistakes: Assuming all-around expertise. The entrepreneurs' forte is usually their own field. They are actualizers and visualizers. Professional managers are better at managing people. Essential: Once the business has taken off, the entrepreneur must find professional managers to take on the people-managing burden.

Selecting the wrong advisers. The most successful entrepreneurs find a personality fit among themselves and their lawyers, accountants, and bankers. Competence isn't everything. Personal style is important in business. While the entrepreneur must learn to talk the language (numbers and money) of bankers and accountants, the best key to a long-term relationship is whether these people fit in with his personal style.

Source: John Mancuso, president, The Center for Entrepreneurial Management, 311 Main St., Worcester, MA 01608.

A Quick Test of Entrepreneurial Potential

Ask yourself these questions if you are considering opening your own business:

1. Do you really have the motivation to do it?

2. Are you psychologically ready to take big risks?

3. Do you have the determination, patience, and courage to persevere?

4. Do you have high levels of intelligence and energy?

5. Were you a leader and organizer as a child?

6. Did your education prepare you for a little bit of everything?

7. Do you have a strong need to succeed, a desire for independence, and an objectivity about your strength and weaknesses?

8. Do you have enough of the right kind of experience?

Source: *Executive's Personal Development Letter.*

Questions to Ask Before You Buy A Small Business

How solid is the current customer base? Avoid any business that depends on strong customer loyalty to the current owner.

Will the current owner stay on for a few months to ease the transition? This helps transfer supplier and customer trust to the new owner and gives immediate assistance on unforeseen problems.

Was the initial planning effective? To evaluate this, look at lease terms, fixtures and equipment, recordkeeping, advertising, marketing, and site selection.

What were the start-up costs? Some sellers try to include these in the selling price. Basic rule: All one-time costs should be absorbed by the owner. Exception: The sale price should reflect the current market value of fixtures and equipment.

What mistakes did the founder make? Could they eventually kill the business?

Problem: Owners selling small, privately held companies often put the wrong value on assets or expenses (or both) for many reasons. Watch out for:

Unreported income on financial reports. Small-business owners have many opportunities to evade taxes.

Hidden expenses: Overly generous benefit packages, payments to family members for nominal services, etc.

Pay scales above or below market rates. Typical situation is a teenage worker receiving pay below the minimum wage standard while friendly officials look the other way.

Property assessed at out-of-date values. Once the business is sold, the property is likely to be reassessed.

Unnecessary assets that can be sold without affecting income. Examples: A vacant lot not needed for expansion, a recreational vehicle carried as a business expense.

The assigned value of family labor. In some cases, it's exorbitant. In others, it's far too low.

Typical outcome after adjustments: Reported income is lowered and the book value of the company rises. Result: Both the buyer and the seller have less room to bargain.

Source: John H. Hand and William P. Lloyd, Auburn University, writing in *MSU Business Topics* and *Straight Talk About Small Business* by Kenneth J. Albert, McGraw Hill Co., New York.

Before Buying A Retail Operation

Don't rely on the store's own financial records. Insist on seeing sales tax records and federal tax returns.

Feel the business pulse in the neighborhood.

Find out why store is for sale.

Spend several days in the store. Note volume and customer profile.

Estimate remodeling and redecorating expenses.

If the image of the operation is to be changed, determine whether inventory will be as valuable as it was to the exisitng owner.

Source: *Small Business Reports*

Advice from the World's Best Salesman

The thing to remember is that when customers come in, they are at least a little scared. They're scared of parting with money, because it comes hard. They all think they're not going to get what they want at a price they ought to pay. But they need what you have to sell.

This means that every day of our working lives, we're in a kind of war. That is, they think we are trying to put something over on them and we think they're wasting time.

Your job is to get them over the desire to hide from you. That's the first thing, because you can't sell a scared person. Look into your own feelings. Are you sore because he interrupted a joke? Does he remind you of somebody you don't like? You've got a war on your hands with your customer, and a war with your own feelings. Don't forget why you're both here: To make a sale that is beneficial to both of you.

The most important thing you can learn is the Law of 250. Everyone knows 250 people in his life. Just ask any wedding or funeral director. He'll tell you that is the average number of people who'll show up. Many of my sales come from people telling other people about me. We're not talking about love or friendship; we are talking hard business. When you turn away one customer with an angry remark or a bad attitude, you're turning away the 250 prospects that he knows.

Satisfied customers are the best bet for future sales. I guard my card file of customers with my life. Put down on those file cards everything you learn about a person: Kids, hobbies, travels, whatever you learn when you talk with a customer. Then when you are trying to sell, lead the prospect into subjects that take his mind off what you're trying to do, which is to trade him your product for his money.

Personalized mail is the best thing that anybody can receive from a salesperson. I used pieces put out by the manufacturers for many years. But now I have my own mailing pieces and I know they get opened and read. Why? Because I fool them. I send each of my customers 12 pieces of mail a year. And each one is a different color and in a different shape envelope. They can't easily identify it as advertising mail. But each one has a very softsell message in there. Important: Don't send your mail out the same time the bills go out.

Use birddogs. I tell every customer who buys from me that I'll give him $25 if he sends in someone who buys a car. I pay out $14,000 to birddogs each year. That means about 550 sales from birddogs, or about one-third of my total. The rule is: Keep your promises and pay. Don't stall on paying a birddog—even if there's a question about whether he did send in the customer.

Take the customer's side if there are any service problems or other complaints after the product is delivered. I fight for him with the mechanics, the dealer, and with the factory. This is the way to make a customer a believer.

It's most important to smile when you don't feel like it. Reason: It's much better to have people ask, "What's he got to smile about?" than to have them notice a long face. Another way to send out good vibes: Share only your positive thoughts, and suppress any negative, unhappy ones. What to avoid: Depressing topics. (Example: News stories that deal only with crimes and violence).

The best smile: The full-faced kind, which includes crinkling around your eyes and wrinkling of the nose. How to develop one: Practice by giving everybody you meet your best smile. (Lips-only smiles look forced and false and don't warm anybody.)

The technique: Even when you're worried,

think of reasons to smile. Before any situation, concentrate on erasing a frown by recalling a happy memory or things for which you can feel thankful. Rule: Worrisome thoughts and good smile don't mix. It is possible to develop a habitually warm smile by working at it. Bonus: A genuine smile can offset the damage done to facial expression by years of scowling and worry.

The chuckle or outright laugh is the most contagious form of a smile. A good laugh takes practice. How to do it: Turn the next smile into a light chuckle. Next time you feel like having an outright belly laugh, let it out. Point: A hearty, uninhibited laugh is immensely appealing, and it makes you feel better, too.

Ways to practice smiling:

Stand in front of a mirror and smile with your whole face. It may feel silly and cause you to laugh out loud, but that can only help.

Put a smile in your voice. How: Smile when you speak to people over the phone.

Source: Joe Girard, the world's greatest salesman, according to the *Guinness Book of World Records,* and author, *How to Sell Anything to Anybody,* Simon & Schuster, New York.

Selling Your Business

When selling a business to another firm, the best written contract offers less protection than good personal chemistry between the seller and the chief executive of the buying firm. A sound relationship cannot be guaranteed in a contract.

What a contract can do: Protect your interests when top management of the buying company is replaced or if sudden financial or personal pressures arise after the closing.

Best approach: Draft the contract you want when making the deal.

The acquisition contract. When it's useful: When you have some financial or emotional stake in the future of the company being sold.

What the contract should cover:

Authority over the day-to-day operations of the company being sold.

Specific limits on the amount of cash flow from the company being sold to the buying company. It's essential to protect a cash generator, unless there is an easy way to get it back downstream again.

Limits on what the buying company can charge for administrative services such as attorney's fees, auditing and other costs. Base the limits on your own company's experience.

Nonrecurring charges (such as damage awards) that are not to be deducted when calculating the earnings of the firm being sold. It's essential when a higher purchase price depends on the firm's future earnings.

Limits on interest charges on loans from the parent company. Alternative: Establish the right to negotiate for better terms from outside lenders.

Language. The purpose of representation and warranty language in acquisition contracts is to avoid potential problems down the road. What terms to consider:

Limited liability up to an amount no greater than the purchase price. What to avoid: The seller gets $2 million for the firm but there remains a product liability claim for $5 million. The seller should carefully avoid any position where he might owe the buyer money some time in the future.

Insulation from liabilities unknown at the closing, even if the condition existed previously.

Example: The sale is closed on December 31. On January 2, a suit is filed claiming that defective merchandise caused injuries the previous November. The buyer will try to tag the seller with the liability, but he can't if your contract is properly protective.

A deductible from any liabilities that are owed. For example, you are not liable for the first $50,000 of any adverse judgment.

Nonaccountability for tax liabilities when they are a result of shifting income from one year to another in a pattern recommended by the seller's accountants.

Accounting methods used to compute earnings of the seller company for earn-out purposes should be no more stringent than those the seller company used when independent.

Example: The buyer institutes last-in, first-out (LIFO) inventory valuation when the seller previously used first-in, first-out. This lowers the tax liability and earnings. Solution: Compute the earn-out by using the FIFO method.

A credit against liabilities that's created by any assets unknown at the time of the closing.

Example: As a result of a class-action lawsuit the firm being sold participated in as plaintiff, it gets $1 million from a group of suppliers. That money can be used to offset any future liabilities.

The right to independent counsel of your own choosing.

The employment contract. When it's useful: The buying company wants you to stay in charge. What to negotiate for:

Authority over day-to-day operations when not reflected in the purchase contract itself.

Termination for cause only, except in the event of death or disability.

The greatest freedom possible to work for yourself or others.

A lump-sum payment of any money due on the employment contract if employment is terminated with or without cause.

Incentive payments for improved performance calculated by uniform accounting methods.

Source: Arthur H. Rosenbloom of Standard Research Consultants, 345 Hudson St., New York 10014.

8
Success Strategies

Assessing Your Own Success

Success in business is usually assessed in terms of economic performance: Income, profits, borrowing power. But as individual high achievers reach high levels in these measurable areas, they look for more challenging situations where money is not necessarily the ultimate goal. They seek situations that offer greater stimulation to their ingenuity or managerial skills. The problem: Measuring their performance.

The best measure: The satisfying sense that all your energies and skills are being tested. Successful business people at every level can describe experiences where they came out feeling really good about the way they handled a situation, and where the monetary aspect was purely secondary.

Reason: Success is a process, not a fixed state. That's true for Olympic champions as well as business executives. A motivated person plays the game because the game itself provides a welcome opportunity for self renewal.

Spur: Once you are in the game, you have to play to win.

Paradox: If you focus on winning, you will lose. Instead: Concentrate on how to go about achieving your objective. Focus on the process.

High performance (and your own recognition that you are performing at a high level) most often happens when you reduce intellectual control of the process. Signs of success:

Work is going well almost in spite of your own efforts.

A feeling that luck is with you. Reason for this performance elation: The ego involvement that leads a high achiever to compete in the first place subsides. Natural drives and talents take over. Result: A feeling that everything is falling into place.

Challenge: Finding the optimum level of stimulation. Beyond a certain point, the pressure is tension-producing and self-defeating. Solution: Self-awareness. Learn to recognize and monitor your own states of tension, alertness, and anxiety. Know: What feels best, and how those good feelings correlate with good performance.

Goal: A balance between a low-key, non-stimulating environment and a situation where you are clearly over your head.

Pace yourself: Truly effective high achievers are able to monitor themselves to achieve a level of performance and a degree of satisfaction that are best for them.

Dealing with obstacles: The skill is learning to get around things that interfere with maximum performance, in not allowing tension-producing situations to intrude. Key: Self-confidence about your own intuition and instincts, even when they may differ from those of others.

Source: Dr. Ari Kiev, a psychiatrist who conducts stress-management workshops for many high-level executives and is the psychiatrist on the U.S. Olympic Committee's council on sports medicine, 150 E. 69 St., New York 10021.

How Solid Is Your Network?

It's not what you know, but who you know. This saying still holds true.

In order for networking to be effective, people must decide what they want from their contacts: Money, power, or fame. Then seek contacts most useful in that area. Expect your services and contacts to be used as well.

The three focuses of networking:
1. Giving and getting support.
2. Exchanging information.
3. Doing business.

Once you've decided on your goals, make a list of 100 contacts. Rank them in four groups.

Group A. Ten vital contacts whose aid you need. You should contact them within the year.

Group B. These contacts may be able to help you in three to five years from now. See them periodically.

Group C. Not terribly important, but make a note to keep in touch with these contacts. It is possible they can help, but it's hit or miss. (Probably 75% of your contacts fall into this category.)

Group D. Cross them off your list. These contacts not only can't help, they can hurt your career.

Questions to ask yourself to evaluate your networking system:

If I got promoted tomorrow, who are three people more advanced than I am in the business world that I would call? Who are three people on my level and on a level below me?

If I got stranded on a trip, either business or pleasure, who are three people I could call to wire me $300?

If you find your own network unsatisfactory, be prepared to invest a lot of time and money for lunches and other social occasions to establish new contacts. Only people who take time for others, do favors, and establish rapport are likely to get help from others.

Networking is not a substitute for skill. Unless you can demonstrate an expertise for good work, people will be unwilling to help.

Source: Alina Novak, Networks Unlimited, Inc., a group set up to help people to increase their contacts to achieve career goals, 150 W. 52 St., New York 10019.

Friendship and Success

Friends nourish our emotional life. But some people have no friends and don't know it. Men often can't tell the difference between friends and acquaintances, sustaining friendships and empty ones. To some people, "friends" are anybody they don't actively dislike.

In a good relationship, both parties experience a positive exchange of energy. Do a cost/benefit analysis on relationships that take up a good deal of your time and energy. Stop seeing the people whose company produces a drained, exhausted feeling.

Friendship allows for giving and for accepting. "Friends" who give but don't allow themselves to accept anything in return often give with resentment, or are giving loans rather than gifts. The "interest" may be to create a sense of obligation in the receiver, or a sense of superiority in the giver. Input needs to match output. Authentic giving is possible only when authentic receiving is allowed, too.

Questions to ask:

Are our value systems compatible? (Or, at least, are they different in a way that is easily acceptable?)

Are we interested in each other's activities? Can we talk about things and ideas?

Can we turn to each other for comfort? Have fun? Feel free to express anger and affection?

Do we respond to each other straightforwardly?

Do we confront each other over controversial personal issues?

Do we derive strengths from our meetings?

Choosing friends:

Typical mistake: We choose friends exclusively among those who do and think exactly what we do and think. These confluent friendships provide no opening on the world, no abrasion against our frame of reference, which might lead to growth. Example: The executive who is working himself to death has no one around to call him a fool because all his "friends" are doing the same.

Men need to understand the importance of man/man friendships. They must learn how to develop close, non-sexual friendships with women, too.

Zero-based budgeting:

Examine honestly whether existing relationships are still supportive. If not, housecleaning and replacement are in order.

A spurt of personal or professional growth usually means outgrowing friends who anchor in old behaviors and outlooks on life.

When making changes—for example, seeking to be straighter in your expression of feelings—seek friendships with people who are further along in the same direction. You don't better your game with people who play less well than you do.

Using friends:

Friendship implies a system of mutual support. "Using" each other is positive so long as the utility value of the friendship is mutually available, clearly stated, and willingly given.

Men deprive themselves of friends by not recognizing them as a support system and by not using them, especially in times of personal crisis. Reason: They tend to limit contact to the rational (superficial) level rather than sharing emotionally. They talk about "things," but not about themselves or about problems that pain them deeply. ("My job is too big for me, and my boss is noticing it.") ("My wife has been sick with cancer for three years and sometimes I wish she'd die.") ("I'm drinking too much.") ("My father just died and I'm scared of growing old, too.") Or, if they do, they mention them only in passing, neither expecting nor eliciting a genuine response. Some emotional outlets can only be provided by friendship.

The bottom line:

Review the portfolio of friends in which you are investing. It is not full enough if you:

Feel alone and cut off when under personal pressure.

Confide mostly in strangers.

Cry or feel sad for others, for example, while watching movies.

Remember, the quickest way to have old friends is to make new ones.!

Source: Gisele Richardson, president, Richardson Management Associates, 2162 Sherbrooke St. W., Montreal, Quebec, H3H 1G7.

How Daydreaming Helps You Succeed

Fantasizing need not be idle woolgathering. Used as mental rehearsals, fantasies have practical payoffs. They can substitute for physical practice when acquiring a skill. Example: Researchers find that individuals who imagine themselves skiing well actually perform better on the slopes.

Three useful applications:

Coping fantasies. Faced with a difficult interview or sales presentation, imagine all the possible questions and answers. Fantasize yourself responding and being alert, relaxed, and effective.

Innoculation fantasies. To help reduce

stress when a decision entails major costs or risks, project yourself mentally into the future. Explore your reactions to the best and worst possible outcomes of the decision. Also: Fantasize how you will overcome setbacks. The fantasy may reveal alternatives you might not have consciously considered.

Self-confidence fantasies. To cure bouts of low self-esteem, invoke past situations that you have handled well. Observe yourself performing skillfully. Use those images as guides for present and future performances.

Recommended: Pack the mental rehearsals with details. Hear the questions and answers. And see the other characters and their surroundings. Keep fantasies positive.

Source: *Turning Around: The Behavioral Approach to Managing People*, by Beverly A. Potter, AMACOM, New York.

Breaking out of A Career Pigeonhole

Technical specialists who want to move toward more general responsibilities should:

Train a replacement. It helps the specialist avoid becoming to valuable to move.

Drop jargon and buzzwords. Ask nonspecialists to read reports and memos. What they don't understand, management won't understand.

Become visible. Run seminars for other managers. Volunteer for assignments. Goal: Become known as versatile and effective.

Develop general management skills. Delegate details.

Source: *Institutional Investor.*

Changing Careers

Fred Papert left PKL Companies (the successor to Papert, Koenig, Lois, the advertising agency he helped found) in 1977 to become president of the 42nd Street Development Corp., a private, not-for-profit development and urban-planning company. Papert offers these views on career-changing, how nonprofit motivation compares with business life, and what idealism is worth in the marketplace.

One immediate result of the change has been a greater degree of measurable accomplishment and autonomy.

Example: It's possible to look at a building owned by 42nd St. Development and say: We're going to convert it to a theater or museum. Then either we do it or don't. To achieve something now, it's not necessary to listen first to dozens of contesting suggestions and plans, as it was in the advertising business.

Why that's a problem: Zeal and a sense of mission are crucial to accomplishing any goal. But too much zeal and mission don't work in business. Committing yourself completely to a proposal that's at odds with the ideas of others (who are just as committed to their opinions) is a losing effort.

New-career advantages: Accomplishments are more enduring, and they happily accord with personal values. There is a certain element of risk in starting out anew. But risk is one of the appeals in any adventure.

Disadvantages: That same risk, of course, remains double-edged. But trading-off with funding sources, whose approval you need, is not so very different from dealing with the conflicting forces in the business world.

To make a career change work:

Focus concentration and will on the goals.

Understand that everything is risky. It's more rewarding in the long run to take risks for meaningful goals than to play it safe.

Source: Fred Papert, president, 42nd Street Development Corp.

A Midlife Switch To Another Career

A major career change during midlife is no aberration. It's now a fact of life for many Americans. One of every three workers is likely to switch careers in a five-year period. The rate climbs higher among executives and other overachievers. More than 40% of several hundred persons sampled in *Who's Who* had undergone a radical change in their work field.

The most likely time for change: Late thirties to early forties age period. Reasons: Midcareer or midlife crises, which lead individuals to reexamine their lives and jobs, are prevalent. At this time individuals are trying to bring personal values into harmony with their work identity. Early symptoms of upcoming change: Divorce, which forces a rethinking of aims and priorities. Entering psychotherapy, which indicates that a person is ready for change.

There's no pattern. Corporate executives, government officials, and academics may start up businesses, venture into new careers, or plunge into the arts. Freelancers, such as filmmakers and writers, may opt for the material success offered by corporations or commercial enterprises.

Career changers are people who are comfortable with risk—switching professions is a risky undertaking. Interviewers find that most career changers (besides freelancers) accept a drop in income and find themselves working harder than before. Family strains and divorce are common at this time.

Bottom line: Career changers report greater enthusiasm and vitality.

Source: *The Big Switch,* by Rochelle Jones, McGraw-Hill Book Co., New York.

Looking Like A Winner

Some people have an unmistakable aura of success because they've really made it. But those on the way up can look like winners if a few basic tactics are followed.

Handling yourself in company:

Don't be cheap. Avoid undertipping or ducking a round of drinks.

Stay current. Read the right papers and mag-azines. And never attend a social gathering without being prepared with something to contribute to the conversation.

Meet important people. Look for chances to make the right contacts and join the right groups, i.e., professional associations, clubs, charities, and so on. Go all out to meet the right people. Don't be bashful.

Be prompt. Try to answer correspondence within 24 hours. It gives the impression of being on top of the job.

Appearances can be just as vital:

Dress well. Go for quality over quantity. Plan ahead. And dress according to what you have to do or whom you have to see.

Act like you belong. Whether you're in a boardroom or at the White House, don't gawk, whisper, or look down.

Look people in the eye. When you do, you automatically take the lead in a conversation. When you don't, you're letting someone else take the lead.

Fatal flaw: Don't be pretentious, untrustworthy, or obnoxious, because you'll make people think you're manipulating the situation. It's tough to get ahead when people can't stand you.

Source: J. Clifton Lundberg, executive vice-president, PRC Technical Applications, 7600 Old Springhouse Rd., McLean, VA 22102.

Are Good Looks a Plus For Executives' Careers?

Recent finding: Being attractive probably helps men land managerial jobs, but it may hinder women.

More than 40% of a group of Columbia University students in the MBA program said in a recent study that they would hire the best-looking man among four equally-qualified managerial candidates. Only 13% of the students picked the least attractive of the four.

Among the women candidates, the prettiest fared worst. Only 13% of the future MBAs chose the best-looking woman. Some 30% preferred the least attractive.

Interpretation: The attractive men were judged to be more masculine, a quality that rates high among managers. But the pretty women were viewed as more feminine, which managers often confuse with passive, indecisive, unstable behavior.
Source: *Management Psychology.*

Success and Body Size

• Fat men command more money and respect than thin ones. A study of 2,356 men, aged 51 to 65, compared income to body weight. Result: The heavy men surveyed earned slightly more than those who are slimmer. Edge: Their bulk conveys a sense of power, strength and capability, which win respect and money.
Source: Robert A. McLean, University of Kansas, writing in *The American Journal of Public Health.*

• Tall men have the edge in business over short men. Generally, tall people are in the most visible and important positions and are starting out with higher salaries and comparably higher job status. This tendency to look at size rather than merit is also true for women in business. The traditional feminine ideal of a petite stature doesn't hold up in business. There, taller women have a distinct advantage. Height, management feels, gives them credibility and has the mixed advantage of intimidating some men, particularly those who are shorter.
Source: *The Height of Your Life.* Little, Brown & Co., Boston.

Dressing for Success

Best advice for males is still to emulate the boss: Conservative-looking suit, white shirt (pale pastels if your cohorts wear them), matching tie. Muted colors connote trust, upper-middle-class status. Black, navy, pinstripe, and chalk-striped suits exude power, competence, authority. Beware: Loud pastels (gaudy); pink (effeminate); gold, green-gray (unflattering); light blues, gray-beige (detracts from presence: You're more likely to be liked than respected). Also out: European cuts, turtlenecks, clashing colors that hint of sloppiness, sports clothes (save them for sports). Buying: Buy for more than one occasion (e.g., blazer with two pairs of slacks, one for business, one for evening wear). Avoid styles or colors that threaten to become overpopular.

Projecting a Confident Image

Many contemporary guides to projecting a powerful personality emphasize packaging. Included are the importance of conservative dress, office location and arrangement, and behavioral gambits designed to place others on the defensive.

But the only valid image of power issues from within. It is based upon a personal sense of worth and security. And it is portrayed consistently by body and voice. Fortunately, efforts to modify outward body language have the added benefit of shoring up inner self-esteem. Among behavioral attributes to examine for possible change are:

Eye contact. The most important aspect is how you respond when others challenge you with a stare or prolonged gaze. Powerful individuals aren't discomfited by the seconds passing as they look into someone's eyes. If you have difficulty, practice with a spouse or close friend. Ask them to catch you unaware.

Space. Try not to move away or flinch when people draw too near, or when they touch you. Take a deep breath, imperceptibly, if you need to force yourself to relax.

Posture. Stand tall, and walk with confidence. Don't try to fake it. If you have poor posture, pursue training (with professional help) in movement, dance, or athletics.

Gestures. Powerful individuals usually keep their hands still or make gestures with their hands and body that are meaningful and deliberate.

Voice. It should be pitched comfortably low and resonate from the chest. If your voice is a problem, find a good teacher. Unaided efforts will sound artificial. Speaking speed, too, is important. Aim at a rhythm that is fractionally slower than normal. It should not be too fast (which can suggest either urgency or the erratic) or too slow (which can indicate deliberateness but also indecisiveness).

Highly recommended: No one can successfully evaluate all of these qualities by himself. Get candid, close friends to rate you on a scale of one to ten in each category. Work on the lowest ratings first. Continue until all approach a ten rating.

Source: *Body Politics: How to Get Power With Class,* by Julius Fast, Tower Publications, New York.

Understanding People Better Through 'Body Language'

Watching people's actions can bring you a lot closer to the truth than merely listening to what they say (which might be a cover-up). This is the "science" of kinesics, or "body language." It can be very revealing. Some outward expressions of inner feelings:

Openness: Open hands, unbuttoned coat.

Defensiveness: Arms crossed, sideways glance, touching-rubbing nose, rubbing eyes, buttoned coat, drawing away.

Insecurity: Pinching flesh, chewing pen, thumb over thumb, biting fingernail.

Cooperation: Upper body in sprinter's position, open hands, sitting on edge of chair, hand to face gestures, unbuttoning coat.

Confidence: Steepled hands, hands behind back, back stiffened, hands in coat pockets with thumb out, hands on lapels of coat.

Nervousness: Clearing throat, "whew" sound, whistling, smoking, pinching flesh, fidgeting, covering mouth, jiggling money or keys, tugging ears, wringing hands.

Frustration: Short breaths, "tsk" sound, tightly clenched hands, wringing hands, fist-like gestures, pointing index finger, rubbing hand through hair, rubbing back of neck.

Winning at Office Politics

Before mapping out a strategy for promotion, a manager must first discover what qualities the company actually rewards. Frequently, these values are unspoken and pertain to the personal style of management.

To discover the unspoken values:

Review the public relations releases about superiors. If, for example, civic organizations or country clubs are prominently mentioned, these activities are valued.

Ask competitors what they perceive. Often, outside people see what insiders don't or can't.

Tune in to office gossip. Find out who the local opinion-makers are, and exchange information with them every now and then. Note: It's better to be on the fringe of several cliques than closely associated with one. Key barometer to check: Current number of job hunters. If many people are looking for a new job, security for everyone is reduced. However, when a manager knows his boss is going to leave, he can move fast to apply.

Look for a mentor. A retiree is best, because he is outside the mainstream of office politics and can chronicle what top managers did to become part of the charmed circle. Active mentors are useful, but also dangerous. Reason: They like to have legions of loyal followers within the company. If anything happens to them, the political fallout can negatively affect their followers, too. The best kind of mentor: One who not only does favors but teaches.

What to do once the unspoken values are discovered:

An aura of integrity is the single most important key to getting ahead. Common problem:

191

Many young employees try so hard to get ahead that they turn everyone off. Point: The fastest way to get undermined by peers is to play up to the boss.

Don't mimic the boss. If anyone's style should be mimicked, it's his boss, the person who can help most politically. Common sense: If the boss and most employees have a master's in business administration degree, the MBA is likely to be an unspoken requisite for getting ahead, although superiors may deny it.

How to handle political problems:

When the boss gives a pointless assignment, do some work, and return it with a detailed report outlining why it won't work. Ask for more direction. Reason: The boss can bow out gracefully and won't feel threatened.

When to go over your boss' head: Only when otherwise there will be an obviously horrendous impact on operations, or the company clearly will get a public black eye. Caution: Going to a boss' superior to complain is extremely risky politics.

What to do if the boss feels threatened. Boost his career whenever possible. If the boss is competent, speak well of him in the hope he will be promoted, making room for you.

How to get ahead of the boss: If he moves ahead, get his job, then jump again by transferring to another company. Then return to the original company at a level above the former boss. Note: Don't be afraid to switch jobs to get ahead. Frequently, it's the only way to get recognized. A person who keeps up his trade contacts can switch frequently without getting a bad reputation. Only those who are hired through personnel departments should limit their moves to once every two years. Advice: Stay at a new job only as long as it is mutually advantageous.

Politically dangerous situations:

When there's a reorganization. Reason: All the power lines are cut, and no one can promise job security or promotion. What to do: The moment there is talk of a reorganization, start looking for another job.

When there's a deterioration in the company's market position unrelated to a general recession.

When top management is old and the rest of the staff is young. Indication: If there are no middle-management jobs to be promoted into, it usually indicates that company policy is to go outside for top managers, not to promote from within.

Source: Marilyn Moats Kennedy, Head of Career Strategies, 2672 Eastwood St., Evanston, IL 60201, and author of *Office Politics* and *Career Knockouts,* Follett Publishing, Chicago.

How to Cope With a Tough Boss

Hard-driving chief executive officers and managers may be monsters to subordinates and treasures to their bankers and their stockholders. At best, such taskmasters can spur subordinates to unexpected levels of performance, adding breadth to executive capacities. At their worst, they are arbitrary, tyrannical, and deliberately cruel. The physical and psychological strain of working for the bullying supervisor takes its toll both on professional and family life.

Guidelines for coping:

Accommodate the boss' weaknesses and strengths. If his long suit is organization, avoid mistakes in that area. If the boss is compulsive about punctuality and schedules, don't provoke his rage with tardiness and long lunches. Do develop strengths to compensate for his weaknesses, for example, in finance, marketing, research and development. It will make you more indispensable.

Swallow your pride. The tough boss is often temperamental and frequently a bit sadistic. Some particularly enjoy humiliating executives in the presence of peers, subordinates, and even family. Keep calm. Maintain eye contact. Rise above the boss' tantrum. Later, let the witness to your dressing down see you looking relaxed and cheerful, giving the appearance that it's all part of the game.

Go for the top dollar. Ill-natured bosses expect to pay for their self-indulgence. Don't let yourself be browbeaten into settling for less.

Master facts. Practice keeping all data relevant to your job in mind and rehearse reciting them on demand. The super-tough boss often prefers grilling you for information rather than listening to your presentation.

Prepare your family. Make sure spouse and children know you may be summoned away from vacations or that you may have less free time to spend with them. Don't let the unpleasant work atmosphere spill over into your family life. Sharing your anxieties and miseries with your family may put a particular burden on your children.

Don't expect praise for accomplishment. Super-tough bosses are never satisfied. Keep records and some proof of your achievements, for example, in surpassing quotas. Don't let the boss' disgruntlement diminish the satisfaction you derive from your own excellence.

Don't neglect your own development. Some tyrannical employers pay high salaries to treat talented executives as flunkies. Set your own work challenges within the organization. Don't let the boss crowd your skills.

Keep your options open. Super-tough bosses generate high staff turnover. Always know something about the next possible job.

Don't burn your bridges. When you quit or are fired, don't yield to the temptation of venting your anger.

Bosses Who Keep Their Distance

Bosses have the same problem as any other person with position, wealth, or power. They are never sure why people choose to relate to them in a positive manner. Is a compliment sincerely felt? Or is it a gambit to gain favor?

Background: Being at the apex of the organizational pyramid, bosses have limited access to the rank and file. Some heighten this isolation by keeping their distance. They don't prize input from their employees. And entrepreneurial bosses are often natural loners. Result: Human contact is limited to people from whom favorable support is neither sought nor accepted.

Ways of breaking through to the boss are often formidable. Best approach: Common sense.

Insight: The boss is a human being, too. See every situation in this light: If you were at work, how would you react to the individual? If you would compliment a colleague, do the same for the boss.

This applies even when the boss makes a positive criticism. If that comment or tip helps you complete a task faster and better, state your appreciation. Compliments should not be interpreted by the boss as buttering-up unless they are excessive or effusive.

How a boss can promote the proper atmosphere:

Be accessible. Show that you can be one of the gang. Caution: Don't overdo it.

Demonstrate willingness to accept the good feelings of employees. How: Thank people when they say something good about you. Don't discount your achievements, and never belittle an employee over a kind word.

Accept an employee's praise so long as you discern no ulterior motive. Some people enjoy conveying kind words. Don't deny them that pleasure.

Foster togetherness through office outings, parties, dinners. In a convivial atmosphere, the exchange of compliments becomes a natural and accepted transaction.

Source: Martin G. Groder, M.D., practicing psychiatrist and business consultant, Durham, NC, and author of *Business Games: How to Recognize the Players and Deal With Them*, Boardroom Books, Millburn, NJ

Criticizing the Boss

Be sure that:

Your superior can handle criticism.

Your relationship is strong enough to take the strain.

You choose a time when things are not hectic, and when there are not likely to be numerous interruptions of the discussion.

The criticism is phrased tactfully and objectively, possibly in the form of a specific suggestion for improvement in one area. It should be accompanied by a compliment about the manager's strength.

Source: *Supervisory Management.*

Are You a Workaholic?

Men and women who feel that everything in life is secondary to work are found in all occupations and in all social and economic classes.

Answer true or false to the following 10 questions to determine if you may be a work addict:

1. Am I a compulsive early riser?
2. When eating alone, do I usually read or work?
3. Do I make daily list of things to do?
4. Do I find it almost impossible to do nothing?
5. Am I energetic and competitive?
6. Do I regularly work on weekends and holidays?
7. Can I work anytime and anywhere?
8. Do I find it difficult to take vacations?
9. Do I dread retirement?
10. Do I truly enjoy my work?

True answers to eight of the ten questions suggest that you, too, might be a member of the ranks of workaholics.

Source: *Workaholics*, by Marilyn Machlowitz, Addison-Wesley Publishing Co., Reading MA.

Dealing with the Workaholic Boss

If your employer makes unreasonable demands on your personal time (for example, he expects you to work on weekends because he does), try to explain to him that you maintain your performance level by relaxing and enjoying your personal time.

If your boss says he understands and agrees with your position, but you still feel psychological pressure to consistently put in long hours at work, the best thing you can do for yourself is to start looking for another job.

Dealing With The Workaholic Employee

The workaholic not only doesn't know when to quit, he also doesn't know when (or why) to take a vacation.

His reasons:

Work is more fun.

So much is going on, or pending, that he simply can't leave.

There's nobody to replace him.

Problem: Far from being a boon to the boss, vacationless workaholics are truly counterproductive. At the point where return on their effort diminishes, that effort can lead to company-wide negative productivity.

Bottom line on workaholics:

They care more for activity than results. Their busy methods are less effective than the simpler, faster, better ways that are available.

They hang on to day-to-day control excessively. Good or bad, that kind of work is hard. They burn themselves out, leaving a gap in the work program not readily filled.

Their unrelenting demands for perfection, and the impossible-to-match example they set in working without a break (or even a pause), drives away good subordinates. Workaholics tend to get the good ones assigned to them because they create, at first, the impression of centers of productive activity. The company can ill afford to lose these promising employees.

What to do about workaholics:

Remember: These are basically very talented people. It's their methodology that's wrong, not their motivation or real value. Solution: Send them away from the arena for a while. How:

Make vacations, at least annually, mandatory. There should be no paid time in lieu of time off.

Train at least one worker in the workaholic's section to take over when he finally does take a vacation.

Try to reach him on an intellectual level, pointing out that work and play are two sides of the same coin.

Source: Robert Moskowitz, time manager, is an author and time management consultant at 6835 Claremore, San Diego, CA 92120.

Workaholics: What Makes Them Tick

Workaholism is caused by an internal set of mechanisms. It's triggered by a controlling parental figure who later becomes integrated as part of the adult's superego. At that point, it commands the internalized child within the adult: Please me, hurry up, work hard, be perfect.

Society and the controlling parent reward the workaholic for this type of compulsive behavior. He's never rebellious. Instead, the workaholic is very goal-oriented and a high achiever. Teachers love him. Parents are pleased. Bosses couldn't be happier. His operating philosophy: I'll prove myself to them even if it kills me. The parental image within him continues to direct his behavior, and he obeys. The pleasurable side of workaholic's personality, the "up" side of life, is stifled and ignored.

Workaholics create a very stressful environment and have the health problems commonly associated with a pressured life-style. They tend not to respect themselves physically. They don't exercise or eat properly, making themselves prime candidates for heart attacks, hypertension, ulcers and other stress-related diseases.

The workaholic is usually inefficient. He brings problems to a job, because he is driven rather than productively busy. The controlling parent in the workaholic won't give him permission to have fun, relax, play, or take care of his health.

Four grades of workaholics (four is the most compulsive personality):

Grade four: This is a type A personality.* He is grandiose, verging on manic.

Grade three: Constantly expresses self-doubt. Example: Why didn't I go to my daughter's graduation? He begins to question the value system learned from the controlling parent. He listens intently to other's complaints about himself.

Grade two: Always in conflict. He recognizes that compulsive behavior is wrong, but is always pulled between opposite poles. Example: He wonders whether or not to answer the phone while engaged in a pleasurable activity.

Grade one: He can't say no at work. He tends to be exploited until he learns to stand up for his rights.

Bottom line: Workaholics must learn to give themselves permission to live as well as to win.

*Type A personality: Has a particular set of personality drives, including an excessive competitive drive, deep-seated insecurities, and often free floating hostility.
Source: Dr. Lawrence Susser, 22 Pelham Rd., New Rochelle, NY 10805.

Handling Difficult People

Everyone has experienced it: Friends who always show up an hour late, colleagues who rarely shower or don't use deodorant, or subordinates who turn in work that looks like it was dipped in the cat box.

If these people are dull, incompetent, and graceless, we write them off as nuisances. But if they are creative or have a spark of talent, personal charm, or other endearing characteristic, we often want to work out the offensive interactions.

However, in most cases, people who consistently behave provocatively toward spouses, mates, colleagues, or employers are really relaying several messages. Those messages are both overt and hidden and often don't augur well for change.

The overt message: I am behaving in an irritating manner to annoy you and to get your attention. I am testing you. I expect you to reject me. However, sympathetic people who place some value on this individual's other traits may interpret it another way. The covert message: Prove that you love me by accepting me the way I am, and I may eventually reform.

The odds are, if you are interpreting such behavior as a plea for love, you are falling into a trap and letting yourself in for additional punishment. Reason: Beneath the superficial irritating message and the apparent need for love and support is a third: I expect our relationship to fail and for you to turn against me because I am unloveable.

If you don't meet the challenger's expectation of rejection, the person will escalate the rudeness, messiness, or other irritating behavior until you are finally forced to give up on the relationship.

Decide how much you want to put up with from such a person. What is the relationship's value to you? How much of your time and energy might you free up by working with or living with a cooperative person instead?

There are, of course, different degrees of this behavior. Rated on a scale of one to ten, a person who is a two might show some signs of this behavior, but it may be intermittent and acceptable. A ten is like coping with an alcoholic—a frustrating effort. This type of person may have had little or no positive attention as a child. Perhaps the only reaction from parents was when something went wrong, and then the child got negative attention. This may be the only kind of attention the prove-you-love-me person can now accept.

Best way to deal with it: Calmly talk about the manner in which you would like the person to behave. Don't wait until resentment collects and you lose your temper. Talk about your unwillingness to accept the status quo. Then set down the consequences to the relationship if the person doesn't choose to meet your expectations. Example: You will be fired from this job. Or: You will never get promoted again. Or: I won't go out with you any longer. Or: Look for another job. If the person hasn't lived up to the behavior goals within a specified time frame, take the promised action!

Source: Gisele Richardson, president, Richardson Management Co., 2162 Sherbrooke St., W., Montreal HRH 1G7, Quebec, Canada.

Working With A Hostile Colleague

Aim: To work together productively. Ways to avoid working at cross-purposes:

Use flattery. Say: Good idea! Expand on the idea to make clear the comment is sincere. Reason: A hostile person often lacks self-esteem, yet needs to feel important, even prestigious.

Resist any temptation to argue. That's where hostile people expect their attitude to lead. Taking the lure will damage efficiency.

Seek areas of agreement, even if it's exasperating. Reason: The alternatives to cooperation are even more troublesome.

Worst reaction to the hostile cohort: Humiliation.

Source: *Security World.*

Dealing with Abrasive Personalities

They are often high achievers, whose potential is undercut by poor relationships with subordinates, colleagues, and bosses. They have an overwhelming need for perfection.

Characteristics:

Intense competitiveness. Tries to dominate others in groups. All differences are taken as personal challenges. Takes charge of projects and is so possessive that all the others feel they can't make any contribution to the project.

Overcontrol. Organizes and supervises too much. Their need for control shows up in their inflexibility and inability to compromise. That's particularly so in abstract principles. To them, losing a little control is the same as losing total control.

Managing them:

Have them recognize the consequences of their behavior. Initiate frequent discussions that focus on the individual's traits. Important: Show the subtle forms the abrasive behavior takes and why people resent it.

Avoid the impulse to strike back when annoyed. Instead: Describe how the person's tactics are irritating. Then point out that they affect other people in the same way.

Center discussions on whether the abrasive person wants to succeed or not. Refuse to argue or respond to his attempts to challenge, philosophize, or debate.

Recognize that this kind of behavior is the result of vulnerable self-image and an extreme need for approval. Such people have to be steered into taking steps that ensure success, not rejection.

When helping these personalities improve their office relationships, give them feedback frequently. Reason: Abrasives often experience considerable anxiety as a result of being forced to move more slowly or because they can't show their competence in the old ways.

Early warning signs:

Watch out for charming personalities. Specifics: Be wary of those who seem to preen, dress perfectly, and pay inordinate attention to themselves.

Be alert to overprecision in speech and manner. An unusually high exactness betrays a great need to control.

Ask for descriptions of past work. Note how many times the word "I" is used and how closely the individual said he had to check the work of subordinates. How did he coach the others? Ask for his views on the limits and inadequacies of others. How does he see faults or human imperfections? How often does he report starting and finishing tasks without the help of others?

Source: Harry Levinson, writing in *The Harvard Business Review on Human Relations,* Harper and Row, New York.

Are You Abrasive?

Three or more yes answers mean that your behavior is abrasive. Six or more yes answers may indicate a serious problem.

Are you condescendingly critical? When talking of others in the organization, do you speak of "straightening them out"?

Do you need to be in full control? Does almost everything need to be cleared with you?

In meetings, do your comments take a disproportionate amount of time?

Are you quick to attack?

Are you reluctant to let others have the same privileges or prerequisites as you?

When talking about your activities, do you use the word "I" often?

Do subordinates admire you because you are strong and capable? Or because, in your organization, they feel strong and capable—and supported?

Do people speak of you as cold and distant when you really want them to like you?

Do you regard yourself as more competent than your peers? Than your boss? Does your behavior show it?

Are you preoccupied with acquiring symbols of status and power?

Keeping Aggressiveness Under Control

For many achievement-oriented individuals, healthy aggressiveness can get out of control. It might become an active, free-floating hostility. Prime symptoms: (1) Compulsive competitiveness, even in relaxed, recreational pursuits. (2) A need to view everything as a challenge. (3) Hypersensitivity that can translate even casual remarks into deadly affronts.

These individuals are often described as quick-tempered. Few of them can conceal the occasional sparks of belligerence that dart from their eyes. If it's a temperamental pattern, change should be attempted. Not only does excess hostility mar enjoyment of life, it also can indicate badly handled stress that, in turn, can harm health. A daily drill to diminish the overly hostile temperament includes:

Accept and constantly remind yourself that you *are* hostile. This can help prevent all but normal outbursts of temper.

Recognize and appreciate the wants and needs of your friends. Strive to check your own sensitivity to possible affronts.

Express thanks for services tendered to you. Do so clearly.

Check yourself when you get wrapped up in your own ideals and standards. Stop judging others solely on your own terms.

Start smiling at people as often as you can. Look for qualities in them that inspire your affection, admiration, and respect. A smile is one of the most powerful tools in overcoming a hostile personality.

Source: *Type A Behavior and Your Heart,* Fawcett Books, New York.

Grappling with Bad Moods

Negative thinking brings on bad moods. You convince yourself, and others, of the truth of your distorted thoughts. Result: A sense of gloom.

Solution: Learn to understand the different ways of thinking negatively. Then use this understanding to control your moods.

Examples of negative thinking:

All or nothing. If your performance falls short of perfect, you see yourself as a failure. But life is seldom all one way or the other.

Overgeneralization. A single negative event looms as a never-ending pattern of defeat.

Discounting the positive. Any compliment meets with the reaction, "They're just being nice." This self-discounting transforms a positive (praise) into a negative.

Magnification of your imperfections. Usually accompanied by minimizing good points.

Forced motivation. You motivate yourself by saying, "I must do that." This air of compulsion leads to guilt when you fall short of your expectations.

Recommended: When you sense yourself falling into these thinking traps, recognize the distortions they produce—and allow for them. This blunts bad moods.

Source: *Mood Therapy: The New Approach to Feeling Good,* by David D. Burns, M.D., William Morrow, New York.

Post-Peak Blues

When people are moving toward a goal, their lives have purpose. But when the task is completed, a sense of meaninglessness often sets in. The time of triumph becomes a time of mild depression. Ways to overcome these blues:

Make plans beyond the completion of the immediate goal.

Get involved with another activity immediately. Don't dwell on your blues.

Accept the feeling of being let down as a sign that you are an emotionally free and creative person.

When to Trust Your Gut Feelings

Gut feelings don't originate in the intestines but in the right side of the brain. That is the brain's nondominant sector for right-handed people, who constitute 90% of the population.

The brain's right side accepts incoming information and matches it against its store of previous experiences. These memories are recorded in the brain like videotapes. The matching process is instantaneous, taking only one-tenth of a second. Suddenly, you're thinking: I've seen this before. Or: I know how this works. Or: I don't really like this guy.

Why they are called gut feelings: That portion of the brain has the power to extrapolate a complete picture, some of it smudged, from a small amount of data. It is also highly visual and has strong links to the sources of emotion.

Result: When the brain's right side starts playing those videotapes of previous experiences, even tiny pieces of them, you receive clear visual information enhanced by emotional reactions. Often these pictures register in your gut.

Example: A seemingly innocent situation may inexplicably produce a gut-clenching feeling of fear. This means that the situation was quickly analyzed by the brain's right side, related to previous experience, and judged to be highly dangerous.

The rational portion of the brain, the left side, perceives no hint of danger. But the right hand system is flashing red alert. Run! Flee!

Not all gut feelings (intuition) take such dramatic form. But they are invariably produced in the same way. It is part of our instinctive system to provide a counterbalance—and complement—to our reason.

The failings of intuition: Although a gut feeling may be based on minimal input, its conclusions feel like knowledge. Intuition can command with authority. Yet it may be dead wrong, diametrically opposed to reality. This leads many people to shrug off their gut feelings.

Dilemma: We can't rationally prove that these gut-level conclusions are correct. We have been trained to select rational modes of thought. In fact, schoolchildren are punished for violating the rules of reason. Given the opportunity, people prefer to distrust their intuition, particularly if there is time for analytical scrutiny.

Example: It's fun to have a gut feeling about a stock in the market. But it's best to check this intuition against all available, rationally computed indicators.

When intuition is valuable: Your gut feelings are a dependable barometer in dealing with people.

Example: You experience bad feelings from a man you have just met. You're not sure why, but you don't trust him. Maybe he reminds you of your crazy brother-in-law.

Harken to those gut feelings. You don't need proof that there is something wrong with him. Just the opposite. Your system is demanding overwhelming evidence that there is something right about him.

Other times to trust intuition: When your past record proves that listening to it pays off. Fact: Intuition can be honed by years of rational study in a particular field. These experiences have stocked the brain with a complete set of videotapes. Little can occur that you haven't recorded in one form or another. Intuition is a creative exploitation of the recorded material.

Some people have a great talent for gut feelings. They often find success in fields in which these gifts are appreciated. Examples: Sales, communications, the arts. They seem to sense the new products that will captivate the marketplace, the type of television shows audiences will watch, and the paintings and sculptures that will become the next rage.

If you and a trusted associate are each working from different sets of information, yet you arrive at the same feeling, you're right on target. That kind of confirmation is highly accurate.

Never ignore a gut feeling that is overwhelming or that signals a possible catastrophe. It doesn't happen often, but when it does, you should trust your instincts. Point: Gut feelings are a form of life insurance. In time of emergency, don't allow your reason to overrule the primal power of gut-tugging warning.

Source: Martin G. Groder, M.D., a psychiatrist and business consultant in Durham, NC, and the author of *Business Games: How to Recognize the Players and Deal with Them,* Boardroom Books, Millburn, NJ.

Are You an Excitement Addict?

Excitement produces a natural high virtually identical to that induced by drugs. Some personalities are hooked on it. Like chronic drug users, excitement addicts live for the thrill of feeding their habit. These people generate their highs by participating in daring actions and deeds.

Symptoms. The excitement addict loves romantic adventures, late-night meetings, gambling for high stakes, speculating in the stock market. Business people who are excitement addicts indulge themselves in imaginative and risky deals. They gamble on concepts and personnel, often hiring unlikely people for adventurous new projects. As their successes become the norm, they seek bolder ways to triumph.

Conversely, these addicts are reluctant to undertake any tasks they consider routine. Daily chores, paperwork, obligatory callbacks are unappetizing to them. Trap: To add tang to these tasks, they procrastinate and/or overload, which creates a pressure situation.

Causes: Excitement addiction follows the classic pattern of any addiction. It is based on substituting something pleasurable (excitement) for something stable and substantial (love, friends, community).

Initial satisfaction: At first, the addiction delivers pleasure at little cost. But as the addiction progresses, the addict must have more and more of the addictive material to gain the same satisfying effect. Words the addicts live by: More is better.

Dramatic situations: Excitement junkies further hype their lives by deliberately fostering dramatic situations. Example: Stirring up trouble at work by being frank and repeating confidential stories told by fellow employees.

Day of reckoning: Eventually, excitement addicts push themselves to the breaking point. Then they suffer the agonies of withdrawal.

How it starts: Excitement addiction stems from a natural stimulation that is triggered by the body's hormones. (Many hormones are involved besides adrenaline.) The condition is independent of drugs, but the ups and downs of the affliction are accentuated by their use.

Who is an addict? Only high-energy people. Their bodies are able to generate large quantities of stimulating hormones.

Stunted areas: Addicts chase excitement while neglecting other essential areas of life.

Examples:
They have few, or no, close personal relationships. They view them as unnecessary and dangerous emotionally.

When faced with a profound loss (a death in the family, the abandonment of a long-term career project), they refuse to grieve. Instead, they indulge in an activity that generates excitement. Point: Excitement deflects and postpones painful considerations.

How they live: Those addicts not heavily ridden with guilt operate in the fast lane. They work and play hard. Spare-time pursuits: Hang gliding, sports-car driving, skydiving. If they are good managers, they can keep themselves strung out for a long time. But traveling down that lane, the addict keeps racing faster and faster.

Bad melodrama: Addicts who are more guilt-ridden slip into a life-style best described as bad melodrama. They cause crises so that they can manage them. Easily foreseeable catastrophes are not prevented. (Indeed, they are nurtured.) The more things fall apart, the more exciting the situation. Addicts must have stimulation, even if it's negative.

Tragic heroes: These addicts are like tragic heroes dragged down by the Fates to total collapse. They are prime candidates for one, or all, of four unpleasant ends. They may:

1. Drop out, quit, or be fired from their jobs.
2. Have either a physical or a mental breakdown.
3. Commit suicide.
4. Commit homicide.

How to spot an addict:
Ask high-energy individuals if they would rather be bored or dead. Those who answer dead are addicts.

In their early stages, addicts appear highly attractive. With their infinite charges of energy, they are vibrant and dynamic. If they maintain their bodies by doing physical exercises, they can be magnificent.

Addicts act in socially approved and encouraged ways. They are doers, meeting life through action. Because of this, they often arrive at advanced addiction before their problem is recognized.

Example: A productive salesperson is the hit of any conference, convention, or party. After years on the road, however, closing a big sale is not enough reward. The salesperson wants to spend more and more time pursuing sexual adventures, financial projects with faint chance of success, and gambling.

Subtle process: The unhappy result takes years to develop. Excitement junkies remain productive, but there is something missing from their performances. Their former creativity is sapped by preoccupation with exciting diversions.

Plight of the entrepreneur: Frequently, under the thrall of addiction, entrepreneurs feed their love of danger. They often gamble on high-risk, long-odds ventures. Obsessed with the drama of these transactions, they reach too far and fall into the disaster they have courted all along. Result: Addiction transforms the entrepreneur from productive to pathological. Solution: Only therapists or business consultants who are former excitement junkies can cure those addicts.

Self-help:

Addicts must analyze what is missing in their lives. Why: They have been compensating for the missing ingredient through excitement.

To restore that missing element: Establish at least one ongoing close relationship.

Cut back on extraneous facets of daily life and build up the weak parts.

Example: A working wife and mother holds a full-time job while running a house, raising three kids, and filling time-consuming church and community posts. The excitement of crises consumes her. Result: She breaks down by developing several ulcers. Remedy: She backs off from her church and community work. She slows down at her job. She devotes more time to her family.

Caution: Sudden withdrawal from excitement addiction is seldom painless. Usually, it involves total collapse in which addicts completely reverse their pattern by sleeping all the time rather than pursuing adventures. For those who keep at the daily grind, withdrawal can take months, even years.

Best bet: Catch addiction while in its early stages. It is easier to cure, and less harm has been done.

Source: Martin G. Groder, M.D., a psychiatrist and business consultant in Durham, NC., and author of *Business Games: How to Recognize the Players and Deal with Them,* Boardroom Books, Millburn, NJ.

Knowing When To Slow Down

It's easy to recognize when you have already pushed yourself too far. You are sick, exhausted, explode too easily, or just feel miserable.

More difficult: Recognizing that you are beginning to overdo it, catching yourself before stress catches you.

There are early warning signs that life is becoming too stressful for your own capacities to adapt to pressure. But we often ignore the signals. Reason: The work ethic tells us to work hard and not pamper ourselves. Instead of heeding the inner voice when it says too much, we answer back: I can handle anything.

The common early warning signals of impending stress:

Any major change in your desire for food, sleep, sex or social interaction. Sometimes, outside events lead you to modify habits. However, when your desires change and you don't know why, your body is trying to tell you something. This does not refer to minor alterations. Something is wrong, though, if you suddenly crave to sleep half the day, can't sleep, lose your desire for sex, can't stand to be alone, or want to be alone all the time.

What to do: When you notice such a change, don't panic. Keep track of your patterns for a while before taking action. Your behavior may correct itself. If it doesn't, get medical help or other professional counseling.

Doubting yourself. When you have been competent for some time in an area, and suddenly you lose your sense of sureness, check your stress level. The mind and emotions play funny tricks. They can make you feel generally inadequate so that you want to give up or try something entirely new. But all you may really need is to reconsider your priorities and learn effective methods for managing the stress.

Strong emotions without apparent cause. Everyone is unhappy for some reason at times. However, when you feel depressed, angry, or irritable and nothing in particular has occurred, your emotions are telling you that you are under more stress than you know how to handle comfortably.

Increased use of alcohol or drugs. A significantly increased use of these substances indicates that you are using them to forget about stress for awhile. This is generally a bad idea. Many find it difficult to avoid escalating alcohol and drug use as the stressful conditions continue.

High blood pressure. Although high blood pressure is related to poor diet, lack of exercise, and heredity, it is also strongly related to emotions. If you are often upset about things, feel out of control, constantly need to adjust to changes at work or at home, and live in crowded conditions in a bustling city, you are more likely to develop this disease. It can lead to heart attacks and other life-threatening conditions. Since it can be symptomless, many people in stress-prone positions now take their pressure regularly.

Headaches, backaches, poor digestion. All of these involve tightening some part of yourself in response to pressures. Your body is signaling that you are storing the tensions you experience and creating additional wear and tear on your human machinery. Repeated consistently, these tensions undermine your health by disrupting the internal balance of your complex, interlocking system.

General fatigue. If you seem to be getting enough sleep and are still fatigued, you may have been pushing yourself for so long that you have undermined your resistance and resilience. Under stress, the body first copes with excessive commitments by putting out more adrenaline. If you continue to overdo it, you are likely to collapse.

Pay attention now. It takes a far longer time to recover from stress-induced exhaustion and disease than it takes to collapse. Many stress-related illnesses (heart attacks, strokes) can be killers. If you survive such an illness, you will be forced to change your habits. Better: Modify your lifestyle while you are healthy.

Source: Kathryn L. Goldman, Ph.D, head of the division of human development Austin Community College, and president, Transformations, counselors in stress management and personal development, 1502 Hilmont Dr. Austin, TX 87804.

Burn-Out Quiz

How close are you to debilitating stress?

	SA	A	N	SN*
Are you fatigued throughout the day?				
Do you speak up less often in business meetings than you previously did?				
Are you forgetting things more frequently?				
Are you tired even after a good night's sleep?				
Does your mind always seem in full gear?				
Do you seem further behind at the end of the day than when you started?				
Are you less patient with others?				
Do you spend less time on hobbies?				

*Score 10 points if the answer is a strong affirmative (SA), 7 points for an affirmative (A), 3 points for a negative (N), and no points for a strong negative (SN).

Are accomplishments seldom pleasing to you? —— —— —— ——

Do you constantly operate at full speed during waking hours? —— —— —— ——

Evaluation: 0 to 15 points indicates you are either totally inactive or have your act together, 16 to 50 shows you are unlikely to suffer from burn-out, 51 to 80 indicates you are on thin ice (burn-out could be close), 86 to 100 means you are a walking time bomb.

Source: *Registered Representative.*

Must You Have A Midlife Crisis?

Much is made of the torments of the midlife passage during the years from 35 to 50.

Is there such a thing as a midlife crisis?

If crisis means change, then life is a constant crisis. But the midlife crisis happens to be a packaged concept, easy to label, write about, and sell.

You reject the concept?

There is no natural law that says you must have a midlife crisis. Men encounter no physiological changes during this period. Women may stop menstruating. But whether that leads to a difficult time depends largely upon their own conditioning. If men or women set themselves up to have a crisis, they'll probably have one.

Are you denying that the age group has specific problems?

I'm certainly not saying that the middle years lack opportunities for problems. By far the most strenuous period of adjustment in our society happens then. Parents see their children reach adolescence. The children work, leave home, take lovers. They challenge the parents, who react with deep conflicts and uncertainties. Is that midlife crisis? Or is it backlash reaction to the adolescent crisis the kids are having?

Most people at middle life also see parents die. Suddenly, they are the older generation. And, at the same time, the family wage earners reach a career plateau. They realize they have gone as far as they will go. They'll never make it to company president.

What happens then?

Here's the danger. We discover that other people share the same problems and so we confirm the discomfort. The midlife crisis is accepted. People then start to function as they believe others expect them to.

This is the real problem. People stop trying to expand their minds and capacities to the limit because they believe in the midlife crisis.

What about mid-lifers who make dramatic changes, such as abandoning a high-paying job for a new lifestyle?

Such individuals are far more likely to be very healthy people whose outlook is changing. They are seeking new challenges, not some kind of crisis. Healthy individuals should not be branded as sick or troubled because they defy the expectations of others.

How do you advise people to make these healthy changes?

The basic steps are the same no matter what the age:

Ask: How did I get where I am? How much of it has to do with early programming—what other people expected and wanted?

Determine your objectives: They may not be related to economics or a career. They may be tied in with more open communication or, perhaps, a better marriage.

Examine how you invest your time and energy. You'll discover that you do many things you don't want to do. Why? Because you feel obligated. Lesson: Stop wasting your resources. Channel your energy in directions that lead to those achievements you desire most.

Recognize that change isn't easy. Making a major change is always accompanied by anxiety. None of us enjoy it.

Are there ways of easing such transitions?

Professional aid can help you articulate hopes and goals. It can also help you change automatic behavior. Stick with those therapies that are very practical as well as action-oriented.

Self-help books can be useful, too, provided you don't believe that they contain magic formulas. Objectives: Discover as well as break old patterns. Make life more interesting. These goals are right not only at midlife, but they will make you a happier individual at anytime.

Source: Dr. Ari Kiev, originator of the Life Strategy Workshops, is a lecturer, former head of New York Hospital's Suicide Prevention Center, and author of 13 books.

Are You in The Right Job?

Most workers fail to appreciate and assess the skills they possess. Most of them remain in jobs beneath their real capabilities because they constantly undersell their skills.

Those people who successfully shift careers are usually initiators who try to shape their abilities to fit into new areas. But, too many workers passively lie back to await the knock of opportunity at their door.

The tools for change:

Write a detailed diary of your life. Brag about your achievements; explain your hobbies; depict the surroundings you find agreeable. Then list those elements you want to include in your future career and those you wish to eliminate.

Enumerate those things you do well and enjoy doing. Experts discovered that a worker's interests and happiness count more toward his ability to do a job well than his or her brains and aptitudes. Seek out those constant elements in each task that make you feel good and productive.

Catalog all your skills. The more you credit yourself with, the greater your chance of landing a better job. A common misconception is that by claiming a wide range of base skills, more jobs will be available to you. The opposite is the case. The higher your level of skills, the more you can carve a niche for yourself. Ideally, a job will be created to suit your talents, which effectively eliminates any other competitors. Warning: Don't fall into the habit of relying on retraining. Most workers can

shift jobs once they understand the nature of their own skills.

Ask: If I could have any job in the world, what would it be? Then ask: What do I want to do before I die? Your responses will help uncover your deepest desires. Then you are ready to start the process of transforming them into realities.

The simplest answer is invariably the best. Counselors have learned that no study or test can match an honest answer to this question: What do you really want to be?

Source: *What Color is Your Parachute?* by Richard Nelson Bolles, Ten Speed Press. Berkeley, CA.

When Not To Change Jobs

There are good reasons for changing jobs. Particularly: Advancement, challenge, and growth potential.

And, there are bad reasons. You shouldn't make a job change if you are motivated solely by the following:

Money. Fatter paychecks don't compensate for job dissatisfaction. Even if you're in financial trouble, the chances are you'll find yourself overextended again in a few months, unless there is a huge salary difference between the two jobs.

Feelings of inadequacy. Insecurity can be a healthy motivator to work hard for skills and experience, which enable you to excel in the present job.

Personality clashes. Get to the root of the problem by talking it through with troublesome co-workers and superiors. There's no assurance that the new job will not offer fresh personality conflicts.

Poor performance. Never leave on a low note, but only when you're on top of your work—an office champ.

Boredom. Maybe all you need is a vacation to get a better perspective on the challenges of the present job.

Source: Don Shilling, Wells Management, 888 Seventh Ave., New York 10019

Should You Stay When The Company is Sold?

Problem: The business has been sold. Should you stay with the new owners? Much depends on the top person in the selling company. His future with the new owners dictates the outlook for everyone else.

Stay if:

The company has a strong market position, good management, and the capability to fend off competitors. Good sign: The new parent company moves the top executive into its organization, with real responsibilities for his old company.

The company is a real moneymaker. Fact of life: Buyers rarely replace managers who are turning a profit.

Start looking if:

The new management pushes the old boss hard to develop long-range plans and to install sophisticated financial controls.

The company was sold for more than its real worth. As soon as the truth comes out, the buyer will start to make major changes.

The seller wants to relax. Also, be alert to a seller who has substantial outside interests. Reason: He may devote more time and energy to personal business ventures, and thus be unwilling to give enough time to making the acquisition work.

There's no acknowledged successor to the top executive, particularly in a family-run business. This is a good sign that the acquiring company wants only the business, not its old management.

Source: *Chain Store Age Executive.*

Handling an Unsolicited Call from a Headhunter

People don't always respond to their advantage to calls from executive recruiters. Reason: They misconceive the intent of the recruiter's calls and therefore are unable to maximize the opportunity.

Basic rules:

Don't read too much into a first call. Most search firms make blind calls in addition to targeted calls to seek candidates and/or recommendations of candidates.

Ask enough questions to determine if the position is worth going after. Good questions: Why is this position open? Why is the company not hiring from within? Much can be learned without making the caller disclose a client company's identity.

Speak up. Don't shrink from self-promotion if the position sounds desirable, even if it's clear the recruiter is making a blind call. Be straightforward.

It's perfectly permissible to say: That job description fits me except that I have only six, not ten, years of experience, but I have been on a fast track. Most recruiters will take the discussion further.

Bear in mind that there is nothing disloyal, immoral, or inappropriate about answering a recruiter's questions. Realize that the recruiter brings potential opportunity (for example, a promotion or more money) that might be of interest not only to you personally but possibly to others you know inside or outside the company.

Don't take it personally if recruiters can't reveal a client company's name. They probably will during a subsequent interview. (Few client companies demand secrecy at that stage.) Feel free during the call to ask questions around the company's identity. Examples: How long has the company been in business? What is its size? Is it profitable? Is the company growing?

Be receptive and courteous to the caller. But use a businesslike manner. Do *not* be overeager.

Highly recommended: If the position might be of interest, take the recruiter's telephone number and ask permission to call back. Reason: To have time to reflect on the job description and to frame good questions (instead of ones that come off the top of the head).

Source: Millington McCoy, partner, Gould & McCoy, executive search consultants, 375 Park Ave., New York 10125

Dealing With the Possibility of Being Fired

In today's rapidly changing economic environment, managers should be as prepared to get fired as to get promoted. Begin to evaluate your position within a few months after you start a new job.

There are three major reasons for getting fired:

- Bad chemistry with immediate superior.
- A change in the company's needs.
- An alteration in the nature of the job.

Personal chemistry is wrong. You should sense it quickly and start making new contacts both within the firm and outside it. You will have a support system if you have to leave.

Problem: You get a new immediate superior and find you are not able to get along. Try to adapt. Otherwise, keep your eye out for other positions.

Change in company need. In an economic cutback, for instance, you may hear that your division's budget is being reduced 10%. However, your chances of being fired are either one in three or one in fifty, not one in 10. You are considered either indispensable or marginal. Understand this beforehand by learning how indispensable your superior feels you are.

How to evaluate your indispensability about three months after your arrival, not when a problem arises:

Write a description of your job functions.

Analyze your strengths and weaknesses, as you would in a resume. Enumerate your achievements.

Ask your boss to look over the evaluation when he gets a chance and to give you his comments. (He will probably be pleased about your concern. This can also help when it's time to ask for a raise.)

If your immediate superior disagrees with your perception of your performance, ask him for suggestions. Try to improve your performance accordingly. Then give him another evaluation in three months.

Alteration in the nature of the job. If your department grows rapidly, needs other skills, or has become too technologically advanced, see if there is a place in the firm where your skills are still needed. Try to learn the new skills and adapt to the altered responsibilities (they may come in handy elsewhere). Put yourself in your boss' position. See if you can figure out whom you would fire and why.

If you feel the day of reckoning is at hand:

Get as much exposure as you can to other executives in the company. In any cutback, firms like to transfer people. If you are respected and liked you may land elsewhere in the company.

Prepare to look for a job while still working.

Analyze your strengths and weaknesses, and prepare a resume.

Get articles published in your field.

Quantify your achievements in detail.

Prepare for job interviews by practicing with your spouse or a friend. Talk about your achievements without sounding too modest or too arrogant.

Make a list of the people you know, where you know them from, where they are now.

Make a list of companies you are interested in. Get information about them.

Become better known in your field. Go to business-related lunches and social activities.

These actions should prepare you to go into action when the day comes.

Caution: Going on job interviews while you are still employed is a calculated risk. Assess your financial position. Stop heavy borrowing and spending. If your company learns you are looking for a job, you will be the first on the list to get fired.

Source: E. Donald Davis, president, THinc Career Planning Corp., 30 Rockefeller Plaza, New York 10112.

First Steps to Take When Out of a Job

If you are suddenly fired, control your anger, anxiety, and guilt until you've left the office. On the way home, decide how you'll tell your family and friends.

Sort out what went wrong and why before thinking about looking for a new job.

Spend the first few days after a firing getting yourself together. Making a lot of calls, blowing your stack at work, and drinking when you're still trying to recover emotionally don't help.

Most important: Deal with financial anxiety. Too much worry about bills hurts your job search. Recommended:

Tell the family they're going to have to cut back. Discuss the specific expenditures that can be canceled or delayed.

Work out an austere family budget, taking into consideration which creditors might allow you to skip or reduce payments.

Calculate how long the severance pay will last, and how long that period can be extended by tapping savings and liquid investments.

Consider taking an interim job. Important: Don't let pride keep you from applying for unemployment.

Plan for the worst. It's smarter to allow for an extended period of unemployment and be surprised than to be disappointed if nothing develops immediately.

Caution: Don't panic financially and put your house on the market, cash in your investments, etc. There's plenty of time to determine whether or not such drastic measures are necessary.

Source: *Sacked: What to do When You Lose Your Job,* by Dean B. Peskin, AMACOM, New York.

Advice for the Unemployed

Get out of the house. Use the library or rent office space. If necessary arrange for research, secretarial, and phone services.

Keep active. Utilize talent. Benefits: Exposure to potentially valuable people and a boost in self-esteem from earning at least a small wage.

Concentrate job-hunting efforts. More than 80% of managerial positions are filled through recommendations. Direction: Cultivate friends and acquaintances, and let them know you are actively looking.

At the interview: Maintain eye contact. Avoid smoking and drinking, even when invited to do so. Never knock competitors. More important: Never arrange interviews for Friday afternoon or Monday morning.

Recommendations: Ignore most help-wanted ads and *all* blind ads. Eliminate: The personnel manager, who usually has no authority. Also: The resume, job application, and screening interview. Why: None of these is a channel to top management.

When You're Ready To Change Jobs

Before exploring a job change, an executive should ask the following questions:

Are all my abilities being used at my current job?

Am I being paid according to my skills and the standard salary scale in the marketplace?

Are there continued opportunities for advancement and promotion? Example: If the boss is only two or three years older, there can be a real problem moving into his position.

Are my family and I happy in our present geographical locale?

If the answer to any of these questions is negative, start quietly to look around for a new job. Do not wait until you are unhappy before looking for the change. When too much time is allowed to go by, you frequently take the first job offered in order to get out of an uncomfortable situation.

Many executives keep their resumes on file with an executive placement service because they are willing to change jobs under ideal conditions. It costs nothing. In addition the search firm offers broad coverage, something executives cannot achieve through their own networks.

Caution: Unless you are currently unemployed, answering advertisements with box number replies should be avoided altogether. Reason: You have no control over confidentiality. Your application, or news of it, may easily get back to your company.

If recruiters publicize your job hunt, they damage their reputation for confidentiality, so you can be assured they will keep it a secret.

Source: Don Howard, president and chairman, Don Howard Services Inc., an executive recruiting firm, 120 Broadway, New York 10005

Assessing Your Place In the Job Market

First consideration: What are your priorities? What financial compensation do you expect? Prestige? Friendship? Responsibilities? Do you know your ego needs? Point: Answers to these questions will determine real commitment in looking for a new job.

Frequently, determination is more instrumental in achieving success than the size of the job market. Key: Never consider the job hunt merely as an escape hatch. Look at it as a plan of action to get the job you want.

Decision to search: Compare your current position with your ideal job. If your current job is fairly suitable, admit it. Not everyone is driven by ambition. Do the intelligent thing to make your position more secure. But, if it doesn't suit you, ask yourself if there is anything you can do to improve it. If you can't, ask yourself whether any outside possibilities might be more satisfactory.

Compare job offers and your current position in all ways: Compensation, type, size and reputation of company, kind of job, type of firm, opportunities in the new job, kind of community in which you want to live. Compare both jobs against the ideal job you have outlined for yourself. You may discover that you should look further.

Once you have decided to switch jobs, it is finally time to ask whether the job market is good or bad. If it is bad, you may want to lie low and wait.

How you learn about the job market: The job market has two parts, the open one and the hidden one.

Open job market: Consists of jobs that are filled through newspaper ads, recruiters, and company personnel officers. Whereas newspaper ads and recruiters represent only a small fraction (some 20%) of the entire market, they can indicate what fields have employment opportunities. Have a discussion with a recruiter. Ask him: What direction is recruiting industry going in, now and for the future? What are the trends, now and for the future?

Hidden job market: Consists of jobs that are not publicized and may not even exist until you call on the right person. Example: An executive vice-president in charge of four subsidiaries may have problems with one. If you meet the executive and discuss your expertise in the field, a job may be created for you to beef up the sick subsidiary. Key: Since the hidden market is difficult to identify, use the open market as a barometer of the entire job market.

While assessing the job market, increase your exposure by publishing articles and joining trade associations and civic groups. They are good job sources.

Side effect: The work you do to assess the job market may project into it. Best part: It entails minimum risk. Reason: Only a very smart boss will realize that when you volunteer to go to a professional conference on a weekend you are in fact looking for a better job. That could inspire your boss to open up a new opportunity for you in the company. Most will only think that you are a dedicated company person.

Critical resource: Learn about the job market within your own company. You may learn more at lunch with a beginner in research than by talking to a secretive senior executive.

Bottom line: Steer a sane path in the job market through frequent self-evaluations. Otherwise, you may find yourself in a new job that is less satisfying than the one you left.

Source: E. Donald Davis, president, THinc Career Planning Corp., the pioneer company specializing in outplacement, 30 Rockefeller Plaza, New York 10112.

The Job Hunt: Opportunity for Growth

A job hunt can do more than land you a new position; it can help prepare you for it.

It is one of the few times in your career when competitors, customers, and suppliers will talk openly with you. Talk to anyone who will see you, even if the position offered sounds unappealing, or even if there's no position available. Questions you can ask—and which will be freely answered—might include: What problem areas would I have at your company? What are its weaknesses?Is the company losing its best marketing man? Does it have production problems? Why does it lose customers? How does it gain them?

You may be meeting people you will want to hire, or avoid hiring, later on in your new job. If you're looking at the customers' and suppliers' sides of a business, you're in a position to make valuable industry contacts.

To gain a more general industry perspective, you might ask: What is the company's marketing strategy? How does it perceive its market? Are customers becoming more sensitive to prices? To services? The company you don't go to work for may have solved problems you'll encounter at another job.

Finally, there's the chance to learn more about yourself. What excites you in a given position? What turns you off? Does the prospect of revitalizing a sales department seem appealing or painful and tedious?

If you get turned down, ask why. What are your weaknesses? Are you projecting negative qualities you don't really have?

experience, temperament, needs and aims. Ultimately, you want to define clearly what the perfect working situation is for you.

Experience. List:

Five things you liked about each job you have held.

Your strengths and weaknesses in each of those jobs.

Your major achievements in each previous job.

Your five best skills, in order of importance.

Temperament:

List what you want in a job. Examples: Fast-track competition, low pressure, creative opportunities, security. Explain your preferences.

Describe the kind of people you prefer as supervisors, peers as well as subordinates.

List the most ego-satisfying aspects of a job. Think these through very carefully.

Needs and goals:

List your family's requirements. Include finances, status, lifestyle, amount of your time available.

Describe your personal goals for the next five and ten years.

Weigh whether you want a lifetime commitment or another step up the ladder.

Ideal situation:

Determine where you want to work geographically.

Explain fully whether you would be happier in a large or small firm.

Identify, with plenty of description, what would really excite you about a job.

Source: Allerton, Heinze & Associates, a management consulting firm that specializes in executive search, 2 N. LaSalle St., Chicago 60602.

What to Know about Yourself Before Writing A Resume

Creative job hunting begins before a new resume is prepared. First step: An in-depth self-evaluation. Includes: A hard look at your

What to Leave out Of Your Resume

The style used for writing resumes has changed over the last few years to make them more persuasive and concise. Goal: Each resume entry should convince readers that they

209

should hire the writer. What to omit:

Photos. A picture may let employers form misleading impressions.

Salary requirements. Why should applicants price themselves out of a job or show that they are a bargain?

Reasons for leaving jobs. These are better explained in interviews.

Date of resume preparation or date available to begin work. Both indicate how long you have been looking for a job. Exception: When looking for seasonal work.

References or a statement that references are available on request. Instead: List them on a separate sheet and adapt them to each individual employment situation.

Empty assurances. All applicants think they are good, honest, loyal, and healthy workers. Demonstrate these qualities through concrete examples during interviews.

Vague references to time gaps. Employers look for holes. Explain them in terms of accomplishments. Examples: Travel to improve a language capability or research a specific project. Caution: Never claim to have been a consultant without proof.

Hobbies and outside interests. Exception: Those that relate to professional interests or show traits that an employer wants. Avoid listing any dangerous or time-consuming activities.

Source: *Resumes: The Nitty Gritty,* by Joyce Lain Kennedy, Suburban Features Inc., Cardiff, CA.

Resume Services

It pays to be skeptical of services that offer to evaluate resumes. Case: Recently, a publishing firm paid a modest fee to have a resume evaluated by one such organization. Unknown to the evaluators, the editors submitted a model resume written by a well-known career counselor. Result: The resume received low marks in the evaluation, which was accompanied by an offer to improve it for a substantially larger fee.

Check Your Own References

Some fine jobs are lost because references weren't nearly as praise-giving as the applicant expected. To make sure that your references aren't damaging or ineffective:

Contact each reference in advance. Explain carefully who will be calling, why, and what should be left unsaid. Reason: Previous employers might offer accidental remarks that could discourage the future boss.

Get a business friend to call and pretend to check your references. Rehearse the questions so he'll sound professional.

If a bad reference turns up and you can't avoid using it, see if you can patch things up with the person giving the reference and arrive at a mutually acceptable description of your professional qualities and previous performance. If that's not possible, prepare the prospective employer in advance. Describe the problem and offer other, more favorable, references at the same company.

Source: *The Executive's Guide to Finding a Superior Job,* by William A. Cohen, AMACOM, New York.

Researching A Prospective Employer

While there is no foolproof method of knowing whether you will be happy and have sufficient opportunity at a prospective job, it pays to investigate. Many employers think that once they offer you a job you needn't know anything more. If they are sensitive to probing, be subtle about it.

Caution: Don't do any type of checking until after you get the offer: At that point, the firm has disqualified all other candidates and is unlikely to withdraw an offer to you.

Once you are chosen for the job, phone the primary interviewer. Say you are delighted about the offer and that you think it would be helpful to talk again about the job.

Before that meeting: Be observant. Talk to the receptionist while you are waiting. Be friendly and exchange pleasantries. Get the employee's opinion of the firm, how long employed, etc. What about John Jones (the department head you will be working for)? You may discover that the firm is a revolving door, or that your department is so obscure no one knows anything about it.

The meeting: First, ask innocuous questions about the pension plan and other benefits. Be inquisitive about neutral subjects. Then ask the real zinger: I could do the job more effectively if I know what problems came up with my predecessor. Can you give me that information? Don't just find out if firing or promoting was involved. Find out why. You'll learn something about the firm's attitude toward employees.

If the person who had your job is still with the company: Suggest that it would be helpful for the two of your to talk, so you might learn how best to serve the company. Again, you are trying to get inside.

Caution: Take this employee's advice lightly. You will always hear some negative points about any job.

Learn about the company's financial position: If it's a public company, get its annual and interim reports. Even large corporations aren't immune to financial instability. If it's a private company, find out who its banker is and the partner in charge of the company audit at its CPA firm. If the owner-managers expect you to take on middle and senior-level management responsibilities, you should be trusted to meet with their financial advisers. Be low key, but impress upon them that your current position is not desperate and you want to feel secure about the offer. If this fails, at least find out about their business plan. Although it may be overoptimistic, it should give you an idea about projected return on investment and the owner's expansion program.

Point: The financial condition of the firm is indicative of the opportunities you will have. If there are few or no profits, there are fewer chances, too, for promotions and raises. Exception: A turnaround situation. There, you are taking a gamble. You should know the odds, for there may be big rewards. However, you may not care to run the necessary risks.

Politics: You want to be hired by someone in a powerful position, not someone on the way out. It's best to be on the right side in company politics, but it may be difficult to discern this position.

Possibility: If you are a professional, use your network of colleagues. Someone is likely to know your boss. Long shot: Find a contact in a competing firm in the same industry. Say: I'm going to be working for John Jones at Acme Screw, and I want to know how he's regarded in the industry.

Upshot: The competition may know Jones is the president's son-in-law, and that it's a dead-end job. If you have been hired by someone on the wrong side of a company power struggle, ask for a transfer.

To get a perspective on how important your department is in the workings of the firm, get the literature it puts out about itself. Get the biographies of the firm's top-management people, too. Find out if any of the officers come out of your field. If you are taking a job as an internal auditor, for instance, you will have better promotional opportunities if several financial people are at the top of the company hierarchy.

The wrong side: Everyone makes a mistake and takes the wrong job occasionally. Best: If you find yourself in the wrong position and can afford to look around again, get out immediately. When you hold a job for only a week or two, it is usually dismissed as a fluke in your employment history if the rest of it is substantial.

Source: Robert Half, president, Robert Half, Inc. executive recruiters, 522 Fifth Ave., New York, 10036.

Getting the Edge On Competitors

When answering a newspaper ad, tailor a covering letter to the ad's key qualifications.

Draft cover letters and resumes to tell a clear

career story with a definite direction and purpose.

Once an interview is set up, learn enough about the company to impress the interviewer with intelligent discussion and questions.

If possible, find out about the person who will actually be conducting the interview. Reveal the knowledge little by little, in a flattering way, as the interview proceeds.

Follow up quickly with a brief note of thanks and interest.

Follow that up with a detailed letter of why you would do well at the job.

Continue to send notes once a week, or so, if the selection process drags on. The notes should accompany something that appeared in print that might interest the recipient.

Getting a Job Out of Town

If you are eager to relocate to another city, take steps to enable yourself to compete better with local residents in that market.

Recommendations:

Get a mail drop in the city of your choice. They are generally available at local telephone answering services. Give them instructions to forward your mail to your current address. This will unquestionably improve the response rate to resumes you send to employers in the chosen area.

Once you get responses, try to schedule several interviews during the same few days. This will make it easier to get a tax deduction for your entire trip and will cut down on your travel expenses.

Avoid asking a prospective employer to pay your expenses. Be honest about where you live now. In most cases, employers will understand that a person eager to relocate to their town and willing to pay his own expenses is a go-getter who should be as valuable as any current resident they might be considering.

Source: Robert Half, president, Robert Half, Inc, executive recruiters, 522 Fifth Ave., New York 10036.

Costs to Check Out Before You Relocate

Before accepting a new job out of state, check out three areas where costs may differ:

Taxes. State and local taxes, which may include a state and city income tax plus sales and gasoline taxes. They are listed in *The World Almanac.* Also evaluate excise taxes on cars, boats, other personal property. (Federal tax rates are the same all over.)

Housing. Here the highest costs are the price of a new home, mortgage rates, and property taxes. Add to this utility and fuel costs plus a homeowner's insurance policy. Trap: Higher use fees for same essential services, such as trash pickup and sewage.

Transportation. Besides auto registration and insurance policy costs, factor in the commuting distances. This may influence choice of house location (and also affect the price).

Checking all the costs may require a personal visit to the city in question with stops at the utility company, Chamber of Commerce, real estate agencies, motor vehicle bureau, and local banks.

Don't worry about food, clothing, and recreation costs; they're not likely to vary enough to affect a decision.

How to Ease Into A New Job

When you change jobs—ease in, even if your mission is complete reorganization.

Priority 1: Get to know your staff. Know who gets things done, who doesn't. How, and how well.

Learn before you leap. Ask questions, solicit advice, don't be afraid to lean on staff in areas you aren't familiar with. Look to making small changes that require teamwork and cooperation, enable you to gauge subordinates, inspire their confidence in you as a learner as well as a leader. Cultivate the dissenters (they care—and usually have something worth listening to); beware of quiet acquiescers: They may be waiting for you to make the first move.

Review your predecessor's records, correspondence, information flows for insight into his priorities, management methods, innovative successes and failures, problem-solving techniques. Be sure you know the realities of your job before you discard his approaches.

Clarify interdepartmental interfaces as rapidly as possible. Look for access or admission to policy and planning committees, pertinent task forces, or other company groups that help give you perspective on overall goals and operations, insight into how your reorganization ideas could affect other departments.

9

Marriage And Family Life

Balancing Business And Personal Life

A talk with Neil Austrian, president of Doyle Dane Bernbach, one of the largest ad agencies in the world and the top winner of advertising awards.

On an average working day, how much time do you spend with your family?

I live in Connecticut with my wife and three children, ages 15, 12, and 9. I'm usually in Manhattan by 8:00 in the morning, if I'm not traveling. Three out of five mornings I have a breakfast meeting with someone at the agency. I usually leave work around 6:30 and am home by 7:30.

When I get home, I spend about an hour on the phone to the Far East or California, places where it's impossible to talk to people during our workday in New York.

We all eat dinner together, even when it's after 8:00, and the kids have already had a few peanut butter and jelly sandwiches. I end up playing with the kids until it's time for them to go to bed.

What are your favorite extracurricular activities?

What we do as a family. We all ski. We spend a couple of weeks in winter doing that in Colorado. We all play tennis. We have a little outboard that we take out for water skiing, fishing, or just having a good time. Every vacation we've taken since the kids were born, we've taken as a family group.

How long a vacation do you take?

I've never had more than two weeks at once. It's usually three or four times a year, maybe a week at a time.

Do you have time to read?

I make time to read. I read history or lighter works that take my mind off business. I also enjoy reading biographies of those who have held high political office here and abroad. I enjoy talking with people involved in politics. It's an intriguing area for me. Of course, I read widely about both advertising and marketing—and almost everything else that relates to my field.

You work hard. Have you resisted becoming a workaholic?

The temptation is there. I could let myself work seven days a week, 24 hours a day, and I'd enjoy it. At the same time, I'd never know my family. I'd wake up some day and wonder what it was all for.

I've found I can balance it. I get the job done at the agency and get the job done at home.

Do you have a few principles that help you run your personal life?

The basic one is to treat people decently and fairly.

In any business, your success depends on how well your people perform, not just on how well you perform. You must have people who want to work with you. They have to respect you, if not like you. The key is to treat employees decently and fairly, just as you would want to be treated.

The Two-Career Marriage: Four Ways it Can Work

• Two equal partners share responsibilities. Careers come first for each, while household chores are done—or put off—jointly. Caution: The partners cannot permit their competitiveness to intrude on the marriage.

• One partner assumes a subordinate position. When a boss marries his secretary, both know their marriage roles. Problem: Shifting roles in any relationship may cause it to founder.

• Personal emotions supersede career drives. Marriage partners sacrifice business opportunities to spend more time with each other. Difficulty: This obsession can become an excuse for not succeeding at work. And this can be a serious mistake, because personal pleasure is often related to professional success.

• Spouses are so aware of each other's needs that they constantly move toward one another. This is the best way of achieving a mix between marriage and career. Devotion to both is mutually reinforcing.

Any of these arrangements will work, however, if both sides are satisfied with the relationship.

Adjustments:

Personal. Redefine your aims and outlook to adapt to a shifting situation.

Joint discussion. Listen as well as talk to your mate. Agree to change if you heard a valid argument for it.

Direct demand. Make one only when you are certain that you are right. Example: If overwork is threatening your home life, decrease the job level, particularly if you are doing work that should be handled by your colleagues.

Taking Work Home From the Office

Any executive with a challenging or demanding job has the problem of taking work home. Sometimes it's necessary. But do it too often and you can jeopardize your health, your home life, and even your effectiveness on the job.

Dangers: When you rely on taking work home, you tend to put off work during the day. You run the risk of becoming less effective during regular hours.

Guidelines:

Take work home only to meet a tight deadline, handle sudden extra work, or compensate for the loss of working time you counted on. If you carry a loaded briefcase more than twice a month, look for ways to delegate more tasks. Streamline your work and distribute the least important part to your subordinates.

If you do bring work home, try to maintain a normal return-from-work routine. Example: Shower, eat dinner, spend time with the kids. Then, instead of relaxing later, find a private place to work.

Source: Robert Moskowitz, author and time-management consultant, 6835 Claremore Ave., San Diego, CA 92120.

Teaching Your Spouse Your Business

Business owners should have their spouses work in the company four weeks a year. Preferred: One week per quarter. Reason: If the owner dies or becomes incapacitated, the spouse will know how to handle key situations and people. Included: Lawyers, accountants, bankers, consultants, major suppliers, and creditors.

Source: Jeffrey P. Davidson, management consultant, 1054 Thomas Jefferson St. NW, Washington DC 20004.

Living With a Workaholic

Intense, driven and competitive workaholics prefer labor to leisure and family pleasures. The addicts generally are active, happy, and healthy. The real victims may be the spouse and children.

Divorce or severe family stress is common among workaholics. The spouses must accept the situation if the marriage is to continue. And they must be prepared to live with a person who is unlikely to change work habits, no matter how many promises he or she makes.

To live with a workaholic:

• Keep contact with his work life. Children should visit his office, store, or lab. Books and toys related to the parent's profession can keep the youngsters involved. Caution: Workaholics can engender similar traits in their offspring. Help the children learn the merits of play and relaxation.

Simplify domesticity. Since the workaholic mate seldom helps around the house, shop by phone, order gifts by mail, and so forth. Use banks that let you pay bills by telephone. Cut kitchen time by using convenience appliances such as a microwave oven, food processor, etc.

Go along on business trips. Take the children along, too, when possible.

Get on the calendar. Workaholics are ob-

sessed with schedules and lists. Make appointments for lunch and dinner. Have the children make them, too. It will help get the message across that the family finds that it needs more attention from the workaholic.

Anticipate spending time alone. Have a social life. Accept invitations, but inform the hostess you're likely to show up at the party or dinner by yourself.

Source: *Workaholic,* by Marilyn Machlowitz, Addison-Wesley Publishing Co., Reading, MA.

Business Techniques for Home Management

Everyone is basically organized. People make the mistake of assuming that clutter is synonymous with disorganization. False. If you can find the item that you are looking for, you are basically organized.

When you are not organized: Reevaluate your system if it takes longer than five minutes to find something.

Separate the problem into components: Instead of attempting to organize all of the closets at one time, choose one closet, then decide which shelf or area to work on first.

Set time limits, and stick to them: Devote an hour two or three times a week to organizing. Once you are properly organized you will be able to maintain your system by devoting only 10 to 15 minutes a week to it.

To synchronize the family: Use a calendar that is prominently displayed and within easy reach of the smallest member of your family. Each member should have his own easily distinguishable color pen.

Other time-saving tactics:

Car pooling. Essential for the busy parent with active children.

Shopping and cooking in bulk.

Using public transit (if feasible). It allows you to do something else (make notes, etc.) while traveling.

Hiring part-time help. It doesn't have to be expensive. Example: A teenager to run time-

217

consuming errands. Recommended: Use another person only to do those tasks that you have put off the longest.

Trading tasks with a friend or neighbor. The person who hates to do laundry may not mind ironing.

Source: Stephanie Winston, a time-management consultant who helps to organize homes and offices, and author of *Getting Organized: The Easy Way to Put Your Life in Order,* Norton Publishers, New York.

How to Change Your Name

Why people change names: Because a surname is hard to spell or pronounce, which can be a handicap in business.

Can a new name be taken without going through a legal procedure? Yes, provided the new name isn't taken on to compete unfairly in business or in connection with an illegal act. Otherwise it is entirely lawful to indulge in an activity under a new name simply by using it. Technically it becomes as much your legal name as the one on your birth certificate. You may use it to open bank and charge accounts, acquire a driver's license, sign contracts, get a Social Security number, or get married.

If an official record is desired: A person can have a name changed in court (usually a state Supreme Court). That will avoid delays in getting a passport or in collecting inheritance and insurance benefits.

What is required: For a court order granting a change, it is necessary to state reasons for wanting the change. Information is required regarding marital status, residence, place of employment, and Social Security number. A person will be asked whether there are any outstanding judgments by or against him, if he has a criminal record, and whether he has ever been bankrupt.

How long: Often a judge will grant it immediately. But if there is doubt about the applicant's good faith, the judge may ask for more data.

Filing: In most states, the original appli-

cation and a copy of the authorization order will be filed in the appropriate court office. And sometimes the authorization order must be published in a newspaper that will be designated by the court.

Costs involved: If a lawyer is used, his fee may be as low as $100, or as much as he thinks you can afford to pay. There is a charge for the newspaper announcement, and, in some cases, there is a modest filing fee.

Replacing a Birth Certificate

The best legal proof of age and citizenship is a birth certificate. Copy of a lost certificate may be gotten from state department of health. In some states the records are kept by city health department. Required at time of application: Name at time of birth, date and place of birth, sex, race, father's name, mother's maiden name. If the birth was not recorded, there are other ways to get a birth certificate. Needed, one of the following: Hospital or physician's record of birth, baptismal certificate, early elementary school records.

Dealing With the New Rules of Marriage

The new social changes, especially women's liberation, are imposing difficult pressures on the marriage relationship. Help for executives in dealing with these changes—in terms of themselves and the employees they manage—is available from Dr. Ari Kiev, eminent psychiatrist and the author of eight books in the field. His observations:

The usual gripes and complaints that erupt when the wife of a middle-aged man begins to work, go to school, or lead a more independent life are merely the symptoms of a much larger struggle that can be solved, says Dr. Kiev. Husband complains about dinner not being ready on time, about the house being untidy, about having to help with the dishes, or his wife being tired and irritable (instead of fresh, adoring, and waiting) when he comes home. In short, he seems to be complaining that the rules of the marriage contract are being changed, making life less comfortable for him.

In fact, says Kiev, he is probably suffering from a lurking fear that he is about to be abandoned. This exaggerated, even childish, notion of what's going on must be recognized and put aside before a healthy, basically good marriage can begin to function well again.

Reality: The partnership rules are changing. The woman isn't threatening to dissolve the partnership.

Then why do men react as if there were a real threat? What most people don't realize, and what goes against the conventional wisdom, explains Dr. Kiev, is that most men are far more vulnerable to threats of being abandoned than women are. So they perceive the threat even when it doesn't exist. Psychiatrists know, he says, that when women think their husbands may leave them, they usually respond by trying to solve problems in the relationship. They try to cement it. Women reach out for counseling and therapy. Men don't.

Reason: The threat is so overpowering for most men (because it springs from their early childhood dependency on their mothers, which gets mixed up with their views of a wife's true role) that many are incapacitated by fear (often they are not even fully aware of this feeling).

How should a husband deal with this change? The first step, says Dr. Kiev, is to understand his role in the problem and the motives behind his reaction. Once he gets that understanding, the problem, in effect, simply becomes less of a problem.

Here is the all-too-common pattern of the husband's reaction: First he encourages his wife's efforts to find independence. Her efforts, on one level, even flatter his ego, and he may brag about her achievements to his friends. Typically, however, the changes accelerate, and he begins to feel that what she's doing is getting out of his control. That's when he begins to feel rejection. (She's ignoring me, he thinks, and if this continues, I'll be left alone and helpless.) So he counterattacks by being quarrelsome, taunting, and threatening.

The hope is, Dr. Kiev says, that once he becomes aware of the pattern, he'll be able to break it, and not overreact to the innocent actions of his wife.

What can the wife do? That's a great dilemma, Dr. Kiev says. If the wife pursues her objective without modification, she endangers the marriage. If she capitulates, she risks her own personal future.

The wife's best route: Pursue the objectives, but she must make clear to her husband that these moves don't represent rejection, let alone a plan to abandon him. That's not an easy course, and there's bound to be a great deal of stumbling. But there is no alternative for a healthy marriage and two successful adults.

Source: Dr. Ari Kiev, psychiatrist, 150 E. 69 St., New York 10021.

Fifteen Tips for a Better Marriage

Few things in life are more worth saving than a good husband-wife partnership. It is still the best arrangement devised for domestic economics, child-rearing, and emotional nourishment. Here are 15 tips that have worked for couples seeking a well-founded, growing relationship:

1. Keep it realistic. Honeymoons may recur, but marriage is a day-by-day relationship between changing humans. Sacrifices and heartaches are challenges you must expect.

2. Don't be afraid to say something nice. Compliment one another on appearance, considerateness, and so on.

3. Show affection. Hold hands, touch, kiss—even in public.

4. Don't let the children divide you. Keep your shared responsibility to the children separate from your responsibility, and loyalty, your mate.

5. Don't let in-laws make inroads. Good relations with relatives are an advantage, but don't let them influence you against your spouse. Talk about the problems that in-laws create—and solutions to those problems.

6. Grow together intellectually. It won't work 20 years later if one partner has progressed while the other slipped backwards. Openly discuss shared goals and the intellectual expectations of one another.

7. Fight when necessary, then forget. Bring things that disturb you into the open—even if it means conflict. Seek solutions. Ultimately, there are no winners or losers. Compromise as much as possible, and then downplay the conflict. The next, far better stage, is making up.

8. Don't confuse honesty and cruelty. Honesty that has no purpose except to hurt the other is a false virtue. Protect your mate's feelings.

9. Be forthright financially. Set realistic expectations about money and its problems. Work toward shared financial goals.

10. Don't let careers diminish the marriage. Overachievers can let careers shut out the spouse. Ironically, bad marriages often diminish the career. Together, work out the right balance. Point: It's easier to get a decent job than a good mate.

11. Do things together. Couples that work and play together, also stay together. (Allow your spouse enough independence too.)

12. Cooperate sexually. Everyone is vulnerable sexually. Talk, explore, experiment. Communicate with one another and protect one another's feelings.

13. Keep talking—even when it's tough. Barriers of silence and nonmeaningful communication only grow and become more impenetrable. The more difficult it seems, the more important it is to keep communicating—especially about communicating.

14. Don't get self-righteous. Each of us has our flaws and inhibitions. A good marriage takes these into consideration. Overlook the petty irritants. If your spouse forgets to screw on the toothpaste cap, just do it yourself, and forget it.

15. Keep positive. Keep the relationship upbeat. Turn problems into opportunities for greater understanding, and work toward creative solutions and projects.

Predicting Marital Compatibility

Birth order influences marital behavior. Certain personality characteristics develop as a result of the individual's placement in the family. Examples: (1) Only children often search for a surrogate parent. (2) First children become self-reliant and goal-oriented. (3) Middle children are competitive. (4) Youngest children are more dependent. Thus, two spouses who have the same birth ranking in their respective families may have the same needs instead of complementary ones. Key: How the power in the marriage is divided. Worst marriage risk: Male only child (highest divorce rate). Best marriage risk: Female only child. Compatible combos: A man who has sisters marries a woman with brothers. A last-born male marries a first-born female. Less compatible: Both spouses are first-born or are the youngest children.

Best unions: The strongest, most resilient marriages are those in which the traditional male and female roles are blurred. Each partner takes suitable responsibilities without blind adherence to rigid sex roles. Women who play the traditional feminine role (centering their lives on their partners and children) have the most difficulty in marriage, according to one large survey.

Top executives tend to be lucky in love as well as in their work, psychiatrists who have been observing them say. Their marriages are more stable. Possible reasons: The ability to persevere at work also helps to keep their marriages together. And the high incomes executive families have cause marriage partners to have fewer conflicts over money.

Rating husbands: Married women today

value most the capacities of affection and emotion in a mate. Switch: When they were being courted, however, half of these women said that the sexual attraction of the male was the strongest influence.

Cohabitation Agreements

Unmarried couples frequently elect to live together with a commitment only to love. But many are now hedging their bets with cohabitation agreements drawn up by lawyers. Point: The agreement specifies what each partner will give toward the upkeep of the house (or apartment), living expenses, and the division of their possessions if they split up. Advantage: Financial arrangements are discussed while the couple is friendly, not during the turmoil of separation.

Special Rules For Second Weddings

Handling a second wedding properly is tricky. The aim: To avoid having guests compare your second wedding with the first one. This can't be totally eliminated, but it can be minimized.

Distinction: Second-wedding rules are determined by the bride's status. It may be hypocritical, but if it is the bride's first wedding and the groom's third or fourth, the bride can have as elaborate a wedding as she pleases, using all the traditional clothes and customs. If it is the bride's second wedding, there are many limitations:

The ceremony: Limit the guest list to members of the families and very close friends of the couple. Ask parents, grandparents, uncles, aunts, siblings, godparents, and a few friends.

Bride's outfit: Avoid a full-length gown and veil. Instead: Wear a street-length or three-quarters outfit and no veil. A bouquet is optional.

Customs: Everyone has a wedding cake. It is absolutely proper for second weddings. However, throwing the bouquet, wearing the garter, and throwing rice are *not* appropriate.

Good news: The reception can be as wild, elaborate, and exuberant as you wish. It doesn't matter who is getting married for the second time.

Socially sensitive guests:

Former in-laws and former spouses: Do not invite them. Exception: If the children of the bride and/or groom are at the wedding, you can invite their grandparents.

Children: Get your former spouse's approval before you invite the children. Then, let the children decide how they feel about attending. If the children are old enough—over 13 or so—you can make them attendants in the ceremony. However, it is improper to ask a seven- or eight-year-old to be an attendant. Reason: The child may not be fully aware of the significance of the occasion. To include such children: Let them be in charge of the guest book or pass the cake.

Gifts: Many guests invited to a second wedding gave generous gifts at the time of the first marriage. Whether you attend or not, it is best to send at least a small gift and note. Reason: These serve mainly as symbols that you approve the new union.

Source: Letitia Baldrige, consultant on executive behavior, president, Letitia Baldrige Enterprises, Inc., 151 E. 80 St., New York 10021, and author, *The Amy Vanderbilt Complete Book of Etiquette*, Doubleday & Co., Inc., New York.

Husbands and Housework

As more wives work, a greater number of husbands are doing more household chores. But they are not enthusiastic about housework. Surveys indicate the husbands' ambivalence:

88% of the men say that husbands should at

least help out around the house.

More than half agree the chores should be evenly divided, whether or not the wives have jobs.

Many husbands undertake such tasks as washing the dishes, shopping, cooking, and cleaning the bathroom. (Insight: Three-quarters of the men believe that bathroom cleaning is the wife's job.)

Many husbands only pay lip service to the idea of helping out. Surprise: The strongest proponents of a woman's right to a professional career are men under 35 years old. Yet, there is still a high percentage of husbands in this age range who do little around the house.

Most husbands believe that the household is better off if the woman stays home to raise the children and care for the house.

Exploring Middle Age Together

Middle age breeds a variety of fears in both men and women. To men, aging places them at a competitive disadvantage at work. They often question if they chose the right career, and they long to be their own boss.

Women watch their children grow up and leave home, while they fear aging as a threat to their attractiveness.

Both sexes face the troublesome realization that it may be too late to accomplish the goals set earlier.

Pressure: Middle-aged parents feel squeezed between generations. They must cope with unwanted urges of envy toward their free-spirited children who have yet to take on worldly responsibilities. At the same time, their own elderly parents grow dependent on them. As their friends and relatives die, the middle-aged are reminded of their own mortality.

Major psychological impact: Abandonment of youthful fantasies of immortality and omnipotence.

New awarenesses:

An increased sense of self.

Partners may feel less competition and rivalry.

The renewed importance of a life centered on self-awareness and self-fulfillment through heightened sensitivity.

Source: *Midlife: Developmental and Clinical Issues,* by Carola H. Mann, Brunner/Mazel Publishing, New York.

Recognizing Your Need for Solitude

The need for privacy is a fundamental physiological need like social contact, hunger, thirst, or sex. All organisms need downtime, the time out from a normal schedule, to relax.

Usually, the greater the stimulation by others, the greater the need for privacy. Continuous stimulation—parties preceded by meetings, followed by family gatherings—produces a need for solitude to compensate. Continuous stimulation is like forcing yourself to eat a big meal right after you have just finished one.

In a family situation where the need for privacy is not accepted and the need for downtime is equated with rejection, people often wind up playing psychological warfare and fighting. This gives them sulking time, which is a negative form of privacy.

At different times in your life, you may find you need different levels of stimulation and privacy, depending on how satisfied or frustrated you are. Sometimes you need more alone-time to think things out, to assimilate, or to be blank.

Physiologically, some people have a high need for stimulation. Others can't tolerate a high level of stimulation without time to digest it.

Be aware of your own time. Structure your needs. Reason: Meeting these needs will help you to conserve your psychic energy.

Situation: Both spouses work. After work, each spouse needs some private time to be alone and unwind. If each recognizes it as a valid need, they can each nap, shower or read the paper. Later, when refreshed, they can get together for some satisfying qualitative time.

If the married couple is out of synch (one needs some qualitative time while the other needs privacy), recognize the difference. You'll be better able to manage stimulation and privacy and negotiate what you need with the people around you. Possibly, for the first hour, one can ignore the other while privately reviewing the day's stimulation. Result: More energy and an eagerness for the time that remains. Both win. If they don't compromise, the result will be fights to get the downtime they need.

Source: Gisele Richardson, president, Richardson Management, 2162 Sherbrooke St. W., Montreal HRH 1G7, Quebec, Canada.

Sexual Hang-ups of Normal Couples

When it comes to sex, there is no such thing as a normal couple. Many who have never felt the need to seek therapy still have hang-ups. And women report more problems than men.

Problems reported by most women:

Difficulty in becoming sexually excited (48% cite this factor).

Trouble reaching orgasm (46%).

Too little foreplay before intercourse (38%).

Problems cited by men:

Ejaculating too quickly (37%).

Attraction to women other than mate (21%).

Too little foreplay before intercourse (21%).

Sensitivity: When asked to guess their spouses' problems, the wives detailed the husbands' complaints accurately. The husbands, however, had difficulty guessing the troubles their wives were experiencing.

The couples who report the most problems engage in sex less often.

Source: Ellen Frank, MSW, reporting in *The New England Journal of Medicine.*

Sexual Decline After Marriage

Diminishing sexual desire after marriage has been traced to a variety of causes.

Prime reasons for this condition:

Wives start to remind husbands of their mothers.

Husbands begin to remind women of their fathers.

Men think of "good" women (their wives) as being "above" sex.

Women lose interest in sex after giving birth to their children.

Men and women believe it is normal that they should lose interest in sex as they get older.

In addition: Sex suffers as the rest of the relationship falls apart because of tension, battling, or indifference. It's neither a new nor an isolated problem.

Treatment of a decreased desire for sex depends on the cause. Marital and psychological therapy are frequently tried. Sometimes specific sexual exercises are recommended in conjunction with other treatments.

Doctors feel that chances of a cure have improved notably in recent years, if the subjects are sufficiently motivated. Lack of attraction based on reality (one mate is obese or one is in love with someone else) is hard to deal with.

Unconsummated Marriages

As many as 7% of all married couples have never experienced sexual intercourse. Reasons: Overattachment to family (either parents or, in second marriages, children); strict backgrounds that fostered the notion that sex is sinful or bad; physical problems, particularly impotence.

Encouraging: Professional counseling has proved effective for two-thirds of the couples treated.

Married Women and Sex

One-third of the women in one survey reported a lack of interest or pleasure in sex. One woman in five had engaged in an extramarital affair. One in four had been involved in two to five affairs. More than three quarters of the married women say that wives should not have affairs. The same percentage were opposed to husbands having affairs.

When wives start earning more money, the resulting increase in their self-esteem heightens their appreciation of sex. Difficulty: The sexual relationship deteriorates as the wife becomes less financially dependent on her husband.

Good news: While frequency of intercourse may diminish, satisfaction is often higher among working wives.

Female sexual peak: Women don't all reach their sexual peak at about age 35, as is commonly believed. Fact: The peak varied with the woman. Some experience the greatest sexual rush in the blush of womanhood, from 18 to 25. Others build slowly toward their peak. Sometimes this crescendo extends 25 years past menopause. Variable factors: The state of the woman's health, the amount of leisure time, the desire to retain romance.

Male stripping: Shows for women are an increasingly common phenomenon, particularly in suburbia. Who attends: Women in their 30s and 40s predominate. Major attraction: Like traditional male-oriented burlesque, the shows offer a chance to laugh, relax, react without self-censorship. Clubs generally discourage men from attending. (The clubs want to provide an environment in which the women feel safe.) Another factor: A sense of power sitting back and watching men perform.

Marital Stress On Vacations

The problem arises because vacationing couples tend to spend more time in closer proximity than is normal. Another aggravating factor: Constantly changing surroundings lead to frequent, unintentional violations of the other person's space. How to deal with it: (1) Plan shorter trips. (2) Include other couples. (3) Don't spend a lot of time in cramped areas like cars, boats, campers, or hotel rooms.

Mates Who Can't Discuss Emotions

Many kind and considerate spouses have one basic flaw: They can't express their feelings or risk revealing tenderness and empathy to their partners.

Problem: This inability to communicate forces the other spouse to become a mind reader. It puts additional burdens on the relationship.

Exception: The reticent partners always make clear their anger. Should anything go wrong, they sound off.

Solutions:

Tell the silent partner the kind of emotional response you expect. It's not easy. Example: When you need comforting, say so. Problem: Usually, this type of personality is not geared to comprehending another person's needs.

Try to understand what makes your partner act this way. Usually, it's the manner in which a person is raised that determines attitudes involving emotion.

Example: People with parents who were hypochondriacs may not be comforting to loved ones who are sick. They think sickness is only an act to gain attention.

Partners often slip into traditional roles to avoid commitment. Women may play protected little girls. Men may act out the role of stoical providers who feel no need to give of themselves. Best: Work on changing yourself to accommodate the silent partner. This may spur the other to match your efforts.

Consolation: The silent partner has plenty to offer besides an inability to divulge feelings. Focus on mutual understanding to play up the healthy, positive elements of your union.

Mixed Messages: Destroying a Relationship

The mixed message is a dangerously effective way to "drive crazy" those you most cherish and regard. The technique: saying yes and then acting in a way that clearly signals no.

Examples: A husband agrees that his wife needs more help, but then he "forgets" to do his weekend chores. A parent agrees to spend more time with a child, but is always too busy with other things when the youngster's appointed hour arrives.

The mixed message is not mean-spirited behavior. It begins when we say what we think the other person wants to hear to avoid hurt feelings or conflict. Underlying cause: A reluctance to express what we feel, think, or expect, fearing that honest communication may damage the relationship. Result: A vicious cycle. Crazy-making messages bring on similar responses, tension increases, and trust is destroyed. Sexual compatibility can seriously deteriorate in intimate relationships. It is ironic that mixed messages arise most often in relationships we genuinely value.

Solution. Don't worry about psychoanalyzing the other person. Eliminate mixed messages by understanding your own feelings.

Also, watch out for these mixed-message syndromes:

Your wish is my wish. This is a false accommodation intended to ingratiate or to avoid conflict. It makes the other person feel guilty or obligated to you.

To love me is to know me. It's a false assumption that those nearest to us can divine our true wants and feelings. This syndrome is symptomatic of dependent people who dread rejection.

I know what you're thinking. This is based on an utterly false notion that one can read an intimate's mind. It enables the ostensible mind reader to project his own thoughts and wants on the other, then blame the partner for not being satisfied.

Source: *Stop! You're Driving Me Crazy,* by Dr. George R. Bach, G.P. Putnam's Sons, New York.

Family Ties and Holiday Blues

People who attach excessive emotional significance to certain holidays are particularly vulnerable to coming down with negative feelings on those days.

All the needs that haven't been met, all the goals that haven't been fulfilled, even the sheer loneliness in their lives, can be ignored for the rest of the year. But not during holidays. On holidays, when merriment is in the air and families are together, the focus on lack of fulfillment is glaring.

Particularly emotion-laden holidays: For some people, Valentine's Day, their birthdays, even Saturday nights. Christmas and New Year's affect more people (of all religions) because so much is made of these holidays that they become impossible to ignore. Expectations of family warmth, intimacy, happiness, and appreciation run high.

Most emotionally evocative aspect of the season: Christmas music and aromas, which can bring back strong childhood memories of family intimacy or lack of it.

People most prone to holiday blues are those who:

Have unsatisfactory relationships with their families.

Live alone and are lonely.

Have had negative experiences of the holidays as children. These experiences may cause negative holiday expectations now. These may turn into self-fulfilling prophecies.

Other holiday traps that affect people negatively: Viewing New Year's Eve as an omen. People who feel unsuccessful or depressed often regard the end of one year simply as a sign of the bad year to come. New Year's Day is a punctuation of the year. Sad or depressed individuals use it to criticize themselves for unmet goals. To people threatened by the idea of aging, the passing of another year can be upsetting.

Holiday behavior that's emotionally costly:

Overdoing gift-giving, party-giving, and similar forms of holiday generosity. Holidays such as Christmas provide the perfect oppor-

225

tunity for people who tend to use up their energies to please others. They give more parties than they can afford, invite more people than they can handle, exhaust themselves shopping for gifts and, generally, put themselves out. The secret hope: To be paid back in love and appreciation from others. All-too-common result: They set themselves up for disappointments.

Uncontrolled holiday highs: Going out every night, seeing more people than usual without the customary rest breaks, drinking more than usual, and getting a lot of stimulation. It all feels good at the time. But the inevitable end to the high feeling is depression. That's especially true for people who need this kind of busyness to obscure or deny their basic dissatisfaction with some aspect of their lives.

A side effect of holiday highs: After all the overstimulation, people find they need to withdraw. Problem: Insecure or depression-prone people may see their friends' healthy need for withdrawal as abandonment. Clincher: Credit-card bills start coming in, adding more weight to these feelings of futility.

How to avert holiday blues:

Plan your expenses to meet your budget.

Redesign your thinking about the holidays. Decide now what you want to get out of them. Examine how much you are doing that you don't want to do. Are holiday invitations being accepted out of duty? Determine whether friends you are spending time with are the people you really want to see.

Determine the most energy-depleting obligations tied in to the holidays and avoid them. Example: It's possible to give up the burden of sending out hundreds of Christmas cards. Instead of allowing them to pile up at Christmas, try keeping in touch with friends (but only those you want to maintain contact with) over the year.

Plan some new activity for the holidays in advance of the season. Go away to an appropriate resort (one that is sophisticated, relaxing, or scenic, depending on your mood) instead of spending your usual Christmas with Mother.

Monitor feelings closely during the holiday season. Turn down invitations from people you really don't particularly enjoy.

Bottom line: The holiday blues can be useful to you. Use them for exploring any dissatisfactions in your life, and for clarifying what you want that you're not getting or what you're getting that you don't want. Then, with these insights, organize your life more positively.

Source: Gisele Richardson, president, Richardson Management Co., 2162 Sherbrooke St. W., Montreal H3H 1G7, Quebec, Canada.

Combating Jealousy

Jealousy is a passion that festers in insecurity. To beat the monster, list:

Five principles by which to pattern your life. Follow them.

Ten good qualities about yourself. Post them so that you don't forget them.

Ten things about yourself that disappoint you. Single out those you can change and work on them. Forget the rest.

Five long-range goals you want to realize. Then enumerate the immediate steps necessary to attain each.

High anxiety can precipitate jealous attacks. Three ways to reduce stress:

1. Relax in a way that's been successful for you in the past. Possibilities: Exercise, meditation, a bath.

2. Imagine the situation that is about to occur. Foresee the possibilities for jealousy. Conjure up positive resolutions.

3. Recall your past achievements. Restore your self-esteem by reminding yourself, "I'm fine the way I am."

Jealous fits between mates can be controlled through reassurance and emotional support. You and your partner must share confidences.

Bottom line: By and large, a trace of jealousy can perk up a relationship. It keeps both partners alert to the desirable qualities in the other.

Source: *Jealousy: Taming the Green-Eyed Monster*, E. Schoenfeld, M.D., Holt, Rinehart & Winston, New York.

Infidelity

The betrayed partner perceives infidelity not just as a transgression against sexual loyalty, but as a deep emotional betrayal. Result: What's under attack, and often destroyed, when infidelity is discovered is one of the cornerstones of a marriage, the trust that the other partner can be relied on.

Who is likely to be chronically unfaithful:

Narcissists, both men and women. Those who have to supply themselves continually with objects and proofs of their own value and strength. Their problem: A disorder in the regulation of their self-esteem. This makes necessary continual nurturing of their self-image from outside sources.

Men who have a need to split women into two groups: Wives, who are pure, and mistresses, who are prostitutes. Their problem: Wives are closely identified in such men's minds with their own mothers, whereas women outside the home can be regarded as sex objects. Trap: Only sex outside the marriage seems to work. Wives are revered and loved, but can't be experienced as real sexual partners.

Least likely to be vulnerable to affairs: Homebodies. People most comfortable in the bosom of the family and a home setting.

Having an affair or two isn't necessarily indicative of a psychological problem. What it is a sign of: Yearning for some fulfillment that is not being provided by the marriage itself or by the partner

Aspects of infidelity that most affect a marriage:

Desire to have an extramarital affair, and acting on that desire.

Communicating the infidelity to one's spouse.

Of the two, communicating is far more damaging to the marriage. It's usually the ultimate in hostility to one's spouse, however rational the reasons may seem for telling, or however accidentally the evidence was left around.

Even if you are planning a divorce, it's wiser not to reveal that the reason is another person. If up to that point you haven't told, don't add unnecessarily to the pain of breakup and divorce by telling. Preferable: Make the reason for seeking divorce general incompatibility. Advantage: Lessening of pain all around, particularly for children of the marriage.

When infidelity is discovered:

Avoid giving the spouse details, however much they may be demanded or however rational, objective, or just curious the jilted one may feel about the rival. And don't rationalize that it's better to tell everything. The less said, the better, about details of the other relationship, the rival's personality, work, age, talents, problems, and feelings. The more the betrayed partner knows about the affair, the greater the pain and rejection.

See a counselor or therapist together with the spouse, at least initially. It enables an airing of some of the grievances that may have led to infidelity in the first place, in a controlled and objective setting.

Project an attitude of acceptance about the distrust and questioning you will face at home, possibly for an indefinite time to come. Be matter-of-fact when confronting regular queries like: Where were you tonight?

If there are children, reassure them that they are still loved. Reason: Children are primarily self-centered. They view the news that one of their parents has been unfaithful as a withdrawal of love from themselves, rather than from the betrayed parent. Handling older children (adolescent and up): Be calm and honest in discussing the matter. But don't go into details. Ask for their understanding. Caution: Don't expect it. All children tend to sympathize deeply with the betrayed parent, particularly if it is their mother.

Source: Leonard Diamond, M.D., a psychiatrist in private practice, 440 E. 79 St., New York 10021.

When a Marriage Needs Professional Help

When should a couple seek professional help?

Ideally, before they're married. Marriage is

one of the most important decisions an individual makes. It's made with virtually no advance information.

It sounds like you're advocating living together before marriage.

Only if it's compatible with your philosophy and moral values. The important thing is to establish what you want from marriage. There are many possibilities:

A haven against the world.

Sanctioned, available sex.

Marital status.

Creation of a family.

A devoted partner.

Some churches insist on premarital instruction before marriage rites are performed. Curiously, the best help often comes from friends and relatives who oppose the match. They, at least, make young people reflect a bit about the decision and the intended spouse. Mostly, people marry solely for love, but highly romantic love is a kind of short-term madness.

When do problems emerge?

The honeymoon phase can last two or three years. At that point, you may wake up one morning, look at your spouse, and think: Hey, I really like this person. If that happens, there's a good chance to build a lifelong relationship. If not, trouble is ahead.

Another critical point is the arrival of a child. Some of the natural childbearing approaches have done a marvelous job preparing the father for the prenatal care and the blessed event. But it's a shock the first time he comes home from work and there's no cocktail, dinner's not ready, and his wife is busy with the baby.

Don't most people marry thinking that they can change the things they dislike in the other person?

That's bound to cause problems. You can alter little habits, such as finger-picking in public. But individuals have basic personality attributes that are difficult to change. If the change has not occurred before marriage, accept it or find someone else beforehand.

The most critical attributes to consider:

How much consideration, affection, and respect are shown to each other.

The quality and quantity of sex.

What the relative dominance and submission needs are (who takes the lead and who follows).

Another extremely important consideration is how much distance and how much closeness both individuals need. Closeness works on two levels:

Sharing space and hours together.

Expressing and hearing feelings, thoughts, and ideas.

Lack of intimacy can cause problems, too. Example: When one spouse expresses heartfelt sentiments and the other responds, That's nice. Did you pay the electric bill? Lack of intimacy and poor communication are the most common marital problems today.

What are danger signs?

When you're frequently irritable with your spouse and you don't know why. When you start thinking about old lovers you could have married. When your spouse always wants to kiss at the "wrong" time. When you escape by watching too much television or, worse, drinking too much alcohol. Infidelity is a danger sign if monogamy is important to you.

When should a couple seek help?

As early as possible. Unfortunately, most people wait until it's too late, until the problems have escalated.

How does a spouse raise the subject of trouble in the marriage?

Be honest and caring since the topic can surprise, hurt, or anger a mate. The first step is to bring it up, and try and understand the problems. You say: Hey, I love you and I want our marriage to work. I want things to feel good between us again. Let's discuss our problems.

When problems are very serious, how helpful is therapy?

If one partner is not motivated, it won't work at all. If one wants help and the other is ambivalent (not sure about going for therapy but also not sure about risking no therapy), great progress is possible.

Can a badly damaged marriage be saved?

I've seen everything work. The real test is whether the marriage gratifies and meets the emotional needs of both partners. Today, if needs are not being fulfilled, people are too ready to leave their mate without making a concerted effort to work out problems.

With the alarming number of marriages ending in divorce, is it still a viable institution?

Absolutely. In fact, I think we're likely to see a swing back to more stable marriages. It's a very old-fashioned notion, but people simply have not been taking their commitments in marriage seriously enough. I think that's going to change, and for the better.

How long does counseling take?

It seems to take either about 10 weekly sessions or about a year. Usually, husband and wife are both involved, but occasionally only one partner is counseled.

Source: Clifford J. Sager, M.D., clinical professor of psychiatry, New York Hospital-The Cornell Medical Center, and director, family psychiatry, New York's Jewish Board of Family and Child Services. He has a private practice at 65 E. 76 St., New York 10021.

A Look at Marriage and Divorce

A successful marriage is a function of one partner's system of organization meshing with the other's. Example: A husband may bring needed order to the life of his wife. His wife may humanize him by bringing emotion into his life.

It often takes many years for a wife to realize that she can have different tastes from her husband and that the marriage will continue to work. (She can even have her own tube of toothpaste.)

The great virtue of some marriages is that both partners retain an important part of their privacy. Trade-off: The basic loneliness of human existence is only partly mitigated by such marriages.

The luckiest people are those who marry their best friends. Unfortunately, because most people consider their best friends to be members of their families, and because there's a taboo against incest, most people end up marrying "strangers." This often leads to dissatisfaction and, finally, to divorce.

Alternatively, one reason many people don't get married is because their early childhood was so good that they're searching for someone to fit the ideal that they have of their parents. It's the sense that they're waiting to meet the person they seem to know from before. They just can't bring themselves to marry strangers.

One phenomenon that sometimes leads to divorce is the one in which middle-aged men sometimes begin to perceive that their wives have become their mothers. Reason: When a boy reaches puberty, his mother is usually middle-aged, so when his wife reaches middle age, he transfers his repressed Oedipal desires onto her.

Married people often feel angry when their friends get divorced. Reason: Marriage is hard work. By getting divorced, the divorcing partners are affirming the belief that they're entitled to be happy and lead a carefree, easy life. The married couple, who entertain this same fantasy but don't act upon it, experience envy and then resentful anger on account of it.

Avoiding Divorce

Today divorce seems to be a trendy cure-all. Couples beleaguered with personal and business difficulties see divorce as an easy solution that is socially acceptable. After the separation, however, the former partners frequently are lonely and depressed.

To avoid divorce by default, be alert to these six snares:

Divorce is not a panacea. It will not cure dissatisfaction with work, a mid-life crisis, or a poor self-image. In fact, divorce robs you of a helpmate at your time of greatest need.

Don't choose divorce because everyone is doing it. A million marriages a year end in divorce court, but because the trail is well worn doesn't mean that it is necessarily the right way for you.

Avoid words that make separation inevitable. The very mention of the word "divorce" in an argument can shatter the fragile bond of marriage. Its repeated use will certainly destroy even the strongest union.

Don't allow one mate to precipitate the split through extreme actions. One partner will sometimes behave so inconsiderately that the other is forced to ask for a separation. Then the inconsiderate partner can claim that it was the other's idea. The best bet is for the abused partner to stand up for the marriage, calling the bluff of the other partner.

Never talk to a divorce lawyer unless both sides are serious. Even an innocent request for legal definitions by one mate can send both partners into warring camps.

Don't be lured by the glamour of divorce. Today's pop culture abounds with couples who have made fresh and constructive starts after shedding their previous mates. In the glitter of their personal successes as actors, entertainers, or sports heroes, the divorces of these stars seem to be a beacon of hope to others. Most of these new marriages are successful, however, only if both partners work very hard at making them so.

Source: *A New Life Plan: A Guide for the Divorced Woman,* by Louise Montagne, Doubleday & Co., Inc., New York.

Divorce Survey

The results of a survey of psychiatrists concerning divorce among their patients:

Who starts divorce proceedings? In 21% of the cases, the man; in 30%, the women. About half of the couples feel instigation was about even.

A majority (54%) claim their second marriages are happier than their first.

Roughly half of the couples say feelings of regret about the divorce are evenly divided. Almost 20% of the men experience the most regrets, while almost 30% of the women do.

Following divorce, 85% of the men had sex with a new partner within six months. Almost half the women waited 6 to 12 months.

More than half the married women polled in another survey have considered divorce at one time or another. Reasons for not following through: (1) Fear that the split would hurt the children. (2) Belief that the marriage would get better. Major sources of marital stress: Money, children, sex.

Divorce Without Lawyers' Fees

Divorce settlements by professional mediators are increasingly being used as more couples recognize it as a practical alternative to long-drawn-out, expensive litigation.

Prime advantages:

A mediator is a well trained, objective third party who can help a couple go their separate ways in a civilized fashion.

The fees are usually a fraction of the cost of legal fees.

It usually takes a few days. Then the agreement is approved by a judge. The parties know almost immediately where they stand.

To find a competent mediator:

American Arbitration Association.

A conciliation-and-mediation-service department, often part of a community's family-court system.

The Family Mediation Association, 2380 SW 34th Way, Ft. Lauderdale, FL 33312.

Women's Educational Level and Divorce

The more years of postgraduate education a women has, the greater her chance of divorce.

Figures from one study:

The divorce rate for women with one year of graduate work is approximately 15%.

For those with two or more years of advanced education, the rate is 19%.

Comparison: About 10% of married female

college graduates end up divorced.

Most precarious: A highly educated black woman and her husband, particularly if he is less educated.

Highest divorce rate (21%): Surprisingly, any woman with less than a high school education.

Source: *Sociological Quarterly.*

Impact of Divorce On Careers

A troublesome divorce saps executives of initiative and diminishes their skills. Consequences: Failing to recognize the emotional trauma of divorce may result in job loss or financial failure.

Roughest period: The first year of the divorce proceedings. Psychologists' advice: Ask for a less demanding job, at least for the time the divorce is being contested. If you own the company, delegate more authority to key employees (which also helps their development).

One-fifth of executives in top echelons of major corporate hierarchies are divorced.

Kids and the Single Parent

Single parents with children under the age of 18 head almost one-fifth of all American families. While 90% of these single parents are women, more men are now seeking custody of their children. Over 10,000 men in 30 states are enrolled in single-father organizations.

How the children respond:

After a breakup, children experience a deep sense of loss. Younger chidren particularly have anxiety problems. If one parent leaves, the child reasons, then the remaining one could walk out too. That would leave the child alone and unprotected.

Boys often have more difficulty adjusting than girls. With a sensible parent and no deep economic concerns, girls make the transition easily, one survey shows. Boys find the going tougher. They bid for attention with more aggressive behavior. This tests the will and nerves of the parent.

Benefits of single-parent homes:

The children mature more quickly.

They are usually more sensitive to the needs and hurts of other children.

Do the advantages and disadvantages balance each other? Yes. Life with a single parent who is at ease with the family is better for the child than a volatile existence with two warring parents.

How Children React To Joint Custody

Joint-custody arrangements, as a means of minimizing the trauma children suffer when their parents divorce, may only add to their misery. Studies show that such plans have three strikes against them. Obstacles:

Having two homes. Giving the home of each parent legal equality doesn't make them into one.

Shunting. Inconsistent rules and life styles are confusing.

Being used. Joint custody creates a situation in which both parents use the children. Example: To carry messages between the two ex-spouses.

Source: *The Levinson Letter.*

Coping With Part-Time Stepchildren

Being a stepparent is difficult. On a part-time basis, when you only see a spouse's children on weekends or vacations, it is usually a no-win situation. You have parental responsibilities, but you're not a parent. Also, the spouse is likely to be of little help because of guilt.

The atmosphere can grow strained, and discipline is next to impossible. Suggestions for easing the situation:

Accept the relationship and its limitations. Recognize that it is difficult for all parties, including the children.

Get to know the children by listening to them. If they're receptive, ask questions about their school life, likes and dislikes in food, music, and pop celebrities and stars. Steer clear of questions that appear to pry into the other parent's life.

Avoid voicing opinions and cracking jokes until you get to know the children well. Grim example: The stepmother who jokes about psychiatry, only to discover that the children's mother has been going to a therapist for years.

Don't try to make everything perfect. That only adds to the tension. Plan special events and outings. Don't try to pack every day with unforgettable experiences. Let them find ways to fit themselves into the rhythm of your home life.

Create opportunities for the children to make friends in your locale. Swimming and riding clubs are places where children meet. An ideal situation would be an acquaintance with another part-time stepparent whose visiting stepchildren are in the same age group.

Decide exactly what you can and cannot accept. Children can be messy, noisy, and inconsiderate. Forbear when possible, deciding which habits you can temporarily put up with. Get your spouse to lay down the law.

Don't let the spouse load all parental responsibilities on to you. They are his or her children, not yours.

When visits are infrequent, keep in touch by adding a few words to telephone conversations or letters.

Ultimately, the best solution is to aim at becoming a friend, not a relative, of the children, sharing their concerns and enjoying their company.

Pointers for Parents

• Child discipline should: (1) Produce the desired change or growth. (2) Preserve the offspring's self-esteem. (3) Maintain a close relationship between the disciplinarian and the child. Punishment that is too frequent or too severe runs the risk of undermining the child's self-confidence or alienating the child from the parent.
Source: *How to Influence Children,* by Charles Schaefer, Van Nostrand and Reinhold Co., New York.

• Children learn fear when they realize certain events are beyond their control. Don't tease or shame a fearful child. It could bring on withdrawal or turn the fear into a form of belligerence. Point: Treat all fears seriously. If a child is afraid of shadows on the bedroom wall, move the bed so that they aren't visible. Best: Discuss openly the fears you had as a child and ways you confronted them. This lesson is reinforced by similar experiences recounted by grandparents.
Source: *Best Practical Parenting.* Meadowbrook Press, Deephaven, MN.

• Prevent pot smoking. Parents who drink heavily or are in other ways dependent upon drugs themselves (such as prolonged usage of tranquilizers) are more likely to rear children with similar patterns, such as a tendency to smoke marijuana. Children are quick to recognize hypocrisy.

• Your children's allowance. Don't cut off or reduce your children's allowance just because they bought something you think was a mistake. The allowance is a learning tool. Like riding a bicycle, they have to fall off a few times before learning to keep their balance. You might point out the disadvantage of squandering money on a flimsy toy that's soon broken. But, generally, a child who no longer has either the money or a toy in usable condition will be able to draw the appropriate conclusion. On the other hand, if children buy something that's really dangerous or seriously inappropriate, you should tell them they can't have it, whether it was bought with money you gave them or with money earned on their own.

• Happiest mothers. Women who gave

birth later in life are happier than those who had children when they were young (16 to 20). Mothers under greatest stress: Those with children under six, or with teenagers. More than half the women who responded to the survey claimed they would feel incomplete as women if they did not have any children.

• The only-child myth: They are selfish, spoiled, and dependent. The facts: Only children test out better than those in their age groups from two-child families. They have an edge in intelligence, achievement, and good conduct toward adults. Differences: Onlies want more education and fewer children. They are less sociable and are fond of solitary artistic and intellectual activities. Parents who choose to have one child rear the child with few sexual stereotypes.

• Happier baby. Dab a little of Mom's perfume on the crib sheet. The baby feels more secure and sleeps more soundly.

• Putting shoes on a toddler is facilitated by placing the child in a high chair. Also, wet the shoelaces slightly before tying them. They stay tied that way. Put plastic bags over shoes before slipping them into boots. This helps the boots go on and it will keep the shoes dry.

Source: *Best Practical Parenting Tips.* Meadowbrook Press, Deephaven, MN.

Baby Shortage Adoption Strategies

Adoptable children are in short supply. Why: Current attitudes toward contraception, abortion, and single parenting are generally more lenient than they were even 10 years ago. As a result, fewer babies are available for adoption through society's traditional channels.

Adoption agencies are not the place to go if you or your spouse are over 40, previously married, in less than perfect health, overweight, both working, already parents, or highly selective about the type of child you want to adopt. Any one of these factors can make you ineligible to adopt a child through an agency.

But children are available for adoption through nontraditional sources. Key: Direct action and some risk-taking.

Today, a pregnant young woman is likely to go to an organization that provides pregnancy counseling. These agencies are good places to focus your search for a child.

To locate these pregnancy-counseling centers, look for ads in youth-oriented newspapers, especially those with an alternative-lifestyle format. Stop in at the student health service of a nearby college. Check the campus newspaper, too. Talk to clergymen, social workers, anyone who works with young adults.

Tell the counselors at the women's clinics that you are personally interested in adopting a child. Ask them to keep you in mind if a woman they counsel is thinking of a private adoption.

Presenting yourself: Prepare a different kind of resume. Include with the fact sheet a picture of yourself and your spouse along with your names, address, and telephone number. Describe your background, interests, and ambitions. Explain why you want to adopt, what a child will mean to you, how long you have been looking.

What you are likely to encounter: Empathy mixed with suspicion. The primary concern of any counselor is the welfare of the expectant mother and her child. By explaining in detail your reasons for an alternative to the adoption establishment, you may be able to convince the counselor and the expectant mother to help you.

Covering expense: Be prepared to help the mother with the costs of her pregnancy. Guideline: Expenses of $5,000 to $7,000 are reasonable. Payments in the range of $20,000 to $40,000 leave you open to a charge of child-buying.

Legal help: The mother needs an attorney to make clear the legal consequences of having her baby adopted. Be ready to bear those costs. Your own attorney must handle matters in a way that ensures that the adoption is strictly legal.

More information: *Beating the Adoption Game,* by Cynthia D. Martin, Oak Tree Publications, San Diego, CA.

Choosing the Right Day-Care Center

Day-care centers, once associated with inner cities or other countries, are increasingly replacing the traditional nannies in many American households.

Tuned to the business world's hours and calendar (8 a.m. to 6 p.m. with weekends and holidays off), privately owned centers are run for profit. Drop-off and pickup hours may be flexible, payment arrangements often are not. A few centers will accept children part-time at reduced fees. Others require full payment whatever the child's hours. And, there is considerable variation in fees.

Age levels: Some centers now accept babies as young as two months. Additionally, more educational institutions—from nursery schools through the elementary grades—are extending their hours and activities to include a day-care program.

Buyers' market: Because of the limited number of private centers in many areas, parents feel some urgency to have their child accepted anyplace, at any cost. Don't give in to that panic. Visit every center that is geographically and financially feasible.

Consider the overall environment:

Ambience. Children need something cheerful, with brightly colored areas, pictures to look at, and a lot of things around to handle. Cleanliness goes without saying. Do a safety check as well.

Approach. Discuss the center's philosophy about child-rearing. It is vital for children to have consistency of approach. If, for example, the center pushes early toilet training and you don't you will have a confused child on your hands.

Activities. Check out the program offered, and its duration. Children thrive on a balance of active and quiet play. If it's structured play, short doses are best. Be sure there is some outdoor time allotted during good weather.

Apparatus. Chairs and tables should include enough small-scaled sets to let three-footers feel at home. Books and toys should be varied and in good condition. One of the great advantages of a top-notch center is that it will offer such things as a well equipped "kitchen area" scaled to size and climbing apparatus, things that space and money usually preclude at home.

Meals and snacks. Lunches must be nutritious. It is to your advantage that they also be hot. Snacks should be regularly scheduled throughout the day. And an infant's feedings should fit in with your master plan.

Ratio of staff to children. Centers are licensed by each state, which dictates the minimum requirements. As a guideline: Federally supported centers must have one staff member per three children under two years of age; one staffer per six two-year-olds; one per eight three- to ten-year-olds. (Note: By most private standards, that's a low standard.)

Staff attitudes. Pay attention to how the center's personnel act toward the children, the facility itself, and you. If they don't respect the center, find out why. There's no reason, though, for not treating the children lovingly, attentively, and as individuals. And, if they treat you only as an obstacle, they aren't doing their jobs either.

Children's attitudes. Observe the others. Are they involved, do they seem happy to be where they are? If they aren't your child probably won't be. Forget it and find another.

Caution: Not all children, especially the under-three-year-olds, cope well under group care. If your youngster gives off excessive anxiety signals after the early stages, it doesn't mean that you, the center, or the child have failed. It probably means that your tot needs the security of home just a little longer.

Source: Janet Spencer Sking, editor-in chief, *Mother's Manual.*

What Your Baby-Sitter Needs to Know

- Where to reach you, a friend, or a relative.
- Emergency phone numbers for family doctor, fire and police departments.

- What, when, and whether to feed the child.
- Bedtime routine: Does the child sleep with a toy or stuffed animal, with any lights left on, or with an open window?
- Where to find: Diapers, fresh clothes, infant feeding equipment.
- How to raise or lower the sides of the crib.
- Any allergies or medical problems the child might have.
- When to expect you home from your engagement.
- How much the baby-sitting fee is.
- How the sitter will get home.

Monitoring Your Child's Development

As two-career households multiply, parents have a more laissez-faire attitude toward child development. This frequently leads to problems. Parents need to find time to monitor their child's development. Reasons: What appear to be problems may be the normal course of behavior development. If you recognize signs of real disturbance or failure to mature, you may be able to remedy the situation before serious problems get a chance to develop.

The major aspects of a child's development to monitor:

Task mastery: Motor behavior, such as walking, building with blocks, school-related behavior.

Social competence: Language skills and social relations.

The key: Normal development is fraught with stress. Although development is not linear, there is an overall continuity. You want there to be more progression than regression.

Outline of a child's development, from 18 months to six years old, as described by authorities:*

Eighteen months: The child is charged with energy and rushes into everything. Expect

*Of course, these are only guidelines. Many children develop more rapidly, others more slowly.

crying tantrums from even the gentlest child. Task mastery: Can walk, run, sit, push or pull toys, turn pages of a large book, scribble. Social competence: Vocabulary consists of words such as mama, dada, and a few names. Child begins to understand the concept of possession. Tends to get absorbed in anything that attracts his attention. Does not relate well to others his age.

Two years: An explorer. Task mastery: Likes to exercise his senses of touch, smell, taste and to play with dolls, books, beads. Social competence: Uses several hundred words. Loves to name things and to be read to. A gentle, docile, conforming age. But socialization between children is not particularly harmonious. Requires considerable supervision. Problem: While the two-year-old is docile, the two-and-a-half-year-old may be demanding, difficult, ritualistic. Example: The two-year-old gets into bed early but may need extra attention. The two-and-a-half-year-old may need all kinds of ritualistic behavior to get him into bed at all.

Three years: Again, there are differences between the three-year-old and the three-and-a-half-year-old child. At three, conformity and comfortable interpersonal relations are evident. A half year later, the child often refuses to obey and is resistant, demanding, strong willed, and insecure. Task mastery: Good balance and control in walking and running at three, but at three and a half the motor skills are less effective and the child often stumbles, trembles, and may develop tics. Social competence: At three, the child can string together words and use them directly with other children. However, at three and a half, stuttering may occur. Big accomplishment: Completion of toilet training. Threes are proud that they can feed and dress themselves, and they enjoy the company of others. Three-and-a-half-year-olds are stubborn and tend to make special trouble for their mothers though they may be sociable with friends and strangers.

Four: Imaginative, wild, and secure. Task mastery: Capable, has good balance, and is able to skip, catch, use roller skates, ride a small bicycle, copy pictures, do cutouts and use blocks. Social competence: Tends to brag,

235

may lie or swear, is obsessed with the word "why," is highly enthusiastic and positive with others, enjoys playing with other children, has strong group identification in nursery school. As the child nears five, uncertainty builds. The child's strong interest is in whether or not things are real. He is more self-motivated, has greater perseverance, is less wild, is better able to stand frustration. Emotionally, the child may be uncertain and highly unpredictable. Begins to have an awareness of good and bad.

Five: Quieter and more conforming than four. Likes to please and obey mother. Has little interest in the new or strange. Attempts only what he can achieve. Loves to be read to, talked to, and informed about the world. Task mastery: Skips, walks on tiptoe, loves tricycles, stilts, roller skates, jump ropes, and acrobatics. Likes to lace shoes and do buttons. Helps set the table, prints name, cuts, traces, draws, pastes, strings beads. Social competence: Loves to talk, answers questions, asks fewer and more relevant questions, gets excited about the prospect of reading, tries to figure things out conceptually, likes to assume responsibilities. It's easy to get child to bed, but he may have frightening dreams and awaken crying. At the end of the fifth year, the child displays polarities, and is hesitant, dawdling and indecisive one moment, then overdemanding and explosive the next. Vacillates between shy and very bold and affectionate. The child is in a constant state of tension, though he may be calmer at school than at home. Physically: May develop headaches, many colds, stomachaches and other pains. May revert to toilet accidents when overexcited.

Six: A paradoxical age; the child lives at opposite extremes. Enthusiasm and naivete alternate with anger and stubbornness. Has difficulty making up mind. Biggest problem: Relationship with mother. Mother was formerly the center of the child's world. Now the child is. This foreshadows the classic adolescent conflict. It's a very trying period for parents. Task mastery: Restlessness results in many accidents, especially for fine eye-hand coordination tasks such as using scissors and hammering toy nails. Attempts to do things that exceed his ability. Loves to draw, builds with blocks, molds clay and mud, begins to read and write, loves to print. Social competence: Talks incessantly, has good pronunciation and grammatical construction, shows great curiosity, may be good on the telephone, loves table games. Conflict with the mother causes many problems. Child loves her, depends on her, and needs her, but when there are difficulties, the child takes all his conflicts out on her. Relationships with siblings and other children are variable. May not be able to tolerate losing. Will break up a game or cheat rather than lose. Extremely jealous and wants to make sure no one gets a bigger piece of the pie than he does. May frequently lie, deny guilt for a wrongdoing, fidget, spill things, even steal.

Public Schooling for Children with Learning Disabilities

Many parents must face frustrating problems with children who are underachievers in public school. In the past, unless the children were seriously handicapped, mentally or physically, there was little recourse except to send them to private schools, a very costly alternative.

Even in private schools, parents quickly discover that lots of attention is given to outstanding students, but poorer students get little notice. If the parent complains, there may even be an effort to expel the child. With academic tenure, strong teachers' unions and increasing evidence of teacher burnout, even teachers in schools specially designed for seriously disturbed or handicapped young people rarely appear to exercise initiative to motivate their poorer students.

Important fact: Many schools have a variety of special resources for poorly performing youngsters that are underutilized because neither teachers nor administrators want to cope with anything but the most routine situations. Teacher conferences, talks with the principal, and letters or complaints usually produce little in the way of real action.

New power for parents: Leverage is now on their side to get a good public school education for their difficult-to-educate child. Federal legislation mandates that every child must receive an education suited to that child's special needs. This contrasts sharply with the past emphasis on a standard education. Eligible children are those with psychological or physical difficulties that interfere with their academic progress.

How to begin: Schools are required to provide (but often don't without prodding) a booklet describing the student's rights and the procedures for implementation. Next step: Request that the school undertake diagnostic testing of the child.

Meet with the school psychologist (or guidance counselor if there is no psychologist). Have a complete summary of what areas are troublesome to your child. Be specific. Examples: Specify long division, not math in general, or writing complete and correct sentences.

Developing the Individual Education Plan (IEP). Assuming there is reasonable evidence of a learning difficulty that is handicapping the child in making academic progress (and the problem is not simply laziness or troublemaking), your case must be submitted to the school's Committee on the Handicapped. The committee is composed of teachers, administrators, parents of learning-disabled children, and specialists such as physicians and psychologists. The law mandates that such a committee be established. The chairperson of that committee, presuming that there is evidence of a persistent learning difficulty, must then designate someone in the school to draw up an IEP. This plan is tailored to the child's needs, not the school's routines.

Possible elements:

Extra tutoring in a difficult subject, or in troublesome areas.

Untimed exams in the regular classroom, or special exams after class.

A shift in teachers (to one known for experi-

ence and skill in teaching the handicapped).

Additional diagnostic testing at clinics, hospitals, or other institutions.

Special assignments in a given class to be carefully graded and discussed and even an untimed version of the Scholastic Aptitude Test, which is crucial for college admission.

The parent must approve the IEP and has the right to be consulted in its formulation. The IEP must establish specific objectives for the upcoming year. Examples: Mastery of working out fractions or spelling at the tenth-grade levels. The committee must monitor the plan to be sure the objectives are being realized. If not, new remedial measures must be taken.

All of these special procedures are paid for by the school. It is important to note, however, that the law does not specify what should be done. Rather, and very sensibly, it specifies the process by which the child gets individualized attention. None of this happens automatically. There is a need for parental initiative in getting the procedure started and pushing to get the critical IEP prepared. Then the plan can move on its momentum, in most cases.

The critical difference between this and what has happened in the past is that children with difficulties are not shunted off to parent-paid private schools or to taxpayer-paid special schools for the severely handicapped. The children are mainstreamed, kept in their regular schools, but with a carefully tailored plan that utilizes, as much as possible, all the learning resources of the school and its personnel. The parents of an underachieving child can't be ignored or volleyed back and forth between teachers and administrators.

Source: Dr. Miriam Lewin, associate professor of psychology, Manhattanville College, Purchase, NY 10577.

Learning Disabilities And Diet

Children with learning disabilities do better when following certain diets, according to studies. The results apply to hyperactivity, too. For the names of doctors in your area pursuing this work, contact Society for Clinical Ecology, Robert Collier, Medical Secretary, 4045 Wadsworth Blvd., Wheat Ridge, CO 80033.

Choosing a Private School

When you decide to send your child to a private school, you commit yourself to a major investment. Make sure it pays off.

For starters: Schools differ in personality almost as widely as do children. Look for the one that will do the most for your child. There should be a good fit between your youngster and the school.

The publications listed below can help you find schools that are right for your child. Write to each school for its catalog, descriptive brochures, and student handbook. They will tell you a lot about the school. But, they're also designed as promotional pieces. Be alert to the kinds of information they omit.

Academics:

Is the school accredited by the state education department or by one of the regional accrediting associations?

What is the student/faculty ratio? The average class size?

Do course descriptions suggest both breadth and depth in the humanities, social sciences, languages, and sciences? Is there an active program in the creative arts? Does the school have a vocational training program?

Reminder: Much learning takes place outside the classroom. Get a feel for the environment (the campus, physical facilities, geographical mix of the student body, arrangements for supervision, counseling, and so on).

Student life:

What kinds of social activities are provided? How extensive is the program? Is there a regular program of cultural events? Are social and cultural facilities available in a nearby community? Are students encouraged to attend these events?

How extensive is the sports program? Does it stress interscholastic or intramural competition?

What health facilities are available for routine illnesses? For emergencies?

Check the student handbook to find out what regulations govern student conduct. Do students develop and administer the code of conduct? Or is the code imposed by school authorities? Is there a dress code?

Visit the schools you and your youngster find most attractive. Drop in on classes in session.

Vist the library, science labs, and classroom. Talk at length with teachers.

Do dormitories have a homelike atmosphere? Opportunities for privacy?

Are meals served family- or cafeteria-style?

The administration:

How long has the headmaster or headmistress been at the school? What is the average tenure of teachers? (Rapid turnover of the faculty suggests that something is wrong with the way the school is being run.)

Question the extent of the school's scholarship program and the basis on which financial aid is awarded. (Most schools have some scholarship money available.)

What are the average Scholastic Aptitude Test scores for the last three graduating classes? What percentage went on to college? Which colleges?

At a school with a large day-student population, what happens to boarding students on weekends and short vacations?

A responsible admissions policy is based on careful analysis of all prospective students' records. If an admissions officer wants to enroll your child before seeing all the records, he may be more interested in your checkbook than your child.

Tuition insurance for child in private school: Many schools participate in insurance programs of this nature. The premiums are included in the annual fee. It provides protection if the child is expelled or drops out of school for any reason and the parent is still liable for tuition.

Useful Private-School Directories

Private-School Handbook lists a wide variety of schools, describes their history, faculty, facilities, and so on. Porter Sargent Publishers, 11 Beacon St. Boston 02108.

The Educational Register is a highly selective list published by Vincent/Curtis, 224 Clarendon, Boston 02116.

The Bunting and Lyon Blue Book, also selective, includes comments about the schools. Bunting and Lyon, 238 N. Main St., Wallingford, CT 06492.

Lovejoy's Prep-School Guide is a comprehensive listing, with editorial commentary. Simon & Schuster, Inc., 1230 Sixth Ave., New York 10020.

Planning Time for Your Children

Kids need parental attention most during their first decade. Irony: This is the very period when many parents are unusually preoccupied with the development of their own careers.

Item: In one survey of 11-year-olds, half the children of working mothers wished their mothers spent more time with them. Even more significant: 30% of the kids with nonworking mothers said the same thing.

In another classic study, fathers estimated they spent 15 to 20 minutes a day interacting with their babies. Reality: The time spent with the babies actually averaged 37.7 seconds per day.

How to make the time spent with your children count:

Focus your attention on the child. Turn off the radio or television. Don't transmit the feeling that you would rather be doing something else. Maintain eye contact. Touch them every so often, too.

Encourage open communication. Don't dominate conversations.

Be willing to help in any way they request.

Keep a positive attitude. Don't belittle what the child offers.

Don't be afraid to spend time leisurely with your child. An afternoon off to take a walk, go on a fishing trip, or read aloud is cherished in the child's memory.

Insight: Usually a single moment of attention when the child needs it is worth substantial amounts of idle time together. Common mistake: Parents believe that a long summer vacation provides all the time together a child requires. Point: Moments given freely when the child yearns for them are far more meaningful. One resort: If you are extremely busy, schedule time with your children. Write the appointment in your datebook. Caution: Never cancel or neglect appointments. It tells the children that your time with them isn't as important as it might be.

Source: *Prime-Time Parenting,* by Kay Kuzman, Rawson, Wade Publishers, New York.

Parent-Child Communication

The ideal family, according to the experts, is one in which both the parents and their children share feelings of achievement, cooperation, and communication. Basics:

Find something at which each child can succeed. Let them know that you are proud of the things they have accomplished.

Listen to your children as if they were your best friends. Start by putting aside 10 minutes a day to devote to this communication.

Cut down unnecessary demands that you make on your children, which you don't enforce. Be sure that what you do ask is explained and enforced. Give your children room to make choices for themselves.

Set limits and stand by them. Let your children know at an early age what the house rules are.

Establish priorities with your children. Allow them to assume some responsibilities

239

for achieving goals. Encourage the children to make some necessary decisions and to live by them.

Have the courage to admit when you are wrong. Children gain in self-esteem when they learn that sometimes *they* can be right.

Family Council

Use regular family meetings to enhance communication between members and help with decision-making. Schedule them at a time convenient to every member. For example, after Sunday dinner. Benefits: They permit every member to have a voice in deciding family rules. Councils with younger children are usually used for teaching. With teenagers they are best for communication, planning and problem solving.

Controlling Anger Between Parents And Children

While few families will admit to it, anger is a constant undercurrent. Parental expectations can conflict with the children's wishes. And children resent limitations placed on them.

Example: Because a son has musical talent, don't expect him to love piano lessons. If he prefers baseball, don't become angry.

Listen to your children's dreams and tell them yours. You'll learn what's important to one another.

Anger also manifests itself in indirect fighting. Children say they'll do something, then don't. They constantly "forget" to do what they are told. They pretend not to hear what is addressed to them. They often act bored and roll their eyes skyward when any instruction begins.

Adults also indulge in this passive anger.

They are notorious for agreeing to do something for a child, then neglecting it. They commonly say, "Of course, dear," without hearing a word the child has said. And they are usually too busy to help a child with a problem that isn't urgent.

To defuse anger, both sides must learn to fight fair. No winner or loser will result, just a positive way of deploying anger.

Learn to express anger and frustration without being cruel.

Pass up things you don't want to do rather than making a promise, then forgetting it.

Make expectations realistic. Don't overload your children with goals they can't possibly meet.

Know and try to understand the strengths and limitations of each other. Then both sides can be appreciated for their very real accomplishments.

Share your sensitivities. Parents: Don't mask them to appear strong. The result will appear to be indifference.

Source: *How to Fight Fair With Your Kids . . . And Win,* Luree Nicholson and Laura Torbet, Harcourt Brace Jovanovich, New York.

Why Children Lie

Most children's lies are really just wishful thoughts, exaggerations, or fantasies. But chronic liars may be revealing deep problems of self-worth, a lack of security, or even a physical disability (such as poor eyesight, hearing, or motor control). Recommended: (1) Treat "tall tales" sympathetically. Say: "That's the way you'd like it to be," or "Wouldn't it be nice if that were really true." (2) Don't invade the child's privacy and force him to lie when he doesn't want to share his thoughts. (3) Be supportive when the child admits to doing wrong, or you will encourage the child to lie the next time.

Bottom line: Fairness, understanding, and reasonable reprimands will discourage lies. Stressful conditions may make lying a way of life.

Friendship Between Children Of Different Ages

Cross-age friendships among children are rarely encouraged in our society. Such friendships are healthy and helpful in developing patience, sensitivity, and nurturant behavior among older children. The younger children learn key skills and behavioral patterns faster than they would normally.

Playing with younger or older children can help children who are bigger, smaller, smarter, or slower than their age group's norm. It also helps those who lack the verbal fluency or athletic skills of their peers.

Negatives: Cross-age associations may encourage bullying or immaturity among older children, or they may engage younger children in activities for which they're not ready. But psychologists feel that the benefits of cross-age friendships outweigh the dangers.

Source: *Child Friendships,* by Zick Rubin, Harvard University Press, Cambridge, MA.

Good Ways for Kids To Earn Money

The best jobs for youngsters are small, independent businesses they can start up and run themselves. Advantages: They will learn the importance of reliability, quality, competition, and salesmanship. Earning money will instill a sense of pride in them that will replace the frustration and boredom experienced by many of today's young people. Children agree. More than 80% of the third-grade schoolchildren polled preferred earning their own money to receiving allowances.

The age to begin depends on the child. A six-year-old child isn't too young to do light chores around the house or to help a neighbor.

Offer help, not interference. Join the brainstorming sessions the children have when considering a job. Let them know they can call on you for advice. Also appropriate: To advance a small loan for the start-up of the venture. Don't make the decisions or bail out the child when problems arise. It's not the success of the business that counts, but the lessons that children can learn from it, including the mistakes.

Good idea: Some children launch job clubs that provide services such as running errands, washing windows, cleaning garages, catering birthday parties, doing lawn work, and many other tasks that adults like to avoid.

Source: *Kids and Cash,* Oak Tree Publications, San Diego, CA.

Children of Successful Parents

An agonizing problem for many successful executives is the failure of their children. Common cause is the parent's inability to distinguish between office and home.

At work, the executive is accustomed to subordinates who comply with his wishes promptly and automatically. Unconsciously, he expects exactly the same response from his family.

Result: This behavior stifles self-esteem and frequently creates resentment. Children are unable to compete, avoid risks, can't survive setbacks. Often they turn to nonachieving peers to win acceptance. Boredom with this kind of existence leads to more severe problems: Alcohol, drugs, avoidance of all responsibility.

Prevention: Conscious effort to keep aware that children are not employees. They need a healthy concept of themselves to reach their full potential.

Simple test: Occasionally ask your children to make a list of their good and bad qualities. If the negatives outweigh the positives in number or strength, it's time to boost their self-esteem.

Source: *Behavioral Sciences Newsletter.*

Finding the Right Camp for Your Child

With 8,500 residential camps and about 450 special clinic camps in the U.S., there is little doubt that there is one to suit your child. Most camps offer comprehensive programs of sports, cultural activities, and skill development in fields as varied as tennis, the performing arts, dressmaking, and gymnastics. Special clinic camps appeal primarily to those who want to concentrate on a single sport, but also include camps for weight watchers, mountain climbers, and salt-water sailors. The trick is to find the right camp for your child.

For starters:

The American Camping Association (ACA) accredits some 2,800 camps in the country, and checks their accreditation every three years. It publishes a *Parents Guide to Accredited Camps** for four regions: Northeast, South, Midwest, West. An index lists the programs and schools, giving them special emphasis. The ACA does not recommend specific camps to parents. It refers them to camp advisory services.

State and regional associations of camp directors across the country provide information about member schools. The Association of Independent Camps (AIC) in New York, for instance, represents 75 private, residential camps in New England and the Middle Atlantic states. Like the ACA, the AIC does not provide advisory services to parents. It offers a free booklet describing member camps.

Camp advisory services, or referral agencies as they are called in the trade, make specific recommendations to parents. They vary widely in character, but "good" agencies have two things in common. They work with a reasonably large number of camps. And they do not recommend any camp unless they have personal knowledge of it. Some advisory services:

1. The Parents League of New York, 115 E. 82 St., New York 10028. It does not visit camps, but has knowledge of several hundred responses from parents whose children have attended them.

2. The Camp Advisory Service, 500 Fifth Ave., New York 10110. Staff members visit camps and report to the counselors. No camp is recommended that has not been checked out.

3. Camp Consulting Services, Ltd., 14 Wesley Court, Huntington, NY 11743. A small agency that provides more personalized service. President Joanna Howe works with 65 camps, which she spends the entire summer visiting, "eating the food, swimming in the lake, doing the whole routine."

Final step: After you have found one or two camps that sound good, ask for the names of parents in the area who have sent their children there and phone them for their opinions. A visit to a camp is rarely possible before the season begins.

Next best: Get the most out of your interview with the director. Ask about the basics: The director's experience and training. Activities program and facilities. Health and safety precautions. Size, age, and experience of the staff (there should be some old hands as well as young ones).

**Parents Guides* are available from the national office: ACA, Bradford Woods, Martinsville, IN 46151.

Hiring a Mother's Helper for Summer Vacation

Vacations are more relaxing for the whole family when a mother's helper looks after the children. The term *au pair* is often used for students who are hired to do this. It is French for as an equal, signifying that the young person is to be treated as a member of the family. Finding the right *au pair:*

Determine what family members expect. Make a detailed list of all duties. It is easy to remove a chore. It causes resentment to add one later.

Be realistic as to how much responsibility the *au pair* must take. Will the parents be absent for the week or on weekends? If so, it is

**Parents Guides* are available from the national office: ACA, Bradford Woods, Martinsville, IN 46151.

necessary to choose an older college student with child-care experience.

Make up a checklist. Include: Cooking (for the children only, or for the family), cleaning, laundry, ironing, etc. Adjust the salary according to the work load.

Pay scale: $55 to $150 per week, with a day or a day-and-half off. (This is suggested by New York's Anne Andrews Agency, which has matched students with families for 45 years.*) At the lower end of the scale are 14-to 15-year-olds, who take on light duties. The scale rises with maturity, responsibility, and skill. However, if the perks are lavish (swimming pool, sailboat, tennis court), take that into account.

Start the search as early as possible. Don't hire if you are not enthusiastic.

*The Anne Andrews Agency, 538 Madison Ave, New York 10022, assists in making countrywide placements.

Tips for Prospective Mother's Helpers

Never settle for a family. Wait for a wonderful one.

List or mention all hobbies, sports, and foreign languages. Examples: Cooking, French, and horsemanship could land you a job in the south of France, where you would ride with, shop for, and feed a child or two.

Ask the mother of a prospective summer family to describe, in detail, a typical day. Be sure that all jobs are outlined and agreed upon before you are hired. Suggestion: If possible, have a trial baby-sitting run.

Pressure on Children: How Much Is Too Much?

Is there more pressure on children today than there was 20 years ago?

Probably. Because there is more anxiety

among parents. Sophisticated parents, especially, are relying too much on what they are reading instead of trusting instincts, genetics, and nature. Years ago there was one book on child-rearing: Dr. Spock's. Today there are experts on every aspect of child development. And the experts often disagree. There are books to get your child walking, talking, and reading earlier, faster, and better, to keep him thin, to help him make friends, etc. All that builds up pressure on parents and children.

Some kids from successful executive families have too much pressure put on them. Others not enough. Some parents expect their kids to be bright, entertaining, athletic, fun, and perfect companions. Other children are virtually unnurtured. No expectations are thrust on them and they are not motivated to perform nearly as well as they could.

Are parents more competitive?

Many parental anxieties over landmarks such as walking and talking are due not so much to competition as to concern that the child is developing properly. But pressuring your child to read before he is ready, just to keep up with your neighbor, is not helpful.

How do you know a child is ready?

Temperament. You can read that in your child's first few years of life. The patterns develop. More active than passive. More motor-oriented than pensive. More shy than sociable.

Do parents who stay available to a child through threatening new situations run the risk of raising less-independent offspring?

No. Knowing what your chld can and cannot tolerate is not the same as being overprotective. The hardest thing for parents to know is when they are needed and when they are not. And this changes over time. Children usually let you know when you are caring beyond their needs.

Does the increasing divorce rate put additional pressure on children?

Definitely. The shifting parental roles, the more complicated sibling relationships, and the varying age groups of children from first, second and third marriages all complicate the lives of children.

College-entrance scores are going down. But most children today seem smarter than their parents were at that age. How do you explain that?

Kids today are 100% more sophisticated and often more creative than their parents were at the same age. But their parents could read better, spell better, and knew more history. Prime reason: today, the school environment has to compete with the hyperstimulation of television, radio, movies and sensational news reporting of rape, incest, and violence. These stimuli have to be controlled for the basic academic input to have an impact.

Are the parents to blame for exposing their children to this overload?

Parents today are not consistent. They pressure a child to do well. But then they're not available to help the child implement the expectations. They don't monitor the children's activities. Then, when problems arise, parents send the kids to psychiatrists instead of being there in the first place to prevent the problems. What is overlooked: Even though kids today are well-informed and sophisticated they are still kids and need parenting.

Are dual-career couples too busy to look after their children?

Successful parents, in terms of both career and parenting, consider the needs of their children in their work decisions. They establish priorities to evaluate career moves.

Parents must recognize that parenting means time and emotional involvement with their child. The fact that many couples are opting to have children later in life, after a career is underway, or not at all, is a good sign. If couples have children when they feel comfortable about it instead of feeling pressured, their children won't be so pressured either.

Source: Pearl-Ellen Gordon, Ph.D., practicing child psychologist, 41 E. 74 St., New York 10021.

How to Talk To Teenagers

Everyone knows that adolescence is a time of turbulence. It's then that parental help is perceived as interfering, concern as babying, and advice as bossing. Dilemmas for parents: How to help when assistance is resented? How to counsel when guidance is rejected? How to communicate with the teenager when attention is taken as attack?

What is really going on: The teenager is trying to remake his childhood personality into a grown-up one with an individual identity, establish new identifications with peers, and adjust to many physical changes. This process takes time and a great deal of trial and error. It also requires distancing himself from his parents.

Helpful guidelines: Accept the child's need for rebellion during this phase of development. Relax in the face of the inevitable. Expect irritating behavior that flies in the face of everything you hold dear. (Example: If scholarship is valued, grades will go down; if neatness is prized, both the teenager's room and personal appearance will become slovenly).

Understand that it is normal for adolescents to behave in an inconsistent and unpredictable manner: Hating parents one minute and desperately seeking heart-to-heart talks the next; trying on new personality types and behavior patterns, then discarding them; worrying about society and the cosmos one minute and becoming overcome with personal agonies and uncertainties the next.

It is not helpful to ask: What's the matter with you? Why can't you sit still? What has suddenly gotten into you? They don't want instant understanding. Don't pretend to know how they feel. They can't believe parents were teenagers or felt the same way.

Confronted with these annoying traits, it's best to develop tolerance, but also make it clear that acceptance does not mean approval.

Never emulate teenagers' language or conduct. They deliberately adopt a lifestyle that is different from their parents. Such emulation drives children into opposition.

Every teenager has some imperfections about which he is overly sensitive. Be very careful not to reinforce them. Youngsters will soon enough torment their peers with terms like shorty, fats, or chicken. The insults cut deeper and last longer when they come from a parent. Even in jest, it's wiser not to tease them.

Teenagers crave independence and react to dependence with hostility. Smart parents make themselves increasingly dispensable to teenagers. The more self-sufficient teenagers are made to feel, the less hostile they will be towards their parents. In talking to your children, emphasize phrases like: Whatever you think. It's your decision. The choice is up to you.

Don't hurry to correct facts. Parents who are always trying to prove how right they are irritate teenagers. When attitudes are hostile, facts are unconvincing.

Let them have privacy. This demonstrates respect. And, by allowing them to have a life of their own, it helps them disengage themselves from parents and grow up. Be aware of, but don't try to participate too eagerly in, their social life. Adolescence requires a distance from the usual family closeness and fraternization.

Don't preach or lecture. Never use reverse psychology or predictions like: You'll never be able to hold a job unless you learn to get up on time.

Avoid confused or contradictory messages. It's better to state a clear prohibition: Sorry, that's out for tonight. Or state a gracious permission or an open choice: You may go if you want. Have a good time.

The most important single rule in talking to teenagers: Do not deny their feelings, perceptions, or experiences. Example: Instead of attacking an adolescent's choice of clothes with recriminations such as: You don't really like that? (which implies stupidity or lack of taste), use noncritical expressions like: You seem to like green. Or: I see you prefer large patterns. Since this does not attack personal taste, the teenager need not defend it. The parent can then say what he prefers, giving the teenager the option of reconsidering the original choice without loss of face.

Also, listen with sympathetic attention. Repeat the gist of what you hear, crystallizing what the teenager may have said vaguely. State your own views honestly, without criticizing the teenager or calling him names.

Source: *Between Parent and Teenager* by Dr. Haim G. Ginott, Macmillan Publishing Co., New York.

Sex in College

About three-quarters of college students have sexual relations by their sophomore year. Also, sexual intimacy among undergraduates increased from 50% in 1970 to 75% toward the end of the decade, a survey of students at 13 colleges indicated. Average age for the first sexual experience: 17 years old.

Other survey results:

More than half of the female students have intercourse five times in a month. Contrast: Only 40% of the male students have sex that often.

Two-thirds of the women term the sex act satisfying. Only half of the men do.

Sex is not rampant. Half of the sexually active students have had no more than two or three partners in their experience.

Source: Joseph Katz, S.U.N.Y. at Stony Brook, and Denise Cronin, Queens College, writing in *Change*.

Teenage Pregnancies

Teenage pregnancies now add up to over a million a year in the U.S. Of these, 600,000 young women go on to have their babies. One of every four is pregnant again within a year. Eight out of ten of the young mothers aged 17 or under don't finish high school. In most cases, they can't provide adequately for their offspring. Their infants are two to three times likelier (than the national average) to die before reaching their first birthday.

Source: *MD*.

At What Age Should a Child Leave Home?

The proportion of young people living at home has risen 25% in the past decade. Reasons: Many can't afford to establish their own homes. Also, young adults are marrying later.

245

This reduces the pressure to find their own places.

Be alert to psychological hangups that could be prolonging the stay at home. Some young people continually fail at school or work so they won't have to leave home. Example: By staying in the house, a child keeps his parents concerned with his problems. This deflects the couple's troubles with each other.

For many children, going away to college is their first leave. This is not always a clean emotional break. Example: children away at school who remain dependent on their parents for money and support are less independent than a working child who lives at home but comes and goes at will.

Those students who live at school grow closer to their parents.

Must all children be pushed from the nest? No. If the child is working and enjoying his own life, then living at home is reasonable.

Source: Dr. Daniel Goleman, a psychologist, writing in *Psychology Today.*

When Grown Children Ask for Money

Assessing the criteria for giving or lending money to one's children is often tricky. Some things worth considering:

Is the request genuine? When approached for money, determine whether the child's request comes from a real need or whether it is a manipulative demand based on dependency or anger. The unspoken demand might actually be: Show me that you love me. Guard against responding through fear that the child might not love you if you don't give in.

Setting conditions: Don't attach hidden strings to a gift or loan: I lent you money to buy a house, and now you hardly ever ask me over. Be explicit right from the start about all expectations attached to the loan or gift.

Set reasonable conditions: Before I lend you $15,000 for a down payment, I want the right to see the house and give you my opi-

nion of it. If I think it's a bad deal, I have the right to say no to your request for a loan because I don't like to get involved in bad deals.

An unreasonable expectation: I'll lend you the $15,000, provided the house is in the right neighborhood. Just as bad: Demanding that in exchange for the money your child spend more time with you.

Basic guidelines:

Lending or giving a child money may mean that you require that he do certain things. It cannot change his feelings toward you.

Spell out loan terms in detail: Make sure both understand the repayment terms.

Giving advice with the money: Guard against telling adult children how to spend their money, whether it is earned, inherited, or borrowed. They must live with the consequences of their decisions.

Sacrificing: Depriving yourself materially to give to your children is usually unsound, at least if done to excess. The practice often breeds martyrdom for the parents and guilt feelings on the part of the children.

Promises and threats: When making a will, once you start thinking about withholding an inheritance, or attaching conditions, be sure the decision arises from adult values and not the need to punish or control.

Beware of using the promise of a legacy or the threat of disinheritance. They may bring about the desired behavior, but they're never worth the trade-off in bad feelings.

Source: Howard Halpern, *Cutting Loose, An Adult Guide to Coming to Terms with Your Parents,* and *No Strings Attached: A Guide to a Better Relationship with Your Grown-Up Child,* both published by Simon & Schuster, Inc., New York.

Dealing With Grown Children on an Adult Level

Guilt and threats are the chief weapons used by older parents and adult children when they find themselves dealing ineffectively and hurt-

hurtfully with conflicts. Recognize the signs that this is happening. It's the first step toward resolving the problem.

Parents are particularly vulnerable to children's accusations of guilt because of the prevalent but false idea that the parents are totally responsible for children's emotional problems, choice of lifestyle, and adjustment to the world. Fact: Parents are not the only influences shaping their children's lives. Aim of children (or parents) in the guilt song and dance: To assume the role of victim, along with the victim's right to reparations.

Most typical guilt provoker used by grown-up children: The parent caused them to fail. (You made me so dependent on you that I have no confidence or ambition. Or: You were always so bossy that I'm afraid to speak up for myself. No wonder everyone takes advantage of me.)

Most typical guilt strategy used by parents: Assuming the martyr's role. (If it weren't for you, do you think I'd have stayed in this marriage? Or: With all the money we spent on your college, that's the kind of job you take! How can you do that to us?)

How parents can get out of the guilt trap: Don't accept the adult child's hostility as valid. Point out that attacking you won't help. Suggest talking about what can be done to help solve problems. Common mistake made by parents: They allow their own childlike fears of rejection and self-doubt to take over, and they accept the accusations. Why the conflict is never resolved: Parents eventually feel like victims and begin provoking guilt in return.

Parents and adult children often use terror tactics as a way of controlling. They back up their efforts to control with rage and threats.

How to deal with fear traps: Recognize that all adults, no matter how old they are, retain an inner child that responds in a terrified way to threats of being abandoned or rejected. Identify the present-day reality of those threats.

How one parent did it: A successful son was habitually threatening to ask his corporation to transfer him across the country unless his parents agreed to baby-sit more frequently. His line: If there are no advantages to staying

here, we might as well move. Finally, the parents realized that their fears were unjustified and tested their offspring's threats. Result: The threats stopped, and he stayed.

Important to remember: Parents tyrannize their children with fear more often than the other way around. (They've had a longer time to practice.) Illusion to avoid: That children are acting out of respect when they are acting, in fact, out of fear. How to tell the difference between the two: When demands, commands, threats, or anger are always necessary to elicit desired behavior from children, it's fear, not respect, that is operating.

Source: Dr. Howard Halpern, author of *Cutting Loose, An Adult Guide to Coming to Terms with Your Parents,* and *No Strings Attached: A Guide to a Better Relationship with Your Grown-Up Child,* both published by Simon & Schuster, Inc., New York.

Coping With the Problems of Elderly Parents

It's a traumatic period—for parents and their children—when the parents get so old that they have to be thought about as children. Here's expert advice from the book *When Your Parents Grow Old,* by Jane Otten and Florence D. Shelly (Funk & Wagnalls, New York).

Time to start worrying about parents isn't when they start forgetting what happened yesterday—but when they stop telling all those stories about what happened years ago. Even psychotic episodes may not mean senility. They can be caused by something as easily correctible as a deficiency in the diet. (Inadequate diet is common among old people who live alone.) Some symptoms that even doctors have been known to mistake for signs of senility can be produced by medication.

If real senility should develop, be cautious about tranquilizers. They can adversely affect an elderly patient.

Don't rush a senile parent into an institution. You'll be surprised how long a person can live an independent life with just a little help—especially if a set routine is followed every day (routine helps the elderly feel safe and secure).

If your mother still scrubs the kitchen floor at age 78, don't bug her about it. If parents insist on living in their old declining neighborhood, don't browbeat them into moving away from familiar things. Even moving to a warmer climate may not be worth the dislocation it involves. If one parent dies, don't force the survivor to move in with you. (Exception: A dangerous neighborhood.)

Things to know in the event of sudden illness or incapacity:

Location of will, bankbooks, insurance policies, securities, safe deposit box (and keys).

Name of parent's lawyer, accountant, insurance company, agent, and policy number. Details of pension and any other retirement plans the parent may have.

If possible, you or a sibling should have the power of attorney, access to safe deposit box, and joint bank account with parent. (These things are hard to talk about with a parent who is in good health, but they are even harder to arrange after a disability or death.)

When payments are due: Utilities, insurance premiums, rent, or mortage. When people are old and ill, they can be absent-minded about paying bills and depositing income checks.

Facts About Aging

• Tired taste buds. Older people often lose their sense of taste and may suffer loss of appetite as a result. Eating foods of varied textures can make up for loss of flavor. Caution: The use of monosodium glutamate (MSG) as a flavor enhancer can triple sodium intake. MSG should be avoided for those on low-sodium diets.

• Learning and aging. A dwindling of learning ability and memory usually does not occur until a person is well into the seventies. Even then, intellectual and physical vigor can be re-

tained. Problem: Often, elderly people have functional loss, brought on by illness, which is confused with mental loss. What keeps the elderly alert: Life style. Those who make an effort to keep learning maintain their ability to do so. Worst: Older people who think they are useless.

• Aches and pains of old age (or even middle age) result from shortening of muscles, especially idle ones. What to do: Exercise regularly, of course. Important: Follow up with stretching routines after 5 to 10 minutes of rigorous exercise to warm up the muscles. Bonus: Increased mobility of joints, especially knees, elbows, shoulders.

Helping Your Parents Financially When They Won't Take Money

Problem: Your parents are faced with inflation and rising home maintenance bills. They refuse to sell their house and are too proud to take outright gifts from their offspring. What can you do?

Solution: Consider a nonamortized bank loan for the parents, using the house as collateral.

How it works:

You negotiate a loan from a bank where a minimum balance equal to the principal of the loan is kept.

The parents pay interest on the loan and you arrange for the principal to be paid back after the parents die and the house is sold.

With the loan, buy annuities for the parents to supplement their income.

Example: A mother is 65 and has a $120,000 house with no mortgage. She gets a loan from her son's bank for 80% of the house's net value ($96,000), at 15% interest. With the money, she buys a 20-year annuity that pays 15% interest. Result: The annuity covers her interest payments and provides her with $1,000 a month. Added benefit: By borrowing on the house, rather than selling it, the woman and her family hold onto its appreciation value

How to Find a Good Nursing Home

Most families postpone as long as possible the decision to use a nursing home. Once the decision is reached, the process of selecting a good facility is so painful that often they move too fast. Good advice: Give parent time to get used to the idea. Meanwhile, investigate every possible choice thoroughly.

How to begin: Get lists of accredited homes from your church, fraternal order, state agency on aging, American Association of Homes for the Aging (Suite 770, 1050 17th St. NW, Washington, DC 20036), or American Health Care Association (1200 15th St. NW, Washington, DC 20005).

Costs: If parent's resources are small, Medicaid may provide financial support for nursing home care. Homes offering complete care in metropolitan areas usually charge more than $1,000 a month (many more than $2,000). Some require a large advance gift or admission fee. (Health insurance sometimes covers nursing homes.) Patients paying their own way may be eligible for Medicaid assistance after their savings run out. Check the rules in your state.

Evaluating a nursing home:

1. Accreditation, license, and certification for Medicare and Medicaid should be current and in force.

2. Best to arrive without an appointment. Look at everything. Building and room should be clean, attractive, safe, and meet all fire codes. Residents should not be crowded (ask about private rooms; sometimes they're available at reasonable extra cost). Visit dining room at mealtime. Check kitchen, too. Visit activity rooms when in session. Talk to residents to find out how they feel about the home.

3. Staff should be professionally trained and large enough to provide adequate care for all residents.

4. If home requires a contract, read it carefully. Show it to your lawyer before signing. Some homes reserve the right to discharge a patient whose condition has deteriorated even if lump-sum payment was made upon the admittance. Best: An agreement that allows payment by the month, or permits refunds of advance payment if plans change.

Find out exactly what service the home provides and which ones cost extra. For example, the expenses of private duty nurses are not included. Extras like shampoo, hairset, can be exorbitant. Make a list of the "extras" your parent will need for a comfortable life. Try to supply some of them yourself.

6. Before you decide on a home, you and your parent should talk with the administrator and department heads. Find out who is in charge of what, and whom to speak to if problems arise.

Tax note: Complete cost of nursing home care for aged is usually deductible as medical expense.

Ways Aged Parents Try to Dominate Adult Children

Many elderly people try to continue the old pattern of controlling their children long after the children are grown. Parents commonly use these verbal tactics:

Judgmental statements. Examples: Your children need more discipline. You are smart to have picked Penny as a girl friend. Real meanings of such statements: You should change your behavior to one acceptable to me. I know what is good for you and will tell you when you are doing well.

Barrage of questions. Real meaning: Parents think they still have the right to ask anything of the child and to expect the child to answer truthfully.

Advice. Real meanings: Child should or

ought to do what the parent suggests. A lack of confidence in the child's ability to think independently.

Teasing, belittling, exaggerating. Examples: Look who is going into business! It looks like you have been sleeping in that dress. Real meanings: Child's ideas are stupid. Child's behavior is unacceptable.

Superiority. Examples: Now, here is how things work. Everybody knows that. Real meanings: Parents still think they are smarter and more experienced.

The overall problem: Relating this way makes the adult child defensive or withdrawn. Shared communication is impossible in such an atmosphere.

Source: *Mother, Father, You: The Adult's Guide for Getting Along with Parents and In-laws,* by Carol Flax and Earl Ubell, Wyden Books, Ridgefield, CT.

Risks When You Pay Domestics Under the Table

It doesn't pay, in the long run. Compensating domestic workers in cash, to avoid taxes and paperwork, is the easy thing to do and is, indeed, very commonplace today. Many housekeepers and janitors, particularly those who are recent immigrants (possibly illegal aliens), even demand this of employers. But it can lead to trouble. IRS agents are quick to turn up at a household's front door, without notice, if they suspect that payroll taxes are being evaded by an employer of household help.

Biggest problem: Social Security (FICA) taxes. They are due from anyone who pays a worker more than $50 in a calendar quarter. There is no effective statute of limitations on the government's ability to collect these taxes.

Penalties for nonpayment are steep. Potential liability: The employer's and the employee's share of the tax due plus interest at 1% a month. In addition: A fine ranging from .5% on underpayment to as much as 5% per month for late filing of returns.

A typical dilemma: A domestic worker is paid in cash. Years later, the worker lacks eligibility for Social Security retirement benefits and points a finger at a former employer. The domestic can prove he worked for an employer through letters of recommendation, holiday cards from the employer's children, or any similar evidence he has kept down through the years.

Or a worker may be injured in the employer's home or place of business and find he has no workers' compensation coverage (which is based on reported wages). The employer can be sued for damages as well as sought out by the IRS and local authorities.

What to do: Offer to raise the hourly pay so the worker will pay taxes without cost to himself, or pay the employee's portion of the tax yourself. If the employee still refuses to put the income on the record (by not providing his Social Security number), insist on paying the FICA tax anyway. Payments can be made in the employee's name to a local Social Security office

Caution: Upon receipt, the Social Security people will quickly contact the employee to get the number, and the employer may lose the employee, if he is an illegal alien, or if for other reasons, he is determined to evade reporting.

Other precautions: Federal unemployment insurance must be paid for employees earning more than $1,000 a quarter. State unemployment insurance and workers' compensation premiums are also due, at least for full-time employees.

Source: Sidney Kess, partner, Main Hurdman & Cranstoun, 280 Park Ave., New York 10017

Helping a Domestic Get a Green Card

To work in the U.S. legally, a foreign worker must have a green card or a working visa from the Immigration and Naturalization Service. Although most domestic day workers either have green cards or are American citizens, live-in domestics are frequently undocumented aliens. If your domestic does not have a green card, it doesn't mean you are breaking the law. That person is. However, in some states there is a penalty for employing an undocumented alien.

Advantages to you of sponsoring a worker for a green card:

You may not be able to get live-in help in some areas without sponsoring them for a green card because demand for help is so high.

You may get a better-caliber worker, because some teachers, nurses, etc. from other countries are willing to work in a live-in capacity in the U.S. for several years to obtain the card.

You are assured of loyalty and good service by live-in help for the one to three years it takes to secure the green card.

Disadvantages of sponsorship:

It's more expensive. Employers often pay undocumented aliens less than the minimum wage (often as little as $100 to $120 a week), since the domestic worker can't complain to authorities. If you decide to be a sponsor, the alien must be paid a minimum wage when he or she returns to the U.S. as a permanent resident. (Cost rises with Social Security and unemployment taxes.)

Once domestics obtain the green card they may leave your employ for higher wages elsewhere.

How to help the employee to obtain the green card: Find an immigration lawyer. Many specialize in one or more nationalities. Your domestics may know one through their own grapevine. Lawyer's fee: $1,200 and up. It's frequently paid by the alien.

You must enter into a contract with the alien on terms of employment: The contract need not fix the time period, just the salary, duties, etc. This is your responsibility. You are not responsible for the alien's character or behavior, despite sponsorship.

Advertise to prove you have looked for a worker who is not an alien, but couldn't find one. Your local state employment agency may also look for an alternative worker.

Success of these maneuvers depends on the receptiveness of individual states to alien labor certification applications. Some take 10 months to decide whether to accept one, since statewide unemployment may be a factor.

Once approved, the alien must usually return to his country to be interviewed by the U.S. consul, who determines if he is qualified to enter. (Political or criminal records, or poor health, may disqualify him.)

Once it becomes time for domestics to go back to their country, advise them to file U.S. taxes for the period they worked. Otherwise, they may be considered lawbreakers. Angle: If they are not approved, and you trust the workers, ask for their recommendation of fellow nationals eager to work in the U.S.

Source: Seymour Magier, immigration attorney, 450 Seventh Ave., New York 10123.

Health Benefits Of Owning Pets

There is strong evidence that owning pets has a specific health value. A recent study shows that of patients hospitalized for heart attacks, those who owned pets were far more likely to survive past the first year than those who did not.*

Others on whom pets have important therapeutic effects: Those who are retired, elderly, or single, as well as children and younger adults with emotional disorders.

Benefits pets offer:

Companionship: Consistent evidence indicates that single, widowed, and divorced people have higher disease rates and die earlier than married people. Pets decrease the isolation, which is hazardous to health. Suitable: Responsive animals like cats, dogs, or birds. Having someone to care for is one of the important reasons for the greater longevity en-

*One test of post-coronary patients showed that of 39 who did not own pets, 11 died the first year. Of 53 who owned pets, only three died the first year. Subsequent tests showed that having a dog (which might have provided crucial additional exercise), was *not* the significant factor: It was having a *pet*.

251

joyed by married people. Prime reason: In biological terms, caring for another may make possible a psycho-endocrine response that results in greater resistance to disease. Small animals can stimulate the caring feelings and actions that human babies evoke. Another function served by caring for a pet: For many, pets can serve as a transitional love object, helping them develop and transfer affections. Depressed people can learn to love others again through caring for pets.

Something alive to caress: Physical contact with another warm body has an important beneficial effect on the cardiovascular system. Some patients in coronary care units experience a marked decrease in irregular heart rhythm when their hands are held by a nurse. Main reason: Touch may decrease arousal of the sympathetic nervous system responsible for elevated heart rate, blood pressure, and blood lipid and sugar levels associated with higher emotional activity. Touching and fondling act as an antianxiety agent. Result: It can decrease progression of conditions like hypertension, stroke, coronary artery disease, and diabetes, usually made worse by consistent emotional arousal.

Something to occupy the mind: Keeping busy has important positive effects on longevity. Lack of meaningful activity can produce feelings of helplessness or depression. Pets provide complexity, interest, and variability to a daily routine and provide stimulus for maintaining that routine. Especially important: Their effect on retired people, who may well become disoriented, in time, without established responsibilities and the daily schedule of duties a pet demands. Suitable: Any animals requiring a routine of daily care.

Exercise: Dog owners have an incentive for going out and walking that they might not have on their own.

Safety: Owning a dog lessens fear of defenselessness and and encourages elderly people worried about crime to decrease their isolation and get outdoors. Feeling safer is a positive health benefit for everybody, and is more relevant than whether or not dogs actually make things safer. Chances are good that they do.

Contrary to prevailing wisdom: A relationship in which one talks seriously and respectfully to one's pet is likely to be a rich one, and one that reflects the emotional capacities of the proud owner.

Source: Dr. Erika J. Friedmann, assistant professor of health sciences, Brooklyn College, and lecturer, The University of Pennsylvania School of Veterinary Medicine.

Choosing the Right Puppy for Your Family

Don't buy a puppy on impulse. Buy it from a breeder, if possible, rather than from a pet store. And make the decision carefully.

First consideration: Type of dog is often more important than size. Many large dogs actually need less room than smaller ones. Original function for which the breed was developed often influences temperament.

Scent hounds (beagle, basset, dachshund, bloodhound). Well suited to city living and children.

Sight or gaze hounds (Saluki, Afghan, Irish wolfhound, Scottish deerhound, greyhound). Among the fastest dogs, they were originally bred for running down prey and killing it. They still need lots of room to be happy.

Sporting dogs (spaniels, setters, pointers, retrievers). Originally bred to locate game and retrieve it. Need a little less room than hounds. But with the exception of Labrador and Newfoundland retrievers, they are not especially protective or good with children.

Working dogs (shepherds, malamutes, huskies, collies, sheepdogs). Probably the most intelligent and protective of all groups. Large (60 to 50 pounds) and used to outdoor work but they adapt nicely to city life if exercised twice a day. Actually require less space than smaller, more active dogs like terriers.

Terriers (Airedale, Scottish, Welsh, West Highland White, fox, miniature schnauzers). The most alert and active dogs. Also tenacious and often aggressive. Need space. Good with children, whose energy they match. Extremely protective (a benefit for older people, as long as they can cope with the terrier's high level of activity).

Toy dogs (Pekinese, toy poodle, Yorkshire terrier, Maltese, Italian greyhound, Pomeranian). Originally developed as playthings for royalty and nobility. Charming companions for adults. But strongly not recommended for small children, no matter how adorable the puppies and dogs may look. They're much too fragile.

Nonsporting dogs—a catch-all group with no special characteristics. Includes unrelated breeds, such as the poodle, French and English bulldogs, Boston terrier, chow chow, Dalmatian, and Lhasa apso. They tend to be good guard dogs and excellent pets.

Most dog owners strongly prefer one sex over the other. General pros and cons:

Males (called dogs by breeders) don't get pregnant. They do fight, wander, chase cars, and display aggressive-dominant behavior toward people.

Females (bitches) are more protective and gentle. They neither wander nor fight but if they're not spayed, they can become pregnant. Even if they're kept locked up, living through their semiannual heat periods is difficult because of all the unwanted attention from neighboring dogs.

Best to see both the pup's parents at the breeder. Chief reason to buy there rather than at a pet store: Not only will the buyer see what the puppy will look like as an adult, he will also be able to judge its genetic inheritance by the health of its parents.

Puppies are best chosen—and make the best adjustment to a new home—when they're 6 to 12 weeks old. At this age, they're so cute that it's hard to choose rationally, even with the knowledge that the choice is one that will have to be lived with for the next 10 or 15 years.

At this age, curiosity is the best indicator of intelligence. Some quick and easy intelligence and temperament tests to help select the best pup of the litter:

Visual test:

Shine a pocket flashlight at the pup.

Show it a mirror.

Roll a ball toward it.

Wave a sheet of white paper.

Drag an object along on a string.

Hearing tests (to be done out of the puppy's sight):

Blow a police whistle.

Clap hands.

Blow a kazoo or noisemaker.

If the pup shows it hears the sound, that's good. If it tries to locate the source, that's excellent.

Body sensitivity is important in training. Gently pinch the puppy's ear between the ball of the thumb and the forefinger. Then push down the puppy's hindquarters, forcing it to sit. Note its reactions. A puppy that doesn't react has little body sensitivity and may be difficult to train because it won't feel corrections. A puppy that whines, cowers, or runs away is so sensitive that it will fear corrections and be difficult to train.

Temperament can be tested by seeing the puppy's attitude toward strangers. Jump right in front of the puppy. It should show neither fear nor anger. Surprise followed by friendliness is a good reaction.

If the puppy has all the traits tested for, with love, patience, and training, it should grow up into a wonderful, rewarding dog.

Note: Don't forget local animal shelters as a source of puppies and older dogs. Many of these animals are pedigreed, too.

Paper-Training a Puppy

Feed the puppy. Then hold it on your lap for ten minutes. Place the dog on paper until it urinates and defecates. Afterward, reward the puppy with a tidbit and praise.

When the dog has an accident, lead it to the soiled spot, jerk on the puppy's collar, and scold it. Then take it to the paper. *Don't* rub the puppy's nose in the excrement.

Be in control. If the puppy deliberately misses the paper by a few inches, it is testing you.

Note: Never fail to reward and praise the dog when it uses the paper correctly.

Dogspeak

Dogs actually have an extensive communications repertory. The standard expressions and their human equivalents:

Rolling over on one side while raising uppermost hind leg: I am showing you friendly respect.

Presenting flank or groin to you: I want to be friends. Note: The forward thrust of canine groin is the rough equivalent of human offering to shake hands and calls for a pat on the head. Caution: First be sure a strange dog is really friendly.

Snarling, wagging a stiff tail: I am feeling aggressive toward you.

Rear shifting of body weight, lowering tail: I am afraid.

Tail-wagging, high and loose: I'm excited, playful.

Bowing, tail-wagging, raising one paw: I want to play so don't take what I do next seriously, even if I bark, snap, or lunge.

Direct eye contact: You're challenging me. I might back down or maybe attack.

Avoiding eye contact: I am demonstrating superiority, and showing my indifference.

Licking, tongue curled back toward nose: I may bite.

Licking, tongue straight out: I want to kiss.

Barking, yelping, growling and making other noises tend to match obvious meanings: Threats, play, pain. When dogs howl along with sirens, singers, or musical instruments, it's not a sign of pain. The animal instinctively is joining in chorus.

Also, some dogs do in fact learn to grin (or grimace), mimicking their human masters by pulling back their lips. And just like humans, a dog can send mixed signals.

Source: Dr. Michael W. Fox, author, *Understanding Your Pet*, Coward-McCann & Geoghegan, New York.

Boarding Your Pets

When checking out kennels in which to board your pet while you're away, look for: Overall cleanliness and general maintenance, indicating the quality of the kennel management.

Cages large enough to permit the animal to lie down and turn around.

Drainage, to ensure the animal doesn't lie in its own waste.

Exercise areas. (Essential for larger dogs.)

Condition of the animals in cages. Boarded pets should have clear eyes and healthy, shiny coats.

Avoid kennels that won't allow you to inspect cages.

Cover in advance: Preference for wet or dry pet food and availability of drinking water at all times.

Care for Elderly Pets

When dogs and cats reach their twilight years, like aging humans, they require some adjustments in their routines. Symptoms of aging in animals include decreased activity, graying fur, deafness, and cloudy (sometimes blue or gray-tinted) eye discoloration.

Ways to help your pet enjoy an active, healthy old age:

Discuss diet changes with the veterinarian. Reduce the amount of food for pets who show signs of obesity.

Take your pet to the vet for regular check-ups. At home, you can examine your pet by checking the mouth for infected gums or teeth, the skin for growths, and the urine for marked changes in amount and color. Warning symptoms: Chronic cough, rapid breathing, and easy tiring could indicate heart trouble.

Offer comforts, including warm shelter, soft bedding.

Remember: Aging animals have less resistance to stress. Avoid sudden changes in their diet, exercise routines, and environment.

Occasional breaches of house-training by an aged dog may indicate the onset of kidney problems. Check with the vet, and consider a reduced-protein diet that is specially marketed for geriatric pets. Do not cut back on the animal's drinking water to reduce trips outside. Pets of every age require ready access to fresh drinking water at all times.

Source: Terri McGinnis, DVM, writing in *Family Health.*

Keeping Your Dog Cool in Summer

Dogs do not tolerate the hot weather well. They need help from their owners to keep cool.

Recommendations:

Fill the dog's drinking bowl with ice cubes and then add a cup of water to it.

Keep a plant mister full of water in the refrigerator and spray the dog periodically. Brush the coat against the grain while spraying. Brushing in this direction allows the cool mist to reach the skin.

When you go out, don't waste electricity by leaving on the air conditioner for the dog. Instead, spray the pet, then put it in the bathroom. The tile floor is a cool place for the dog to lie. Leave a bowl of ice cubes for it to lick and chew.

If you must leave the dog in the car, park the car in the shade and open the windows a couple of inches.

Don't shave the dog's coat. The fur acts as insulation from the heat and protects the skin from sun and insect bites. It's fine to clip a long-haired coat, however.

Source: *Pat Widmer's Dog Training Book,* by Patricia P. Widmer, David McKay Publishers, New York.

Dealing with An Angry Dog

First, face the animal squarely. Pick up a stick or stone, and yell at the dog if it advances. Don't throw your weapon unless the animal is within easy reach. Keep the hand poised and back away slowly. Don't turn your back on the dog or try to run. Signs of weakness might spur it to attack. Also, never charge at the animal. It's far quicker than you.

Lower Veterinary Bills

Be meticulous about your pet's diet, exercise, grooming, and training to avoid as many problems as possible.

Find the veterinarian who will give the most service. Is the office open weekends? Do after-hours emergency visits cost extra?

Are there free clinics in your area? Some communities offer free rabies shots and sponsor neutering clinics.

Take your pet for annual checkups. Problems spotted early can be cured more quickly.

If you have more than one animal, ask your veterinarian for a discount if you bring them all in at the same time.

Don't bring a new pet into the house before having it checked first by a vet.

Keep a good animal-medicine handbook at home for treating minor problems. It's also helpful in spotting serious symptoms.

Learn to do grooming chores like nail clipping and ear cleaning.

Use the phone to get advice from your vet.

Following surgery or another treatment, ask if your pet can recuperate at home rather than at the animal center.

Find out the charges before treatment begins. It may be possible to spread the payment over a period of time.

Ask about anything on the bill you don't understand.

Allergic Pets

Dogs and cats are allergy-prone to many of the same substances that bother humans. Symptoms: Excessive scratching, watering eyes, sneezing, wheezing, hives (and other skin disorders), and digestive upsets.

Common causes: Fleas, mites, pollen and mold spores, dust (possibly from a clay-type litterbox filler), drugs and medications, chemicals found in household products such as detergents, paint, etc., or insect powders.

Recommended: If symptoms persist, consult a veterinarian. Note: Frequently, reactions are not immediate and may not appear until several days after exposure to the offending substance.

IO

Home Ownership

Inspection Checklist Before Buying a House

Most home-shoppers know that it's a good idea to have an engineer check out a house for major defects before buying. But the buyer should precheck the structure so that he can direct the engineer to report on specific details.

Start in the basement, where defects are the most obvious. Check walls for inward bulge, cracks or crumbling mortar, fresh patches and high-water marks. Check floor for signs of leaks, seepage, or damp odor. Look for a hidden sump pump, indicating frequent flooding.

Use a pocketknife to probe for termites or decay. If knife goes in easily, the wood is rotten. Other danger signs on joists: Marks of water seepage from kitchen or bathroom above. Pulling away from supporting masonry. Notches more than one-third into the joist for pipes. If joists are propped up, find out why.

Check basement pipes for corrosion. Hot-water pipes should be copper, preferably insulated. Coldwater lines should be copper or plastic.

Check fuse box for power adequacy (16 to 20 circuits with circuit breakers needed for an 8 to 12 room house).

Study house from outside for sag, alignment of walls, missing mortar, broken bricks, cracks in walls. One tipoff to trouble: Extra-wide mortar joint on the stair steps may show house is shifting.

Siding: Aluminum is a plus. If it's wooden, look for peeling that shows walls hold too much moisture. If windowsills are freshly painted and the rest of the house is not, paint may be covering rot.

Check roof for broken/missing shingles, tar paper bubbles, broken patches. Check metal sheathing around chimney and ventilators. Should be watertight and made of nonrusting material. Look for leaks or breaks in gutters. If possible, check attic for watermarks on underside of roof.

In the house, check for warped doors that won't close, rattly doorknobs, creaky floor or stairs, loose tiling, inadequate plumbing, too many electric cords in an outlet. Check closets and storage space for adequacy. Water heater should be 30 to 40 gallons if gas, 60 if electric.

Examine walls and ceilings for repaired cracks (may indicate structural problem) or patches (may indicate leaks from above).

Source: *How You Can Become Financially Independent by Investing in Real Estate,* by Albert J. Lowery, Simon & Schuster, New York.

What to Ask a Seller

Is the house built on a landfill? If it is, it may be settling and may continue to sink, causing cracks in the plaster and more serious, recurrent structural problems.

Is the foundation's exterior surface waterproofed?

What's the R factor (the ability to resist heat flow) of the insulation? Good ratings: R 22 for ceilings, R 13 for exterior walls. For colder climates: R 38 and R 19.

Are windows insulated or double-glazed?

Has the house been protected against termites? Look for written proof from a pest-control firm.

What is under the wall-to-wall carpeting?

Is the waste system hooked up to a city sewer?

What is the inside diameter of the water pipes? Acceptable: ½ inch for feeders, ¾ inch for main runs.

Are major appliances and heating and cooling units on separate electrical circuits?

Evaluating a Neighborhood

The house or apartment seems perfect. But will the dwelling continue to be perfect?

What to check: Transportation facilities.

Police and fire protection. Traffic. Street lights. Garbage collection. Zoning laws. Water supply. Sewerage. Schools. And so on.

Possible nuisances: Smoke. Soot. Dust. Odors. Caution: Don't judge by a Sunday-only visit.

Useful: Find out from a local insurance broker about fire and burglary claims.

Most important of all: Neighbors. Call on a few to ask about the area.

Alternate Ways To Finance a House

There are several variations on the conventional long-term, fixed-rate mortgage.

Flexible-rate mortgages: The most popular are the renegotiable-rate mortgage (RRM) and the variable-rate mortgage (VRM). General terms:

Interest-rate review and, if necessary, revision up or down every three, four, or five years, up to a total contract term of 30 years. The rate changes (generally limited to increases of 0.5% or 1%) are tied to a specific index, such as the Federal Home Loan Bank Board's.

The maximum total increase over the life of the mortgage usually is five percentage points.

RRM calls for negotiation of each change. VRM changes are automatic.

Added cost: A one-percentage-point increase on a 30-year mortage adds 63¢ to monthly payments for each $1,000 borrowed. Monthly payments on a $60,000 30-year mortgage increase by $37.80 (63¢ × 60). Assumption: The homeowner will meet the increased costs with inflation-cheapened dollars, from a larger personal income.

Wrap-around mortgage: A contract between buyer and seller that combines old financing (the seller's own first mortgage) and new financing (provided by the seller). The seller collects payments from the buyer, including interest on the total financing, from the seller, and applies part of it to the first mortgage. The seller gets a slightly higher rate of interest on the spread between the old mortgage and the wrap-around rate, and the buyer gets a loan below the market rate.

Second mortgage: A buyer who is unable to assume the seller's mortgage without assistance obtains secondary financing, to be repaid over time. What to calculate: Whether the second-mortgage's high-interest cost, when combined with the assumed first-mortgage cost, is more or less than the current market rate for new first-mortgage financing.

Land contract: The buyer makes mortgage payments directly to the seller, who retains title to the property until the mortgage is retired.

Lease-purchase agreement: The purchase price is agreed upon, but the closing date is delayed until the buyer obtains financing. Meanwhile, the buyer occupies the house at a stipulated monthly cost, part of which may be applied to the purchase price.

Installment sale: The buyer pays for the house over three or four years.

Land lease: The house is bought, but the seller retains ownership of the land. The contract must contain a long-term property lease giving the house owner the option to buy the land. Value: Buyer's down payment and monthly payments are smaller.

Equity sale: Low-interest mortgage financing, generally one-third less than the market rate, is given to the home buyer in exchange for a percentage of the profit (usually one-third) when the property is sold.

Interest only: Smaller monthly payments for a specified period, with principal paid when the property is sold or refinanced.

Balloon mortgage: Payment of interest only or scheduled amounts that do not retire the mortgage over its full term. The balance of the balloon is paid in full when the mortgage matures. Assumption: The house is sold or refinanced when the balloon is due.

Longer mortgage terms: To 40 years and more. Particularly applicable for lower-priced houses.

Variations: Leases with options to buy. Low first-year interest, with increase in each of the next three or four years. Low-interest bridge loans for buyers who haven't sold their homes.

Source: Sal Nuccio, president of Nuccio Organization, financial consultants, 60 Algonquin Rd., Yonkers, NY 10710, and author, *The New York Times Guide to Personal Finance.*

Pros and Cons Of Adjustable Mortgage Loans

Adjustable mortgage loans (AMLs), also known as adjustable-rate mortgages, can now be used by virtually every kind of mortgage lender. They are good financing instruments and may help to solve the housing crunch. Reason: Lenders can definitely lend and borrowers have an affordable way to borrow. Also: Neither takes undue risk. The risk is shared.

Major difference between the new AMLs and the older variable-rate mortgages (VRMs): AMLs have no cap on the upward movement of interest rates over the life of a loan (although there is a 2% cap on annual changes in the rate.) Result: If the interest rates rise, your mortgage interest may go up by the same amount. On the other hand, your mortgage could drop sharply if rates go down (lenders don't have to drop your mortgage rate, however).

Although the note can vary at any time and by any amount, the lender must peg its mortgage interest rate to a rate known to the public and not controlled by the bank. Example: It could be pegged to the Treasury-bill rate but not to the bank's prime.

Lender restraints:

Many states' banking laws provide ceilings on raises in a given year.

The competitiveness of the mortgage industry will result in sweeteners. Example: A bank may limit yearly raises to a maximum of two percentage points.

Borrower disadvantage:

With AML financing, a home purchase will

not be as inflation-proof as it once was.

Barring a lender- or state-imposed cap on interest rate rises, carrying costs could skyrocket.

The bank has the option of increasing your interest rate but not your monthly payment, and extending the payment period to 40 years.

Example: If your monthly payment is $400, of which $375 is interest and $25 is principal, and interest rates go up, the bank may keep your payment at $400. But it may make the interest payment $380 and the principal payment $20 and extend your payment period accordingly.

A severe swing in interest rates could result in what is known as negative amortization.

What can happen: Say your monthly payment is $400 for 20 years at 12%. Interest rates soar to 18%. The bank, seeing that it would have to raise your payments to more than $600 to amortize your mortgage in the same 20-year period at the higher rates, decides to keep your monthly payment at $400 but make that purely an interest payment (no principal). Each month, the principal that you are not paying accumulates, with interest. If the interest rates stay near 18% for any period of time, you will owe a substantial balloon (lump-sum) payment after 20 years instead of owning your house free and clear.

Recommendation: Ask your bank if it will give a fixed-rate mortgage. Despite the use of AMLs, fixed-rate loans are not dead. Preference: Fixed-rate loans, if and when they are available at a reasonable premium over AML rates. The competitiveness of the mortgage industry should keep them alive for some time. Option: Some lenders may offer you the choice of an AML or fixed-rate mortgage. Whether to pick an AML at the lower starting rate or a fixed-rate mortgage at higher interest depends partly on where you (or the people you rely on for financial advice) see interest rates going over the long term. But if the lender offers you an AML at 13% or a fixed-rate mortgage at 15%, grab the fixed rate at 15%.

Source: Thomas L. O'Dea, head of O'Dea and Co. Inc., investment real estate consultants and publishers, *Carolina Real Estate Journal.*

Family Partnership for Financing Home Purchase

It may be the best way for many people to buy a home—certainly a lot better than asking relatives for loans.

How it works: Form a partnership in which relatives participate in raising the cash for the purchase price. At some future date, the house is sold or refinanced and the proceeds used to pay off the partners, including a share of any profit.

How it differs from a loan: The partnership, not the resident, owns the house. Each partner has equity participation. Also: Profits may be treated as capital gains. Interest earned on a loan would be taxable as ordinary income. Added benefit to the buyer: No payments are due until the house is sold or refinanced.

Source: *Real Estate Investing Letter*

Questions to Ask Before Signing Mortgage Papers

Because it is such a long-term contract, conditions that may seem minor when signing a mortgage loan contract can end up costing a lot of money during the life of the agreement. Some typical mortgage clauses to negotiate before signing:

Payment of "points": Percentage of the amount of the loan paid to the lender at the start of the loan. Banks and thrift institutions have no statutory right to charge points. Their presence may reflect competitive local market conditions. And when interest rates are high, points are common. They're inevitable when rate ceilings exist. Recommended: Try to negotiate on points.

Prepayment penalties: Sometimes as much as six months' interest or a percentage of the balance due on the principal at the time loan is paid off. With mortgages running for 25 or 30 years, the chances of paying them off early are relatively high.

"Due on encumbrance" clause: Makes the first mortgage immediately due in full if property is pledged as security on any other loan, including second mortgages. Not legal in some places and usually not enforced when it is legal. Request its deletion.

"Due on sale" clauses: Requiring full payment of loan when property is sold.

Escrow payment: The popular practice of requiring a prorated share of local taxes and insurance premiums with each monthly mortgage payment. The bank earns interest on the escrow funds throughout the year and only pays it out when taxes and premiums are due. Amounts to forced savings with no interest.

Have lawyer check state's law to see if interest on escrow-account money is required. (It is, in several states.) If not, try to eliminate escrow—pay taxes and insurance on your own.

Other alternatives to escrow:

Capitalization plan, in which monthly tax and insurance payments are credited against outstanding mortgage principal until they are paid out to the government or insurer, thus lowering amount of mortgage interest.

Lender may agree to waive escrow if borrower opens an interest-bearing savings account in the amount of the annual tax bill.

Option of closing out the withheld escrow payments when the borrower's equity reaches 40%. At that point, the bank figures, equity interest will be a powerful incentive to keep up tax payments.

Source: *The Consumer's Guide to Banks,* by Gordon L. Weil, Stein & Day, Braircliff Manor, NY.

Figures to Check At Real Estate Closing

Monthly payments.

Per diem figures for utilities, taxes, and/or interest.

The broker's commission.

The rents, security deposits, and/or interest on deposits that have not as yet been transferred.

A charge for utility bills already paid.

A charge for loan fees already paid.

A contractor, attorney, appraiser, or some other party to the contract who has not been paid.

Tax Break On Property Taxes

If real estate taxes are paid *after* the year you sell your house (because the amount of tax for th property year wasn't known at the time of the sale) you can deduct your share of the taxes *either* in the year of the sale *or* in the year the tax is paid, whichever produces the greatest tax advantage to you.

When the New House Is a Lemon

A home buyer may be able to get out of the entire purchase contract if the seller has misrepresented a house with many serious defects.

Normally, when defects show up after the buyers move in, they can sue for damages. Some state courts have ruled that two reasons for suing to void the entire sale are: (1) Misrepresentation of an important aspect of the house. (2) The presence of many serious defects.

One case: The builder had assured the buyer that there would be no water problem. But the house was flooded soon after the closing. The court said the related damage would be impossible to repair.

Source: Chastain v. Billings, 570S. W. 2d 866.

Save on Title Insurance

Many title insurers have a special reissue rate for property on which they've written a policy within the past five years. Advantage: A full title search is not necessary. Savings can be considerable. Companies usually don't mention the special rate unless a customer asks.

Special "inflationary endorsement," a clause that can be added to the homeowner's title policy, provides that the insured's protection will be adjusted for any inflationary increase. Maximum benefit: 150% of face amount of policy at the time of writing.

Source: David Schechner, attorney, 80 Main St., West Orange, NJ 07052

Misconceptions About Title Insurance

Insuring the title to property does not mean the title can never be lost. What it does mean: If you lose title, you will be compensated. No matter how thorough a title search is, legitimate claims against it can pop up. Without title insurance, the cost of defense must be borne by the person being sued. With insurance. the cost is borne by the insurance company.

A title search is not the same as title insurance. It's merely an investigation of records to find out who seems to be the lawful owner of a particular piece of property.

Suppose your property is taken away because proof develops that some other party has the rightful claim. Usually you are insured for the price of the property.

Protect Mortgage Point Deduction

"Points" paid to get a mortgage loan may not be immediately tax-deductible.

Interest must actually be paid to be deduct-ible by cash-basis taxpayers, which most individuals are. In one case, the Tax Court held that, since the points were deducted from the loan proceeds, they weren't actually paid, thus no deduction could be claimed that year. The deduction would have to be taken pro-rata as the mortgage was repaid.

Problem: The typical real estate closing statement mixes up credits to the buyer and amounts actually paid.

Solution: Pay the points by single check to the lender. Don't lump the payment in with other payments.

Learning to Build Your Own Home

With the costs of home construction sky-rocketing, the economics of building your own home look increasingly attractive to people thinking of a second home, or for people who have $150,000 to sink into construction, but a desire to live in a $250,000 house. Problem: Mastering the skills required to build a house.

One solution: A course in one of the do-it-yourself homebuilding schools proliferating now. The courses: Up to three weeks, in which everything from plumbing and wiring to budgeting is taught. Also: Specific construction skills. Example: How to convert a house to a solar heating system.

Cost of courses: $350 to $500. Saving: Since labor, on average, represents 50% of home construction costs, a saving of up to 50% is theoretically possible.

Recommendation: Look into a middle route between contracting out for construction work and doing it all yourself. Possibility: Find an amateur homebuilder with low overhead costs willing to negotiate an arrangement whereby you do some of the work, and the builder does the rest.

Caution: Finding mortage money for do-it-yourself homes may be difficult now.

Note: The work is always more time consuming than expected. Rule of thumb: Plan to spend 1½ hours for every square foot of living space you are working on.

Checklist for Move To a New House

Arrange for the utilities (gas, electric, water, etc.) to be turned on in the new house or apartment a few days before you move in.

Install the telephone a month before you move (or as early as is feasible).

Enroll your child in the new local school.

Open savings and checking accounts promptly at a bank in the new neighborhood.

Notify companies of change of address (insurance, credit card, magazines, etc.)

If you are moving to a new state, check to see if your auto coverage is applicable.

Notify the IRS of the move both at the time of the move and again when you file your income tax.

Have pharmaceutical prescriptions renewed before moving so that adequate amounts of medication will be on hand.

Ask the previous occupant for a list of reliable local service people (electricians, plumbers, carpenters, etc.) and good nearby stores.

Moving outdoor plants to a new home: For a long move, place them in a plastic bag and cover with wet straw or weeds. If you know in autumn you'll be leaving in the spring, use a spade to cut a deep circle around a shrub or young tree to sever the roots and outline the rootball.

The Cautious Way To Buy a Condominium

Experience in buying and selling several single-family homes doesn't alert you to all the things to look for in a good condo deal.

Your lawyer must read the covenant of condominium (also called the master deed or declaration of condominium). Clauses in a covenant are non-negotiable; all participants must have the same wording. There are traps that could make it more desirable to walk away from the the whole deal. Specifics:

Resale restrictions. The condo association (the governing body of owner representatives that owns and maintains common areas such as hallways, parking lots, and swimming pools) may have a 30-, 60- or 90-day right of first refusal. That delay could cost you a sale. Worse: Federal Housing Administration, Veterans Administration, and other government-insured mortgages are not available when there are certain resale restrictions. Your resale market could be cut significantly.

Use restrictions. Does the covenant permit owners to rent their units? If you are buying the condo as an investment: You must be able to rent. If you are planning to live in a unit: You may want this restriction. Other use restrictions: Children, pets, window decorations, even the type of mailbox you can use.

Sweetheart deals. The most common one is when the developer owns the common areas and leases them back to the association. Disadvantage: Such leases are usually long term and include escalator clauses and pass-alongs that could cause big jumps in your monthly association fees. Another variation: The developer does not own the common areas, but has a long-term contract to manage them. The best deal for the buyer: The condo association owns all the common areas. All management agreements with the condo association should strictly control costs and contain termination provisions.

Potential problems that won't show up in the covenant:

Subsidized fees. Developers of newly built condos often manage common areas for a fee until most of the new units are sold. To speed sales, the developer may keep the management fee below cost. Then, when the condo association assumes management, the owners' monthly costs soar. Prudent comparison: Check fees charged by similar condo associations in the area.

Construction problems. Before you buy, have an engineer inspect the condition of the entire property, if feasible, not just your unit. Reason: If the condo association has to make repairs, you will be assessed for the cost. Suggestion: If you are buying a unit in converted building, ask the condo salesperson for the engineer's report. Most converted buildings need one to obtain financing.

Best times to buy: Prices are lowest during the pre-construction sale of new units, or early in the conversion of a building. Risk: If you buy too soon, you could end up as one of the few owners. As long as units remain unsold, your investment will not appreciate. What to do: Check the price and demand for similar units in the area.

Source: Thomas L. O'Dea, O'Dea and Co., Inc., investment real estate consultants 285 S. Stratford Rd., Winston-Salem, NC 27103.

Suggestions for Condominium Hunters

Look for a building about to undergo conversion. If you sublet an apartment in it, you get first crack at buying the apartment.

If you have a trouble getting a mortgage, look for a condominium developer who has a mortgage commitment from a lender.

Rent a portion of the condominium apartment to a friend. This helps meet the monthly payments.

When Buying a New Condominium

Buying a condominium is more complicated than buying a house. Reason: The purchase is really for two separate pieces of property, your unit and the property held in common. Before signing any contract for a new condominium, which is harder to check out than an established condominium, buyers should study the prospectus for any of these pitfalls:

The prospectus includes a plan of the unit you are buying, showing rooms of specific dimensions. But the plan omits closet space. Result: The living space you are buying is probably smaller than you think.

The prospectus includes this clause: The interior design shall be substantially similar. Result: The developer can alter both the size and design of your unit.

The common charges set forth in the prospectus are unrealistically low. Buyers should never rely on a developer's estimate of common charges. Instead: They should find out the charges at similarly functioning condominiums.

Common charges include: Electricity for hallways and outside areas, water, cleaning, garbage disposal, insurance for common areas, pool maintenance, groundskeeping, legal and accounting fees, reserves for future repairs.

Variation on the common-charge trap: The developer is paying common charges on unsold units. But these charges are unrealistically low. Reason: The developer has either underinsured, underestimated the taxes due, omitted security expenses, or failed to set up a reserve fund.

The prospectus includes this clause: The seller will not be obligated to pay monthly charges for unsold units. Result: The owners of a partially occupied condominium have to pay for all operating expenses.

The prospectus warns about the seller's limited liability. But an unsuspecting buyer may still purchase a condominium unit on which back monthly charges are due, or even on which there's a lien for failure to pay back carrying charges.

The prospectus makes no mention of parking spaces. Result: You must lease from the developer.

The prospectus is imprecise about the total number of units to be built. Result: Facilities are inadequate for the number of residents.

The prospectus includes this clause: Transfer of ownership (of the common property from the developer to the homeowners' association) will take place 60 days after the last unit is sold. Trap: The developer deliberately does not sell one unit, keeps on managing the condominium, and awards sweetheart maintenance and operating contracts to his subcontractors.

The prospectus specifies that the developer will become the property manager of the functioning condominium. But the language spelling out monthly common charges and management fees is imprecise. Result: The owners cannot control monthly charges and fees.

Source: Dorothy Tymon, author, *The Condominium: A Guide for the Alert Buyer,* Golden-Lee Books, Brooklyn, NY.

Condominium Emergency Reserves

Make sure the board of directors sets up a contingency reserve for emergencies. It should be at least 3% of the annual operating budget for newer buildings and 5% for older ones. Danger: A major assessment on very little notice when an emergency arises if no reserve is set aside.

Source: *The Condominium Community,* The Institute fo Real Estate Management of the National Association of Realtors, Chicago.

Condos vs. Co-ops

When you purchase a condominium you own real property, just like when you buy a house. You arrange for your own mortgage with the bank, pay real estate taxes directly to the local government, pay water bills individually, and have an individual deed.

When you buy a cooperative apartment, you are participating in a syndication. A corporation is formed, shares are issued, and people subscribe to the shares. The corporation raises money, takes out a mortgage, and owns the building.

Maintenance charges for a condominium are likely to cost 50% of a cooperative's charges for an equivalent building. The reason: The maintenance on a condominium covers only the common area upkeep. That includes: Labor, heating oil, repairs, and maintenance of the playground, swimming pool, and other community areas. Co-op maintenance fees cover those same items plus mortgage payments, local real estate taxes, utility and water bills.

Capital improvements: If an extensive, major repair needs to be made (such as the replacement of a roof or boiler), the board of managers of a condo cannot borrow funds from a bank unless it receives the unanimous consent of the condo owners. Problem: If a dozen owners are content to live in a dilapidated building, improvements must be funded through maintenance cash flow, which may be very expensive. In a co-op, the board of directors can take out a second mortgage to fix a roof, plumbing, or other major problem. Individual co-op shareholders cannot easily obstruct the board.

Delinquency in paying maintenance fees can be handled more expediently in a co-op than in a condo. In a co-op, an owner who doesn't pay maintenance fees can be evicted almost immediately. The person is served with a dispossess and can be evicted within days. In a condominium, a lien must be placed on the apartment and then a foreclosure proceeding is brought. It could take two years to get the money, and it is a difficult legal proceeding.

Exclusionary rights: Since a co-op is considered personal property, not real property, prospective tenants may be rejected by the co-op's board of directors for any reason whatsoever except race, creed, color or national origin. Reality: As long as the co-op board members don't state the reason, anyone can be excluded for any prejudice. Problem: A tenant may have trouble subletting a co-op if the co-op board members don't approve of the new tenant. In a condominium, each owner has the right to sell or sublet to anyone the person wants, subject only to the condo's right of first refusal, which is rarely exercised.

From the entrepreneur's point of view, a co-op can be more advantageous if the building at the time of the conversion date has a low-interest mortgage. Reason: When a building is converted into a condominium it must be free and clear of all liens. In a co-op, the former financing can be kept intact.

Source: David Goldstick, senior partner, Goldstick Weinberger, Feldman, Alperstein & Taishoff, 551 Fifth Ave., New York 10017

Condo/Co-op Insurance

Many people who own cooperative or condominium units may be taking a risk they are not aware of. If there is a serious disaster from a fire, flood, or other catastrophe, collective insurance may not be enough to restore the dwelling. In that case, each owner would be assessed to pay for expenses above the liability coverage.

Solution: For a small fee, tack coverage for uninsured damages onto your regular policy, which normally covers the contents of your unit and improvements. Suggested coverage: $25,000. The cost is negligible.

When buying a unit, ask the project's board of directors how much liability insurance they carry in case of an accident on the common ground. Most projects do carry adequate amounts of this type of coverage.

Source: Richard Hess, executive vice-president, Schiff-Terhune, an insurance brokerage firm, 8701 Wilshire Blvd., Beverly Hills, CA 90211.

Traps in Homeowner's Insurance

Many home buyers hastily purchase homeowner's insurance to qualify for their mortgage. Problem: They don't understand the choices involved in insuring a home.

Basic insurance: If a fire or other catastrophe destroys your home, you get the replacement cost, which is enough to rebuild the home to its original state. You carry at least 80% of the replacement cost. What you don't get: The market value of the home so that you can go out and buy a similar one. Land value and neighborhood are inherent in market value, yet unrelated to replacement cost.

Carry at least 80% of the home's replacement value. If you don't, the insurance company penalizes you by the percentage you underinsure.

Example: You have a $100,000 house, and carry only $60,000 on it. That is three-quarters of the $80,000 required. If you have $20,000 worth of damage from a fire, you will get only $15,000, or three-quarters of your damage. If you were insured for $80,000, you would get full coverage.

How to ascertain replacement cost:

Most insurance companies will inspect your house if it is worth over $100,000.

Your broker has a replacement-cost guide. This determines the cost of the average home by computing the number of rooms and square feet. It is an educated guess.

If your home was custom built, get an independent appraisal.

Replacement cost versus actual cash value: Replacement cost is only useful when you rebuild your house. If you decide to walk away and buy another house, you will only get actual cash value. What it is: Replacement value minus depreciation.

Example: You have a 50-year-old home worth $100,000 and $80,000 worth of insurance. You might get only $40,000 if you decide not to build, because depreciation could take away as much as 50% of the payment. (Depreciation computed by an insurance company is not related to depreciation for tax purposes. Depreciation is rarely in excess of 50% on a home.)

Inflation protection: Most insurance companies automatically increase coverage by whatever it costs to rebuild a home in your area. This automatic increase has been running about 10%.

Check out: Whether inflation increases are

granted annually, semiannually, or quarterly. Problem: If inflation is running 10% and you have a disaster after six months, you may have insufficient coverage. Best: Ask for an endorsement that increases protection quarterly. It costs little. Some insurers don't charge for it.

Other coverage included in a homeowner's policy:

The cost of staying in a hotel or renting a temporary apartment or house while your own home is repaired. Coverage: Up to 20% of insurance of the home's contents (furniture, china, clothing, etc.). Coverage: 50% of the insured value of the house.

Third-party liability: Protection in case anyone is injured on your property. Example: A party guest slips on a rug and breaks an ankle bone. Or: Someone is injured through some action of yours off your property. Example: You hit someone with a golf ball.

Appurtenant structures: A garage or shed. Coverage: 10% of home coverage.

Theft away from home: This covers a suitcase stolen from your locked car, etc. Caution: This coverage is limited and optional in some states.

Examine policies for restricted coverage on jewelry, furs, silverware, fine art, money, and securities. Schedule high-value items so that you and the insurer agree on value before there is a loss.

Keep accurate records of your possessions. Don't keep the records where they can be destroyed with the rest of your home.

Seek the broadest coverage possible within your budget. Some homeowner's policies are little more than fire-insurance contracts. Caution: No homeowner's policy covers floods. Flood coverage must be obtained separately. The best policies, known as all-risk policies, cover nearly everything and take the burden of proof of coverage away from you. They make the insurance company prove it is excluded from the contract.

Example: A deer jumped through a picture window. The deer panicked and tore through the house. The entire interior was destroyed since the deer either broke or bled on nearly everything. A standard policy would not cover this incident. Under an all-risk policy, the company must pay unless it can prove the incident falls within a specific exclusion from coverage set out in the policy.

Look for credits for higher deductibles, particularly percentage deductibles.

Example: You insure your house for $100,000. Instead of getting a $500 deductible, you can get a credit for a ½% deductible. However, realize that when the amount of the insurance is raised 10% the next year, your deductible will rise proportionately, from $500 to $550.

Look for credits for burglary and fire alarms.

Look into companies that pay dividends.

Source: Judith L. Robinson, CPCU, vice-president of general insurance brokers H & R Philips, 622 Third Ave., New York 10017.

How Much Fire Insurance Do You Need?

Most standard homeowners policies will pay the full value of the policy only if that value is 80% or more of the replacement value of the house. If coverage is below 80%, the maximum payment is limited to the replacement value minus a depreciation charge (usually quite large) figured according to the age of the house. The burden of keeping coverage to at least 80% of replacement value rests with homeowner. Advice: Increase coverage annually, to keep up with inflation.

Keep Insurance Ahead of Inflation

Keeping insurance coverage ahead of the inflation rate can be difficult. What to do:

Keep homeowner's coverage at a minimum of 80% of current replacement cost.

267

Take replacement cost policies for furnishings and other possessions. These reimburse for the cost of the replacement at prices in effect at the time of the loss.

Use a health-care cost index to figure how much more coverage you'll need, rather than an inflation index. Over the past five years, the rise in medical services has outstripped inflation. (Watch the newspaper for the monthly Consumer Price Index report, which breaks down medical costs.)

Jewelry, furs, and silver pieces should be included, piece by piece, on your homeowner's policy. Increase deductibles on cars and homeowner's comprehensive coverage. It will cost more if something is stolen or destroyed by fire, but premiums can significantly lower.

Gaps in Your Homeowner's Coverage

Most homeowner's and renter's policies do not cover you against liability in some common situations, including:

Claims connected with a business operated from your home. State law requires "residence employees" to be covered for injury by workers' compensation. This might include a babysitter who comes in regularly, or a teenager hired for a special project.

Bodily injuries or property damage arising out of deliberate actions by a family member below the age of 14. Note: Physical damage caused by a child under age 13 is covered, but only up $250 or $500 per accident.

Claims arising from the use or ownership of an airplane.

Accidents with recreational vehicles.

Accidents with any motor vehicles owned, rented, leased, or borrowed.

Motorboats with more than 50-horsepower engines, outboards with 25 or greater horsepower engines, sailboats over 26 feet.

Suggestion: Some of these risks can be covered by an umbrella policy. Cost: About $100 for $1 million of coverage. And you will gener-

ally be required to maintain $50,000 or $100,000 worth of coverage under both your homeowner's and auto liability policies. Certain risks, like home businesses and residence employees, must be insured separately.

Trap for Joint Property Owners

If you own property in joint tenancy or some other form of co-ownership, make sure all the co-owners are listed on any insurance policies that cover the property. Reason: If there is a fire or other casualty, and the insurance company finds out about the co-owners who are not listed, it may argue that the loss is not fully covered.

Example: If you are the only owner listed and it turns out you have only a half interest in the property, the company may argue that it is only responsible for your half of the loss.

If this happens to you, be prepared to sue. The court will probably agree to reform the policy and add the name of the missing co-owner. You must show:

The name was left off by mistake, not to mislead the insurance company.

The insurance company was not prejudiced. That is, it would not have had some reason for rejecting the policy if it knew who the co-owner was.*

*Gebhart v. American Consumer Insurance Co., 185 N.Y.L.J., No. 34, P. 16

Mistakes When Filing Insurance Claims

Failure to accurately calculate losses. It's hard to believe, but many people can't accurately determine their losses—whether by damage or theft. Reason: They fail to maintain effective accounting and record-retention procedures to document the losses. It's not uncommon to hear of a situation where a theft loss amounted to $250,000 but the claimant could only substantiate $100,000 of the loss.

Overstating the loss. This is a subtle problem. If a claimant purposely overstates the loss to the point where the insurance company could question his integrity, the latter will take a hard line. Generally, if the claimant takes a fair position, the insurer will still bargain over the loss claim but will be more reasonable.

Underestimating the loss. This sounds like a contradiction of the above, but it's not. Immediately after losses are claimed, adjuster will ask claimant for an estimate of the damage, not an accurate, justified number. The insurer requires such a rough estimate, but be wary of providing a number before taking time to get a reliable estimate. If the adjuster reports a number that's too low and then must go back later to the insurer and restate it much higher, his credibility and yours are hurt. He looks foolish. Those hurt feelings can make future loss negotiations tricky. So tell the adjuster about any problems in coming up with a number.

Guidelines for photographing household possessions:

Use an instant-copy camera, to get the job done to your satisfaction in a day.

Photograph everything you own. Open cupboards to show contents. Even objects that appear to be inexpensive and ordinary may be costly to replace.

Don't forget the boiler, water heater, and pump.

Mark the backs of the photos with model and serial numbers and other pertinent information.

Unstack pots and pans and group small appliances together when shooting kitchen appliances.

Put silver and bric-a-brac on black velvet material to make them look as valuable as they are. Shoot them with color film.

Don't neglect the bicycles, tools, and barbecues in the garage.

Get exterior shots of shrubbery and other landscaping, which are generally covered by insurance.

File the pictures, along with receipts and related documents, categorizing them by room.

Store the file and the insurance policy in a bank safe-deposit box.

Photographic Proof Of Insurance Claims

To speed up an insurance claim in case of fire, flood, or other damage to your home, a photographic record of your possessions is the best means of establishing proof of loss.

Check your policy. Items such as the building itself will probably be compensated for to the extent of replacement cost. However, furnishings (for example, sofas and silverware) are usually covered under the heading of actual cash value (ACV). With a photo, you have documentation that an old and valued chair is worth the $500 you claim rather than, say, the $5 the insurers may offer.

Liability for Injuries To Uninvited Guests

Courts in many states are more likely than ever to hold an owner responsible for injuries to a visitor. That's so even though the person was on the property without an invitation. The old distinction between an invitee (someone asked onto the property) and licensee (someone on the property without an invitation) is breaking down. Traditionally, invitees would be awarded higher settlements for damages.

Now courts in about one-third of the states ignore the distinction between an invitee and licensee and hold the property owner responsible for keeping the property safe for both invitees and the self-invited.

Now: Salespeople, whether they contacted the customer before their visit or not, are generally treated (by courts recognizing the distinction) as invitees.

Law When Trespassing Children Are Injured

A property owner or contractor may be liable for damages if a child is hurt on the property (or by unguarded machinery) even though the child trespassed. A "No Trespassing" sign isn't enough.

Example: A swimming pool should be surrounded by an adequate fence and a locked gate.

General rule: The attractive nuisance doctrine in the law makes the property owner responsible for trespassing children who are too young to understand the dangers.

Special problem: Protection while construction work is being done or when machinery is left unguarded in a residential area (or near heavily traveled streets).

Before You Renovate An Old House

The positive aspects of renovating an old house are enticing: A sense of accomplishment, an outlet for creativity, and the possibility that it will be a good investment. However, the experience of returning a house to its former glory can be frustrating and overwhelming to anyone who attempts it for the first time without proper understanding.

The worst aspects, according to old-home buffs:

Not knowing what you are getting into.

Living amid the chaos of reconstruction for very long periods.

Some things to consider when buying an old home to renovate:

Choosing the right neighborhood is the most important element on the investment side. If many homes are being renovated in your neighborhood, chances are good that your choice will be expensive. Best: Find a neighborhood where one or two homes have been renovated on your block and several more a few blocks away. There is a strong possibility that the neighborhood will blossom and values will rise.

Speak to owners of similar homes in your area before you purchase. Concentrate on the steps they took.

Get a good engineer's report about the home, and focus on foundation, plumbing, electrical and mechanical systems. These are the most difficult to restore. Choose an engineer with considerable experience in old homes.

If you want a modern interior and expect to gut most of the house and substitute modern fixtures, find a house that's just a shell. Reason: Old homes with fine architectural details such as a marble mantels and restorable wainscotting cost more.

Don't put your last penny into a down payment and take a big mortgage. The fixing-up process can be extraordinarily expensive even if you expect to do much of the work yourself. Expenses vary nationwide, correlating most closely with labor costs in your area.

Don't get an architect to draw up a master plan for your house immediately. It usually takes a while to know what you want out of a house. Unless you have lived in it at least six months to a year, you will probably make expensive mistakes.

Learn how to deal with contractors. You can't do everything yourself. You must hire experienced people. Read the contract. Make sure the contractor is bonded. Possibility: If you are fairly handy, call in a professional to do a small portion. Watch carefully. You may be able to finish the job yourself.

Gutting an interior can be done easily by anyone. All you need is a crowbar, sledge hammer, old clothes, and elbow grease. Most homes can be gutted in a weekend. Keys: Hire neighborhood teenagers to help. Find a dumpster for the plaster.

Don't be discouraged by broken beams, crumbling interior plaster, or even a leaking roof. As long as the exterior walls and the foundation are solid, shabby interiors are secondary.

Study local zoning laws before you make major changes. Reason: Removing a pipe or a wall frequently requires a building permit. However, after you get the permit, your tax assessment will be raised, probably by as much as the value of the renovation. Important: Be prepared to try negotiating with tax assessor.

Most expensive changes: Changing the location of the kitchen or bathrooms. Why: Plumbing. Don't do it if you can possibly live with things where they are.

Way to boost resale value: Organize a walking tour of restored homes in your area. These walking tours are great sales tools.

Source: Benita Korn and Patricia Cole, directors, the Brownstone Revival Committee, Inc., 65 Liberty St., New York 10005.

How to Deal With Home Improvement Contractors

The key to protecting yourself when hiring a contractor for major alteration is thoughtful contract negotiation. Even contractors with good reputations sometimes get in over their heads. It's especially important now that improving the home has become more attractive than buying a new one.

Consider an attorney when:

The job is very complicated or expensive.

Modifications to an existing house will require the structure to be open to the weather for an extended period.

The nature of the property (swampy, rocky) makes unforeseen difficulties likely.

A thorough check on the contractor's references is impossible.

Be specific about what work you want done, how and with what materials.

Don't settle for normal contract language about the project being done in "a workmanlike manner." Reason: Homeowners' standards for work they want done are often higher than common trade practice.

To avoid misunderstandings, refer in the contract to architect's drawings, where possible, and actual specifications.

Include a schedule against which to measure work's progress. Use calendar dates.

Example: Foundation and framing to be completed by March 1. Roughing-in by April 1. Sheetrock by May 1. Woodwork and finish work by June 1. Push for a penalty clause if the work is completed late.

Example: All work to be completed by June 1. If, however, work is not completed by July 1, the contractor will pay the homeowner $100 a day thereafter.

Including a payment schedule in the contract. Typically, a contractor gets 10% of the negotiated fee upon signing a contract. Then, partial payments at completion of each stage of succeeding work.

Your aim: Withhold any payment until contractor actually begins work on your house. Then hold down succeeding payments as much as possible, so that contractor does not earn his profit until his work is completed.

Make contractor responsible for abiding by local building codes. If you assume this responsibility, make the contract contingent on your ability to get all necessary building permits. Safety point: Make sure the final payment is contingent upon approval of the work by municipal inspectors. Typical issue: Fence is 4½ feet high because of rough terrain, but town insists on 4-foot maximum.

Work out procedure to amend the contract. If an unforeseen problem crops up (example: subsurface boulders obstruct the laying of a new foundation), or if the contractor honestly underestimated his costs, it will be necessary to renegotiate terms. If you try to hold a contractor to unreasonable terms, he will cut corners, stall, or walk off the job.

The contract should have a clause that describes how changes will be made. Typically:

271

All changes above $100 must be agreed to in writing by both parties to the contract.

Contrary to popular myth, an attorney is not necessary to modify a contract. How it's done: Write on a separate sheet: Notwithstanding anything else in the contract to the contrary, we agree as follows. . .(specify the contract modification). Then, both parties sign the modification.

Financing clauses: If the contract submitted by a contractor contains provisions for financing your home-improvement project, cross them out. Instead, always do your own financing. Terms of lenders working with contractors are usually stiff. Often they give the lender a second mortgage on your house—sometimes without your realizing it. That can leave the homeowner without leverage to force correction of bad workmanship.

Getting out of a contract: It's possible to insert a clause saying what damages you will pay if you cancel a project before work begins. But once work does begin, you should see it through to completion. Courts favor contractors in cases where homeowners want to break off a project halfway through.

Insurance: Contractor should show you the document from his insurance company covering workers' compensation. Reason: Standard homeowner's policy does not cover workers (except, in some states, an occasional babysitter). Fix responsibility for repairing wind, rain, or fire damage as well as possible vandalism at worksite.

How to Live Through A Home Renovation

Remodeling has become even more important recently because of high purchase prices and mortgage interest rates and the growing trend toward restoring old homes nearer to city centers.

Too many people have an idealized notion of what a renovation entails. To minimize frustration and disappointment, recognize from the start that the project will:

Cost more than you expect. You may find that you are paying much more than your neighbor paid to remodel just two years ago. Rule of thumb: Add 20% to the most conservative estimate.

Take longer than you have been told it will. Assume that everything that can go wrong will.

Be more disruptive to family member's lives than you can possibly imagine. Renovating, especially if several rooms are involved, is very messy. And there is no way to make it neat.

Once your expectations are realistic, you can begin to minimize the discomfort. Best defense: Move out (or don't move in) while the demolition and other heavy work are going on. If you must live in the middle of a renovation:

Complete as much work as possible in summer. At that time, you can send children to camp or to visit relatives. Workers can leave bulky supplies and equipment outside. Don't hold off until winter in the expectation that it will cost less because it's off-season. Interior renovation goes on all year long. And prices seem to go only up.

Use a professional you can communicate with and trust to get the job done in a reasonable period. This could be an architect, architect-builder, builder-designer, or designer-contractor. Most important: Rapport with you. Problem with some architects: Overoptimism, which can take the form of not leveling with clients about how time-consuming, costly, and messy the project will be.

If you have a competent supervisor, stay away from the house as much as possible.

Be realistic in deciding what to have professionals do and what to do yourself. Almost all the jobs required in a remodeling can be done by an intelligent, reasonably handy amateur. Few are exceptionally difficult. Problem: Each task can take an enormous amount of the time, in some cases months, especially if you hold down a full-time job.

Use experienced workers for heavy work: Demolition, basic carpentry, wiring, plumbing and masonry, floor scraping and refinishing.

If you want to cut costs by doing some things yourself stick to: Wallpapering, painting, stripping, sanding, tiling (vinyl, asbestos, ceramic), and laying parquet-wood floor squares (messy, but not hard).

To find the best skilled workers, get names from the previous owner of the house or apartment, neighbors, realtor, bank.

Do the remodeling in stages. Get a couple of rooms finished, clean, and livable quickly. Best first choice: Children's rooms. It helps if they have a place to play that keeps them out from underfoot while the rest of the work goes on. If the renovation is easy on the children, the parents will have it easier too.

Make sure supplies and workers are ready at the same time. This is especially important when doing the kitchen. Reason: If the job is well coordinated, you will be without a functioning kitchen for only two weeks. Key: Order cabinets well ahead. If they are custom built, plan a six-to-eight week lead time. Don't tear out wiring and plumbing until you know the cabinets are on the way.

Keep the place relatively clean. Sweep up every evening, even if the workers are coming back the next day to make a new mess. You will feel better. When bedrooms are being redone, move all your clothes and belongings out. Even if you put your things in drawers, the plaster dust will infiltrate.

Every week or so, invite friends over. If there is no place to sit, spread a tablecloth on the floor and have a picnic. If there is no kitchen, serve takeout food. Nice touch: Fresh flowers amid the debris.

Source: Richard Rosan, architect and president, the Real Estate Board of New York, 12 E 41 St., New York 10017.

Home Improvements That Increase Resale Value

Some improvements may not add as much to the property value as you paid for them. Example: A $15,000 pool or tennis court added to a modest house in a middle-class neighborhood may boost market value only $3,000 to $4,000. Better bets: Improvements that add top dollar value. Examples:

Outside. Paint-job, lawn, driveway, gutters, things people notice first when shopping for a house. General impression is that entire house has been well cared for.

Inside. The kitchen is the most important room for enhancing resale value. Everything spent to improve a kitchen will be close to 100% recoverable on resale. What buyers look for: Complete and proper arrangement of appliances, adequate storage and counter space, good lighting and bright, cheerful yellow or white colors.

Next most important room: The bathroom. Installation of a second bathroom will repay in increased resale value 100% of its cost or better; a third bathroom will repay about 80% of cost.

A garage can be a strong selling point if it is structurally sound, clean, and uncluttered. Basement: Dampness indicates foundation and drainage defects. Naturally, this turns potential buyers off and lowers value considerably.

Asking price. Call in a professional appraiser to determine fair market value. Then tack on 10% to establish asking price.

Source: *The Optimist's Guide to Making Money in 1980's*, by Jerome Tuccille, William Morrow & Company, New York.

Tax Benefit From House Repairs

Repairs after a fire or flood can be tacked on to the original purchase price of the house when the house is sold. That reduces the capital gains tax. Also added to the purchase price: General home improvements, including the cost of materials for do-it-yourself jobs. Caution: Keep invoices to document claims for the IRS.

Source: Phillips et al. v. Comm'r, TC Memo., 1979-239, 6/25/79.

Buying a Home Pool Without Getting Soaked

Backyard pools are growing in popularity as high gasoline and motel prices keep more people at home. While buyers must still proceed cautiously, there are now plenty of reputable pool dealers around. The industry itself has set standards and flushed out many fly-by-nighters.

Caution: Do not expect to recoup or better your pool investment when selling the house. Real estate brokers consider pools neither a plus nor a minus. Pools frequently reduce the resale value, but can be very attractive to some buyers.

Costs: Traditional 16 by 32-foot pools that are in the ground now start at $25,000. Basic aboveground pools begin at about $5,000. Do-it-yourself pools are cheaper, but are often shoddy. Also budget for: Annual chemical costs (about $400). Higher electricity charges. Winterizing.

Drawbacks: Pools require considerable maintenance. Neighbors often expect pool privileges. Some neighbors may complain about noise, drainage, and safety. Fencing the pool can be expensive.

Defensive strategy: While the pool is being built, order additional liability insurance coverage. About $100 a year buys extra liability protection of $1 million.

To find a builder: Ask neighbors with trouble-free pools. Other sources of referrals: Home contractors, swimming pool managers, a national trade group.* Have builders take you to other pools they have built, and ask owners about any problems.

From initial inquiry through completion, the job can take from two weeks to two months. Much depends on what the builder finds when excavating. Underlying rock, for instance, will slow process. But, on average, construction itself takes three to four weeks. Watch out for contractors who will not sign an agreement for a firm completion date. Reason: Pool contractors tend to take on too

*National Swimming Pool Institute, 2000 K St. NW, Washington, DC 20006.

many summer jobs and push leftovers into the next season.

Best materials: A Gunite concrete liner, using pneumatically applied concrete, is best. Vinyl liners often tear. They do not fit right. Stainless steel, aluminum, and partly wooden liners are all adequate. Fiberglass is suitable for smaller pools only.

Equipment: A premium-priced filter, plumbing, and pool heating equipment are worth the cost in the long run. Do not buy both an electrical heater and a cover that heats with solar energy.

Body comforts: Plan for a sauna or hot tub in the original design. It probably will add less than $3,500.

Financing: Bank loans run about 19%. They are easily available.

Paying the builder: Do not hand over more than 10% up front. Leave a big payment, at least 25%, until the day of your final inspection and acceptance. Do not forget to ask for the winter pool cover.

The latest fad: Shallow pools. Advantages: A pool 3½ to 5 feet deep saves $1,000 and up in building costs. And children do not have to be watched so carefully, provided that they know the pool is too shallow for safe diving.

If the pool turns out to be more trouble than it is worth, fill it in and plant grass.

Selling Your Home And Buying Another

There isn't any quick answer to the question of whether to sell your home first or buy another first. Too much depends on market conditions in your area and on your individual circumstances. Consider several key factors first.

If you sell before you buy:

When there's a seller's market, you have a strong bargaining position. Negotiate for time with the buyer. If your bargaining position isn't strong, delay the closing a few months by making a price concession.

If the buyer must close the purchase right away, ask him to rent the house back to you until you are able to move. To calculate whether it makes sense to pay rent on your own home: Compare the cost of living in temporary quarters, such as a motel. Then, factor in the cost of moving twice plus the storage costs on furniture and other belongings that you will have to pay.

If you buy before you sell:

When there's a buyer's market, the seller might be flexible about the closing date. Consider offering the seller a short-term note, secured by a second mortgage on your present home, to cover the down payment on the new place until the old one is sold.

A bridge loan can sometimes provide the cash for a down payment on a new home before you close on the old one. But banks usually require that you have a contract of sale on your old home, unless you or your broker have a very strong relationship with a local bank. Banks also want assurance that you have enough equity in your old home to cover the loan and some sort of escrow arrangement to make sure the loan is paid off when the sale of your old home is closed. Rates for a bridge loan: ½% to 1% above the prime, subject to local rate limitations.

Consider renting out a newly acquired home until your old house is sold and you are ready to move in. Of course, you will have to keep the rent low, since you can only offer a month-to-month tenancy.

Tax break: Otherwise nondeductible expenses, such as depreciation on the house, can be used to offset the rental income. But aside from interest and taxes, do not write off expenses that exceed rental income. Bear in mind that you are not renting the house as an income-producing property, but as a convenience.

Caution: You should not treat the house rental as a profit-oriented activity in order to boost your deduction. Reason: When you sell one home and buy another at a higher price, you can defer the tax on your gain. To qualify, the two transactions have to take place within 2 years, and both the old house and the new one must qualify as your primary residences.

Should you turn the new house into income property before you move in, you could lose this tax break.

The option solution: You might be able to nail down a deal on a prospective new home without actually taking title to it, and then take your time about selling your old one. Here's how:

First, locate the house you want to buy. Work out acceptable terms with the seller. Then, offer to pay the seller for an option to purchase the house on the terms you have already worked out.

To decide how much to pay for such an option: Compare the cost of your alternatives. How much would it cost to rent temporary quarters, store property, move twice? What would it cost to carry a bridge loan (interest, recording fees, service charges, etc.)? How much of a price concession does your broker think you would have to offer to get a potential buyer of your home to be flexible on the proposed vacancy date?

If the seller is hesitant about offering you an option, point out some of the advantages to him:

If you exercise the option (which you are likely to do), he gets to keep the option fee plus the agreed-upon price.

If you let the option lapse, he keeps the fee and still gets to sell the house.

If the seller is concerned about appreciation in real estate values between the time you purchase the option and the time you exercise it, it may be worthwhile to build in an escalator clause. This could be a flat-rate clause, raising the purchase price by say, ½% for each month. Or it could be tied to a mutually acceptable price index.*

An option arrangement gives you maximum flexibility in selling your old home. Knowing you can purchase a new home on agreed-upon terms makes it easier to evaluate the offers you get for the house you are trying to sell. In addition, there's a tax break: Later on, when you eventually sell your new home, the option cost is added to the purchase price to offset against any gain on the sale.

*The Bureau of Labor Statistics keeps track of changes in home-purchase prices as one of the components of the Consumer Price Index.

Real Estate Brokers' Jargon

Open listing: The owner reserves the right to sell the property himself or to retain brokers.

Exclusive agency: No other broker will be hired as long as the original broker is retained (usually for a specified period), but this doesn't prevent the owner from selling the property himself.

Exclusive right to sell: The broker gets his commission whether the property is sold by the broker, the owner, or anyone else.

Multiple listing: Brokers combine to sell properties listed with any member of the broker's pool. They split commissions between the listing and selling broker.

If no time is specified, the listing is good for a "reasonable" time. The owner can revoke the listing at any time before the broker has earned his commission, provided he acts in good faith and doesn't revoke when negotiations have been substantially completed.

If a time is specified, the agreement will end as stipulated. It continues only if the owner waives the time limit by accepting the services of the broker, or if the owner acts in bad faith (as by postponing agreement with a buyer until after the time limit). In some states, the owner can revoke only up until the time the broker has put money and effort into the listing contract.

If nothing is said, the broker will earn his commission on finding a buyer ready, willing and able to buy on the terms specified. The owner should ask for a provision under which payment of the commission will depend on closing the deal and full payment.

Selecting an Agent To Sell Your House

Avoid the trap of listing property with a relative or friend in the real estate business. Seek out an experienced, full-time agent, preferably one who specializes in your type of property or neighborhood.

Watch out for supersalespeople. They often push easy properties. If you feel uncomfortable with the agent, or there's some hangup about the property, find someone else.

The real estate office is important, too. It should be attractive, easily accessible, and open seven days a week for residential business. The agency should be a member of a multiple listing service and well regarded by financing sources. Note: Try to speak with the head of the firm. If you call in cold, you will get (and be stuck with) the broker who is on duty that day.

When to Watch Your Broker Closely

A company or individual listing property for sale with a real estate agent may find it's no longer listed after an offer is turned down. Reason: The agent is trying to make the commission by temporarily taking the property off the active list in the hope the owner will give up and accept the offer. The agent may keep other agents from sending around prospects by removing the file or spreading word that the property has been sold.

When Not to Take A Broker's Advice

Don't rely too heavily on a real estate broker's opinion on how much your house is worth. Conventional wisdom: The broker wants as high a price as possible to maximize the 6% commission. Reality: A broker makes more on quick sales than big ones. A fast commission of $5,400 on a $90,000 sale is much more attractive than $6,000 on a $100,000 sale that takes months to make. Advice: Check out a broker carefully before giving an exclusive. Look into prices of recent sales in the community.

Reducing the Broker's Fee

Discount real estate brokers charge significantly less than conventional brokers. The difference: Discounter appraises the house, lists and advertises it, shows pictures to customers, helps arrange mortgage. The homeowner actually does the showing. While showing is time-consuming, it is also the easiest part of the conventional broker's job.

Buyers Who Back Out at The Last Minute

Selling a house can be a problem when the potential buyer makes the deal contingent on the sale of his own house. After months of waiting, your deal may fall through.

Solution: Include a kick-out clause in the sales agreement. This enables the seller to keep the house on the market until the sale is completed. If another buyer makes an offer, the original buyer has 48 hours to decide whether he wants to buy the house or not.

Getting More For an Old House

An old house (built 1920 to 1950) can be sold as easily as a new one. The right selling strategy and a few improvements may raise the selling price significantly. That's the advice from Mary Weir of Rumson, New Jersey. She has bought, refurbished (on a grand scale) and resold more than 50 houses. Her suggestions:

Invest in a complete cleaning, repainting, or wallpapering. Recarpet or have the rugs and carpets professionally cleaned. (Approximate cost for a four-bedroom, three-bath house: $2,500 to $3,000.)

Get rid of cat and dog odors that you may be used to but potential buyers will notice.

With trend to smaller families and working wives, it may be desirable to convert and advertise a four bedroom house as two bedrooms, library, and den.

Exterior of house is crucial. It's the first thing buyer sees. Paint or replace shutters if necessary. Clean and repair porch and remove clutter. Repaint porch funiture.

Landscaping makes a great difference and can sell (or un-sell) a house. Get expert advice on improving it. (Approximate cost: Anywhere from $100 to $1,000.)

Good real estate agents are vital to a quick sale. There are one or two top people in every agency who will work hard to show houses and even arrange financing. Multiple listing lets these supersalespeople from different agencies work for the seller.

Is Your Property Assessed Too High?

The effective real estate tax is the tax rate multiplied by the assessed value. There's not much an individual can do about the tax rate, but assessment can often be challenged successfully. Requirements: Owner must show either that the property is overvalued or that the assessment is higher than on comparable property in the same area.

When to ask for a reduction:

Just before making necessary repairs of damages that have lowered the value.

Local tax records err in description by overstating size or income.

Net income drops due to factors beyond owner's control.

When the price paid for the building in an

arm's length transaction is lower than the assessed value.

What to do:

Determine the ratio of the assessed value to the present market value. Compare against average ratios of similar properties recently sold in the same area. Sources: Ratios available to public in tax districts. Real estate brokers, professional assessors can also be consulted.

Check tax records for a description of the property income.

Consult a lawyer on the strength of the case, whether it can be handled by an informal talk with the assessor, how much it will cost if a formal proceeding and appeal are necessary.

Minimizing Taxes On Sale of a House

While most people know that no taxes need be paid on profits of $125,000 or less from selling a home if you are over 55, not everyone is aware of other tax opportunities connected with house sales. They include:

Profits on any sale of house are taxed at a favorable rate. Only 40% of the profit need be reported as income.

Profits on a house sale that are reinvested in another house within 2 years will not be taxed until the new house is sold.

How this works: When calculating the profit made from selling the second house, deduct from the purchase price of the second house the profit made from the sale of the first home.

Homeowners who move more than once in 2 years for job-related reasons can take advantage of a special tax break. Normally, people buying and selling more than one house in 2 years may only defer capital gains from the sale of the first house. However, homeowners who can show that they sold two or more houses in 2 years because of job changes can defer gains on the sale of all houses. It is up to

the taxpayer to prove to the IRS that the moves were job-related. (And the taxpayer also must meet strict criteria for deducting moving expenses.)

Financing Your Own House Sale

As mortgage rates remain high, an increasing number of homeowners are enticing buyers with offers to finance the sale themselves. By offering financing, sellers may make their house so marketable that outside financing will be unnecessary. Bonus: The commission saving is substantial.

Caution: Although financing the sale of a house is simple in principle, sellers should have the advice of a lawyer who specializes in real estate.

Four basic methods:

• First mortgage: If you are trying to sell a $100,000 house that has no mortgage (a rarity), and the purchaser can afford only $40,000 cash down, then the purchaser simply gives you a first mortgage for $60,000 which is paid out over an agreed-upon interest rate. In case of default: You keep the cash and foreclose on the house.

• Second mortgage. If you are trying to sell the same $100,000 house with an existing $50,000 first mortgage, a second mortgage reduces the cash that a buyer would need. How it works: The purchaser assumes the first mortgage and gives you a $20,000 down payment. The purchaser then gives you a second mortgage for $30,000. Interest rate and maturity date are negotiable. Caution: Many existing first mortgages held by institutional lenders contain a "due on sale" clause, which prohibits the sale of the house without the consent of the leader. Typically, such consent is given only if the interest rate is substantially increased.

• Wrap-around. Similar to second mortgages. Using the same numbers as in the second-mortgage example, you get a $20,000 down payment, but instead of taking back a $30,000 second mortgage, you take back an $80,000 wrap-around mortgage (the amount of the first mortgage plus the remaining $30,000 of the sales price). Advantage: Defaults are quick to catch because the buyer makes all payments directly to you, and you pay the first-mortgage portion to that lender. Another advantage: The interest rate on the wrap-around is calculated on the entire $80,000, even though the $50,000 first-mortgage portion may be a lower interest rate. Result: You receive the interest average, giving you a higher yield on your $30,000 portion.

• Leasing with purchase option. Lease payments may be applied to the purchase price, an amount agreed on when the deal is made. Best approach: Make the term as short as possible. Why: Should another prospective buyer come along with ready cash, you won't be hindered by long-term contract. Advantage of purchase options: Since you are still the owner, you can depreciate the house as a rental unit.

Source: C. Gray Bethea Jr., vice-president and general counsel, CMEI, Inc., 300 Interstate N.. Atlanta 30339.

Taking Back A Second Mortgage

A tight mortgage market can force many home sellers to provide home buyers with second mortgages in order to complete sales. In their rush to sell, many homeowners are sticking themselves with poor deals. All-too-common bad terms:

Accepting payment for 50% of a house's sale price in annual payments over 30 years.*

Charging an interest rate lower than the going mortgage rate.

Cementing the deal with an informal note.

Considerations before taking back a second mortgage: Is it absolutely necessary? The ans-

*New Law: No longer need to defer 70% or more to get an installment sales break.

wer can be positive when it's urgent to unload the house or when the interest rate you are getting makes the deal a good investment.

How to protect yourself:

Check home buyers' credit references.

Require that buyers put up a minimum of 15% of the cost of the house.

Take back a second mortgage from someone who will occupy the house.

Record the transaction in the county office. While doing this, file for a notice of default. What it does: The county office will inform you if the buyer defaults on his first mortgage. That gives advance notice of probable foreclosure action, and he may default on the second mortgage.

Keep a receipts ledger for payments received, to strengthen your case if a default ends up in court.

Make the mortgage payment period as short as possible. A good idea: Some home sellers take back a six-month second mortgage just to give a buyer time to find permanent financing.

Insist on an adequate (high) interest rate.

Stipulate that the second mortgage is negotiable. Meaning: You can sell it, if you prefer to keep more liquid assests. Average discount on face value: 10% to 15%. Money-saving idea: Get the home buyer to agree before-hand to pay the discount points.

Include a "due and payable at default" clause. Protection: This means the entire mortgage becomes due if a buyer defaults on a single payment. Benefit to the seller: Pressure on the buyer to keep up with payments.

Include a "due on sale of property" clause. Protection: Prohibits the buyer from selling the house and passing the second mortgage on to the new owner, who might be less solvent.

Terms to avoid:

Those that result in your note being subordinated to other debts of the borrower.

Don't permit the home buyer to automatically extend the loan without renegotiating it.

Don't let the buyer pay interest, but not principal, over several years. Only by collecting principal do you commit the buyer to future payments.

Important: Learn about the local laws and

going interest rates for second mortgages. Object: Identify the minimum terms that make a sale acceptable to you before a buyer offers terms of his own. Sources of information: Realtors, mortgage brokers, attorneys, title companies, and banks.

Source: R.S. Peck, president, The White Company, a realty broker, appraiser, and investment firm, 14583 Big Basin Way, Saratoga, CA 95070.

Renting Your House If You Can't Sell It

Problem: You're committed to moving, but you can't sell your home at the price you want because high mortgage rates are scaring off buyers. Solution: Stop trying to sell, and rent your house instead.

Key advantage: Renting out your house turns it into a business property. This entitles you to deduct operating expense, maintenance, and repairs, and to depreciate the property. Result: A $200,000 house with an estimated life (for tax purposes) of 40 years yields an annual deduction of $5,000 for depreciation, on top of the amount you put in to maintain it. Extra: If you rent the house furnished, the furniture, too, is depreciable.

Note: When establishing a depreciation schedule for a rented home, the IRS requires that owners compute the value of a house by taking the lesser of its fair market value or its purchase price plus the value of permanent improvements made. The depreciation schedule itself is supposed to stretch over the remaining useful life of the house. That figure depends on both the age and the condition of the dwelling.

Drawing up a lease:

To retain the option of moving back into the house on short notice, lease on a month-to-month basis.

Stipulate which redecorating, maintenance, and repair costs will be borne by tenants. Usual terms: Owner pays for major repairs, renter for minor work. Set limits on what redecorating the tenant may do.

Spell out the conditions under which you may evict your tenants.

Make the renter pay for utilities.

Include an option to buy *only* if it is essential to rent the property.

Don't rely on a standard lease form. Consult a lawyer to draw up the papers.

Consider hiring a property manager to handle your home if you will be located far away. (Property-manager fees are tax-deductible.)

Consult your accountant before setting the rent. Reason: A low rent may permit you to take a tax loss, which could be more advantageous than added rental income. Caution: Drastically undercharging on rent to create a tax loss will be disallowed by IRS.

Source: Ronald Vukas, executive vice-president, the Institute of Real Estate Management, 430 N. Michigan Ave., Chicago, IL 60611.

Finding Reliable Tenants

Referrals are the best bet. For the owner and tenant to have a mutual friend will give the renter a greater sense of responsibility.

Check with local large corporation for families in transit who need temporary housing.

Advertise in the newspaper. List your phone number, but not the street address (to protect your privacy).

Energy Savings In the Home

There are a number of simple maintenance chores to attend to before getting into high-cost energy-saving investments in insulation, solar energy, etc.

• Plug the holes. Weather stripping, caulking, patching foundation cracks are always worthwhile. Adding storm or combination windows in front of existing window sashes may be cost-effective, depending on circumstances. Replacing existing windows with double-glazed units can rarely be justified on the basis of cost alone in temperate areas of country. Double panes are also tough to replace if broken. Tip: If your windows are equipped with screening, but lack storm sash, covering them with plastic sheets looks awful, but works well. Don't make the house too tight and stuffy, however. It's not comfortable, and can lead to moisture buildup, rotting, and mildew inside walls. Really tight houses may need a small fan (more like a kitchen range fan than the large attic fans in many older homes) to draw out moisture from time to time.

• Check the furnace. Caution: Don't depend on oil-burner service people to keep it clean. Even if they do, they'll only handle cleaning once a year. That's not enough.

There are several devices available for checking burner efficiency. Contact your local gas utility (the person to talk to usually has a title like "energy conservation liaison"), county energy conservation office (many areas have them), or plumbing and heating contractor for test. Utilities and government offices do it free; contractors charge about $30.

Have the contractor change the oil (or gas) burner nozzle for the spring and summer. A smaller nozzle cuts the burning rate 30%. It saves fuel (especially in hot air or water systems).

Heating system modifications. Units that close the flue when the burner is not operating are rarely cost-effective at current prices ($400 installed).

Other system modifications to consider first: (1) Old, open circulating hot-water systems (the expansion tank is under the roof, and vents to the outside) should be converted to pressurized systems with a circulating pump and expansion tank in the basement. (2) Zoning heat (to reduce flow to all but bedroom area at night) may be worthwhile to do at same time. (3) Fan on hot air furnace should be wired to continue running when the furnace burner is off—that increases the electrical bill slightly, but improves comfort and cuts

fuel bills by decreasing stratification (hot air at top of room, cool near floor).
(4) Day/night thermostats, or even computerized units to change desired temperature at various times during the day, are usually cost-effective—especially if you're about to replace old thermostats anywhere due to normal wear. (5) In-flue heat exchangers are usually worthwhile ($150 to $300 installed), especially on older furnaces (plenty of waste heat in flue to capture) and where heat can be ducted to nearby living space. Problem: Units require frequent maintenance and cleaning. The task is messy, but simple and worthwhile.

• Radiators. Oldest are best. Cast-iron radiators even out the flow of heat from furnace, circulate air in rooms by convection. Leave them uncovered and undraped (drapes should end at the bottom of a window, or fall behind the radiators). Covers, if you insist on them for looks, should offer wide spaces for air flow in front and above radiators themselves. Avoid covers with solid tops. Paint radiators a flat black. Shiny silver cuts efficiency.

• Hot water heaters. Often set at 160°. Cut to 140° if you have dishwasher (you may have to insulate hot water line to distant kitchen; low-cost kits are available from builders' supply houses), 110° without dishwasher. Consider a booster unit to heat water for dishwashing only (see plumbing contractor). Average family uses 26,000 gallons of hot water per year. That takes more energy than refrigerator, TV, stove, freezer, lights combined.

• Air conditioners. Buy units of correct size for room. Common mistake: Buying a bigger unit because it costs only a few dollars more. This wastes money in the long run. Keep filters clean—change them once a month in summer. Install the air conditioner on the north side of the building, if possible. Reason: It's the side that keeps the coolest in the summer. Central air conditioning: The condenser should be on the north side for the same reason. If located elsewhere, shield it from the sun.

• Sign of wasted heat: Quickly melting snow on the roof of the house indicates that heat is being lost because of poor attic insulation.

• Test for air leaks: On a windy day, hold a lighted candle near the frames of doors and windows. If the flame flickers, there are leaks that need sealing.

• Don't plant tall evergreens on any side of the house but the north. Otherwise the sun's warming rays will be blocked in the winter.

• Energy-conservation trap. Too-tight insulation reduces air circulation, which increases humidity and allows bacteria to breed. Solution: A dehumidifier.

• Wrap up your water heater. An average 14% of the heat from a water heater escapes into the house, lowering the heater's efficiency and raising cooling costs. Solution: Install insulation, which shouldn't cost very much, around the heater. Energy savings should pay for the kit within a year.

Source: *The Family Handyman.*

• Quartz heaters. Advertising claims are greatly exaggerated. Their energy efficiency is about the same as other electric space heaters. Ads implying that quartz heaters are a technological innovation are nonsense. They have been on the market for over 20 years.

• Attic fans. Proper use: When evening temperatures drop, open house windows and turn on the fan. It will draw in the cool night air. Next morning, shut off the fan, close all windows, and draw all drapes. The temperature in a well insulated house will stay comfortable all day. Attic fans are relatively inexpensive (about $500) and they use only a small portion of the energy of central air conditioning.

• Save hot water. Shower: Remove the shower head, and insert a common washer inside the threaded end of the head, as far as it will go. Then reattach the head. This will cut water flow by half. The cost is about 10¢. Or use a plastic or metal water restrictor that fits behind the shower head and doesn't decrease spray intensity. Taps: An aerator will reduce water flow by 50%. (Brass disk aerators last longer than rubber or plastic ones.) Dishwasher: Wash only full loads. Don't rinse the plates beforehand, just scrape them clean.

• Energy-saving cooking. Rules: (1) Use the smallest pot and the least amount of water possible to speed up cooking time. (2) Bring water to a boil on high heat, then cook on medium heat. (3) Match the pot size with the size of the electric-range element. Discard wobbly pots with uneven bottoms. They don't distribute heat evenly and can cause accidents.

• Plug up the damper in your fireplace with insulation or wood. Saving: $20 to $45 a year for snowbelt areas.

• Seal holes in the attic floor where pipes, ducts, and exhaust fans cut through. Potential saving: $25 to $80 each year.

• Extend caulking or weather stripping beyond windows and doors. Other areas worth looking into: Baseboards, wall outlets, pipes, wires and vents. Covering heating or air conditioning ducts that pass through unfinished attics or basements alone can save up to $100 a year in heating and $35 a year in central air conditioning for many houses.

• Roofing in warm climates. Consider aluminum asbestos-fibrated roof coatings that reflect heat. They cost more to install, but there's sizable saving in air-conditioning costs when the aluminum is compared to black asphalt (which absorbs heat).

Window Treatments That Save Energy

The most successful window coverings are light-efficient, energy-saving, and decorative.

Some of the options:

White, tightly woven shades, which run on tracks that are permanently affixed to the window. They block out and reflect the heat of the sun. Yet they permit sufficient daylight to minimize any additional lighting requirements.

Venetian blinds along with tightly woven draperies provide good alternatives to shades, although they are more difficult than shades to keep clean.

Reflective film coating on window glass reflects 80% of the sun's heat. Coating can cut air conditioning costs by as much as 50%. In winter, insulating film reflects radiant energy back into the room rather than allowing it to escape through the glass. That cuts the heating bill slightly.

Thermal-lined draperies and window blankets are coming back in the form of gauzy sheers, draperies, and valances. These "period styles" reduce heat loss.
Source: *The Designer.*

Energy Tax Credits For Homeowners

Residential energy tax credits totaling $4,300 are now available to homeowners, tenant stockholders in cooperatives, and members of condominium management associations. Point: Credits are worth more to the taxpayer than an equal amount in deductions because credits reduce the tax bill on dollar-for-dollar basis. Limitation: The credits are available only for work that is done on the taxpayer's principal residence.

Renewable energy credit is available for 40% of the first $10,000 spent on alternative energy systems, such as wind, solar, and geothermal power. (Maximum credit: $4,000.) The cost of labor used to install the system is included when computing the credit. Typical qualifying items: Solar collectors, heat exchangers, windmills.

No credit is available for: Woodburning systems or for the cost of a conventional furnace that is used to back up a renewable-energy system.

Passive solar energy systems are a problem area. These systems use south-facing windows to catch the sun, massive masonry walls to retain heat, awnings and draperies to provide shade. Point: The energy credit is available only for those elements of a passive system that serve no other decorative or structural function. A masonry wall is not eligible for the credit. But glazing on the wall is eligible. Other ineligible items: Windows, skylights, greenhouses, awnings, drapes.

Conservation credit: 15% of the first $2,000 spent on insulation and other means of energy conservation. (Maximum credit: $300.) Typical qualifying items: Storm windows and doors, caulking, weather stripping, automatic furnace ignition systems and flue-opening controls. Point: The expenditure must be made on a house that was substantially completed before April 20, 1977. No credit is available for any part of the cost of significant renovation done after that date. That is so even if the purpose of the renovation is to make the house more energy efficient.

Both the energy and the conservation credits are available retroactively for work done after April 19, 1977 (although the maximum renewable energy credit for the years before 1980 is $2,200).

Save Money and Fuel With Wood Stoves

Wood stoves are fast becoming a cost-efficient supplementary means of heating houses.

Cost: $150 uninstalled to $1,000 installed. Wood itself is sold by the cord (128 cubic feet usually cut into two-foot-long pieces and split in half). Price varies by locality. You can save money by doing the cutting, splitting, and stacking yourself. The local parks department may let you cut wood for free to save the department cost of having it cut and hauled.

Rule of thumb: The median range for the heating value of wood is about 25 million BTUs per cord. A well insulated house of 2,000 square feet in a relatively cold climate requires about 100 million BTU's per heating season (about four cords per winter).

Calculate the economic logic of switching to wood heat, by estimating how much you can comfortably reduce oil consumption by putting a wood stove in your living room. If the saving over two or three winters adds up to more than the cost of buying and installing a wood stove, plus the cost of four cords of wood per winter, a stove is a good idea.

Shortcomings: Wood stoves usually mean chillier upstairs bedrooms. Also, you must dispose of ash and remove creosote from the pipe connecting the stove to the chimney.

Alternative Fuels For Stoves And Fireplaces

Fuel substitutes for fireplaces and wood-burning stoves:

1. Compressed wood logs.
2. Pelletized fuel made from fibrous organic material. Caution: Wood-burning stoves must have insulated linings or be air tight cast iron to use pelletized fuel. The heat generated hits 1,800°F. It works best when burned with wood or coal.
3. Coal produces twice as much heat as seasoned hardwood.
4. Combinations of hardwood chips and coal chunks processed with an organic resin binder.
5. Newspaper logs don't produce as much heat as coal products, but they are very cheap. All you need is wire to bind newspaper tightly together (or purchase a newspaper roller).

How to Burn Wood More Productively

Heating a home safely and efficiently with wood requires more than a stack of logs and fireplace. The ground rules:

Price: To be cost-effective, one cord of wood should cost no more than 150 gallons of fuel oil.

A cord is 128 cubic feet of logs, including air spaces between them. This is the standard commercial measure for wood, but prices vary widely. Example: Four-foot-long green logs are much cheaper than shorter dry ones. But the latter come ready for the fireplace. (The others must be dried and cut.) Advice: It's best to buy green wood in late spring or summer. It will dry in six months, in time for winter use.

Types of wood: Harder woods yield more heat. Included: Oak, ash, and beech. Less efficient: Magnolia, cherry, Douglas fir. Least: Poplar, spruce, willow.

Stoves: The most efficient stoves use baffles, long smoke paths, and heat exchangers to extract as much heat as possible. They are more expensive than simpler types. But, in the long run, they save money. A wide variety of wood-burning (and multi-fuel) furnaces is available for central heating systems. Caution: Check local restrictions. Some furnace types are not allowed in certain states.

Fireplaces: Except for emergency use, open fireplaces are mainly for aesthetic value. Reason: They are essentially poor heaters. Homeowners who want the best of both worlds should consider installing efficiency-improving modifications or combination fireplace-stove units.

Source: *Heating with Wood*, U.S. Department of Energy, Washington, DC.

A Quick Course On Insulation

One of the most rewarding energy conservation efforts, in terms of savings and comfort, is home insulation. But, despite the rewards, over 90% of American homes are inadequately insulated.

While the ideal time to insulate a house is during construction, insulation can be added to existing homes in several ways. It will cost the homeowner nothing in the long run because of substantial savings in heating and air-conditioning costs.

Because of the variables (particularly energy costs, house type, location, and exposure) a homeowner cannot predict the precise savings for a given house or how long the payback period is for the insulation work. A good installation, however, generally pays for itself within four years.

The reductions in heating and cooling costs thereafter are pure savings. The bonus is a draft-free house in winter, a cooler house in summer, and a quieter home the year around.

Two types of insulation:

• Batts (four to eight-foot lengths) and blankets (rolls): Placed between wall studs and roof rafters.

• Loose fill: Blown in between roof rafters and into hollow walls through holes bored from the outside.

How it works: Insulation's R value is the measure of the insulation's resistance to seasonal heat loss or gain. The higher the R-value, the greater the resistance. You should try to exceed the minimum standards dictated by the climate in your area. The New York State minimum standards:

Roof or attic R-19
Floors above outside spaces or garage . R-19
Exterior walls R-11
Floors above unheated spaces R-11
Foundation walls in heated basement or crawl space R-5
Heating ducts in unheated spaces R-5

The typical R values of the more commonly used materials:

Inches of Thickness

Loose fill:						
Fiberglass	5	5½	8½	9½	13	16½
Rock wool	4	4½	6½	7½	10	13
Cellulose	3	3½	5½	6	8½	10½
Batts and blankets						
Fiberglass	3½	4	6	7	9½	12
Rock wool	3½	4	6	6½	9	11½
R Values:	11	13	19	22	30	38

Total insulation of an existing one-family house (exterior walls, floors, and attic) should cost $1,500 to $3,500. Variables: House size, design, and the type of material used.

Tax credit: 15% of the cost of all energy-conservation efforts, including insulation. The maximum total credit: $300.

Financing: Favorable terms for financing insulation work and other energy conservation expenses are generally available through utility companies and from banks.

Source: Sal Nuccio, president, Nuccio Organization Ltd., financial consultants. 60 Algonquin Rd., Yonkers NY 1070, and author, *The New York Times Guide to Personal Finance*.

Places to Insulate

Ceilings with cold spaces above them (for example, the attic or the roof).

Exterior walls and walls between heated and unheated areas.

Floors over unheated or outside spaces.

Walls of a finished basement or of a basement that is heated.

Aboveground part of foundation or basement wall.

Superinsulating Homes To Slash Fuel Bills

Energy-conscious contractors in the U.S. and Canada are building homes that require little or no gas, oil, or electricity for space heating. Cooling bills, too, are greatly reduced. Basic concept: Superinsulation. It maintains temperatures by using the heat generated by appliances, lights, water heaters, even human bodies. Modest backup heaters are usually available too.

Cost range: 1% to 3% above standard building expenses, including land. Key elements:

Solar orientation: North-south axis. Most solar windows are on the southern wall, where incoming sunlight provides maximum direct heating .

Triple-glazed windows: For heat retention without loss of light or views.

Heavy insulation: In all floors and ceilings.

Double-wall construction: For all exteriors, the large inner cavities filled with insulation.

Air-infiltration barrier: A 6 mm polyethylene sheet fastened to framing lumber during construction.The barrier prevents heat leakage and keeps condensation from reducing effectiveness of insulation.

Air-to-air heat exchanger: Located at the point where stale air is drawn out and fresh air in, it transfers 80% of outgoing heat to the incoming air.

Entrance hallways: At doors to baffle and help contain icy blasts.

Designs of superinsulated homes differ little from conventional houses, except for the concentration of windows on the south wall.

Superinsulated homes in Springfield, VA, average 230 gallons of fuel oil in a year for heat. Comparison: 1,200 gallons for neighboring homes. Payback period: About 18 months.
Source: *Civil Engineering.*

Insulate, But Don't Suffocate

Recently, there has been an emphasis on improvement of building insulation to save energy and money.

But insulation can be too good. When a building is airtight, chances are that moisture can build up within walls and in attics and roof spaces, causing structural members to rot and, in some cases, to collapse.

Adequate ventilation is required in all buildings. In addition to allowing moisture to escape, it prevents carbon dioxide buildup, eliminates odors, dilutes toxic gases, reduces stuffiness, and maintains comfortable temperatures in warm weather.

In Dortmund, West Germany, a 30-year-old man died of carbon dioxide poisoning in an apartment that he had made airtight by adding wall insulation and weather stripping to windows and doors. All outside air had been shut out.

Because of tighter construction, the amount of humidity in a new house is usually higher than in an older house.

Most attempts to avoid moisture buildup indoors have been ineffective. Use of vapor barriers, siding, or soffit vents and ventilation of a building's outer walls have disadvantages. Water vapor can pass through the wall and ceiling insulation and condense within the insulation material itself. That reduces its insulation value and could freeze within the walls in winter.

How can you insulate your home adequately and still avoid moisture buildup? Ventilation from the inside to the outside through the use of mechanical exhaust fans has proved effective and requires that only a moderate amount of air be exhausted.

For all practical purposes, an exhaust rate of 20 cubic feet per minute for each 1,000 cubic feet of space is needed. Thus, for a home of 2,000 square feet floor area and an eight-foot ceiling (16,000 cubic feet), use an exhaust fan with about 320 cubic feet per minute minimum rating. Such a fan could be used as an exhaust in the kitchen, the bathroom, the laundry room, and wherever else moisture accumulates.

Usage: Depends on the size of the family. The larger the family, the more often the fan would be on.

How Utility Meters Work

Both electric and gas meters operate on the same principle. Each has several dials with pointers that tell you how much of the product you are using.

Electric meter:

It has five numbered dials. The pointers on three of the dials turn clockwise, while the other two go counterclockwise.

It is read from left to right. The pointer always registers the number it has just passed. Example: If the pointer rests between three and four read the number as three. This holds true even if the pointer is touching the four but has not gone past it.

The numbers taken off of each of the dials give you the reading of the meter at that moment. When it is read again (usually in a month), you know how many kilowatt-hours of electricity have been consumed.

Meters can be wrong. Electric meters can wear out or be damaged during an electrical storm. A dramatic increase in your electric bill should signal a call to the utility company.

Gas meter: It is read exactly the same way as the electric meter. Difference: It has four dials. The pointers of two turn clockwise, while the other two go counterclockwise.

Fire-Detection Systems For Your Home

The danger of house fires hits a peak in winter as families spend more time indoors and heavy demands are put on heating and electrical wiring systems.

The best defense: A combination of smoke, heat, and ion detecting alarms installed throughout the house. Cost: About $200. They can cost up to $2,000 for sophisticated units that alert police and fire departments.

What the three basic detector units sense:
• Opaque smoke from a fire.
• A rise in temperature.
• Electrically charged particles (ions) that are produced in the earliest stages of most house fires.

The three types are often packaged together. All can be bought to run on house current or on batteries.

What is available:

Smoke alarm. Cost: Often less than $10 per unit, including an alkaline 9-volt transistor radio battery. Requires a new battery every six months or so. Drawback: Will not detect some types of fires as quickly as an ion detector will. Good for rooms used for entertaining.

Heat detector. Cost: Under $25. Most often hooked up to house current, not operated by a battery. A household unit is normally set to go off at 120°. Drawback: A fire may get out of control and give off toxic fumes before the home heat sensor sounds the alarm. Best locations: Kitchen, storage areas, furnace room, garage. In remote locations, they can trigger an off-site alarm that will continue ringing even after the sensing element is consumed by fire. (Some battery-powered smoke and ion detectors can be equipped with transmitting devices to do the same thing, but they are not always available.)

Ion detector. Cost: $15 to $40 (including the battery). Note: The cheaper versions sometimes use an expensive 11.2-volt silver-zinc battery, which is hard to find. Best: A unit run on a 9-volt radio battery instead. Disadvantage: It's so sensitive that it can be set off by moderate cigarette smoke, fireplace heat or even kitchen fumes. Best locations: Bedrooms, upstairs hall, furnace room.

Battery versus house power. Ionization and smoke detectors powered by house current are most expensive and more difficult to install than battery units, especially in older homes. They must be equipped with standby rechargeable batteries; otherwise they won't protect during power outages (a period when fires often start, since candles are being used and power lines get knocked down, sending sparks flying). Nevertheless, most families eventually tire of the battery-changing routine, or they put off changing a dead battery for weeks. Best: A mix of power sources as well as detector types. Suggested:

House current in remote locations. Example: The attic.

Batteries in units that are easy to reach. Example: The ceiling of a front hall, within arm's length of stairway to second floor.

How many? Professionals can sense household air flows and use fewer units to provide adequate protection. Do-it-yourselfers should aim for a unit in every room, except bathrooms, and one at both the bottom and the top of every staircase.

Note: Consider buying an extra battery-powered smoke detector that can be carried when traveling, for protection in hotels. The units are lightweight and can be placed atop a hotel-room cabinet, near the ceiling.

Carpet Fire Hazard

Acrylic carpets are gaining popularity among consumers. Reasons: They're colorfully attractive, look like wool, wear like nylon, resist fading and are easy to clean. Caution: they are also extremely flammable. Advice: Look at the label first. If an acrylic carpet's fiber is at least 20% modacrylic, then it is flame-resistant to a degree that is at least comparable with other materials.

Checking on Water Purity

Advice from Armando Balloffet and Patricia Gillens, experts on drinking-water quality.

Detecting impurities in drinking water requires a technical analysis. Taste has nothing to do with it.

Three types of impurities that require different types of testing:

Physical impurities: Soil, sand, or clay.

Biological impurities: Bacteria and other microorganisms from nearby sewers or other unsanitary water sources.

Chemical impurities: PCB, chloride, or pesticides from nearby landfills, industrial sites, etc.

How to test: If your water is supplied by a public water company, call the utility and ask them to test it. They should come to your home. If you doubt their results, request a look at the analysis. Check it against the minimum standards available from the Environmental Protection Agency (EPA).

To test private well water, call the local health department. It generally has test facilities. However, their testing facilities are usually restricted to biological impurities. If you are concerned about chemical impurities, it costs a few hundred dollars to get a sample tested at a private laboratory.

Reason to test: A landfill or industrial site near your well. Otherwise, such contamination is rare. If you are near such a site, the hydrology of the area (which way the water flows) may make it possible for you to live as close as a block away from the source of pollution and still have clean water.

If the water does prove to have impurities, the bacterial ones are easiest to solve. Boiling water destroys these microorganisms. Alternatives: Clean or disinfect the well.

Chemical problems are tougher to solve. Consult the EPA. You may have to use bottled water. Chemical impurities sometimes flush out of the well or soil with proper rainfall and treatment. However, it can take years.

The EPA does not recommend the use of water filters, which usually use carbon filters to purify water and to alleviate these problems. It's hard to tell when the carbon no longer functions. When that happens, a sudden buildup of pollutants can get into the water, and bacteria can slough off the filter.

Source: Armando Balloffet, hydrological engineer, Trippette-Abbet-McCarthy-Stratton, 655 Third Ave., New York 10017, and Patricia Gillens, sanitary engineer, the Environmental Protection Agency, 26 Federal Plaza, New York 10278.

How to Minimize Flood Damage

Flooded basements can be "good." If a flood reaches your property, water inside will equalize underground pressure outside and prevent collapse of the basement walls. Don't pump out the basement until the flood recedes.

If you have no second floor: Remember, water inside a building often gets no higher than two or three feet. Use high shelves for valuables (including furnace motor).

Keep underground fuel tank full. Otherwise, it can buoy up to the surface, causing foundation walls to collapse. (If no fuel is available, fill the tank with water.)

Home Security Checklist

• Use door locks with pick-resistant cylinders. A solid wooden door can take a well-constructed mortise dead bolt lock. If there is any glass in the door, or within 36 inches of it, try a double-cylinder locking device that requires a key to get out as well as to get in. Reason: The burglar can't smash a window and open the lock from the inside. Caution: Check with your local fire and building departments to make certain there are no regulations that prohibit this, especially in multiple dwellings.

• Window locks. Use an inside jimmy-proof locking device. The window frames should be in good condition. There's no use locking windows if the frame can be jimmied.

Although windows are easy to break, the sound attracts attention and many burglars avoid it.

In less-populated areas, the breaking of windows may go unheard. Solution: Invest in security glazing material. This permits the outside glass to break, but the intruder runs into one quarter inch of Plexiglas. Unless he's willing to expend a lot of energy, he won't get in. It's expensive, but you don't have to reinforce all windows, just those offering easy access.

• Any windows you never open should be pinned with penny nails placed through holes drilled at edges of sash. Block patio doors with screws in top track.

• Secure the garage door from the inside with a padlock through a hole drilled in the track. Don't use photoelectric-cell automated doors. Better: A good bar with a key lock or an electronically operated door with at least two radio frequencies.

• Trim shrubbery around the house to three feet or less, especially around windows and doorways. Reason: Shrubs can act as shields for an attacker, or as an observation point for those looking to see if anyone's home.

• Don't leave anything around the yard that could make entry into the house easier. Swimming-pool ladders, lawn furniture, even gardening tools could be used to gain entry.

• A full inventory of your valuables, with photographs, will help police use the National Crime Information Center to track down your lost goods (which probably will be fenced quickly out of state).

• Get a jump on the thief: Ask for a security assessment by your local police department. In many areas, this involves marking valuables with your Social Security number and the initials of the police department. Such identification helps police secure convictions of burglars. Serial numbers are good to know, but too often are accidentally duplicated by manufacturers.

• Stamp "Do Not Duplicate" on keys. It's not foolproof, but it helps to hinder unauthorized key copying. Also use locks that require very hard-to-get key blanks. Some blanks are secure, that is, licensed keymakers don't stock the blanks; they must be acquired from the lockmaker. There is a delay—not long, but worthwhile. Don't leave a key under the doormat or in the mailbox. When keys are lost: Have all locks changed immediately.

• When signing important papers, use an *italic* pen. It's very hard to forge.

• If you awaken to find a burglar in your home, pretend to be asleep. Sleepers usually survive a robbery.

• A woman living alone should *not* put her first name on the front door, the mailbox, or in the telephone book.

• Use the peephole in your door.

• Close your drapes or blinds when dressing or undressing.

• Check all window locks before going to bed.

• Always have your keys ready to unlock the door when you get home, so you can get in fast.

• Set up a simple signal system with a friend, e.g., three rings on his phone to indicate you need help.

• If you lose your purse or wallet go home with somebody. Reason: The thief will know your address and may have your keys.

• Obscene calls. Unanticipated bonus of a telephone answering machine: a fast hang-up by the caller and no return calls.

• Before letting someone in who says he's from the gas company, cable-television company, or any other service, see proper identification. Never admit anyone who simply flashes a police badge. A police officer must also show his police identification card, which has his photograph on it.

Making Burglars Think There's Somebody Home

You've heard it before, but you're probably still not doing it—leaving lights on when you leave the house. And even if you are leaving lights on, you're probably leaving only one—in the living room.

Some better ideas: Use several electronic timers that can be programmed to go on and off at various times during a 24-hour period. Avoid the simple ones that only make one on-off cycle a day; not versatile enough. Scatter them in various front and back rooms and upper and lower floors.

Put adequate lighting outside—illuminating doors or vulnerable windows. Especially: Those entrances that aren't fully visible from the street or from a neighbor's house. Important: Make sure those outside lights can't be easily turned off by the burglar. And that means they should be sufficiently inaccessible so he can't reach up and unscrew the bulb!

Lights alone aren't very effective. Reason:

Thieves who are "casing" affluent neighborhoods today assume that residents will leave some lights on. Best to add noise to the burglar resistance list.

One way: Connect a radio to the timers. Even better: Make a tape recording of "household" noises. Include dog barking in inventory of sounds. Be sure the recorder and tape can rewind automatically, or the technique will fail.

When you're away for a long period, inform the police. Stop all deliveries. Maintain the appearance that the house is occupied. Leave shades and drapes in their normal positions. Don't have the phone disconnected (get vacation rates instead). Have a neighbor park his car in your driveway.

What a Burglar Thinks About Alarm Systems

Michael Weaver, in Walla Walla prison, tells what he learned about burglar alarms in his years of dealing with them professionally—mostly successfully. His from-behind-bars report:

Systems to avoid:

Door and window alarms. They are usually turned on by key when the last person leaves the premises. The alarm systems monitor all the doors and windows. If anyone tries to open them, an alarm sounds. These systems aren't only worthless, they are an invitation to the burglar. Reason: They are visible (tape on windows and contact points around doors), so the burglar knows what he has to deal with. He may simply enter and leave through a roof vent or he may use a jumper wire to "fool" the electrical system.

Electronic eye alarms: These rate no better than door and window alarms. They operate like automatic supermarket doors. When an invisible beam is broken, a silent alarm is tripped. Since the eye can be moved and aimed easily, it can be shifted to cover doors, windows, walls, or a safe. Like door and window alarms, these systems are easy to breach using optical equipment to discover their position from a safe vantage point. Once the burglar spots them, he just works around them.

Effective alarms:

Proximity alarms. Microphones are placed throughout an area and are activated when the premises are empty. They are sensitive to any noise they are programmed to register. One weakness: The last person to leave will activate the system. If anyone wishes to return, he must telephone the monitor, giving a code number and the length of time he expects to be in. If a burglar spots this, he may place a miniature recorder near the phone and learn the code. Solution: Code numbers, security information, and schedules must be protected and changed frequently.

When and Where Burglars Strike

Most vulnerable time: Daylight hours, when both husband and wife may be at work. Nearly half of all burglaries happen during working hours. Most burglars are in and out of a house within about 15 to 20 minutes and won't risk being trapped above or below the ground floor. Especially vulnerable areas: Dining room, living room, kitchen, ground-floor bedrooms. Strategies: Pack valuables in unlikely looking cartons, store them in attics or closets, the more inaccessible the better. Avoid overdone tricks like jewelry in ice trays.

If You Catch a Burglar in the Act

Never try to cope with a burglar yourself. Even master burglars may kill if confronted. If you enter the house and suspect a burglary has

occurred (or is occurring), get right out and call police from a neighbor's home. If the thief surprises you, be passive; follow his orders. Don't try to save your valuables or catch him.

Weapons: In general, forget them. They're dangerous. The chances of being where the gun is when you confront a thief are rare.

What to Do When the Police Arrive

Have a list ready of items missing. Give a reasonably correct estimate of the value of what was stolen. Don't exaggerate. Reason: Your later statements may be discounted. State the time of the burglary. If you were away and don't know, don't make a wild guess. Let the police try to figure it out. Have answers to questions police will ask: Are you sure doors and windows were locked? Who else has keys to the premises? Are there any people that you suspect? Do you carry burglary insurance? Have you already notified your insurance company? Do they have investigators working on this too?

Numbers Not to Use For a Combination Lock

Many lock combinations (those which can be adjusted) are set to the user's birthday, Social Security number, phone number, or some other obvious set of digits. And crooks know that. In "casing" a potential burglary site, sophisticated thieves gather all the obvious numbers, and usually open the safe quite easily.

Recommendation: Don't use a related number. Memorize the digits and don't put them in "safe" places. Experienced burglars know where to look for them.

Selecting a Watchdog

Depending on the amount of time you are willing to spend training the dog and your available space, some breeds you should consider are:

German shepherds: They are the best big watchdogs and are highly intelligent. They need a large outdoor area and lots of exercise.

Airedale terriers: Fine watchdogs, but they may become aggressive if mistreated. They are gentle with children.

Terriers in general: Best small watchdogs. They will bark at anything out of the ordinary and attack anything that upsets them, regardless of the odds.

Doberman pinschers and Russian wolfhounds: Generally, they are too aggressive for home guard duty. Tough to train, they suffer from one-owner syndrome. (They usually obey only one family member and ignore or even menace the others.)

Pointers, setters, spaniels: Obedient but too passive for watchdogs.

Dachshunds: Aggressive and loud, they're surprisingly effective.

Choosing the Right Glue

With the bewildering array of glues available today, it's often difficult to know which kinds to use. Guidelines:

China, plastic, glass, ceramic, toys, costume jewelry: A cyanoacrylate adhesive. Brand names: Elmer's Wonder-Bond, Krazy Glue, Perma Bond.

Fabrics: A spray adhesive such as Scotch Spra-Ment. Or a rubber cement such as Best Test.

Leather: Contact cement.

Metal: An epoxy. Note: It comes in two tubes, the contents of which must be kneaded together.

Paper: Rubber cement.

Plexiglas: Ethylene chloride solvent. Brand name: Weld-On 4.

Common Plumbing Problems and Solutions

Hot-water problems:

Too long a wait. The tap may be too far away from the water heater. Cures: Either let the water run until hot, or have a small plug-in water heater installed near the tap.

Shortage. The water heater may be too small for your family's needs. The thermostat may be set too low, or it may not be operating.

Rusty. Could be caused by corrosion to the tank. More likely: Silt or mud has accumulated in the tank bottom. Clue: Tank rumbles. Cure: Turn off the heater, drain and refill.

Toilet problems:

It doesn't flush completely. The flush ball in the tank isn't being lifted high enough. Cure: Adjust the lift mechanism so it pulls the ball higher.

Tank won't refill. The flush ball isn't fitting correctly into the outlet. Cure: Adjust the rod guide.

Condensation on the tank. Insulate the tank's interior with a liner. Bonus: This reduces the amount of flush water needed.

Water "runs" after toilet refills. Cures: Align the flush ball with the outlet, and lower the float level setting. Also: Check the outlet for leaks.

When the Home Freezer Stops Running

Check first for a defective wire or dead electrical outlet. If that's not the problem, call for repairs. If the freezer can be fixed in less than a day, the food inside is probably safe.

Should the freezer be out for more than a day: Take space in a local locker plant where frozen foods are stored (if neighbors can't help out). Or put dry ice in the broken freezer, and keep the freezer door shut. Fifty pounds of dry ice will preserve frozen foods for several days. Place the dry ice on the top shelf of an upright freezer. In a chest freezer, lay a protective layer of heavy cardboard over the frozen food. Then put the dry ice on the cardboard. Caution: Wear gloves when handling dry ice. Keep room well ventilated.

Once the freezer is fixed, examine its contents. Food can be safely refrozen if it is not completely thawed and if it still has ice crystals. Most foods will have a bad odor if spoilage has begun. When in doubt, throw it out.

Humidifier Health Hazard

Humidifiers may make you think you're healthier, but research shows no real benefits. Patients with obstructive lung diseases often feel worse under humid conditions. Caution: Organisms growing on humidifiers can produce allergic symptoms (shortness of breath, cough, fever, malaise). Preventive steps: (1) Central units: Remove the scale that forms, as often as once a week. (2) Consoles: Wash with detergent weekly. (3) Cool-mist vaporizers: Empty and wash every day. (Note: Steam vaporizers don't pose health problems, but they can be a burn hazard.)

Having a Garage Sale

Be the first to open for business. If competing sales open at 8:00 a.m., begin at 7:00. Sixty percent of the customers arrive before 10 a.m. By noon, it's 70% to 90%.

Suggestions:

Price-label all merchandise. Uncertainty about prices stifles impulse buying.

Display goods in plenty of open boxes and on long tables. (Improvise with long boards mounted on boxes.) Avoid high stacks. They make browsing difficult and look disorganized.

Anything that's good sells better if it has been cleaned. Wash all china and crystal. Display them on a white tablecloth. Polish old furniture. This attention shows you value the items.

Play any radio or television that works well.

Have on hand:

Thirty-five dollars in nickels, dimes, and quarters to make change.

A tape measure.

Wrapping material to make it convenient for customers to carry off their purchases.

Source: *The Great Garage Sales Success Book* by Ryan Petty, Provision House, Austin, TX.

Storage Space You Didn't Know You Had

Behind the drywall and panelling in your home lie countless spaces between the two-by-four studs to which the finished walls are attached. Some of these cavities are stuffed with wires and pipes. But others are empty and ripe for exploitation.

Examples: Cavities can be used for open shelves in children's bedrooms; useful cubby holes in kitchen; a second medicine cabinet in bathroom.

How to take advantage of this space: Diagram the empty between-stud spaces in all your rooms.(Or get a carpenter to do it.) Use this diagram as the need for extra space arises.

Note: Only useful for inner walls. Outer walls, of course, need that space to hold the insulation.

Better Gardening

• Cut mowing time. A 36-inch mower does the job in half the time it takes an 18-inch one.

• Fertilizer from your fireplace: Wood ashes make an excellent soil conditioner and natural fertilizer for delphiniums, lilacs, peonies, and roses.

• A hemlock hedge is unrivaled as a natural, graceful means of protecting your privacy. Advantages: The hedge is disease free, requires no fertilizer, and holds up well through snow, extreme temperatures, or drought. To start a hedge: Plant four year-old seedlings about two feet apart. Once the desired height and fullness are reached, cut back annually on the year's growth. Best: A hedge about six feet high.

• Miniature roses flourish indoors and bloom every six to eight weeks throughout fall and winter. Potted rosebushes grow to 12 inches high with one-inch blossoms. They need at least four hours of sunlight a day or 12 hours of fluorescent light. Bushes should be moved outside and planted (in their pots) for at least two months every spring, summer, or early fall.

• Repotting a houseplant. Moisten the soil well. Wait an hour. Then up-end the pot and rap it on something hard. The dirt ball should drop out, intact. Before transplanting it in a bigger pot, cover the drainage hole with plastic mosquito netting. Reason: It stops soil runoff, but doesn't take up space as pebbles do.

• Geraniums in winter. Keep the pot on a sunny windowsill and the flowers will continue blooming throughout the winter. Southern exposure is best, with at least three hours of direct sun daily. Care: Between waterings, the soil should be permitted to dry out. The plant should also be misted every few days. A standard houseplant fertilizer should be added to the soil about once a month. To encourage growth, snip straggly stems and blossoms that fade. For consistent foliage, rotate the pot.

• Free citrus plants. Press plump, moist seeds from any citrus fruit into a rich potting mixture, and place on a windowsill which is warm and gets bright light. Keep soil damp. After two months: Transplant seedlings. Lift gently with two spoons. Place each in a two-inch pot in fast-draining soil mix. When the root ball fills the pot, transfer to a four-inch pot. Move again when necessary to successively larger pots. Keep mature plants in indirect light. Feed annually with a half-strength fertilizer. Citrus plants grown inside have glossy dark leaves, but no flowers or fruit.

• Basic birdfeeding rules: (1) Feed birds in the fall only if you intend to continue during the winter. Reason: If they depend on a known supply of food, they won't gather their own. (2) When on winter vacation, leave an adequate supply or use regulated feeder device. (3) To prevent cats, squirrels, and other animal from endangering the birds, place the feeder at least 5 feet above the ground and 15 feet from trees.

• To kill weeds and grass growing in driveway and sidewalk cracks: Pour household bleach in the cracks. The vegetation dies and is easily pulled out. The bleach keeps it from growing back. Also effective: Saturated salt, or rock salt dissolved in water.

Gardening Catalogs

Free:

Bountiful Ridge Nurseries, 102 Nursery Lane, Princess Anne, MD 21853. Ask for the Herbst Seedsman catalog.

Breck's 6523 N. Galena Rd., Peoria, IL 61614. Containing color photos of tulips and bulbs, shipped directly from Holland.

Brittingham Plant Farms, Salisbury, MD 21801. Berry plants and a planting guide.

Burgess, Box 3000, Galesburg, NI 49053. Complete outdoor gardening catalog.

Burpee's Seed, 4721 Burpee Building, Warminister, PA 18974. Over 1,8000 varieties of vegetables, flowers, fruits, shrubs, and trees.

Conner Co., 105 N. Second St., August, AR 72006. Strawberry plants.

Dean Foster, Hartford, MI 49057. 220 varieties of strawberries, blueberries, and grapes.

Earl May Seed & Nursery Co., Shenandoah, IA 51603. Ornamental plants, vegetable seeds.

George W. Park Seed Co., 372 Cokesbury Rd., Greenwood, SC 29647. Flowers and vegetables.

Harris Seeds, 51 Moretib Farms, Rochester, NY 14624. Seeds of all kinds.

Jackson & Perkins Co., 1 Rose Lane, Medford, OR 97501. One of the very best gardening catalogs.

J.W. Jung Seed, Randolph, WI 53956. Some 1,200 varieties of flowers, vegetables, fruits.

Kelly Bros., 802 Maple St. Dansville, NY 14437. Trees, plants, fruits, etc.

Mellinger's 2310 West South Range Rd., North Lima, OH 44452. Seeds, plants, other garden items.

Musser Forets, Indiana, PA 15701. Evergreen, hardwood seedlings, etc., all geared for the home gardener and field planting.

Olds Seed Co., Box 7790, Madison, WI 53707. Flowers and vegetable seeds.

Putney Nursery, Putney, VT 05346. Ferns, herbs, perennials, orchids, etc.

Spring Hill Nurseries, Tipp City, OH 45366. Perennials, including a indoor-plant section.

Stark Bros., Louisiana, MO 63353. Vegetable seeds, dwarf and full-sized trees.

Stokes Seeds, 1171 Stokes Building, Buffalo, NY 14240. Ninety-five varieties of tomatoes.

Thompson & Morgan, Box 100, Farmingdale, NJ 07727. Some 4,000 varieties of garden seeds.

W.J. Unwin Ltd., Farmingdale, NJ 07727. Some 1,000 varieties of flower, vegetable, and plant seeds.

Others:

Gilbert H. Wild & Son, 181 Joplin St. Sarcoxie MO 64862. Peonies, irises, day lilies.

Lilypons Water Gardens, 102 Hougar Rd., Lilypons, MD 21717. Lotus plants, water lilies, water gardens, etc.

Naturalists, Box 425, Yorktown Heights, NY 10598. Herbs plus medicinal plants.

Rex Bulb Farms, Port Townsend, WA 93868. Hundreds of lilies.

Van Ness Water Gardens, 2560 N. Euclid, Upland, CA 91786. Water liles and other aquatics.

Wayside Gardens, 90 Garden Lane Hodges, SC 29695. Trees, shrubs, roses, etc.

White Flower Farms, Litchfield, CT 06759. One of the most versatile and beautiful catalogs.

Hints for the Home Handyperson

• If the nails split the wood, dull the points. Put the nail head against a hard metal surface and tap the point once lightly with a hammer. If blunting doesn't work: Drill a small pilot hole first, slightly smaller than the diameter of the nail.

• Aluminum nails are better than the conventional galvanized steel kind when building a home or an additional room. These nails cost more, but they prevent red rust streak on wood siding and put off the need for repainting.

• Loose screws. To tighten them, place a small piece of nylon fishing line in the screw or bolt hole. Insert the screw or bolt all the way. Result: The resilient nylon locks the screw firmly in place.

• Refrigerator maintenance: Vacuum the accumulated dust and dirt from cooling coils and the compressor motor. Lubricate the compressor according to the manufacturer's manual. Check for loose mounting hardware under the compressor. Also look for damaged electrical contacts. Replace any worn rubber door seals. Be sure the refrigerator is level. Important: Leave enough space behind the refrigerator for ventilation of cooling coils (and easier cleaning).

• Air conditioner maintenance for window units: Replace the air filter. Vacuum the evaporator and condenser coils. Lubricate the fan motor with a few drops of SAE nondetergent motor oil. Note: When reinstalling a unit removed during the winter, set it so that it tips slightly to the outside. This makes the water drain toward the condenser coil.

• When replacing fuses, use the S-types rather than Edison-based fuses, to reduce the danger of overloading the wiring. Reason: With S-types, it's harder to put in a size that's too large, which creates a fire hazard.

• Painted-over wallpaper requires extra effort to remove. What to do: Rough up the paper's surface with coarse-grained sandpaper (the grade sold for electric floor sanders). Score the entire wall. Then use the liquid remover or steam. As the remover penetrates, scrape off the painted paper with a wide-blade putty knife or special scraper.

• For overhead sanding on ceiling or upper walls, fashion a longhandled sander from a floor-wax applicator. Steps: Unscrew the wing nuts that attach the applicator pad to the handle. Wrap a sheet of sandpaper around the pad. The sandpaper is held in place when the wing nuts are screwed back into place.

• Cleaning windows. Buy a commercial glass cleaner to get the spray bottle, but after you have used the liquid up mix the cleaning compound yourself. It costs only a fraction as much. Formula: 3½ quarts of water, a pint of rubbing alcohol, and ½ cup of sudsy ammonia. Many people add a few ounces of vinegar, but tests show that doesn't really help.

• Scatter kitty litter or coarse sand on icy walkways. Why: Salt and de-icing chemicals harm grass and plants. Litter granules and sand improve the condition of the soil by providing aeration as well as better drainage.

• Service your snow thrower. Reread your owner's manual. Be sure that all moving parts turn freely. Lubricate the areas of friction. Remove the spark plug to check for carbon deposits on the gap. Replace an old or worn plug. Now, start the engine for a trial run. Before the snow falls: Mark hidden obstacles along the pathways with sticks topped by flags. This enables you to avoid them when they are buried under the snow.

• Roach remedy: Old-fashioned boric acid (available in powder form at local drugstores). Sprinkle the boric acid around the perimeter of the infested room and on sink counters. It will take seven to ten days to work.

• Eliminate mice in the country home: Before leaving for the season, spread ordinary cloves around kitchen pipes, doors, and windowsills, or use mothballs. Reason: Mice don't like strong smells so they'll avoid the area (and you won't have the problem of emptying traps or fearing poison around the house.)

• The north side of a roof often outlasts the south side many years. Reason: The north side is less exposed to the sun's harmful rays. Bot-

tom line: Reroof only the side that needs it. (Note: The same advice works for repainting.)

• TV interference is often caused by an electrical transmission from a household appliance. Recommended: (1) Plug the TV into a TV-interference suppressor, which is available at most TV and radio shops. (2) Install new grounding conductors from a washer and dryer to a cold-water pipe or other grounding electrode. (3) Tighten the connections at the rear of the TV. (4) Replace antenna wire.

Source: *Electrical Construction and Mainteance.*

• Washer and dryer maintenance: Tighten loose hardware and belts. Repair tub leaks with silicone sealant or epoxy. Replace frayed belts and leaking pump or tub seals. Lubricate pulleys, drive shafts, and other moving parts by following the manufacturer's instructions. Prime cause of machine breakdowns: Worn control switches.

• Beat the cost of buying commercial household cleaning products at the supermarket by making them safely at home. Common ingredients include baking soda, vinegar, salt, and many others. Write for *Recipes for Home Care Products,* 83 P&AS Building, Clemson University, Clemson SC 29631.

• Bird droppings mar the beauty of decorative redwood or cedar fences. To prevent the birds from perching: Attach three small screw eyes every few feet along the top of the fence. Run lengths of lightweight plastic fishline through each eye. Result: Three strands of line running along the top of the fence. Point: Since birds can't grab the thin plastic fishline with their talons, they won't land on the fence. Bonus: From a distance, you won't even be able to notice the fishline.

• Longer-lasting job. Paint adheres better to siding that has been washed. Wet the siding, using a long-handled brush dipped into a bucket of trisodium phosphate. Rinse with water. Dry with a squeegee.

Source: *The Family Handyman.*

• Refrigerator odors. How to remove a persistent smell: Take everything out. Sponge the entire inside with a solution of one-quarter cup of salt in a pint of water. Then sponge again with a 5% ammonia solution (one part ammonia to 20 parts water). Leave an open box of baking soda in the refrigerator for a few days. Then replace with a new box, if necessary. (This works for freezers, too.)

• Moving large appliances across the floor. Squirt liquid dishwashing detergent around the feet of the appliance. With this lubricant, the appliance will glide smoothly across the floor when you push it. Bonus: The liquid can be mopped up easily.

• Furniture care. To cover superficial scratches in dark wood, apply iodine two or three times. After it dries, polish with a hard paste wax. To remove white rings on tables, use a mix of fine ashes and olive oil. Put the mix on the ring, then rub until the white disappears.

Source: *House & Garden.*

II

Shopping for Your Money's Worth

Commonsense Shopping

Avoid unnecessary and random buying by preparing a shopping list first.

Try to buy from one of the many discount or factory-outlet store selling quality merchandise.

Look into joining a consumer-buying cooperative for basic foodstuffs if one is being organized in your neighborhood. Rule: Make sure you like the people you'll be dealing with and that you, or some member of your family, really can put in the time required (a co-op usually requires its members to put in a few hours of service a month to help run it).

What Supermarkets Don't Tell You

Supermarkets usually place the most expensive items at eye level, where they are more likely to be selected on impulse. Recom-

mended: Look at the entire group of products before deciding on a purchase, unless you have a preference for a specific brand.

Generic items can offer real savings, but quality varies widely. Best bets: Products such as household bleach, which, by law, must contain specific ingredients common to all brands. Trap: House brands and national brands may actually be cheaper, when on sale, than generic brands. Point: Comparison shop.

The Art of Bargaining

Getting a better price can be rewarding economically and psychologically. How to do it successfully:

Be discreet. A shopkeeper won't reduce a price if he's worried that the special value will be made public.

Confine most bargaining to the privately owned shops. However, don't write off supermarkets and department stores. Occasionally,

299

managers of these stores will bargain, especially on slightly damaged merchandise or goods that are older and hard to dispose of.

Make it clear to the shopkeeper that you are a serious shopper who intends to spend money. Select several definite articles and several tentative purchases. Ask the shopkeeper for the total cost before writing the bill. As he completes his tally, begin some tongue-clucking and head-shaking. Then, softly ask the merchant if that price is the best he can do.

If he says it is, bargain by offering to pay in cash. This method usually works only if the purchase price exceeds $100.

If the shopkeeper still refuses to bargain, leave everything on the counter and begin to walk out, slowly; this ploy may prompt him to reconsider. However, less hard-core bargainers may wish to buy a few of the items anyway and leave the bargaining at that.

Source: *A Shopping Guide to the Lower East Side,* by Ellen Telzer and Sharon Greene, 2 Grace Court, Brooklyn, NY 11201.

ized purchasing. Imagine that you will have to explain to the person why you chose a particular gift, and, inevitably, you will tailor the present to fit the person. For instance: Here's a scarf to match your eyes; no one looks better in this shade of blue. Or: You're the most organized person I know; that's why I picked this executive datebook. If the explanation you speak into your internal ear sounds flattering, write it on the gift card. Bonus: Your friend gets a gift plus the feeling of being noticed and appreciated.

Shop off the beaten path. You will find more inspiration and less commonplace items if you check out the local antique stores, old book and print dealers, museum gift shops, crafts fairs, and yard sales. Train yourself not just to react to something you like but to match interesting objects with a friend's tastes and needs.

Source: Letty Cottin Pogrebin, *Ms* magazine editor and author, *Growing Up Free: Raising Your Child in the 80s,* McGraw-Hill, Inc., New York.

Stalking the Perfect Gift

What's the most wonderful present you received last year? Or how about the five best gifts you've received over your entire lifetime?

If both questions draw a blank, you are not alone. Few of us remember past gifts because we haven't often received material things with meaning beyond the event that inspired them. We know we got something from so-and-so for a birthday, anniversary, or holiday. But all those baubles and bottles of Scotch are quickly forgotten because they rarely connect with an inner self.

Think of all the dollars you have spent on family, friends, and business associates whether lovingly, impulsively, or dutifully and consider how little the money bought in terms of emotional impact, enhanced intimacy, or personalized pleasure. Resolve to do gift-giving differently by following six principles:

Use this foolproof technique for personal-

When the Seller Wants Cash Instead of a Check

A request for payment in cash should put you on the alert. People requesting cash may be doing so:

1. To cheat the IRS.

2. To steal from their partners or employers.

3. To avoid complying with insurance, worker compensation, or other statutes.

Two reasons paying cash may mean trouble:

1. When your contact is stealing from his partner or employer, you may be held liable for the money and be a party to the crime.

2. If a large sum is involved and the IRS finds out, you may be called in for a full IRS audit.

To protect yourself: Request a receipt. If refused, have a third party witness the transaction. Then, have the witness sign a letter detailing the transaction and certifying he was a witness to it. Have the letter notarized. This will serve in the absence of a receipt.

If you are unable to have a witness, write a letter to the party who performed the work, detailing what was done and what was paid. Keep a copy of this letter. This is the weakest form of protection.

Best means of protection: Make sure that before making a large cash payment you go to a bank and make a corresponding withdrawal.
Source: Dan Brecher, Esq., 230 Park Ave., New York 10017.

Precautions for Mail-Order Shoppers

(1) Allow at least three to four weeks for delivery. (2) If item is a gift, be specific in instructions for gift card. Include the recipient's name and address as well as your own. (3) Carefully read descriptions of products in catalogs, and note size, weight, contents, etc. (Pictures can be very misleading.) (4) Keep shipping label as proof of purchase in case of dissatisfaction. (5) Inspect items as soon as they arrive to see if everything is enclosed and undamaged. Note: If complaints to the company about quality of goods, misrepresentation of the product, etc., go unanswered, write the Postal Inspection Service, 475 L'Enfant Plaza West, sw, Washington, DC 20260. To investigate fraud: Write the Bureau of Consumer Protection, Federal Trade Commission, Pennsylvania Ave. & 6th St., NW, Washington, DC 20580.

Before Signing a Credit Contract

Provision for liens against personal property: This gives the lender the right to take possession of almost anything you own to satisfy a delinquent loan.

Confession of judgment: By signing, you waive all rights to defend yourself.

Wage assignment: It gives the lender the right to attach your paycheck.

Attorneys' fees: You agree to pay any of the lender's legal fees.

Acceleration payments: If a payment is missed, the loan falls due.

Quirk in Law on Repossession

Having a law-enforcement official around when pressing a claim is not necessary, and it can be a very bad idea when a seller is trying to take possession of an item that was used as collateral for a past-due debt.

The Uniform Commercial Code stipulates that the *creditor* can take possession of the item. It says nothing about the use of a law enforcer.

In fact, one state court recently decided that a repossession was illegal, specifically because a police officer was along. The ruling: The officer's presence implied state action and was unfairly oppressive.
Walker v. Walthall, 588 P.2d 863.

Catch-22 for Consumers

New big-ticket appliance doesn't work, and no one will be home to wait for the serviceman. Nor (in most states) is the retailer obligated to take it back (because the manufacturer must be given a chance to make repairs). What to do: At time of sale, get seller to accept a carefully worded statement, written on the receipt, that if for any reason the buyer is not satisfied, the appliance may be returned or exchanged. Further, this will be done at seller's (or buyer's) expense, within a certain number of days and/or on a weekend (or whatever time is convenient for the buyer). The statement becomes part of a binding contract.
Source: Dan Brecher, Esq., 230 Park Ave., New York 10017.

301

Consumer Rights in a Billing Dispute

Customer does not have to pay the disputed amount.

It's not necessary to pay finance charges or interest on the amount involved, while it is in dispute. (However, the creditor can use the disputed amount in deciding whether the customer reaches a credit limit.)

A creditor may not close the account because of the customer's refusal to pay the disputed amounts.

Creditor may not threaten to jeopardize the customer's credit rating because of failure to pay.

If the creditor does not agree with the consumer complaint and states the reasons for believing there has been no billing error, the consumer has at least 10 days to pay the contested amount before the company can report the account as delinquent to credit bureaus or anyone else. Note: If the normal duration for payment of undisputed charges is longer (if, for example, the retailer allows 30 days to pay a charge), then the customer must be given at least that much time to pay the contested amount.

Customer can delay action further by writing a second letter in reply to the company's explanation.

The creditor company forfeits the amount in dispute, plus any finance charges computed on that amount up to a maximum of $50, whether or not there has been an error, under these circumstances:

It fails to answer a complaint letter within a 30-day period.

It does not notify the customer of its decision within two normal billing periods (90-day maximum).

It violates any other consumer rights.

If the customer is wrong: Entire amount owed must be paid, plus finance charges accrued while the amount was in dispute.

Source: *Give Yourself Credit (Guide to Consumer Credit Laws)*, Superintendent of Documents, U.S. Government Printing Office, Washington, DC.

Getting Satisfaction if Merchandise Is Defective

Dealing with defective merchandise is greatly simplified by adequate preparation. Basic rule: Save receipts, warranties and all other papers. After analyzing the defect and deciding on what kind of compensation you want, it's time to act.

First step:
Meet with the salesperson or store manager. Describe the problem. Give him copies of the paper work. Then ask for a replacement or other compensation.

Be polite but firm. In response to whatever excuse the merchant may offer for a defective product, repeat your demand like a broken record.

Further recourse:
Write to the manager, going over the points made in the conversation.

Include in the letter copies of the sales slips as well as a statement of your intention to refer the matter to the Better Business Bureau, a consumer agency, or the manager's office superior.

If that fails:
Write directly to the president of the company, not the customer relations department. For information: Manufacturers of products are listed in the *Thomas Registry*. Names of executives and addresses of companies are in *Standard & Poor's Register of Corporations*.

Recount the facts and demand for compensation. Once again, include copies of all the paper work.

Last resort: Call a consumer agency. They are usually listed under municipal agencies in the telephone book. State consumer appeal offices are generally in the attorney-general's office.

There are 140 Better Business Bureaus in the country and more than 100 consumer hot lines. Complete listings of hot lines are available from Call for Action, Inc., 575 Lexington Ave., New York 10022. Phone: (212) 355-5965.

Traps in Appliance Service Contracts

Don't assume that all appliance service contracts are worthwhile. A study shows that the average yearly repair bill on washing-machine models ranging from one to ten years old came to only $49. That is $6 under the cost of a typical repair contract.

The study finds that the chance of needing a repair on an appliance in any given year is only one in five. Over the life of the machine, a service-contract holder will in all probability be paying out much more in insurance than the person is ever likely to collect in actual repair services.

Understanding Product Warranties

Before buying an appliance or other mechanical product, check the fine print if necessary to determine who is actually warranting what. In most cases, the merchant you are dealing with is not even required to be a helpful middleman. Customers usually must assume the burden of returning a defective product, at their own expense, to some distant factory for service.

Source: *The Better Business Bureau Guide to Wise Buying.* The Benjamin Co., Inc., New York.

Appliances: Repair or Replace?

Appliance repair people are becoming scarcer by the year, and the cost of service calls has gone through the roof. Consumers face a difficult decision over whether to repair appliances or opt for new ones. A survey of appliance marketers and repair people disclosed what life expectancy appliances have and how to determine whether they are worth fixing.

Televisions. The big, old American sets (like Zenith and RCA) frequently lasted ten years. Today, most sets last from five to eight years. After that, the set will start needing a new high-voltage transformer, a new picture tube, and a new tuner. It's best to replace the television at that point.

Television repair. It costs from $250 to $300 to repair or replace the picture tube of a color television (including parts and labor). It costs more to replace the tube of a 13-inch or 19-inch color television than of a 23-inch set. Reason: Most color replacement tubes are rebuilt from old tubes. And there are more 23-inch tubes around to salvage because that size used to be more popular.

The most expensive television set to repair is the Sony. Repair people find it the most difficult to work on, and its parts are hard to get. Picture tube replacement can cost $400.

Air conditioners. They should have a life expectancy of ten to twelve years. Two problems may arise at that time: The compressor fails or the Freon leaks. If Freon leaks, don't expect a repair person to fix it permanently.

Refrigerators. They have the same time span and problems as air conditioners.

Dishwashers and washing machines. They last ten to twelve years.

Longest-lasting. items: Stoves, vacuum cleaners.

Rule of thumb: When repairs cost 50% of the price of a replacement, it's time to get rid of the appliance.

If you are going to repair: Try to deal with authorized service centers. They have a better knowledge of individual brands. Furthermore, you can be sure with an authorized service center that you are getting the right parts.

When buying a new unit: The best buys on appliances can usually be had at discount appliance stores or through buying co-ops. The discount stores advertise loss leaders to get you into the store. Go with the advertised special.

Alternative: Rebuilt appliances. They come with complete warranties and are generally below the discount house's prices.

303

Big Screen TV

Before buying a video-projection system (four- to seven-foot diagonal picture), be aware that plenty of space is required. The projector type also has complex wiring that must be hidden. The dim lighting required for a sharp image may inconvenience nonviewers. Note: The screen should be washable in order to avoid fingerprint damage.

Choosing an Air Conditioner

When buying an air conditioner, ask:
How many days a year am I going to use it?
How expensive are my electric-utility rates?
Point: In the Northeast, people use air conditioning only about 90 to 120 days per year. However, electric costs there are the highest in the country. Result: The extra cost for an energy-efficient air conditioner is worth it. However, in the Midwest, where usage is similar, utility bills frequently run less. Therefore, it may be much less cost-effective to buy a very efficient air conditioner. And as for the South, where electric rates are low but the days of use are high, the energy-efficient air conditioner may be a sensible buy.

Consumer preference: In the East, where costs are high, central air conditioning for the home is dwindling. Key: There is no need to cool your whole house when you are only in one room at a time. Result: Room air conditioners are coming back.

Efficient air conditioners: All models are given an Electrical Energy Rating (EER). The range of EERs is 5.5 to 10.5. The higher the number, the more efficient the unit. In some states, such as New York, the lowest legal efficiency is 7.5. You pay extra for models in the 7.5 to 10.5 range.

Another advantage: Efficient units can build up your cooling much faster. Example: A 10 × 10 room can be cooled in 20 minutes with an inefficient air conditioner. With a 7.5 or higher rating, the room can be cooled in 10 minutes.

How large a unit you need depends on the size of the room or rooms you want to cool. To do an area of 1,200 square feet, you need 24,000 BTUs. You may also need a more powerful air conditioner if your windows face south or west.

Installation: Have a professional do it. Many air conditioners are advertised as quick mount (easily installed by the consumer). Problem: The air conditioner will work, but it's not airtight, and therefore won't give you the most efficient air conditioning.

Heat pumps: They bring the heat generated by air conditioners into the house for use in cold weather. Where they are useful: In states such as Florida, lower Texas and California, where it doesn't get too cold. Extra cost: $100. In areas where it freezes regularly, they are useless.

Source: Victor Vergil, president, Wholesale Appliances, 33 Taylor Reed Pl., Glenbrook, CT 06906.

Cooling Your House Without an Air Conditioner

Install an attic propeller fan. It should be 26 to 36 inches in diameter and thermostat-controlled. How it works: Hot air rises to the attic. When the temperature in the attic exceeds the thermostat setting, the fan automatically turns on and pushes the air out of the attic.

Best fan usage: When the temperature is lower at night and in the early morning, shut off the fan, close the windows, and draw the blinds. Retain the evening's coolness. Result: A precooled home for the next day. If the home is reasonably well constructed, it should stay cool for most of the day. Help: Keep the shades or blinds and curtains closed to prevent the sun from shining directly into the house.

Oscillating fans: These are those standalone fans, which people have forgotten how to use properly. Best: When the outside temperature is lower than the inside temperature, open the windows and let the fans move the air in. When the air inside is cooler, keep the windows closed and the fans turned off.

Landscaping: Use it partly to shield a house from the sun's heat. Example: Deciduous trees on the south side of a house are a benefit in summer.

Tinted glass: Reflects sunlight. There are also drapes that reflect the sun's rays. Alternative: Mylar, which adheres to the glass. These are relatively expensive, but may prove cost-efficient on the south side of your house.

Source: Peter Flack, president, Flack & Kurtz Consulting Engineers, 475 Fifth Ave., New York 10017.

Buying a Microwave Oven

Microwaves are not good for all foods. They cannot replace conventional ranges. Special features are not really necessary. Most top-of-the-line microwave-oven owners do not use the temperature probes, humidity-control programs, or other options. Best buy: A basic model, with only four or five power settings.

Buying a Garbage Disposal

Opt for a more expensive, one-half horse-power model. Lower-powered disposals can't shred bones, corncobs, fruit skins, and other tough materials.

Spend extra for batchfeed units. They operate only when the cover is securely locked into place. This added safety feature is especially good for families with young children. More costly, but highly recommended, are garbage-disposal models with noise-reducing insulation and automatic unjamming mechanisms.

Buying a Refrigerator

Best: Models with freezers on top. Side-by-side models are expensive and their shelves are too narrow. Those with freezers on the bottom often are less efficient. Common error: Buying a refrigerator that's too large for the family. Three people can make do with a nine-cubic-foot refrigerator and three-cubic-foot freezer.

Using Your Freezer Efficiently

Just over three-quarters full is the optimum load for freezer operating efficiency. Jam-packing the freezer retards the flow of air needed for cooling. Corollary: Understocking the freezer is just as bad; it merely wastes energy.

Phones: Buying vs. Renting

Now that it is legal, consumers should buy their phone instruments, rather than renting them from the phone company. The cost of purchasing a phone equals approximately eight months of the phone company's rental fees. The normal service life of a phone is 30 to 40 years.

Trap: It is sometimes hard to get repairs made on owned phones. Reason: It's hard to determine whether a phone is not working because of a fault in it or in the company lines. As a result, no one does repairs.

Solution: Rent at least one phone. If a private extension goes dead, disconnect it, and see if the rented unit works in that connection. If it does, you know the fault is with your private phone. If the rented extension does not work, you can be almost certain the fault is with the system and can report the problem to the phone company, requesting immediate repairs.

Source: Robert DeRosa, president, Bridging the Gap Through Communications, telecommunications consultants, 38 Yale Terrace, Blauvelt, NY 10913.

Cordless Telephones

As the popularity of cordless telephones grows, prices are dropping and user sophistication is increasing.

Basic attraction: Cordless phones eliminate the need for extensions. How: They can be carried around anywhere in the house and even outdoors. And, while they initially cost much more, there are no monthly charges, as for extensions.

How they work: A base station, about the size of a standard telephone, plugs into any phone outlet. The base relays calls the user makes from a smaller, portable handset.

Disadvantages: Except for more expensive models, the handset isn't effective farther than 440 feet from the base. Cheaper models allow users only to answer calls, not initiate them. Also: Household wiring may interfere with reception.

Buying a Telephone Answering Machine

Telephone answering machines range in price from $70 to $700. Avoid the cheap models. If they last a year, you're lucky.

Better: Pay $400 to $500 for a machine that you can expect to last 10 years with minimal maintenance.

Make sure the machine:

Uses a cassette recorder. Many users find that reel-to-reel recorders are inconvenient and temperamental.

Is voice actuated, so the answering machine

starts and stops at the beginning and end of each message.

Has an amplifier. Then it can pick up quiet messages.

Remote pickup: For persons who get a lot of messages, it may make sense to pay a few hundred dollars more to get a machine that allows for remote retrieval of messages. (You call your number and use an electronic sound-emitting device to activate a replay of the messages over the phone.)

Source: Robert DeRosa, president, Bridging the Gap Through Communications, 38 Yale Terrace, Blauvelt, NY 10913.

How to Check Phone Bills

Local service: Periodically, ask the phone company for an equipment inventory form—which provides a complete listing of every item included in the local service portion of the bill. If any part of it is not clear or if any code or abbreviation isn't understandable, check with the phone company's business office. If it can't supply you with what you need, ask the phone company's marketing department for it.

If there are any problems in getting the inventory, tell the credit manager that no further bills will be paid until they furnish the itemization. If an error is found, claim a retroactive refund. It is up to the phone company to prove the claim incorrect.

Keep careful records of the service changes that have been ordered. Also, issue written orders to the phone company for moves, changes, installations, and disconnects. You are entitled to credits for any disconnected equipment. Telephone equipment is billed in advance. Refunds should be made for unused service within the month when the disconnect is made.

The phone company's meters aren't infallible. If you pay only a single message unit charge for a call of any length to any point in the metropolitan area, it may be practical to tally every local call dialed. If that total count is different from the phone company's count, request a credit.

Long-distance toll charges and telegrams. If you find an unverified telegram on the phone bill, call the business office for a copy of the message to substantiate the bill.

On long-distance calls, look for distant numbers which aren't familiar. Keep a log of the calls dialed. If a number is not familiar, call the phone company's business office. If you are sure the call isn't from you, it will be instantly removed from the bill. The telephone company will then call that number and try to find out who made the call. If you're not sure about it, the phone company will take the number and call back in a few days, giving the name of the called organization or residence. If you're still not convinced, have them remove the charge from your bill. They will promptly bill it back if they find it was made on your line.

Source: Frank K. Griesinger, president, Frank K. Griesinger & Associates, Inc., 1412 Superior Bldg., Cleveland, OH 44114, and author, *How to Cut Costs and Improve Service on Your Telephone, Telex, TWX and Other Telecommunications,* McGraw-Hill, New York.

When Not to Buy High-Priced Batteries

Expensive alkaline batteries are usually not worth the extra cost when used in calculators, flashlights, etc. Low-cost carbon-zinc batteries bounce back well after occasional use for *brief* periods.

When the Tag Says 'Do Not Remove'

"Do not remove this tag under penalty of law." These words on tags attached to bed mattresses, pillows, cushions, upholstered furniture, etc., serve as a warning to manufacturers and dealers. As purchaser, however, you may remove tags if you wish. It is best to leave them on until you are satisfied with the purchase. Once you have removed the tags, the merchandise cannot be returned.

Before You Buy a Safe

Most home safes on the market today are designed to protect against either fire or theft, but not both. So, unless you are willing to break your bank account for a dual-purpose supersafe, the best solution is to buy one of each type. Manufacturers suggest welding the theft safe inside the fire safe, and then bolting the whole thing to a concrete wall or floor.

What to look for:

Burglar-resistant safes. You generally get what you pay for. Minimum advisable specifications: A half-inch-thick solid steel door and quarter-inch-thick solid steel walls. (Aim: To prevent a thief from peeling away the walls with a crowbar.) Also: Make sure the safe has a relocking device in addition to a good-quality lock. If the lock is tampered with, the device automatically relocks the bolts.

Fire-resistant safes. Recommended for most homes: A safe that can withstand a temperature of 1,850° F for two hours.

Prices depend on the size of the safe, the specifications of the materials, or the rating of the model. And, for burglar-resistant safes, the complexity of locks and relocking devices adds to the cost.

Money saver: A used safe. The cost is 20% to 40% lower than comparable new ones.

Safe Ratings

Underwriters' Laboratories rates safes for function. Those labeled A, B, C, and D are fire resistant. "A" offers the least protection. Burglar-resistant safes carry the designations E, F,

G, and H. The "H" gives the highest degree of protection from forcible entry, but little protection against fire.

Point: Know the difference. Safes look alike, but an experienced safecracker can spot and open a fire-resistant safe in minutes. And sheer bulk is no indication of burglar protection. Fire resistant safes are massive because of heavy insulation.

Reminder: Don't keep your valuables in a safe that is light enough to transport easily or one that has wheels. If you can move it, so can a burglar.

Source: Robert B. Murray, Murray Safe Co., writing in *Security Management*.

Twenty Top Reference Books

The most useful reference books, according to students at Columbia University's Graduate School of Journalism, are:

The Bible
Dictionary of Dates, Keller.
Dictionary of Miracles, Brewer.
Dictionary of Modern English Usage, Fowler.
Dictionary of Slang & Unconventional English, Partridge.
Familiar Quotations, Bartlett.
Handy Book of Literary Curiosities, Walsh.
Harvard Dictionary of Music, Apel & Daniel.
Home Book of Verse, Stevenson.
National Geographic Atlas of the World.
New Columbia Encyclopedia.
Popular Fallacies: A Book of Common Errors, Ackerman.
Reader's Encyclopedia, Benet.
Roget's International Thesaurus.
Webster's Biographical Dictionary.
Webster's New Collegiate Dictionary.
Webster's New Dictionary of Synonyms.
Webster's New Geographical Dictionary.
Who's Who in America.
The World Almanac.

Selecting a Portrait Artist

You can have a portrait done for as little as $250 to as much as $30,000 or more. In addition to sitting for an artist, people are commissioning paintings of their spouses, children, pets, boats, automobiles, airplane—with or without themselves.

Recommended:

Look at the work of many portrait artists.

Shop price, as well as style. There are no hard-and-fast rules concerning what an artist charges. If you like the work done by two different artists, don't be afraid to haggle. Best way: Pit one against the other.

Use an art gallery to help you find the right artist. There are galleries specializing in the work of portrait artists in the major U.S. cities. They can show you the work of many artists and put you in touch with the one you choose. (Many local galleries can be helpful, too.)

Ask the artist who he's done portraits of in the past.

Give thought to clothing and pose well beforehand. If you have a photograph of yourself that you like, show it to the artist and see if he can duplicate it in oil.

Don't be afraid to make suggestions to the artist.

The bottom line: While commissioning a portrait isn't quite the same as buying furniture or an appliance, you have to ask yourself many of the same questions about being comfortable with it. After all, it's going to be staring at you from the wall a long time.

Choosing the Right Musical Instrument

An increasing number of adults are learning to play instruments, but some run into problems because they plunge ahead too quickly. The basics:

Decide whether you want to play in a group

(string, bass, or drums require one) or on your own, and choose the instrument accordingly.

Don't choose an instrument that you'll have trouble carrying.

Select a teacher who genuinely enjoys giving lessons to an adult.

Prices: Brass instruments and woodwinds that are adequate for beginners run between $200 and $300; violins cost over $300, and most pianos over $1,000. Private lessons usually cost between $10 and $32 an hour.

Taking Care of a Piano

Get your piano tuned at least every six months, more frequently if it's new. Ideal: Cool, dry room, away from direct sunlight and not close to radiators, air conditioners, or vents. Put it at least four inches away from the wall to allow the sound to get out. Get a professional cleaning every three years. Don't do it yourself. Dangers: Mothballs or spray inside the piano.

Choosing a Christmas Tree

Scotch pine and Douglas fir are most popular because they are nicely shaped and retain their needles well. Most pines and firs have good needle retention. Spruce loses its needles quickly.

Check for freshness by bending needles. They should be springy. If they break, the tree is not fresh. Bounce the butt of the tree on the ground. If needles fall off, the tree is dry. The bottom of the tree stump should be moist and sticky. The tree should have a good green color, a nice fragrant woodsy odor, be dense, and have sufficient limb strength to support the ornaments planned for it.

Cleanliness: The tree should be free of foreign matter such as vines, moss, lichen.

Shape: The butt of the tree should be clean under the lowest group of branches and cut smoothly at the bottom. There should be a full, symmetrical shape, with branches trimmed to taper toward the top.

Until the tree is to be placed in its indoor location, keep it in water in a shady area outside. Cut two inches off the bottom to help water absorption. Indoors, place the tree in a well-secured stand with a water well. Add water each day.

How to Buy Caviar

Caviar from sturgeon is top of the line and most expensive. Three grades (beluga, osetra, sevruga) all come from the same fish. Beluga is biggest grained and most expensive; color is black or gray. Osetra grains cost somewhat less and are almost the same size, brown to golden in color. Sevruga grains are much smaller and least expensive.

The freshest, best caviar is packed with mild salt, labeled "Malossol." So is pressed caviar, which is top-grade caviar, too "ripe" to pack in whole grains. A best buy, it is very rich tasting, authentic (served widely in Russia), and, unlike whole-grain caviar, it can be stored in a freezer.

Bottom of the line: Strongly salted caviar that is sold in jars.

How to serve: Figure ¾ of an ounce per person. Serve whole-grain right out of the tin atop crushed ice, pressed caviar at room temperature. Surround both with small plates of lemon wedges, chopped onions, chopped egg whites, chopped yolks. Spoon some caviar into thin-sliced black bread, toast, or thin pancakes (blinis) and let guests add whatever they want (nothing is necessary).

Don't shun red-colored salmon caviar, which is delicious and far less expensive. Best tasting are the smaller-size grains from silver salmon rather than more common Ketovya or chum salmon caviar, which is often artificially colored.

Good Low-Priced Wines

Price isn't necessarily an indicator of quality in wine. Yes, superb wines are costly, but not all costly wines are superb.

Safest way to buy foreign wines: Rely on a good shipper. (The name appears on the neck or body label.) The shipper acts as the consumer's sampler and taster. By buying better vintages from a selection of vineyards, they maintain good consistency from year to year.

Reliable shipper names to remember when buying French wines: Louis Latour, Louis Jadot, Alexis Lichine, and Joseph Drouhin.

For French and German wines: Peter Sichel and Frank Schoonmaker.

When buying reasonably priced domestic wines, there are two price levels to choose from:

Premium California wines. Two reliable producers are Beaulieu and Robert Mondavi.

Standard price range: Charles Krug and Christian Brothers are names to remember.

How about sherry? Many people are switching to it from martinis and other hard-liquor cocktails as an aperitif. Good Spanish sherries cost very little more than California brands. Two good buys: Tio Pepe and Dry Fly.

In general, heavily advertised foreign wines and sherries are overpriced. If you like Mouton Cadet, try a red Bordeaux from one of the French shippers. Substitute a German Liebfraumilch for Blue Nun, or a California rose for the popular Lancer's.

All the brands (both foreign and domestic) listed above are available just about everywhere in the U.S. Anyone sticking to these tried and true choices is unlikely to go wrong.

General guidelines for businesspeople who want to explore wines without the penalty of serving a really bad bottle to guests:

Be wary of white wines over three years old and red wines older than five years. They may have turned the corner—become oxidized through age. This warning is particularly important for people living in parts of the country where wine isn't widely drunk. The turnover there is slower than in California and New York, and bottles stay longer on the shelves. Be careful. (Top-flight wine, how-

ever, requires considerable bottle age before it is ready to drink.)

Before buying a case (usually 10% cheaper), the invariable rule is to buy a bottle and taste it. Especially important when a local liquor dealer is offering a "special." People who don't trust their own taste shouldn't feel hesitant to ask someone who knows about wine to sample it and give an opinion. The friend or business associate who is asked will be flattered.

In the long run, the best rule is to seek a dealer who can be trusted and learn to rely on his judgment. In almost every city, there is a liquor store that is trying to build up its wine business. Give it a try. Name or describe a wine that you have enjoyed (or save the label) and ask the dealer to suggest another like it. If he knows his business, he will produce something equally good.

Final thought: Don't overlook some of the good, inexpensive jug wines produced in this country. Many guests now prefer a glass of chilled white wine as a drink before dinner. Keep a jug of Gallo Chablis Blanc or Sauvignon Blanc in the refrigerator.

Storing Leftover Wine

Storing in the refrigerator, even overnight, hurts its quality. But freezing the wine in its original bottle does not. Problem: After thawing, sediment may increase slightly. Solution: Decant the wine before serving. Never freeze a full bottle. There must be enough space for the wine to expand.

Source: *The Wine Spectator.*

Buying Champagne

More and more countries are bottling bubbly, but there is only one champagne. It is bottled and shipped from France's Champagne

310

region, about 90 miles east of Paris. Americans have a genuine taste for the real product, buying more than 8 million bottles annually. Price: $15 to $40 each.

Champagne: Mixture of white wines that acquires the characteristic bubbles when a blended wine is allowed to ferment a second time in the stoppered bottle. Both red and white grapes are traditionally used. (Blanc de blanc champagnes are made exclusively from white Chardonnay grapes.)

Vintage: Premium-priced. From a single year's harvest when the grapes are deemed exceptional.

Non-vintage: More than 85 percent of all champagnes. A combination of the current year's grape harvest and reserved wines. Each house blends the ages, tastes, and aromas to reflect its particular style.

Tete de cuvee: Superior blend of rare and costly wines in especially designed bottles. For connoisseurs who will pay about double the price of non-vintage wine from the same house.

Champagne tastes range from very dry to sweet. Details:

Brut: Very dry, ideal for general entertaining, with any course of a meal, or as an aperitif.

Extra dry: Semi-sweet. Goes well with desserts, fruits, and after meals.

Dry: Sweet, a cocktail replacement.

Serving champagne: A bottle will fill generously six glasses. Allow one glass per person for a champagne toast or as a dessert wine; one to two glasses if serving the wine as a pre-meal cocktail; and one-third to half a bottle for a champagne evening.

Cooling: Thirty minutes in an ice bucket is ideal, or keep it in the least cool section of the refrigerator for several hours.

Stemware: Long, thin-stemmed egg- or tulip-shaped glasses are ideal. Avoid the wide-mouth "champagne glass." It lets bubbles and bouquet dissipate too quickly.

Pouring: Handle the bottle gently with one hand and unwind and remove the wire muzzle with the other. Grasp the cork firmly. Tilt the bottle at a 45° angle. Twist the bottle, not the cork. You should get a soft pop. Wipe brim and bottle carefully, but don't wrap it in a towel. Rotate the bottle a quarter turn between each pour to avoid dripping.

Storing: Keep bottles on their sides in a cool, dark place. Champagnes are sold mature; storing won't improve them. Properly stored, champagnes will keep five years or more. Open bottles can be recorked with a device available at a bar supply store.

Connoisseur's Guide To Beer

Beer lacks the subtlety and distinction of wine, but it often tastes better with simple or spicy food. The three basic types:

Lager: Also called pilsner, it's America's most popular variety. Pale gold in color, light in body, it's flavored with mild to light hops and is fairly high in carbonation. Alcoholic content by volume: 3.4% to 4.2%.

Variations:

Dark lager: It's sweeter tasting. The color comes from the use of roasted barley in the brewing process. Alcoholic content: About 5%. Caution: Cheaper dark lagers are colored with caramel.

Bock: A heavy, dark lager with a slightly sweet malt flavor and a strong hop taste. It's traditionally brewed in the winter for consumption in the spring. The color comes from heated barley, although artificial coloring agents are common. Alcoholic content: 10% to 12%.

Steam: Indigenous to California. It takes its name from the steam raised in its special brewing process. The special taste is produced by barley malt, the only flavoring used (many domestic lagers are made from a malt of barley mixed with rice or corn). It has a sharp, hop-like taste and full body. Alcoholic content: Same as regular lagers, 3.4% to 4.2%.

Ale: It's more romantic and fuller bodied than lagers and has a heavier hop flavor.

Variations:

Common or stock ale: Flat tasting. Alcoholic content: 4% to 5%.

Cream ale: Slightly bitter. Light. Alcoholic content: 5% to 6%.

Strong or brown ale: Sweet tasting. Sometimes highly carbonated. Alcoholic content: Up to 10%.

Stout: Dark and bitter. Alcoholic content: 5% to 6%.

Malt liquor: By definition, any American-brewed beer with an alcoholic content over 5%. It's usually a lager-type beverage, with a slightly bitter taste.

Choosing beer:

Read all labels skeptically. Terms like ale and premium, which in the past told how a beer was brewed, have long since gone flat with advertising overkill.

Avoid beers that have been on the shelf longer than eight weeks, if you can. Point: The lower the alcoholic content (lightness), the shorter the shelf life. Ask your dealer his storage policy. Also: A beer consistently refrigerated is more likely to keep than one stored at room temperature.

Bottled beers taste better than canned beer according to everyone but can suppliers.

Beer and snacks:

Eating potato chips or other greasy snacks with beer deadens the palate. Pretzels, nuts, and other salty snacks have the same effect.

Source: *The Great American Beer Book*, by James D. Robertson, Caroline House, Ossining, NY.

Shopping for the Best Stereo Value

You can spend up to $8,000 for a stereo system. The music that it will produce will be extremely high in fidelity. However, it will not be ten times better than a system that costs one-tenth of that.

Rule of thumb: Above $1,000, the return falls off markedly. Midpriced systems ($600 to $1,000) offer the best value.

If you do want the best: Buy expensive speakers first.

Watch out for hard sales tactics. Make certain that the components you are auditioning are all played at the same sound volume. (The more loudly a component is played, the better it will sound at first.) Bring your own records to the stores.

Listen alone, without a salesperson.

You can almost always swing a better deal by purchasing the entire system at one place.

Selecting a Phono Cartridge

It's the smallest component in the system and the most important one. What it does: Clings to a groove at very high speeds, wiggling back and forth at the rate of 20,000 times per second, responding to peak amplitudes of 2/1000 of an inch (and average amplitudes of two-millionths of an inch), and to acceleration forces of 1200 to 25000 G. No astronaut has ever been put to similar stresses. Sound advice: Don't skimp on the cost, which at most is a mere fraction of a total system's value. Prices vary over a range as wide as the cartridge's performance, from under $50 up to several hundred dollars. Payoff: The better the cartridge, the better the sound, and the less the wear and tear on your records.

Your present cartridge may be obsolete, even if you regularly replace the stylus and the sound seems to be coming out right. Reason: Records have undergone major changes in the past few years. Old cartridges can no longer track them very well. Many cartridges cannot accept the new stylus shapes.

Good Second-Hand Stereo Components

Buy used high-grade equipment through the active hobbyist market. Owners of high-end equipment maintain their gear very well. And the components usually show their highest rates of failure when they are brand new.

So the purchase of good used equipment carries relatively little risk. Exceptions: Tube-type equipment, cartridges, and turntables.

If buying used, pay no more than 75% (and preferably no more than 60%) of original list price for equipment approximately one to two years old.

Used components worth looking for include: Acoustic Research, Dahlquist, Denon and Infinity, Levinson, Linn Sondeck and Threshold. Hobbyists put these systems on the market because every new advance is important to them, not because the systems are lemons.

Records to Play When Testing Speakers

- Sopranos Birgit Nilsson and Elisabeth Schwarzkopf. (German Electrola-EMI 1-C 187-00786/7 and 1-C 187-01307/8.)
- Great Conductors. (German Telefunken 6.4205 AW.)
- Flutist Ingrid Dingfelder. (Nonesuch Records H-71388.)
- Lorin Maazel conducting the Cleveland Symphony in Richard Strauss' *Ein Heldenleben*. (CBS Masterworks M-34566.)
- Herbert von Karajan conducting the Berlin Philharmonic in Puccini's *Tosca*. (Deutsche Grammophon 2707121.)

An Alternative to Separate Components

Since the late 1950s, getting a good sound system has meant shopping around for the right mix of components—speakers, tuner, amplifier, tape deck, and turntable.

Now, however, a variety of top-name stereo makers are beginning to make good-quality compact stereos, with all the components except the speakers squeezed into one box.

This is because new technology now per-

mits more powerful and better-sounding compacts. Also: The cost of separate components has risen to the point where many buyers have been priced out of the multiple-component market. That's especially so, for example, for shoppers looking for a second stereo for their country or beach houses.

Compacts sell from $100 to $800. Best bargains are in the $300 to $500 range.

The cheapest compacts have all the shortcomings of the 1950s models. Money spent on most expensive compacts could be better used for separate components.

Taking Care of Your Stereo System

Lengthen the lives of components by making sure they don't get overheated. Symptom: Equipment becomes too hot to touch comfortably. Problem: Internally generated heat. Check overdriving, inadequate ventilation, and maladjusted circuits.

Preventive maintenance. With the power off, give all stereo control knobs a full twist, and push in all buttons. This simple procedure helps to keep all contact points clean and avoids maintenance problems later.

Remove the wrapper from record albums. In time, the cellophane will shrink and cause albums to warp.

Salvaging damaged tapes: Tapes and cassettes that have outside coatings and/or backing materials that are dried out usually cannot be revived. To make the tape playable long enough to copy it: Put in an airtight container with wet blotting paper for 24 hours.

Tape Buyer Beware

- Avoid buying prerecorded tapes from record clubs. The editions that the clubs put out are inferior to the standard tapes or record

313

reproductions. You're better off making your own tape of a record if you really want it.

• Counterfeit cassettes, inferior in quality and durability, are flooding the market in many cities. To avoid them: Buy only from reputable record and tape dealers. Be skeptical of big price markdowns. Check package for spelling and graphics errors.*

High Fidelity.

Taping Old Records

When tape-recording old 78 rpm records, use specialized equipment to filter out scratches and other bothersome noises the record has picked up over the years.

Most important: A phono-cartridge stylus specially designed for the wider grooves of a 78 rpm record. SAE, Garrard, and Burwen (now part of KLH) make equipment that removes sharp ticks and pops.

Employ a dynamic noise filter to get rid of continuous surface noises.

To help approximate the nonstandard equalization of old records, use an octave-bond equalizer.

Good Pictures Without Expensive Cameras

There's a simple way to assure passable focusing without expensive, battery-draining electronics if your camera has a lens with a focal length no longer than 58 mm (35 mm or 38 mm is better).

For slides: Use Ektachrome 200 and set the lens focusing ring for 10 feet and the shutter speed for 1/250 in the sun (1/125 in shady areas outdoors, or when it is cloudy).

For prints: Use Kodacolor 400 and set the shutter speed for 1/500 in the sun, 1/250 in the shade. The method does not work as well when using slower but more vibrant Kodachrome or Fujichrome film.

How it works: Under normal bright-light conditions, the lens will operate at f/8 or f/11 rather than at its wide-open setting (usually f/1.8). When focused for 10 feet, all objects from the very distant to about five feet away will appear sharp as long as the final print isn't enlarged beyond five by seven inches.

This is exactly why simple nonfocusing cameras like the Instamatic give such good results for casual use, especially outdoors.

Note: Slides are enlarged far beyond five by seven inches when projected, but, because people sit some distance from the screen and because slides offer more of a contrast than prints, the human eye is tricked into thinking the picture is sharper than it really is.

Self-Focusing Cameras

For about 25% above the cost of a manually focused camera, amateur photographers can get a self-focusing model, which produces an excellent picture almost every time. Bonus: Those who shoot many pictures can recover the extra cost rapidly by saving on the development cost of out-of-focus negatives. Drawbacks: You can't change lenses. Certain situations fool the autofocus mechanism. Some models won't operate in very low light.

Three systems on the market:

Image matching. Light reflected off the subject creates images on two small mirrors inside the camera. One rotates until both images match. That determines the focus. Drawbacks: The manual override is complicated to use and won't operate in low light. This limits the use of the built-in flash, a standard feature on all these cameras. Exception: The Fujica Auto Focus shoots out its own light beam and works in total darkness.

Infrared detecting. An invisible light beam bounces off the subject, and its reflected density is translated into the proper focus. But highly reflective objects fool the system. The only solution: Change camera angles. Advantage: Operates in poor light (also has a built-in flash) and on low-contrast subjects.

Sonar. The sonar bounces an inaudible sound wave off the subject. Drawbacks: Doesn't work when shooting through glass. Sometimes focuses on the wrong object. Advantages: Manual override is easy. The auto-focus isn't affected by the amount of light and refocuses as fast as the user can push the button. Reminder: Expensive film must be used, while other self-focusing systems use standard 35mm film.

Bottom line: The sacrifice in flexibility is worth the price for those who don't have much interest in developing sophisticated photography skills.

Source: *Medical Economics.*

Camera Cautions

• Film that is advanced too rapidly generates static electricity, which leaves streaks and fog. Fix: Advance film slowly and carefully.

• Old prints shift and lose colors as dyes change with age. Fix: Display photos out of direct sunlight. Store them in a dark, dry, well ventilated area.

• Moisture-bred fungus spots on slides and negatives. Fix: Use film cleaner, which is sold at photo-supply stores.

• Mold permanently damages unprocessed film. Keep film sealed until just before using. Process it quickly after exposure.

• Erratic exposure readings can be caused by the camera meter's cold battery. Solution: Carry spare batteries in an inside pocket and replace PX-13 batteries with the cold-resistant PX-625.

• Camera cleaning: (1) Use special liquid lens cleaner and lens-cleaning tissue to remove fingerprints or smears. Put liquid on the tissue, not the lens. (2) Use a soft lens brush to remove dust. (3) Clean battery contacts with a pencil eraser to get rid of any buildup of deposits.

• If your camera is used near the seashore regularly, consider having it cleaned by a professional. Otherwise, interior corrosion can occur in hard-to-reach areas. Everyday maintenance when shooting pictures by the ocean: Wipe the metal parts of the camera at least twice with a fresh, damp, soft cloth. Then, run a silicone-saturated cloth over the metal. Use a moistened lens tissue to clean the glass.

• Using your camera in cold weather: Prevent condensation on the lens or viewfinder when bringing it in from the cold. Condensation causes fuzzy pictures and sometimes contributes to mechanical problems. Solution: Put the camera in a plastic bag when coming in from the cold. Condensation will form on the bag, not on the camera.

• Never be without spare batteries for the new electronic cameras, flash units, and motor winders. Always have the exact type of battery required. When the camera calls for sets, replace all batteries at once. Remember: The system is only as strong as its weakest cell. Before installing new batteries, rub all terminals with a rough cloth (or pencil eraser). This wipes away any oxidation that could mar performance of the batteries. Protect spares from extremes of climate. Wrap them in plastic and keep in dry, shaded areas in summer. Cold weather: Tuck them in a warm inner pocket.

• Airport x-rays at security-check stations can damage your color film, despite what signs usually say. Problem: One pass-through may be harmless, but on a multiflight trip the cumulative effect of radiation causes tints to turn. Solution: Remove film from a carryon at checkpoint, and ask a guard for a manual-visual inspection. Caution: While the Federal Aviation Administration requires U.S. airline personnel to comply, you may have to haggle for this favor overseas.

• In-flight photos. Get a window seat on the shaded side of the plane, up front (clear of wing and distorting engine exhaust). Don't hold the camera against the window (vibrations will cause blur), and don't angle it (glass reflects).

Use a shutter speed of at least 1/250 and a filter that minimizes blue-sky haze to sharpen scenes on the ground. Warning: Since some countries ban in-flight photos, inquire before takeoff.

Preserving Photographs And Slides

Store prints in a baked enamel steel container. Second choice: A box made of heavy-duty, acid-free paper. Photo dealers have a selection of both.

Keep the storage area below 70° F and under 50% humidity. If possible, filter the air.

Use 100% rag paper for mounting prints. Avoid transparent sheets made of polyvinyl chloride. It fuses with the photographs.

Check with your dealer to make sure that album pages are made of chemically inert materials.

Contrary to popular belief, mounting slides in special glass sandwich mounts increases their tendency to fade. The cardboard or plastic mounts provided by most photo finishers are best.

The Best Men's Clothes For Your Build

• For short men, the pinstripe contributes to an illusion of height. The vertical line formed by the classic three-button jacket will enhance the illusion, as will pockets that point inward and upward. No cuffs on trousers.

• Dark suits will make heavier men look lighter. Best for men of ordinary height is a single-breasted jacket with a center vent. A double-breasted jacket is suitable for taller men of any weight.

• Clothing for very thin men should underplay vertical lines and emphasize horizontal dimension. Contrast colors above and below the waist, as long as the difference isn't extreme. Two or more layers of clothing on the torso add weight to the appearance. Examples: A sweater under a shirt (the top of the sweater showing at the open neck of the shirt). Vest over the shirt, jacket over the vest. Even a muffler tossed around the jacket.

• For men with problem legs:

Bowlegged: Stick to wider trousers, altered to move the crease toward the inside of the leg.

Knock-kneed: Wear pants with tighter legs. Move the crease toward the outside to deemphasize the triangle effect.

Short legs: Avoid wide pants. Stick to short jackets.

• Quick test for jacket length. Stand with arms hanging straight at sides, hands curled inward into half-fists. Bottom of jacket should touch the palms.

• New pants often are the wrong length after they're taken home. Guidelines: (1) During a fitting, wear your own belt. (2) Look straight ahead into the mirror, never down at the tailor. (3) Be sure the waist is neither too loose nor tight so pants' legs aren't affected by hiking them up for comfort. (4) Wear the shoes you'll regularly wear with them. Often overlooked: Be sure the crease runs right through the center of the kneecap.

• Overcoats. The proper length: A little above or below the knee, not directly on it. A coat that reaches below the knee makes the wearer look taller and slightly slimmer. To get a taller, leaner look with a parka or car coat, choose one about the same length as a jacket (but no shorter).

• Sweater styles. Thin men: Avoid tight-fitting sweaters with narrow-legged slacks. Best: Boat and cowl neck styles in bumpy and cable knits. Less flattering: Mock turtle and scoop necks, dropped shoulders. Heavy-chested men: Avoid all bulky sweaters. Best style: A V-neck, with set-in shoulders. Also good: Turtle and mock turtle necks.

Source: *Dressing Right,* by Charles Hix, St. Martin's Press, New York.

Buying a Custom-Made Suit

Off-the-rack suits are getting more expensive, making custom and made-to-order suits increasingly attractive buys. Difference between the two:

Custom suits. A number of fittings are required, so custom suits are more expensive and custom tailors are usually found only in the largest U.S. and foreign cities.

Made-to-order suits can be completed in one or two fittings. Advantages: (1) Greater choice of fabrics and design, better fit and tailoring than ready-made suits. (2) Greater availability, lower price than custom suits.

Two well-known stores offer made-to-order suits around the country:

• Brooks Bros. (Special Order). Customers can choose fabrics and be fitted at all Brooks stores, and traveling representatives service 45 other cities. Made-up jackets are available to try on.

From a customer's initial fitting to the collar-baste stage (final fitting and alterations) takes around six weeks. Finishing the suit takes about two weeks more. For steady customers whose measurements are known, the store ships the suit when finished without the final trying-on.

• Saks Fifth Avenue (Made-to-Measure). There are no traveling representatives. Customers can be fitted at any of its 26 branch stores around the country. Choice: Over 500 fabrics in six basic styles ranging from European traditional to American contemporary. Finished suits are usually ready in six weeks, with only the waist buttonhole left for the final fitting.

Custom suits are a practical luxury. (Englishmen keep custom suits 10 years or longer.) English tailors send representatives to the United States and they advertise their advance schedules in *The Wall Street Journal.* Two to four months required for the first suit, less for subsequent ones.

Custom details:

Pattern lines must match everywhere. Pocket flaps must match jacket.

Lapel points must be sharp and neat. Undercollar should be made of felt and handstitched.

Seams should not pull or pucker. They should be neatly finished inside.

Armholes should have shields.

Buttonholes should be handstitched.

Lining should be handstitched.

Precaution When Buying Custom-Made Shirts

Write down the details on your receipt. Include: Color, style, collar, monogram, etc. Don't accept the store's receipt with its code letters. Clerks make too many mistakes, and it's too hard to remember what you ordered until delivery.

Buying Clothes Made of Down

Down has superior insulating properties because it traps warm air and forms protection against heat loss. However, outerwear made of duck or goose down varies in how much warmth will be provided. General rule: The higher the "fill-power rating," the better—and warmer— the garment. Down rated at 700 cubic inches is warmer for its weight than down with the standard 550-cubic-inch measurement.

Shopping for Well Made Jeans

Features to look for: (1) Double rows of stitching along the seams, pockets, and fly. There should be 8 to 10 stitches per inch. (2) A heavy-duty metal zipper with a reputable brand name—Talon, YKK, Scovil. (3) Metal rivets or reinforced stitching at stress points (pocket corners, bottom of zipper, belt loops). (4) At least five belt loops. (Three of the five must be in the back, one of those at the center seam and one over each back pocket.) The most popular jeans are made of denim. The heavier the cloth, the longer lasting. Fabric weights are not always listed on the label. For longest life, buy the jeans that feel heaviest.

Prolonging the Life Of Clothes

(1) Hang jackets on wooden or plastic hangers that approximate the shape of the human back. (2) Remove all objects from pockets. Leave unbuttoned. (3) Keep some space between garments to avoid wrinkling. (4) Allow at least 24 hours between wearings. (5) Use pants hangers that clamp onto trouser bottoms. Remove belt before hanging pants.

Instead of Having Your Suits Pressed

Frequent pressing by a tailor is harmful to fabric and reduces the life of suits. A good practice is to put them on hangers in cool air, giving creases and wrinkles a chance to hang out. If that doesn't work: Use a hand steamer (weighs 15 ounces, costs about $20). Fill with ordinary tap water. Plug into electric outlet. Steams for 15 minutes on one filling. Needs no ironing board; any flat surface will do. Cover the surface with an old folded sheet.

When Buying Shoes

Advice: (1) Shop in the afternoon, because the foot swells as the day goes on. (2) Fit should be snug, but not tight (with ¼ inch extra room in toe area). No gap between ankle and shoe when walking. (3) Inner soles should have adequate cushioning.

Custom-Made Shoes

Custom-made shoes are indeed expensive, but they last for years and are extremely comfortable and good-looking. The price of the first pair includes sculpting a wooden last to the exact shape of the customer's feet. The shoemaker keeps the last for the customer's lifetime.

In the U.S.:

Church's English Shoes Ltd., 428 Madison Ave., New York 10017, and 9633 Brighton Way, Beverly Hills, CA 90210. Custom shoes and boots for men in calf and exotic leathers (antelope, lizard, wild boar). Golf shoes. Delivery: Three to six months.

In London:

John Lobb, 9 St. James St. Shoes and boots for men and women. Delivery: Two to four months.

Trickers, 67 Jermyn St. Shoes, boots, and embroidered slippers. Delivery: Six months.

The Safe Way to Dry Wet Shoes

Simply stuff them with newspaper and allow to dry overnight at room temperature. Mistake: Placing shoes near the radiator to dry: It saps the leather's essential oils. Recommended: Waterproof leather footwear with mink oil and silicone spray. Be sure to apply substances evenly to avoid mottled coloring.

Buying Western Boots

• Western boots are designed to fit differently from other types of boots. Guidelines for buying: Always get the longest, narrowest pair you can wear. They should be snug only at the instep and slip a little at the heel when you walk. Toes: Touch, but never push against the inside of the boot when you stand. Key: The boots should feel comfortable almost at once.
Source: *Consumer Life.*

• A new pair will fit better if they are worn

for several hours immediately after a saddle soaping and polishing. Myth: Cowboy-type boots should first be worn wet for a good fit. Fact: The fit is no better than with saddle soaping. Also, if they are shrunk with water, the wearer can't take them off before they are dry.

Source: Louis Luskey, Luskey's Western Wear, Ft. Worth, Texas, quoted in *RetailWeek.*

Buying a Hairpiece

Wigs made up partially of human hair are expensive, but are better than synthetics. They tend to last twice as long (one to four years). Reminder: Suit a new hairpiece to age. A full head of hair is incongruous for an older man. Hairpieces need professional cleaning, reshaping, and coloring every two weeks. Best: Buy two hairpieces so that one is always in tip-top condition.

Discount Shopping In New York City

New York City is the best place in the world to buy quality apparel and accessories, at any price.

To be a good shopper, you must be well informed about values. Before you visit discount stores, check your local department and specialty shops for comparative values.

Basic rules of discount shopping:

Buy carefully. Avoid impulse purchases, since returns can be difficult.

Be prepared for communal dressing rooms and a lack of ambience.

Know your size.

Frequent one or two shops that sell the kind of apparel you like to get good service.

The best places to shop for discount apparel in the city:

Women's wear:

A. Altman: 204 Fifth Ave.; 182 Orchard St.;

1341 Second Ave.; 530 Central Ave., Cedarhurst. Top-quality imports, with some designer labels.

Bolton's: 225 E. 57 St.; 1180 Madison Ave.; 2251 Broadway; 43 E. 8th St.; 53 W. 23 St. Specializes in designer and medium-to-better-priced women's wear. Lots of closeouts and good discounts are available.

Damages: 169 E. 61 St. Important European couturier names, at unheard-of-prices.

European Liquidators: 1402 Second Ave. Imported designer clothing at 30% to 60% discounts.

Gucci on 7: 2 E. 54 St. Substantial discounts on last season's shoes, dresses, blouses, boots, bags, etc. Men's wear is also sold here. Some luggage.

J's Advance Apparel: 491 Seventh Ave. Mainly jobbers for small retailers, they open up for private customers, offering designer labels at 40% to 50% discounts.

Labels for Less: 1116 Third Ave.; 639 Third Ave.; 130 E. 34 St.; 130 W. 48 St. Cater to young women. Discounts range from 20% to 35%.

Paris Fashions: 270 W. 38 St. Jobbers to the trade. Discounts at around 50%.

Arthur Richards Factory: 79 Fifth Ave. Specialties are women's suits, jackets, skirts, and pants. They also sell men's apparel.

S. & W.: 165 W. 26 St.; 283 Seventh Ave.; 291 Seventh Ave.; 287 Seventh Ave. Top discounts on a variety of merchandise from well known manufacturers and designers. Specialties include coats, gowns, handbags, blouses.

Stanrose Dress Company: 491 Seventh Ave. Calvin Klein labels are a favorite here. Discounts run around 80% on new, seasonal merchandise.

J.S. Suarez: 67 E. 56 St. Sophisticated, top-quality domestic and imported handbags and wallets. Discounts are between 35% and 50%. The merchandise is excellent.

Sue's Discount Dresses: 638 Lexington Ave. Discounts at about 40%.

A special suggestion: On Saturday, from 10 a.m. to 3 p.m., visit any of those buildings on Seventh Ave. (from 36 St. to 39 St.) where the leading New York manufacturers have lofts. Ask the elevator starter which of the manufacturers are open for business. If there are none open in their building, they will tell you which buildings nearby do have manufacturers open. The following buildings are the ones most likely to accommodate you:

498 Seventh Ave.: Sportswear and moderately priced apparel.

500 Seventh Ave.: Coats.

512 Seventh Ave.: Coats and moderately priced apparel.

530 Seventh Ave.: Better-known labels.

550 Seventh Ave.: Top-designer labels.

Shopping on Orchard Street: It's off the beaten path, but it's well known as a bargain hunters' paradise. On the Lower East Side of Manhattan, it runs from Houston St. to E. Broadway. On Sundays, the street is closed to traffic. Best places to shop:

S. Beckenstein, Inc.: 125 Orchard St.; 118 Orchard St.; 130 Orchard St. A unique operation with fine fabrics for women, men, and the home.

Feminique: 143½ Orchard St. Top designers are featured at a substantial saving.

Fine and Klein: 119 Orchard St. Discounts of 40% on handbags, attache cases, and wallets. Fabulous selection.

Giselle: 143 Orchard St. Clothes by eminent designers. Discounts are between 30% and 40%.

Shaia Galapo: 161 Orchard St. In addition to a vast selection of discounted Dior handbags, there are Harve Benard, Crazy Horse, Main Street, and Gloria Vanderbilt labels at good discounts.

Unlimited Pret a Porter: 121 Orchard St. Seasonable clothes at 30% to 40% off regular prices.

Women's shoes:

The following is a listing of stores where you can buy top-name shoes at discounts of 15% to 30%.

Discount Shoes: 1185 Madison Ave.

Emotional Outlet Shoes: 242 E. 51 St.; 91 Seventh Ave.

Eti-Quette: 860 Lexington Ave.; 103 W. 44 St.

Flair's Edge: 110 Orchard St.

FM Bags and Shoes: 126 Ludlow St.

Jerri's: 538 Second Ave.

Lace-Up Shoe Shop: 119 Orchard St.

Shoe Express: 1420 Second Ave.

Men's clothing:

Moe Ginsburg: 162 Fifth Ave. Good variety in domestic and imported suits, overcoats, jackets, and slacks.

Gorsart: 122 Duane St. Discounts of 20% to 25% on suits, tuxedos, raincoats, shirts, ties.

Andrew Pallack: 120 Fifth Ave. A wide assortment of men's clothing at prices that are about half of the suggested retail price.

Eisenberg & Eisenberg: 149 Fifth Ave. Full range of men's clothing. Alterations are free.

Saint Laurie Ltd.: 84 Fifth Ave. Classic men's apparel, all made by Saint Laurie, at top discount prices.

Sussex: 895 Broadway. Almost wholesale prices for top-quality suits, sport coats, trousers.

Harry Rothman: 111 Fifth Ave. Strictly retail, but prices are discounted on everything.

Barney's: 7th Ave. at 17th St. In a class by itself. It has the widest variety of men's apparel of any store in New York. They don't discount, but Barney's has major sales twice a year.

Buying Furs at Wholesale

Shoppers can find unusual bargains in furs purchased directly from wholesalers.

How it works: Unlike most other wholesalers, fur manufacturers do a lot of their business directly with the consumer. Reason: They need the cash flow. Don't expect wholesale prices. But those you're quoted will be from 30% to 40% below the retail price.

Where to go: Virtually all the country's fur manufacturers and wholesalers are clustered in a small area in New York City (in the neighborhood around 7th Ave. and 30th St.). Advantage: Because the outlets are so close together, shoppers can easily compare prices.

Tactics: Before selecting a coat or jacket, do some homework by looking at what's available at the local department stores. Don't settle on a coat at the first manufacturer you go to. Not only do prices vary, but so does the quality of skins and workmanship.

When you go to a manufacturer's showroom, you may find that a coat to your liking is already in stock. If not, the wholesaler will make one to your specifications. If you are dissatisfied with the finished product, few manufacturers will argue about it because they can sell it to another customer. Caution: Check this point before making a deposit.

Shopper's checklist:

Examine the inside of the coat to make sure the skins are not dry.

Look at the label. Every fur product selling for more than $5 must have a label, according to federal law.

Ask about the fur's country of origin. Canadian sable, for instance, can't be sold as Russian.

Once you have bought a coat, keep it in good condition by hanging it away from the heat. Use a large hanger. Don't squash it in the closet. Let it hang loosely. Clean furs regularly, and keep them away from chemical sprays.

Wholesale Fur Dealers In New York City

Alixandre, 150 W. 30th St., (212) 736-5550.

Bossis Furs, 330 Seventh Ave., (212) 695-3050.

Christie Bros., 333 Seventh Ave., (212) 736-6944.

Michael Forrest, Inc., 333 Seventh Ave., (212) 564-4726.

L.J. Freiman (fur hats only), 350 Seventh Ave., (212) 244-4017.

Oliver Gintel Furs, 333 Seventh Ave., (212) 736-5573.

Goldin-Feldman, 345 Seventh Ave., (212) 594-4415.

HBA, 350 Seventh Ave., (212) 564-1080.

Jan Originals, 307 Seventh Ave., (212) 255-4800.

Laurence H. Kay Furs (Christian Dior), 345 Seventh Ave., (212) 695-8340.

Levitt-Charles Parras, 350 Seventh Ave., (212) 244-7091.

Mohl Furs, 345 Seventh Ave., (212) 736-7676.

Tepper Collection, 370 Seventh Ave., (212) 244-8755.

Wagner Furs, 150 W. 30th St., (212) 736-8552.

Fur Coat Care

Use a neck scarf to protect the collar from the discolorations of cosmetics.

Never spray a fur with perfume or cologne. Perfume contains oils and alcohol is in cologne, neither of which is good for a pelt.

Avoid chain belts. The friction causes damage. Better: A leather belt, with nonmetallic buckle.

Never pin flowers or jewelry onto a fur.

If caught in a rainstorm, dry a fur by hanging it on a large wooden hanger away from heat. Pick a spot where the air circulates freely. Never use an electric blow dryer under any circumstances.

Best thing for a fur coat: Wear it. The body's heat helps maintain the fur's shape.

Toughest, best-wearing furs: Mink and Alaskan seal. Sable is also very durable.

Storage:

For short periods at home, hang the coat in a closet away from light. Leave some space around it so that the fur can breathe.

Never store fur in a cedar closet or with moth repellent.

Never cover fur with plastic. It dries the skin and causes rot in a silk lining. Use a loose dark fabric cover that is open at the bottom.

In warm weather, place your coat in a good furrier's vault. Storing it at home exposes it to heat, humidity, moths, other insects, and home air conditioning. All of these things are harmful. Added incentive for away-from-home fur storage: Your coat is safe from housebreakers.

Getting Your Money's Worth from Dry Cleaners

Bagging is important. Heavy plastic wrappers and lavish use of tissue paper maintain a garment's shape both on the conveyor belt and in your closet.

Make sure there is someone on the premises to stitch falling hems and replace buttons. Ask if the service is included in the price.

French dry cleaning is a meaningless term. It may only mean a higher price.

Not every disaster is the cleaner's fault. Many garments are poorly manufactured and mislabeled as to fabric content.

When the cleaner *is* at fault, expect to get back only the current market value of a garment. Do not expect the cleaner to give you the garment's replacement value.

A sign announcing not liable for goods left over 30 days shouldn't be taken at face value. It may not hold up in court.

Better dry-cleaning results: Pin a note on any stain. The note should mention what may have caused the stain. Stains most difficult to remove: Nail polish, lipstick, suntan lotion.

Before You Hire A Moving Company

When a mover gives you an estimate, it is based on a guess as to how much the goods weigh. No matter what the quotation, you won't know the actual cost until your goods are actually loaded on the van, weighed, and delivered to your new home. Then the price you must pay is what the mover tells you, regardless of any previous estimate.

How accurate is the guess? One way to find out is to ask for the moving company's performance record. That record, which the law says must be given, will show how often the final charge was higher than the estimate. It also shows how often goods were lost or damaged and how often shipments were picked up or delivered late.

For in-state moving, it is sometimes cheaper to use local movers because their rates are not regulated by the Interstate Commerce Commission. They may be willing to cut prices.

Always shop around. And try to get a fixed contract price. Always read the small print of the contract so that you know what damages the mover is liable for, whether the insurer can limit the amount paid for goods lost, stolen, or damaged, and extra costs.

For a long move, your shipment is weighed at highway weigh stations that are usually far from your home. It's possible to follow the van to the weigh-in station to observe the scales and to receive a copy of the gross-weight ticket.

Do movers cheat? Some do. They may load extra men on the van when your goods are being weighed. Or they may have an empty van weighed with an empty gas tank, then fill the tank after the shipment is loaded.

Moving: How to Do it Yourself

Planning ahead is the single most important requirement for do-it-yourself moving without disaster. The professional mover can pack your possessions in one day. The ordinary family that tries the same thing is courting serious trouble. It is a mistake to leave all the packing for the last minute and then face the loading, driving, and unloading. Packing should begin at least four weeks ahead of time.

Renting a truck: It is important to get the right size truck, neither too small nor too large. Truck-rental companies can assess your needs from a description of how much and where you are moving. The basic twelve-foot panel truck can move two to three rooms of furniture. Fourteen-foot: Three large rooms. Sixteen-foot: Four rooms. Eighteen-foot: Five to six rooms. Twenty-foot: Seven to nine rooms.

What it takes to drive one: Usually the same amount of skill it takes to drive the family station wagon. Many trucks are equipped with automatic transmission, power steering, and power brakes.

Costs: Vary from city to city and by season. Charges are highest during the peak moving months of July and August.

General price range for truck rental: $40 to $60 per day plus 15¢ to 22¢ per mile for a local move. If the move is between cities, companies often use an unlimited mileage rate. The mileage cost is built into the price (for a limited number of days and a maximum number of miles).

How to pack: Pick the most convenient and roomiest area to create an assembly line for packing. Store all materials (cartons, packing paper, and marking pens) there. Recommended: Buy cartons from a moving company rather than scrounging boxes from grocery and liquor stores. They are much better suited for the job and well worth the $50 they may cost.

Label every carton and the room each goes to in the new dwelling.

Pack out-of-season items first. Examples: Quilts and winter clothing in the summer.

Pace yourself. Pack for a few hours each day and call it quits.

Avoid putting too much in a carton. Pack heavy items (such as books) in small cartons. Large cartons are good for holding big, bulky items that are not heavy (pillows, blankets etc.).

Use newspaper to wrap glassware and silver. Caution: For delicate china, ceramics, lamp shades, or items that will be smudged by newsprint, use newspaper that does not have print on it. It is available from any paper-supply house and it's inexpensive. For wrapping small quantities of china or ceramics, use a newsprint pad (without print), which is obtainable for a few dollars from any art-supply store. Lamps: Remove shades. Pack separately, each in its own carton. Plants: Pack them last.

Load the truck on the last day, right before moving.

Put heavy appliances (refrigerator, washer,

dryer, etc.) in the truck first. Place them in the back, next to the cab, and tie them down to the slats on the sides of the truck. Put smaller items (blankets, pillows, lamp shades, etc.) inside the large appliances, to save space.

Load heavy furniture next. Tables go in top down, on a heavy pad or blankets. Remove table legs if possible.

Stand mattresses and box springs along the sides of the truck. Between them: Put long, fragile items (mirrors, pictures, etc.).

Keep all items close together to eliminate sliding. Stuff furniture pads or blankets between them to avoid scratching.

Important details:

Keep careful records of moving costs. They are tax deductible. Include: Expense of house-hunting trips before the move, temporary living costs, packing and crating charges, the truck fees.

Consider selling some of the bulkier items of furniture (piano, desk, chest, etc.) and buying new ones later. Depending on their quality and condition, the additional weight and space taken up by moving them could be more than offset by selling and replacing them. Or: Consider donating large but inexpensive items to charity. Keep receipts for tax purposes.

Make a personal inventory of all household goods and their worth before the move. That facilitates collecting insurance in case of theft or damage en route.

Source: William Proud, director of marketing, Avis Rent a Car's truck division, 900 Old Country Rd., Garden City, New York 11530.

Getting Your Money's Worth from Lawyers

Problem: The lawyer's quoted fee seems high. Solution: Shop around and negotiate the lowest possible fee. Stress that the case is routine (if it is). Get a contract or letter specifying the fee or how it will be calculated, the services covered, and the payment schedule.

Problem: You can't afford the fee. Solution: Tell the attorney in advance. He may reduce it and/or extend the payment time.

Problem: The final fee seems too high in relation to the work done or the case's outcome. Solution: Get a breakdown on what was done, how long it took, and the charge for each activity. If still not satisfied, bring the dispute to the arbitration board (if there is one) of the local bar association. If a lot of money is involved, get legal help on how best to present case to the bar's board. Or you can threaten litigation.

Problem: A lawyer neglects a case. Solution: Let the attorney know you're unhappy. Get an explanation of what's been done so far. If this doesn't work, tell him you're considering reporting him to the bar association and the lawyer review board. You can also dismiss him and hire another attorney.

Problem: The lawyer is incompetent. Solution: Bring the matter to the bar association's grievance committee. A decision in your favor is ammunition for a malpractice suit. If you go to court, you can recoup losses in civil cases. In criminal cases, a malpractice finding may entitle you to a new trial in addition to a monetary award.

Problem: A lawyer mishandles your property. Solution: This could have been avoided by having the lawyer provide regular and detailed accounts of the money, property, or other assets entrusted to him. After the fact, threaten and/or institute a malpractice suit. If the settlement doesn't cover losses, apply to the client security fund of the bar association. This reimburses clients victimized by lawyers.

Source: *A Client's Manual*, by Joseph C. McGinn, Prentice-Hall, Englewood Cliffs, NJ.

Pros and Cons Of Legal Clinics

Good news: Many legal clinics do provide excellent, low-cost service in routine matters such as simple wills, uncontested divorce, etc.

The bad news: In cases requiring legal analysis and experience, their performances range from very good to very bad. Fees in tricky cases may equal or surpass those of traditional law firms.

Hiring a Lawyer For a Court Case

Many executives who deal confidently with attorneys in the normal course of business feel unsure of themselves when a matter goes into litigation. Here is frank advice from Milton R. Wessel, a trial lawyer who practices in New York and teaches at NYU.

Selecting counsel. The best trial lawyers don't necessarily work for the biggest firms. Many of them are with smaller ones where the chances for broad experience are greater. Choose the lawyer, not the firm. Trial law is a specialty. Seek out counsel with trial experience in the field. A local trial attorney who's familiar with the court where the case will be tried is usually best. If represented by a lawyer from out of town, most courts usually require local counsel, too.

Negotiating the fee. Avoid contingency arrangements. A fee based on time spent is safest, but get assurance that rates won't change during the period of litigation without prior discussion. Costs quoted can be deceiving. A $50-per-hour fee for a lawyer fresh out of law school is no bargain. Better to pay much more for an experienced senior partner who knows how to get work done in one-tenth the time. $25 per hour for law firm's paralegals is too high if they perform a file clerk's job.

Questions to ask. Many law firms have more than one rate for an attorney. Are you getting the best price? Travel time: How much is charged for a day spent away from the office? How many hours count as a day? Are you charged for a whole day if only part is used for your case? What if the trip is for more than one client? Is there a charge for weekends and holidays if the lawyer doesn't work? Tourist or first-class travel? Who pays for the lawyer's meals and entertainment? Disbursements: Are secretarial and messenger work handled as disbursement or overhead? How are duplicating documents in the law office charged?

Client's rights. Law firms are a business like any other. It's proper to demand good service, protest excessive costs, keep lawyers on their toes without compromising their professionalism. Ask for the litigation plan in advance. Who will do what and when? Hold the law firm to the plan. Your counsel should stay with the case from beginning to end, supervise internal administration (including billing), as well as represent your company in court.

Get itemized monthly record of charges. The record should list everyone working on the case, hourly rate, and time spent. Watch for signs that people already familiar with your company's business are being replaced by staff who must be educated at your expense.

Question overtime closely. Somebody's work is being done during regular office hours; why not yours?

Costly delays can pile up when trial lawyers on opposing sides exchange "professional courtesies" to accommodate personal or vacation schedules. Don't accept postponements unless they will clearly help the case.

Be sure counsel knows enough about your business to handle any questions arising in the courtroom.

Trial lawyers tend to be cynical, need to be sold on the merits of a client's case. The more confident an attorney is that the client is right, the better his performance.

Five Ways Some Lawyers Steal From Clients

1. Inflating expenses in negligence cases. Research is a popular dodge. Where the lawyer's fee is one-third of the settlement on a contingency basis, inflated expenses are trimmed off the top before the split.

2. Inflating billable time when the client is paying by the hour. Some large firms create impossible quotas on billable time.

3. Commingling of funds. Collecting money due the client, then putting it in his own account—not the escrow account into which it should go. He gets the interest, or uses the money and pays the client later.

4. Playing cozy with an insurance adjuster. Where a settlement should be $7,500, he agrees to settle for $7,000 if the adjuster will tell the client the settlement is $6,500. The lawyer pockets the extra $500.

5. Telling you that he can "fix" the case for a set sum. There's no fix needed, because the case is solid, and the lawyer simply pockets the "bribe."

When to Sue an Attorney for Malpractice

The legal profession is entering its own malpractice crisis. The number of suits against attorneys is increasing and the availability of malpractice insurance is decreasing.

Ground rules for considering a suit against your lawyer:

Where malpractice is charged in connection with litigation, the client must show that the litigation would have ended with a result more favorable to the client except for the attorney's neglect.

Where the attorney fell below the standards of skill and knowledge ordinarily possessed by attorneys under similar circumstances, expert testimony is needed to support the charge. And the standard may be affected by specialization (which raises the standard of care required), custom, and the locality. Locality and custom can't lower the standard, but they may be used in defense to show that the procedure or the law involved is unsettled.

Best way to avoid malpractice charges (and costs of a suit):

Good communication between lawyer and client.

Avoid creating a situation where the lawyer is handling serious matters for personal friends. The tendency is to deal with them on a more casual basis.

The attorney should give an honest opinion of each case, good or bad. The client shouldn't press him for a guarantee as to the result, and a value on the claim.

All fee arrangements should be in writing.

The attorney should spell out the scope of his responsibilities, including appeals, and a limit should be placed on costs.

The agreement should provide for periodic payments, unless the matter is one involving a contingent fee, and for withdrawal, if there is a default in payment.

Selecting an Insurance Agent

Insurance is an arcane and sometimes tedious field, but some research will help you make useful comparisons when your insurance agent suggests a particular program. Don't rely on him to sell you the right policy. Be informed so that you can make qualitative judgments of the products. You want to know what value you will get per dollar of premium.

When comparing policies, look for:

Amount of coverage.

Exclusions from coverage, if any.

Size of deductibles (that part of any loss claims you must pay first).

Other terms and conditions.

The difference between an agent and a broker:

An agent represents the companies whose policies he sells. All agents are independent except those who represent companies that deal directly with the public. Example: Allstate and GEICO have employee-agents, while others, like State Farm and Liberty Mutual, use agents under exclusive contract to represent only them.

A broker represents you and other clients when dealing with the companies from whom he buys policies on your behalf.

An agent or broker's expertise is usually in either life or property/casualty. If he handles both, he may not have equal competence. However, if he's with a large organization, there should be adequate backup support available to him.

Selecting an agent. Interview all agent-candidates (after checking the companies with which they deal).

Sources:

Referrals from friends.

Large, reputable insurance companies who list their agents in the Yellow Pages.

Large and established agencies and brokerages. Avoid part-time and marginal agents.

To avoid payment and refund problems: Always keep proof of payment. Most state laws view brokers and agents as insurance-company representatives in premium transactions. Therefore, when you pay the salesperson, you are paying the insurance company. The receipt should indicate that the insurance firm is contracting to provide the specific policy and is crediting the premiums paid to the agent.

Potential problems:

Policy cancellation for nonpayment of premium. If you can prove you paid the agent, it is up to the insurance company to collect the money. You are legally insured.

No insurance. You order and pay for protection, but a policy never arrives. No problem: You are insured if you can produce your receipt (as above).

No refund. If your insurance agent neglects to send money due you because of a canceled policy or reduced coverage, request the money directly from the insurance company. They are obligated to pay you. (However, if your broker or agent cashes your refund check, proving the forgery may delay your payment.)

Be cautious of an agent who gives a super-low premium quote. He may be tricking you. When the bill comes, the premium may really be much higher. If the insurance quote seems too low, ask for it in writing, with full particulars. If you are refused, find another agent.

Policy replacement. This may be suggested by competent life insurance people to improve your protection or reduce the cost. However, a greedy agent knows he will get a higher sales commission for the first few years if you replace a life policy. So compare the old and new policies carefully and consult with experts.

Clean sheeting: Salesman fails to report a health condition that would make the applicant uninsurable. When the supposedly insured makes a claim, the lie comes to light and the company refuses to pay. Defense: Ask to see the health report that the agent sends to the company. This should note any pre-existing conditions.

Stacking: Selling a client more coverage than he or she needs or can afford. Defense: Don't carry more than one policy with the same coverage. Double coverage is not allowed by most insurance companies.

Scare tactics: The "buy now because you may not be able to get insurance later" pitch. Defense: Don't deal with an agent who arouses suspicion. Ask for a complete explanation.

To get recourse for a problem that your agent or insurance company will not resolve, file a complaint with your state's insurance commission.

When Not to Trust An Insurance Company

Life insurance is controlled by state, not federal regulations. Consumer protection varies around the country. (25% of U.S. insurance companies are domiciled in Arizona, 10% in Texas. Both states have low capitalization requirements.) Bankruptcy disasters could leave beneficiaries with worthless policies.

Be wary if a company isn't qualified to sell in New York State, which has very tough standards.

Keep a sharp eye on the insurance company's reported investment results. Ask to see the latest results when buying a new policy.

Avoid companies that are floating commercial paper to fund policy loans or to pay dividends.

Find out about the company's capital surplus position. A healthy company will have capital surplus equal to about 7% of total life insurance liabilities.

Some companies do not offer immediate low-interest loans. Watch out for clauses that begin: The company may defer the loan . . . (Look for the clause that contains the interest rate.)

Surrender payment: Is there a waiting period between the time you cash in the policy and when you receive the money? It can be a six-month delay.

Installment interest: Some companies offer beneficiaries the option of receiving benefits in installments. Watch out for low interest rates.

Insurance Often Bought Unnecessarily

A standard homeowners policy usually covers stolen purses and wallets, lost luggage, and property taken in car break-ins. It can also cover many off-beat accidents. Example: Damage to a power mower that you borrowed from a neighbor. Also: Trees, shrubs, fences, or tombstones damaged by vandals or motor vehicles. Property lost or damaged while moving.

American Automobile Association members have automatic hospital and death benefits if they are hurt in a car accident.

Many clubs and fraternal organizations have life and health benefits.

It's possible to collect twice on car accident injuries: Once through health insurance and again through the medical payments provision of auto insurance.

Family health policies usually cover children away at college. Check before buying separate policies.

327

Insurance Policies To Avoid

Insurance policies that should be avoided, because the premiums are too high for the coverage they provide:

Flight insurance. Does it make sense to have more coverage for dying in a plane crash than any other accident? If it does (perhaps to help assuage fear of flying), buy accident coverage or an accident rider for plane travel on your life policy instead of a policy for each flight.

Rental car insurance. Waiving the deductible on collision coverage costs an extra 1% a day. It may be covered anyway by the driver's own policy. If the car is rented for business use, any damage is tax deductible, except the first $100. Common tax error: If one rents for personal use and doesn't buy the collision damage waiver, then has an accident and has to pay, that's technically not tax deductible. Why? Because it isn't the driver's own car. Most people probably deduct it anyway as a casualty loss.

Mortgage insurance. It's often structured so that the borrower is paying interest on the insurance premium. Buy decreasing term insurance instead.

Source: Israeloff, Trattner & Co., CPAs, 11 Sunrise Plaza, Valley Stream, NY 11581.

Before You Buy Boat Insurance

The policy should cover ice, freezing, and racing damage.

Include protection and indemnity coverage. Reason: A boat can be sued much like a corporation ashore. Personal homeowners insurance won't protect it from confiscation to satisfy an award against it.

The policy should cover use of the boat in all planned geographic areas.

Ask about discounts based on owner experience, Power Squadron courses, automatic fire-extinguishing systems, diesel engine, etc., may lower your costs.

12

Collecting for Pleasure and Profit

Beginner's Guide To Big-Time Auctions

Fewer and fewer people are intimidated by auctions. During an Americana sale, for instance, where items went on view about a week before the auction, many of the people had never even been to an auction house before, and knew little about the procedure.

People now realize that auctions are a good way to acquire items for a collection. Attending one can be like going to a museum or an art show, only better, since you can actually handle the merchandise.

While the glitter and social aspects of auctions have attracted attention in the press, that is merely part of the excitement. The other side: Many items are now within the reach of a broad collecting group. Some two-thirds of all items auctioned in 1980 by Sotheby Parke Bernet, the internationally famous auction house, cost under $1,000.

Don't feel pressured to bid: Not all who attend auctions are high-powered collectors or specialist dealers. People come for the thrill of the exhibit or to learn about *objets d'art*.

Then they may start collecting. Some 25% to 50% of the people at the auction are there just to watch. At times there may be only a dozen serious bidders at the sale. On other occasions, 50 to 100 bidders may compete on a single lot (one item). Exception: Very important sales, such as those of Impressionist paintings selling from $100,000 to over $1 million, are reserved for known collectors and dealers, and are so conducted. Tickets may be available to onlookers for seats in an auxiliary auction room, equipped with videoscreens and loudspeakers. The average session lasts two hours, with a lunch break between morning and afternoon auctions. Sessions for outstanding, extensive collections have been known to last several days.

If you are interested in acquiring an item: Get the auction house's catalog for the appropriate auction. Cost: $7 to $15 for a single catalog. A year's catalogs in your field of interest: $35 to $75. Look at the low and high estimates for the items you like. Examine the items during the period of time they are exhibited before the auction. Use the services of the auction house, if you need to. What's available: Customer-service representatives who walk the exhibit floor and tell people whether certain pieces are good examples of a particular style, or may be less desirable. Also, catalogers and experts who can tell you which are the best objects in the sale.

If you are thinking of starting a collection: Catalogers and experts can advise you which pieces are good ones to start off your collection. Point: Some education and homework are necessary before you plunge into collecting. The expert may point to a repair in an Oriental carpet or a restoration in a piece of furniture that might make it serviceable for a home but not appropriate as a cornerstone for a serious collection.

Learning about pricing and periods: Visit a few dealers' stores. See the prices they want for comparable items. Compare them to the auction estimates. Another idea: For items to decorate your home, such as furniture, rugs, and porcelain, look at what department stores charge for similar decor, especially modern reproductions. Example: A good-quality, 18th-century Georgian chest of drawers sells for no more than a modern reproduction of the same piece (about $800). Paradox: While the antique may appreciate in value, the reproduction will probably depreciate.

A few weekends of looking through antique stores and at modern reproductions as well as at catalogs will give you a good sense of the price levels of various objects. You may not be able to figure out what a rare specimen from Chippendale's workshop costs. But that is for a serious collector. You should be able to determine the price of a mainstream chest of drawers.

Getting set: Arrive at the auction about 30 to 45 minutes early, to get a good seat so that you have a good view of the auctioneer and, more important, to let the auctioneer have a good view of you. If you are interested in a specific piece, the chronological catalog will give you an idea of when it will be put on the block.

Bidding against the dealers: It is not the cloak-and-dagger trap some people make it out to be. Why: Dealers have to resell that object through an antique store, or wholesale it to another dealer. Key: As a consumer, you have the edge, since you are not looking for a

large profit (up to 100%). Therefore, even if you pay more than a dealer pays, you still have a bargain in terms of what the item might cost you retail.

Paying up: The auction house tacks an additional 10% commission onto your purchase. Therefore, if you buy an item for $3,000, expect to pay $3,300. No one will ask beforehand whether you can afford your bid, but when you settle after the auction you pay immediately, using cash or a personal or certified check. You don't need identification. The auction house calls your bank on the spot.

Source: David Redden, vice-president in charge of marketing and sales coordination, Sotheby Parke Bernet Inc., 1334 York Ave., New York 10021.

Antique Auction Do's and Don'ts

"Antique" means that an object is 100 years old or older.

Examine the items carefully at the pre-sale exhibition. (Take along a tape measure and flashlight.) Beware of wooden furniture with legs made of wood that differs from the surface. Chances are someone has put the piece together from two or more pieces.

When an item catches your interest, ask the attendant what price it is likely to bring—usually a pretty good estimate.

If you can narrow your choice down to one item of each type, you don't have to attend the auction. Simply decide on the maximum you are willing to pay and place the bid in advance. If a piece isn't up to your price, the auctioneer will award it to you at the next level of bidding. Example: If your bid was $250 but the bidding stopped at $175, you will get the piece for $200.

If you cannot narrow your choice down to one item of each type and you must be physically present at the auction, find out what time the first item on your list will go on the block. Rule of thumb: Most auctions clip along at about 100 items an hours. Hence, if you are planning to bid on Lot 121, you can arrive an hour after the auction is scheduled to begin.

Buyers do best in June, July, August, and December, which are slow months at most auction houses.

Auctioneers never take anything back. They are not responsible for bidder's errors. If in doubt, bring an expert along.

Don't be overeager. It encourages bids from "phantom" buyers, bidding you up. Best not to open the bidding.

Art for Love and Profit

A good collector must first have passion for what he's collecting. Every culture has collectible antiquities. But without passion, it's impossible to judge their beauty or value. It's worth cultivating that passion. Reason: A good collector ought to be able to return 10 to 20 times his investment every 10 years.

First law of collecting: The more one knows about a field, the greater the likelihood of recognizing value. It is not essential to have a great artistic eye, although truly great collectors do, but it is essential to heed what the experts say. Point: Time is the collector's major investment, not money.

What to do: (1) Start by reading books on the history of your field of interest. (2) Choose a specialty. (3) Go to galleries and educate your eye to recognize subtle differences between objects. (4) Take courses. (5) Find the smartest people in the field and pick their brains on a continuing basis. (Note: The reason most investors fail is that they don't spend enough time educating themselves.)

Where to find the smartest people: In the art field, they are usually artists, museum curators, top dealers, and critics. Unlike the stock market, where insiders can't publish what they know, art-market insiders must publish to do business. Result: It's much easier to learn about collectibles than about stocks. Artists have shows, museum people write monographs and collect for their institutions, dealers exhibit, and critics write.

When to buy: When at least three of these experts are talking about the same artist or the same group of paintings. General rule: When insiders talk about something, it's probable that its value will increase shortly thereafter.

How to buy: Either through dealers or at auctions. Auction prices are generally lower, but are cash deals. Most dealers allow collectors to get several works with a down payment that equals the price of one work at auction.

Sound advice: Buy the best works of an artist or movement to guarantee maximum flexibility should liquidation become necessary. Top works are quickly salable and give the collector a powerful negotiating position, too.

Two different buying strategies:

1. Buy unrecognized art. This can be risky, but it offers the biggest potential payoff. Rule of thumb: When other collectors of equal talent think a fellow collector has gone off the deep end, it may be an indication that he's on to something big. Reminder: It may take seven years or more for the market to catch up with unrecognized great art.

2. Buy recognized art. More information is available and reputations have already been established. It's easier to make intelligent buys. Strategic point: When the experts begin to moan that prices are getting too expensive. (Background: All collectors tend to buy in tiers. Those who buy a work at $1,000, for example, are unlikely to pay $5,000 or $10,000 for a similar object.) This creates buying opportunities. Hint: Good deals can be made by buying from prescient collectors, who like to boast they bought an object when it was cheap.

How to increase the value of an existing collection: Publicize it. How: (1) Give showings at your home. (2) Lend art objects to museums. (Note: Inclusion in a museum show increases a painting's market value by 5% to 10%.) Warning: Museums damage about one out of every 10 paintings entrusted to them. (3) Seek press coverage.

Added bonus: Publicity gives the collector admittance to dealers' back rooms, where the best deals are often found.

What to expect:

Collecting often requires a modification of lifestyle. Many collectors wear old clothes longer, go to second-class restaurants, and generally pinch pennies so they can pour all their extra money into their collection.

Downside risk in collectibles is usually less than in stocks. Reason: Artwork can always be donated to a museum for a tax deduction. Secondly, even if a work's market value shrinks, the collector still gets the benefit of living with a beautiful object. Note: Novice collectors must expect to fare poorly the first two years. After that, their collections should begin to appreciate.

Source: Barbara and Eugene Schwarz, collectors of American postwar art, and American art, pottery, and photography.

Collecting Art Prints

Over the past 25 years, art prints made between 1850 and 1950 appreciated 25% a year on average. To get into this market, an initial investment of $40,000 is sufficient. This will purchase 10 investment-quality prints at auction. A collection of 20 to 30 works from the same period, school or artist can be acquired for between $100,000 and $200,000.

Basics of collecting prints:

Concentrate on editions limited to 250 prints or fewer.

Always buy at auction. Dealers buy at the same auctions and then mark up prints 100%.

Use prices from previous auctions to determine bidding levels. Bonus: Prints sell regularly. That gives them easily determined market value and makes them among the most liquid of collectibles.

Don't overspecialize. Reason: Dealers and other collectors can demand unreasonable prices when they hold the prints needed to round out a collection. Instead: Buy 15 to 24 prints by several artists of the same period. To avoid attracting attention, decide which artists to buy and acquire works by all of them from the beginning.

Hold the prints for at least five years to get maximum gains.

Lend the prints to galleries, museums, schools, and other public institutions for exhibition. This helps create interest among other collectors.

Source: Robert E. Penn, financial manager of Danoes Ltd., writing in *The Journal of Portfolio Management.*

An Expert's Guide to Fine Prints

Prints are original works of art that are limited in number and usually signed by the artist. They include etchings, lithographs, silk screens, aquatints, woodcuts, drypoints, and combinations of techniques. Artists use the techniques they find most interesting at the time.

Cost: A great print can cost from $50,000 to $200,000, depending on the artist and the importance of the work. The cost is related to the quality of the image, condition of the paper, and rarity of the print. Paramount: Choose quality artists and the finest examples of their works. Run-of-the-mill works do not go up in value, not even the works of famous artists.

Quality: Training your eye to examine the quality of the impression is essential. Never purchase a poor impression of a great print. Although Old Master prints such as a Rembrandt, Piranesi, or Durer are extremely valuable, they require enormous study. How to tell: Look at as many impressions and slides as possible, for a basis of comparison. Do your homework by going to museums, print houses, and auctions.

Learning the market: Over 24,000 prints may be sold at auction in one year. Dealers and print galleries account for thousands more. Many artists are as famous for their prints as for the rest of their works.

Major artists' prints are described in *catalogues raisonnes*. These catalogues detail pertinent information about each of an artist's prints, with illustrations at various stages, edition size, and the varying states of a particular print. Example: Norwegian artist Edvard Munch printed many of his woodcuts in different color combinations, and he used different types of paper, making it possible for investors now to collect many different images of the same subject. You should know the differences among them and which ones are more valuable. How: Consult art dealers, read books, attend lectures, ask questions of curators and auction personnel specializing in a particular field.

Patience: It is essential in building a collection. Most serious collectors of prints know each other and are known to auction houses as well as the dealers. Part of the joy of collecting fine prints is the hunt for rare and wonderful pieces that can be appreciated when seen in the context of a meaningful collection.

The availability of great prints is, of course, well known to those in the field. The prints become harder to obtain each year. Reason: They are highly sought after by museums, institutions, and collectors. The increasing rarity and worldwide interest in this medium has caused a tremendous escalation of interest —and prices—in the print market in the last decade.

In today's society, collecting has become a worldwide phenomenon. For centuries, prints were made by many major artists, but they never realized high prices. In recent years, they have outperformed almost all collectibles, and they have certainly appreciated faster than most stocks. Point: Prints, like all collectibles, do not pay dividends. It is of primary importance to buy what you like. The purpose of collecting is to visually enjoy the prints, providing that there is quality in the print to enjoy.

How to care for prints: Avoid keeping them in direct sunlight. Make sure prints are framed properly, using acid-free paper and Plexiglas, which filters out ultraviolet rays that are harmful to paper.

Source: Nelson Blitz, print collector and member of the acquisition committees of the Museum of Modern Art in New York and the Israel Museum.

Collecting Fine Photos

The fine-photography market is in an nascent stage similar to a promising growth stock. Many feel it is the most exciting segment of the world of art collecting. Their view: Fine photos may someday command prices many times current levels, even comparable to the prices of fine paintings.

Availability of masterpiece-quality photography is excellent. The very best photos, by nearly every great photographer, can be purchased. The most outstanding works are in $10,000 to $20,000 range. Paintings of similar quality command from $100,000 to $1 million.

Demand is likely to grow more strongly than it has in the past, as collecting and displaying photographs gains acceptance. The pace of sales is picking up momentum. Reason: More art lovers can afford to collect masterpieces of photography than nearly any other art form. It has also become more fashionable and is attracting a new audience.

Learning about fine photographs: As in all art collecting, it is best to get a firm understanding of the periods and styles of photography. Then choose one or two that you enjoy the most. It is fairly easy to get acquainted with the best. Bonus: You may find it makes you more interested in history.

Periods in photography:

1837 to 1850. When the daguerreotype was first perfected in France and salt-print photographs were first developed in England.

1850 to 1860. The great period of French photography.

1860 to 1880. Height of topographical photography: Exotic photos of China, India, Egypt, and Japan. Also the beginning of the careers of great American photographers such as Carleton E. Watkins and William Henry Jackson.

1880 to 1900. End of the topographical period and the beginning of pictorialism. Important photographer: Peter Henry Emerson and his naturalistic photography.

1900 to 1920. Photo-Secessionist Period: Alfred Stieglitz, Edward Steichen, Alvin Landon Coburn, and Gertrude Kasebier.

1920 to 1930. In Europe, the beginning of the avant-garde group: Laszlo Moholy-Nagy, Man Ray, Andre Kertesz. In the United States, the beginnings of photojournalistic social realism.

1930 to 1940. Height of photojournalism: Erich Salomon, Berenice Abbott, and Margaret Bourke-White.

1940s. Advent of color photography.

Key: As in all art collecting, masterpieces will appreciate faster and more steadily than works of middle-range quality.

Scarcity: Some photographs are extremely rare. Great 19th-century photographs are in editions of only three or four. Superb French 19th-century photographs are even rarer. Reason: In the 19th century, there was no market for photos, so limited editions were made only for friends. In addition, many have been destroyed.

Contrast: Today's photographers often make as many prints as needed to meet the demand of people who will buy them. Important collecting point: Buy only prints made by the photographer, not those commercially produced. As each edition of 10 or 20 prints made by a recognized master is bought, the price of ensuing editions may go up. Example: Ansel Adams has made over 1,000 prints of Moonrise, Hernandez, N.M., his most popular work. Yet, it still brings the highest price of any of his works. Obviously, scarcity is *not* necessarily a factor in price.

Alternate ways to collect photographs: Buy stereographs (three-dimensional photographs), illustrated books, pictures with subjects that particularly interest you (such as automobiles, boats, or birds), special movements, themes such as portraiture, nudes, or interiors.

Don't expect your attic collection of family photographs to gain in value. Portrait photography was the rage in the late 19th century. Everyone had portraits taken then. Unless the photographer is well known or the subject matter is of unusual interest, the only thing the family photograph album is good for is nostalgia.

Source: Daniel Wolf, photograph dealer, head of Daniel Wolf, Inc., 30 W. 57th St., New York 10019.

Group Investments In Fine Photos

Group investments in fine photos can provide a hedge against volatility in the pricing of one or two artists. An investment group of five or more people can buy a wide variety of photographers and periods.

In one such case, the group agreed to hold the prints for appreciation for five years. In the meantime, each member keeps one or two prints in his home, with the option of exchanging them for others if he tires of them. Sidelight: If an investor grows so fond of a particular print that he wants to keep it, he can purchase it from the group at the current market price.

Source: Jill Rose, photograph dealer, 1040 Fifth Ave, New York 10028

Art and Antiques As Investments

Buying an unknown artist's work for under $100 and realizing a fortune after the artist is recognized is an exciting fantasy. The realities, though, may be quite different.

Buying art solely as an investment is riskier, in many cases, than the stock market. Most art decreases in value. Over 95% of the first one-person shows in New York (or any major city) in any given season are from artists never heard from again.

With those cautions in mind, here are some ways to enter the art market.

Buy art only because you "experience" the work, have a strong reaction to it, and want to live with it. That way, if it goes up in value, you have everything to gain. If the value doesn't increase, you have the pleasure of living with it.

Educate your eye. Go to museums, galleries, take courses, get subscriptions to art or antiques publications. Since art is a new status symbol, there's a lot of visual pollution—hack work that can attract naive buyers.

Don't buy a painting because it matches the sofa.

Don't buy a painting because your neighbors are collecting "names" like Picasso or Miro.

Don't blindly follow the critics. Time is the only test of art. A critic's tastes may veer in different directions at different periods. Just because experts endorse an artist now doesn't mean they'll favor him in 10 or 20 years.

Don't be afraid to sail against the wind. Some of the biggest fortunes in art or antiques have been made by people who weren't afraid to buck the trend. (Tastes change: Paintings by the big names of the 1880s, such as Meissonier and Bourguereau, went for $65,000 back then. In the 1960s, they were down to $4,000.)

Look for periods and artists that please your own eye, but are not popular at present. Reputations change with time. Some dealers believe early Spanish painting (up to the Baroque era) is being neglected and may eventually be reevaluated.

Find reputable galleries. Get the names through a dealers' association or by recommendations from respected acquaintances who are collectors. There are first-rate galleries in many cities.

Don't be intimidated by the mistaken idea that good galleries carry only "superstars." Galleries must develop fresh talent. Some galleries specialize in new artists. If it's an artist's first one-man show, it's possible to buy a work for under $1,000.

Learn to identify that elusive characteristic called quality:

The painting is in good condition. It has not been heavily restored or retouched.

It has a history that adds to its lustre. (It was in a museum or important collection.)

It gives you a wonderful feeling.

Bargaining is not uncommon. Sometimes you are wasting your time—the price is non-negotiable.

Best time to make a gallery deal: May or June. Dealers are more receptive because they want to unload their inventories and make buying trips to Europe and elsewhere to purchase more art and antiques.

Develop a relationship with your art or antiques dealer. Once he knows your taste and pocketbook, he may give you first pick of new works. Many dealers enjoy helping to build an outstanding collection.

Getting a better buy at auctions: Study the catalog and check presale estimates. Determine the works you intend to bid on and the maximum price you intend to pay for each purchase in which you are interested. Don't deviate from these plans.

Source: Milton Esterow, publisher, *Artnews, Antiques World,* The Art Newsletter.

Collector Bargains In American Antiques

No matter what you pay for fine new furniture, its market value drops the moment you take possession. Moreover, new furniture costs continue to soar. Prime reason: Scarcity of fine woods. Two years ago, a quality manufacturer paid $40,000 for one walnut tree. That extraordinary log was shaved into veneer for top-of-the-line pieces. (The problem isn't new: The densest, finest cabinet wood the world has known, plum-pudding mahogany from Santo Domingo, was almost gone by the late 1700s).

Instead of new furniture, undervalued American antiques are the better buy. Many are priced competitively with new furniture. Other pieces, expensive but not exorbitant, are good bets to appreciate within a few years. Moreover, the workmanship is excellent. What you choose will have aesthetic as well as monetary value. Examples:

Federal. Circa 1815 to 1835. Formal and austere. Often in Hepplewhite and Sheraton styles. A Connecticut dealer finds it "grossly underpriced." Representative price: $700 to $1000 for a sturdy Sheraton worktable.

Late Federal. Known as Empire. Massive, often large in scale. Relatively unpopular. If it pleases your eye and your house can take a large piece, it may be a bargain. (Recommended by a Midwestern museum curator.)

Gothic Revival. Victorian style from the last quarter of the 19th century. One Texas dealer says it is "undiscovered by 75% of the antique-buying public." Good pieces, he finds, can be bought for less than $1,000.

Wicker. 19th and early 20th centuries. Both fancy and austere styles. Unpainted wicker is worth more than painted. Look for paper labels, which enhance value.

Patented furniture. Example: Folding chairs from the late 19th century. George Hunzinger's work is well known and expensive. But hundreds of other cabinetmakers held patents too. Most pieces bear a label or mark and can be traced through patent records.

Although it is expeditious to get in on the ground floor of a style, beware of investing too enthusiastically at first. Reason: When a style resurfaces, it takes even the experts a while to distinguish the best from the mediocre. Eventually the inflated, poorer items will drop in price. Examples: Some arts and crafts, and 19th-century oak. A California dealer says that oak rolltop desks, which brought $2,000 not long ago, are selling now for $1,000, when they change hands at all.

Recommendations:

Look for the style you want in an area where there is little demand for it. Examples: French 18th-century furniture in California. Middle-range Windsor and other country furniture at city, not country, auctions.

Examine a piece very carefully. Pay special attention to construction, the state of inlay and veneer, and signs of dry rot or infestation.

Buy the very best, the absolute top of the line, insofar as your funds allow. The masterpiece is always underpriced.

What Makes A Book Valuable?

Not all first editions or rich-looking, old, leather-bound volumes have much value. Collecting fine books takes a lot of knowledge. It best suits book lovers, not general investors. Reason: Books, in most cases, haven't appreciated as quickly or as much as most art, stamps, and rare coins.

It's a gamble to buy contemporary first editions and expect they will increase in value. For instance: A first edition of John Steinbeck's *East of Eden,* in good condition and with a dust jacket, is worth a couple of hundred dollars. But if you go out and buy a first edition of a current Ann Beattie novel and expect it to appreciate, after a couple of decades you may find it's worth no more than you paid for it. Value increases according to how future literary critics rank new author Beattie and what the demand is for her early books.

Book rarity: It often bears little or no relationship to value. Example: A first edition of an obscure 19th-century poet with only 200 copies extant may have no value. But John James Audubon volumes or Samuel Johnson's *Dictionary* appreciate every year even though they are plentiful.

Condition: This is very important in determining value. A perfect dust jacket can make the difference between a $500 book and a $1,500 one.

To keep books in condition, store them away from sunlight and humidity. If they get worms, museums and libraries offer fumigation services.

Best strategy for collecting books: Buy books that dovetail into a single concept. Examples: 20th-century American literature, Western Americana, science books, nautical books, Victorian children's books. Reason: Once the collection becomes large enough (say 250 volumes), the whole collection frequently becomes more valuable then the sum of its parts.

Trends: As with paintings, different periods generate different amounts of interest. Currently, American 20th-century authors are in vogue, as in Western Americana. Ernest Hemingway first editions go for several hundred dollars, J.D. Salinger about $100, and F. Scott Fitzgerald even more. However, although 20th-century literature has been increasing in price significantly faster than inflation, it will probably slow down soon. Collecting popular categories is always expensive and may not prove to be the best use of funds.

Undervalued periods and authors have greater potential for appreciation. Aldous Huxley, Robert Louis Stevenson, Nathaniel Hawthorne, James Fenimore Cooper, Stephen Crane, and Edna St. Vincent Millay are all out of vogue now. You can probably assemble a collection of their first editions at a reasonable price.

An author's inscription adds hundreds of dollars to the value of the book.

Books with artwork tend to outpace the market. Especially interesting: Victorian children's books, and botany books, Audubon books, and architecture books. Reason: There is a double-edged market of book collectors and people who want to sell the pictures for framing.

Myths about fine and rare books and first editions:

When an author dies, the value of the books goes up. Not necessarily. Demand is the key factor. There are exceptions. When John F. Kennedy was shot, first editions of *Profiles in Courage* skyrocketed. However, their price has since come down.

Limited-edition book clubs are a good way of collecting. Not true. These books rarely increase in value.

Any book more than 50 years old is valuable. False. Bibles must have been printed before 1615 to be worth much. Encyclopedias are worth more new than old.

You can pick up bargains at flea markets and in yard sales. Rarely. Even fleamarket dealers know the value of any first edition. The only way to find something under market value is to educate yourself very well.

To find out whether a book you own is valuable: Contact an auction house or fine-book dealer. Information needed: (1) The name of the book. (2) Its condition. (3) The place it was published. (4) Any distinguishing notes (autograph, dedication, etc.).

If you want to sell a book or a collection: You can use an auction house or a bookstore that deals in fine books. The advantage of a bookstore is that you'll be paid immediately and the price is preset. At an auction house you may have to wait months before the sale, and you may be disappointed with price you get.

Source: Peter Mallary, expert in Early Americana, Sotheby Parke Bernet, 980 Madison Ave., New York 10021; George S. Lowry, president, Swann Galleries, Inc., 104 E. 25 St., New York 10010; Judith Lowry, first-edition expert, Argosy Book Store, Inc., 116 E. 59 St., New York 10022.

Buying and Keeping Leather-Bound Books

Basics for buying and keeping old volumes bound in leather:

Before purchasing a leather-bound book, check its condition carefully. Essentials: Be sure no pages are missing. Make certain the book has not already undergone commercial restoration. Trap: If leather is brittle or powdery, reject the book. It cannot be restored adequately.

Remember that old leather bindings need special care. To aid preservation: Clean away dust with a soft brush. Apply leather protector (potassium lactate). When dry, apply a small amount of leather dressing (either lanolin or neatsfoot oil).

To repair a valuable leather-bound book, seek the services of an expert craftsman, not a commercial bookbinder. Best bet: Write to the Guild of Bookworkers, 1059 Third Ave., New York City 10021.

Profit in Postcards

From the 1880s until the 1920s, collecting postcards was just a popular hobby. Now, interest in postcards is growing rapidly. Price range: Most cards that collectors want are still under one dollar. Yet prices are rising. The most desirable ones have gone up 25% each year for a decade. Some are now considered investment vehicles. Examples: An Alphonse Mucha postcard, advertising the bicycle product Waverly Cycles, sold for $3,000, a record.

Building a collection: Start with a theme. It could be history, fashion, or street scenes.

Criteria for choosing: Condition is very important. The card should be clean, with no creases, tears, or missing pieces. In the U.S. before 1907, it was illegal to write anything but the address on the back of a card. For collection purposes, if writing appears on the front, in a space reserved for it, fine. But if a message is scrawled over the picture, that lowers the value.

Keeping the collection in shape: Most are stored in shoe boxes, but shoe-box paper is not acid-free. (Acid destroys paper.) Albums should be of acid-free paper, too. As to the new albums, with clinging plastic sheets that hold a card in place, we don't know how effective they are for storing postcards. I keep my cards loose, in steel filing cabinets, and handle them very carefully, with clean hands.

Sets and series: In general, each card of a complete set is worth 1½ times more than a single of that set.

Expensive categories:

Foreign propaganda postcards. Example: The bigoted cartoons made in Germany after Adolf Hitler came to power. Incidentally, Hitler had artistic approval of all cards made in Germany. Either the cards pleased him, or they weren't printed. Cost: $25 and up.

Art Nouveau and Art Deco advertising images. Cost: $8 to $20 each.

Finding cards: Card collecting is international. Hobby clubs are everywhere. Our club meets monthly and has a newsletter, guest speakers, and card exchanges. We sponsor two shows a year.

Selling cards: If you have inherited a sizable collection, take it to a show or a dealer. Dealers are hungry for good merchandise.

The hottest collectibles: Photo postcards. They were usually taken amateurishly by family members. The developing was done at home, and the cards were printed on postcard-backed printing paper. These cards flourished from the turn of the century up until the 1940s. The least desirable in this hot category are photos of proud parents with their new baby. They are in the one dollar range. A fine example: A butcher shop, with the butcher posed with his wares. Value: $10 to $15.

Source: Leah Schnall, dealer, and president, Metropolitan Postcard Club, 401 E. 65 St., New York 10021.

Collecting Baseball Cards

Prize baseball cards rose in price by 500% in just two years. A 1910 Honus Wagner has sold for $12,000. The American Tobacco Co. issued the cards. Wagner, a vehement anti-smoker, sued successfully to have his image withdrawn. Only 561 cards were printed. Other valuable players: Nap Lajoie, 1934, $6,500; Jim Konstanty, 1951, $2,500; Mickey Mantle, 1952, $1,700. If you collected run-of-the-mill cards in the 1950s and 1960s, they are worth $2 to $3 each now.

Valuable Autographs

Signatures of famous people are collector's items that hold their value in good times and bad. But autograph collecting is not limited to just signatures. Look for signed letters, documents, manuscripts, and photographs.

How to start:

Scout local dealers and collectors. Auction galleries often specialize in autographs.

Search through attics and antique shops.

Write to celebrities who appeal to you and request their signatures.

Most valuable:

Rare signatures. For example, the autographs of Button Gwinnett and Thomas Lynch Jr. are now worth $100,000 each. Reason: They are both Founding Fathers who died shortly after they signed the Declaration of Independence.

Signatures from Hollywood's Golden Age of 1920s and 1930s. An autographed photo of Clark Gable is valued at $200. A handwritten letter from Greta Garbo may be worth more than one signed by Abraham Lincoln. An autographed Garbo photograph fetches up to $1,000.

Sports heroes. The only field of real value is baseball. Top signatures: Babe Ruth and Lou Gehrig. Suggestion: For the autograph of ballplayer enshrined in the Hall of Fame, write to him: c/o The Baseball Hall of Fame, Cooperstown, NY 13326.

Famous criminals. An autographed photo of Al Capone sold recently for $750. A document signed by Adolf Hitler brings $500. A deportation order signed by Adolf Eichmann is currently valued at twice that price.

Historical documents. These vary in value according to the occasion. General Eisenhower's signed announcement of victory in Europe changed hands for $45,000. A document signed by Napoleon goes for $500.

For further information: Write to the renowned autograph dealer Charles Hamilton for his brochure, *How to Sell Your Autographs,* 25 E. 77th St., New York 10021.

Other Autograph Resources

The Universal Autograph Collectors Club, Box 467, Rockville Centre, NY 11571. They offer an informative publication that appears six times each year.

Manuscript Society, 429 Daisy Ave., Pasadena, CA 91107. Annual membership includes a quarterly publication.

Leading dealers:

Academy Book Store, 10 W. 18 St., New York 10011.

Antiquarian Book Sellers Center, 50 Rockefeller Plaza, New York 10020.

Archives & Historical Autographs, 119 Chestnut Hill Rd., Wilton, CT 06897

Cambridge-Essex Stamp Co., 500 Eighth Ave., New York 10018.

Edmunds Book Shop, 6658 Hollywood Blvd., Hollywood, CA 90028.

James Lowe Autographs, 667 Madison Ave., New York 10021.

Kenneth W. Rendell, Inc., 154 Wells Ave., Newton, MA 02159.

Kover King, Inc., 120 W. 44 St., New York 10036.

Lion Heart Autographs, 150 Fifth Ave., New York 10011.

The Scriptorium, 427 N. Cannon Dr., Beverly Hills, CA 90210.

Postage Stamp Bargain Hunting

Begin by reading the standard stamp catalogs and several books on stamp collecting, too. Then get to know your local stamp dealers. Compare the prices that your local dealers are quoting with catalog prices. When you find a bargain, check the stamp for its condition and, if it's satisfactory, snap it up.

The process is slow and time-consuming. But stamp collections assembled on a bargain basis appreciate on the average of 15% a year.

Stamps being hunted by collectors:

British and Commonwealth Nation stamps. Their values are climbing rapidly.

Stamps whose demand will increase because of anniversaries coming up soon. Example: In 1976, shrewd collectors saw that the next year, on the 50th anniversary of the occasion, the 1927 stamps honoring Lindbergh's flight across the Atlantic would soar in value. They did. Target: Stamps commemorating events with round-number anniversaries coming up.

First day covers. These are stamp-bearing envelopes put out in very limited numbers to be postmarked at one post office only the first day a stamp goes into circulation.

Offbeat philatelic items. Trick here is to guess what stamps are not valued now that will be valued in future. This game comes close to pure speculation, but winners are handsomely rewarded financially and psychically.

Remember: You must buy at retail and sell at wholesale prices. Therefore, consider the dealer markups, which are as high as 50%. Generally, markups are less for expensive stamps and more for the inexpensive ones.

Collectibles Under $500: American Art Pottery

Shortly after the Civil War, American art pottery originated in a Cincinnati factory named Rookwood. As a reaction against the Industrial Revolution, it was deliberately meant to be artistic rather than commercial. Art pottery features striking glazes. Some pieces are handthrown, while others are machine-made and glazed by artists.

Prices: Depend on the maker and where you find the piece. Why: You may find very important pieces in good New York galleries like Jordan Volpe, but they may cost thousands of dollars. However, since many people are unaware of the value of art pottery, you may find pieces for under $100 at country auctions and garage sales.

Before buying: Research to develop your eye.* Some museums have collections of American pottery.

For the best collection: Find a style you like and a price range you are comfortable with. Point: Since they are not masterpieces, you must get a group of similar pieces to look impressive. Possibilities: All the same shape with different glazes.Or, all the same glaze with different shapes.

Some important styles:

Rookwood: 1880 to 1949. Decorative vases

---

*A good reference book is *The Guide to American Art Pottery* by Ralph and Terry Kovel, Crown Publishers, New York.

and tiles. The early pieces are handpainted and signed by the artist. Those pieces sell for up to $10,000. Caution: Some pieces marked with dates from 1880 to 1886 and impressed with the Rookwood symbol are actually copies made in the late 1960s. But you can still buy legitimate pieces for around $500.

Ohr: 1883 to 1906. Handmade pottery with unusual, eccentric and delicate shapes. Many resemble today's modern art. Prices are going up very quickly for the work of this man who called himself the world's greatest potter. There's great collector interest in these pieces. You can still buy small pieces for $500.

Grueby: 1897 to 1920. They made natural and organic shapes in art pottery and tiles. Most famous: Cucumber-green matte glaze. Few sell for less than $1,000, but you might find small pieces for $500.

Clifton: 1901 to 1910. These are signed and dated. If you are lucky, you may find one for $200. Look for Crystal Patina and Indian Ware. They are getting rarer, as many have been broken or lost (a common problem).

Teco: 1902 to 1923. The Teco glaze (almost always a matte green) is not nearly as important as the form of the piece. The factory produced art tiles for Frank Lloyd Wright. There are still some pieces for under $500.

Niloak: 1909 to 1946. All pieces have been handturned from multicolored clays. Cost $90 to $300.

Fulper: 1910 to 1935. Mass-produced but individually glazed. You can still find pieces for under $500. Major pieces sell for as much as $2,000.

Source: Barbara Schwartz, ASID and Barbara Ross, ASID, principals of Dexter Design, 133 E. 58 St., New York 10022, an interior design firm that serves both the office and residential market. They also advise clients on art and collecting.

Collecting Classic Perfume Bottles

A 1930s Guerlain bottle and a two-ounce L'Air du Temps bottle have sold for $300 each. What to look for: Was the bottle produced by Baccarat or Lalique? Check the bottom for their names. Is the stopper ground glass or plastic? Is the particular perfume still being manufactured? If not, the bottle will be worth more. Is the bottle unusual, beautiful, or amusing? Does the bottle still have the label? Do you have the box it was packed in, and perhaps a bit of the original fragrance?

Collecting Political Americana

Political Americana is a rapidly growing hobby. Two categories:

1.Presidential campaign artifacts. Examples: Buttons, posters, related mementos.

Commemoratives or historical political materials from before the 1820s when presidential aspirants didn't campaign. Examples: Inaugural souvenirs, patriotic textiles, coins, etc.

Highly prized items: Those dealing with the most popular political figures. And the rare leftovers of obscure candidates.

The most popular memorabilia: The early presidential candidates such as Andrew Jackson, Abraham Lincoln, William Jennings Bryan, Theodore Roosevelt, Eugene Debs, and Al Smith. Also, Franklin D. Roosevelt, Harry Truman, John F. Kennedy.

Candidates with the least available material: John Quincy Adams, John Tyler, Martin Van Buren, Horace Greeley, Levi Cass, John Davis, Franklin Pierce.

How to begin collecting: Gather indiscriminately at first. This teaches you about American political-campaign history. Aid: Keep a comprehensive scrapbook during the current campaign season while publications are full of anecdotal accounts of past politics. Save only genuine materials. Resist fakes, no matter how showy.

Auction catalogs detail price trends for different items. To buy catalogs, write: The Americana Mail Auction, 4015 Kilmer Ave., Allentown, PA 18104.

Collectors' club: American Political Items Club, c/o Robert Fratkin, 2322 20 St. NW, Washington, DC 20009.

More information: *Collecting Political Americana*, by Edmund B. Sullivan, Crown Publishers, New York.

Tomorrow's Classic Cars

Auto collecting requires much less than the $50,000-or-so price of many models now considered classics. Instead: Purchase those that many experts see as classics of the future. Examples: Lotus Europa, Lotus Elan, Jaguar E-Type or 140. Also: Mini Coopers, Triumph TR-3s, MGAs, and Bugeye Sprites. Caution: The classic car market is unpredictable. Note: A car must be restored to near-perfect condition to command top prices.

Source: *Autoweek.*

Collecting Rare Paper Money

Although some collectors spend thousands of dollars for bank notes, a collection can be started for as little as $100.

What makes the notes valuable:

Condition of the bills. Professionals have a strict grading system, with perfect new notes given at UNC (uncirculated) or CU (crisp uncirculated) code at the top.

Rarity. Scarce American bills have the most value.

Unusual serial numbers. Examples: Notes with all one number (22222222). Or, with numbers in sequence (12345678). Or, with very low numbers (a note normally worth $1,500 sold for $11,500 because its serial number was 0000002).

High face-value of unstable countries in Asia and Africa. Why: These countries often

341

outlaw exportation of money. This creates shortages and drives up the value of the bills. Rule of thumb: When collecting foreign bills, avoid low-denomination notes.

Bonus for bank-note collecting: The notes are easy to mail or carry, which is important in reaching overseas markets.

Best market for buying or selling notes: Fellow investors in the United States.

More information: The International Bank Note Society, c/o Milan Alusic, Box 1222 Racine, WI 53405; The Society of Paper Money Collectors, Box 4082, Harrisburg, PA 17111.

Identifying Counterfeit Gold Coins

The output of counterfeit coins has risen sharply.

To avoid getting stuck:

Study real examples of the coins you're in the market for.

Buy only from accredited coin dealers. Experienced dealers can spot even the best counterfeits.

Be especially wary of buying rare coins overseas.

If in doubt about a coin, have it authenticated by the American Numismatic Association Certification Services, 818 N. Cascade, Colorado Springs, CO 80903.

Getting the Most For Old Gold and Silver

The formulas that dealers use to determine what they'll pay you for gold and silver items are closely held secrets. Warning: You'll never get the full market value. Often, they'll offer more than half. Advice: Get at least two appraisals before selling.

Determining factors:

Weight and purity: Fourteen-karat gold is 58.33% pure. Eighteen-karat gold is 75% pure. Twenty-four karat gold is 99.9% pure. Sterling silver is 92.5% bullion.

Cost of doing business: The appraiser's time, overhead, smelting costs, and profits are all informally figured into the price quoted.

Market trends: With highly volatile bullion markets, the dealer has to second-guess what prices will be when he's ready to sell.

Antique value: Rarely a consideration, since most jewelry and flatware are worth more melted down. Reminder: Appraisers care nothing about family heirlooms or design. But most of them can recognize pieces that are worth more than their bullion content.

Fair price: For bullion by weight, 65% to 75% of the going rate.

Investing in Diamonds

Investment-grade diamonds are an alternative to gold, silver, and collectibles as a hedge against inflation and hold up particularly well in periods of recession. Diamonds are less volatile than precious metals. (Reason: DeBeers has a virtual monopoly on the wholesale diamond market.) Some international investors find diamonds attractive because they are very easy to transport and can often be sold without any record. However, diamonds are also a much more complicated investment than silver or gold.

Determine whether the investment fits your needs. Diamonds can only bring capital appreciation. If you need income, choose something else. Financial planners recommend that investors keep no more than 10% of their net worth in diamonds.

Expect to hold on to diamonds for at least two years. In an unusual year, like 1979, diamonds appreciated fast enough to outpace both inflation and the dealer's commission. But normally, even with good appreciation, you must hold it for two years to make it pay.

Study the grades and characteristics of diamonds. Each one is unique. Your investment is only as good as the quality of the stone. Investment-grade stones should be certified by an independent lab such as the Gemological Institute of America. Avoid dealers who don't provide certification.

Diamonds are rated on four characteristics, which determine their value and liquidity:

Carat weight: A carat is 1/5 of a gram, or 1/142 of an ounce. Diamonds over a carat offer more liquidity. Historically they have had the greatest appreciation. Some firms warn against buying any stone under a carat for investment. However, others believe that half-carat stones and larger will be the next group to experience a large price runup.

Avoid stones that are under half a carat. It is doubtful that they will have any major price rise. Trap: Diamonds that are just short of a carat (.96 to .99). They are much less valuable than a one-carat stone.

Color: The finest stones are white. Stones are grades from D to Z (colorless to murky yellow). Conservative investors believe H to be the lowest worthwhile investment. Some risk-oriented investors believe I and J will have some future appreciation. The top grades are the most liquid.

Clarity: There are flaws in all diamonds. Flawless means there are no imperfections visible under a microscope that magnifies ten times. VVS1 and VVS2 have very slight flaws seen under a 10x microscope and are considered sound. The lower quality VS1 and VS2 stones are shaky investments, since they are much more plentiful than VVS1 and VVS2 diamonds.

Cut: The cut of a diamond is extremely important in determining its value. The greatest demand is for round, brilliant-cut stones. The depth and symmetry of the stone should be in proper relation to each other to maximize the brilliance.

Expect dealers to charge a percentage over the wholesale price. That charge can vary from 5% to 40%. The wholesale price varies also. Despite quotations, which now appear in *The Wall Street Journal* each Monday, dealers may ask different prices. Reason: The quota-

tions are approximate. Check for the best price.

Colored gems are a very speculative investment. Although rubies, emeralds, and sapphires have appreciated along with diamonds recently, there is no uniform grading system for them, and their prices are extremely unpredictable. But some investors believe that their scarcity may eventually make them an even better investment than diamonds.

Source: Issac Jaroslawicz, vice-president, NYDEX (New York Diamond Exchange), 10 W. 47th St., New York 10036, and Barry Rosenblum, president, and Peter Pizer, chairman, Diamonds Under Glass, 163 South St., Hackensack, NJ 07601

Caring for Diamonds

Even though diamonds are the hardest natural substance, they require special care to prevent damage and to keep them looking their best. Suggestions: Remove rings when doing manual work. Have your jeweler periodically check the mountings.

It is also important to clean diamonds at regular intervals. Methods:

Using mild detergent and warm water, you should rub it with a soft brush and dry with a lint-free cloth.

Soak for 30 minutes in a 50-50 solution of cold water and ammonia.

Dip the diamond into a commercial liquid cleaner, which is available from jewelers.

Use an ultrasonic cleaner, which is also commercially available.

Hidden Pitfalls In Jewelry Insurance

Insuring good jewelry specifically against theft can be costly if the loss results from another catastrophe. Problem: Once a sepa-

343

rate schedule covering the theft of particular pieces is added to the policy, the same valuation formula is used to determine reimbursement for loss of those pieces due to any other cause.

Example: A $20,000 ring lost in a fire is reimbursed at its full appraised value (to the policy limits). However, if the ring were insured against theft under a separate schedule for $10,000, reimbursement after the fire would be only $10,000.

Recommended: If the chance of having jewelry stolen is slight, consider not insuring it against theft.

Source: *Insurance Marketing.*

Selling Family Jewels

Avoid retail jewelers who won't offer much more than 20% below wholesale value. Better: Offer the jewels on consignment through a jeweler who takes a 10% to 15% commission. Best: Sell by advertising in newspapers and spreading the word among friends and associates. Caution: Don't keep jewels at home or list home address in an ad (a surefire bait for burglars). Important: Have a third party hold the jewels until the buyer's check clears (including cashier's checks). Next best: Offer items through a reputable auction house. They provide free appraisals and estimate the likely price. Auctioneers receive a 10% commission.

Selecting a Jewelry Appraiser

Avoid appraisers whose fee is a percentage of the jewelry's value. They are too likely to overappraise to boost their own fees. Additional trap: The owner's insurance company won't pay the overvaluation if the piece is lost. Note: Frequent appraisals are essential if

insurance coverage is to keep up with inflation.

Treasures in Your Attic

• Check your junk. Look for: First-edition books, old records, real fountain pens, 1950s comic books, original Popeye memorabilia, and so on. Before you price or sell the object, see what some antique and junk shops are charging. Reason: Only a professional can see the difference between worthless pieces and those that are valuable. Good guides: *Kovel's Complete Antiques Guide* (Crown Publishers, 1 Park Ave., New York 10016), and *Insider's Guide to Antiques, Art and Collectibles* (Cornerstone Library, 1230 Ave. of the Americas, New York 10020).

• Antique slot machines now sell for $1,500 or more and have been appreciating at 10% to 30% per year. Most states permit individuals to own slot machines but not to put them into commercial gambling use.

• Those old fishing lures with wooden bodies, handpainted finishes, glass eyes, hook hangers, and metal lips have been replaced by modern plastic bait paraphernalia. Now they are increasing in value as collectibles.

More information: The National Fishing Lure Collectors Club, 707 West Ave., Austin TX 78701.

• Antique trade cards have been collected as works of art since their introduction in the early 1880s. These colorful, tiny billboards of the past were created by American manufacturers who needed to advertise their products. The cards were distributed by local storekeepers. The front of the card is a once-novel, full-color illustration of the product, usually surrounded by children, beautiful women, or domestic animals. The back invariably contains stirring sales copy. Rare cards, including Currier and Ives editions, bring $10 and up.

Source: *American Collection.*

• Doll collecting is no longer child's play. A French turn-of-the century Bru Bebe, purchased 10 years earlier for $600, sold at auction in 1979 for $6,000. Though prices of china dolls are soaring, cloth and rag dolls are still affordable and likely to rise in value. Finds: Dolls made by Lenci and Chase.

Source: *American Collector.*

Establishing the Value Of Your Collection

Even if you don't plan to sell the objects, an evaluation is useful. Reasons:

As part of estate planning.

For insurance purposes in case of theft, fire, or flood.

For use as deductible donations.

Guidelines for exploring the value of potential collectibles:

Determine if the item is a collectible. Check encyclopedias of collecting to see if your object is included. Important: Keep the dominant design motif in mind, because many collectors specialize. An antique mirror ornamented with an eagle may be worth one price to a mirror collector, but a different one to an American eagle specialist.

Visit museums and historical societies. They won't price the object, but they can help you identify it and offer opinions about its age, authenticity, and in many cases, famous collections extant. Also, visit antique dealers to price similar items.

Prepare the piece for evaluation. Don't do more than take a color snapshot and have several prints made. Without expert assistance, never clean, repair, or alter a piece. That is likely to impair and reduce its value, especially if it belongs to one of those categories whose devotees prefer signs of aging.

Check potential value. The best method is to get an expert appraisal. Caution: Never settle for a single assessment, especially if the appraiser might be a potential buyer. Look for appraisers who charge a specified fee. Avoid those who want a percentage of the item's estimated value, which is a temptation to overestimate the piece. Best bet: Consult a member of the American Society of Appraisers. Write for their free directory: American Society of Appraisers, Dulles Airport, Box 17265, Washington, DC 20041.

Ask the art dealer for records on the prices paid at auction for any work by an artist you are in interested in acquiring. A good dealer will have a market catalog if any of the artist's work has been auctioned fairly recently. And that's the best guide to reveal value.

Other possibilities: Check the prices in catalogs. For traditional collectibles, there are excellent guides to recent prices. For newer specialties, catalogs range from highly professional to spurious. Remember, all prices quoted are estimates. You may be able to get more or less, depending upon current demand and also geographic locale. (New York is the antique center; the Midwest is best for memorabilia.) You can also send a photograph of the piece to a reputable auction house.

Safeguarding Collectibles

You may regard your collectibles—paintings, porcelains, stamps, coins, old books, jewelry, etc.—mainly for the enjoyment they bring you. But with their values soaring, there are precautions you should take.

Recommendations: Keep an up-to-date listing (both at home and in your safe-deposit box) of when and where each item was bought and what was paid. Include, too, a full description (with photo, if possible) of the item that should cover its history, current appraised value, any additional costs incurred, and where it is kept.

Keep the bills of sale in your safe-deposit box.

It may be desirable to store your smaller collectibles in a safe-deposit box. Check if the bank or the insurance policy insures the item while it's in a vault.

Learn from the experts how best to keep

your collection clean and resistant to temperature changes, and what the best methods of storage are. (Good books are available for guidance for almost every type of collectible.)

Mark the collection somehow with your name, Social Security number, or other identification, to help recovery of your valuables if they are lost or stolen.

Protect rare coins by using Plexiglas or Mylar holders. Caution: Avoid using cheap plastic holders made with polyvinyl chloride (PVC). Reason: The vapor emitted from these holders turns copper coins green, which reduces their value.

Cleaning delicate antiques. To wash valuable porcelain objects, use equal parts of high-quality ammonia and water. Rinse and dry with a soft cloth. Note: If the objects have gilt trim, *don't* use ammonia. Instead: Use a mild synthetic detergent and warm water. Rinse with distilled water, and dry with soft cloth. For delicate glass or crystal, wash with warm soapy water, then air-dry. Don't rinse off the soap, which serves as a lubricant.

Cleaning antique rugs. Vacuum once a month, using a machine with a low-suction or brush attachment. For gentler cleaning: Use a carpet sweeper. In cold climates, throw the rug upside down on the snow. Tap softly on the rug with a broom handle. Take up the rug and see the dirt and dust left on the snow. Note: Don't try this with fragile, worn rugs.

The Basics Of Collecting Plates

Collectors' plates are now one of the mainstay categories of the collectors' market.

Why: Plates can be beautiful. As works of art they are small, easy to display, and are not difficult to move.

Collecting rules: With the rising interest in collectibles, there are signs of glut in the collector's plate market. So, buy carefully:

Limit the selection to plates whose "edition limit" has been announced. The limit announcement should be in numbers. Don't buy anything in which the limits are vague, for example, "firing days."

Avoid plates decorated with copies of original work done by artists for other purposes.

Aim for decorations by artists with good reputations in the collectors' plate world.

Buy plates when they're first issued. You'll get the best bargains if you do this.

Ask the dealer if you can take the plate on a trial basis for several days to see if, in addition to buying the plate as an investment, you actually like living with it on display. Like all collectibles, it may be difficult to sell, and you may have to live with it for a long time. And plates, although they provide much pleasure to the eye, don't collect interest or dividends, unlike savings accounts and stocks.

13

You and Your Automobile

Motorist Do's and Don'ts

• Don't use dealer financing plan to buy a car. Borrowing from a bank, a credit union, or against an insurance policy costs much less.

• Don't buy a factory-installed AM/FM radio. They're priced too high and not very good. Instead, order the least expensive AM radio plus stereo speakers. This provides the necessary wiring. Then buy and have installed a quality radio and speakers.

• Best time to buy a car is after the first severe winter weather of the year, especially snowstorms. Sales are slow then, and automobile dealers are very eager to move their stock.

• Testing new car for leaks: Put some clean white paper (shelf paper is good) under the whole car at night. Don't worry about clear spots, which are likely to be moisture which has condensed around the air conditioner. Oily pink leaks are likely to be transmission fluid. Dark leaks are engine oil. Dry pink leaks are gasoline. Engine coolants leaks depend on what color the coolant is, either yellow-green or pink.

• Fanbelt adjustment test: Press your thumb down on the belt at the midpoint between the pulleys. You should be able to press the belt in about a half-inch by pressing down moderately. (If more or less, an adjustment is necessary.) Also, always carry an extra belt in the trunk.

• Synthetic lubricants are a better buy in the long run than natural products. Advantages: Better reduction of friction and absorption of engine contaminants. Users report as much as 50,000 miles driving between oil changes. And there is little evidence of wear on engines that have logged 250,000 miles.

• Radial tires signal impending trouble before they blow out. Early warning signs: Difficult or erratic steering, rough ride under normal conditions, or a bulge on the tire.

• Sell your old car yourself rather than trade it in. The dealer will only allow wholesale value on the car or even less.

• Lengthen the life of old windshield-wiper blades by rubbing the edges with a knife or the striking part of a matchbook cover. This exposes the softer material underneath and improves wiping ability.

347

• Preserve the car's finish by washing it with cold or lukewarm water. But never wash the finish with hot water, which may damage the finish in some way.

• Run the air conditioner at least 10 minutes every week. This procedure will maintain coolant pressure and avoid costly air conditioner breakdowns.

• When you stop for service, get out of the car and watch gas station attendants carefully, particularly if you have an out-of-state license. When the oil is checked, make sure the dipstick is inserted all the way. Reason: Some attendants may show you a dipstick that indicates oil is low, then use an empty can and pretend to add a quart of oil.

• Never fill up while gasoline station is getting delivery of fuel. Reason: Gas pumped in stirs up sediment that has settled on the bottom of the dealer's tanks. Recommended: When traveling, get gas where the truckers do. They usually know which are the good stations.

• Bargain tires marked "blems" are perfectly serviceable except for minor cosmetic blemishes on the sidewalls.

• Clean corrosion off battery terminals. Use a wire brush or steel wool to scrape battery posts and cable clamps. Clean the top surface with a mild solution of baking soda and water. (Don't let it seep under cell caps.)

• Prevent wind resistance, which cuts performance up to five miles per gallon, by keeping the car windows closed while driving.

• Extended auto-service plans aren't a good deal. Typical luxury-car contract covers very little. Owner pays full cost of tuneups and other maintenance plus a deductible for each repair under warranty (engine, drivetrain, etc.). Also, the owner is locked into using the dealer's repair shop.

• Substitute for dry gas on cold winter mornings when you can't get the car started: Denatured alcohol, a pint per tankful, into gasoline tank. Cheaper, too.

• Sports cars and two-door cars are much more likely to be stolen. Least likely: Four-doors in all sizes, from subcompacts to full size.

• A dealer's emblem doesn't have to be af-fixed to your car. When ordering, specify no emblem and make sure the instruction shows up clearly on the order. When you speak with the dealer on subsequent calls about one detail or another relating to delivery, remind him about the emblem so he doesn't go through with that procedure, which is almost automatic.

• Diesel fuel and gasoline shouldn't be mixed. Despite the advice of some diesel-car manufacturers, recent evidence shows that this practice is dangerous. Temptation trap: Wintertime addition of gasoline to increase diesel fuel combustibility for easier starts.

• Caring for radials: Rotate radial tires differently from bias tires to insure that they wear evenly. Bias-plys are changed front left to rear right and front right to rear left, in an X. Radials are changed front left to rear left, and front right to rear right, in two parallel lines. The bottom line: Don't mix radials and bias-ply tires. If you must, use radials as rear tires. Never mix radials and bias-plys on the same axle; the combination is dangerous.

• Start the car in neutral, not in park. Reason: There is less drag on the engine.

• Don't turn your wheels while waiting for traffic to clear before making a turn. Recommended: Keep the wheels pointing forward until you actually begin to move into the turn. Reason: If your car is hit from behind, it will go straight ahead rather than into the path of oncoming vehicles.

• Overheated car. When caught in traffic, if needle on indicator moves up or red light comes on, car can probably make it to the next service station if these steps are followed: (1) Turn off air conditioner. (2) Turn on heater to draw heat away from engine. (3) Put transmission into neutral (when stopped) and race engine slightly. Note: Check water level as soon as possible. If it's adequate, thermostat may be malfunctioning.

• Tire-changing aids. All-purpose penetrating oil helps loosen lug nuts crusted with rust. Keep a can in the trunk. Also helpful: Lifting and positioning the spare is easier with leverage. Place X-shaped lug wrench flat on the ground. Roll the tire onto it. Then, using the wrench as a two-footed crowbar, raise its other legs until the tire and lugs match up with each other.

- **Shock absorbers.** The sure sign they should be replaced is when they begin to look damp and oily. Reason: Absorbers are filled with fluid. After 40,000 to 45,000 miles, the seal holding the fluid usually gives out.

- **Keep a golf tee in your car tool kit.** Two suggested uses: (1) When removing contact points on the distributor, slip the tee into the hole in the advance plate. This keeps the just-removed screws, which could slip out of your hand, from dropping through the hole—a mishap that requires removing the entire distributor. (2) When working on the distributor, plug the tee into the end of the vacuum line while setting engine timing.

- **Scam.** A class of costly car-care products, called "sealer/lusterizers," is said to help preserve your car's exterior finish. But this claim has *not* been substantiated, at least to the satisfaction of automakers and chemical producers.

- **Rustproofing** is advisable for any new car that you plan to keep for three or more years in a corrosive climate (generally the Northeast, Snowbelt, and coastal areas of the Southeast). Note: The rustproofer should apply the spray at a pressure of 960 pounds (or higher). Otherwise the material may not adhere properly.

- **Automated car wash** may do more harm than good. Reasons: (1) Rotating brushes, if adjusted for down-sized cars, may apply too much pressure to a full-sized model and scratch the finish. (2) Many car washes use recycled water. The salt picked up from previous washings can hasten rusting. (3) Hot-wax processes can damage vinyl tops. Bottom line: Old-fashioned washing, done in the shade, is safest. Never wax vinyl tops.

- **Removing a bumper sticker.** Apply heat to the sticker. Use a cloth dipped in hot water or a hair blower. Caution: Don't hold the blower too close if the sticker is on the trunk. It could melt the paint. After the sticker is off: Wipe away the adhesive residue with mineral spirits. Note: Usually mineral spirits will not remove car paint. But before applying it to a prominent painted surface, test on a hidden part of the car.

- **Exploding batteries.** Car batteries can release explosive hydrogen fumes. (There are over 8,000 battery explosions each year.) Accidents are most likely in winter, when drivers are trying to start dead batteries with jumper cables. Safety rules: Don't smoke while attaching cables. Take off battery caps to vent gases. Remove ice before attaching cables.

- **Gasoline poisoning rise.** It's another effect of inflation, striking inept siphoners. Hospitals report a twelvefold increase in poisonings. Caution: There's no *right* way to transfer gas by sucking on a tube.

- **The safest color for cars and trucks** is yellow. It is most visible under almost all traffic conditions, particularly in fog or hard rain and at twilight. Second best: Light green. Both yellow and light-green vehicles are two to four times more visible than dark-colored cars and trucks under poor driving conditions.
Source: *Minnesota Department of Safety.*

- **Carbon-monoxide poisoning** is suspected as the cause of many of the annual 14,000 fatal single-car accidents for which there is no other apparent reason. Protective steps: Have the car's exhaust system inspected on an overhead rack twice a year, or whenever the muffler or tailpipe is damaged. Drive with a front vent or window open to let in fresh air. (This helps ward off highway hypnosis, too.) Danger signs: Shortness of breath or a slight headache while driving may indicate carbon monoxide inside the car.
Source: *The Road Ahead.*

Making the Best Deal On a New Car

Determine a fair price by figuring what that car costs the dealer. This can be done by subtracting the markup on the base sticker price (before options are added on) and then subtracting the markup on the options.

The markup on base sticker prices generally is as follows:

10% on economy cars (Chevette, Omni, Fiesta).

12% on subcompacts (Pinto, Monza).

15% on compacts (Nova, Volare, Fairmont).

16% on sporty cars (Camaro, Firebird).

18% on intermediates (Malibu, Cutlass, Granada).

20% on smaller luxury cars (Monte Carlo, Grand Prix, Thunderbird).

22% on full-size cars (Caprice, Galaxie).

25% on luxury cars (Cadillac, Lincoln).

25% on pickups and vans.

The markup option is as follows:

30% on appearance and convenience items (vinyl roof, air conditioning, power windows, radio).

20% on performance items (radials, five-speed transmission, heavy-duty suspension or cooling system).

After subtracting the markups to determine dealer cost, add $125 for dealer overhead. Add on freight charges (itemized on the sticker) and also $100 profit for the dealer (he'll still get an additional 2% rebate from the manufacturer). The final figure is what you should pay for the car you want. Shop around until you find a dealer who'll sell it for that price (give or take $100). Don't be pressured to take a car that is loaded with unnecessary options from the dealer's inventory.

Which Cars Bring The Most Injury Claims

Imported small cars are more dangerous than large models. This is confirmed by the record for insurance claims filed by persons injured in crashes.

Is the economy worth the risk? 45% of the general public think so. Contrast: Of corporate executives asked the above question, 83% said the small cars are worth the risk.

Other groups polled who also opted overwhelmingly for the riskier small cars: Investors, lenders, federal regulators, Congressional members and aides.

Source: *The Highway Loss Reduction Status Report.*

Used, Late-Model Gas Guzzlers

Big cars are generally considered to be safer and more durable and comfortable than small cars. Also, they can carry more passengers. A recent model could cost $2,000 to $6,000 less than a new small car ($4,000 to $7,000 less than a new large one). Depending on the alternative new-car purchase being considered, it would take from 4 to 20 years of extra gasoline costs to offset that initial saving.

Ideal buyer: The person who drives about 12,000 miles a year or less, requires generous passenger and trunk space, enjoys comfort and luxury, and cannot resist a true bargain.

Buying privately: The price should be about midway between wholesale and retail. New-car dealers may charge the full retail price, but you may get a better car, because they generally keep for resale the best cars they take in trade. Also, they usually can service what they sell. Refer to the monthly National Automobile Dealers Assoc. Official Used-Car Guide. It lists trade-in (wholesale), loan, and retail values for each make and model and the value of extra equipment.

Caution: Discontinued models and unpopular or unusual imports may be very attractively priced. But it may be difficult to find repair parts for them later.

Used-Car Inspection Checklist

Examine the interior for signs of wear. A worn clutch or brake pedal in a low-mileage car could mean that the odometer has been set back.

Inspect tires for uneven wear.

Sight along the sides of the car. If the line is uneven, or if the car has been painted, the car may have been in a serious accident.

Press down on the fender. If the car keeps bouncing, it may need new shocks.

Take a 15-minute test drive. Try out all controls and equipment. A slow-sinking brake could mean that there's a leak in the system. If the car moves forward at a slight angle, don't buy it. Watch for gear slippage (shift back and forth between forward and reverse several times), poor acceleration, unusual noises.

Source: *Everyone's Money Book,* by Jane Bryant Quinn, Delacorte Press, New York.

Buying a Car From a Rental Firm

Large car-rental firms sell their fleet's better used cars to the public.

The cars sold are predominantly the previous year's models. Range: From subcompact to station wagon. Check the national organization of car-rental firms for the sales locations. Since there isn't a complete selection at a specific location, call the nearby one first. They may be able to tell when a certain model will arrive or offer to get it from another location.

Caution: Prices and warranties can vary dramatically from firm to firm.

Since there is much suspicion about the abuse rental cars take from poor drivers, buyers are supplied with a record of all service that's ever been performed on the car. Policy: If $700 or more has been spent on repairing body damage or on recurring maintenance problems, then the rental company will not sell the car to the general public.

Some firms give a weekend rental period, enabling a potential buyer to test the car. This gives the buyer the opportunity to get an independent opinion about the car and to review its service record. The price of the weekend's rental can be applied to the car's cost.

Leasing vs. Buying

No matter what car-rental agencies claim, leasing costs about 20% more over three years than a direct purchase.

Misconception: Leasing provides tax breaks not available from ownership. Truth: All business driving expenses are deductible, no matter who owns the car.

Leasing does make sense when:

The owner of a company uses the car mostly for business. Caution: Personal use of the car has to be paid for.

The business needs several cars, but lacks the cash to cover the down payments. Leasing also helps keep the balance sheet healthier.

The trouble and time required to buy and maintain a car are headaches. A lessee can just order a car, swap it for a loaned one when necessary, and get a new car every two to three years automatically.

An accident has forced you into the assigned-risk pool and insurance is going to cost a lot more. The leasing companies may provide coverage for less.

Details: (1) Full-maintenance contracts are usually not worth the cost. (2) Check the contract carefully for surcharges on driving over a certain number of miles a year. (3) Evaluate a lease for total costs, not just the monthly payments.

Options on a New Car: How to Decide

The value of an optional feature depends on how, when, and where most of the driving will be done.

Important for everyone: Options that make the car safer, such as steel-belted radial tires. They hold the road better, provide better fuel economy and longer life. Another important safety feature: Day/night mirror.

Important, but not essential:

Disc brakes. Stand up to repeated hard use under big loads, but are not really necessary for city driving.

Cruise control. Great advantage for long distances regularly. Sets pace and helps avoid speeding tickets.

Air conditioning. Important for comfort

and for car's subsequent resale value. (Nobody wants a used car without air conditioning.)

Radio. Recommended for resale value, even if not a high-priority extra.

Heavy-duty suspension system. Makes the car feel taut and firm and holds the road better. Little initial cost and little value on resale. Important for car owners who are going to carry heavy loads, or who love to drive and are sensitive to car's performance. Not important for those whose car use is limited mainly to trips to the supermarket.

Power seats. Extremely useful feature for drivers who go long distances regularly. Permits moving the seat back. Allows arm position in relation to steering wheel to be manipulated and fine-tuned. In some ways a safety factor because it helps ward off fatigue.

Adjustable seat back. Some form of this is highly recommended. Wards off fatigue and thus is a safety element.

Tilt steering wheel. Another aid in fine-tuning the driver's relation to car and therefore recommended as a safety factor. Important for large or short people.

Electric door locks. Key unlocks all doors simultaneously. Button locks all doors at once, including trunk lid. A convenience. Makes it unnecessary to open each door from outside in bad weather. When driving through dangerous neighborhoods, provides immediate security with the touch of a button.

Options with problems:

Sun roof. Redundant if a car has air conditioning, and not as comfortable. Disadvantages: Noise and buffeting as wind hits. Problem of water leakage.

Power windows. Recommended for drivers who use toll highways regularly. Caution: Power windows can be dangerous to small children and pets.

General rules:

Buy accessories that relate to the character of the car. A very lightweight car does not require power steering or power brakes. But the purchase of a heavy car without power steering (and such cars are still made) is a mistake many drivers regret making for the sake of economy.

Consider where and how car will be used. Distances. Neighborhoods. Weather.

Decorative options. Important to the car's resale value. The plainest, unadorned model is not necessarily the one that will save money in the long run. Chances are the used car buyer wants more pizzazz. Best to buy upscale rather than down to insure optimum resalability.

Pros and Cons of Front-Wheel Drive

Cars with front-wheel drive have four advantages over rear-wheel-drive cars: (1) Better gas mileage. (2) Smoother ride. (3) More trunk space and rear seat room. (4) Better handling under most conditions. But note these conditions:

Better traction can sometimes make these vehicles unwieldy when changing direction on slippery roads.

Front-wheel skids can usually be corrected by slowing the car enough to allow the front tires to regain traction.

Don't put a sandbag or two in the trunk to improve rear traction in snow. The extra weight in the rear actually lessens traction on front-wheel-drive cars.

Snow tires are effective on the front wheels *only*.

Front tires wear out much more quickly from the work of both driving and steering, thus mandating frequent rotation of tires to keep tread wear even.

Choosing the Best Car Engine

Diesel versus gas: Diesels don't make sense for everyone, despite the fuel savings they represent. Disadvantages:

Diesels usually cost more than gas engines.

They have an unpleasant smell.

They are noisier.

Advantages:

Greater fuel economy. Seven additional miles for every gallon of gas.

In the event of gas rationing, the crunch might not extend to diesel fuel (as was the case in 1973-74 fuel crisis, when it was readily available).

Maintenance is lower.

Resale value is greater.

Best customer for a diesel: Someone who drives a lot, goes long distances, and for whom fuel cost is a significant factor. Also, someone who won't be bothered by the odor. Diesel is a doubtful choice for the driver who doesn't travel heavily. Annual net saving on fuel will be very small. Payout for a heavier traveler (30,000 miles a year or so) comes more quickly, justifying the extra cost.

Large versus small engine: The big-engine gas hog can be more economical, depending on the work it's asked to do. An eight-cylinder engine moves weight with much less effort than a small-cylinder engine. It also runs more smoothly, with fewer vibrations. Reason: Greater number of pistons provides a harmonic balance.

Getting the Best-Value Car Sound System

The basic components of a high-quality car stereo system are an AM/FM tuner, a tape player, an amplifier (optional but recommended), speakers, and an antenna.

Rule: No auto audio can equal the performance of fine home equipment. The car compartment is small, besieged with engine and traffic noises, and surrounded with competing electrical signals. And all of this in a moving environment.

A welter of technical and personal choices dictate the final package.

General guidelines:

Shop around. Car audio components are of-ten discounted. Check mail-order houses for best buys, but be prepared for added freight and C.O.D. charges and shipping delays. Essential: Deal with reputable businesses and buy name brands.

Make sure you can exchange or return components in case they prove incompatible or do not fit into the car. Remember each unit must be installed and may require custom mounting accessories.

Keep personal tastes in mind. Rock and country music fans usually prefer stronger bass ranges. Classical music requires good mid and treble.

How to allocate your spending: 40% to 50% for tuner/tape player, 25% to 30% for amplifier, 25% to 30% for speakers (unlike home gear, for which half the recommended expenditure may go for speakers alone). Depending upon your normal driving locale, an antenna may cost from $5, for a perfectly adequate 31-inch whip antenna, to $100 for a signal-boosting, automatically retractable antenna.

General recommendations:

Components are a better deal than manufacturer-installed original sound equipment. Good manufacturer-installed gear can cost $700, a price that will usually bring you far better sound if spent on components.

Try to find a dealer that has set up a sound room to hear and compare different systems.

New-car buyer strategy: Buyers planning to purchase components should insist on a delete-option clause, eliminating the installed radio cost.

In-dash versus under-dash components. Under-dash components are easily installed. Overriding disadvantage: A thief can slip out the under-dash gear as easily as an ashtray. Choose in-dash tuner/tape players unless you want to stow the components in the trunk each time you leave the car. (If you still prefer an under-dash system, SONY components are top-notch ones.)

The tuner/tape player: Unless you have a small fortune invested in eight-track tapes, choose a cassette player. Cassette technology is advancing fastest and the cassettes can be used on home equipment.

Amplifiers: Most auto-sound packages

benefit from amplifiers that strengthen bass and high-treble tones. Problems:

Amplifiers are bulky and often must be installed under a seat or in the trunk.

Unless your tuner has a bypass circuit permitting you to plug into the preamplifier, your costly amplifier will only boost the distorted output of the built-in amplifier.

Smart buying: Look for amplifiers measuring power in watts (W) per channel in terms of distortion (THD). Goal: About five watts per channel at 1% distortion or less. To get this, the amplifier may require 50 watts per channel because few operate at better than 10% efficiency in a car.

Bi-amplifiers: They offer separate power boosts for bass and treble ranges. Bi-amplification may be called for when separate bass and treble speakers are installed.

Speakers: Speakers must be compatible with amplifiers. Their power capacity should be slightly higher than amplifier. Example: Get 60w speakers for a 50w/ch amplifier. One way to be sure of speaker/amplifier compatibility is to purchase them as a package.

Stereo sound requires at least two speakers. Many enthusiasts choose four. Nondirectional bass speakers are best placed in the factory cutouts in the rear window shelf. Next best placement: In rear doors. Treble speakers can be mounted in front door panels or under dash.

Installation: Unless you are highly skilled electronics hobbyist, have the auto-sound system professionally installed. Allow $50 to $100 for installation, and get a satisfaction-guaranteed agreement.

Source: Jay Jennis, J&J Corp., automotive distributors, 10 Milltown Court, Union, NJ 07083.

When Purchase Involves a Trade-in

The buyer who trades in one item for another is also a seller. He might have to pay damages for any misrepresentation about the item traded in.

One car buyer traded in what he thought was a 1970 Mercedes. Even the title said so. But it turned out to be a 1968, and the court ordered him to pay the difference in value. 18 UCC Reptr 75; 570 SW 2d 542.

When the New Car Turns Out to Be a Lemon

If something is wrong with a new car, the owner must give the dealer a reasonable number of chances to fix it. Exception: If something major goes wrong within the first few miles, the buyer has the right to insist on another car.

Buyer's right: If the dealer does not, or cannot, fix the defect within a reasonable time period and the defect substantially impairs the car's value, the buyer can demand a replacement or the money back.

What to do: Except in the case of full warranties, a buyer who wants a replacement or the money back must officially give the car back to the dealer under a procedure called "revocation of acceptance." To revoke acceptance, the buyer must deliver the car to the dealer, provide a written explanation of the reasons for the return, and inform the dealer that the insurance and registration are being cancelled.

Prudent advice: If the car has been financed through the dealer, inform the bank or finance company that further payments will not be made until the problem is resolved. If the loan is direct, the buyer may wish to continue to make payments to avoid the possibility of being sued. But the lender should still be told in writing who has the car.

If the dealer has any inclination to settle the dispute, the revocation of acceptance should work. The only practical alternative is to hire an attorney.

Source: *Down Easter's Lemon Guide,* Bureau of Consumer Protection, Augusta, ME.

Understanding Car Warranties

Auto warranties usually contain language that seems to limit liability to the repair or replacement of defective parts. But this will not bar a lawsuit based on personal injuries caused by a defect. Also: If the car company or dealer refuses to make repairs called for by the warranty, it may be held liable for any subsequent property damage. Some courts have even extended liability for damages when the company tried to correct the problem and failed. 2 ALR 4th 576.

Taking a Car Manufacturer to Court

A little-known federal law, the Magnuson-Moss Warranty Act, can make a big difference for car purchasers who get stuck with a lemon. Reason: If the manufacturer won't live up to its warranty obligation, you can sue and collect attorneys' fees, in addition to your other damages. Result: Complaints that ordinarily wouldn't justify a lawsuit because of the expense of litigation are now worth pursuing.

Mark Silber, an attorney who has handled a number of these cases, answered questions about suing car manufacturers.

When does it pay to hire a lawyer in an auto-warranty dispute?

When you have had no satisfaction from the dealer or from the auto manufacturer's zone representative. We generally get three kinds of cases:

The company wants to keep trying to fix the car, even though numerous repair attempts have been unsuccessful.

The company insists that the car is operating "within specifications," although the problem persists.

The problems are so massive that fixing the car would amount to remanufacturing it, and what you would end up with is a rebuilt auto instead of a new one.

How do you decide if a case is worth taking?
I have four guidelines:

• The car must currently have a substantial impairment that affects its safety, reliability, or market value.

• The problems must have arisen during the warranty period.

• The purchaser must have visited the dealer at least five times about the problem.

• There must have been at least two attempts to work things out with the manufacturer.

Is the litigation long?

Most cases are settled. Very few are tried to completion. A fair number are settled after a trial has begun but before a verdict is handed down.

What does it cost to get the lawsuit started?

Often, there is an initial consultation fee. Cost: $35 to $50. If the case is worth pursuing, there may be a retainer of $450 to $750, depending on the size and value of the vehicle and the extent of the problem. As mentioned, the settlement or verdict usually includes reimbursement for attorneys' fees.

How do I locate a lawyer who handles these cases?

The Center for Auto Safety in Washington, DC, keeps a list of attorneys who handle auto warranty cases. They can be reached at (202) 659-1126.

Source: Mark Silber, an attorney in private practice, 10 Station Pl., Metuchen, NJ 08840.

Rules for Driving Small Cars Safely

In a severe crash between a large car and a small one, those in the small car are eight times more likely to be killed. Defense strategies:

Wear seat belts. A belted occupant of a small car has the same chance of surviving as the unbelted occupant of a big car in a crash between the two.

Keep your lights on at low beam full time to increase visibility.

Be aware that light poles and signs along the road may not break away as designed when hit by a lightweight compact car.

Respect the inability of larger vehicles to maneuver or stop as quickly to escape a collision.

Better Gas Mileage

Use radial ply tires, and keep them inflated to maximum recommended pressure. Other advantage: Tires will last longer.

Make sure that the alignment and balance of the wheels are true.

Use 10W-40 oil, a more slippery oil than number 30 or 40. It reduces piston resistance.

Change your driving technique: Never accelerate energetically. Try never to use the brakes. (Less possible in city driving than elsewhere.) Instead: Stay well back from the car ahead. When it slows, take foot off the accelerator and glide down. Stopping the car completely and having to start up uses much more fuel. In city driving, where a full stop is apt to be necessary, try not to jam on the brakes.

Park indoors on cold nights. Fuel efficiency for the first five miles of driving with a cold engine is half what it would be had it been kept warm overnight. (Cold oil in the engine is a heavy, gelatinous mass that is resistant to the movement of the engine. When warm, oil becomes slippery and parts move with less friction.)

Turn off engine when waiting instead of letting it idle. An engine running at idle speed for as little as one minute uses more gasoline than it takes to start it up again after it's shut off.

Buying a Gasoline Container

For most households, a 2½-gallon can is sufficient. What to look for: A tip-proof container of noncorrosive metal or plastic. Flame

arrester: A fine wire mesh in the spout. A place to store the pouring extension. Safety considerations: Before buying, check out the local fire code with the fire department. Allow for gas expansion: Leave at least two inches of space. Store the container away from the house or garage, out of direct sunlight. Except for the trip home from the gas station, don't carry filled containers around in your car.

Car out of Control: What to Do

Brake failure on a downhill grade: First pump the brake to build up pressure. Shift into low gear, and gradually apply the parking brake. Last resort: Bring the car to a stop by sideswiping a guard rail, a snowbank, or bushes.

Simultaneous failure of power brakes and power steering: Steer firmly and brake hard. It is still possible to maintain control without the power-assist system, which is usually where the trouble lies.

Gas pedal sticks: Brake and turn the ignition to OFF (not to LOCK).

Safety Seats for Children

Ninety percent of the young (under 5 years of age) children killed in car accidents each year would have survived if they had been in safety seats. Reason: They can slip out of full-sized seat belts or be knocked out of an adult's arms by any impact.

For infants, experts recommend a molded plastic bucket that holds the baby securely with its back towards the front of the car to protect the child from flying glass. When they are too big for that model, graduate to a child seat. These face forward, have racer-type harnesses, and are padded.

Two types: Tethered (a strap gets anchored to the car) and non-tethered. Both are safe when properly installed. Shop for one that's been crash-tested by the manufacturer. Safest place to install: The center of the back seat.

Driver's Rights When Stopped By a Police Officer

When stopped by a police officer while operating a car (or other motor vehicle), you have certain rights.

The officer can only stop a vehicle for an infraction, not for an indiscriminate safety check. Exceptions: A police roadblock, or a consistent search of every 100th or 1,000th car for information purposes.

If halted for a relatively simple traffic violation, like running a red light, it's illegal for an officer to search you or your vehicle. Sometimes an officer will ask consent to search ("Mind if I look through the trunk?"). You don't have to give permission. If he searches anyway, complain later.

If you're arrested for not producing an insurance or registration card, for instance, the officer can make a body search and search the area within your reach.

A complete search of your car may be done only at the police station even if you are arrested. Otherwise, an officer must have a warrant that specifies exactly what is sought and where. These are your constitutional rights.

Source: Robert I. Kalina, Esq., 230 Park Ave., New York 10017, specialist in criminal defense.

Commuting By Motorcycle

Sixty miles per gallon lures many people to ride motorcycles. The fear of falls, accidents, and ridicule are potent deterrents.

Getting started: Buy a bike that has enough power to hit 80 on highways, but won't be too much to handle.

Learning to ride: Get an experienced rider to help you. Alternative: Buy the bike from a dealer that gives lessons. Find an empty parking lot or schoolyard in which to practice. Balancing is the hard part of riding a motorcycle.

Expect stares. The bike rider in a business suit is still an unusual sight. Carry a canvas shoulder bag; it's easier to manage than an attache case. Also, carry a poncho and keep a set of old clothes in the office in case of rain at quitting time.

Cautions: Drive defensively. Watch every vehicle for unexpected turns and stops. Don't drive in bad weather. Ruts, potholes, and cracks in the road are dangerous, too.

Security Tips for Motorists

How thieves steal cars in less than a minute: (1) Push a flat instrument (putty knife) down next to window (near lock)—tripping the lock in an instant. (2) Jam a hardened screw into the ignition lock. (3) Yank it out. (4) Insert a screwdriver and make contact with the now-exposed wires. (5) Zoom away.

While you can't save your car from a determined pro, anti-theft devices discourage the youthful and unskilled crooks, who are responsible for about 70% of all stolen autos. Basic protection: (1) Locks for doors and parts, especially trunk and hood. (2) Reinforcers for ignition locks that also disable steering and/or transmission. (3) Car stoppers that kill the ignition or clog the fuel line after the thief starts the car. (4) Alarm systems. Best: Passive alarms that engage automatically and go off within a few seconds to a couple of minutes after the driver's door is opened. Some insurers offer lower premiums for cars with these alarms.

Parking precautions: Park car in a supervised parking lot or in a well lit, heavily trafficked area.

Avoid parking in the space at the end of the block. Reason: Professional car thieves with tow trucks can easily remove your auto. Helpful: Turn your steering wheel sharply to one side or the other. That locks the steering column and prevents the car from being towed from the rear.

In bad neighborhoods, keep doors locked, windows open no more than a crack, and at a red light, keep car in gear for a fast takeoff. (More important if waiting in a parked car.) When disabled, tie a white cloth to antenna, then wait inside car with doors locked and windows up. Be wary of accepting help from strangers. If another car ever tries to force you off the highway, forget the dents and scrapes —resist and keep blowing horn in short blasts to get attention and help. Head for gas station or any crowded place.

A Car Thief's Advice on Foiling Theft

No car or truck is immune from thievery, but professional thieves tell police that there are ways of making the heist harder.

Recommended:

Don't rely on factory-installed alarms. Reason: Repair manuals that detail how they work are available in libraries.

Use combinations of systems. Example: An alarm with an ignition cutoff switch hidden under the dashboard or in the glove compartment.

Replace standard door-lock buttons with tapered ones. Caution: They won't stop professional thieves, but they deter amateurs who are responsible for most of the country's car thefts. Best: Doors on the Saab must be opened with a key.

Leave only the ignition key when using parking lots. And don't tell the attendant how long the vehicle will be parked. Also note the mileage.

Learn how to remove and replace the distributor rotor. The car won't run without it. This easy maneuver should be standard when the car is left unattended for over a day.

Car Clinic

Engine misses at all speeds. Clean out fuel lines and fuel carburetor inlet filters. Have carburetor float level checked.

Engine misses while idling. Adjust either fuel mixture or carburetor.

High-speed missing. Could be low or erratic fuel pump pressure, a clogged or damaged carburetor, fuel line or filter problems or, frequently, just a bad tune-up.

Poor acceleration. Check the carburetor, throttle linkage, float setting, timing, spark plugs, and breaker points.

Engine cranks, but doesn't start. Check both the electrical and fuel systems. Moisture in the ignition system can be the problem. The starter or neutral safety switch in the automatic transmission may be defective.

Engine starts hard. Most often an ignition problem, either a weak spark, open or grounded coil circuits, fouled spark plugs, or worn spark-plug cables. Check the battery and fuel supply, too.

Car won't start in cold weather. Most often the automatic choke is stuck open. But moisture in the fuel line, or using too heavy a grade of oil, can also cause problems.

Car won't start even when engine is warm. Check for a choke stuck in the closed position, a flooded carburetor, or vapor lock.

Source: *Automobile International.*

Persistent Stalling

If a complete tune-up fails to solve the stalling problem, look for:

Dirt or water in the fuel lines, filters, or carburetor.

A clogged or restricted positive crankcase ventilation valve.

A poorly adjusted automatic transmission.

Improperly set throttle linkage or accelerating pump stroke in the carburetor.

Source: *Automobile International.*

Ignition Checkup

Remove all spark plugs and examine for wear. Bad sign: Heavy carbon buildup in the gap. Replace those that are worn.

Disconnect the plugs' cables. Replace those that are brittle, cracked, or corroded. Note: When installing new cables, seat them firmly in the distributor cap.

Examine the distributor cap for cracks or corrosion on the terminals.

Check the distributor points for pitting, oxidation, or oil residue. Replace points where necessary.

Look for wires stripped of insulation. A bare wire can cause a short circuit, which kills the engine.

Avoiding Transmission Problems

Bad driving habits that hurt an automatic transmission:

Shifting into reverse or park when the car is moving.

Keeping the car from back-rolling on a hill by revving the engine in gear, rather than using the brakes.

Parking for long periods with engine running and transmission engaged.

Racing the engine for more than 10 seconds with the drive wheels stuck in snow or sand.

Maintenance for automatics: Check the transmission-fluid level with each motor-oil change. The fluid should be the color of cherry soda. If it is dark, change it.

Bad habits to avoid when driving a manual

transmission: Riding with a foot on the clutch pedal. Racing the engine when letting out the clutch.

Maintenance for manuals:

Tighten the clutch pedal if it has more than a half inch of play. Sign of clutch wear: Shuddering or jerking in the transmission when you let the clutch out.

Again, check the transmission fluid level with every oil change.

Alternator Troubles

When the generator light comes on, there may be a dead battery in your future. What to look for:

Loose or broken fan belt. Caution: A loose belt won't always trip the warning light. Dimmer headlights and slower clicking of the turn signals are sure signs of alternator trouble. Point: It's the alternator that keeps the battery charging.

A break, blown fuse, poor connection, or open circuit in the wiring.

A defective or improperly adjusted voltage regulator.

Special problem: A noisy alternator that still functions is usually caused by worn bearings, a loose fan-belt pulley, loose mounting bolts, a worn drive belt, or an open or shorted electrical connection.

Source: *Automobile International.*

Replacing Shock Absorbers

The next time your car's shock absorbers need replacing, consider buying better ones. Benefit: Handling and performance you never dreamed existed before.

Best choice: A heavy-duty model, which is about 30% stiffer than the factory installation. There's little loss in ride quality and much better stability and handling.

Special choice: A super-duty model, which is twice as stiff as normal. It's excellent for cars that are frequently driven on highways and around town. Avoid: Competition and off-road shocks, unless the vehicle is used only for these purposes. Exception: Sports cars, for which they are a good choice.

Expensive alternative: Air shocks, which can be adjusted for stiffness. Consider them if you frequently haul heavy loads or a trailer, or like to hot-dog off-road.

Bottom line: Even factory replacement shocks will feel stiff at first because you are used to the mushy feel of the worn-out ones. Give yourself time to adjust to high-performance shocks.

Source: *Automobile International.*

Quick Fix for Bad Auto-Radio Reception

Poor car-radio reception usually means trouble with the antenna.

Simple adjustments you can make: For FM, adjust the antenna height to exactly 31 inches. For AM, adjust the trimmer. The trimmer is a small adjustment screw found on the back or side of the radio. (In General Motors cars, it's behind one of the knobs.)

To make the adjustment: Pick a weak station at the high end of the dial (near 1500). Then turn the trimmer until the reception is the loudest. If poor reception persists, the antenna cable may be corroded or improperly connected to the car fender. Cleaning off the rust and tightening the antenna mounting can sometimes help.

Windshield antennas don't suffer from the same problems, but they have other drawbacks. They're more likely to pick up engine noises, and reception can fade out when the car changes direction.

Source: *Motor.*

Winterizing Checklist

Check battery charge and water, antifreeze level and strength.

Look for wear on snow tires. Reminder: Maintain correct pressure for best traction and durability.

Check brakes and brake fluid.

Replace worn windshield wiper blades.

Refill window-washer reservoir with a no-freeze solution.

Spray dry lubricant on door latches to prevent freezing.

Test run heater and defroster. Check for leaks that could let carbon monoxide into the car.

Carry an ice scraper in the glove compartment and a piece of old carpet in the trunk for traction on icy spots.

Source: *Steering Wheel.*

Cold-Weather Starting

Starting a car quickly and efficiently in cold weather requires a special approach. The steps:

Turn off all electrically powered equipment such as the lights, heater, and radio.

Slowly press the accelerator pedal to the floor. Do this only once if the outside temperature is 10°F or higher. Press the accelerator twice if the temperature is below 10°F. Release the accelerator.

Turn the ignition key to start. Keep your foot off the accelerator.

If the engine fails to catch within 15 seconds, turn off the ignition. Wait 30 seconds. Press the accelerator to the floor. Again, try to start the car with your foot off the accelerator. Never pump the accelerator pedal. You will flood the engine with gasoline. And the failed attempts at starting will drain the battery.

After the engine is going, allow it to idle for 30 seconds. Then give the accelerator a quick press. This releases the idling speed mechanism and slows down the engine.

Winter Driving Safety

Reinforced tire chains on the rear wheels reduce braking distance on ice by 50% (compared to regular tires).

Conventional snow tires without studs actually are slightly inferior to regular tires for stopping on ice.

Radial tires offer no advantage over regular tires when driving on ice. On snow, they help only if they have special snow treads.

Small, light cars have less start-up traction on ice than standard-size cars. But they perform somewhat better when it comes to braking on ice.

The Best Way to Wash Your Own Car

Bypass the machine-equipped car wash. Doing it yourself: Fill one bucket with a mild detergent and another with clear water. Run the suds over the car with a thick terrycloth towel. Wash a small section at a time, starting at the top. Rinse each section with another towel dipped in the clear water. Then wipe the section semidry with a third towel. Avoid: Harsh detergents that dull finishes. Also: Never blast the car with the hose on full force. This procedure drives the dirt into the paint.

Repainting Your Car

A quality paint job is so costly ($1,000 to $2,000 and up) that it's usually better to trade in your car for a new model. Nonetheless, a fine repainting is the best way to spruce up a prized vehicle.

Suggestions:

Check out the local paint and body shops. Visit auto shows where these shops often display their best work. Get recommendations from friends.

Inspect prospective shops for organization of the work area, cleanliness, and good lighting.

Suggestions:

You can save money by doing some of the preparations yourself. But unless you're an expert, don't get involved in paint removal or sanding. You can handle the time-consuming chore of removing the chrome and trim. Do some of the masking yourself, especially around the interior, trunk and hood.

Discuss the procedure to be followed with the shop foreman. Once the paint has been chemically removed and the necessary body work completed, top-quality shops will lay on three or four coats of primer. Wet-block sanding follows, and then several more light coats of primer.

When the paint is applied, a few light coats are followed by four or five heavy coats. More is not always better. Paint starts to get brittle as it gets thicker.

The car must remain stationary for several days (ideally, it will sit for several weeks) before the buffing takes place. In the final stages, the car is wet-block sanded with number 600 sandpaper. Then it is buffed by hand and machine.

Source: *Autoweek.*

After the Collision: Repair or Replace?

Determine the clean, adjusted-for-mileage value of the car according to a recognized wholesale guide (such as the *Automotive Market Report*, or *AMR*, Automotive Action Publishing Co., Pittsburgh, PA).

Divide the repair estimates (made by at least two reliable garages) by the adjusted wholesale value. Result: The replacement percentage. Example: Average repair estimate: $1,600. Clean, adjusted-for-mileage value according to *AMR*, $3,212. Replacement percentage = 49.8% ($1,600 ÷ $3,212).

If replacement percentage runs 25% or less, repair the unit. 40% or more, replace the unit.

You and Your Automobile

Between 25% and 40%, make a repair-or-replace decision.

Also take into account:

Economic cost of extensive downtime for major repairs. (Remember, parts for current-model-year cars are usually in short supply early in the model year.) Include cost of a rental car, availability of a pool car (least expensive alternative), or cost of reimbursing the driver or using his personal car.

Visible repairs diminish resale values. Small dents can be hammered out without affecting resale value. But large damaged areas should be replaced to make the repair less visible at resale.

Possible bad effects on morale of the driver of an extensively repaired vehicle.

Source: Peterson, Howell & Heather, fleet management consultants, P.O. Box 2174, Baltimore 21203.

Cutting the Cost of Car Repairs

Automobile repair costs are soaring at a rate unusual even for these times. Car owners can do better than just hold the line, if they adopt a vigilant attitude every time they deal with a garage.

Behind the dramatic spiral in car repair costs: The cause is more than the increased prices for parts, often given as an excuse by repair personnel. Flattened car sales, for one thing, have placed pressure on dealers to widen shop margins. More complicated cars are not helping either. Many shops do not know how to fix plastic parts or solid-state electronics. They subcontract the work, then add on their own profit.

Some of the increase, perversely, is a result of pressure the insurance industry is placing on car manufacturers to make accident repairs cheaper. And the insurers are getting such things as two-part doors, which can be repaired in sections, avoiding the charge for a whole new door.

In turn, repair centers and garages are buck-

ing the pressure. They claim that the expensive new equipment they must buy (such as frame straighteners or tools to handle front-wheel drives) is boosting their capital costs. Besides, they say, more mechanics are unionized these days and bargain hard for exorbitant rates. Dealers also claim that warranty and recall repairs are forcing them to do a lot of costly work for nothing.

Target: Labor costs. Shops placed one-third of the tag on labor 15 years ago. It is now usually two-thirds of the bill. But despite unionization, mechanics' rates have not risen that fast. Nationwide, the average service-shop labor rate is $18.63 per hour. Yet dealers in major cities charge $40 per hour. Even small-town dealers charge $25.

Trick: Shops use flat-rate manuals to figure labor charges. The costs are based on expected time for particular repairs. But the job is often done in much less time by the lowest-rated mechanic in the shop. Trap: No bill adjustment.

Suggestion: Writing out the specific repair needs ahead of time and giving the list to the service manager (keep a copy for yourself) can help control bill padding. But one longtime Midwestern car dealer says: I don't know of a really honest repair shop in the country today.

Best: Search out a respected garage run by an independent mechanic or repair organization. Joseph Innes, car-use director for the National Highway Traffic Safety Administration (NHTSA), says a survey revealed that high-powered dealer service-managers tend to pad bills and miss customer needs. Independents have a better reputation with the public.

Problem: A new car's warranty may be voided if maintenance and key repairs are not done by the dealer. But it can pay to consult an independent and have him write out exactly what the car needs. His $25 charge may save hundreds of dollars.

Become a bug on preventive automobile maintenance. There are a growing number of specials around. Example: The promise by Firestone to keep your car's steering aligned, free of charge, through 50,000 miles of new tire use.

Start by buying a car with a good record of

repair frequency. Some foreign subcompacts were low on average repairs a few years ago, but in a few cases new models are lemons. Ask for the actual maintenance record when you buy a used car. Rental agencies provide them. Dealers and individuals who really wish to sell a car can often do better than they pretend.

Learn to repair: Adult-education courses are now offered at many high schools and junior colleges. A car owner can at least learn preventive maintenance.

Divide your outlays: Some shops, such as those run by Sears, J.C. Penney, and K Mart, often do routine maintenance quickly, without bill padding. Using them for routine repairs and maintenance leaves only the complicated repairs for the dealer. But don't let that warranty expire.

Avoid extended warranty contracts: The latest studies show that they are very expensive. They have hidden limits. Labor costs may not be covered adequately. A plan may require you to pay first and be reimbursed later, and it may not cover repairs if you move.

Garage personnel: They are tough, and they respect toughness. Look for points of leverage. Examples:

Business relationships: Perhaps your firm's fleet cars are purchased from, or repaired by, the dealer.

Higher-level protest: Dealers deny it, but direct protests to the carmaker often work.

Protests should start at ground level, however. Contact the local Better Business Bureau, consumer fraud offices, action-line columnists for the media, and local or regional officials with the NHTSA, Federal Trade Commission, and Department of Justice. Repair garages that wish to stay in business will bow quickly to such pressure.

Cut Auto Insurance Costs

Shop around: Rates can vary as much as 100%, depending on the coverage desired.

Don't overbuy collision and comprehen-sive coverage: The average driver files a collision, fire, or theft claim only once every 10 years or so.

Use bigger deductibles: Increase of $50 in the deductible can reduce comprehensive coverage cost by up to 30%, collision by 10% to 20%.

Eliminate duplicate coverage. Don't buy medical payments coverage if the family already has adequate medical insurance through job-related benefits.

Take advantage of discounts that insurance companies offer for low mileage, driver education courses, and geographic location. Most common saver: Insuring a second car on same policy as first vehicle.

Source: *Money.*

Reducing the Repair Bill When the Car Breaks Down

Tell the police the least expensive thing you can think of when they ask what's wrong with the car, because that's what they'll tell the garage. If the garage thinks you know what you're talking about, there's less chance of being cheated.

Try to stay with the car while repairs are done. The mechanic needs only a minute to concoct an engine malfunction. Best to ask the mechanic to return the old part before putting in a new one. This prevents him from reinstalling the old unit.

Ask the mechanic for an estimate of the job and ask him if he has the proper parts. If he doesn't have the parts or is uncertain about whether he can get them, you can save time and cash by picking them up yourself.

The job will get done faster if you keep after the mechanic. Otherwise, the car may sit for several days and you may get charged for hours of labor that never occurred.

Don't opt for the most expensive repair. If the car can be made to go with a less-than-perfect repair, do that and wait till you get home to have it fixed properly.

One way to speed along the repair is to have a repair manual in the car. These books are published for virtually all cars and are available at dealers and some bookstores. Read it and bring it out if the mechanic looks at the car and starts talking about many hours of work and costly repairs.

Insist that the bill itemize separately the charges for towing or road service, replacement parts, and labor.

How to Collect Full Auto Insurance Benefits

Expedite your insurance claim—and increase your chances of a fair settlement—by keeping careful records of the accident.

Guidelines:

• Immediately set up an orderly file containing police reports, repair estimates, hospital bills and copies of claims submitted.

• Document everything in writing. Write a follow-up letter confirming any telephone conversations with insurance company representatives. Include the date and the names of the persons with whom you spoke. File a copy.

• If the insurance company stalls, check your policy to see whether your coverage includes use of a rental car during the settlement period. If so, rent one. By spending the company's money, you may speed up the claim.

Source: The National Insurance Consumer Organization, 344 Commerce St., Alexandria, VA 22314.

Handling a Fender-Bender Accident

Common situation: A family member has a minor accident, a fender-bender. No one is hurt, and car damage is less than $200. The decision is made not to file an insurance claim, since it might result in higher insurance premiums for years to come. But this might create a problem:

When another party is involved, if the insurance company is not notified within the time limit there is no liability coverage. This could be dangerous if the other party files a lawsuit a month or two later. One way to cover yourself: Send the company a certified letter informing them of a minor automobile incident, and write that you believe no claims will be filed. Helpful: Offer the other party about $50 in exchange for a written release from liability.

Best Insurance Deal for Teenage Drivers

Your teenager has just gotten his driver's license. You are thinking about getting him a car, but you are confused about how to insure him if you do.

Typical questions:

Should you register the car in your name or his?

Should you get him his own insurance, or add him to your policy?

If you have your own business, should you give him access to a company car and cover him with the company's insurance?

Factors to consider:

The cheapest way to insure a teenage driver is to restrict his time on the road. Reason: Insurers make a distinction between principal operators of cars and occasional drivers. A principal operator is someone who drives a car more than 25% of the time it is on the road. Cars whose principal operators are high risks (teenagers and specifically teenage males) cost the most to cover. Restrict a teenager's driving time to 15% to 20%.

If you opt to give your teenager unrestricted access to a car, insurance generally will cost the same regardless of the car's registration and regardless of whether the teenager is covered under the parent's policy or his own.

However, in some states the highest rated car will take on the underage driver classification.

When the car used by your son becomes the second car in the family, you will get a 15% discount by adding the car to your own policy. If your family has two cars, the overall discount percentage will be reduced by putting a third car on the same policy.

Liability is the key consideration in deciding whether to insure a teenage driver with his own policy or his parents'. If a teenager injures people or property in an accident, his own insurance should be broad enough to cover him sufficiently. If the teenager is covered under his parents' policy, however, they are likely to be sued.

The person who has his own business and lets his teenager use a company car will save the most in insurance premiums. Reason: The rates do not increase because the owner's teenager drives a company car.

Risks of this approach:

If the teenager injures people or property in a company car, the company can be sued.

If the teenager has an accident, or even if he does not, the insurance company may have second thoughts about renewing the company's automobile coverage.

Source: Marvin I. Sameth, CPCU, president, Kurtis Sameth Hill Inc., 9 E. 38 St., New York 10016.

How Insurance Rates Jump When Teens Take The Wheel

Rates with and without the teenager as principal operator of a family car in a Chicago suburb:

For six-month coverage

	Without teen	With teen
Liability	$ 68	$241
Medical	5	12
Collision	49	196
Comprehensive	14	32
Total	136	481

Source: R. James Young, price manager, Allstate Insurance Co., Allstate Plaza, Northbrook, IL 60062.

Tax Angles When Parent Buys Youngster's Car

Sales tax: If you buy the car in your name and then give it to him, you'll get a sales tax deduction on your federal tax that will be worth more to you than to the child.

Interest deductions: If you buy the car on time, the interest deductions are yours even though you later gave away the car.

Before You File A Liability Suit

About 55% of those hurt in traffic accidents receive nothing from the liability system. The percentage is even lower for malpractice or faulty products suits. Considerations:

Your lawyer's fee could be one-third of the cash award, plus expenses.

Cash is dispensed only after the claiming process is completed. Some insurance companies delay in the hope that you will accept less out of court.

Damages paid for "pain and suffering" are influenced by the amount of your medical bills, resulting in extended medical treatments.

The lengthy treatment and court procedures encourage you to dwell on your injury and delay your rehabilitation.

What to do:

Deal with reputable lawyers.

Brace yourself for an emotional roller coaster once you file suit. While 95% of the personal-injury suits are settled before trial, those settlement negotiations are as tense as a court case.

Be sure your lawyer details all the facts of any proposed settlement. That should include his fees and costs. Once you agree to a figure in court, there is no second chance.

Source: *The Lawsuit Lottery*, by Jeffrey O'Connell, The Free Press, New York.

14

Travel

Pros and Cons of Group Travel Tours

Best reason to choose a package tour: Economy. Saving can amount to several hundred dollars per couple. Food and drink on chartered jets tends to be better than on commercial flights, but space is more cramped. Chartered air-conditioned buses between airports and train stations are a big convenience and eliminate need for constant tipping in foreign currency. Warning: Chartered deluxe European express trains are pleasant, but by no means express. They are frequently sidetracked for the real express trains.

Tours also save time on planning and organizing and are especially helpful to those who have not traveled to a country before or do not speak the language.

Minuses for package tours: Rushed sightseeing schedule. Be wary of promises of full American breakfasts. They're usually poor quality. Probably better to stick with a traditional roll and coffee in Europe.

Tip: Save coupon books for gourmet dinners at restaurants on special nights. Pay cash for light suppers when you're tired or have had a late lunch.

Best tour to pick: One sponsored by a local professional, cultural, or educational group. Usually assures you of finding compatible companions.

Precautions When Paying for a Charter Tour

Make out check to escrow bank account, usually found in small print in tour operator's brochure. Put destination, dates, and other details on the face of the check. Write "For Deposit Only" on the back. Reasons: Tour operator must deposit check in that account. Purchaser is protected against cancellation of the trip, failure of the tour operator or travel agent. If agent objects to the procedure, find another agent.

Questions to Ask About Resort Packages

Read the fine print closely and question the travel agent at length. Both are essential. The kinds of little extras tacked on to a package vary widely. Typically included: Free transfers, hotel taxes, tips, meals, welcome cocktails, guided sight-seeing. Other things to determine in advance: How far is the resort from the beach and the city center? How crowded will the sports facilities be? What about cancellations?

Travel Bargains to Turn Down

If super cut-rate tickets are offered by a travel agent (or even an acquaintance), be aware that they are probably stolen. The airlines are using computers to track down these illegal tickets. The user faces the embarrassment and inconvenience of confiscation, detainment, and possible legal action.

Trip Cancellation Insurance

Worth considering if serious health or personal problems threaten to interfere with vacation plans. It assures refund of prepaid vacation money upon presentation of a doctor's certificate. Premiums start at about $4 per $100 of coverage. Some policies cover vacation interruption as well as cancellations.
Source: Herbert Teison, publisher, *Travel Smart.*

Choosing a Cruise

Focus on a cruise with a compatible group of people. People over 60 generally take longer cruises. People on summer cruises are usually 15 to 20 years younger than those on winter cruises.

Compare capacity of the ship's main lounge to number of passengers. If lounge is relatively small, there will be uncomfortable fast meals and guests will scramble for seats at entertainment performances.

Visit the ships you are interested in while they are in port. If you have never taken a cruise before, make the first one a short one. Cabin advice: Choose one near the waterline, in the center of the ship, for minimum motion-sickness problems. Prices are lower than for top-deck staterooms, too.

Get a complete rundown of on-board activities. Some lines operate nothing more than floating casinos.

When to sail: Christmas, February, and March are the peak periods for the Caribbean, and reservations should be made up to a year in advance. Budget cruises are available at other times.

Booking tactic: A small deposit holds an option on a room when you book far in advance for the busiest times. Good deals: People with flexible vacation schedules can get bargain rates at the last minute when the ship still has a few empty cabins.

New wrinkle: Fly-cruise deals that take your from major cities to the port of departure with almost no additional charge for air fare.

Caution: Even no-tip cruises involve some tipping. Other typical extras: Bar bills, shore excursions, shopping, port taxes, film, new clothes. And gambling losses.

Cheaper cruises: Have your travel agent request To Be Assigned (TBA) accommodations. If lower-priced rooms are overbooked, you can be "bumped up" into luxury cabins at the nonluxury rate.

Beating Air Fare Increases

"Buy" the tickets immediately, even if they won't be used for months to come. How it works: Customer arranges with travel agent to buy now, at the current price, but doesn't have to pay until just before the trip. If the trip is cancelled, the customer resells ticket (at a profit, if prices rise). And there's no loss if prices go down. Note: Not all agents will accept delayed payment. Shop around for one who will cooperate and who will track down the bargains. Be prepared to forgo convenience for flight discounts.

Cancelled Airline Tickets

Check monthly credit card statement carefully to be sure that proper credit is given when travel plans are changed and tickets (or portions) are unused. Recommended: (1) Request a refund receipt. (2) Make a note of the ticket numbers and date they were returned. (3) If the charge is not corrected on the following month's bill, call the credit card company's service number and request a temporary credit.

Boarding the Wrong Plane

Airline regulations allow for reimbursement of air fare to passengers who accidentally board a wrong flight. The refund also covers the return flight. Note: Passenger may have to pay the round-trip price and then later apply for what the airlines call a futile flight refund.

Best Tour Seats on a 747

Ask for rows 11 through 18. Best visibility and smoother ride. For nonsmokers: Reserve a seat at least five rows in front of a smoking section for smoke-free air. Extra leg room: Sit in first row of a section or just in back of exits.

Bending the Rules About Carry-on Luggage

Many planes actually provide space for larger luggage than the official 45-inch maximum size. Some can accommodate 60-inch carry-ons. Most allow travelers to hang garment bags in coat compartments. First-class passengers usually get more carry-on space than those passengers in tourist class.

Lost Baggage

The best way to make sure an airline does not lose your baggage: Carry it on the airplane with you. (Alternate: Take along less baggage.)

When you must check your bags:

Place name-and-address tags on the inside and outside of each bag. Airlines supply them at ticket counters. (Use a business, not personal address.) Remove all old baggage-check tags.

Place a note inside each bag that tells where you are heading on your trip and the dates you will be there.

Lock your bags. It won't prevent theft (luggage keys are often interchangeable), but it will keep a bag from opening accidentally.

Carry on the plane such items as medicine, jewelry, your contact lens equipment, and any other small irreplaceable items.

When checking in at the airport, make sure that correct baggage checks (for destination and flight number) are attached to your luggage.

Avoid flights where you change planes and airlines. Reason: Transfers account for 40% of lost baggage. If that proves impossible, don't check your baggage through (make arrangements to recheck it between flights).

To minimize the risk of having your baggage stolen, get to the baggage claim area as soon as possible after landing. Put some instant identification on your bags to set them apart (a red stripe down the center, or a plaid ribbon).

If your luggage fails to appear, notify the

369

baggage-service personnel immediately. Then fill in the proper tracing form. If you don't file the claim promptly, the airline may deny the loss, particularly if damage is involved.

If your baggage doesn't arrive on the same flight, it's likely to show up on the next one. (Ninety-five percent of those that do show up arrive within 24 hours.)

Insurance: The federal government recently increased the amount per bag for which airlines can be held liable (from $500 to $750). But if your bag and its contents are worth more, consider additional insurance. Buy extra-valuation insurance at the check-in counter. Or get an all-risk policy from your own insurance broker. It covers loss or damage to baggage, along with coverage in the event of illness or accident. Check your homeowner policy for baggage insurance. Recommended: Make an inventory describing each bag and its contents. Keep this with you, separate from the baggage.

Flying With a Cold

Take a decongestant before the flight to help clear ears and sinus passages. If the cold is severe: Continue taking decongestants, as prescribed on the label, during the flight. Consider postponing the trip. Alcohol and wines can cause nose and throat problems.

Source: American Physical Fitness Research Institute, 824 Moraga Dr., West Los Angeles 90049.

How to Avoid Jet Lag

Don't change your watch or habits for brief stops.

Stay at an airport hotel with 24-hour food service and a quiet room.

Schedule meetings soon after you arrive if you get there before end of your normal working day. Example: An executive regularly flew from California at 8 a.m. to the East Coast, arriving at 5 p.m. New York time. He knew

from experience that he'd have problems "getting started" the next morning, so he scheduled his meeting at 6 p.m., just after he arrived, since it was only 3 o'clock for him.

For longer stays, be fully rested before departure. Don't rush to the airport. Plan arrivals as close as possible to your normal time for going to sleep. Don't take pills or alcoholic beverages. They hinder the deep sleep vital to recharging mentally.

Don't plan important hard work for the first or second day of a long trip.

When traveling, wear comfortable, loose clothing and shoes. Exercise during the flight. (Isometrics, etc.) Don't overeat or drink heavily.

Important tip: If crucial work must be done immediately after arrival, precondition your mind and body to the destination's time zone for several days before the trip.

Combating Air Travel Fatigue

Before takeoff:

Food and beverages. Eat and drink lightly for 24 hours before a flight. Recommended: Salads, fish, chicken, wine. Avoid: Liquor, bon-voyage parties.

Forty-eight hours before departure: Ask the airline for a special severe hypoglycemia (low blood sugar) on-flight meal. You will probably get a nice seafood salad from the first-class galley, even if you have an economy ticket. On boarding, remind the chief flight attendant about the special meal you ordered.

Clothes: Wear loose-fitting clothing. Bring slip-on shoes. Reason: Long hours of sitting can cause swelling of the legs and, especially, of the feet.

Women: If possible, plan a plane trip within 7 to 10 days after the onset of the menstrual cycle.

Medication: Take an adequate supply and a copy of your prescriptions. A note from your doctor can often avoid hassles with over-zealous customs officials.

In the air:

Avoid consuming all the food and drink offered. Alcohol, nuts, soft drinks, and other foods that have empty calories can cause a swing from high to low blood sugar. You go from feeling great to feeling tired, cramped, and headachy.

Don't do important business work while flying. Reason: Decision-making and complicated paperwork add to an already increased stress level. Better: Accomplish as much as you can before departure. Aboard: Read non-demanding work-related material. Preferred: Relax by reading an absorbing book.

At your destination:

Changes of time, space, and place can cause a feeling of dislocation. Continue following the airborne guidelines of moderation suggested. Realize that your tolerance level for everything from decision-making to dining are below average while on a short trip abroad.

Source: Warren Levin, M.D., and Howard Bezoza, M.D., World Health Group, 5 World Trade Center, New York 10048.

Plane Travel and Heart Strain

Even with pressurized air, being in a plane is similar to being at an elevation of about a mile and a half. The heart works harder, and the very dry air inside the plane means that more carbon monoxide is absorbed into the blood from tobacco smoke, putting even more strain on the heart.

Higher Damages for Airline Accident Victims

Accident victims on international airline flights may be entitled to higher damages than the standard warning on most tickets suggests.

Most airline tickets list damage limitations of $10,000, $20,000, and $75,000. The limit that applies depends on which airline you are flying, the route that is taken, and where the accident occurs. It may also depend on the price of gold.

Background: The $10,000 and $20,000 figures are based on an interpretation by the Civil Aeronautics Board (CAB) of two international treaties (the Warsaw Convention and the Hague Protocol). The $75,000 limit is based on an agreement that the U.S. negotiated directly with the major airlines. It applies only if the treaty limits are lower. But are they?

The $10,000 and $20,000 figures were set by the CAB in 1974, based on the then-official gold price of $42.22 an ounce. The CAB's own lawyers, in an internal document, pointed out that there was no longer any legal basis for using this price. Nevertheless, the CAB has failed to take action. At today's gold prices, the treaty limits would be much higher.

What a claimant should do: Don't settle for the limit on the ticket. Once the issue is properly presented in court, liability may well be recognized in terms of current gold prices, says aviation lawyer Marc S. Moller. The possibility of such a ruling is already a factor when airlines negotiate settlements with knowledgeable attorneys.

Other ways around the limitations:

Showing willful misconduct on the part of the airline.

Attacking the adequacy of the printed warning on a ticket.

Showing that the accident victim never got a ticket with the printed warning on it. (This sometimes happens with chartered tours.)

Source: Marc Moller, partner, law firm of Kreindler & Kreindler, 99 Park Ave., New York 10016.

Making a Hotel Honor Your Reservation

Overbooking is now a common hotel practice. How to make sure your reservation is honored:

Insist that your travel agent give you the actual hotel confirmation number. Beware: A travel agent's voucher is the weakest form of proof. It lacks official acknowledgment from the hotel.

Best: Guarantee payment for a reserved room in advance. How: Give the hotel your credit card number for billing even if you may not show up.

You can cancel this reservation if you notify the hotel in advance. Usually, such cancellations must be made a couple of days before the reservation date. Ask the hotel clerk for details when confirming.

What if your confirmed reservation is still completely ignored? Make a fuss, even to the point of being embarrassed. Rooms have a way of materializing for those who demand them loudly.

Source: Steven Birnbaum, travel editor, *Playboy,* and editor, *Houghton Mifflin's Travel Guide,* Houghton Mifflin Co., Boston.

Telephone Calls from Hotel Rooms

Hotels frequently add their own operator assistance fee to the normal cost of a phone call. What to do: Charge intrastate calls to your credit card or tell the operator to charge the call to your residence telephone number. Both of these procedures will eliminate the hotel surcharge.

Hotel phone surcharges abroad for calls to the U.S. can be triple the amount of the actual costs. Recommended: Ask the switchboard operator what the long-distance surcharge is. If it's unreasonable, make the call from a pay phone.

Saving on Hotel Bills

Ask hotels for their corporate rate. All chain motels, and many individual hotels, have them. Bonus: Business people on personal trips can use the corporate rate, too.

Example: If the range of rates is $45 to $70,

the corporate rate might be $50. That means $50 or less, never more, even if the hotel assigns a deluxe room.

Make arrangements in advance, not at check-in time. To be eligible for corporate rates, a few hotels require a minimum number of visits per year. But many give them to any travelers who write ahead for reservations using their companies' letterheads.

Weekend discounts are often available at hotels and resorts that cater to business travelers during the week. Three-day packages may offer a 30% saving and include extras such as theater tickets, drinks and tours.

Quick Way to Check a Hotel Bill

Adjust the amount of the tips so every item that's added to the bill ends up with the same digit. Example: Tip odd amounts to have the bills for all meals end in the numeral 6. Result: It takes only a moment to skim the list for items that don't end in 6, and, thus, don't belong on your bill. Point: The odds of an accidental 6 occurring on the bill are 9 to 7 in favor of the traveler.

Hotel Guest's Rights

If it's necessary to extend your stay longer than planned, remember that a hotel cannot evict a guest if that guest has paid his bill or established credit.

Holding Down Phone Bills While Traveling

Resist the temptation to use credit cards to charge telephone calls. They can increase the price of a call by as much as 500% over the direct-dial method. One reason: The initial charge on a credit card is three minutes, not one minute.

Develop the habit of calling WATS information at (800) 555-1212 before phoning a hotel, airline, or other large service company. Information knows if a company has a free 800 number.

Source: Frank K. Griesinger, Frank K. Griesinger and Associates, Inc., Suite 1412, Superior Bldg., Cleveland 44114, a management consultant who specializes in communications.

Traveler's Tipping Guide

Waiter: 15% of the bill (not including tax).

Captain: 5%. Note: If diner writes tip on the check, the waiter gets it all, unless the diner specifies how it is to be split. (Example: Waiter, $5; captain, $2.)

Headwaiter who seats diners: $5 or $10 or more at intervals for regular patrons. He should be tipped in cash.

Sommelier: 10% of the wine selection or 5% if the wine is expensive; $2 or $3 is a good tip.

Bartender: $1 minimum or 15% of check.

Hatcheck: 50 cents to $1 per couple.

Restroom attendant: 50 cents.

Doorman (to get taxi): 50 cents normally. $1 in bad weather or rush hour.

Other staff at a restaurant that is regularly used should be tipped once or twice a year: Hosts, switchboard operators (where the restaurant provides telephone service).

Nightclubs: Headwaiter should get $2 to $10 per person, depending on the impression the party host wishes to make on his guests. (Higher tip usually ensures better service.)

Limousine service: 15% to the driver. If service charge is included in bill, tip an additional $5.

Hotels: Valet, room service, bartender should get about 50 cents, depending on amount and quality of service. Bellboy: 50 cents per bag. Chambermaid: $1 per day.

Sports arenas and racetracks: A $5 tip to an usher will often give you and your guests access to unused reserved seats.

Source: Restaurateurs Vincent Sardi, of Sardi's, and Tom Margiatta, co-owner of the Four Seasons.

Tipping Overseas

When leaving the U.S.: Tip skycaps 25 cents to 50 cents a bag.

On a package tour: Even if tips are "included," employees may not know it, so play it safe. Bellhops: 25 cents a bag. Waiters: No tip necessary if it's a different one each meal. But if it's the same waiter for the whole stay, a dollar or two on the first day with the promise of the same at the end will usually guarantee top service. Tour Manager-Guide: $8 per person per week, $12 for 10 days. Local guides: 50 cents per person for a full day.

Touring on your own: Depends on the city and country. In Athens, 18 cents to 25 cents (6 to 8 drachmas) each time the doorman hails a cab for you; $2 to $5 a week for the concierge of a hotel; 30 cents per bag for the bellhop, $3 per person per week for the chambermaid.

In restaurants: Usually there's a 15% service charge, so no tip is necessary. But round off the total to the nearest whole currency denomination, as long as it doesn't add more than 5% to the bill.

For no tipping at all: Try Australia; tipping is not the custom there, or Iceland, where the 15% service charge covers all gratuities.

Tipping on a Cruise

One good rule of thumb for tipping on a vacation cruise: Figure 5% of the ticket cost for gratuities for couples. If traveling alone, budget 7½%.

Whom to tip, how much, and when:

Cabin steward. $1.50 to $2.50 per person per day. Depends on how helpful he's been and how expensive the cabin was. If there's a cabin boy, give him about half of what the steward gets.

Waiter. $1.50 to $2.00 per person per day. If the busboy has been particularly attentive, give him a little something. Otherwise, his share comes out of the waiter's.

Maitre d' and gym and pool attendants. Optional. Key: How much special attention they provided.

Deck steward. Tip each time he performs a service or at the end of the trip. Do whichever seems more appropriate.

Waiters and bartenders in the ship's lounge. 10% of tab in each case. Wine steward: 10% to 15%.

Hairdressers, barbers, etc. The same tip that you would give on land.

Officers. Never.

When to tip: If it's a short cruise, tip on the last evening. If it's a two-week vacation, tip at the end of the first week. If your voyage lasts longer, gratuities should be given every two weeks.

Caution: Before tipping anyone, check with the ship's purser to make sure that gratuities aren't automatically added to the bill when service is requested.

What Car Rental Agencies Don't Tell You

Reserve a car smaller than you actually want. Chances are it won't be available. If the agency doesn't have it, they'll give you a larger one at the small car price.

Many rental companies give the police your name, address, and your home state license number if the car you rented gets a ticket.

Be wary if the car rental agency asks for the name of your auto insurance company. Chances are they're giving you only secondary liability insurance coverage. That means their insurance is exhausted (and your own premiums will go up).

Does the price include fuel? Dry rate means the customer buys the gas. Find out where it's cheapest. Fill up there, too, before dropping the car off.

Special restrictions or charges for one-way rentals.

Special weekend or weekly rates.

When luggage space is important, make sure the reservation spells it out. (A compact or intermediate model may still be suitable.)

Special corporate discount. Comparison shopping on this could hold surprises.

Your airline may have a special fly/drive package.

The policy in case of car trouble.

In case of accident, does the contract include primary liability coverage? (In California and Florida, only secondary coverage is required.)

Car-Rental Myths

Myth: Small rental companies don't have dealer networks to service users efficiently. Fact: Many smaller companies are building impressive rental networks in major cities.

Myth: If a rental agency is cheaper in one city, it will be cheaper throughout the country. Fact: Rates vary substantially from city to city.

Myth: You always save by taking advantage of discount rates. Fact: Discounts are usually offered on the most expensive models, which may easily cost 30% more than smaller vehicles. Corporate discounts may have restrictions.

Myth: Weekend rates apply only on Saturday and Sunday. Fact: Many agencies stretch out weekend rates to cover several days.

Source: *Travel Smart for Business.* Communications House, Dobbs Ferry, NY.

Before Buying a Foreign Car Over There

Sometimes the savings aren't worth the hassle and wasted time.

What to check out:

The specifics of any security deposit required by the government of the country in which the car was made. Example: West Germany requires a deposit as assurance the car won't be resold in that country by an American buyer. Key point: Find out when the deposit will be returned. One buyer waited six months for his $950 to be returned.

Cost of marine insurance to cover shipping of the car, and casualty insurance if car is to be driven before shipping.

Whether initial tune-ups are included in cost. Example: One buyer found out that the 1,000-km. checkup and adjustment was not covered by the purchase price. Cost: $150.

Other factors to consider: (1) Savings pocketed by not renting a car while in Europe (if automobile is used on vacation before shipping home). (2) Possibility of damage not covered by insurance during its voyage home.
Source: *Medical Economics.*

Pros and Cons of Using Credit Cards Overseas

Using credit cards in foreign countries can produce savings on currency conversion. Credit card companies convert at the wholesale rate, which is 3% to 5% better than individuals pay. Diners Club and Carte Blanche pass full benefit along to cardholder. Visa and American Express pass along most of it. Master Charge keeps it all.

Be aware that you're speculating in foreign exchange—though it's rarely with really big dollars. The charged item will cost more if the dollar falls between purchase date and preparation of bill. It will cost less if the dollar rises.

When to Turn Down a Duty-Free 'Bargain'

Check the prices at duty-free shops against prices in local stores. The airport and dockside shops generally charge higher, rather than pre-

vailing, prices for their products. In addition, only top-of-the-line products are sold, meaning that the prices are high to begin with.

Suggestion: Buy only heavily taxed items in these stores.

Tax Refund for Shoppers in Europe

American tourists whose European purchases are for their own personal use can obtain refund of value added tax (VAT), which ranges from 8% to 33% of the purchase price. How to do it: When leaving the European country where the purchase was made, ask the customs official to stamp the receipt. After returning home, mail all receipts back to stores, enclosing U.S. address so purchases can qualify as "exports." Best to arrange for this while you're still in the store. Most will agree to make a refund.

How to Keep out of Trouble with Customs Inspectors

Get an invoice for everything you buy, no matter how inexpensive. Even if you purchase it at a local bazaar or flea market, get something in writing. A scrap of paper with a foreign name or stamp and any legible receipt is admissible proof of a transaction.

Make sure local sales taxes are listed separately on invoices. Taxes on purchase are not subject to duty. But if they're not listed clearly, the amount may be construed as part of the price, thus raising the duty.

List items first that have the highest rates of duty so they will come under the per-person exemption. Always list clothing under the legal exemption to avoid high duty. Jewelry should also be ranked up high on the exemption form. It should always be declared if it was purchased abroad, even though it's been worn. Items with relatively low rates of duty (about 7%): Cameras, radios, and perfume.

When you leave the U.S., give the Customs officer a list of any foreign-made items you are taking with you, like a Japanese camera, Swiss watch, etc. Otherwise, when you reenter the country, Customs officials will assume that these items were just purchased abroad. They may charge full duty on them unless a certificate of registration is produced.

Traveling from developing countries: Recently enacted Generalized System of Preference rule lets the traveler bring in normally dutiable items duty-free from 98 countries and 40 dependent territories. (Details: *GSP & The Traveler,* available at all U.S. Customs offices.)

Gambling Junkets: The Real Cost

People who enjoy gambling in somewhat more than modest amounts should consider the many "free" junkets offered by most Las Vegas hotel-casinos. If a person is known to be a high roller, chances are he already knows about these all-expenses-paid trips to the Nevada resort, because the casinos recruit such players for their junkets.

But a person who has not established such a reputation can get the free RF&B (Vegas hotel talk for room, food, and beverages) by calling or visiting the offices of various Las Vegas hotels situated in major cities. Although these offices are also there to book rooms and tours for people who are willing to pay their own way, they serve to steer the big shooters to Vegas on the free, chartered flights that arrive every day.

There's no trick to getting aboard, except that the junketeer must show a willingness to risk, though not necessarily to lose, substantial sums of his own cash.

How much? A top-flight hotel-casino such as Caesar's Palace wants the first-time junketeer to come with at least $5,000 to bet. (That's for the player and a spouse or friend.)

But, as one junket manager put it: "People go there with the idea of beating the casino without playing—eating the gourmet food in the half-dozen restaurants, having the room with the sunken tub, drinking all that free booze. But they don't want to put their money at any peril. So the guy takes $500 worth of chips, thinks nobody is looking, gives his wife $400, she runs to the cashier's window, and he puts the $100 in his pocket. But that won't work, because everybody in a casino is watched by stickmen, croupiers, pit bosses, and cameras. It's all recorded on their markers and—through the ceiling—on film or tape.

"So if the customer tries to pull that, it goes on his record: Stiff! Don't invite again."

It's strictly business. The obligation of the junketeer is purely to give the house the opportunity to win his money.

Some casinos will settle for less than the $5,000 minimum. But depending on the length of stay and the quality of the hotel, that amount could vary. Some don't even ask to hold the money but settle for a look at a checkbook or savings account passbook to establish that the player is good for the agreed-upon amount.

Once a player becomes known as a heavy bettor, he will usually find (1) that he is in demand for free trips to other casinos, including those in the Caribbean, Monte Carlo, and (2) that he won't have to put up his own money but can get credit up to a limit from a casino.

Typically, play works this way: The player deposits his money with the casino on arrival, then goes to whatever game he wants to play. At such front-rank establishments as the Grand, he is expected to buy at least $500 **worth of chips at a time. He gets the chips by identifying himself to the croupier and signing a marker against his deposit, just like in a bank.** These markers become the record of his style of play.

Players are rated A, B, or lower. But below C +, the player won't be asked back. An A-rated player is strictly black-chip from the shoulder. In Vegas parlance, that means he bets at least $100 (black chips) on opening bet (from the shoulder). A C+ bettor bets $50 from the shoulder and never much less later on.

What shows your pattern and therefore your reputation is the opening bet style. It isn't what a player builds up to that matters. A small initial bet that produces winnings and subsequent bigger bets doesn't rate a player highly. "He's playing with our money, and that doesn't make him a genuine high roller," says the junket manager. "If he bets $25 of his own but $100 of the house's, there's nothing wrong with that, because at least we can get our money back. But that's not what it's all about."

What it is really about, is the house getting a chance to win the player's money. The casino doesn't provide the $300 or $400 a day worth of food, drink, lodging, and entertainment for fun. If a player wins by betting big with his own money, that's fine. He'll look happy on the premises, tell his friends at home about it, and almost certainly come back and allow the odds to work themselves out. (That is, let the house get his money back—and more.)

As long as a player with a plunger reputation can afford to keep coming back he is assured all kinds of extra special treatment. Every first-rate hotel has a resident host or equivalent, a kind of concierge who arranges restaurant and show reservations (the best seats) not only at the junket hotel but at others in town. All the big hotels have reciprocal arrangements, because they want the players to be happy.

Test for Loaded Dice

Fill a tall glass with water, drop each die in gently. Repeat several times, with different number on top each time. If die turns when sinking so that same two or three numbers always show up, it's loaded. Less obvious test: Hold die loosely between thumb and forefinger at diagonally opposite corners. Loaded dice will pivot when weighted side is on top. The movement is unmistakable.

How to Spot a Card Cheat

A recent gambling survey indicates that cheating takes place in 10% of card games. Some ways to protect yourself:

When shuffling cards, never take them entirely off the table, either for the riffle or for squaring the deck.

Get into the habit of cutting the cards at least once during the shuffle by pulling out the bottom half and slapping it onto the top.

If you suspect marked cards, riffle the deck and watch the design on the back. If the cards are marked, some lines in the design will move like an animated cartoon. In an honest deck, the design will stand absolutely still. The player to suspect: The one who keeps his eyes glued to the backs of the cards—especially the hole card in stud poker and the top card of the deck in gin rummy.

Sit with your back against the wall.

Source: *John Scarne's Newsletter.*

When Gambling Losses Are Tax-Deductible

Gambling gains are taxable, but the profits can be offset by gambling losses. Gambling establishments are required by law to report large payouts to the IRS; however, it is up to the individual to establish the amount of any losses.

Here's how IRS says it can be done:

Keep an accurate diary showing names, dates, types of bets, names of witnesses, and dollar amounts.

Save verifiable documentation: Betting tickets, canceled checks, credit records, bank withdrawal slips. Also: Hotel bills, airline tickets, gasoline credit cards, and other records that show you were at gambling locations.

Get affidavits or testimony from responsible gambling officials attesting to your losses. Rev. Proc. 77-29.

Playing Blackjack To Win

Blackjack is a game that lends itself to a system. Here are some of the best techniques, according to expert John Scarne.

When dealer's upcard is:
A two, three, or four: Hit with 12 or less. Stand with 13 or more.

Five or six: Hit with 11 or less. Stand with 12 or more.

Seven, eight, or nine: Hit with 16 or less. Stand with 17 or more.

An ace or ten: Hit on 15 or less. Stand on 16 or more.

Caution: These are best odds only. There are no winning odds. Also, the odds assume a full deck. They change as cards are played. They should be used only when the deck is fresh or when you haven't kept track of cards played.

Proper splitting of pairs (to make two hands out of initial two cards) can pare the house's blackjack advantage from 5.9% to 5.4%. Useful rules:

Split twos and threes when the card the dealer is showing is a two, three, four, five, six, or seven.

Never split fours, fives, or sixes.

Split sevens when the dealer's upcard is five, six, or seven.

Always split eights unless the dealer's upcard is nine, ten, or an ace.

Always split nines unless the dealer's upcard is a ten or an ace.

Always split aces, even when casino rules permit you to draw only one card to each split ace.

Never split tens. Exception: If casino rules require that both of the dealer's cards be dealt face up, split tens when the dealer's count is 19. Under most conditions, this turns a house advantage of 5.9% into a player advantage of 1.71%.

Caution: These rules are also based on a full deck of 52 cards. Odds change as the deck is played.

Source: *Scarne's Guide to Casino Gambling,* by John Scarne, Simon & Schuster, New York.

How to Have a Good Day at the Races

Where to be. Best: The boxes, leased for the season, mostly by horse owners. Only a private arrangement with the boxholder will give you access. A big tip to the usher won't help most outsiders.

Next best: The clubhouse section. Available to anyone willing to pay an extra dollar or two over the grandstand (tourist class) price. The clubhouse is a little cleaner, closer to the finish line and the paddock area (where the horses are walked and saddled before each race).

Sitting in the grandstand is not all bad for the occasional racegoer. The ambience can be fun, and the seats are comfortable.

Neither clubhouse nor grandstand admission entitles you to a seat, however. So reserve seats in advance, especially on weekends. (If you don't have a reserved seat but find an empty one, fold a sheet of newspaper into the seat slats. This indication that the seat is taken will almost invariably be respected.)

Alternative: Most major racetracks have tiered, glass-enclosed clubhouse dining rooms. Food is fair and the tables provide a comfortable view of the races. (Closed-circuit TV also available.) It's okay to keep a table for the entire afternoon even though you walk away to the betting windows, etc. Table reservations are always advisable.

Getting there. Traffic jams, in and out of the racetrack, are inevitable. Arrive early or very late. Regular parking lots will usually leave you some distance from the entrance gate. Preferred parking lot (at a moderate surcharge) is better. Valet service is convenient going in, but inevitably means a lengthy wait on the way out, when the track is crowded. (Recommended only on weekdays.)

Horse selection tips. Watch the horses close up being saddled and walked in the paddock area. (Bring lightweight binoculars or rent them at the track.)

Favorites: Betting on favorites is the simplest way to give yourself a chance to be a small winner—or, more likely, a small loser. (Approximately one favorite in three wins.) Indiscriminate favorite betting is a losing proposition. Statistics indicate that younger horses (two- and three-year-olds) provide a somewhat higher percentage of winning favorites than do older horses. Betting these will moderately increase your chances of coming out slightly ahead.

Weight: It's very important and often overlooked, especially in short races. The occasional bettor should look with keen interest at lighter-weight horses in any race.

Jockeys. Average bettor overestimates the importance of the big-name jockey. An apprentice, who has not yet made his reputation, is given a five- to ten-pound weight advantage. This and the fact that less money is bet on his mount because of its rider means a better payoff if the apprentice wins.

Post position. An inside post position is a big help. Each horse between yours and the inside rail around a full turn means your horse runs an extra full horse's length to the finish line. Of course, there is usually more crowding close to the rail, and at some tracks the footing on the inside is a bit softer, hence slower. Still, on balance, the horse in a position to "save ground" has a definite advantage.

Previous race. Horses tend to react adversely to very strong efforts. (The great Secretariat, for example, was beaten three times by much inferior horses—each time in a race that followed an unusually strong effort.) In addition, a horse that has just run an unusually good race will be heavily bet the next time it runs.

Traveler Beware

• Don't fly within 12 hours after dental work. The change in atmospheric pressure can cause severe pain.

• First-class air travel. Not worth the 30% premium unless the flight lasts more than four hours.

• You shouldn't pay the 8% federal tax on air fare if you're flying from one U.S. city to another U.S. city in order to catch a flight to another country. You may have to show the agent the foreign ticket.

• Don't take the night train Channel crossing to Paris. It is very uncomfortable and travelers just do not get much sleep or rest. Better: Cross the Channel by plane or try the enjoyable ride by hovercraft during the day.

• Carry your medical history. Fold a one-page summary of health data into your passport. What it should include: Blood type, allergies, eyeglass prescription, medications currently being taken, any pre-existing health condition.

• Don't buy travel insurance at airports. Coverage is much more expensive and rates vary from city to city. Better: Buy directly from insurance company.

• Confirm airline reservations when the small box in the center of the airline ticket is marked "RO." It indicates that the travel agent has only requested a seat, and wait-listing status is a possibility. A confirmed reservation is indicated by an "OK" on your ticket.

• Alcohol has more punch during an airplane flight than on the ground. Reason: Body fluids evaporate quickly in the pressurized dry cabin. And under pressure the alcohol absorbs more fluids in the intestinal tract, thus making itself felt more quickly. Alternative: To reduce the dehydration of a long flight (six hours or more), drink three or four pints of water.

• Nonsmoking travelers. If the airline's check-in clerk says the nonsmoking section is filled, be insistent. The airline must supply nonsmoking seats to all passengers who request to be put in that section.

• Separate passports for family members. Husband, wife, and each child over 13 years old must have their own individual passports, even when they are traveling together.

Preventing Diarrhea While Traveling

University of Texas Medical School researchers have discovered that the primary ingredient in Pepto-Bismol (bismuth subsalicylate) can help to prevent the most common traveler's ailment. A group of new students in Mexico received four tablespoons of the medication four times a day for 21 days. Others were given a placebo. Diarrhea developed in 14 of 62 students on medication, versus 40 of 66 students on the placebo.

Eating Safely In the Tropics

Skip fruit unless you peel it with your hands. Eat food freshly cooked and still hot when served. Don't trust mayonnaise, dressings, custards, and cream fillings. Hard-boiled eggs are okay if you break the shells yourself. Warning: Spice doesn't decrease contamination.

Protecting Yourself Against Muggers

The best defense against becoming a crime victim is to avoid a setup. Muggers, like most people, don't take more risks or work harder than they have to. Point: They choose victims who seem easy to handle. And they create situations that make the attack simpler.

Chief defense: Don't allow yourself to be distracted, isolated, or simply stopped on the street by a stranger. Muggers prefer victims who have stopped moving. They use every technique to accomplish that: Asking for directions, a match or a handout.

First and most important rule: When spoken to by a suspicious stranger, don't stop. Move away quickly. Don't slow down to watch an argument or any other commotion on the street. Fake street fights are a favorite way to set up a robbery.

Defensive tactics:

Walk down the middle of the sidewalk near the street. Be wary of corners and doorways.

Reduce the possibility of being grabbed from the shadows. Hugging the curb permits you to see around the corner while at a distance. Be alert to someone hiding between or behind parked cars.

Walk a couple of extra blocks to take a safe route, especially late at night. Keep to known neighborhoods. Identify in advance where the places of refuge are, in event of trouble.

Look ahead up the street (not down) to see what's happening. Be alert, especially to people loitering or moving suspiciously. Example: Two men up ahead who suddenly separate and begin walking apart. They could be preparing to set you up.

However foolish or rude it may seem, don't get on any self-service elevator if there's somebody at all suspicious on it. Never let an elevator you are on go to the basement. How to avoid it: When entering an open elevator, keep a foot in the door while pressing the floor number. Keep your eyes on the elevator indicator. If the arrow is pointing down, don't get in.

Don't get into a self-service elevator late at night without making sure nobody is waiting on an upper floor to intercept you. How to do it: Push the top floor elevator button, but don't get in. If the elevator does not stop on any floor on the way up or down, it's safe.

Avoid places where gangs of juveniles congregate. They can be more dangerous than professional muggers because they will often hurt a victim rather than take the money and run.

Get into the habit of automatically saying excuse me when you bump into someone on the street. Say it no matter who's fault it is.

Never show money in public, whether at a newsstand, market, bank, or getting out of a cab. Muggers are watching.

If you are mugged:

Cooperate. Above all, communicate the willingness to cooperate. Keep calm. It can help relax the mugger, too, which is crucial. Reason: If a mugger is pointing a cocked revolver, nervousness on his part could be fatal to you. Ways to calm the situation: Say something reassuring, or ask a distracting question that establishes the mugging as a businesslike transaction. Example: You can have anything you want. Do you mind if I just keep my driver's license?

Never move suddenly. Tell the mugger where your wallet is and ask: Do you want me to get it, or do you want to get it?

A woman mugger with a knife or gun can kill just as easily as a man. Letting macho feelings interfere with cooperating is suicidal.

Don't show the slightest condescension or hostility. Be careful of your tone of voice. Cooperating with disdain can set off violence. Best attitude to project: You've got to earn a living too. Or: I don't hold this against you at all, times are tough.

Don't make jokes. They are too risky, and the chance for misinterpretation is too great.

Avoid direct or steady eye contact.

If a mugger is particularly hostile, be super-cooperative. Offer money or possessions he has overlooked.

Bottom line: Always carry mugger money. Keep $25 to $100 in your pocket as insurance. A happy mugger is much less likely to do harm than one who comes away empty-handed.

Source: Ken Glickman, director, Civilian Defense Training Center, 61 W. 23rd St., New York 10010.

Traveler's Security

Nothing puts a damper on a vacation faster than having your money stolen. Basic precautions:

Keep only the amount of cash you will need for a day or two, and divide it up among family members. Keep the rest in traveler's checks. Never put all your cash or traveler's checks in one place or one pocket.

Leave credit cards you won't need at home.

Use a thin wallet, and put it in an inconspicuous place (never in your back pocket).

Don't drop off your room key at the hotel desk until you check out. If the hotel has a duplicate key for your room, tell them you want it. When you're at the pool or beach, put your key in your bathing suit, not on a chair or in your robe.

Burglar-proof your hotel room when you're out: (1) Ask the maid service to make up the room as early as possible. (2) Leave the TV or radio on and the do-not-disturb sign on the door.

Good place to hide things in the hotel room: Under the rug beneath the bed. If it's difficult to get to, it will also be difficult for the burglar.

Don't use a "pickproof" lock on hotel dresser drawers. That lets the burglar know precisely where your valuables are.

Do buy a travel lock to attach to your hotel room door. Cost: About $12. Too many people have access to hotel keys.

As you leave the hotel room for dinner, insert a small piece of paper low down in the door. If it isn't still there when you return, it means that someone has entered the room. What to do: Go back and get someone from hotel security to enter the room first.

Thieves Who Prey on Travelers

A stranger engages the traveler in conversation while an accomplice walks off with the luggage. Recommended: Keep bags in view at all times—in airport lounges, restaurants, while checking in at hotel, etc.

A thief listens in the hotel hallway for the sound of a running shower, then quickly picks the lock (or uses a passkey). Particularly vulnerable: Hotels without chain locks on doors. Prevention: Carry a wedge of wood and place it under the door while showering.

381

15

Health

Little-Known Health Hazards

• Aluminum cooking pans should be thrown out if corroded or marked with pits surrounded by white deposits. New evidence indicates that food cooked in corroded aluminum pans absorbs the metal. Possible results: Impaired kidney function, brain and nerve cell problems, and behavioral abnormalities.
Source: *The New England Journal of Medicine.*

• Foam insulation releases formaldehyde gas after installation in a house. Effects on those susceptible: Respiratory problems, eye irritation, skin rashes, nausea, headaches, dizziness. What to do: Some local health departments test for formaldehyde in the air. Many private laboratories provide the service for a modest fee.

• Electric blankets are a hazard to people with occlusive arterial disease. Uncontrolled heat may lead to gangrene by increasing metabolism but not circulation.

• Hair dye hazard. Paraphenylenediamine, a common ingredient in hair dyes, has been found to damage the lens of the eye. Some

89% of the long-term hair-dye users tested had developed cataract problems. The extent correlated with the frequency and duration of use.

• Alcohol and allergies. Sensitivity to foods may increase when they are consumed with or at around the same time as alcohol. Have physician check further when allergy to alcohol is suggested. It may actually be allergy to a food.

• Mascara hazard. Bacteria buildup in opened tubes of mascara leads to eye infections. Prevention: Discard all open containers of mascara after six months or less.

• Caffeine can produce the same symptoms as anxiety neurosis: Insomnia, muscle twitching, headache, restlessness, and irritability. Drinking three or four cups of cola, coffee, or tea daily is probably okay, but more can result in bad side effects. Note: Some headache remedies contain caffeine and boost intake considerably.

• Prescribed drugs can cause more harm than good if combined with other medications or even some foods. Recommended: Ask the doctor about what should and should not be taken with all prescriptions you and family members are given.

• Vitamin C and aspirin should *not* be taken together. Studies at the University of Southern Illinois indicate that combined heavy doses produce excessive stomach irritation, could lead to ulcers.

• Use eyedrops sparingly, especially commercial brands. Reason: They relieve redness by constricting blood vessels so eyes will look whiter. If used frequently, varicose veins can develop and eyes will become permanently reddened.

• Kidney failures may be brought on by overuse of analgesics. Frequent cause of damage: Mixture of aspirin and phenacetin or acetaminophen, which is found in many painkillers sold over the counter as well as by prescription.

• Toxic common plants. Plum pits, apple seeds, apricot pits, morning glory seeds, English ivy, American ivy, holly, hyacinth, hydrangea, lantana, Japanese yew, delphinium, Virginia creeper, lily of the valley, daffodil bulbs, azalea, rhododendron, rhubarb leaf blades, sweet pea, wisteria, nightshade, Jack-in-the-pulpit, water hemlock.

• Ice water can be harmful for people with heart disease. Reason: A sudden drop in body temperature can cause an additional strain on the heart. Chilled water poses no danger to most people. However, it can cause stomach cramps if taken right after strenuous exercise, at which time the body's internal temperature is elevated.

Source: *Prevention*.

• Steak, the most popular entree at business meals, contains more saturated fat (and less unsaturated fat) in an average serving than other meats. Federal health officials have urged Americans to cut back on saturated fats to help lower the risk of heart disease and cancer. Suggestion: Eat desirable alternates such as ham, pork, liver, chicken and turkey. They contain far less saturated fat and have a more favorable balance of unsaturated fats. Most fish have even less saturated fat.

Source: *Executive Fitness Newsletter*.

• The elderly may have different reactions to some medications than younger people.

Reason: Slower metabolism often results in accumulation of drugs in the liver (such as sleeping pills). Can cause an overdose. Antidepressants may cause confusion, loss of appetite, tremors, or anxiety.

• Cut flowers sometimes contain high levels of pesticides. If inhaled, they can cause, in the short run, headaches, blurred vision, and muscle weakness. Recent study: 18% of flower arrangements were polluted.

• Acupuncture needles can cause hepatitis. Recent problem: Six patients treated by acupuncture at a Florida clinic developed hepatitis because the needles had not been properly sterilized. Solution: Insist on disposable needles. (The Florida clinic now uses them.)

Source: Health Devices Alerts, 5800 Butler Pike, Plymouth Meeting, PA 19462, semimonthly.

• Avoid using a copper utensil that puts the metal directly in contact with food. Why: Copper poisoning, which can be lethal. Basic rule: Use only lined copperware. Check the lining periodically. When it becomes worn, have the pot relined (or stop using it for food). Safer: Maximize heat efficiency without risk by using copper-bottom pans. Beware: Utensils made of brass (which contains copper).

Source: *How Safe Is Food in Your Kitchen?* Charles Scribner's Sons, New York.

• Biking hazard. Standard, narrow, hard leather bicycle seats may compress nerves in the pubic area, leading to impaired sexual responses in men and possibly women. Recommended: If necessary add extra seat padding. Also: Give the seat a more downward slant.

Source: *The New England Journal of Medicine*.

• Nonstick cookware remains controversial. Key component: Fluorocarbon resins. They impart traces of fluorides to foods, making them toxic to fluoride-sensitive persons. Safety first: Never overheat food in nonstick utensils. And be sure to discard the cookware when the nonstick coating becomes scratched, or if the cookware either chips or peels.

Source: *How Safe Is Food in Your Kitchen?* Charles Scribner's Sons, New York.

• Toxic metals can build up in tap water overnight because they leach out of the plumbing. Defense: Run the tap for a few minutes. In water-scarce areas, shower first, then make the coffee. Use the cold tap for food and beverage preparation. Hot water, far more corrosive, contains greater amounts of dangerous debris.

Source: *How Safe Is Food in Your Kitchen?* Charles Scribner's Sons, New York.

• Hazard at health clubs. Steam baths, saunas, and hot tubs induce certain strains on the body. In the circulatory system, there is an increase in blood pumped and pulse rate but a decrease in circulation time. Meaning: The heart sends more blood to the skin for cooling purposes and less to the vital organs. Even the feeling of relaxation following the exposure to heat may be merely relief that it's over. Up-shot: Heat treatments should be used only by those with strong hearts. They are not advised for people with hardening of the arteries, hyperthyroid conditions, heart or lung disorders.

Source: *Executive Fitness Newsletter.*

• Being too thin is as dangerous to your health as being too fat, according to the results of a 24-year mortality study. The researchers were surprised at the finding. They speculate that skinny individuals smoked more than fat ones and that may have had some effect on the statistics. Note: There is a thin line between healthy trim and unhealthy emaciated.

Source: National Heart, Lung and Blood Institute, 9000 Rockville Pike, Bethesda, MD 20014.

Health Fallacies

• All-in-one vitamin supplements are misleading as to the amount of the nutrients they provide. They supply 100% of some nutrients, trace amounts of others, and leave out some vital minerals and vitamins altogether. Problem: Consumers think they are receiving ample supplies of vitamins and minerals. This tempts them to disregard the need for a balanced diet.

Source: Dr. Helen A. Guthrie, professor of nutrition, Pennsylvania State University, University Park, PA 16802.

• Breast infection developed while nursing babies doesn't mean that nursing should be discontinued. Fact: Nursing with the affected breast helps treat the infection, which is called mastitis. The milk is not tainted by the breast infection.

Source: Dr. Audrey J. Naylor, Director of the Lactation Clinic, University of California at San Diego, Box 109, La Jolla, CA 92093.

• Doubtful drug. Medical authorities and government agencies are stepping up warnings about so-called vitamin B^{15}. The Federal Drug Administration says it has no therapeutic value, and at least one doctor, Victor Herbert of New York's S.U.N.Y. Downstate Medical Center, says B^{15} may even be harmful. No standard formula exists for the drug, which is also known as pangamic acid or Pangamate.

Source: *ACSH News and Views.*

• Rash after receiving penicillin is not always an allergic reaction. The rash is often a result of the illness. True allergic reactions: Hives, swelling in throat, joint pain, chest constriction.

Source: *The Harvard Medical School Health Letter.*

• Milk may not help ulcers, says an eminent gastroenterologist, although it's traditionally prescribed as a buffer for the stomach. It is now known that the calcium in milk stimulates secretion of acids that aggravate ulcers. Antacids with high buffering capacity are better. (People on low-salt diets should select antacids with low sodium content.) Food also acts as a buffer. Ulcer patient should have food in the stomach at all times. Important to eat often, but not large quantities.

• Corrective shoes for children with foot problems seldom do any good. Reality: Children outgrow most lower-limb deformities without special treatment. Some severe cases may require operations, casts, or splints. But the records show that sole wedges to cure pigeon-toes or corrective shoes for flat feet, bowlegs, or knock-knees do not correct the basic deformity.

• Covering a public toilet seat with paper may be fastidious, but is not necessary. Diseases are rarely transmitted by toilet seats.

Source: *Medical Aspects of Human Sexuality.*

• Buffered aspirin, contrary to its advertised benefits, doesn't alleviate the stomach and digestive problems many people have with plain aspirin. Tests show digestive problems are about the same with regular aspirin and buffered aspirin. But a test group that took *enteric-coated* aspirin had practically no digestive problems.

Source: *The New England Journal of Medicine.*

• Cholesterol: Not all bad. One form, high-density lioprotein (HDL), is associated with decreased risk of heart disease. HDL helps block the production of the more dangerous form of cholesterol, low-density lipoprotein (LDL), which clogs the arteries. Long-distance runners, joggers, moderate drinkers, and the college-educated are more likely to have high levels of the beneficial HDL. Reason: College-level education promotes nutritional awareness and proper health-care habits. But overweight individuals, heavy smokers, and the less educated have more LDL, increasing their risk of atherosclerosis.

• Dark circles below the eyes are probably hereditary. There is no medical basis for the myth that fatigue and lack of sleep cause these dark areas.

Source: *Journal of the American Medical Assn.*

• Acupuncture doesn't relieve all types of pain. It does help: Low back, shoulder, neck, and knee pain. (Areas close to the trunk respond best.) Osteoarthritis in certain joints. Muscle contraction and migraines. Pain related to nerve injury. It often alleviates psychological pain, such as acute depression.

Source: *Free Yourself From Pain,* by Dr. David E. Bresler, Simon & Schuster.

Keeping Your Cool in the Summer Heat

Make a planned effort to increase your (and your family's) heat tolerance. The key is to improve your sweat rate, the rate of evaporation of water from the skin's surface. Best ways: Slowly build up your stamina by taking walks in the sun or working out. Typical result: Within one to two months, a doubling or tripling of your evaporation capacity.

Replace lost water by drinking large amounts of cool water or other beverages. Four or five glasses is not too much for four hours outside on a hot day. (Professional tennis champion Roscoe Tanner now drinks 12 glasses of water before a tennis match.) Sugared drinks, including orange juice, probably help because they also provide an energy pickup. Stay away from: Alcoholic beverages (even cool mint juleps) and heavily iced drinks.

Overrated: Gatorade. It is useful only for a few individuals who lack adequate amounts of potassium in their systems. Salt tablets are usually unnecessary and can be dangerous. Most Americans consume about four grams of salt daily, 10 times the amount lost on a hot day.

Keep the skin surface cool. Almost any method works, including dousing the head, swimming, bathing, and applying ice packs. Wear loose, light clothing.

Recognize the onset of heat-injury symptoms. Heat exhaustion does not strike unannounced. You will feel sick before you collapse. Do not push that sick feeling the way a jogger pushes pain. Death can occur when blood temperature rises to 105°.

Although injuries due to heat are usually temporary, strokes and heart attacks do tend to occur with more frequency during unusual heat.

Do not pamper yourself. If you have built up your sweat rate and are under 50 years old, you should be able to play a set or two of tennis at high noon in a city like Houston with no ill effects.

Do not count on air conditioning to protect you. Some units fail when the temperature reaches 110° or more, and individuals may be better off outdoors. Also okay: Moving from ice-cold air-conditioned buildings or cars to the hot street and vice versa, as long as the transitions do not trigger heat-injury symptoms in you.

Source: Reuel A. Stallones, M.D., dean of the School of Public Health, University of Texas Medical School, Box 20186, Houston 77025, who has done heat-injury research on Army recruits, and Virginia Gill, Ph.D., assistant director of the Public Health Dept., 414 E. 12 St., Kansas City, MO 64106.

When You Need a Tetanus Booster

Tetanus boosters are required every 10 years for resisting infection by the tetanus organism colostridiam. In the event of a wound, especially from a puncture, get a booster shot immediately if it's been as long as five years since your last one.

Problem: Once you have been infected, medical techniques against tetanus are only marginally effective. Mortality rate: 40% to 50%.

Symptoms: Rigid contractions of the facial muscles (lockjaw), followed by muscle contractions in the arms, torso, and legs. Time: 5 to 10 days after injury. Since the lungs are affected, the cause of death is asphyxiation.

Treatment: Use of a respirator, muscle relaxants, and tetanus antitoxins. Allergic reactions to tetanus antitoxins are rare. However, there is no test to predict such a reaction (called tetanus toxoid). If a serious reaction results, it must be treated with adrenaline.

Bottom line: Tetanus is easy to prevent but perilous to cure. Keep up to date on shots.

Source: Dr. Arthur Reingold, medical epidemiologist, the Center for Disease Control, 1600 Clifton Rd. NE, Atlanta 30333.

Health Do's and Don'ts for Parents

• Your negative attitudes about tooth care could be dangerous to your children's teeth. Don't encourage children to think tooth problems are inherited and trips to the dentist are thus a waste. Misconceptions frequently expressed by parents: I was born with soft teeth. I'll lose my teeth at an early age because my father did. I thought gums were supposed to bleed. False teeth don't look so bad, and they don't get cavities.

Source: *Your Mouth Is Your Business,* by Hyman J.V. Goldberg, DMD, Appleton-Century-Crofts, New York.

• Mouthwash is not for kids. Young children, attracted by its pretty colors and nice smells, may be tempted to drink it. Special problem: Popular brands of mouthwash contain roughly twice the amount of alcohol found in beer and wine. Suggested: Keep mouthwashes out of reach of young children.

• Children's medication. A major factor in the amount of dosage is determined by the child's weight and height, not age.

• Allergies and bed-wetting. Allergies to cow's milk, chocolate, eggs, grain, or citrus fruits can make children wet their beds. How: These foods swell the bladder and keep its outlet from closing properly. The allergy also brings on deep sleep, which inhibits the child from getting up during night to go to the bathroom. Cure: Once the allergy-causing food is withheld from the child, the problem rights itself.

Source: Study conducted by James C. Breneman, M.D., chairman of the food allergy committee of the American College of Allergies, 2141 14 St., Boulder, CO 80302.

• Deafness in infants can now be determined as early as the first day of life. High-risk babies are given a crib-o-gram. Ordinarily, the handicap isn't discovered until a child is two years old. By that time, much of the prime language-development period is over. The new test prevents problems of delayed diagnosis. Pioneer: Dr. F. Blair Simmons, Stanford University, Palo Alto, CA.

• Bronchitis and pneumonia in infants increases in proportion to their exposure to cigarette smoke. Reason: Secondhand smoke can trigger respiratory symptoms or worsen them in many individuals who are sensitive to tobacco smoke. Note: Asthmatic children whose parents smoke often improve when the parents quit and the home air is freed of smoke.

• A special blood test is recommended for babies whose mothers ate undercooked meat or were exposed to animal droppings during pregnancy. The test diagnoses taxoplasmosis. Unchecked, taxoplasmosis leads to mental retardation, blindness, and epilepsy in the child.

• Children's vision should be checked before they are one year old, then once more before the youngster starts school. Biannually thereafter. Early checkups help identify congenital diseases and developmental problems, including poor focusing, poor convergence, and amblyopia (which is a medical condition that can cause one eye to stop functioning altogether). Parents should be alert to early symptoms of eye trouble: Squinting, eye-rubbing, redness, tearing. Problem: A child who has never experienced clear vision will regard his own fuzzy eyesight as normal.

• Expectant mothers: Avoid caffeine. While the FDA does not consider the substance a drug, it is a stimulant that has a druglike effect. Recent FDA studies with pregnant rats indicate that caffeine consumption, at a level equivalent to two cups of coffee a day for humans, delayed growth in offspring.

• Children and sugar. Hyperactive children react especially badly to sugar. Even average consumption (3 ½ tablespoons per day) aggravates mean and nasty behavior. That sugar behavior association applies to normal children as well. Recommended: Limit children's intake of candy, cake, and soda. Encourage: Fruit, nut, and juice consumption.

Source: *Prevention.*

How to Help a Stutterer

When talking with someone who stutters (or has some other speech impediment), these things will put him more at ease:

Don't try to supply the word he's stuck on or try to complete the sentence. You'll just frustrate the speaker, especially when your suggestion is wrong.

Focus on what's being said instead of how it's being said. Resisting the temptation to interrupt shows that you value what's being said.

Phrase questions so they can be answered with short and direct responses.

Try not to react to the speech problem. Do this by maintaining eye contact and listening patiently.

Reminder: Stuttering and stammering are common in children and usually disappear as they grow older. There's no reason for concern unless the problem continues or worsens in elementary school. If it does, consult a speech therapist.

Source: Susan Wildman, speech therapist, Los Angeles, writing in *Teacher.*

Being Left-Handed

Left-handers comprise 4% to 10% of the American population. Male lefties outnumber female by two to one. The actual number of true left-handers may be much larger. The others were trained in babyhood to use their right hands. Left-handers have it tough in school (doing the opposite of what the teacher demonstrates), the military (rifles are designed for the right hand), and opening doors. But in case of stroke (or other brain damage), many have a great advantage. About half of the lefties have speech control on both sides of the brain so damage to one side is easily compensated for. Surprise: both the mentally retarded and the academically superior include more left-handers than the general population.

More information: The Aristera Organization, 9 Rices Lane, Westport, CT 06880.

Aging: The Process, and How to Delay It

Our life span is fixed. Scientific advances are increasing our life *expectancy*, not our *span*. Anthropologists say it has been the same for about 100,000 years. Without disease, most of us will die between ages 73 to 97.

The good news: We can all die in good health. More and more major diseases have been eliminated as causes of premature death. The breakdown of cells is an ongoing process. While we can't live longer, we can live better.

Aging is not a real term. There is no such thing. It is a composite of dozens of factors.

Specifically, it is the process of losing things: Hair, elasticity, strength, memory, eyesight, job, friends and, finally, life itself.

The rate of loss differs among individuals. For some people, it is a gradual process, taking place over 20 years. For others, it is good health to death in 20 seconds. In fact, any time frame is arbitrary.

What you can do: Some aspects of aging can be controlled or modified, and others cannot.

Examples:

Cataracts, gray hair, and loss of elasticity are not modifiable.

Physical vigor (cardiovascular reserves), mobility, and memory can usually be retained or improved. The way to modify them is through training.

Select those aspects of aging that most concern you, and work on improving them. Practice. You will only get better at what you work on. There is very little cross-transfer. If you concentrate on improving your memory, don't expect positive changes in other areas. However, the more areas you choose to modify, the more you can delay the onset of old age, and shorten the span of infirmity.

Prerequisites for staying young while getting old:

Relative good health. Taking proper care of yourself (nutrition, exercise, rest) is useful, but health is primarily a function of good genes. If your parents live to a ripe old age, chances are you will too.

Comfortable income. The anxiety caused by money worries is as detrimental to older people as it is to younger ones. It helps to have the freedom to pursue enjoyment, as well as to meet basic needs.

Companionship. Social connections are extremely important in staying productive. Be it a spouse, old friends or, even better, newer acquaintances, people to talk with and do things with are valuable assets.

Mental involvement. Have a positive outlook. The single most important factor in staying alive and alert is to stay plugged into the society. See what is happening, know what is going on. Have plans for tomorrow and further into the future. Wake up every day with a full program. Be too busy. Always run a little be-

hind. Despair and boredom are the real killers.

Source: Herbert R. Mayes, age 81, former editor of *Good Housekeeping* and *McCalls's*; Arthur Schechner, president of Schechner Corp., 241 Millburn Ave., Millburn, NJ 07041, and an expert on nursing homes; and Dr. James F. Fries, associate professor of medicine at the Stanford Medical Center and coauthor of *Vitality and Aging*, W.H. Freeman & Co., San Francisco.

Popular Remedies That Can Hurt You

Heavy use of over-the-counter medications (those that are freely available) can frequently exacerbate existing conditions and even create new problems. Common examples:

Aspirin: Daily ingestion of aspirin can cause small erosions on the surface of the stomach. Possible result: Bleeding, iron-deficiency anemia, even predisposition to ulcers. Discard old aspirin. Pills exposed to air absorb moisture. Decomposition releases acids that seriously irritate the stomach.

Antacids: They often mask symptoms that should be brought to a doctor's attention. Antacids with calcium carbonate may cause kidney stones or acid rebound (the acid returns in an even more aggravated condition after the medication wears off). High amounts of sodium in other antacids (sodium bicarbonate) are dangerous for individuals with high blood pressure, heart trouble, or on low-salt diets.

Nasal decongestant sprays can be addictive. Reason: With repeated use, more and more spray is required to shrink the swollen vessels in the nose, which cause stuffiness. Advice: Do not exceed the recommended dosage. If you are already hooked, an ear, nose, and throat specialist can inject small amounts of cortisone to help cure the stuffiness and break the habit.

Eyewashes: The ones that constrict the vessels in the eye have a rebound effect, too. After their effects wear off, redness may return in even more severe forms. Eyewashes may also mask early signs of glaucoma.

Staying on the Safe Side of Tranquilizers

Prescription tranquilizers have become one of the most widely used drugs in America. Result: The incidence of tranquilizer addiction is rising. It frequently comes about by following the doctor's orders.

Symptoms:

A need for more and more pills.

Blackouts or other incidents of increased sensitivity after intake of moderate amounts of alcohol.

Getting prescriptions for tranquilizers from two or more doctors.

How to avoid addiction:

Question your doctor's prescription for tranquilizers in the first place. Examples: If the medication is for a physical symptom, ask the doctor why tranquilizers are appropriate. If the prescription is to treat insomnia, ask the doctor about alternative treatments through diet and exercise. Point: Some physicians see tranquilizers as the answer to all their patients' problems.

Don't exceed the prescribed dosage.

Each time you renew the prescription, first consider alternatives for treating your ailment.

If you feel vulnerable to addiction, contact *Pills Anonymous*, a self-help group, Box 473, Ansonia Station, New York 10012.

Getting a Good Night's Sleep Without Pills

Sleep problems—from clinical insomnia to the occasional night of restless slumber—can be cured.

The first step in the cure is to become aware that you're not alone—and that something can be done. Most people have some sort of sleep problem. Dr. Frank Zorick, former clinical director of the sleep disorder center at Cincinnati Veterans Administration Hospital and the University of Cincinnati, offers advice on solving sleep problems.

Occasional insomniacs, Dr. Zorick says, usually contribute to their problem by worrying that theirs is a serious disorder—and a symptom of even more sleep problems in the future. By occasional, Dr. Zorick means anything from one sleepless night a week to one a year. In most cases, sufferers should dismiss those symptoms. They are usually caused by nothing more than some specific and temporary stress or anxiety.

How do you know when your occasional insomnia has become a chronic disorder?

"To be a chronic problem, the loss of sleep must have a real effect on your daytime functioning," says Dr. Zorick. "My usual question is, 'What would you be doing differently during the day if you were getting eight hours' sleep at night?' In other words, what benefit would being able to sleep bring them?"

Sometimes, Dr. Zorick will find that a person is simply not sleeping as much as he thinks he should, but that his daytime functioning is not adversely affected. In those cases, the patient probably is trying to sleep more hours than he needs to.

Dr. Zorick's prescription for the occasional insomniac: Condition your sleep environment. Learn to associate your bed and your bedroom with sleep.

How to do it? Dr. Zorick suggests:

Pay attention to bedroom conditions, such as light, heat, noise. Shut off telephones if necessary. Keep temperature cool (around 68°). Make sure your mattress and your sleep clothing are comfortable.

If you don't fall asleep right away, get up, leave the bedroom, and go do something else. Don't lie awake thinking about it. Staying in bed for hours trying to get to sleep accentuates the problem. You begin to associate your bed and bedroom with trying to sleep instead of with sleeping.

Stick to a regular bedtime schedule. Go to bed at the same time every night—weekdays and weekends. Some insomniacs have the idea they'll catch up on missed sleep on the weekends. You can't do it. Trying to do it simply disrupts your biological rhythms.

As for other popular sleep inducers or aids, Dr. Zorick has this to say:

Sleeping pills. Doctor-prescribed sedatives are very useful in temporary situations where a particular emotional or physical upset is the cause of the insomnia. Problem: Tendency to become dependent on them, and a worsening of the quality of sleep as more pills are used.

How to handle pills: Use for no more than a week or two. Expect that the first night or two after stopping the pills will be very disturbed sleep. That's perfectly normal. Expect it and accept it.

Nonprescription, over-the-counter sleeping pills are absolutely useless. Studies have shown "sugar pills" to be just as effective.

Exercise. Early in the day is okay. Late in the evening is too stimulating. Exception to the rule: Sexual activity, within a comfortable relationship where no tension or anxiety exists, is helpful.

Caffeine. Coffee, tea, soft drinks act as stimulants. Avoid completely.

Alcohol. May help you get to sleep but interferes with quality of sleep. Wears off after several hours.

Widely advertised insomnia cures like vibrating beds, prerecorded cassette tapes, sleep masks? Dr. Zorick says, "Fine, if they relax you."

Side Effects of Sleeping Pills

Hypnotics (drugs prescribed to help you fall asleep and stay asleep) stay in your bloodstream for a long time. If you take sleeping pills for a week, the accumulation in your system will be four to six times what it was the first morning. Be aware of any decrease in your abilities (such as hand-eye coordination). Be especially careful about driving if drowsy.

They can interfere with other drugs you are taking. Let your doctor know if you are taking another medication of any type.

If you have respiratory problems, impaired liver function, or you are elderly, there are increased risks in taking Dalmane or barbiturates.

Pregnancy precautions: Barbiturates and chloral hydrate (one particular kind of sleeping medication) both pass through the placenta to the fetus. Dalmane and Quaalude taken by pregnant women have been linked to birth defects.

People Who Are Always Tired

Chronic fatigue may be generated by stress, a low-grade infection, anemia, a glandular disturbance, malnutrition, excess weight, or serious organic or mental problems.

Recommended: Avoid sleeping pills or pep pills, which only complicate the problem by creating drug dependence and don't treat the cause.

What to do: (1) Increase morning energy by eating a low-sugar, high-protein breakfast. (2) Avoid sweet snacks! They give a quick rush of energy, followed by a letdown. (3) Develop a regular exercise routine to increase stamina. Contrary to the belief that exercise saps energy, it exhilarates, relieves tensions, and has a tranquilizing effect, allowing more restful sleep. Note: Overworked muscles cause an unpleasant, short-lived tiredness, easily cured by rest. Caution: Know your own body's needs and don't overextend yourself. (4) Schedule your most arduous tasks for your peak times. Some people work best early in the day, others later.

Midafternoon Fatigue

Many people go through a valley of fatigue, which occurs for a couple of hours between 1 p.m. and 4 p.m. each workday during prime working time. How to avoid it:

Start with a physical checkup by your physician. Get an eye examination, too. Eyestrain is a prime cause of fatigue.

Rearrange the day. Schedule challenging or pleasant tasks for the midafternoon.

Check the physical environment, especially temperature, humidity, sunlight, and air conditioning. See if there's a correlation between these and your personal energy levels.

Vary the morning routine. Take a 15-minute coffee break in midmorning. Get away from the desk at lunch time for at least an hour.

Cut down on your lunchtime food and drink.

Source: *Marketing Communications.*

Is Aspirin Good for Your Heart?

Since aspirin interferes with clotting, the FDA recommends its use, under doctor's orders, to prevent strokes in males who have shown stroke symptoms. Contrary evidence: Tests by the National Heart, Lung, and Blood Institute found no proof that daily intake of aspirin prevented second heart attacks. Their finding: Deaths were actually higher for the aspirin group than for the placebo group.

The Dangers of Megavitamins

Professional opposition to megadoses of vitamins, based on continuing research in nutrition, is growing in the face of a trend to consume more and more vitamins in ever-larger dosages.

Old advice that is still best: There is no reason to take more than the recommended dietary allowance (RDA) of any vitamin, except for relatively rare individuals who cannot absorb or utilize vitamins adequately.

What a megadose is: 10 or more times the RDA . This is the level at which toxic effects begin to show up in adults. Even in cases of actual vitamin insufficiency, megadoses are not generally prescribed. Therapeutic doses are generally smaller than 10 times the RDA.

Some of the medical problems adults may experience as a result of prolonged, excessive intake of:

Vitamin A. Dry cracked skin. Severe headaches. Severe loss of appetite. Irritability. Bone and joint pains. Menstrual difficulties. Enlarged liver and spleen.

Vitamin D. Loss of appetite. Excessive urination. Nausea and weakness. Weight loss. Hypertension. Anemia. Irreversible kidney failure that can lead to death.

Vitamin E. Research on E's toxic effects is sketchy. But the findings suggest some problems: Headaches. Nausea. Fatigue and giddiness. Blurred vision. Chapped lips and mouth inflammation. Low blood sugar. Increased tendency to bleed. Reduced sexual function. (Irony: One of the claims of Vitamin E proponents is that it heightens sexual potency.)

The B vitamins. Each B has its own characteristics and problems. Examples: Too much B^6 can lead to liver damage. Too much B^1 can destroy B^{12}.

Vitamin C. Kidney problems and diarrhea. Adverse effects on growing bones. Rebound scurvy (a condition that can occur when a person taking large doses suddenly stops). Symptoms: Swollen, bleeding gums, loosening of teeth, roughening of skin, muscle pain. Vitamin C is the vitamin most often used to excess. Some of the symptoms of toxic effect from Vitamin C megadoses:

Menstrual bleeding in pregnant women and various problems for their newborn infants.

Destruction of Vitamin B^{12}, to the point that B^{12} deficiency may become a problem.

False negative tests for blood in stool, which can prevent diagnosis of colon cancer.

False urine test for sugar, which can spell trouble for diabetics.

An increase in the uric acid level and the precipitation of gout in individuals predisposed to the ailment.

Better than vitamin pills:

• Four portions a day of grains (either cereal, bread, or pasta).

• Four portions of fruits and vegetables (including at least one fresh fruit or vegetable or fruit juice.)

• Two or three portions of milk and milk products.

• Two portions of meat, fish, poultry, eggs, dry beans, peas, or nuts.

For people who don't eat properly or want nutrition insurance: Take a regular multivitamin capsule containing *only the RDA* of vitamins.

Source: Dr. Victor Herbert, author, *Nutrition Cultism: Facts and Fictions,* George F. Stickley Co., Philadelphia. He is chief of the hematology and nutrition laboratory at the Bronx Veterans Administration Medical Center and professor of medicine at the State University of New York Downstate Medical Center.

Natural vs. Synthetic Vitamins

Vitamins sold at health-food stores are more costly than synthetic ones. Are they more potent than the synthesized ones? Facts: The processing of natural vitamins often weakens or destroys potency. Most contain high amounts of synthesized vitamins anyway. The spoilage risk is greater without preservatives. Best bet: Pharmaceutically produced vitamins. They are cheaper and more accurately measured.

Source: Dr. Robert Nirschl, writing in *World Tennis.*

Storing Vitamins Safely

Properly kept, vitamins remain stable for four years. Capsules or sugar-coated pills hold up better than porous, pressed tablets. Long-term storage: Keep unopened containers in the refrigerator. Take out a three-month supply at a time. Don't keep vitamin bottles that have been opened in the refrigerator, kitchen, or bathroom. Condensation builds

up in those places. Best: Store tightly capped containers in the linen closet or in any other cool, dark, dry place.

Extra Vitamins

Under certain circumstances, you need to take more vitamins than usual. Example: Dieters, pregnant women, heavy smokers (who often lack vitamin C), heavy drinkers (B-complex), elderly people (both C and the B vitamins), and people taking oral contraceptives or cortisone drugs (vitamin B[6]). Advice: In all cases, consult a physician.

Good and Bad Ways to Remedy A Zinc Deficiency

Zinc deficiency in the diet is much more widespread than most people realize. As much as 70% of the population may have a zinc deficiency, including infants and children. Possible consequences: Stunted growth, impaired healing and diminished sense of taste.

What to do: Eat food with high levels of zinc, such as fortified cereals, red meat, liver, eggs, cheese, shellfish.

Beware of pharmaceutical zinc supplements. Too much zinc (more than 15 mg. per day) can create a copper deficiency, which can lead to other health problems.

Handling Medical Emergencies

Persons who are first on the scene at an emergency have a special responsibility. What to do:

Check the victim's breathing. Use your finger to make sure that the tongue is not blocking the respiratory passage. If necessary, turn the head to one side to allow spit and vomit to drain away.

Stop bleeding by pressing clothing against the wound.

Protect the victim from further harm, but move the person only if there is danger at the spot where the accident occurred. If the victim is conscious, have him lie down and remain still.

Treat for shock by keeping the victim warm but not hot. If injuries permit, loosen tight clothing and place him on his back, with legs elevated 18 inches.

Caution: Do no more than you know. People not trained in first aid can sometimes do more harm that good. If you are the most qualified person available, stay with the victim and send someone else for help.

Source: *Emergency Handbook: A First-Aid Manual for Home and Travel,* by P. Arnold, Doubleday & Co., New York.

First Aid Checklist

• Spotting a choking victim. Someone who is choking shows the same symptoms as a heart-attack victim. They take on a bluish cast, sweat freely, and appear apprehensive, even frantic. Difference: The heart-attack victim can usually explain what's happening. The person choking can't say a word. Point: If ever you are choking on something stuck in your throat, point to your mouth.

• Burn treatment. Minor burns should be soaked in tepid, not cold, water or, worse yet, ice. Reason: The use of extreme cold on the sensitive burned skin can result in an ice burn in addition to the one already received.

Source: Burn Unit, New York Hospital, Cornell Medical Center, 525 E. 68 St., New York 10021.

• Emergency dressings can be fashioned out of sanitary napkins. Cut the sanitary napkin to the right size and let the wound drain into it.

• Strains and sprains. Apply an ice pack for the first 24 hours to relieve swelling. Follow with warm compresses or heating pads to increase blood flow and stimulate healing in afflicted area. Rest and take aspirin for the pain. If pain, swelling, or discoloration persists, see a doctor.

• Foot blister. Wash it with soap and water, and puncture it with a sterile needle to let the fluid drain out. Protect the area with a bandage. Important: Don't remove the skin over the popped blister. Reason: It protects the tender new tissue underneath.

• Getting a ring off a swollen finger. Lubricate the finger with oil or grease. Then begin winding soft, strong string around the finger. Start at the top joint near the nail. When you reach the ring, pass the string between the ring and the finger using a tweezer prong to push it through. Now unwind the string from the palm side of the ring, pushing the ring up with each revolution. Caution: Don't use this method if the finger is swollen from infection, or is badly cut.

Source: Dr. Morris Leider, writing in *Journal of Dermatological Surgery*.

Heat vs. Cold for Easing Pain

• Use heat (heating pad) and muscle relaxation (a hot bath) for chronic pain. Drawback: Heat deepens feelings of depression. Cold works best for acute discomfort. Apply ice directly to the source of the pain for its numbing effects. Trap: Both heat and cold work on the neural transmitters that regulate pleasure and pain and may influence your feelings.

Source: *Free Yourself from Pain,* by Dr. David E. Bresler, Simon & Schuster, New York.

• **A heating pad should not be used on a bruise or other injury until at least 48 hours after the accident. If used earlier, the heat will increase the swelling. Ice or cold packs are better at first. (For arthritis or other noninjury aches and pains, heat is fine.) Caution: Don't use heat for more than 20 minutes at a time. And never go to sleep while the heating pad is** on. Risks: Skin burn, electrical fire. Don't use: When asleep, with sensitive skin, with poor blood circulation, if elderly, if diabetic, on areas treated with heat-producing medication (liniment). Important: Never put next to bare skin. Never place under the body, where heat can build up. Suggested: Instead, use a hot-water bottle where possible.

• Crushed ice applied for 30 minutes is still the best remedy for swellings and sprains. New chemical ice packs just are not as effective. Added nuisance: The covering splits easily and the leaking chemical leaves white spots on clothing. Also: The real thing stays cold longer and releases cold faster than the chemical ice packs.

• Cold compresses in an emergency: Use frozen food pouches from the home freezer.

The Not-So-Simple Headache

Headaches are as complex as they are common. For some people, tension can bring on headaches. For others, relaxation can cause the head to pound. Mysteriously, most migraine sufferers are women, but cluster headaches (severe pain around an eye) occur almost exclusively in men.

The three major types of headaches:

1. Muscle-contraction headaches (including the familiar tension headache) cause a band-like ache or pain at the base of the skull. Severe cases can last months or years.

Treatment: Many include common analgesics (aspirin, dextropropoxyphene, or ethoheptazine), sedatives, tricyclic antidepressants, or physical therapy (with local injections of anesthetics and corticosteroids).

2. Vascular headaches (including migraine and cluster headaches) result from dilation of blood vessels and cause pulsing pain (often on one side). Most migraine sufferers inherit the affliction. Others can get toxic vascular headaches from systemic vasodilation caused by

fever, alcohol, or nitrate intake, carbon dioxide retention, etc.

Treatment: Taken early enough in a migraine attack, the natural alkaloid ergot acts to constrict blood vessels and relieve pain. Sedatives can also help. Aspirin usually doesn't work, except in mild cases.

Prevention: Physicians usually prescribe doses of methysergide maleate (Sansert R), cyproheptadine (Periactin R), or BC 105 (Sandomigran), to decrease the vascular changes that bring on migraines. Lithium therapy sometimes works to prevent cluster headaches.

3. Traction and inflammation headaches are caused by brain tumors, aneurysms, strokes, and other serious illnesses, or by disorders of the eyes, ears, nose, throat, and teeth.

Treatment: The medicine's focus must be on the underlying disease.

Acupressure for Headaches

Relief from tension, vascular, and migraine headaches is possible through a form of acupuncture known as acupressure.

The technique: Exert very heavy thumbnail pressure (painful pressure) successively on nerves lying just below the surface of the skin at key points in the hands and wrists. As with acupuncture, no one's sure why it works.

Pressure points to try: The triangle of flesh between the thumb and index finger on the back of your hands (thumb side of bone, near middle of the second metacarpal in the index finger). Just above the protruding bone on the thumb side of your wrist.

Self-Massage for Headaches

The throb of a headache can be most distressing. However, there is a quick and easy way to relieve yourself from one. It's not by

395

taking aspirin or any other chemical. Self-massage does it, in two stages. Method:

Sit down. Become aware of your breathing. Let your head hang forward. Press with your fingers, particularly your thumbs, into the aching area. Inhale and press in. Exhale as you release the pressure. Press and rub all around the painful spot. Now press and rub all parts of the head.

Be sensitive to yourself. Let your mind rest. Stop thinking. Work systematically from the top of your forehead down to your chin. Press along the scalp line, press all parts of your forehead, your eyebrows, under your eyebrows, close your eyes and let your hands cover them.

Relax. Massage in a circular motion your temples and your cheeks. Exert pressure by pressing along your sinuses and nose. Continue the same motion around your ears. Cover the ears for silence for awhile. Leave no part of your face untouched.

Massage your scalp as if you were washing your hair. Gently pull your hair too. Go back to the aching area and massage it. Make sure that your tongue has been behind your front teeth, to relax your jaw. This first stage should take a few minutes.

The head-roll: Now get down on your hands and knees, or in a crawl position. Lower your head to the floor. Upon contact with the floor roll your head forward and back. Repeat this about 10 times. This will release tight neck and shoulder muscles.

When your head and neck feel loose enough, roll them also in diagonals and circular patterns. After rolling your head for a few minutes and massaging your head, you will feel refreshed, alert, and relaxed.

Source: Leslie Cerier, a personal fitness counselor who works with corporations and educational institutions, 235 W. 102 St., New York 10025.

Battling Migraines

The best way to deal with recurrent, intense migraine headaches is to try more than one solution. Chronic sufferers (estimated at between 8 million and 12 million Americans) can try one or more of the following:

Keep a headache diary. Note the times a headache starts and stops and what you were doing, eating, and thinking. The records help a doctor evaluate the condition and help patients discover causative factors.

Avoid aggravating foods and drinks. These include edibles containing tyramine (nuts, chocolate, aged cheese), sodium nitrate (frankfurters), and alcoholic beverages.

Headache sufferers who are on birth-control pills: Consider switching to another contraceptive method.

If aspirin doesn't provide relief, ask your doctor about propranolol (marketed by Ayerst laboratories under the name Inderal), now considered the safest, most effective antimigraine medicine on the market.

Get more opinions. Ideally a neurologist should verify that the condition is indeed a migraine.

Buying Contact Lenses

Constant wearers of conventional eyeglasses—especially bifocals—may find contact lenses nothing short of miraculous in terms of quality of vision, convenience, cost, and appearance. But there is an annoying, at times painful, break-in period.

They're not for everybody. Those with mild myopia (nearsigntedness), who wear glasses only occasionally or at theaters, sporting events, or to watch TV, probably shouldn't bother. And people who have good distance vision but wear glasses only for reading because they have developed presbyopia (farsightedness) won't benefit from them, either.

But the lifelong, all-day glasses wearer should consider the investment in money, time, and discomfort, because the payoff, as one person put it, "is like getting brand new eyes."

Where to get them? Most likely, where you get your present glasses. Ophthalmologists

(MD eye specialists) may do it all: Refract, prescribe, and dispense the lenses on their own or through a lab. Optometrists (lens and glass specialists) work the same way or with their own or other optical stores. These arrangements vary with local law and custom.

Don't get caught up in local and professional differences. The ophthalmologists obviously can perform many functions that optometrists can't, so everybody ought to visit one occasionally regardless of where glasses and lenses are bought. But optometrists usually are more experienced at fitting glasses and lenses than opthalmologists, and are involved with eye diseases, medication, and surgery as well as with the prescribing of glasses and lenses.

Which kind—hard or soft? Hard lenses are cheaper. Also, hard last longer, usually give somewhat sharper distance vision, can give correction for a higher degree of astigmatism than soft ones, and are easier to handle, clean, and use.

Soft lenses are much easier to get used to, but trickier to learn to handle, more easily damaged, require sterilization, and must be replaced more often.

Best bet: Try a pair of hard ones first. Give them more than the recommended time adjustment—at least three months. By then the wearer knows the benefits and problems. You'll probably find them far superior to glasses.

Then, if the discomforts persist, along with the benefits, try a pair of soft ones. For anyone who requires good vision for work and play (sailing, tennis, etc.), the cost and the bother of getting the right kind are well worth it.

Bifocal wearers usually can replace their complicated spectacles with a pair of contact lenses and a simple pair of magnifying reading glasses.

Important: Don't use sprays (deodorant, hair, food) after inserting lenses. Also: Make sure there's no soap or shampoo on fingertips. Wear lenses while shaving to avoid contaminating them with after-shave products applied with the hands.

Don't wear the soft contact lenses in a chlorinated pool. The chemicals can be harmful to the lenses. Hard lenses may be lost in the water.

Ocean water also increases deterioration.

Lake water is easier than saltwater on the lenses.

Waterskiing: Easy to lose a contact if you take a spill.

Sailing: Perfect sport for contact lenses. Reason: Unlike glasses, contacts don't get fogged up or splashed.

Tennis, riding, baseball: No problem. If the lenses pop out or give you problems during these activities, it means that they are poorly fitted.

The birth-control pill can affect the comfort and fit of contact lenses. It causes a shift in hormonal balance. This sometimes changes the shape of the eye's cornea. Result: contact lenses no longer fit. Instead, they cause discomfort, tearing, and redness. This condition is also experienced by women coming off the pill. They experience cornea change from cessation of the hormonal influence. Have your lenses adjusted by an ophthalmologist.

Buying Sunglasses

To test for lens irregularities, hold glasses at arm's length toward a surface with both horizontal and vertical lines, such as a paned window. If lines waver when glasses are moved up and down, or side to side, the glasses are imperfect. Lens colors that offer the best protection: Medium-dark gray or green.
Source: *Body Language.*

Exercises That Relax Your Eyes

The eyes have it. Sometimes, the eyes have had it. The controlled eye movements necessary for reading are strenuous and demanding.

Artificial light is stressful to the eyes. The eyes often get tired, overworked, and overstimulated. Tense facial or neck muscles and poor head/neck alignment are often responsible for poor eyesight and eye fatigue.

Exercises to do during the day to take advantage of natural lighting: If you wear contact lenses or glasses, remove them. Starting in the constructive rest position, lie on your back with your knees bent and the soles of your feet flat on the floor. Your arms can either be crossed over your chest or open above your head. Close your eyes. For a moment or two, just breathe. Let your thoughts go. Breathe naturally. Gradually, let your breathing get slower and deeper. Take your time. Then, as you inhale through your nose, imagine that the air fills your whole head. As you exhale through your mouth, imagine that the air leaves through the back of your neck. Attempt five minutes with this visualization.

While your eyes are still closed, slowly cover them with your hands. Return your concentration to your breathing. Then uncover your eyes. Repeat 5 to 10 times. Allow yourself several breaths between covering and uncovering your eyes.

Return to the visualization and the eye-covering sequence. Then rest.

When you are ready, slowly open your eyes. Don't move. Relax. Ask yourself: How am I feeling? How is my vision? My body? My mind? After a moment or two, as slowly as possible, turn your head to the right. Do not try to see. Instead, passively look at each molecule of space that passes by. When you have turned your head as far to the right as you comfortably can, pause and take a slow, deep breath. Now, turn your head as slowly as you can and as far to the left as is comfortable. Pause again for a complete slow, deep breath. Repeat this sequence five times. After the first sequence, you need not pause, just continue at a tortoise-like pace. Slowly bring your head back to center. Rest.

Both the eye-covering and head-turning exercises can be performed from a sitting or standing position.

Source: Leslie Cerier, personal fitness counselor, 235 W. 102 St., New York 10025.

Removing Ear Wax

Wax protects the inside of the ear. But sometimes it hardens, resulting in diminished hearing.

Caution: Never try to get out the wax with sharp objects; for example, match sticks or bobby pins. They could puncture an eardrum. Probing the ear with cotton-tipped swabs can drive the wax deeper into the ear until it hits the drum.

Instead, put several drops of hydrogen peroxide, or mineral oil, into the ear twice a day for two or three days. Then irrigate the ear canal with a soft ear syringe filled with lukewarm water. This washes out the softened wax. To prevent a recurrence, repeat the irrigation procedure every two or three months. Better yet: See your doctor.

Source: *The Ear, Nose and Throat Book*, by Stanley N. Farb, M.D., Appleton-Century-Crofts, New York.

Causes of Ringing in the Ears

Ringing in the ears (tinnitus) can be a disabling condition. Variety of causes: Presence of a foreign body or wax in the ear canal, perforation of the eardrum, infection-related fluid buildup, allergic or drug reaction, prolonged exposure to a loud noise. Other possibilities: Chronic disease or condition such as abnormal blood pressure or a growth in the head or neck area. Recommended: See your own physician and an ear specialist.

More Information: Better Hearing Institute, 1430 K St., NW, Washington, DC 20005.

How to Improve Your Hearing

A simple exercise to improve your hearing and to help you relax:

Lie on the floor in a quiet room with your

knees flexed and the soles of your feet flat on the floor.

Breathe slowly and deeply through your mouth.

Close your eyes.

Cover and uncover your ears several times until your head and neck area feel relaxed.

Massage your ears. Pull gently on both earlobes and all parts of the outer ear. Indulgently massage the inner rims of the outer ear.

Rest quietly. Now sounds are received with a clearer sense of hearing.

Source: Leslie Cerier, personal fitness counselor, 235 W. 102 St., New York 10025.

Protecting Your Ears

Hearing protectors should always be worn when shooting *any* guns—hunting, skeet shooting, or target shooting. Risk: Permanent hearing loss and constant incurable ringing in the ears. In addition: The unprotected are more prone to fatigue, slowed reflexes, anxiety attacks, and heart problems. Good protectors sell for under $10. Note: Homemade cotton earplugs furnish almost no sound protection.

Coping With Hearing Loss

Hearing loss is a complex disability. Most people don't even realize it when the person they're trying to communicate with has a hearing problem. Reason: Many sufferers don't let on about their hearing loss. They either do all the talking to avoid responding, or they do none.

Hearing loss is as much a problem for the speaker as the listener. Many of those who lose their hearing late in life develop negative attitudes toward themselves based on their previous perceptions of deafness. Example: If someone believed deaf people are slow-witted, he may easily look down on himself when he is overtaken by the disability.

People who become hard of hearing also grow more dependent on others. This quickly alters their self-image. Other anxieties: The hard of hearing often worry about having missed something (they probably have) and are tempted to avoid social situations.

Basic steps if you think you have a hearing loss:

Have your hearing tested at an approved center. If the test shows a problem, be honest with yourself and admit it.

Visit a hearing counselor who has experience in working with people who have hearing impairments.

Be direct. If you have trouble hearing someone, say so: Enunciate more clearly, please. I'm hard of hearing. Or ask him to take his hand away from his mouth or to speak more slowly. The hard of hearing are often too hesitant to say these things and, in the end, communication suffers.

Evaluate hearing aids in a noncommercial environment (such as the New York League for the Hard of Hearing).

Get the opinion of a qualified doctor. You may need medical intervention to prevent further deterioration of hearing.

Keep pace with advances in technology. There are now shake-awake alarm clocks, telephone amplifiers, doorlights for doorbells, TV adapters that provide subtitles for some programs, and theaters that have headphones for the hard of hearing.

Caution: Don't feel sorry for yourself. If you become hard of hearing, you must find substitutes for old activities. The faster you do so, the easier the adjustment will be.

Getting Teeth Capped

Capping is an elaborate, dramatic, and expensive technique in dentistry.* Most people who are concerned with keeping their teeth

*Caps, crowns and jackets are synonyms referring to a restoration that completely covers the tooth, usually a gold thimble or cap covered by porcelain.

will have several crowns in their lifetime. Teeth are capped when there has been so much decay or so many fillings that there isn't enough tooth structure left to hold fillings. Aesthetics is another good reason for capping.

Crowns are used to construct fixed bridges (rather than removable dentures) to replace teeth that have been extracted.

First consideration before capping: Finding an experienced dentist. Caps that aren't done right can accelerate the breakdown or loss of teeth.

Main problem: A somewhat increased difficulty in maintaining gums. The margin between the tooth and the cap becomes an area a little more susceptible to the formation of plaque and inflammation of gums. The point: Having caps means that more effort is required in maintaining gums.

Fit: Ideally, the cap should end above the gum. This makes it much easier to clean. Problem: Having cap margins visible isn't as aesthetically pleasing as having them invisible. A dentist may take this aesthetic consideration into account where front teeth are concerned. But where such small differences can't possibly show, it's a mistake to insist on caps whose margins are shoved under the gum since this will make proper maintenance of gums much harder.

How long caps should last: Caps last anywhere between five and 20 years or more. In a relatively healthy mouth, properly maintained, they last indefinitely. Porcelain or gold material can break down, requiring a new cap in less than 10 years. If treatment is unsuccessful: The tooth can be lost because too much bone has been destroyed, or the tooth may decay under the crown.

Most important variable: The way the patient maintains the gums. There is no question that proper care can double or triple the life span of crowns.

How to make caps look real: Each tooth should vary slightly in shape, position, and color. The total composition should be one of balanced variety, not perfect symmetry. Avoid the gleaming, artificially white teeth that so many entertainers choose. Natural teeth are not white.

Teeth should conform geometrically to the shape of a head or emotionally to the body type, sex, or personality of the patient. There is no such thing as feminine or masculine teeth.

Source: Dr. Arthur Brisman, 31 Washington Sq. W., New York 10011.

Root Canal Work

The cost is high, but root-canal work (endodontics) is worth the time and money.

It's less painful than the toothache that sent you to the dentist in the first place, and root-canal work saves the tooth by removing the diseased or infected pulp. That keeps other teeth from shifting.

The procedure: You get a local anesthetic. The dentist drills a hole in the enamel-covered part of the tooth to get to the pulp (nerve and blood vessels in the root). He removes the infected pulp, using miniature files, and fills the empty canal with a sealer.

Usually, several visits are necessary to remove all the pulp, but you are left with your own comfortable tooth, which is no longer painful or sensitive to either hot or cold substances.

Orthodontia for Adults

Adults who need braces may decide to forego this dental treatment out of embarrassment. However, more than aesthetics must be considered. Neglect that results in loss of teeth is too steep a price to pay.

Recent advances in orthodontia have produced devices that can be worn in back of the teeth, where they are virtually invisible. If braces are prescribed, check with your orthodontist on this lingual treatment, and keep smiling.

Questions Your Dentist Should Answer

Remarkably few patients ask:
What treatment is planned?
What are the alternatives?
Costs? Method of payments?
Courtesy: If the dentist consistently leaves you waiting too long for your appointments, talk it over. Your time is valuable, too.

Dental Do's and Don'ts

Toothbrushes. Use two or more in rotation so that they can dry out properly. Soft nylon is best. Natural bristle brushes take longer to dry. If not used properly, they can damage gum tissue because bristles are too firm and coarse. Angled brushes may help in reaching some areas. Caution: Too-vigorous brushing can wear grooves in tooth enamel. When used correctly, a toothbrush will not abrade tissues or teeth. And hardness of the bristles is not as significant as the way the brush is used and the time spent brushing.

Dental floss: Unwaxed floss is better because it absorbs particles.

Flushing devices: If used with too much pressure, device can damage tissue, force debris into periodontal pockets, and cause inflammation and infection. Use at half the recommended pressure.

Pain perception is less in the morning than in the afternoon, according to recent research. Suggestion: Schedule dental appointments early in the day.

Avoid over-the-counter tooth whiteners. Reason: They contain highly abrasive ingredients that remove tooth enamel after prolonged use.

A tooth knocked out in an accident can be saved. When a child falls and loses a tooth, wrap it in a wet cloth, and bring it and the child as quickly as possible to the dentist. Reimplantation works best with children (sometimes works with adults, too).

Playing the trumpet or trombone can correct a bad bite. However, playing flute or piccolo can make it worse. Saxophone can work either way.

Bad teeth don't cause headaches, bursitis, or anything like that. But jaw and tooth pains may be "referred" pains that originate in other areas.

Preventing Gum Disease

Gum disease causes teeth to fall out as it destroys roots and supporting bones. About 90% of tooth loss in people over 40 years old is due to gum maladies.

Symptoms:
Gums bleed easily.
Gum tissue swells.
Teeth become loose and move apart.
Cause:
The irritation of gum and bone by plaque, a sticky, hard-to-see film. It's made up of decomposed food and living bacteria, which must be cleaned from the teeth every 24 to 36 hours.

Best means of plaque removal:

Brushing. Do it regularly with a soft or medium nylon toothbrush. Concentrate on the juncture of teeth and gums. Hold the brush at a 45 degree angle. Use short, horizontal (almost circular) strokes. Don't stop brushing if bleeding begins. Plaque removal reduces bleeding.

Flossing. Clip off an 18-inch length of unwaxed dental floss, and curve it around a tooth's edge. Bring the floss around the tooth until it meets resistance from the gum. Scrape the tooth's edge from the top to the gum at least three times. Repeat for every tooth surface. Be patient: Flossing is tricky. It takes practice to do it quickly and effectively.

Advanced cases of gum disease require surgery to remove pockets where food and bacteria collect.

Source: *Your Mouth Is Your Business: The Dentists' Guide To Better Health*, Appleton-Century-Crofts, New York.

401

Tooth-Decay Culprits

Cream-filled chocolate cookies cause 50% more cavities than pure sugar, according to a National Institute of Dental Health Research study on laboratory animals. Runners up: sugared cereals and sugar-coated candies. (These have the same cavity-causing rate as pure sugar.) Worse than sugar: Potato chips (84%), caramels (73%), chocolate bars (72%).

No surprise: All sugar-containing foods cause tooth decay to some extent.

Of interest: Dicalcium phosphate (a food additive that improves consistency or reduces tartness) reduces sugar's cavity-creation ability.

Good news: Research with animals shows that cheddar cheese retards some sugar-producing bacteria and acids that cause tooth decay.

Emergency Toothache Remedies

• If immediate dental help is not available, take aspirin and try sucking on an ice cube. If a filling is lost, put oil of clove on a small piece of cotton and pack it into the cavity. Common mistake: Applying heat. Reason: If the pain is the result of an abscess, heat can help to spread the infection.

Source: *Emergency Handbook: A First-Aid Manual for Home and Travel,* Doubleday, New York.

• Try rubbing ice between your thumb and index finger on the same side as the aching tooth. Massage until the area feels numb or seven minutes have passed, whichever comes first. The intense cold often is as effective as acupuncture or novocaine.

What to Expect from a Good Dentist

A thorough examination, which includes full-mouth X-rays (18 separate pictures) and a plastic impression of your teeth so the dentist can study their shape and their relation to one another. The dentist must probe the gums and also examine the tongue and interior of the mouth.

Full cleaning of plaque deposits.

Clear explanation to the patient of how to maintain the health of the gums, teeth, and mouth. (Even if patients say they know how.)

Description of what is going on in the patient's mouth and why. Also: What to expect in the future.

Effective recall system that brings the patient back to the dentist's office regularly (at least every three months) for cleanings.

More than one treatment room and a strong support staff. Reason: A dentist who personally does the cleaning and makes the X-rays is likely to be inefficient (and also may be charging more for cleanings and X-rays).

An orderly schedule. For some kinds of intensive work, be prepared to spend a good many hours at the dentist's office. The dentist who can take you anytime for regular work without regard for efficiency may be careless in his professional work.

The dentist spending some part of every week either teaching, in a hospital, or in another clinic situation where he's kept in touch with other skilled dentists, new techniques, and experimental procedures.

Source: Dr. Arthur S. Brisman, associate professor at New York University's College of Dentistry, is in private practice at 31 Washington Square W., New York 10011.

Denture Problems of Older People

The older person whose dentures hurt too much to wear may need a change in diet and life style, not new dentures.

Reason: A dry mouth and tissue fragility are the most frequent causes of denture problems. They are caused by loss of body water, aggravated by the use of tranquilizers, antihistamines, and diuretics. Depression and calcium or protein deficiencies produce these changes too.

Solution: Add vegetable soups (with some meat), bran, and yogurt or cheese to your daily diet to rebuild oral tissues. Boil meats and eggs to make proteins easier to digest. Exercise and social activities help by increasing blood flow and warding off depression.

Relief from Jaw Pain

Five exercises to ease discomfort:

Start by opening the mouth wide, then closing it. Do this repeatedly and as rapidly as possible.

Continue the same motions, but now place the palm of your hand beneath the chin when opening the mouth, and above it when closing. This offers a slight resistance.

Repeat the same two steps with a sideways motion of the lower jaw, first doing it freely and then doing it against the resistance of the palm of the hand.

Go through the same steps with a motion that protrudes the jaw.

Chew a piece of gum alternately on each side of the mouth, then in the center of the mouth. Do each for three to five minutes.

Repeat every exercise five times twice a day during the first week. In each successive week, increase the number by five, to a maximum of 25 twice a day.

Source: Patricia Brown, RN, writing in the *American Journal of Nursing.*

Symptoms of Thyroid Trouble

People under heavy pressure often develop symptoms caused by stress or depression such as heart palpitations, sweating, insomnia, and even general apathy. In some cases, these problems can result from a much more troublesome ailment: Thyroid dysfunction. If the true cause isn't discovered and proper treatment begun, permanent damage can result.

Thyroid problems that can be confused with stress or depression:

Hyperthyroidism: Overactive thyroid. Symptoms: Sweating, often accompanied by intolerance of heat; heart palpitations; nervousness; irritability; insomnia; weight loss despite a good appetite. Treatment can involve surgery, drugs, or use of radioactive iodine to destroy thyroid tissue.

Bulging eyes may also be a side effect of a malfunctioning thyroid gland. They can be unsightly as well as uncomfortable. The eyelids become shortened. The exposed portion of the eyes is subject to drying. They are less protected from dust and injury. Plastic surgeons can correct the condition by lengthening the muscles that control the lids, thus allowing them to come together.

Hypothyroidism. Too little thyroid hormone. Symptoms: Intolerance of cold, thickened skin, hoarseness, constipation, weight gain, general apathy and fatigue, emotional changes that are easily confused with depression. Treatment: The simple and safe use of a synthetic or natural thyroid hormone.

Source: *The Harvard Medical School Health Letter.*

Colds: What You Don't Know Can Hurt You

Doctors cannot cure a cold, but sufferers can help themselves by keeping in mind what is known about the ailment. Essentials:

Chills don't cause colds, but they encourage existing viruses to multiply.

Colds spread most effectively by direct contact and are most contagious in their early stages before the symptoms are even noticeable.

The body's process of curing a cold requires about the same energy as hard physical labor. Advice: Keep vigorous exercise to a minimum so your energy goes toward fighting the cold.

Taking vitamin C may help. Advocates suggest one to three grams a day at the outset of a cold and 500 mg. daily throughout its duration.

Avoid stress during a cold. It reduces antibody production in the nose and mouth.

Don't numb pain by drinking alcohol.

Source: *Executive Fitness Newsletter.*

How to Fight The Common Cold

Your own body's defenses work better than pills or liquids from the drugstore.

Reasons: The inflammation that causes a stuffy nose, sore throat, congestion, headache, and general discomfort is a sign that antibodies are fighting the infection. A low-grade fever (below 100° F) helps to keep cold germs from spreading and multiplying. Treating these symptoms slows down the healing process.

Home treatment: Consume liquids to soothe your throat and prevent the dehydration that comes with a fever. Stay warm by bundling up. Cold viruses can't multiply rapidly when there's a slight fever, so don't attempt to bring one down. Get plenty of rest.

Source: *Cold Comfort,* by Hal Zina Bennett, Clarkson N. Potter Publishers, New York.

Treating Sore Throats

Most sore throats are caused by viruses, which cannot be combatted with antibiotics like penicillin. Avoid antibiotics unless you are certain you have a bacterial infection. Why?

The side effects are capricious.

A heavy reliance on antibiotics can create an allergy to them.

Overexposure to the drugs enables some bacteria to develop resistant strains.

How to differentiate between a viral and a bacterial infection: A throat culture. A swab of infected throat mucus must be taken by a doctor and sent to a laboratory for testing.

Sore throat cure: Rest and drink plenty of liquids.

Useless steps:

Gargling with mouthwash or salt water. It never reaches the infection, which is at the back of the throat.

Anesthetic sprays or lozenges. They may ease the sore throat pain somewhat, but they do not help cure the disease.

Source: *The Ear, Nose, and Throat Book,* by Stanley N. Farb, M.D., Appleton-Century-Crofts, New York.

Tonsils: In or Out?

The old practice of removing infected tonsils and adenoids is no longer followed. Only chronically infected tonsils and adenoids are taken out today. Acute infections are treated with antibiotics.

Myth: Tonsillectomies for adults are more dangerous than for children. Fact: Adults may have more discomfort afterward, but the operation is so simple it can be performed with a local anesthetic.

Note: Most adult have no adenoidal problems. Normally, adenoids begin to shrink at the onset of puberty and are gone by the age of 17.

Source: *The Ear, Nose, and Throat Book,* by Stanley N. Farb, M.D., Appleton-Century-Crofts, New York.

How to Beat the Hay-Fever Season

Hay fever strikes with virulence when the air is heavy with ragweed pollen at summer's end. Some ways to evade the invisible pollen:

Sleep late. Pollen is borne aloft by rising air currents in the morning.

Don't exert yourself. The heavy breathing from exercise causes you to pump pollen into your system.

Beware of swimming pools. Reason: Pollen gathers on the water's surface, where it is easily taken into a swimmer's eyes and nose. A solution: Wear protective goggles and nose plugs.

Mix a mild solution of salt water to dash in your nose several times each day during the hay-fever season. It washes away collected pollen.

Two inhalant preventive drugs: Cromolyn sodium and beclomethasone. Relief for those who have hay fever comes from antihistamines. The latest: Clemastine fumarate. Sold by prescription under the name Tavist-1. Length of effectiveness: 12 hours.

How to Avoid Back Pain

Most back problems originate in the lumbosacral joint, the lowest disc in the spinal column. "Ruptured discs" usually occur in this joint. Specifically: The disc, which shields nerve tissue from your vertebrae, ceases to function. Result: Vertebrae pinch your nerves, causing excruciating pain.

To avoid this: Exercise! Exercise is more important if you're a desk-bound executive. You must learn to sit properly, too.

Sitting:

At the office: Use a straight-backed chair. Sit with your back at a 90° *angle to the chair seat.*

At home: In addition to sofas and easy chairs, have some straight-backed chairs. Make sure to use them.

Driving: The next time you buy a car, consider the seating. Look for the same qualities in car seats you would look for in a desk chair.

Exercise:

Walking: Keep your stomach in. Reason: The spine straightens when you do; the head rises; the shoulders go back; and chest volume broadens.

Jogging: Jogging is good for the cardiovascular system, but unless you use good shoes, and the right running form, it's bad for your back. Reason: It jolts the vertabrae. Better: Swimming and bicycle riding. (Preferred: A stationary bike.)

Stretching: To keep your back limber, perform the exercises below three times a day.

This can be done in your office, and should take no more than 20 minutes.

1. Push your buttocks back in the chair. Straighten your upper back. Place forearms on the arms of the chair. Lean forward as far as you can, then lean back. 25 times.

2. Sit on the edge of your chair. Straighten back. Hold head erect, chin in. Place feet about 18 inches apart. Keeping back straight, reach down sideways with your right hand, and try to touch the side of your right foot. Do the same with your left hand. Alternate 25 times.

3. Stand with your body against the desk, legs apart. Place your hands on the desk. Now touch with your forehead the surface of the desk. Then come smartly to erect position. 25 times.

4. Stand with your feet apart, arms at sides. Reach downward as far as possible with your right hand, and then your left hand. Alternate 25 times.

Source: Dr. Jesse Schmidt Manlapaz, a neurosurgeon specializing in head and disc problems, Danbury Hospital, Danbury, CT 06810.

First Aid for Backache

To relieve sudden back pain that results from stress, strain, or overwork, here are some simple exercises:

Lie on your back with knees bent and feet flat on the floor. Using both hands wrapped around one knee, slowly pull that knee up to your chest. Do ten times with each leg.

Assume a sitting position on the floor with legs extended. Now place your right heel atop your left knee. Using your right hand, push your right knee gently down toward the floor. Do ten times. Repeat with the left knee.

Other techniques that work:

Lie on a slanted board with your feet elevated and head down. This can relax the tightened muscles that cause a backache.

Apply heat to the affected areas with a heating pad, a hot-water bottle, or soak in a hot tub.

Ice is sometimes more effective. Massage the sore area with a plastic bag full of ice cubes until the area is numb.

A corset gives support to relieve pain. Remove it when the pain subsides.

Because of its anti-inflammatory qualities, aspirin is a helpful drug for back pain. For an acute attack, codeine can be prescribed, for prolonged periods. But be careful, you can become dependent on it.

One of every four back problems is caused by foot problems. To protect your feet and your back:

Wear flexible shoes that don't constrict your feet.

Replace shoe heels that are run-down.

At home, go barefoot as much as possible.

When sitting for long stretches of time, rotate your feet and wiggle your toes.

Don't wear tight socks. A sock should be three-quarters of an inch longer than your foot.

Women must not wear extremely high heels with pointed toes for long periods—if at all. Because of high heels, four times more women than men have foot problems. Example: Forty times more women require bunion surgery. Maximum heel height for women's shoes: Two inches.

Two exercises to strenthen your feet:

Walk on the outer edges of your feet, taking short steps.

Stand lock-kneed, with legs crossed, like scissors. Distribute your weight evenly on both feet. Hold this stance for a minute, then reverse the position of your feet.

Source: *How To Beat a Bad Back*, by Shirley Linde, Rawson, Wade Publishers, New York.

The GI Series

GI stands for gastrointestinal. What the doctor wants is a special X-ray examination of the stomach, esophagus, and intestines as an aid in diagnosing diseases such as ulcers, colitis, gallbladder problems, and cancer.

How it's different from an X-ray or fluoro-scopic examination: The stomach and digestive tract can be seen as a special liquid preparation, which the patient has previously swallowed, is passing through them. The liquid contains barium, which cannot be penetrated by X-rays. Since the surrounding areas are penetrated by X-rays, the barium silhouettes the intestinal areas, sharply defining them.

Barium: It resembles a milk shake, but has a chalky flavor. The patient drinks it at about 8 a.m., after having eaten nothing since midnight. During the next several hours, the barium passes through the digestive areas, which show up in the X-ray and are observed through a fluroscope. The patient experiences little or no discomfort.

Cost and time: A GI series is not normally included in a routine physical checkup. It is ordered only when there is a suspicion of an ulcer or other intestinal ailment. The charge varies, depending on the extent of the examination and the time necessary for it, but may run anywhere from $100 to $300 or more. A general physician does not usually perform such tests, but he will refer the patient to a specialist, such as a radiologist or gastroenterologist.

Causes of Heartburn

Acidic gases from the stomach flow up into the sensitive esophagus. This produces a burning sensation. Normally, a muscular ring closes to prevent the flow of acid. But certain foods and drinks loosen this muscle. Prime offender: Coffee. Next worst: Alcohol and smoking. Also: Fried foods, fatty meats, spices, oils, and chocolate.

Nervous Stomachs

The nervous stomach is a folk myth. It is not the result of eating food that "does not agree with you." Fact: Irritable bowel syndrome bedevils some 22 million Americans.*

Symptoms: Recurrent diarrhea, constipation, or bouts of both.

The cause is a combination of the following: Stress. A high-fat, processed-food diet. Irregular meals. Intermittent dieting. Dinners as the main meal of the day, after the stomach has been under stress for 8 to 10 hours and it is at its most acidic.

Treatment: Regular meal times. Healthy breakfasts, and moderate lunches and dinners.

Increased fiber intake through the consumption of a wider variety of fruits, vegetables, and grains. Reduced caffeine usage. Regular exercise.

* About one-third of all those between 30 and 40 years old. And, it's three times as prevalent in women (particularly working women) as in men.

Hiccups: Cause and Cure

Hiccups come from eating fast, swallowing hot foods, disorders of the stomach, and sometimes from psychological stress. They are caused by spasmodic contractions of the diaphragm muscle. Time-honored remedies for ordinary hiccups:

Breathe into a paper bag, thus accumulating carbon dioxide.

Swallow a teaspoonful of sugar. That also increases the carbon dioxide level.

Hold breath as long as possible, or gargle while holding breath.

Put a pinch of salt on the back of the tongue.

Try to cough or sneeze.

While another person holds a finger in each of your ears, hold your nostrils closed with one hand while drinking a glass of water slowly.

When due to minor causes, hiccups will usually respond to one of the above measures. For severe and persistent hiccups, a doctor may have to administer a tranquilizer intravenously or even inject a sedative solution into one of the phrenic nerves which stimulate the diaphragm muscle so as to relax the spasm.

Foods That Cause Intestinal Gas

Belching: Foods that lower pressure of the sphincter (the one where the esophagus meets the stomach) should be consumed in moderation. Examples: Whole milk, high-fat foods, peppermint, chocolate, orange juice, alcohol (especially aromatic after-dinner drinks, such as brandy). Chewing gum and smoking cigarettes also increase gas because they each cause more air to be swallowed.

Using antacids one to three hours after meals can help control gas. Use of cimetidine (trade name: Tagament) reduces acid secretion, which lessens upper-intestinal gas. Although these drugs are generally safe, as with any drug, protracted use may have side effects.

Flatulence: Normally, in the process of breaking down food material for excretion, the colon produces several odorless gases (hydrogen, carbon dioxide, and, in about one-third of the American population, methane). Excessive malodorous gases are created when proteins, fats, and carbohydrates aren't fully broken down and fermentation occurs. Beans, bananas, apple and grape juices, nuts, and raisins are among common offenders. Difficulty in breaking down milk sugar (lactose) can also produce tremendous amounts of gas and diarrhea.

Although no one is sure why, it is interesting to note that methane-producers are associated with 85% of all cases of cancer of the colon, which is the commonest form of cancer in America.

Source: Gerald Friedman, M.D., 2 E. 85 St., New York 10028.

How to Avoid Constipation

Evaluate your diet. A lack of roughage (leafy vegetables, fruits, whole-grain cereals and bread) can be the cause. Eating dates, figs, or prunes is helpful. Fluids are necessary. Recommended: Water, milk, fruit juice.

Consider daily tension as a cause. Worrying about being constipated can make it worse. When you are tense, talk things over with a close friend. If the problems are serious, consider professional help.

Train your body to eliminate regularly. This usually solves the problem.

Do not rely on laxatives. Reason: The bowels become less and less sensitive to the irritants they contain, and over a period of time laxatives cause constipation. Caution: Children should never be given laxatives. Instead: Administer an enema.

Caution: Constant constipation can be a sign of serious disease. If it persists, see a doctor.

Source: *Emergency Handbook: A First-Aid Manual for Home and Travel,* by P. Arnold and E. Pendagast, Doubleday & Co., New York.

Hiatal Hernia

This condition, associated with overeating, obesity, injury to the stomach, or a congenital deformity, is fairly common, especially in older people. Symptoms: Chronic heartburn or indigestion. Cause: A weakness in the diaphragm, which allows the stomach to move up into the chest area alongside the esophagus. Stomach acids are not tolerated by the esophagus and some minor, but discomfort-producing, damage may result. Treatment: Taking antacids, establishing a light diet, avoiding raw fruits and vegetables and juices, and keeping the head elevated at night. Surgical repair is major surgery.

Ulcers: New Light on Causes and Treatment

Popular image: The typical victim of a peptic ulcer is a hard-driving businessman. Fact: Not so true now, if it ever was. Males between ages 45 and 64 are the most vulnerable group. But when all ages are considered, as many women as men now have ulcers.

Also surprising: Age itself is no barrier. Ulcers are frequent among retired people. But they also afflict teenagers. And the incidence of ulcers is not higher in cities than in small towns.

A hopeful sign: Hospital admissions for peptic ulcers declined 24% from 1970 to 1977. But it's still a big problem: Currently, about 300,000 new cases are diagnosed each year; 350,000 patients are hospitalized; 50,000 have operations; and 6,000 die.

How ulcers occur: Almost everyone suffers now and then from the temporary discomfort of stomach gas or heartburn. It is the normal result of overeating: A buildup of excess stomach acid.

Not so normal: A painful peptic ulcer that develops in some people, especially those under stress. The gastric secretions wear away the tender lining of the stomach or, more commonly, the even more delicate duodenum, which is the first segment of the small intestine.

Instant effect: Fierce, burning soreness. (An ulcer is, literally, a raw wound.) The condition usually is not readily relieved by drugstore antacids.

Ulcer terminology is sometimes imprecise, but according to doctors:

Peptic ulcers are, all-inclusively, those ulcers found anywhere in the digestive system.

Duodenal ulcers are peptic ulcers in the duodenum. They are more than twice as common clinically as gastric ulcers. Soreness is concentrated in the area of the navel.

Gastric ulcers are peptic ulcers in the stomach.

Worst case: A perforated ulcer. The acid eats through the organ wall, allowing contents to spill out into the body cavity, threatening life. Blood transfusions and an operation are usually necessary. Bad news: Incidence is rising among women, though it remains stable among men.

Why ulcers happen: Excessive gastric acid is secreted, especially at night, when the stomach has the least need for it. Usually lacking food to digest, the hypersecreted digestive juices attack the visceral tissue.

What triggers hypersecretion: A genetic predisposition combined with emotional distress, illness, or other trauma, especially in older persons. Chronic causes: Excessive use of alcohol (the leading trigger of ulcerating hypersecretion), aspirin, cigarettes, and coffee.

Encouraging note: A developing ulcer is easy to diagnose. And even advanced ulcers respond to a new pharmaceutical, Tagament, which represents a new era in ulcer treatment. How it works: Checks gastric acid secretion for long periods, especially through the night. Limitation: Recommended only for duodenal ulcers.

Source: Dr. Arthur S. Lobel, gastroenterologist and peptic-ulcer consultant at Red Bank Medical Associates in New Jersey; The National Center for Health Statistics, Federal Center, Building 2, 3700 East-West Highway, Hyattsville, MD 20782.

Prostate Disorders

The male's prostate gland seems to cause an inordinate amount of trouble. Most of it is not serious. The gland surrounds the base of the urethra (the tube that emerges from the bladder and carries urine). By squeezing fluid into the urethra, the prostate helps nourish and transport sperm.

Major disorders:

Acute prostatitis. An infection that's accompanied by a sudden onset of fever, pain at the base of the penis, and uncontrolled dripping of a cloudy fluid from the penis. It can be diagnosed through a urine specimen. Treatable with antibiotics.

Benign prostatic enlargement. By age 60, almost all men have some degree of enlargement. Symptoms: Difficulty in starting the flow of urine, decreased force of the urinary stream, dribbling of urine after voiding seems to be completed, and increased frequency of urination. Caused by an overgrowth of

glands, it's usually treated surgically. Note: Most procedures do not result in impotence.

Cancer of the prostate. Grows at a slow pace. Not likely to spread excessively or cause death. Removal of the obstruction is the usual treatment. In the more malignant type of this cancer, radical prostate surgery and radiation treatment may be employed. Most prostate growths can be felt during a standard exam, which should be done at least annually if a man is over 50 years old.

Preventing Prostate Trouble

Until 50 years ago, prostate disorders were extremely rare. Modern culprit: Too much fat in today's diet. Best prevention: Reduction of total calories, especially those from meat and dairy products. Substitute more fruits and vegetables in the daily menu.

Prognosis: This is no sure cure, but a delaying action on the discomfort and danger of prostate problems.

Source: *Executive Fitness*.

Impotence as a Sign of Illness

• Impotence is not always a psychological problem. It is often the symptom of disease.

In a recent study of men with periodic impotence, three-quarters of them had illnesses. Most common: Diabetes. Note: Both younger and older men had illnesses, indicating that impotence among young men is not automatically psychological.

Insight: Even when a disease causes impotence, there are psychological ramifications. Example: Fear of failure, which may prolong the condition.

Source: Study by Drs. Sallie Schumacher and Charles Lloyd, Bowman Gray School of Medicine, Wake Forest University, Winston-Salem, NC 27109.

• Impotence is often found in males suffering from high blood pressure. Many patients think the problem is related to the drugs they take to control hypertension. Fact: The drugs do not affect the frequency of successful sexual intercourse, nor does sexual performance vary according to the dosages of the medicines.

Source: Elijah Saunders, M.D., Provident Hospital, Baltimore, MD 21215, reporting in *Medical Aspects of Human Sexuality.*

Pros and Cons Of Vasectomy

According to the most recent studies, vasectomies have no effect on the production of testosterone or other hormones. The body still produces both sperm (which is reabsorbed by the body) and seminal fluid (which is ejaculated).

Vasectomies are considered so safe and simple that they're generally performed under local anaesthetic in a doctor's office or in a clinic. The doctor makes one or two incisions in the scrotum through which each sperm-carrying tube (vas deferens) can be lifted out, cut, and closed, thus blocking the passage of sperm. The operation takes 20 minutes. Cost: $100-$250 (depending on clinic or physician). Usually covered by Blue Shield or other private medical insurance. If it is performed on Friday afternoon, most men can go back to work on Monday. Best to wear an athletic supporter and to avoid heavy labor for a week to 10 days. There may be some discomfort for several days. Usually ice packs and aspirin provide all the relief that is needed. Contraception is still necessary for the first 10 to 12 ejaculations after a vasectomy—until two samples of semen, generally taken a week or two apart, show no sperm.

Physical after-effects:

Sperm antibodies develop in about 50% of vasectomized men. One type of antibody immobilizes sperm. The other causes sperm to agglutinate (clump together). These antibodies may prevent restoration of fertility in men whose vasectomies have later been reversed. But it is not yet known for what length of time these sperm antibodies go on being produced—and under what conditions the body stops producing them.

Increased cholesterol and atherosclerotic placque. The results of an experiment on monkeys at the Oregon Primate Research Center, which concluded that vasectomies produced increased cholesterol and atherosclerotic placque, were widely publicized. However, there were only five monkeys in the experimental group and the monkeys' diet contained twice the cholesterol found in an ordinary human diet. This study will have to be refined and repeated on a much larger scale before any firm conclusions can be drawn. Meanwhile, a low-cholesterol diet may be desirable for vasectomized men.

Reversibility. Vasectomies can be reversed —sometimes. Although major surgery is involved, microsurgical vasotomy (reconnecting the tubes) is the technique when remarriage or another major life change makes a man decide to father children again. Some doctors claim a 40% to 50% success rate on vasectomy reversals (provided the wife is fertile, of course). This figure will probably rise as microsurgical techniques continue to become more sophisticated.

More information: Association for Voluntary Sterilization, 708 Third Ave., New York 10017.

Facts About Artificial Insemination

Artificial insemination is now used by about 15,000 couples annually. About 10,000 children are born from the procedure each year.

Who uses it:

Couples in which a fertile husband cannot impregnate his wife for physical or psychological reasons.

More commonly, partners in which the woman is fertile but the male sterile. Also:

When males have a low sperm count, a blood incompatibility with the wife, have had a vasectomy or are known carriers of genetic disease. The sperm in these instances comes from male donors.

Who are donors: Volunteers chosen by professionals at the sperm bank. This is the center where specimens are stored, usually in a frozen state. Likeliest candidates: Professionals (such as doctors or medical students), lawyers, and Ph.D.'s. Often they are married men with children. Why: They are proven fertile.

Donors always remain anonymous. However, the parents select specimens according to traits of the donor (blonde hair, blue eyes, etc.)

Procedure: The woman has two or three inseminations from the same donor during a menstrual cycle. Cost: About $65 per insemination.

Drawbacks:

The legal status of the child is questionable in many areas. Only 15 states have laws declaring the children as legally belonging to the parents. Result: Many parents are secretive about the process to avoid legal battles.

The procedure may have to be repeated for several months before conception occurs. The length of time varies from one individual to another.

The emotionally charged procedure can be tough for the husband. This happens to even the most understanding and rational of men. Solution: Psychiatric counseling.

More information: The New York Fertility Research Foundation, Fairmont Medical Bldg., 1430 Second Ave., New York 10021.

Understanding Menopause

Menopause is said to cause so many problems for women at midlife that its advent is universally dreaded. Latest studies indicate, however, that menopause has been much maligned. Menopause is not a contributing factor to many of the common midlife dysfunctions, reveals a survey of women between the ages of 43 and 53. How menopause affects a woman depends on her previous life history.

Since menopause signals the end of childbearing, those women who have never borne children, but wanted to, often suffer more than those who have children. The most deeply affected mothers are those who had depended on child-rearing as a vital part of their feminine identity, self-importance, and status.

Social position heavily influences a woman's attitude toward menopause. The middle and upper classes often feel liberated at midlife. Their children move out of the house and the mothers are free to pursue their various interests. They join the work force, pick up a discontinued education, and so on. Lower-class women, who may lack personal resources, are harder hit, according to the new studies. Regardless of class, however, the woman who has devoted her life to her children experiences the greatest sense of loss and uselessness when they depart as she reaches midlife.

Depression, long considered a concomitant of menopause, is *not* inevitable. Once linked to the common midlife hormonal changes that occur in a woman's body, depression usually has purely psychological roots. Midlife itself does not make a woman susceptible.

Altered hormone manufacture is responsible for the hot flashes that occur during menopause. The decrease in estrogen induces the increased production of other hormones, which trigger the rushes of body heat. While embarrassing to many women, the symptoms usually go unnoticed even by friends and close acquaintances.

All sorts of other complaints have been blamed on menopause. They include insomnia, irritability, headaches, dizzy spells, and diminished sexual interest. But most are symptoms of anxiety or depression brought on by psychological reasons. And menopausal conditions do not necessarily precipitate anxiety.

Menopause does affect sex life—for the better. Free from the anxiety of pregnancy, women enjoy increased sexual satisfaction.

Menopause is supposed to bring back memories of unpleasant experiences, perhaps guilt or regret over an earlier abortion. Again, there is no proof that menopause inspires this melancholia.

True, menopause can be a difficult time. It's a particularly troublesome time for women with low self-esteem. It is an undeniable sign of aging in a culture in which the young are held in high regard. But the anticipation of menopause has proven to be more destructive than the experience. Most postmenopausal women agree that the condition is controllable. That's especially so for those who have supportive husbands, families, and friends.

Source: *Midlife: Developmental and Clinical Issues*, Brunner/Mazel, New York.

Contraceptive Update: Choosing the Best Method

Despite reports that development of an oral contraceptive for men is imminent, a pill for men is at least several years away. But other new contraceptive techniques are coming into use. And older ones are being improved.

There are new ways to help determine which days women are fertile and infertile. How the new rhythm techniques work: By reorganizing changes in body temperature and cervical condition. Big advantage: None of the side effects related to drugs or barrier devices.

Simplest guide: The lowest body temperature during normal waking hours. Known as the basal body temperature (BBT), it is taken immediately after waking in the morning. When the BBT rises and stays elevated for three days, a woman is beginning an infertile period that lasts until menstruation.

Other methods use signs of ovulation as a guide to fertile periods, and still others use a combination of signals. Caution: Because these natural methods are not 100% accurate, many couples combine them with backup contraception.

Oral contraception. Effective about 99% of the time. Unwanted reactions (nausea, high blood pressure, etc.) still persist, and the medical community is divided over their seriousness. For some women, the low-dosage minipill eliminates most side effects, but effectiveness is also reduced.

Women over 35, especially those who smoke, are overweight, have a history of heart, blood, or liver trouble, or have had any form of cancer, are usually advised not to take any birth-control pill. And barrier devices rather than the pill are best for nursing mothers, to avoid affecting their milk.

Intrauterine devices (IUD). New IUD models are small. Some are impregnated with minute amounts of copper and progesterone to enhance efficiency. But they still can cause side effects, some serious. Examples: Cramping, pelvic infection, painful intercourse. Women who want children later in life are discouraged from using IUDs because, in some cases, they can lead to sterility.

Prophylactics. No side effects, but condoms are effective only 90% of the time. Problems: Improper use, occasional breakage. Best: Store condoms in a cool place. Never lubricate them with petroleum jelly; it weakens them.

Spermicides. They cause no greater side effect than perhaps a local irritation. Alone, they are about as effective as prophylactics. But effectiveness is greatly enhanced when the two are used in combination.

Diaphragms (with spermicides). Effective about 80% of the time. Rare side effect: Bladder infection. Diaphragms are especially useful for women who want intercourse but are nursing or menstruating.

Cervical caps. Available only from physicians authorized to conduct tests on this modern adaptation of an old device. The thimble-sized rubber cap can be left in place longer than a diaphragm.

Sterilization. Effective over 99% of the time for men and women. For men, the operation is much simpler, but new surgical techniques have greatly simplified it for women. Drawback: Sterilization is irreversible for women and only sometimes reversible for men.

Source: International Fertility Research Program, Research Triangle Park, NC 27709, and the National Center for Health Statistics, 3700 East West Highway, Hyattsville, MD 20782

Taking Care of Your Feet

Basically, the amount of trouble you are likely to have with your feet depends on the shape of the feet you inherit.

Problems, causes, and cures:

Hammertoes are anatomical deformities. The tips of the toes dip toward the ground. Result: The tips develop painful calluses, the joints develop bumps on top. Cure: Shoes with high toe boxes. Ultimate cure: Have the hammertoe corrected and realigned by having microsurgery (a minimal incision), a procedure that can be done in the doctor's office.

Bunions develop when a toe moves in one direction and the bones linking the toe to the foot (the metatarsals) move in another direction. Cure: Ambulatory microsurgery can eliminate the bump. The bunion is shaved down. How: A microincision is made, and a tiny surgical burr is inserted through the incision to reduce the bump. This can be done in the office. Patients can usually return to work the following day. Pain is minimal. Point: Pumice stoning the skin off a bunion is ineffective.

Corns result from a lack of fat padding between skin and bone. Cure: Artificial pads help. Or, the bone under the corn can be smoothed down so that it does not rub against the shoe. This is also done by microsurgery, and usually allows patients to return to work the same day. Avoid liquid corn removers. Reason: They are mild acids, which burn away healthy skin, too. For a major foot problem, see: Ambulatory-trained surgical podiatrists familiar with microsurgery. Cost for treatments: Varies from $200 to $1,500. They are usually covered by most health insurance plans.

Source: Dr. Louis Shure, a podiatrist/foot surgeon, 144 E. 84 St., New York 10028.

How to Trim a Callus

Soak the foot in soapy water for 10 to 15 minutes. Dry it, then rub callus area gently with a moistened pumice stone or buffing pad. Apply moisturizing lotion to help soften skin. Repeat this routine several times a week and remove callused skin progressively. Important: Never use razor blades to remove calluses. In severe cases, see a doctor.

Preventing Varicose Veins

Varicose (swollen) veins usually occur in women's legs. Ways to prevent them: (1) Don't stand or sit for long stretches. When traveling, take walks every half hour. (2) Put your feet up periodically. (3) Don't wear clothes that impede circulation (tight underwear or jeans, knee socks with binding elastics, etc.). (4) Exercise the legs by dancing, jogging, bicycling, swimming, walking, playing tennis. (5) If you spend long periods of time on your feet, wear support hose. (6) Pregnant women should wear support stockings and they should try to either lie down or rest their legs several times a day.

Acne: Not Just Kid Stuff

Although most common at puberty (because of the production of androgen, a sex hormone), acne also afflicts millions of adults.

413

While there is no cure, there are ways to control it:

Wash face thoroughly two or three times a day, using a greaseless cleanser. Follow it with an astringent.

Try a gentle peeling medication. It's available over the counter and from dermatologists. Caution: Some people find that it irritates their skin.

See a dermatologist if you have deeply embedded blackheads, whiteheads, pustules, or cysts. Don't try to remove them yourself, lest you injure your skin permanently.

Topical antibiotics (liquids applied to the face) work well against papules or blackheads. Systemic antibiotics (taken orally) are available by prescription only. Tetracycline is most commonly used. Caution: Tetracycline should not be taken by pregnant women or nursing mothers. It can affect the baby's teeth. It also gives many women vaginitis, since it alters bacteria in the intestinal and genital tract. It may also increase vulnerability to sunburn, because the bacteria in the skin change as well.

Unrelated to acne: Eating chocolate or greasy foods, taking vitamins, having sex, using makeup (but acne sufferers should avoid makeup that is greasy and blocks the opening of the oil glands).

Acne and Women Athletes

Medical evidence shows that women who exercise heavily develop more severe acne than those who do not. Reason: Vigorous exercise produces increased amounts of male hormones for at least 30 minutes following a workout. The hormones cause the oil glands to produce increased amounts of oil. Some ducts carrying this oil to the skin surface are blocked. Bacteria in the pores convert the oil to free fatty acids. They cause redness and swelling in the skin. Recommended: Remove blackheads. Wash thoroughly twice a day with bland soaps.

The Best Soap for Each Type of Skin

For normal skin: Ivory soap. For oily skin: Transparent soap or a detergent-based soap. For dry skin: Superfatted soap. Avoid so-called "natural" or fruited soaps. They offer no benefits and may not be as pure as Ivory.

Preventing Premature Wrinkles

In general, what is good for your overall health is good for your skin. Vigorous exercise, for instance, can help postpone wrinkling by increasing the thickness and elasticity of the skin.

Special care is desirable:

Don't drink excessively. Too much alcohol causes dilation of the facial blood vessels and results in red spots.

Avoid prolonged exposure to the sun. The same ultraviolet rays that promote tanning also dry the skin and can cause cancer.

Cut down on smoking. It impairs circulation and encourages wrinkling.

Keep living quarters humid, especially in the winter when central heating reduces interior humidity.

Avoid crash diets. Rapid weight loss causes skin to sag.

Avoid squinting. It lines the face.
Source: *Executive Fitness.*

Keeping Your Skin Young

Wash your face after exercise to remove perspiration. It causes moisture loss and creates a dry condition.

Use moisturizing cream to protect your face from wind and sun exposure. Also apply it after showering to lock in moisture.

Rinse with warm instead of hot water.

Absence of oil glands around the eyes causes tiny lines to form. Use cream or petroleum jelly, gently massage from the outside corners toward the nose and eyelids.

Protect lips from exposure with a lip balm or sunscreen lotion.

Ice water stimulates skin circulation and tightens the pores, giving a younger look. Therefore, submerge a clean face into icy water for 20 seconds once a day. (The time underwater can be increased as the skin becomes comfortable with the tingling sensation caused by the icy water.) Then, lightly pat (don't rub) the skin dry, and lightly spray your face with sparkling mineral water.

Getting Rid of Acne Scars

The skin's own healing ability is the key to eliminating or reducing the unsightliness of acne scars. There are three types of scars:

1. Pits: Ranging from tiny dents (sometimes indistinguishable from pores) to deep, ragged craters.

2. Hypertrophic: Fibrous, discolored thicknesses.

3. Atrophic: Thin, slightly depressed patches.

Such scars can be caused by any acne lesion, such as blackheads, pimples or red, boil-like inflammations. None pose a health threat, but the scars cause some individuals to live with a private, unnecessary anguish about their looks. Treatment is most effective after the acne-prone years, which occur from the mid-teens to the mid-twenties. Usually only a few visits to the dermatologist's office are needed. The three favored treatments at present are:

Dermabrasion. The most widely used technique, it sands the afflicted area down to the level of most scars. Following a consultation and a photographic session (for a before-and-after record), the patient is given a general painkiller (usually Demerol), and then a local anesthetic (a skin refrigerant). The abrasion is performed with a wire brush or a diamond-dust stone, which is attached to a device resembling a dentist's drill. Scarred tissue and surrounding areas are abraded to ensure uniformity of skin color and tone afterward. Upon healing, the skin will return to its normal texture, minus the scars and some superficial wrinkles.

Once scraped, the face is a raw, draining lymph until the scab forms about two days later. There may be initial pain and itchiness. The scab falls off in about two weeks (plan to take a two-week vacation during the scabbing period), followed by a couple of months when the skin is slightly pink and tender. It's essential to avoid the sun during this period. The healing process goes on, unnoticeably, for about a year.

From dermabrasion, expect elimination of most superficial pits and 50% to 80% improvement of deeper scars. Cost: $500 to $1,500. Risks: Infection, gouging (during the abrasion), hyperpigmentation (discoloration) if the skin is exposed prematurely to the sun.

Dermabrasion is not recommended for: Hemophiliacs or individuals allergic to anesthetics or metals. The treatment must be used with extreme caution on dark-skinned people, including blacks, Orientals, and Latins, because of the increased likelihood of hyperpigmentation.

In severe cases, dermabrasion may be repeated, but no more frequently than once a year. Or it may be combined with one of the localized scar-removal methods (such as excision or pit incision).

Excision. This procedure surgically removes the entire scar, including the depression, after which the wound is sewn up along skin lines. The fine stitches are removed five to seven days later: Cost $50 to $250. Risk: Minimal.

Pit incision. It removes the base of the acne pit with a tubular surgical instrument. As the wound heals, the pit floor moves upward and into plane with the skin surface. Cost: $50 to $250. Risk: Minimal.

Limitation: Antiscarring treatment is usually confined to the face and is far less effective on other acne-vulnerable areas, such as the neck, back, torso, or buttocks. These areas heal less easily than facial tissue, and treatment can lead to additional scarring.

Source: Dr. Rabin M. Sarda, formerly a clinical instructor in dermatology at New York Hospital, Cornell Medical Center, in private practice at 337 E. 50 St., New York 10022.

The Sun and Your Skin

Sun damage is cumulative, starting with childhood exposure. Once a certain amount of damage has been done, there is a potential for developing skin cancer. If you have been a beach-goer all of your life and stop at age 45, the potential for skin cancer is nevertheless already there.

When the sun's effects begin to show: By age 50, at least. People who have soaked up the sun a lot will show wrinkles and possibly swollen blood vessels on the cheeks.

What can be done about sun-aged skin: Very little except, possibly, the radical method of dermabrasion. Prevention is really about the only way to avoid the harmful effects of the sun. The most serious of those effects: Skin cancer, particularly malignant melanoma (a malignant mole), which spreads internally and, unless caught early, is fatal. There are additional factors that may cause malignant melanoma besides the sun, but the sun is the major cause.

Less serious forms of sun cancer: Squamous cell, which can spread internally, but is usually limited to the skin area. It is curable. The most common is basal cell carcinoma. It occurs most often on the face. If treated early, it is usually not harmful.

Symptoms to watch for:

Any progressively growing skin lesion must be checked by a physician. There are, however, many skin spots that develop after age 40 that have no relation to cancer. Watch for bleeding discoloration, sudden growth, or other changes in old spots. Pay close attention to the development of new ones. The average person has about 40 moles on the body. Any changes, such as itching or bleeding, in any one of them should be checked by a doctor immediately.

Most susceptible are people who:
• Are fair-skinned.
• Tan poorly.
• Have red or blonde hair.
• Are blue-eyed.

How to prevent sun damage:

Avoid excessive sun exposure. Sun is most damaging between 11 a.m. and 3 p.m.

Use a sun block when in the sun. There is evidence that sun blocks help prevent skin cancer and retard the aging effects of the sun. Get sun blocks with the highest protective number, preferably 15 or greater. Good ones: Coppertone Supershade 15, Total Eclipse 15, Presun 15. It's essential to reapply the sun block after going into the water or after a set of tennis.

Don't use sun reflectors. They have a tremendous potential for increasing sun damage to the skin.

Be aware of medications you are taking. Some can make you more sensitive to sun. Examples: Tetracycline, diuretics, and major tranquilizers (such as Thorazine or Stelazine). They have the potential to cause a bad burn from an amount of sun that would not ordinarily be harmful. Reason: They have substances that cause skin to absorb more of the sun's radiation.

Wear protective clothing that is thick and tightly woven when shielding yourself from sun at the beach. Thin and sheer clothing allows harmful radiation to penetrate through to the skin.

What to do about a bad burn:

Apply cool compresses and calamine lotion to the area. Or take an over-the-counter antihistamine (such as Chlortrimeton) to relieve itching. If more severe symptoms take place (swelling of the face or extremities, for example), it is important to see a doctor.

Recommended:

People over 40 who are fair-skinned and have had a considerable amount of exposure to the sun should consider seeing a dermatologist for a checkup once a year.

Poison Ivy

A woeful affliction, poison ivy is caused by skin contact with an oil found in the ubiquitous ivy, poison oak, and poison sumac. The painful, blistering, itchy rash can result from brushing against the plant, petting a dog with fur contaminated by the plant's oil, or even standing in the smoke of burning poison ivy leaves.

The rash usually develops in 6 to 48 hours after contact. Prevention: Wear protective clothing, especially on the legs, when in the woods. If you've spotted any of the offending plants, throw your clothes in the washer and take a shower immediately. If a rash appears, consult your doctor. Severe cases: Cortisone in either pill or cream form is highly effective. **Source:** *The Runner.*

Getting Rid of Warts

For a simple, universal viral infection, warts have inspired an extraordinary number of bizarre cures. Our ancestors had recourse to witches and toads. Many contemporaries have tried hypnosis and therapy. People burn warts off with cigarettes, and slice them off with razors. Teen-agers often try to bite off the blemish, which is unfortunate because the likely result is the spread of warts to the face, lips and inner mouth. None of the above are recommended.

Causes: Warts are tumors caused by a virus. They are most active during the years of puberty, but anyone—from infants to elderly people—can get them.

We don't know exactly what causes warts to appear. They are contagious, but at a low level. This means that repeated contact is needed, and infection is slow to occur. Trauma may trigger the appearance of warts, whether the trauma is an injury to the site where the warts occur or an emotional upset. One theory holds that everyone always carries a wart virus, but occurrence results only with a breakdown in the immunological system.

There are five different types of warts:

Common: Bumpy. Occur most often on hands and fingers.

Filoform: Tiny, fingerlike projections, usually found on the face.

Flat: Small, barely raised tumors. Clustering on the neck or the back of the hands.

Plantar: Flat, rapidly clustering blemishes. Occur only on the soles of the feet. Because of their location and the discomfort to the patient, they are the most difficult wart to treat.

Genital: Occur on the skin and mucus membranes of the genital region. Sometimes spread through sexual contact. Parents sometimes transmit warts to infants' genital areas while diapering them.

Cures: Over-the-counter wart removers are generally ineffective. They are sometimes sufficient for a small common wart. If the drugstore cure hasn't worked in a week or two, see a physician.

Eliminating warts requires complete destruction of the virus that caused them as well as the tumor itself. All current treatments are performed in a doctor's office. Usually, a single visit to the doctor will suffice.

Among the treatments currently in use:

Electro-dessication: After an injection with a local anesthetic, the area of the wart is burned with an electric needle. This is the quickest and most widely used treatment. The aftermath may be a slight, brief pain. The wound heals in a few days.

Acid plasters: Applied with an adhesive, these are painless but can require two to six weeks for full healing. Usually used to get rid of plantar warts. Acid plasters must be prescribed by a physician, who teaches the patient how to replace them as needed.

Blistering solution: An extremely powerful agent, it softens the wart and surrounding tissue, which then falls off.

Dry ice (applied) or liquid nitrogen (sprayed): These also induce blistering, followed by softening and dropping off.

Podophyllin: This drug arrests cell replication and destroys a wart by stopping its growth process. The medication can be very painful to surrounding tissue.

417

In the future, a wart vaccine may become available. Such an immunizing agent is currently available in a crude form, but tests presently indicate that it is no more effective than a placebo.

Source: Dr. Rabin M. Sarda, formerly a clinical instructor in dermatology at New York Hospital, Cornell Medical Center, in private practice at 337 E. 50 St., New York 10022.

Why Hair Falls Out

The four general causes of hair loss are:

Heredity. Each individual's hair growth pattern is a unique, genetically determined phenomenon, like fingerprints. Unfortunately, genetically inspired hair loss is both the most common and most permanent cause of baldness. Men are prone to the spread of bald patches, beginning over the temples, the center of the brow, or on the pate.

Systemic problems. These include severe vitamin deficiency, major illness, prolonged fever, cancer, thyroid imbalance, and anemia. Medications, including some anticancer drugs, cause hair loss. New mothers occasionally have postpartum thinning. Systemic hair loss problems are normally temporary. Once the underlying condition is corrected, hair returns to normal growth and quality.

Localized infections and reactions. Severe infections and seborrhea (dandruff) can lead to temporary patchy baldness. Hair straighteners, shampoos, and other cosmetics can destroy hair through an allergic or irritant reaction, also temporary.

Alopecia areata. A fascinating condition about which we know virtually nothing. Alopecia is a Greek term meaning baldness (of sheep and birds as well as humans). It may occur on part of, or over the entire scalp. Sometimes all body hair disappears. When localized, alopecia is temporary. The more widespread the condition, the more likely that it will be permanent.

When hair begins falling out, particularly if it is accompanied by other symptoms, see a physician. It may be an early warning of a disease whose treatment will end the hair problem as well.

Source: Dr. Rabin M. Sarda, formerly clinical instructor in dermatology at New York Hospital, Cornell University Medical Center, is in private practice at 337 E. 50 St., New York 10022.

Three Medical Tests to Have Regularly

Blood pressure. At least annually. Untreated high blood pressure can cause heart attacks and strokes. Get this test from your doctor, or buy a simple do-it-yourself device. You can even get tested in some supermarkets and drugstores which are equipped with coin-operated machines.

Glaucoma. This is a fluid buildup behind the eyes, which can lead to blindness. Get checked by an ophthalmologist at least every four to five years. Glaucoma examinations are especially important after age 40.

Pap test. Women should have this at least every two years to check for cervical cancer. It's treatable if caught early.

Source: *Surgery: Your Choices, Your Alternatives* by George Crilie, Jr., MD, Delacorte Press, New York.

Do-it-Yourself Medical Tests

Self-diagnosis has been made easier by a proliferation of do-it-yourself medical testing devices for a variety of ailments. Among them:

Blood pressure: Stethoscope and cuff kit are available at any department or discount store for around $20. More sophisticated devices, with digital readouts: $100 and up.

Bowel cancer: The Guaiac Test, available through some local offices of the American Cancer Society, analyzes for blood in the stool.

Pregnancy: A kit available at drugstores gives a moderately reliable diagnosis in two hours.

Baby breathing: This device monitors for irregular infant breathing to warn against crib death. Can be rented from hospitals.

Urine tests: For diabetes. At drugstores, the cost is about $3.

Coming soon: Blood tests for anemia and cholesterol levels; electronic dental hygiene kits; emergency medical equipment similar to that used by paramedics.

Diagnosing Diabetes

Diabetes is the third leading cause of death in the country, after heart disease and cancer. The disease is an inability of the body to handle sugar. It appears at two times:

Juvenile: Strikes children and young adults (10% of the cases). Control: Regular injections of insulin.

Maturity: Occurs in middle age and beyond. More common and less dangerous. Control: Weight loss through diet and exercise. Usually, oral medication or injections are required.

Who gets it: The risk of diabetes in adults doubles with every ten years of life and every 20% of increased body weight. Women run a greater chance of contracting it than men. Many victims have diabetic relatives.

The symptoms in children: Rapid weight loss, fatigue, nausea, abnormal thirst and hunger. In mature adults, if uncontrolled: Weight gain or loss, tiredness, scaly or itchy skin, circulatory impairment.

Caution: For some adults, the disease is only uncovered during a routine physical examination.

Top U.S. Diagnostic Clinics

A day at a diagnostic clinic can be as useful as a day with a business consultant who knows the right questions to ask. The clinics use the latest techniques to screen and test for a broad spectrum of problems and potential problems. At the end, a physician gives the patient a thorough review of the results. Typical follow-up: Individuals are motivated to stop smoking, change their diet, or lose a few pounds. Many return for another run-through of the tests to see the improved results.

Twelve top U.S. clinics for diagnostic physicals:

Vincent Astor Diagnostic Service, New York Hospital, Cornell Medical Center, 525 E. 68th St., New York 10021, 212-472-5753. Appointment: Two weeks in advance. Exam: Three to four hours.

Cleveland Clinic, 9500 Euclid Ave., Cleveland 44106, 216-444-2200. Appointment: Six to eight weeks' notice. Exam: One day, or two half days.

Executive Health Examiners, 777 Third Ave., New York 10017, 212-486-8900. Branch facilities in Stamford, CT, Morristown, NJ, with affiliates in 500 cities. Appointment: Two weeks' notice. Exam: Two to three hours.

Greenbriar Clinic, White Sulphur Springs, WV 24986, 304-536-1110. Appointment: One year in advance. Exam: Two to three days.

Lahey Clinic, 605 Commonwealth Ave., Boston 02159, 617-261-2200. Appointment: Four to six weeks' notice. Exam: One to three days.

Life Extension Institute, 1185 Ave. of the Americas, New York 10036, 212-575-8300. Institute has over 800 affiliates. Appointment: A few days' notice.

Mayo Clinic, 200 S.W. First St., Rochester, MN 55901, 507-282-2511. Appointment: One year's notice. Exam: One day.

Ochsner Clinic, 1514 Jefferson Highway, New Orleans 70121, 504-834-7070. Exam: Three days to one week.

Palo Alto Clinic: 300 Homer Ave., Palo Alto, CA 94301, 415-321-4121. Appointment: Four weeks' notice. Exam: One day.

Scott-White Clinic, Scott-White Hospital, Temple, TX 76501, 817-774-2111. Appointment: Three weeks' notice. Exam: Two days.

Scripps Clinic, 10666 N. Torrey Pines Rd., La Jolla, CA 92037, 714-455-9100. Appointment:

Two to three weeks' notice. Exam: Two days.

Strang Clinic, 320 E. 15th St., New York 10003, 212-475-6066. Appointment: Two weeks' notice. Exam: One day.

Should You Choose Outpatient Surgery?

A growing number of simple operations are being performed without postoperative hospitalization.

Prime benefit: Saving money. Even with medical insurance, patients generally pay 20% of their hospital bill. In the case of plastic surgery, a popular outpatient operation, hospitalization costs may not be covered by insurance at all.

Psychological benefit: In the case of older people, in particular, leaving the familiarity of their home and spending a night or more in a strange hospital is traumatic. With outpatient surgery, they can be back home within hours, thus limiting the potential trauma.

The most common procedures performed where you can usually (but not always) leave after just a few hours of recuperation:

Tonsillectomy.

Minor plastic surgery.

Abortion.

Skin-growth removal.

Vasectomy.

Hand surgery.

Eardrum repair.

Removal of a cyst.

Diagnostic viewing of bladder and urine ducts.

Vein ligation.

Some cataract operations.

Outpatients do not have the constant medical attention offered by a hospital stay. They should check out the following on their own:

Is the surgeon associated with a good hospital in the area? Can the doctor perform the operation in that hospital?

Does the surgeon have admitting privileges with a good hospital that will allow you to be transferred there in case of complications?

Is the admitting hospital nearby?

Is the doctor's assistant qualified to administer anesthesia?

Is there a recovery room where you can rest for a few hours?

Is there a full-time registered nurse present during surgery and during the recovery period?

In the case of a private surgical suite, is the facility approved by any regional agency? (There is no government organization that regulates them.)

Be aware that outpatient surgery may be undesirable if you have physical problems like persistent hypertension or psychological problems. Also, most outpatient clinics use only local anesthesia. If you insist on a general anesthetic, you may find there's no alternative to a hospital stay.

Pros and Cons of Walk-in Emergency Clinics

Fast-growing development in health care: Walk-in clinics open 12 or more hours a day and located in shopping centers. They handle minor emergencies and routine medical complaints. More than 150 are already operating in over a dozen states, and the number is expected to zoom.

Advantages: The new clinics combine the after-hours availability of a hospital emergency room with the more pleasant atmosphere of a doctor's office. No appointment is needed. Waiting time is usually under 10 minutes. Costs are often only half of what a hospital emergency room would charge.

Disadvantages: Most won't file insurance forms. That's left to the patients. Some encourage excessive lab tests to pad profits. Many don't have the sophisticated equipment that hospitals do to handle more serious emergencies.

Note: If you use one of the clinics, be sure a record of the treatment is sent to your regular doctor.

The Safest Blood Transfusion

Be your own blood bank. Most hospitals allow patients to donate their *own* blood prior to nonemergency surgery. It can safely be refrigerated until you need it. Many operations require about three pints. Advantage: Despite careful, significantly improved techniques, a donor's blood will never be as safe as your own.

Know Your Rights When Entering a Hospital

All the civilized ways of making life dignified and graceful disappear when people enter a hospital, just the time they need those things the most. Important: To know the courtesies to which you have a right when in a hospital. More important: Your legal rights as a patient. Specifically:

Considerate and respectful care. Examples: Being included in conversations about your case and the way doctors and other personnel carry on in your presence. Having curtains drawn around your bed when being examined. Not being awakened in the middle of the night to be given a sleeping pill. None are legal rights, but they are essential courtesies to insist upon. Recourse if these rights are violated: Speak up assertively, or have a friend or relative do it for you. Or: Contact a patients' representative that many hospitals have as ombudsman for patients. Where to find them: In the hospital admissions booklet issued to new patients. (It may be near the bedside telephone; if not, ask for a copy.)

All current information concerning diagnosis, treatment, and prognosis of your condition, in terms you can understand. (Legal right.)

Information from the physician to enable you (or the surrogate decision-maker if you are too ill) to give informed consent before the start of any procedure or treatment. This in-cludes any medically significant alternatives to a treatment, if they exist. Consent must be given before you are sedated. You have the right to withdraw consent if you change your mind. If you change your mind about giving consent: Get the original consent form back and destroy it. (Legal right.)

The authority to refuse treatment if you are not convinced it is necessary. The right to a full explanation of the consequences if you do or if you don't have it. (Legal right.)

Privacy in all examinations and consultations pertaining to your case. Example: if you are in a teaching hospital and you object to six students watching while the doctor performs your examination, you can refuse permission for them to be there. If students try to examine or treat you against your wishes: Ask to see the head of the department and remind that person that the attending physician and the hospital (as well as the students) are liable for any unauthorized exam or treatment. If you have been led to believe that the person examining or treating you is a doctor, and you later discover the person is a student, you can bring suit for fraud or misrepresentation. (Legal right.)

Confidentiality. Information relating to your care and condition should be discussed only with those medically involved in it. Where confidentiality may be a problem: In large teaching institutions where cases are necessarily discussed at conferences. If there are special reasons for wanting strict confidentiality (concern for employment prospects or damage to career), be sure to tell the physician at the outset. (Legal right.)

If a hospital doesn't have facilities to treat you, expect it to arrange for your entry into a hospital that does. It can't just discharge you. (Legal right.)

If any part of your treatment is going to be medical experimentation, you must be advised beforehand. To protect yourself from experimentation without your consent: Look for any dramatic change in treatment that the doctor hasn't prepared you for. And ask questions. (Legal right.)

The medical information in your records. The actual papers belong to the hospital (or the doctor), but the patient has the legal right to the information in them. Ask to see the records if the hospital won't give them to you. If the hospital balks at letting you see records, check the state law requirements. In some states, a lawyer's help may be required to get access to records, while others allow patients direct access. Some state hospitals and all federal hospitals must provide patients access to records, under the Federal Privacy Act and the Freedom of Information Act. (Legal right.)

When your child is the patient: If you want to stay with the child and the hospital discourages or refuses it, get the doctor to write a note advising it. Most hospital authorities are unwilling to refuse doctors' orders. Argue that you can't give a fully informed consent (a legal right) to the child's treatment if you can't be with the child to monitor reactions and make the proper judgment. Be quietly insistent. There are solid practical and emotional reasons for staying with a small child in the hospital, unless it is medically unfeasible.

Before signing in: Appoint a surrogate decision-maker who will look out for your interests and deal with the hospital staff, and who must be consulted whenever there are questions and decisions to be made about the treatment. (That's particularly important should you not be in condition to make those decisions.) Examples: A spouse, parent, child, brother, sister, lover, friend. Be sure the doctor caring for you knows who that surrogate is. It should be someone who is capable of putting your interests and comfort above all else and is not afraid to demand action or question authority.

Specific suggestions for patients and their families:

Do not agree to any diagnostic tests without clearly understanding their purpose and necessity. Reason: Threat of malpractice suits has led many doctors (and hospitals) to practice "defensive medicine." They schedule every conceivable test when only a few are truly relevant. (If the same tests have recently been performed by your own doctor, try to substitute those.)

Check medical insurance before tests or hospital visit. It may be possible to take some tests as an outpatient. But many policies cover only those that are done in the hospital and within a specified period before admittance. Note: If admittance is postponed, you are liable. Also check coverage on things like private vs. semiprivate rooms (most are written for semiprivate) and private nursing (if coverage is skimpy, the family could take the day shift).

Avoid going into a hospital on Friday, if possible. Reason: Nothing significant is ever done on weekends. Often the staff is skimpy and any emergency occupies everyone. Weekend patients pay generously for two days of bed rest and poor service.

Upon admission, ask to see the "Patient's Bill of Rights." Most good hospitals now publish these as part of the preparatory material offered to all patients.

Find out what medication has been prescribed (doctor should explain), and what it looks like (mistakes can occur). Also: How often the medication should be taken (again, watch out for errors). And what it is intended to do (including possible side effects). These are safety measures that will also make it easier to understand charges that appear on your bill.

If specialists are called in, ask why they are needed and what their credentials are. Also determine if there is an alternative specialist at the hospital in case the first is not satisfactory to the patient.

If surgery is being considered, get a second opinion. Blue Cross and other insurance plans not only pay for this, but encourage it as a good way to avoid unnecessary surgery. If it's a tie, get a third opinion.

Question any of the items on the hospital bill that you do not understand. Patients and their families are entitled to an explanation of all the charges, whether or not they are covered by insurance. The financial department of the hospital can explain what typically is or isn't covered by Medicare, Medicaid, Blue Cross, and other insurance plans. They will also clarify the terms under which payment is expected from the patient.

Source: Florence Janovic, co-author of *The Hospital Experience*, Bobbs-Merrill, Indianapolis, IN.

Understanding Hospital Talk

A hospital patient may have considerable difficulty understanding some of the jargon used by nurses and other hospital personnel. Here is what some commonly used terms mean:

NPO—Sign placed by the bed of a patient who is not to get anything to eat or drink.

Emesis basin—Basin brought to a patient who is sick to his stomach.

Ambulate—Take the patient for a walk.

Force fluids—Encourage intake of lots of liquid.

Void—Urinate.

IV—Intravenous.

OOB—Out of bed.

IPPG—Intermittent Positive Pressure Breathing Machine to aid the breathing.

HS—Medication before sleep.

BP—Blood pressure.

HR—Heart rate.

Medication schedule:

QID—4 times.

TID—3 times.

BID—2 times.

OD or QD—Once a day.

QOD—Every other day.

What to Ask a Surgeon

To protect against unnecessary surgery, ask the physician hard questions *beforehand*.

What are the risks?

What is the mortality rate for this operation?

How long will it take to recover?

What is the likelihood of complications? What sort?

Are there ways to treat this condition medically?

How many people have you seen with similar symptoms who have chosen not to have surgery?

How many of these operations have you done in the past year?

Always get a second opinion.

The Ultimate in Fat Reduction: Plastic Surgery

Fat-reduction surgery removes a layer of fat. But like any other major surgical procedure, there are real hazards, not the least of which is that the result may not be what you imagined.

There are three commonly performed types of fat-reduction surgery. All three require hospital stays of up to a week and are performed under a general anesthetic.

Tummy tucks. (Abdomenplasty): This operation is major abdominal surgery and is equivalent to a gall-bladder operation. In this procedure, the surgeon removes fat and skin down to the abdominal muscles. The cosmetic change in appearance comes mostly from the removal of loose skin. Tummy tucks are most effective when performed on people who have lost a great deal of weight or women who have loose, stretched-out skin following pregnancy. The natural elasticity of their skin has been lost, thus creating folds of loose skin, which the surgeon removes. The prominent scar is usually placed at the pubic hairline. The pain is similar to any major operation, but rapidly lessens after the first day or two. Normal activity can be resumed, with caution, in ten days to two weeks. Insurance: It generally covers the hospital stay (four to five days) and a portion of the surgeon's fee.

Thighs and britches. (Lipodystophy): For people with excess tissue on the upper thigh (called riding-britches). Like an abdomenplasty, this leaves big dark scars in the creases of the upper thighs, prominent enough to be visible in a high-cut bathing suit, but not in a pair of shorts. Insurance: It usually does not cover the cost of the hospital stay (five to seven days) or the surgeon's fee.

Breast-reduction surgery. (Gynomasta): Up to six pounds of fatty tissue can be removed. The scar runs around the nipple and down past the areola. Insurance: It usually covers the cost of the entire procedure for women. Since very few men suffer from the discomfort of very large breasts, it is difficult to get an insurance company to cover.

How to decide if plastic surgery is for you:

Choose the surgeon very carefully. See before-and-after pictures of other patients. Get recommendations from friends. Be wary of doctors who promise miracles and tiny scars. Such promises can rarely be kept.

There will be prominent scars. Before having the surgery, you must decide which really bothers you more—sagging skin or visible scars.

The surgeon cannot change your basic appearance. The only thing he can do is alter it.

Source: Dr. Henry Zackin, plastic surgeon, 525 Park Ave., New York 10021.

Cosmetic Surgery For Men

Plastic surgeons are seeing a great increase in the number of men seeking cosmetic surgery, including face lifts.

Next to eyelid surgery, it's become the most commonly performed cosmetic operation chosen by men. The prognosis for good results varies dramatically with facial type. Certain facial types lend themselves far better to this surgery than others. People with well-defined longer faces, good bone structure, and well-defined necks are likely to have far more striking results from a face lift than will a person with a very short or nearly nonexistent neck, and a very rounded face. (Face-lifting involves the neck area in an important way because skin there has to be redraped and pushed upward to get rid of jowls.)

Optimum result: Look eight to ten years younger. Good surgery should not produce a masklike effect, the usual result of a surgeon's effort to get the last millimeter of loose skin taken up. Aim: A plastic surgeon who goes for a natural look and who won't try for maximum, or extreme, results.

Effect on beard: The beard area of the neck will move upward and back, with the result that there will be some space behind the ears that will have to be shaved. Sideburns will be somewhat closer to the ear. Incisions are in front of the ear, within a natural fold, and continuing upward into the scalp above the ear. Incision scars, when healed properly, are not normally noticeable. The recovery period is roughly two weeks. Swelling and discoloration of the neck and face will be mostly gone in this time. They should disappear completely in a month. Stitches in front of the ear are removed in five days' time. Stitches in scalp are removed within ten days to two weeks after the surgery.

Cost: Twenty-five hundred dollars to $3,500 for face lift alone. If additional corrective surgery is needed, such as the procedure to get rid of serious jowl problems, called "muscle sling," the cost is greater. (At present, medical insurance generally will not cover the cost of this kind of purely cosmetic surgery.)

Other kinds of cosmetic surgery being done on men: Hair transplants and, to a far smaller degree, nose surgery.

Choosing a plastic surgeon: It is better to choose someone who is not limited to a particular cosmetic surgical procedure. Especially true in the choice of rhinoplasty surgeon. Reason: Surgeons renowned for their "noses" tend to give the same nose to everyone, regardless of facial structure.

Source: Dr. Henry Zackin, 525 Park Ave., New York 10021.

Plastic Surgery After an Accident

Someone who is hospitalized after an accident and needs cosmetic surgery usually will be offered the services of the plastic surgeon the hospital has on call that day.

If that particular surgeon doesn't seem like a good bet: Ask the hospital for a list of plastic surgeons affiliated with it, and choose one. Or: Ask your doctor to recommend a good one. Remember that not all injuries need the immediate attention of a plastic surgeon. Example: A broken nose. It can be attended to by a plastic surgeon three or four days later, unless the patient is in very bad shape.

Problem of scarring: Plastic surgeons have a harder time making scars disappear on young patients than on older ones. Young skin is smooth and shows scars more prominently. The wrinkled texture of older skin makes it more possible to conceal scars. Techniques that reduce scars: Reoperations, to make the scar smaller. Also: Dermabrasion (sanding), to blend the scar into surrounding skin.

Source: Henry Zackin, M.D., plastic surgeon, 525 Park Ave., New York 10021.

Mistakes Made by Plastic Surgeons

Many problems that disturb patients who have just had cosmetic surgery go away with time. Others may require additional surgery for correction. Common errors:

Nose: When a doctor removes too much bone and cartilage from a nose, it must be rebuilt. Or, when cartilage and bone removal aren't balanced properly on both sides, the nose appears to be asymmetrical.

Eyelids: When too much skin has been removed from the upper eyelids, the patient can't close the eyes properly. Related problem: If the lower eyelid is pulled down because too much skin was removed, new skin may be grafted onto the area to correct it. Lesser problem: The surgeon has left a pouchiness or excess loose skin around the eyes. Remedy: The operation must be redone to remove the excess skin.

Rule: It's much easier to correct problems that result from too little being done than to correct problems where too much has been done.

What to do: Revisit the surgeon, who can help you determine if the problem is one that will pass in time. If the problem is obviously more serious and the surgeon is uncooperative, consult another doctor.

Way to prevent a problem beforehand:

Determine before undergoing surgery what the doctor's attitude will be if the results are unsatisfactory. How: Ask questions. A reasonable bet is a doctor who says: If it can be made better, it will be.

Source: Dr. Henry Zackin, M.D., plastic surgeon, 525 Park Ave., New York 10021.

Getting the Best Medical Care

Patients and their families manage their medical problems by finding a good physician and, on occasion, getting a second opinion. For good medical care, much more initiative and responsibility must be taken. Even the best doctors tend to limit their interests to a small part of a patient's total problem, leaving someone outside the doctor's office to tie the rest together.

In effect, there is a medical system that contains doctors in various specialties, their office managers, hospitals (and their various subdivisions), clinics, and insurers—to mention the most obvious parts of the system. Getting well requires somebody who can make the system work for you. Unfortunately, if you try to cope with only one part (i.e., a doctor), you may not obtain the proper care.

Evaluating a doctor's advice: Even the best physicians wear blinders. They see illness in familiar terms, given their own specializations. Thus, even well-trained psychiatrists often approach depression as entirely "psychiatric" in origin, when numerous physical diseases may cause depression (e.g., an ovarian insufficiency).

The patient (or the family) often must be the one to take the initiative in checking out alternative diagnoses. In addition, it's useful to seek specialists who will have a different viewpoint. Many symptoms can have a variety of alternative causes, with each symptom residing within a different medical specialty.

Other doctors: In asking your family doctor, or another health specialist, about referrals, you should ask about more than professional qualifications. For many patients, it's important to have a doctor who is not harsh or threatening, is easy to talk to, and even someone they can telephone. Ask about the disposition and personality of the referred physician. Often, your doctor will know more about this person and how he treats patients than the original recommendation suggests.

The doctor-patient relationship: Most patients fail to clarify their new doctor's system. A typical problem (particularly with many specialists) is that their nurse and receptionist have been trained to protect the doctor —at all costs. Straightforwardly ask your doctor how you can get in touch with him or her, what hours and under what circumstances you can telephone, and the receptionist's instructions about letting calls through to the doctor. Ask the doctor or the receptionist how office visits are booked. If you have had a long wait, find out how many patients have the same appointment time or what the odds are that the doctor won't be there because of hospital calls or visits. Take this into account when deciding if you can spend time waiting to see the doctor. At the least, you will be prepared for the wait.

Find out how to handle prescriptions. Can your pharmacist call the doctor? During what hours? Or does the doctor prefer to call the druggist? The nurse? Who will set in motion this particular coordination?

Finally, consider your relatives to be part of your health-care system. Clarify with the doctor the relatives who can call seeking information. Determine the information the doctor can properly give them about your condition.

Medical insurance:

Obviously, it pays to check in advance with your employer about what is, or isn't, covered by insurance. It often saves time and grief to have the right forms with you when you go to the doctor so they can be filled out and signed at the time of your visit. This saves endless calls and expedites your reimbursement.

Planning a hospital stay:

Patients hospitalized for one type of diagnostic test or medical procedure may have other ailments. Hospital stays are not only costly, they are highly traumatic. It may take the patient's, or his family's, initiative to get as many procedures done during the period as possible. Usually one doctor has ordered the hospitalization. But when other specialists and doctors want additional tests taken, the patient should take responsibility for contacting the doctors so that all their requirements are coordinated and no unnecessary tests are ordered.

When the patient is very sick: A family member or friend may have to represent the patient. Modern hospitals like to discuss diet, nursing, and other instructions with a patient's representative when the patient can't speak up or he lacks initiative.

Planning the discharge: Again, hospitals have social-service departments that are supposed to arrange for needed home care. Often, the patient may not need medical attention, but there is no one at home to provide normal care and feeding. While the hospital staff has the contacts, there may be ambiguous questions about whether the care is covered by the patient's insurance or benefit program. Again, someone must represent the patient, seek a favorable interpretation for the ill person, and perhaps get the physician to order home care (which may then place it under the insurance plan).

When social service isn't effective, it may be necessary to extend the hospital stay until all arrangements for home care have been completed. Since hospitals are under strict surveillance to limit hospital stays to the absolute minimum (to keep insurance costs down), a patient's threat to refuse to be discharged may stimulate the hospital to provide home care.

Given the legitimate need of the hospital to minimize the length of a stay, some patients (those who are very frail, or whose recovery is delayed) may have to take the initiative to get their doctor to request a longer stay. Again, the system requires someone to take action or the results will be by formula.

Coordinating specialists:

Some doctors who have patients with multiple diseases will consult specialists. But don't take this for granted. Often, the patient or his representative consults a specialist on his own and confronts one doctor with the diagnosis of the other to assess its implications. This can be especially true when psychiatrists and other medical specialists are involved.

While most doctors are very alert to possible drug interactions, don't be afraid to ask how a medicine prescribed by one doctor for an ailment interacts with other medical prescriptions. Glaucoma patients, for example, have to be very careful about the medicines they receive for other problems.

Bottom line:

While it would be nice when you are sick to put yourself completely into the hands of an omniscient, caring physician who will tend to everything for you, most doctors have neither the time nor the inclination to do so. A great responsibility for good care continues to rest with patients and their families. They have to oversee how the medical system delivers its services.

Source: Dr. Miriam Lewin, associate professor of psychology at Manhattanville College in Purchase, NY.

Hospital Mistakes

Hospital stays can be dangerous. Some 36% of those in one study suffered ill effects from drugs or therapy prescribed by their physicians. And 9% of the adverse reactions were life-threatening (2% of the patients actually died). In another study, 36 mistakes were found in the treatment of 5,612 surgical patients. Causes of the surgeon's errors: Over-optimism, haste, desire for perfection.

Source: *The New England Journal of Medicine.*

When to Get a Second Medical Opinion

A doctor persists in saying the diagnosis is tentative or presumptive. Or, if the doctor requests more and more tests.

The patient's health does not improve.

An ailment is diagnosed as rare or as an emotional disease.

The doctor says the condition requires long-term treatment.

Surgery is recommended.

The prognosis is unfavorable.

It is possible that in any of the above circumstances the doctor may be correct. No patient need be embarrassed in seeking another opinion, however, even if the doctor opposes it.

Source: *Talk Back to Your Doctor,* by Dr. Arthur Levin, Doubleday & Co., New York.

Verifying a Doctor's Credentials

Check the doctor's background in the *Directory of Medical Specialists,* available at most libraries. What to look for: Where the doctor served as resident (postgraduate training). Key: A residency at a prestigious hospital means more than graduating from a famous medical school.

When to Sue For Medical Malpractice

A medical malpractice suit is high-risk litigation. That means a vast majority (80%) of tried cases result in a verdict in favor of the doctor. Point: Consult a lawyer who is a specialist in the field. Unless the case involves a serious injury brought on by a doctor's negligence, it will be discouraged.

Finding an expert: Check with your family or business lawyer. From those names recommended, select a specialist with a demonstrably successful track record. Note: After the first consultation, the specialist should be able to give you an educated opinion on your chances of winning the suit.

Procedure: The lawyer will need supporting testimony by an experienced doctor to prove that your complaint was caused by negligence. Exception: If the negligence is blatant.

Pitfall: Prepare for perhaps years of psychological turbulence. Morality and credibility are often at issue. But the financial award can be substantial, particularly in urban areas where jurors favor plaintiffs.

Costs: Cases are prosecuted on a contingency basis. Generally, you pay nothing during the course of litigation. With a favorable settlement, the attorney's fees and costs are taken off the top. Lawyer's fees vary from one-third to 50% of net recovery. (Most states have contingency limits.)

If you lose: Traditionally, you owe the lawyer expenses (usually at least $5,000). If you can't afford the costs, your lawyer may bow out.

Source: Irving O. Farber, a specialist in malpractice suits and a partner in the law firm of Meiselman, Farber, Stella and Moran, 205 South Ave., Box 229, Poughkeepsie, NY 12602.

Health Insurance: How to Determine Adequate Coverage

Most of the shortcomings in medical insurance occur because buyers are unfamiliar with what is available in the market. They don't have a checklist of questions to ask. Even many brokers are unaware of the pitfalls in some policies. So read the terms of the contract before you buy. Once you have a policy, fighting for additional payments is very frustrating. Therefore, have the right policy in the first place.

Many hospitalization and surgical policies do not cover the entire cost of a hospital stay or surgery. Example: Many plans only cover a semiprivate room up to $200 a day. Many surgical plans, such as Blue Shield, insure operation costs on a national average basis. Therefore, if you have an operation in New York,

Boston, or San Francisco, you are apt to have significant out-of-pocket expenses since doctors there charge considerably more than in, say, Kansas City.

To supplement such plans, get a major medical with a sizable deduction that "wraps around" your primary hospitalization and surgical coverage. These policies can enable you to have a private nurse or specialized care in many cases.

In areas where Blue Cross/Blue Shield is noncompetitive in price or benefits, and there is no prepaid group plan such as a Kaiser-Permanente or Health Insurance Plan (HIP), get a comprehensive major medical plan from a private insurer.

Read the terms of the insurance contract to determine what the insurance company will pay for each situation. Private insurers often use the phrase "reasonable and customary charge" to limit what they will pay for operations and doctor's services. Reasons: The insurer wants to discourage victims of illness from visiting very expensive specialists for any minor complaint. However, "reasonable and customary" falls within a fairly wide spectrum and is negotiable up to a point. Limitations are not absolute.

Example: A New York resident flew across the border to Montreal for a gallbladder operation. He was able to prove that the operation with the cost of the flight was cheaper in Canada than a doctor and hospital in New York. The insurance company found the case convincing and paid air fare and all bills.

However, some insurance firms establish inside limits or scheduled benefits of various operations. Each situation is described with the sum the insurance company gives for room, board, and the surgery. Read these carefully. Check out how these limits compare with actual practices in your region. If possible, avoid these policies and stick to the reasonable and customary policies. Obviously, you get what you pay for. Policies with inner limits are cheaper, but the cost differential is minimal.

Look into the limits of major medical insurance. Are they lifetime or per cause limits? How they work: If you have a $250,000 lifetime limit and get cancer treatments that use up the $250,000, you are not able to collect money for treatments when you get a heart ailment the next year. But if you have a per cause limitation of $250,000, the insurer will pay up to the limit, $250,000, for the heart ailment after you use up $250,000 for cancer. If you get any other disease, then you can obtain still another $250,000 for treatment.

Check out the extent of coinsurance. Few companies will pay 100% of all medical treatment. They want the consumer to undertake some of the payments, partly to avoid malingering. Therefore, they make you pay 20% of the second $2,000, $5,000, $10,000, $50,000, or even an unlimited amount. The insurance company picks up the other 80%. Naturally, you want to avoid policies with large coinsurance clauses. With extensive hospitalization for a major illness, you could wind up being $10,000 or even more out of pocket. If your 80/20 coinsurance is limited to $2,000, you will only be a maximum of $400 out of pocket.

Source: Leon Sicular, president, Leon Sicular Associates, benefit consultants, 350 Fifth Ave., New York 10118.

Fighting Back When an Insurance Claim Is Denied

Even though the bureaucracy of a giant insurance company may seem intimidating, it's often worthwhile to challenge the company when reimbursement for a medical bill is denied or inadequate. An employee-benefits consulting firm recently found that health claims submitted were erroneously processed over 60% of the time.

Dealing with health insurers has become so complicated (particularly for people covered by two or more policies) that a new type of service industry has sprung up. Within the last five years, several companies have been formed to help people cope with the huge amount of paperwork that accompanies large

medical and hospital bills.* Their services are targeted at elderly people covered by Medicare, who also have supplemental private insurance (often called Medigap policies), and at successful executives, who are too busy to be bothered filling out stacks of forms.

Usual charge: $45 to $50 an hour. A consultation over billing problems connected with a lengthy hospital stay might be $75. While that might seem steep at first, the service can get you significantly more benefits.

It is also possible to challenge a health insurance company on your own. Most carriers have a fairly straightforward appeals process.

Blue Cross and Blue Shield of Greater New York is typical, although policies among companies do vary. At Blue Cross, a complaint is first reviewed by someone at a level higher than the examiner who made the initial determination. If the consumer is still dissatisfied, the complaint is reexamined by an examiner with a technical background (such as a nurse or lab technician). Next, the complaint is sent to the company's medical advisory staff of physicians. Top level of review: The physician who serves as the company's medical director. Only 1% to 2% of challenges ever get this far.

Under the Employee Retirement Income Security Act (ERISA), subscribers can file appeals within 60 days after the complaint.

Officials in charge of claims handling at insurance companies suggest putting a complaint in writing. That usually gets a more searching review than a gripe made over the telephone. (Many claims-handling departments, though, will accept collect calls from dissatisfied customers, or will call back at company expense.)

When challenging a company's reimbursement decision: Include as much pertinent information as you can. Specifically: past bills and doctors' treatment records, if you have them. Sometimes, a dispute is resolved in a consumer's favor when a doctor provides additional details.

Example: Blue Cross, under one of its com-

* The companies include: MediClaim Inc., with offices in Oakland and Santa Cruz, CA; Mediform, in Cleveland, and the Health Claims Assistance Company, in New York City.

mon contracts, will pay only $425 for gall bladder surgery. But it paid an extra $280 when the doctor repaired the patient's ulcer at the same time.

Some battles concern new or experimental medical procedures. Example: The use of elaborate new home equipment that tests the blood-sugar levels of people with diabetes. A company might challenge the use of the equipment, which costs $500, compared with 20 cents for the standard paper-strip tests. But if the physician argues that the machine is necessary because the patient needs a very accurate reading, the decision might be reversed.

If you are still unhappy after exhausting the internal appeals process within a company, you can take your dispute to the peer review committee of the local medical society. The committee has no formal legal power to overturn either the insurance company's finding, or the doctor's fee, that both you and the company feel is higher than customary. But its findings are frequently followed up.

Another complaint route: Appeal to your state insurance department. While some experts say these agencies are not set up to handle consumer complaints, others find that they can be very powerful allies. One company's experience: 13% of the complaints about medical reimbursements filed with state insurance departments were found to be justified, and the company's decision reversed.

Final step: Take the company to small claims court. While tedious and time-consuming for the consumer, it is even more inconvenient for the insurance company. Result: The insurer doesn't put up much of a fight, and the subscriber emerges victorious.

Winning an Argument With Medicare

Millions of people are covered by Medicare, but only a fraction ever challenge the insurance system when they feel their reimbursement has been too low. Even though only 2% of beneficiaries who disagree with the findings of Medicare claim examiners file appeals, raising questions can pay. Roughly 50% to 60% of those people who do request a review of their claim are successful, according to experts.

Most disputes arise with claims submitted under Part B of Medicare. For an additional monthly premium of $9.60, it complements Part A, the basic policy that covers major medical expenses such as hospital stays. Part B pays for such things as doctor bills, diagnostic tests and X-rays. But it does not cover routine physical checkups and tests, prescription drugs, glasses, or hearing aids.

The Health Care Financing Administration, which operates Medicare, contracts with various insurance companies to handle reimbursement of claims. The companies, which differ from area to area, are usually the nation's major insurance carriers.

Any dispute about reimbursement under Medicare Part B is between that person and the designated insurance carrier in the area. But if the patient has assigned payment of the bill to the doctor (that is, if the doctor accepts the Medicare payment), then it is up to the physician or other professional to handle the dispute.

One very good reason not to routinely accept the decision of the insurance companies' claim examiners is that the decisions are frequently wrong. Each month, every state calculates its own Medicare processing error rate. Research has shown that the error rates have ranged from 2% in South Carolina to 14% in Massachusetts.

The General Accounting Office found that the insurance company handling claims for most of the New York metropolitan area had erroneously underpaid 13% of claims. Later studies found that nationwide, Medicare underpayments outnumbered overpayments by almost four to one.

Two-step appeals process:

First step: A written request can be filed for an informal review determination with the insurance company.

Second step: If the outcome is not satisfactory and the claim is for at least $100 (or if all of the individual's claims within a six-month period total at least $100), request a fair hearing held by outside attorneys hired by the insurance company.

The insurance companies urge people to furnish as detailed an explanation as possible when submitting their appeals. Include: Copies of doctor bills and treatment records. Why: Insurance companies say that they are often not privy to medical information that is necessary in order to make an informed decision, usually because physicians fail to provide such details.

Appeals generally fall into three major categories:

Uncovered services, such as private nursing care, which are not eligible for reimbursement.

Doctor bills that are not fully covered because they exceed the prevailing reasonable charge.

Services that a medical review panel has found to be not medically necessary.

Uncovered services are usually cut-and-dried, with no opportunity for argument. But there is room for compromise with high doctor charges. Sometimes, for example, a physician will characterize an office visit as routine. But the examination may have been more extensive than indicated, and thus eligible for higher reimbursement as a comprehensive visit.

The same is true for Medicare guidelines that determine whether a particular treatment is medically necessary. The parameters may indicate that patients in a nursing home are eligible for only one visit a month from their personal doctors. But sometimes an unusual situation, such as a flare-up of heart trouble, may justify five visits a month.

Sometimes, the amount at stake in an appeal will be relatively small. Postoperative visits to an ophthalmologist after cataract surgery, for example, are frequently not reimbursed because the surgeon does not indicate the purpose of the visit. Often, the claim examiners incorrectly assume that the visit is for a routine service, and they deny reimbursement. Example: For eyeglasses, which Medicare does not cover.

But sometimes the stakes are much higher. Example: An 86-year-old woman received extensive medical and psychiatric treatment after she was raped. She was denied payment for her psychiatric care on the ground that it was not medically necessary. It took the active intervention of a family member to plead this case. A review was conducted, finding psychiatric treatment a medical must. Result: Ruling reversed.

Often, people who have private medical insurance in addition to Medicare are confused about which company to submit their bills to first. Generally, Medicare is the primary insurer. It pays the basic bills first, and should therefore receive them before the company providing supplemental insurance.

In some states, the insurance company handling Medicare claims will automatically forward the unpaid portion of the bill to the company providing supplemental insurance. But everywhere else in the country, consumers are expected to do the paper work themselves.

Collecting More on Your Company Health Policy

Health insurance policies are not etched in stone. There are contractual provisions in the insurance policy that are negotiable.

Most companies give health insurance to engender goodwill among employees. Many problems in collecting the maximum due you are a result of incompetence or of negligence on the part of the administrators in your company who handle insurance benefits. They may be too busy or unaware of how to get more for you.

Three ways to improve your ability to collect:

Know the insurance contract and all its provisions. Be aware that everything is negotiable. Example: Home health care by someone other than a registered nurse or practical nurse is not covered in the policy. Contractually nothing needs to be said, but administratively an alternate source of home health care could be covered. It is really a question of negotiation.

Have the company's insurance broker help negotiate with the insurer. He is the one who is making the money from selling your company the policy. He also has more leverage than you do with the insurance company. If he is unwilling to help, encourage your company to switch to a more cooperative broker.

Set up a liaison. The individual in your company in charge of claims should have a good working relationship with the insurance company. Reason: If the settlement is too low or doesn't fully cover your needs, the claims person at your firm can make a better settlement. After all, the insurance company is selling policies.

Strategy: If your claims person is uncertain whether you can get more compensation for an ailment or treatment, ask for permission to contact the broker. The broker should know the terms of your contract and be familiar with the people at the insurance company. He should have an idea of how to get the claim paid, especially if it's a legitimate claim but a trifle unusual.

Take advantage of situations where both spouses are covered at their jobs by group insurance policies to increase your benefits.

Example: You both have Blue Cross to cover hospitalization and, in addition, you both have major medical. Typically, the major medical has a $100 deductible. The insurance company will pick up 80% of the next $2,000 and 100% thereafter. However, if both spouses coordinate their policies, you could wind up using the other's policy to pay that remaining 20% of the $2,000.

Don't expect to make a profit by having several insurance policies. Years ago many health insurance policies were not coordinated and it was possible to get duplicate payments. Today all plans are coordinated so you can't get duplicate payments.

Trying to make specifically unallowable treatments allowable: This is between the doctor and you. For instance, if you want to claim cosmetic surgery necessary for health reasons,

consult your doctor. If he won't go along with it, you are not going to get anywhere with the insurance broker, the personnel at your office, or the insurance company.

If you are stuck with a flawed company policy and find you have huge deductibles and other uncovered expenses, take out a personal policy that coordinates with the company's.

Source: Leonard Stern, president, Leonard B. Stern & Co., an insurance consulting and brokerage firm, 65 E. 55 St., Suite 303, New York 10022.

Report on Health Maintenance Organizations

People who have switched to a health maintenance organization (HMO) for company-paid medical care are generally happy with the decision, according to a nationwide survey. In an HMO, the subscriber is entitled to unlimited medical care from a group of doctors for a flat fee.

Key findings:

Of those surveyed, 86% said they are satisfied with the quality of the doctors, even though under the HMO concept they don't get to pick their physician.

Complaints about long waiting times and impersonal service were not any higher than those voiced by a similar group of workers *not* in an HMO program. Of those responding, 13% complained about waiting time and 12% about impersonal care.

Source: Survey by Louis Harris & Assoc., reported in *Business Insurance*.

Midwives and Medical Insurance

Before choosing home delivery, rather than hospitalization and doctor's care, check out the company medical insurance plan. In some states, Blue Cross/Blue Shield won't cover midwifery, on grounds that the hospital routine, although more expensive, is safer.

Phobias and Manias

Ablutomania: Incessant and compulsive washing of the hands and body.

Acathisia: Feeling of impending disaster if one sits down, conviction dreadful things will happen to self or other nearby.

Acrophobia: Fear of heights.

Aelurophobia: A dread of cats.

Agoraphobia: Abnormal fear of open spaces.

Agromania: Irresistible desire to live alone or in the open country, away from everything and everybody.

Aichmophobia: Fear of needles and other pointed objects, such as knives, arrows, spears, scissors.

Algophobia: Fear of pain.

Amathaphobia: Fear of dust.

Arithomania: An obsession with numbers, an irrestible impulse to count. Examples: The number of cats that pass a given point, the number of steps from home to office, the number of tiles on a bathroom wall and floor.

Astrophobia: Fear of storms, thunder and lightning in particular.

Bathophobia: Fear of being at a height and having the impulse to jump or fall to one's death.

Cenophobia: Fear of auditoriums, large halls, places with very high ceilings.

Claustrophobia: Fear of being shut in an enclosed place.

Contrectation: Desire and impulse to touch members of the opposite sex, which might be the first move toward a sexual act.

Ecdysiasm: Exhibitionism, the impulse to disrobe in public.

Entomophobia: An unreasoning fear of insects.

Gynecomania: Insatiable male sexual appetite, an impulse to assault women.

Gynephobia: Aversion to being with or associating with women on any level.

Hydrophobia: A dread of water.

Kainotophobia: Fear of change or of going to a new place.

Kakorrhaphiophobia: Fear of undertaking anything because of possibility of failure.

Mysophobia: Dread of dirt, of being contaminated, often accompanied by excessive desire to wash hands.

Nosophobia: Irrational fear of illness.

Nyctophobia: Fear of night, of darkness.

Ochlophobia: Fear of crowds.

Pathophobia: Fear of contracting a disease.

Pyrophobia: Dread of fire.

Xenophobia: Fear, distrust, and suspicion of strangers.

Zoophobia: Fear of animals.

Hypochondriacs

Hypochondria is one of the most misunderstood psychological problems. What it is: A concern with one's body or physical symptoms which is so excessive that it becomes a primary preoccupation. Why it is destructive: It drains a person's energy and causes suffering that may be as bad as the real thing.

Major misconceptions:

Hypochondriacs are fakes. The pains and other symptoms hypochondriacs think they have are real to them and cause suffering. What they suffer from is psychological anxiety rather than physical pain.

Hypochondria is a fear of illness. Hypochondriacs aren't afraid they have an illness. They are convinced they have one. In fact, hypochondriacs are often brave rather than fearful. This is evidenced by their eagerness to submit to any number of treatments, diagnostic tests, even operations, which might verify the presence of the imagined disease as well as cure it.

Hypochondriacs suffer from psychosomatic symptoms. Hypochondriac and psychosomatic illnesses are not the same thing. Difference: People with psychosomatic symptoms have real physical illnesses with psychological causes. Hypochondriacs' illnesses exist only in their mind, not in their body.

Common cause: An early childhood spent in an atmosphere of illness, either of an invalid parent or grandparent, or of one who was chronically ill. Much talk of illness in the household during childhood.

What the symptoms do: Gain attention, sympathy. A majority of hypochondriacs have learned from childhood that complaining about symptoms almost always will capture attention and sympathy.

Signs of hypochondria:

Excessive preoccupation with any part of the body or all of it. Example: A health-food freak who has a full-time concern with cooking, preparing, and eating health foods, and a constant preoccupation with vitamins, pure and organic foods, etc.

Enormous amount of time spent exercising and thinking about working out. Example: People who spend more time thinking about jogging than about their business or occupation. In particular, watching their bodies' reactions (taking their pulse or breathing rate).

Doctors' visits scheduled more often than normal. Especially going from one doctor to another because of a belief that the previous doctor doesn't really understand the "illness," or hasn't done anything constructive about it.

Complaints of feeling stress. Stress symptoms very often are symptoms of hypochondria.

Another category: Closet hypochondriacs, who won't go to doctors. They don't trust physicians and are secretive about their complaints. This person often confides all complaints to one person, usually a spouse. Most frequently, men are closet hypochondriacs. Reason: They see their symptoms and preoccupations as weak and unmanly although their suffering is as intense, perhaps more intense, than that of overt hypochondriacs.

Age when onset of hypochondria is likeliest: Men, in their thirties; women, in their forties.

What hypochondriacs should do: Find somebody intelligent and patient to whom they can talk. The key is to recognize that hypochondria is an expression of hunger for affection and attention. Even better: Find a good doctor willing to talk about the problem. Difficulty: They are hard to find. Most physicians can't offer the proper amount of listening time a hypochondriac needs.

What a good medical doctor can provide: A thorough physical examination, to remove any doubt that the hypochondriac's symptoms have a real physical basis. Particularly useful: A psychiatrist, who is better than a psychologist or a therapist in this case. Point: Psychiatrists have the medical, as well as the psychological, authority to address themselves to a patient's practical fears. Therapists and psychologists are not qualified to assist a person medically.

Next step: Hypochondriacs should bring themselves to believe the doctor and begin to accept the fact that their certainty of illness has no physical basis.

Important to remember: Hypochondriacs are ill, despite the fact that the illness is without a physical cause. Also: Hypochondria can be enormously expensive to hypochondriacs who, in search of help, often spend small fortunes on doctors and medicines.

What they need most of all: Sympathetic attention and encouragement to find out what the symptoms and physical concerns really express.

Source: Robert Meister, author of *Hypochondria: Toward a Better Understanding,* Taplinger Publishing Co.

The Importance of Nonsexual Touching

The human warmth that everyone longs for is much more than a psychological exchange between people. Physical contact is one of the most important contributors to the feeling of inner warmth. So important is touching, that people who don't get enough of it often use psychological or emotional contact as a replacement. Point: Everyone needs physical contact with other human bodies.

Examples: Young children deprived of the touch of gentle human hands are disease-prone. Their central nervous systems fail to develop properly. Deprived adults often suffer generalized depression, discomfort, and edginess.

Ineffective substitutes for touching:

A tendency to take far more showers and baths than are actually necessary. Purpose: To obtain the physical warmth they provide.

A more significant substitute: Sexual activity. Why it happens: Most people tend to mistake their basic desire for skin-on-skin physical contact for a sexual impulse.

Key: Physical contact itself is of value, whether or not there is personal attraction or tenderness between the people who touch each other. It's a romantic fallacy that only people who care about each other deeply can have gratifying physical contact.

The better way: Couples should try to negotiate some simple skin-on-skin caressing or cuddling when on a casual date, instead of hurling themselves into immediate sexual activity. People who get enough warm exchanges are likely to be less obsessed with sex. The surprising discovery for many: Cuddling is much more intimate than sex. That's the major reason why people who are afraid of genuine intimacy prefer to move immediately into sexual activity, without too many preliminaries.

Who profits most from increased skin contact:

Cardiac risks. Well-being and longevity increase for heart patients who are lucky enough to have partners who provide regular physical contact.

Type A, hurry-up or driven personalities. They usually can be slowed down by increasing their level of skin contact. Possible forms increased contact can take: Regular massages. But preferably, skin-on-skin cuddling or touching.

Unconscious patients show a marked improvement in their vital signs when someone holds their hands or strokes them. Even more significant: This works even when the hand-holder is a stranger.

How to get enough skin-on-skin contact:

Recognize the symptoms of touch deprivation: Irritability, sadness, or depression.

Accept the fact that touching gratification can come even where there is no particular tenderness or genuine sexual interest.

Create situations that make skin contact easy. Couples often unconsciously make direct physical contact harder by wearing nightclothes or sleeping in twin beds. Instead: Sleep in close proximity, in positions comfortable for both partners. Mistake married people often make: Withholding touching, cuddling, or other skin-on-skin contact as a way of punishing a partner during hostilities. Trap: Cutting off one's partner from physical comfort also means cutting one's self off.

Be aware of a greater need for physical comfort during times of crisis. When there's a break in a love relationship, either through illness, divorce, or death of a partner, the period of transition can be made easier by obtaining regular doses of skin-on-skin comfort. Even simple massage helps.

Remember: Skin-on-skin contact is important in itself. It is not simply a sexual prelude. Touching need not lead to sexual activity to be greatly satisfying.

Source: Gisele Richardson, president, Richardson Management Co., management consultants, 2162 Sherbrooke St. W., Montreal, H3H 1G7, Quebec, Canada.

Using Music as Medicine

Beyond its pleasures, music can be put to practical uses. Researchers have discovered that properly chosen selections can change moods, boost working efficiency, even increase physical strength. Music to avoid: Heavy rock and roll can reduce strength. And a steady diet of atonal, discordant modern music can cause depression, nervousness, sleeplessness, and impotence.

Ways to use music:

When depressed: Listen to pieces that are even sadder in spirit (Mahler's *Kindertotenlieder,* blues, tragic opera areas), then gradually progress to more lighthearted works.

When hyperactive: Tune in to energetic selections (Sousa marches, disco, jazz), then ease yourself down with calmer pieces.

To fall asleep: Play works by Bach (especially *Goldberg Variations,* written for an insomniac patron).

To get started in the morning: Listen to perky pieces (Sousa's *Stars and Stripes Forever,* Mozart's operatic overtures, Berlioz's *Hungarian March*).

Source: *Executive Fitness Newsletter.*

Nervous Breakdowns

Nervous breakdown is a nonmedical term that the lay public uses for a serious psychological condition. Since it is not a medical term it has no precise definition. Result: Many people worry that they are having a breakdown when, in fact, they are experiencing something much less serious.

People who are aware enough to be concerned about whether they are having a breakdown are usually not having one. Fact: People in the throes of a nervous breakdown have their feelings of self-concern and self-awareness so immobilized that their ability to analyze and worry about their condition is frequently impaired. It is often those around them (relatives, friends, and colleagues) who first recognize the seriousness of their condition.

Through popular usage, the term nervous breakdown has come to indicate a significant interruption or cessation of the individual's ability to function. Its effects on the victim's life are devastating and widespread. It cannot be assumed that the condition will get better by itself with the passage of time, the way other acute psychological reactions may.

Main characteristics of those having a nervous breakdown: Persistent inability to do things they previously had no trouble doing. Don't confuse this with a passing depressed mood or even a longer period of functioning below par.

Example: A person who is suddenly, and for no discernible physical reason, unable to get up and go to work for weeks at a time is having a serious interruption of function. In all likelihood, this is a breakdown. A person who cannot face getting up and going to work for one day, but who resumes function the next day (even though still depressed and disturbed), is not having a breakdown.

Feeling very depressed, anxious, or disturbed, even for a long period, does not indicate a nervous breakdown.

Symptoms: Psychological: Sleeplessness or continuous sleeping, loss of appetite, agitation, inability to concentrate.

Physical: Bowel function ailments (colitis, diarrhea, etc.) in conjunction with psychological symptoms. Many people have bowel dysfunctions that do not signify a nervous breakdown.

What the breakdown means: Nervous breakdown signifies just that. It is a breaking down in the functioning of the individual's mental and physical systems. Because it is an imprecise term, it may include many psychiatric conditions, such as depression or psychosis, which a psychiatrist would be able to accurately identify and treat. People who have not been evaluated while they are suffering a nervous breakdown should be seen afterwards to determine their vulnerability to future episodes. Nervous breakdowns differ from other kinds of mental disorders by nature of the acute way they manifest themselves. Other conditions such as depression and schizophrenia are more insidious in their development.

Suspicion of a breakdown: Whether the problem is your own or someone else's, first see the family doctor, particularly if there are any physical symptoms. The doctor may prescribe antidepressant medications (which can be highly effective) or refer you to a psychiatrist.

If symptoms of nonfunction are so obvious that there is no doubt a breakdown is occurring, see a psychiatrist. What a psychiatrist can provide: Correct diagnosis, enlightenment about the meaning and cause of the symptoms, psychotherapy, and appropriate medication. It is important for people who are vulnerable to having breakdowns to learn the danger signs. Reason: To get help before they are in serious trouble and overwhelmed by the symptoms.

Source: Leonard Diamond, M.D., a psychiatrist in private practice at 440 E. 79 St., New York 10021.

Finding the Right Psychotherapist

Most business people have more difficulty seeking aid for personal problems than for business difficulties. The same characteristics that make them special as leaders and problem solvers (independence and decision-making) stand in their way when they need professional help for their own troubles. However, short-term goal-oriented therapy has become acceptable.

Signals that indicate help is needed:

A recurring problem that consumes time, energy, or good feelings. Example: A problem with a family member that remains unsettled, or a dilemma with a subordinate that crops up again and again.

A lack of communication with a spouse or other important people.

Deterioration of sex life.

A sense of futility or ever-increasing pressure from which there appears to be no relief in sight.

An ailment that you sense may be psychosomatic. Or an obvious psychosomatic manifestation, for example, hypertension, ulcers, or migraine.

Any untypical behavior, such as increased anger, increased drinking, extramarital affairs, or other stress-related behavior.

When shopping for a therapist, look for someone who:

Does short-term therapy.

Sets objectives with clients (for example, reducing alcoholic drinking, ending child abuse, and so forth).

Establishes a time frame in which to accomplish the goals.

Can establish a rapport. The therapist should be at least as smart and powerful as the client to avoid the client's temptation to manipulate the therapist.

Is caring, competent, and ethical. If any of those traits are missing, don't get involved.

Caution: If you interview ten therapists and don't find the right one, you may be seeking a guru with a magic cure, or trying to prove that nobody really can help you after all.

To get a shopping list of possible therapists, consult a doctor, a hospital, a management consultant (most have family-therapy resources), and friends.

Therapy can be terminated when the clear objectives that were established during the first meeting have been achieved. Make sure those objectives were not too vague. Goals like improving relationships or becoming happier are not measurable.

Source: Gisele Richardson, president, Richardson Management Associates, Ltd., 2162 Sherbrooke St. W., Montreal H3H 1G7, Canada.

Learning Not to Smoke

Willpower has less to do with kicking the cigarette habit than acquiring the skills to stop smoking. One widely successful treatment uses a gradual, self-directed learning program.

First, plan to stop smoking during a relatively stable period in your work and social life. Understand your smoking habits by keeping a simple diary that records how many cigarettes you smoke daily and how badly you want each one. Score the craving on a scale of one (automatic, boredom) to four (powerful desire). Firm up your commitment by enlisting a nonsmoking buddy to call up and encourage you several times a week.

Phase out the cigarettes in three stages:

1. Taper. Heavy smokers should reduce to 12 to 15 cigarettes daily. If that's your present level, then reduce to 8 or 9 a day. Use a smoke suppression drill, a mental learning process, each time you have an urge to smoke. Begin by focusing on the craving; then immediately associate it with a negative effect of smoking,

such as filthy lung passages, clogged, fatty arteries, or skin wrinkled and aged by carbon monoxide and nicotine. Next: Relax and imagine a peaceful scene. Follow up with a pleasant image associated with nonsmoking (smooth skin, or greater vitality).

2. How to withdraw. One week before your scheduled quitting date, smoke only four cigarettes a day. Smoke two cigarettes in a 15-minute period. Wait at least an hour, and then smoke the other two. While gulping down the cigarettes, concentrate on the negative sensations: Scratchy throat and lungs, foul breath. Keep up negative thoughts for at least five minutes after finishing the last cigarette.

3. Quit. When a smoking urge arises, conjure up the negative image, relax, and follow it with a pleasing fantasy. Also, call your nonsmoking buddy for moral support.

Note: Never label yourself a failure. If you have a relapse, return to the tapering phase, and try the procedure again.

Source: *The American Way of Life Need Not Be Hazardous to Your Health,* by John Farquhar, MD, W.W. Norton & Co., New York.

More Bad News About Smoking

• Filter cigarettes may be more hazardous to health than regular ones. Reason: Carbon monoxide, which is present in larger amounts in filtered smoking, is more dangerous than the nicotine and tar that are filtered out.

A recent study of almost 8,000 smokers showed that the average filter smoker died three to four years earlier than other smokers. Risk: Increased cardiovascular disease.

Source: Health Insurance Institute, 1850 K St., N.W., Washington, DC 20006.

• Pipes and cigars are not as dangerous to smokers as cigarettes. But they pose more of a hazard to nonsmokers working nearby. Reason: Smoke from both is higher in gaseous and particulate compounds than smoke from cigarettes. Critics charge that passive smoking is equivalent to smoking one to 10 cigarettes a day. Note: The tobacco industry counters that breathing cigarette smoke is actually not hazardous to the health of nonsmokers.
Source: *Executive Fitness Newsletter.*

• Male smokers were found to have a greater percentage of sperm abnormalities than nonsmokers. Reason: Smoke products cause genetic damage to sperm cells.

• Cigarettes kill sleep more than coffee does. Recent experiments reveal that smokers take longer to fall asleep and spend more time awake during the night than nonsmokers and coffee drinkers. Cheering: Sleep improves dramatically beginning the first day smokers kick their habit. Surprised by the discovery that coffee had little effect on sleep, researchers surmised caffeine addicts build up a tolerance to the drug. Nicotine users apparently do not.

Source: Pennsylvania State University's sleep lab experiment.

Staying Smoke-Free After You've Quit

Frustration, anger, loneliness, or depression often triggers the urge to start smoking again.

Reach for a person instead of a cigarette. Research has shown that friends who quit smoking together and called one another daily were still not smoking after six years.

Even a few drinks can sabotage attempts to stop smoking. In one study, smokers were given similar-tasting drinks. Those who received drinks with a higher alcohol content smoked more.

Can Hypnosis Help You to Stop Smoking?

How does hypnosis help an individual stop smoking?

Hypnosis is a state of hyperawareness. It is

exactly the opposite of sleep. This is not fully understood by the public. In a hypnotic trance, your ability to focus attention is freed from distractions. By helping a person mobilize this extraordinary power of concentration, hypnotists enable their subjects to bring their will to bear on a single, clear goal, in this case, nonsmoking.

Does it work for everyone?

No. About 30% of the population cannot be hypnotized at all. Of the remaining 70%, 15% are very hypnotizable and 15% are capable only of light trances. The rest fall somewhere in between.

How do you tell if a person can be hypnotized?

Over the years, some reliable indicators have been discovered. The most accurate one is the eye-roll sign. Have someone observe you. First, gaze straight ahead. Then, roll your eyes up and into your eyelids. The further upward the eyes move, the more hypnotizable you probably are.

What happens when a person goes to a hypnotist?

It's a single, 45-minute session. First, we give tests to determine hypnotizability. We take a personal history to determine that the patient possesses reasonable mental health. The technique won't work on people with major personality disorders because they have too much difficulty concentrating. About half an hour is devoted to the treatment itself.

What does the treatment consist of?

In the most general terms, it involves the implantation of a set of premises in the psyche. These are positive expressions of the will to protect the body and to celebrate its well-being. It's far more effective than dire don't smoke warnings.

What's the success rate? Does it depend on how hypnotizable a subject is?

Surprisingly, no. In the short term, about 80% of the high-trance types will stop. But these people are very sensitive to their surroundings. For example, if you live alone, receive little support for your effort, or associate mainly with smokers, it's likely that you will backslide. People on the lower end of the hyp-

notizability scale who stop in the short run are more likely to stop forever.

All told, about one out of three hypnotizable people quits completely. They never smoke again after the session. It's a lower rate than many claims you read about, but it's a good result. Remember, these are hard-core smokers who have repeatedly tried to quit and have failed.

How can an individual find a reputable hypnotist?

Go to someone with medical training, ideally a psychiatrist or psychologist with some experience in other behavior-modification techniques.

Can people use hypnosis to reduce smoking?

You either smoke or you don't. It's a life-or-death issue. You cannot negotiate it.

Source: Herbert Spiegel, M.D., a pioneer in the use of hypnosis to break self-destructive habits. A former three-pack-per-day smoker, he teaches psychiatry at the College of Physicians and Surgeons, Columbia University, New York 10027.

How to Stay on a Diet

Identify the cues that start you thinking about eating. Common ones: TV commercials, walking into the kitchen. Control the impulse.

Inactivity, tension, anger, frustration usually lead to impulsive eating. Deliberately select an activity to replace the impulse: a fast walk, exercise, a bath, a nap, etc.

Eat only in one place in the house. Make it a firm rule.

Put food directly on a small dinner plate. Don't use serving dishes during meals.

A glass or two of water before each meal diminishes the appetite. The colder the water, the better.

Hot soup eaten slowly at the beginning of a meal gives the brain's satiety center time to switch your appetite off before too much is consumed. Try this technique at lunch and the afternoon snack urge is lessened.

Eat slowly. Stop for a few minutes during the meal.

Hunger is satisfied by bulk, not calories. Keep uncooked vegetables and fruit, bouillon, bran, rice, vegetable juice around. Keep desserts and other high-calorie foods out of the house.

Never skip meals to compensate for unscheduled eating. Resume standard diet instead.

Never "reward" youself with forbidden foods (not even to celebrate a weight loss).

Don't discuss your diet with anyone. It's boring. And it's often looked on as a challenge to tempt the dieter to cheat.

Weigh yourself daily first thing in the morning.

Don't combine eating with other activities, such as reading or watching TV.

When dining out: Have bread and butter removed from the table. Always order a la carte so you don't feel obliged to eat everything you've paid for. If salad comes with the main course, eat it before the main course (with lemon juice or dash of vinegar and oil).

How to Stop Food Binges

The majority of binge-eaters are women. (Men turn more often to alcohol.) The crisis stages when the binge-eating habit usually starts:

For women: The teens, pregnancy, and over 45.

For men: Adolescence, starting a new career, and 45 or older.

Binge-eating is also becoming more of a problem for businesswomen tackling both a career and a family.

Another problem common to both sexes: Often executives begin to binge when their goals are greater than their achievements. Sometimes they are competitive with very successful parents and they see themselves as losing the contest.

Ways to understand your unconscious reasons for losing fat and starting to lose weight:

Examine your fantasies of what life will be

like once you become thin. Many people think they will no longer be shy. Don't count on it. The danger: You will be disappointed and put the weight right back on. You have to be realistic about what changes you can expect in your life when you are thin.

Separate the reason for eating from the act of eating. The two most common unconscious reasons for not losing weight permanently are: Equating food with love, and fear of intimacy. Many overweight persons were taught by their parents that eating well meant they were good, hence loved. Fear of the opposite sex, particularly being close, also leads to binge-eating (particularly in the 20 to 30 age group).

Be honest with yourself about the real reasons for personal failures. Recognize that if you were thin, you still might not have gotten the promotion. Think again about why you were not promoted. Don't use your weight as an excuse.

Essential: In planning your diet, allow for eating binges. Work with this tendency to cheat, which all overweight people have. Alternate dieting with small eating binges. The fat person's psychology is best suited to this method of weight loss.

Source: Dr. Joyce Bocka, 500 Newfield Ave., Stamford, CT 06905. Her book, *The Last Best Diet Book,* is published by Stein & Day, Scarborough House, Briarcliff Manor, NY 10510, $10.

Myths About Food

Myth: Watermelon is not nutritious. Fact: It is rich in vitamins A and C and contains iron.

Myth: American cheese is more nutritious than skimmed milk. Fact: This cheese contains high levels of saturated fats, which are linked to heart disease, and of sodium, which contributes to high blood pressure.

Myth: Corn syrup is a harmless sweetener. Fact: It contains no nutritional value other than calories and promotes tooth decay.

Myth: Apple juice is a very nutritious drink. Fact: It contains only small amounts of vitamin C. Orange, tomato and vegetable juices are more healthful.

Salt Talk

How harmful is salt? Answer: It depends. A majority of the population (about 80%) can handle large doses. The average daily intake per person is about 4,500 MG. Contrast: The body demands only 200 MG. The excess is passed from the body in normal waste.

Where salt is a problem: In the other 20% of the population, excess salt stays in the blood. One result: High blood pressure (hypertension), which can bring on a heart attack or stroke. Best bet: Avoid salt. Reason: Most people don't know if they are among the susceptible 20%.

Other reasons to avoid salt:

There is already plenty in many foods on most regular diets.

It builds up thirst, which means greater consumption of liquids and a higher rate of water retention.

Source: *Executive Fitness.*

Safe Diet Drugs

Two diet aids safe enough to be sold without a prescription have been approved by a government review panel. They are:

Phenylpropanolamine. A medication that works on the hypothalamus, a portion of the brain. It helps convince your body that you are not hungry. It is sold as tablets and time-release capsules.

Benzocaine. The ingredient in cough lozenges that numbs sore throats, benzocaine, is sold as a gum. It anesthetizes the taste buds on your tongue, which dulls your appetite.

Advantages: Unlike some other diet drugs, both phenylpropanolamine and benzocaine are nonaddictive. Also, they cannot be abused to get high.

Cautions:

They should not be used by children.

The daily dosage of phenylpropanolamine must not exceed 150 mg. Preferably take in three doses of 50 mg. each.

If you have any disease or are under medication, check with your doctor before taking a diet aid.

Fasting to Lose Weight

Short 24-hour fasts rarely reduce weight permanently. Reason: The weight you lose is primarily in fluids, which your body restocks as soon as you begin to eat again.

Longer periods of not eating do result in weight loss. But they are serious business and require serious attention. Point: People who simply stop eating, but otherwise go about their ordinary business, jeopardize their health.

To fast for more than 24 hours:

Have a check-up and put yourself under a doctor's care.

Drink water to avoid dehydration.

Take vitamins and mineral supplements.

Drink fruit juice, so you get a minimum amount of glucose. Reason: A shortage of glucose results in a chemical imbalance known as ketosis, which results in nausea and dehydration.

Rest to conserve the little energy your body does generate.

Avoid activities that require a quick reaction time.

When going off your fast, only gradually begin to eat again.

Dieters' Mistakes

Many dieters choose foods that they think are low in calories but actually are high. One example: Vanilla ice cream has fewer calories than orange sherbet. And vanilla ice milk has fewer calories than frozen yogurt and costs about one-third less.

Don't take it for granted that a product labeled imitation is lower in calories. Example: Imitation sour cream is actually higher in calories than real sour cream (31 calories per tablespoon vs. 20).

Diet Advice for Women

Women who diet lose weight sporadically. Reason: Water retention. Female hormones increase the body's tendency to retain water. Women also have less muscle mass than men. Therefore, the spaces between muscle and skin tend to fill with extracellular water. High-salt diets, antibiotics, birth-control pills and anti-inflammatory drugs all tend to aggravate the situation. What to do: Stick to the diet, decrease salt intake, and cut back on carbohydrates. Exercise can help by flushing out some of the fluid around the muscles.

Were You Born to Be Fat?

Are fat people metabolically different from thin people? Researchers recently found that red blood cells of obese people use 22% less energy than those of normal people. Conclusion: The caloric requirements of these cells were reduced. Implications: The caloric needs of obese people may be less than normal, so they gain weight while not eating more than the average person does.

High-Fiber Diet as Preventive Medicine

A high-fiber diet is good preventive medicine. The importance of fiber in your diet cannot be overstated.

Fiber is the bulk, the roughage, needed by the intestines to move its contents through the digestive tract. Fiber cannot be absorbed or digested. It is not fattening unless eaten in excessive amounts. Fiber acts like a sponge in the stomach. It prevents and relieves constipation, binds toxins, dilutes bacteria, and absorbs water. It also keeps the stool moist, soft, and bulky.

Fiber is found in whole foods, particularly in whole grains such as brown rice, barley, kasha, millet, and wheat berries; in legumes such as peas, soybeans, black beans, lentils, and lima beans; and in fresh fruits and vegetables. Whole grains actually have more fiber than fruits and vegetables.

Cancer of the colon, prostate, and breast, and other disorders such as diverticulitis, appendicitis, hemmorrhoids, and varicose veins are all related to a high-fat diet. A diet high in fiber will be low in fat. Those who switch to a high-fiber diet lose weight, keep cholesterol levels down, and need no laxatives.

A good way to judge if your diet is rich in fiber is to check your stool. If it floats, all is well. If it sinks, you need more fiber in your diet.

Unfortunately, bran, the fiber found in whole grains, is milled out in processing. This leaves refined carbohydrates such as white rice, white bread, and white pastas calorie-rich and nutritionally poor. Whole grains are rich in the B vitamins, as well as iron, zinc, and folacin.

Bottom line: A low-fat, high-fiber diet keeps you healthy and regular.

Source: Leslie Cerier, a personal fitness counselor who works with corporations, educational institutions and individuals, 235 W. 102 St., New York 10025.

How Healthful Are Health Foods?

The popularity of health and diet foods shows that many Americans are conscious of their physical fitness. However, some health food may be just marketing gimmicks. Traps:

Sugar. The trend is away from refined sugar toward such natural sweeteners as honey and the fructose syrups and powders. Fact: All sweeteners are transformed into blood sugar (glucose). They all have the same calorie content (four per gram). They all combine with bacteria in the mouth to cause dental cavities. Sole advantage: Pure fructose aids the diabetic. It takes longer to become blood sugar, thus reducing the chances of overload in the blood stream.

Bottom line: Use any sweetener, but in moderation.

Diet candies. Many contain the same ingredients disdained by purists, including: Hydrogenated vegetable oil, imitation honey, artificial colors and flavors. Also: They are almost half sugar. Advantage: Some have slightly more protein than a normal candy bar. Drawbacks: Same fat, carbohydrate, and calorie counts as other sweets. In addition, they ordinarily cost considerably more than the nondiet variety.

Diet cookies. Most are baked from the same ingredients as other processed foods. Primarily: Corn sweeteners, hydrogenated shortening, refined (enriched) flour, and salt. Also: They are more expensive. Caution: Some contain raw brown sugar. Raw sugar can be unhealthful. It contains filth usually removed in the refining process.

Vitamins. Natural and synthetic vitamins are equal nutritionally. Exception: Vitamin E, where the natural form is preferable. Natural Vitamin E: It is called *d*-alpha tocopherol. The synthetic is *dl*-alpha tocopherol. It's the letter *l* after the *d* that provides the only clue to the synthetic.

When Alcohol Is Good for You

• People who consume about three alcoholic drinks per day have lower mortality rates than do abstainers or heavy drinkers. Nondrinkers are more likely to die of coronary heart disease, while those consuming four or more alcoholic drinks per day are more often done in by liver and lung ailments and car accidents.

Source: *Lancet.*

• Menstrual cramps can occasionally be eased by a red wine concoction. Recipe: Put a chamomile teabag in a cup and soak it with two tablespoons of red Burgundy wine. Pour in boiling water and allow to steep for several minutes. Drink. Repeat two or three times an hour.

• Two glasses of wine a day can supply about half the nutritional need for chromium. Many Americans are deficient in this important mineral. Low chromium levels have been linked in animal studies to abnormal heart rhythms, metabolic disturbances, and other severe problems. Chromium depletion in Americans is probably caused by their heavy consumption of refined white sugar and other highly processed carbohydrates.

Drinking moderate amounts of wine may also help prevent heart attacks by helping to clean cholesterol from arteries. And there is good news for nondrinkers, too: Plain grape juice is also a good source of chromium.

Source: Study by Drs. M.E. Jennings and J.M. Howard reported in *Lancet.*

Alcohol Without Hangovers

Some hangover discomfort is caused by congeners (toxic chemicals formed during fermentation). Vodka has the lowest congener content, gin next. Blended scotch has four times the congener content of gin. Brandy, rum, and pure malt scotch have six times that amount; bourbon eight times.

Retard the absorption of alcohol by eating before and during drinking (especially foods containing fatter proteins, such as cheeses).

Use water as a mixer. Carbonation speeds the absorption of alcohol.

If you get a hangover anyway, the only known cure is rest, aspirin, and time. An endless roster of other remedies—ranging from cucumber juice and salt to a Bloody Mary—has more to do with drinking mythology than with medical fact, although according to psychologists who have studied hangovers, if you believe in a cure, it may help.

Early Signs of Problem Drinking

Gulping first drinks to get the effect of the alcohol.

Reluctance to discuss alcohol consumption.

Increased tolerance. An alcoholic has to consume more for the same effect.

Loss of control, blackouts, sneaking drinks (drinking before a party and then acting restrained during).

Alcohol's Effects on Sex

Scientific proof is piling up confirming alcohol's adverse effects on both male and female sexuality. Examples:

Secondary impotence developing in the male in the late 40s or early 50s has a higher incidence of direct association with alcohol consumption than any other single factor. (*The Human Sexual Response,* by Masters and Johnson.)

Intensity of female orgasms, as measured by vaginal pulses and blood volume, goes down as blood alcohol levels rise. (Experiment by Dr. Vincent Malatesta, Univ. of Georgia.)

Male erections are weakened as more alcohol is consumed. (Experiment at Rutgers University, NJ.)

Why? For males, alcohol stimulates the liver to produce an enzyme that destroys testosterone. For females, there has been no definitive research on the relationship between hormonal function and effect of alcohol.

Source: *Executive Fitness.*

Alcoholics Anonymous

In the U.S., alcoholism is the third greatest killer, after heart disease and cancer. It is a progressive illness and can never be cured. But it can be arrested.

No one who has become an alcoholic ever stops being an alcoholic. Abstaining for months or even years doesn't prove than an alcoholic can begin to drink normally or socially. With the first drink, the habit becomes active again. *There is only one solution:* Stay away from alcohol totally.

Alcoholics Anonymous (AA) is a worldwide fellowship of people who help one another stay sober. They offer immediate help, day or night, to anyone who has a drinking problem and wants to do something about it. Since the members are all alcoholics, they have a special understanding of each other. They know there are no former alcoholics or ex-alcoholics. But they do know that alcoholics can become recovered alcoholics.

Anonymity is inherent in the AA program. Only first names are used. Even those names are not disclosed outside of the group. No records of address, age, occupation, etc. are kept. No member signs anything. And there are no rules for attending meetings. People come and go, or stop attending altogether. No questions are ever asked. No member ever says to another: This is what you should do. Recovered alcoholics sometimes say: This is what I did.

When an alcoholic approaches AA, the person is not asked to stop drinking for a week or a month. Request: Don't take a drink for just 24 hours. The theory is one day at a time without a drink.

Motto: If we feel the urge for a drink, we neither yield nor desist. We merely put off taking that drink until tomorrow. That's the philosophy behind AA, which is made up of local groups of men and women in thousands of communities.

AA does not recruit members, nor does it solicit or accept outside funds. The small sums necessary for its existence are donated by those who attend meetings, where a hat is passed.

Telephone numbers of local AA members can be found in the telephone directory. A call will bring help immediately. Or write to: General Service Office, Box 459, Grand Central Station, New York, NY 10017. The response comes in an unmarked envelope.

Psychology of the Problem Drinker

There are at least 10 million alcoholics in America. Half of them are married and have children. About 80% are employed. Thus, every alcoholic affects the emotional health or well-being of many other people.

What makes them tick: Being anxious people, drinkers use alcohol to calm themselves. Hitch: In the early stages of alcoholism, drinking causes acute anxiety.

Drinkers harbor anger. Passive ones direct this anger inwardly and often self-destruct. Aggressive drinkers lash out at those close to them.

They delude themselves by denying that they have a drinking problem. They disdain remedial efforts.

They ride an emotional roller coaster, up one day and down the next. Actually, this is a manifestation of their deep depression. The up periods are mood swings to avoid depression.

Problem drinkers have social problems. Common gripe: I can't get along with anyone, myself included.

Problem drinkers have sexual problems usually linked to identity. Example: Many male alcoholics drink to fit a macho image. Similarly, women drink to prove their warmth and femininity. Unresolved question: Who am I?

Source: *How to Live with A Problem Drinker and Survive,* by Dr. Gary G. Forrest, Atheneum, New York.

Compulsive Gamblers

Most compulsive gamblers can be cured—and in a way that benefits both them and their employers.

The majority of out-of-control gamblers are in the $30,000-plus income brackets. Also, most of them are college-educated, intelligent, and aggressive.

Symptoms: No control of personal life, reckless borrowing, and bad-check writing to cover losses. Business failures, broken marriages, theft, or embezzlement frequently follow. Depression and suicidal tendencies are common.

Treatment works in at least half of the cases. Group support, available through Gamblers Anonymous,* and strict budgeting are part of the cure. Frequently, therapy helps and, in some cases, hospitalization.

Best permanent solution: Turn the compulsive gambler into a workaholic. It offers the chance to build up self-esteem and to meet challenges that suit the gambler's aggressive personality.

Important: No cure is effective until the individual completely stops all gambling-related activities.

*Local groups can be found in the telephone book.
Source: *MD Medical Newsmagazine.*

Successful Men Who Die Young

The leading causes of death for male executives in their forties and fifties have been determined to be cancer and degenerative diseases of the heart and liver.

The odds: A 50-year-old male executive who doesn't get much exercise but who smokes and has mildly high blood pressure has about a 15.5% chance of dying in the next 10 years. Source: A Life Extension Institute computerized *Health Risk Profile* of a hypothetical executive.

Causes, in descending order of probability: Heart attack, lung cancer, cirrhosis of the liver, highway accident, stroke, cancer of intestines and/or rectum.

To reduce the odds:
Not smoking can add 1½ years.
Exercising can add one year.
Not drinking can add 8½ months.
Driving with seat belt can add 6 months.
Losing weight can add 3½ months.

Source: Dr. Ronald E. Costin, medical director, the Life Extension Institute, sponsors of the Staywell Corporate Preventive Health Program, 1185 Ave. of the Americas, New York 10036.

Work Habits That Lead to a Heart Attack

Making the job and financial success your first priority. Putting health and personal needs at the bottom of your list.

Spending evenings, weekends, and holidays at the office because you feel your family's financial health is more important than their emotional well-being.

Taking your briefcase home on evenings when you don't stay late. Reviewing each day's problems at home every night.

Agreeing to every request. Never saying no.

Accepting every invitation to serve on a committee or sit on a board.

Using lunch as merely a midday setting for a business conference.

Taking shorter vacations than you're entitled to.

Refusing to delegate authority.

Working at least 12 hours a day.

Smoking, drinking and overeating at night as a reward for putting in a hard day.

Associating mainly with friends and business associates who also smoke, overeat, and drink heavily.

Avoiding exercise because it's a waste of time.

An executive who has already slipped into nine of these twelve habits is a likely candidate for the Coronary Club.

Best first step to escape the high-anxiety life style: An exercise program.

Source: Joseph Arends, MD, Wayne State University, writing in *Security management.*

Why Exercise and Moderate Drinking Help the Heart

Physical exercise and moderate alcohol consumption are connected to high levels of a blood protein, which guards against heart ailments.

Danger: Cigarette smoking and obesity are linked with lower amounts of blood protein.

The blood protein is called high-density lipoprotein (HDL). It binds to cholesterol in the blood and carries the cholesterol through the arteries. Cleansing the cholesterol from the blood prevents it from forming blockages that cause heart disease.

Source: National Heart, Lung and Blood Institute, Building 31, 9000 Rockville Pike, Bethesda, MD 20205.

Lessening the Risk of Heart Attack and Stroke

Heart attacks and strokes are both linked in part to common factors you can control. Steps to take:

• Check blood pressure regularly. Early detection and treatment of high blood pressure has played an important part in the declining number of strokes in the U.S. About two-thirds of stroke victims have either high blood pressure or diabetes (detected by a blood test and also treatable).

• Eliminate excess body fat. Shifting to a low-fat, low-cholesterol diet is best. Avoiding obesity is important to lower blood pressure and to reduce levels of harmful low-density lipoproteins, which deposit cholesterol on blood-vessel walls.

• Exercise regularly. It holds down body weight, promotes the production of beneficial high-density lipoproteins (which combat cholesterol buildup), and seems to decrease the tendency of blood to clot.

• If you smoke, stop. Stopping can decrease the risk of stroke by 50%.

Avoid birth-control pills if you are a woman who smokes or has high blood pressure. Other women who use the pill may increase their risk of a stroke from one in 10,000 to six in 10,000.

Source: *The Health Letter.*

• Hugs prevent heart disease. Recent research concluded that lab animals receiving physical stroking every day developed arteriosclerosis (hardening of the arteries) at one-third the rate of animals given no special attention and the same high-cholesterol diet. The key to prevention may be reduced stress.

• Fish oil lowers the blood's cholesterol level. Recent test: Oil from fresh salmon was substituted for saturated vegetable oil in the volunteers' diet. Result: After four weeks, cholesterol levels dipped, triglycerides dropped and the blood showed signs of reduced clotting. Lesson: Those worried about cholesterol and heart disease should eat more fish. Fishes rich in oil: Bluefish, flounder, haddock, halibut, mackerel, pollock, salmon, sardines, and shad.

Early Warning Signs of a Stroke

A sudden, temporary weakness or numbness of the face, arm, or leg.

Temporary difficulty with, or loss of, speech. Or trouble understanding speech.

Sudden, temporary loss (or dimming) of vision, particularly in one eye.

Double vision.

Unexplained headaches, or a change in the pattern of your headaches.

Temporary dizziness.

A recent change in personality or mental ability.

If you notice these signals: Call your doctor. Quick action can prevent more serious problems.

Number one cause of strokes: High blood pressure.

Handling a Heart Attack

A heart attack signals its arrival in these ways:

A crushing, searing pain in the middle of the chest, which may move quickly into the shoulders, arms, and neck.

Sharp pains in the pit of the stomach.

Fainting spells, dizziness, sweating, nausea, troublesome breathing.

The uncomfortable chest feelings associated with heartburn or indigestion.

Warning: You can die waiting for an episode of "indigestion" to subside. If you suffer severe chest discomfort for more than two minutes, call your doctor immediately. More than half of all heart-attack deaths occur within three hours of the first signs.

Be prepared: Keep the telephone numbers of your doctor and nearby hospitals within easy reach. Also, when you're ill, it's best to have a close friend or family member present to ensure that actions will proceed in an orderly manner. Best: A person who will not panic. Preferable: One of the millions of people in the country who have been trained to administer cardiopulmonary resuscitation.

Since no action taken by a layman will ease a heart attack, first priority should be given to getting to a hospital. If your doctor can't be reached, call a hospital emergency unit, or ask a friend to rush you to the hospital by car.

If during this time you collapse or stop breathing, and/or your pulse stops, a companion trained in cardiopulmonary resuscitation can exert pressure on the chest to get the heart and lungs going again.

Caution: No one should try this life-saving technique unless he has been properly trained.

Reducing Chances of a Second Heart Attack

Recurrent rate in U.S. now averages 45%. Among the patients of Dr. Meyer Friedman, author of *Type A Behavior,* the rate is 10%. This is what he tells them to do:

Diet? Yes, low fat. Eat mainly both fish and fowl. People cheat anyway, says Friedman. But no heavy meals at night and no exercise within two hours of a meal.

No smoking.

Moderate exercise. One hour a day, every

day, rain or shine. No high altitudes and absolutely no running or jogging, which Dr. Friedman regards as something of a national disaster from any therapeutic standpoint, especially for cardiac patients. Why? Because Americans tend to be fanatics about everything they do, even relaxing. We jog our way to emotional stress.

Heavy drinking (more than two jiggers a night) is also out.

Another way of life: Essential for the success of his program, says Friedman. He trains patients in contingency planning—ways to avoid situations that most commonly trigger heart attacks.

Rehearsal for emergencies is also definitely part of the new routine for survival. Feel the pain at night? You have five minutes to do something about it. Know just whom you are going to call—call your regular doctor or another one. Rehearse carefully.

Modifying behavior: Reduce the self-generated stress that prompts the coronary condition in the first place. Recognize yourself in Friedman's description of Type A people, the ones he identifies as most prone to heart attacks?

Excessive drive. Aggressive, though often they don't know it. Above all, obsessed by time urgency and by getting more and more things done in less and less time. (Time-sickness, Friedman calls it.) Continuously upset by traffic jams, by people who don't explain things fast enough, or by anything that impedes them.

Changing such behavior is not easy. But with professional help it can be done, particularly if the person realizes that it is literally a matter of life and death not to give in to 5 o'clock frenzy, to relax at lunch, to seek consciously to be alone at certain times of day.

Where to start: Remember your successes. Ask yourself, were you ever promoted or did you get a raise because you were impatient? Did things faster? Were hostile or aggressive? This will give you confidence to begin thoughtful self-analysis.

How to handle travel: Some 20% to 30% of all heart attacks occur just before or just after travel. Friedman trains his patient/executives to contingency plan for a business trip. Say he's going to New York for an important conference on Monday, March 12:

Monday, March 5. Executive starts cleaning desk in preparation for the trip. By the time he leaves work on Friday, the desk is clear except for the plane tickets.

Sunday, March 11. He flies to New York. Goes straight to hotel. Does not pick up the phone. Takes a mild tranquilizer and goes to bed.

Monday, March 12. Tranquilizer, conference and back to the hotel.

Basic pattern to follow: Hotel. Meeting. Return to hotel.

How Heart Specialists Care for Their Own Hearts

A survey of the personal regimens of top heart experts:

Eat two or three meatless meals a week.

Eat fish and chicken rather than beef.

Have high-roughage, low-cholesterol breakfasts.

Skip dinner when the pounds creep up.

Avoid dairy products.

Swim two or three times a week.

Exercise rather than attend meetings.

Try to live in a pleasant atmosphere at home and at work.

Check blood pressure three times a year.

Bicycle to and from work.

Eliminate high intake of fat from the diet by eating fewer animal products, less refined sugar, and more fiber-rich foods.

Practice muscle relaxation.

Sex After a Coronary

Highlights from a study of the sexual behavior of 100 couples, in which the husbands are recovering from heart attacks:

Some 76 of the 100 couples resumed sexual activity, with 22 retaining the precoronary frequency, 49 decreasing and 5 increasing.

Greatest fear of the wives: The strain of the sex act would induce a new heart attack, or even death.

Some wives used the husband's condition as an excuse to terminate sexual relations which were previously unwelcome.

About half of the couples who resumed sexual activity now enjoy a closer emotional relationship. Many found their husbands more loving and caring.

Most wish they had been given detailed instructions by the physician concerning sexual activity following a heart attack.

Source: Chris Papadopoulos, M.D., chief of cardiology, South Baltimore General Hospital, writing in *Medical Aspects of Human Sexuality.*

Cure Rates for Six Kinds of Cancer

Cancer is not an automatic death sentence. The cure rate for some types is 100%. Details:

Bowel cancer: Recurrent abdominal pains. Cure rate: Over 50%.

Breast cancer: Lumps in the breast. Cure rate: Nearly 100% after mastectomy.

Cervical cancer: Vaginal bleeding. Cure rate: Nearly 100%.

Lung cancer: Heavy coughing, shortness of breath. Cure rate: 6%.

Prostate cancer: Difficulty passing urine. Cure rate: Over 50%.

Skin cancer: Skin ulcers that fail to heal. Cure rate: Nearly 100%.

Source: *International Management.*

Colon Cancer

Prime victims: Adults over 40 in industrial nations. Particularly: Those with polyps, inflammatory bowel disease, or a family history of colon cancer. Early detection is imperative. Important: By the time discomfort is felt, the disease is likely to be beyond cure. Interesting: Mormons, who shun coffee, tea, and alcohol, have substantially lower rates of colon cancer than the rest of the U.S. population.

Source: *The Health Letter.*

Skin Moles and Cancer

Skin moles are usually benign. However, changes can signal the onset of melanoma (cancerous growth). Warning signs: Change in color, shape, size, or texture. Redness around a mole. Easy bleeding.

Sex and Cancer

Sexual activity may help to prevent prostate cancer. Theory: Sex hormones build up during abstinence and possibly reduce the prostate cells' immunity significantly.

Exercise and Cancer

Those who exercise regularly may be less susceptible to cancer. A German study reveals that sedentary people contract cancer six times more frequently than the physically active. Similarly, experiments with mice indicate that the growth rate of tumors is twice as great among inactive animals as in those that exercise on a treadmill for 20 minutes daily.

Source: *Executive Fitness Newsletter.*

Cancer Survivors

The cancer survival rate is increased in patients who are able to articulate their feelings of anger, fear, and depression. Patients in one study who talked about their emotional state outlived those who couldn't express their emotions by three to one. Suppressing negative feelings may negatively affect hormones necessary for recuperation.

Source: Johns Hopkins University School of Medicine.

Obesity and Cancer

Obesity increases a woman's chance of developing breast cancer. And, it pays for those overweight victims to trim down even after a mastectomy. Cancer patients who weigh less than 140 pounds have a 62% survival rate five years after breast surgery. Those who are over 140 pounds, or overweight according to body size, have a five-year survival rate of 49%.

Cancer Insurance

Such policies are probably unnecessary. Reason: Buyers, mostly the elderly, are better covered by Medicare or a general policy. Moreover, prospective buyers, not familiar with the statistics, often do not know the hard questions to ask. Note: Many reputable insurers reduce benefits if coverage is duplicated. The buyer pays twice, but receives no additional reimbursement. Alternative: If supplemental insurance is needed, buy a policy that covers *all* illnesses.

Source: *Prevention.*

Can Your Mind Make Your Sick Body Well?

Techniques using mental imagery in the treatment of cancer were pioneered by Dr. O. Carl Simonton, a radiation therapist practicing in Fort Worth, TX. Hundreds of medical spe-

cialists have been trained in Dr. Simonton's method. Theoretical basis: That cancer results from a failure in the body's immunizing mechanisms, which is triggered by emotional stress and the sense of personal loss.

Dr. Simonton emphasizes that mental imagery is a supplementary disease-fighting technique. It should be used in conjunction with traditional therapy for cancer (or other diseases). Also, proper application requires counseling from trained specialists. Essentials of Dr. Simonton's mental imagery technique:

Sit in a quiet, softly lit room, in a comfortable chair, with your feet flat on the floor and eyes closed. Key to all else: Total relaxation.

Mentally picture the cancer in your body, using either symbolic or realistic images. View the cancer cells as very weak and confused. Remember: The body's white blood cells naturally destroy thousands of cancerous cells during anyone's lifetime. Thus, recovery now will also enlist your body's natural defenses to restore its health.

Visualize the medical treatment going to work in your body. For radiation therapy: Imagine a beam of millions of energy bullets hitting all the cells in its path. Healthy cells quickly repair themselves. But the weaker cancer cells cannot survive the deadly beam. For chemotherapy: Imagine the drug as a poison that strong cells resist. Weak cancer cells, however, can't resist the lure.

Picture your body's white blood cells as a vast army that surrounds and destroys the cancerous cells.

For pain, picture the army of white blood cells racing toward the discomfort, soothing it away. Command your body to heal itself.

Imagine yourself well, rid of the disease, full of energy, reaching your goals in life. Envision family members doing well, too, and your relationships becoming more meaningful. Concentrate on powerful reasons for being healthy.

Congratulate yourself for participating in your own recovery.

Frequency of mental imagery routine: At least three times a day.

Source: *Getting Well Again,* by O. Carl Simonton, MD, J.P. Tarcher, Inc., Los Angeles.

16

Fitness And Exercise

Choosing the Right Exercise Program

Exercise fads have taken the place of dance fads. Jogging, running and cycling have their adherents. Popularity, however, is the worst criterion to use in choosing an exercise. Reason: An effective program must be tailored to the aims and abilities of the individual.

Key criteria:

Physical capacity. Age, medical problems, and individual quirks can make some programs desirable and others dangerous. Example: Running and jogging can be highly destructive to previously injured knee joints.

Temperament. The exercises or athletics must become a routine part of life. Your choice must fit your favored style: Solitary versus team workouts, high-intensity or long-duration exercises, competitive versus noncompetitive sports, etc.

Personal goals. Possible objectives are reduction of stress and nervous tension, weight loss, a buildup of muscles, flexibility and suppleness, a buildup of strength, power and endurance, relaxation. Usually best: An exercise program that combines two or more different sports.

Exercise precautions:

Get a medical checkup. Anyone over 35 years old who has a cardiac risk factor (for example, people who are overweight, smoke, have high blood pressure, etc.) should have a stress electrocardiogram. Individuals over 45 who have been leading chair-bound lives (most executives, for example) should build up their exercise routines gradually.

Buy good equipment and protective gear. Examples: Shoes with well-padded heels for jogging, eye protectors for squash and racquetball, knee pads and elbow pads for fast-action sports played on hard surfaces. A woman should always wear a good support brassiere.

Matching the exercise to the goal:

Reduction of stress and nervous tension. Take part in challenging physical activities and high-intensity exercises that last for at least 30 minutes. Frequency: Three times a week. Locale: Away from home or office. Pick a structured sport conducted outdoors or in a gym.

451

Athletics that offer acceptable outlets for aggression (such as tennis, basketball, etc.) can be helpful to improve the cardiovascular system. Essentials: Stimulate the body's use of oxygen and drive the heartbeat rate to 70% to 85% of your maximum (as determined by a cardiac stress test). Pace: Ten minutes to one hour. Recommended: Energetic walking, jogging, running, swimming, rope-skipping, rowing, playing handball, racquetball, or basketball, wrestling, taking judo or karate.

Weight loss. An exercise program is only a minor supplement to a sound diet. You have to work off 3,500 calories to lose a pound of fat. That's the equivalent of five hours of swimming the butterfly stroke, nine hours of playing table tennis, more than five hours of running. Exercises tone and firm muscles through repeated action. Recommended: Calisthenics, cycling, jogging, running, rope-skipping.

Muscle buildup. Weight-training, playing football and soccer, climbing and doing isometrics are all recommended activities.

Strength. Suggested activities are weight-training and doing isometrics (use lighter weights/resistance and more repetition).

Power and endurance. Alternate high-intensity bursts of exercise with rests to improve power. Increase duration to achieve greater stamina. The ability to work through pain is a must. Recommended: Playing basketball, cycling, running, rope-skipping.

Flexibility and suppleness. Bending, twisting, stretching for a few minutes each day. Recommended: Doing calisthenics, yoga, karate, judo, fencing, wrestling.

Source: *Vegetarian Times* and *The Health Letter.*

Two Ways to Test Your Own Fitness

• Take your pulse while resting or sitting. Then, hop 25 times on one foot, then on the other. Immediately take your pulse again. Sit two minutes, take pulse again. If you are fit, the pulse should rise by about 50 beats per minute right after hopping. After two minutes, it should fall to 5 to 10 beats of the prehop pulse.
Source: *Lifegain,* by Robert F. Allen, Ph.D., Appleton-Century-Crofts, New York.

• Run and walk comfortably as far as possible in 12 minutes. If winded, slow down until you catch your breath. Then pick up pace again until time is up. Measure: Less than 1 mile indicates poor fitness. Best: 1.25 to 1.5 miles (if over 50 years of age), 1.3 to 1.55 miles (if 40 to 50 years), and 1.4 to 1.65 (if 30 to 39 years).

Making Time for Exercise

Park the car farther away from the office or train station and walk.

Quit taking elevators. Payoff: Daily climbs of 18 floors or more will increase fitness, studies show.

Eat lunch in a restaurant at least 10 blocks from the office, and stride briskly both to and from.

Instead of driving to the shopping center, walk there. If it's too far, ride a bicycle. If there's too much to haul home, make a second trip.

Carry your own golf clubs. And skip the golf cart, even if you're the lone walker in your foursome.

Source: *The Cardiologists' Guide to Fitness and Health Through Exercise,* Simon & Schuster, New York.

Before Signing a Contract With a Health Club

Inspect club at the time of day you'd be most likely to attend; how crowded are pool, sauna, exercise rooms, etc? Make certain all facilities that are promised are available. Avoid clubs that require long-term contracts. Once a contract is signed and termination is desired, it's usually possible to avoid liability for the full term of the contract by notifying the club by registered mail, paying for services already rendered, and a small cancellation fee. Check local consumer protection agency on rules. Don't be pushed into a hasty decision by a low-price offer. Specials are usually repeated.

Result: The way the left hemisphere of the brain received and processed information, serial processing, improved significantly for the group that participated in the exercise program. Limitation: No improvement, however, was noted in parallel processing (creative ability).

Source: *Engineering Times.*

Exercising in Polluted Air

Polluted air poses special problems for runners, cyclists, and other urban exercisers. The workout and expanded lung capacity allow greater inhalation of carbon monoxide and other dangerous substances.

If you can't avoid pollution, it helps to maintain an adequate intake of antioxidants. Prime ones: The food additive BHT and vitamins E and C. Of these, vitamin E is the most potent antioxidant. Important: Taking vitamin E won't immunize you from pollution damage. But a vitamin E deficiency can increase your chances of being harmed.

No definitive guidelines exist as to the effects of different pollution levels on exercisers. Performance is lowered, of course, partly because some pollutants reduce the amount of oxygen carried by red blood cells to muscles. But exercise also helps increase the rate at which carbon monoxide is cleared from the bloodstream.

Source: Dr. Gabe Mirkin, writing in *The Runner.*

Exercise and Your Mind

Exercise can sharpen your thinking. A Purdue University study that tested two groups of men (average age 42) tells the story.

The experiment: One group exercised 1½ hours a day, three times a week, for four months. The control group remained sedentary.

Sex and the Athlete

Does sexual intercourse before an athletic contest help or hurt the athlete? Answer: It depends. Sexual activity does sap strength and drive. Excessive indulgence results in fatigue and apathy. However: Abstinence creates increased sexual tension. This induces a time-consuming search for gratification. Bottom line: The search for sex is often more debilitating to an athlete than the act itself.

Source: Edward Colt, M.D., Columbia University College of Physicians and Surgeons, New York City, reporting in *Medical Aspects of Human Sexuality.*

Exercises That Can Hurt You

One should be careful in selecting an exercise plan. Correct breathing and posture during exercise are essential. Improper exercising can cause or aggravate injuries. Even basic exercises can be dangerous:

Toe-touching: Doing this with the knees in a locked position and with a rapid bouncing action places tremendous pressure on the lumbar vertebrae. This could result in lower-back pain. Allow your knees to bend slightly, and remain in a hanging-over position for three complete slow, deep breaths. Then straighten slowly. Repeat this three times. Do it without bouncing.

Leg lifts: Performing these while lying on your back and raising both legs at the same time can cause the pelvis to rotate and lead to swayback (the problem of lower-back lordosis). Eliminate this exercise.

Sit-ups: Doing these with straight legs can also contribute to an increased curvature of the lower back. For the abdominal muscles to get a real workout, bend your knees, keep your feet flat on the floor, fold your arms over your chest, and curl up to only a 30° angle from the floor.

Deep knee-bends: These can cause injury to knee cartilage. Bending the knees so that they are directly over the feet and the thighs are parallel to the floor will not cause injury.

The important thing to remember is that any repeated movement done in an unnatural position can create problems. Two key areas of the body to be concerned with are the knees and the lower back. If an exercise is painful, perhaps you are doing it improperly, or it is too advanced for you. Or: It may be simply a dangerous exercise.

Source: Leslie Cerier, a personal fitness counselor who works with corporations, educational institutions and individuals, 235 W. 102 St., New York 10025.

Cause and Treatment of Sports Injuries

• Running injuries. More than half of America's 20 million runners suffer injuries from their sport. Most common: Friction within the large joints and flat feet. Antidotes: Wear only those shoes designed for running. Do at least 15 minutes of pre-running stretching exercises. Don't overdo it. Running six miles isn't twice as good for you as running three miles. Best reason to run: It makes you feel better.

Source: Dr. Charles Gudas, director of podiatric education and training, University of Chicago Medical Center, 5801 S. Ellis Ave., Chicago 60637.

• "Runner's knee." How the bottom of your foot hits the ground determines if you will suffer from "runner's knee." Cause: Landing on the outside part of the bottom of the foot and rolling to the inside. The lower leg twists inward while strong knee muscles pull the kneecap outward. This causes the back of the kneecap to rub against the thigh bone. Solution: Arch supports to limit rolling-in motion and isometric muscle exercises to move kneecap inward.

• For painful heels, insert a sponge-rubber heel pad in your sneaker for extra cushioning and transfer of your weight forward. For a heel spur (a calcium deposit that will show up in an X-ray), cut a hole in the insole under the spur, then cover it with a sponge-rubber pad. **Source:** *Tennis.*

• Long-distance runners should avoid the use of aspirin in hot weather. Reasons: Aspirin causes dehydration through excessive sweating and urination. It may also inhibit thirst. Result: Risk of heat stroke, with nausea and dizziness. It can also provoke exercise-induced asthma. Substitutes: For localized pain, apply heat, cold, or other physical therapy. **Source:** Dr. Herbert L. Fred, director of Medical Education at St. Joseph's Hospital, Houston 77002, writing in *The Runner.*

• Swimmer's ear. Sometimes water soaks the ear canal, making it conducive to bacterial infections. Problem: Earplugs are often too loose or so snug they irritate the skin. Prevention: After swimming, place four or five drops of isopropyl alcohol in each ear. It will dry the remaining water droplets, creating an inhospitable environment for bacteria to breed.

• Leg cramps from bicycling can often be avoided by drinking a pint of water before a long ride and a pint an hour while riding. Also helpful to avoid cramps: Eating low-fat, high carbohydrate foods. Training hard, no more than once every 48 hours. Getting an expert to check the position of the bicycle seat. **Source:** *Bicycling.*

• Racquetball wrist is becoming a widespread malady. Prevention: Shift from heavy racquet to one of the new light, fiberglass models. Treatment: Rest followed by wrist-strengthening exercise.

• Cyclist's palsy can result from extended bicycling. Symptoms: A numb feeling in the hands, combined with poor finger coordination. Cause: Constant pressure on the ulnar nerve in the palm of the hand. Cure: Stop biking for a while.

• Tennis toe: A painful swelling of the first

and sometimes the second toe. It's frequently accompanied by discoloration under the toenail. Cause: A shoe that is loose in the heel or too short in the toe. The player's toes then jam up in front when he stops short. Treatment: Cold compresses and aspirin to relieve the pain. Buy properly fitted tennis shoes, and, most important, wear only one pair of socks at a time (cotton or wool).

Source: Dr. John F. Waller, Jr., Lenox Hill Hospital's Institute of Sports Medicine and Athletic Trauma, New York, NY.

• Asthma attacks can be brought on by running. What to do: Continue running. The exertion actually helps reduce the effects of the attack. Ask your physician about Cromolyn, an inhaled powder. It prevents asthma attacks three-quarters of the time when taken just before running.

Source: *The Runner.*

Ten-Minute Guide to Relieving Office Fatigue

Today's executive is often plagued with aches and pains caused by business pressures. The following exercises can bring quick relief and can be performed in the privacy of your own office. They concentrate on different areas of the body. If they are *all* done as part of an exercise regimen, they will provide overall relief.

Face: Using the thumbs only, move along each eyebrow line from the bridge of the nose outward, stopping every one-quarter inch to apply heavy pressure for about 20 seconds. Again using only the thumbs, repeat this motion from the base of each nostril, along the cheekbone, to the top of the ear. Using the four fingers of both hands, follow the hairline from each ear to the center of the forehead, still applying heavy pressure every one-quarter inch. Place the index finger behind each ear, and then follow the ridge that is behind the ear up and around to the front of the ear, using periodic pressure as indicated above. Approximate time: 2 minutes, 45 seconds.

Neck: Drop the chin to the chest. Slowly roll the head toward the right shoulder until it touches. Continue the rolling motion until head points backwards and the base of the scalp touches the top of the spine. Then slowly roll the head toward the left shoulder until it touches the top of the shoulder. Finish the exercise with the chin resting on the chest. Repeat the exercise twice and then do it in the opposite direction three times. Approximate time: 1 minute.

With the shoulders straight and motionless, turn the head to the right, looking over the shoulder as far as possible. Muscles should feel taut. Hold this position for a count of five and release. Repeat this head turn in the opposite direction. This exercise should be performed five times. Do it five times on the left side and five times on the right side. Approximate time: 50 seconds.

Forearms: Extend the right arm in front of you, palm down. With the left thumb, follow the line of the middle finger along the forearm, stopping every one-quarter inch from the wrist to the elbow to apply heavy pressure for 20 seconds. Turn the arm over, palm up. Follow the middle of the inner forearm, using the same periodic pressure technique from the elbow to the wrist. Repeat this exercise on the left arm. Approximate time: 4 minutes.

Shoulders: Raise the right shoulder to touch the right ear. Hold this position for a count of five and release. Repeat with the left shoulder. Complete this cycle five times. Then raise the shoulders in a shrugging motion in order to touch both ears simultaneously. Hold this position for a count of five and then release. Repeat this exercise five times. Approximate time: 50 seconds.

Waist: While standing, press the lower part of your body against the side of the desk or other similar surface. This will force the pelvic area to remain immobile during the exercise. Twist the upper torso back and forth. Do this while rapidly swinging both arms, fully extended, from left to right. Repeat this exercise approximately 12 times. Approximate time: 45 seconds.

Spinal-fluid circulation: Raise the right arm as if hailing a cab and, at the same time, raise the left knee. Lower the arm and knee and immediately raise the left arm and right knee as if marching in place. Repeat this cycle, going through the movements at a brisk rate, 15 times. Approximate time: 45 seconds.

Source: Suzanne Castro, physical therapist, 35-03 29 St., NY 11106.

Yoga: Five-Minute Office Routine

Most exercise programs aimed at improving physical and mental tone are too time consuming for executives. Exception: Yoga. Practitioners find that 10 minutes per day will do the trick (and do it so well that you may soon voluntarily expand the time you spend on it). Here's a five-minute routine for starts that you can do in your chair or standing beside your desk:

Chest expansion (2 minutes): Standing with heels together, slowly bring arms up so they are straight ahead of you, palms turned outward. (Feel elbows stretching.) Bring arms straight back on a line with shoulders and then upward, as high as you can. Then, slowly and carefully, bend backward at the waist. Keep arms high, knees unbent, head back. Hold for a slow count of five. Next, bend forward as far as you can (don't strain), holding arms high, head down, and neck relaxed. Hold for count of ten. Straighten up a bit and extend left leg to the side. Bend forward at the waist, aiming forehead toward left knee. (Bend right leg slightly.) Hold for a count of ten. Repeat, bending toward right. Straighten slowly, draw right leg in, unclasp hands, and relax. Repeat entire routine. This is good for tension in spine, legs, shoulders, and elbows.

Head twist (2 minutes): Sitting at your desk, place elbows close together, put head between hands (hands over ears), and close eyes. Place clasped hands on lower part of back of your head. Slowly and gently push head forward until chin touches chest. Keeping arms still, turn head, resting chin in left hand and gripping back of head with right hand. Turn head very slowly as far to the left as you can. Don't move arms. Repeat, turning to the right.

Simple spinal twist (1 minute): Sitting, cross right leg over left. Then, while gripping back of chair seat with right hand, cross left arm over right knee and grasp left knee. Slowly twist head and trunk as far to the right as possible. Hold for count of ten. Resume original forward position, holding chair and knee. Relax and repeat once. Next, crossing left leg over right, twist to the left side twice.

Back stretch (1 minute): Sitting toward chair's edge, extend legs outward, bend forward, and hold upper calves firmly. Bending elbows outward, pull trunk down, and relax all muscles, including neck, so head hangs down. Hold for count of 20. Straighten up slowly, rest a moment, then repeat, holding lower calves or ankles, if possible.

Result: Fifteen minutes after you complete this set of exercises, you should begin to feel a surge of mental and physical energy.

Source: *Yoga for Personal Living,* by Richard L. Hittleman, Warner Books, New York.

Quick, Deep Relaxation

You can banish intense stress with a simple technique that provides deep relaxation in less than a couple of minutes. Payoffs include reducing the risk of cardiovascular disease and also easing tensions, which induce such unwanted habits as smoking and overeating.

Developed by Stanford University researchers, the deep-relaxation technique proceeds as follows:

Muscle relaxation. Lie or sit comfortably in a quiet environment and close eyes. Right-handers begin with the right hand (left hand for southpaws). Tense the hand, clench fist, then let it go loose and relaxed. Continue tensing and relaxing your body's right side: Forearm, upper arm, shoulder, foot, lower leg, upper leg. Repeat on the left side. Next: Relax hip muscles and let the wave of relaxation flow upward through the abdomen and chest. Keep breathing low, in the diaphragm. Move the relaxation upward through the shoulders, neck, jaw, and face, with special attention to muscles around the mouth and eyes. Tell your entire body to feel warm and heavy. End the muscle phase by imagining a cool sensation around your forehead.

Mental relaxation. After the muscles are relaxed, let the mind grow calm. Don't fix on thoughts; let them pass through. If any thought recurs, eliminate it by saying "no" softly, under your breath. Imagine a peaceful blue sky or the sea (blue is an especially relaxing color). Follow your breath as you inhale, and exhale it naturally.

To use these techniques: Start with a couple of muscle-relaxation sessions daily. Fifteen to 20 minutes each are ideal, but you'll get results with only three minutes. Follow up with the mental technique. As you grow accustomed to the feeling of loosened muscles and a calmed mind, you'll be able to induce them in as little as 30 seconds.

Source: *The American Way of Life Need Not Be Hazardous To Your Health,* by John Farquhar, M.D., W.W. Norton & Co., New York.

Relieving Tension With Isometrics

Simple exercises to do in your office that will help you to transfer emotional pressures into tension-relieving physical activities:

Place the palms of the hands together and push hard.

While seated, take hold of the sides of the chair seat and lift. This flexes the opposite arm and back muscles from the prior exercise.

Lean forward against a desk, with your feet three to four feet away and hands on top of the surface. Do two slow push-ups.

Simplest of all, at the end of each telephone call, squeeze the receiver as hard as possible for a few seconds before hanging up. Alternate hands every other call.

Schedule a short walk about every hour. Don't wait until you become conscious of the tension. Take the walk every hour as a preventive measure.

Source: *Executime.*

Breathing Exercises That Make You Feel Better

The way your body functions and the state of your health are affected by the way you breathe. Here are some exercises developed by experts.

To ease chest-cold congestion:

Inhale deeply, hold breath for 15 counts.

While holding your breath, rest your fists at the sides of your ribs, with your elbows pointing back.

Lightly pound your ribs. Move from top to bottom and back again.

Exhale. Repeat several times.

To stimulate the digestive process, this exercise should be done at least once a day:

Sit comfortably on a chair or floor with your hands resting on your thighs.

Inhale deeply. Exhale in two stages. First, pull in the stomach to push out most of the air. Then, give the stomach muscles a fast contraction to complete exhaling.

Release the stomach, and allow the air to flow in naturally.

Repeat the exhalation process.

Continue the exercise so that you are inhaling and exhaling at a rapid rate.

To prevent ear-popping while traveling in an airplane:

Tilt your head back slightly. Open your mouth and yawn. Inhale as much air as possible.

Exhale through the mouth, and then swallow.

Repeat as often as necessary.

To prevent seasickness, start this breathing exercise at the first sign of queasiness:

Tilt your head back. Inhale until your lungs are about three-quarters full.

Press your tongue against the roof of your mouth. Hold your breath for seven counts.

Look slightly downward. Vigorously exhale half of the breath. Pause. Then exhale the rest of the air.

Repeat as necessary.

Even pain can be managed by breathing. Point: Concentrate on the methods of breath-

457

ing, not on the pain. Methods:

Inhale deeply as soon as you feel pain.

Immediately breathe out forcefully through your nostrils.

Take another deep breath, and push out the air.

Breathe in and out to help force the pain from your body. Take longer and deeper breaths as the pain diminishes.

Source: *Total Breathing,* by Philip Smith, McGraw-Hill, New York.

Exercise to Correct a Pot Belly

Exercise abdominal muscles. Pull muscles in, tighten, and hold 8 to 10 seconds at least once an hour (while standing, sitting, walking, waiting for elevators). At home, lie on back, bend knees. Hook toes under a piece of furniture, lock hands behind head, and curl forward until shoulders are 10 inches off the floor. Hold for 2 seconds. Repeat 10 times at each session.

Exercises While Driving

(1) Double chin: Lift chin slightly and open and close mouth as though chewing. (2) Flabby neck: Move head toward right shoulder while looking straight ahead at the road. Return head to center, then toward left shoulder. (3) Pot belly: Sit straight with spine against back seat. Pull stomach in and hold breath for count of 5. Relax, then repeat. The exercise also relieves tension and helps fight sleepiness.

Inconspicuous Exercises

Four simple exercises can help relax tension and keep neck, shoulder, back, and belly muscles in tone. Try these, keeping the back straight:

Rotate shoulders, forward and backward.

Tilt head and focus eyes just below right shoulder, then stretch neck and arc head and eyes up, around, and down to just below the left shoulder. Repeat, left to right.

Very slowly, tilt head and touch left ear to left shoulder, raising it only as needed, then alternate, right ear to right shoulder. Raise both shoulders, tensed, to ears, then let the shoulders drop as low as possible.

Pull in the abdominal muscles, tighten them, and hold for a count of eight without breaking. Then relax, breathe into the abdomen, and repeat.

Source: *Body Language.*

Mild Exercises That Ease Arthritis

There's no magic cure for arthritis, the painful, degenerative joint disease. But experts believe that inactivity aggravates stiffness and makes it more difficult for arthritis victims to move.

One answer:

Exercise can cause a substantial decrease in pain within two to three weeks, if it's done regularly for 15 to 30 minutes a day. How:

Avoid violent exercises that jolt and bounce the body. Reason: They put unneeded strain on joints.

Stretching and elongating exercises, which emphasize large, sweeping movements, help most. These include a set of circular movements for the arms and rotating movements for the shoulders and neck. Important: Do mild back and side bends, which stretch the body and the length of the spine. For legs: Try deep knee bends, stretches, supine exercises with legs in the air, and walking.

Routine: It's important to do the exercises at the same time every day so the momentum of habit can override psychological resistance on difficult days.

Hot baths: Beginners should begin by exercising after a hot bath. Reason: It makes the joints more supple and less tender. Be cautious though: Too hot a bath can make you lethargic or dizzy.

Muscle setting: When a joint is so painful or stiff that it's virtually locked, flex or contract the muscle, then relax.

Tests: The alleviation of pain should be noticeable. In addition, measure the areas directly above and below the afflicted joint with a tape measure. Enlargement after several weeks means the muscle has grown bulkier—and stronger.

Source: *Buster Crabbe's Arthritis Exercise Book,* Simon and Schuster, New York.

Simple Warm-up Exercises

What trainers recommend:

Toe-touching. Bend forward from the waist, with the knees flexed slightly. Hold the stretch for 30 seconds. Let the arms hang loose, and gradually increase the amount of stretch in the leg and hamstring muscles. Don't force yourself to touch the floor.

Thigh-muscle stretch. Kneel down. Sit back on your legs. Lean as far back as is comfortable. Then extend one leg in front, and lean back further. Goal: To get your back flat on the floor.

Seated stretch. Place feet together, with knees apart. Lean forward, and grab the feet, stretching the inner thigh muscles as you do. Hold for 15 seconds. Rest 30 seconds. Repeat. Goal: Getting loose enough to touch chin to toes.

Developing flexibility is a slow process. Stop before hitting your pain threshold.

Source: *The Cardiologist's Guide to Fitness and Health Through Exercise,* Simon & Schuster, New York.

Running and Calories

How far you go, not how fast, determines the number of calories burned off. Example: A 160-pound man who runs a mile in 10 minutes and 40 seconds uses 99 calories. He burns off only 11 more calories by running twice as fast. Key factor: Your weight. A 220-pounder burns off 135 calories per mile at a 10:40 pace. A 120-pounder burns off 75 calories.

Source: *Journal of the American Medical Association.*

Calories Used per Hour In 20 Activities

Activity	Calories
Bicycling (5 MPH)	150-250
Bowling	200-250
Calisthenics	250-450
Cardplaying	75-125
Cooking	125-200
Dancing	250-450
Driving a car	75-125
Gardening	250-325
Jogging (5 MPH)	450-500
Making beds	200-250
Reading	75-125
Scrubbing floors	200-250
Skiing (downhill)	350-500
Swimming	230-325
Tennis (doubles)	250-350
TV-viewing	75-125
Typing	75-125
Walking (3 MPH)	200-250
Washing dishes	125-200
Writing	75-125

Every pound taken off is equivalent to 3,500 calories burned.

Walking Instead of Jogging

Walking can be as good as jogging for lowering cholesterol, improving general health, and reducing the risk of heart attack. Reason: Walking increases high-density lipoprotein (HDL) in the blood. (HDL is a blood component that clears the bloodstream of cholesterol rather than helping to deposit it on artery walls.)

To get the benefits of walking:

Do it regularly. At least five times a week. But it's best to do it every day if possible.

Walk briskly. A stroll will not do the job.

Take long walks, preferably at least half an hour at a time.

Walking provides psychological benefits, too:

Relieves depression. While the exact reasons for this are unknown, it's not just fresh air and the great outdoors that alleviate depression. There is a physiological effect on the brain chemistry. Current theories attribute it to amines (a chemical compound in the neurotransmitters) or endorphines (a painkiller released by the brain).

Reduces anxiety. Walking is a good constructive way to dissipate anxious energy that is not being used. Using this energy constructively makes people less tense.

Adjusts bad sleeping patterns.

Aids in building self-esteem. Brisk walks stop people from accepting the idea that their bodies are deteriorating. It shows them they can choose to be healthy.

Creates a sense of exhilaration. While people assume that a long walking regimen will tire them out, they find, instead, that they have more energy to get to work and feel less aggressive when going home. They stop barking at their spouses. In part, there's an increase in energy because of improved circulation and more oxygen in the system. Walking is a general toner for the body and mind—the whole system.

How to Buy An Exercise Treadmill

A treadmill in the home improves physical condition without a trip to a gym or a health club. Drawback: It gets monotonous.

Cost: Motorized models are priced from $450 to $1,275 (for a top-quality model).

Treadmills powered by the runner are less expensive, but not recommended. Reason: A motor-driven belt gives a more controllable workout, which makes it safer and, in the end, more efficient.

Features to evaluate:

Speed. For the young and fit, a top speed of 8 mph is recommended. Others: Start at 1.5 mph to 5 mph.

The elevation. A 5% to 10% grade range is more than enough. Anything higher isn't good for the legs. Treadmills without any elevation-adjustment force you to run longer for the same exercise benefits. But motorized adjustment of elevation is an unnecessary luxury.

Running surface. A rubber-covered smooth plate is best. Certain cheaper models have metal rollers under a rubber belt, which lends a strange feel to the running surface.

Controls. They should be accessible while running. Some models offer remote control, which is an extra feature you may want to consider.

Idea: Purchase a darkroom clock with a sweep second hand and an adjustable timer. The big luminescent dial is easier than a stopwatch to keep an eye on while exercising.

Source: *The Cardiologists' Guide to Fitness and Health Through Exercise,* by L.R. Zohman, MD, A.A. Kattus, MD, and D.G. Softness, MD, Simon & Schuster, New York.

Skipping Rope Instead of Jogging

Skipping rope is three times more effective as an exercise for the cardiovascular system than is jogging. Example: In ten minutes of skipping rope, you can achieve the health benefits of a half-hour jog. Aim: 100 skips a minute for ten minutes (each day). Recommended: A leather rope, with ball bearings in the handles, and a gym mat or other other soft surface.

This kind of exercise provides a hardy workout. Start slowly. Procedure:

The right length rope is long enough to

reach from armpit to armpit when you stand on it. The heavier the rope, the easier it is to manipulate.

Jump only high enough for the rope to slip under your feet. Land lightly on the balls of your feet. Wear sneakers or padded exercise shoes.

At first, jump easily until you feel winded. Don't exceed three minutes of jumping.

When winded, stop and walk until you are breathing normally. Then resume jumping. Point: To jump for longer and longer periods of time without resting.

Goal: 10 to 15 minutes of continuous exercise. To reach it, increase the time of continuous jumping by a minute a week.

Cool down by walking or doing stretching exercises. Caution: Check with your doctor before starting the program if you are overweight or over 35.

Don't take little jumps in between the real ones.

Vary the exercise. Jump with both feet. Then use one foot at a time.

Choosing a Scuba Diving Mask

Over 70 models of masks are available. Most important consideration: Proper fit. The mask should have a tight seal and be comfortable.

Don't buy a mask only on a friend's recommendation. The contours of a face and head are like fingerprints—everyone's are a little different.

To assure proper fit: Place the mask lens on the palm of the hand; gently press the mask to the face. Inhale through the nose. The seal should cling to the face.

If the mask passes this test, strap it on, and move the head and body vigorously to see how it feels. (This can be done at the store.)

If the fit isn't right or the mask leaks, don't rely on tightening the strap. The strap should merely keep the mask from falling off; it won't prevent leakage if the mask doesn't fit properly.

Keeping the mask out of harsh sunlight and chlorinated swimming pools will make it last for years instead of just a season. (Silicone seals last longer, but cost a great deal more.)

Scuba Diving Safety

Smart scuba divers: (1) Stay in good shape. (2) Practice in a pool. (3) Maintain equipment carefully. (4) Stay alert to changes in environment such as surf and current conditions. (5) Dive with a partner, and communicate with each other while diving. (6) Constantly monitor their location relative to the boat or beach. (7) Are willing to abort a dive if environmental or personal conditions are not right.

Buying a Bicycle

• Common myth: For top performance, a bike must have 15 or more gears and be fully equipped with all the most expensive components.

• Fact: Four to five gears are best. More just add weight and increase the chances of a breakdown. And any adequately designed components are fine. Performance depends mainly on the rider's strength and technique.

• Other guidelines for good riding:

Saddle height. When the pedal is at its lowest point, the leg should be almost fully extended. Then make minor adjustments for comfort and greatest power.

Tire pressure. Compromise between rock-hard tires that roll easily (but bumpily) and soft ones that ease road shock. Avoid maximum tire pressure for most leisurely riding. It is meant for racing on a smooth surface.

Brakes. Too sensitive an adjustment is unsafe, causing skids on steep hills and slippery pavement. Conscious pressure should be required to lock the wheels.

Shoes. Running or tennis shoes are poor choices. Best: Cycling shoes with cleats. Ped-

461

als should have toe straps. Goal: To pull up as well as push down on each pedal stroke.

Source: Ray Guest, racing and touring cyclist, writing in *Bicycling.*

• Bikes for kids. A too large bicycle is a safety hazard. Buy to fit and trade up as the child grows.

Source: *The Better Business Bureau Guide to Wise Buying,* Benjamin Co., Elmsford, NY.

Choosing a Karate School

Karate as a hobby is great for developing endurance, speed, agility, and the constructive, harmonious interplay of mind and body. But there are some injuries, usually minor, such as sprains and bruises. Beginners will be exercising muscles that ordinarily are rarely used.

There's a wide variety of types and styles. Gentlest is *Tai Chi Chuan*, a kind of boxing practiced widely in China and now here, principally for exercise and health with little thought of actual combat. A few steps up the scale is *Aikido*, a Japanese system aimed at neutralizing rather than damaging an opponent. Further up are a variety of vicious styles, featuring punching, kicking, and chopping, such as the Korean *Tae Kwan Do.*

Visit schools of each type and observe a few classes before deciding. Talk to the instructors. Least expensive introduction is a course at a community college.

Stick to well-established schools. You'll probably be required to sign up for periods of three months or more at a time. Try to avoid signing an installment contract that must be paid even if you drop out.

Improving Your Golf

Off the golf course: Practice 30 minutes a day. Technique: Spend 15 minutes with a different club each day. Aim: To perfect the han-

dling of that club and improve your confidence with it. Spend the second 15 minutes each day swinging a heavy-weighted driver. That stretches your back, shoulder, and arm muscles. Helps you stay limber.

On the golf course (physical aspect): Concentrate always on square contact with the ball. Logic: You're swinging a one-pound club to hit a 1.62 ounce ball. This requires touch and timing more than strength.

On the golf course (psychological aspect): Resist the mounting emotional pressures built into the game. Point: Each hole is guaranteed to build emotional pressure, as you aim first for the wide fairway, then for the smaller green, then finally for the tiny hole.

Many players set standards too high for their play. As a result they press harder on each succeeding hole. That's counterproductive.

Source: Pro Bob Toski writing in *Prime Time* magazine.

Warming Up for the First Tee

Most golf pros concur that the drive from the first tee is the key shot in a round. Why: The tension of anticipating the game is highest. And the shot indicates what the entire round will be like. Suggestions:

Do stretching exercises to loosen the muscles and relax the body.

Gather several clubs in your hands and swing them. Their weight makes a single club feel light. A weighted attachment for a driver serves the same purpose.

Practice shots: Hit a handful of shots with the driver. Some pros swing easily at first, others go at it as hard as they can. Object: To get a comfortable feeling for the club and ball.

Think positively. Imagine the ball flying straight down the fairway.

Best bet: Don't put everything you have into that first tee shot. Swing with about three-quarters of your power. By about the sixth tee you should be warmed up enough to be swinging at 95% to 100%.

Improved Backswings For Older Golfers

Backswings get shorter as golfers get older. When the swing gets too short, you'll lose distance, accuracy, and consistency.

Remedies:

Hold the club lightly. Reason: Too tight a grip tenses the arm and shoulder muscles and restricts the backswing.

Put more weight on your right foot, especially on full swings with woods and longer irons. Result: A head start on your swing and less weight to shift.

Turn your chin to the right (or to the left, if you're a southpaw) as you start your backswing. If it throws your timing off, cock your chin in the direction of the backswing before you swing.

Better Putting

• Accelerate through the ball. Make sure your follow-through is longer than your backswing. Practice short putts, concentrating on feeling your putter accelerate.

• Be consistent in your speed.

• To judge distance of the backswing, use your right big toe (or the left toe if you're left-handed). Take the putter back to your right big toe, accelerate the clubhead through the ball, and see how far the putt rolls. Then gauge from there how long your backswing should be for the putt you are facing, and how far inside or outside your right big toe you should take the putter back.

• Think of the swing as a pendulum.

• Strike the ball solidly with the sweet spot of the putter. To find the sweet spot, dangle the putter between your thumb and forefinger, holding it lightly and letting it swing. Then, with your other forefinger, tap along the blade until the putter head rebounds straight back. That's the spot—mark it.

• Never look up until the ball is out of your sight, or until you hear it drop into the hole.

This will keep your upper body from moving.
Source: Tom Watson, playing editor, *Golf Digest*.

• Putting error. Golfers' eyes often follow the club's backswing rather than staying on the ball. To correct this: Turn the ball so the brand name is on top. Then keep your eyes on it.

Golfing in the Rain

Clothing: Get a good rain suit (two-ply Sanforized denim cotton is the best. It's lightweight, breathes, and doesn't make noise.) A cap with a peak will keep raindrops off your glasses. Carry some extra towels, a dry shirt, and extra socks. Waterproof your shoes.

Clubs: Keep the hood over your bag and stuff a towel in it. Keep friction tape in your bag to cover the grips. (Do this before you set out, since rules prohibit altering clubs once a round has begun.)

The game: Play defensively. Hit the ball higher off the tee. Don't hit it too hard, especially with the irons. Grip down on the club, restrict your swing a little.

The course: On the greens, check the amount of water. A light film can cause putts to run farther and break less. More water: The putt will roll less and break less.

Buying Flexible Clubs

Flexible clubs should be considered by golfers now struggling with a stiff-shafted set. Flex gives more impact, and the swing is easier. Shaft guidelines:

Length of average drive (in yards)	Club shaft to buy
240 plus	X (extra stiff)
210-250	S (stiff)
175-220	R (medium)
160-185	A (flexible)
under 160	L (ladies)

Cleaning Golf Clubs

Rubber grips seldom need more than a periodic washing with a liquid detergent, followed by a thorough rinsing with lukewarm water. If the grips are getting slick, use a scouring powder with a small hand or fingernail brush and brush vertically. Very slick grips may require replacement.

Leather grips are wetted with lukewarm water, then brushed with a liquid detergent. Place the soapy grip under running water until all the bubbles disappear. Then pat dry with an old, lint-free towel. Apply a leather conditioner or preservative. Let dry overnight.

Shafts made of chrome just require a quick wipe with a damp rag. Then a light coat of metal polish or wax for winter storing. For light surface rust: Buff off blemishes with extremely fine (.000) steel wool. On old graphite shafts: Follow the buffing with a coat of furniture or carnuba paste wax.

Wood heads should have their faceplates carefully cleaned with a brush and water. Follow immediately by a thorough drying and a coat or two of furniture wax. To protect against wintertime moisture: Lightly buff head with .000 steel wool. Then, with your finger, quickly apply a light coat of polyurethane.

Iron heads are quickly cleaned by soaking them for a few minutes in water. Then follow with a vigorous brushing. Use .000 steel wool to eliminate rust. Next: Apply a coat of chrome polish or wax.

Don't forget to clean the golf bag. Shake out loose grass and dirt. Wash with a liquid detergent. Use saddle soap on zippers for smooth sliding.

Source: Ralph Maltby, writing in *Golf Magazine*.

A Golfer's Diet

Eat about two or three hours before you play a game of golf. This gives your body time to digest the meal. Insight: The digestive process draws blood to the stomach, thus denying it to the muscles needed for playing golf.

Best: Fruits, vegetables, all natural foods that are moderate in calories but high in carbohydrates (grains, seeds). Point: Carbohydrates deliver jolts of energy for the golf round.

Shun hot dogs and candy bars. They pack little nutritive value and provoke thirst.

What to drink:

In hot weather, take in enough fluids to maintain your normal body weight. Best drink: Cold water. Mineral water is good since it supplies minerals lost through heavy perspiration.

If golf is to follow a long plane ride, drink plenty of liquids during the flight. Why: The dry air of a pressurized plane cabin dehydrates you faster.

Avoid salt tablets. The body conserves salt even during periods of heavy perspiration. And consuming too much salt contributes to hypertension.

Better Tennis

• It's possible to change the way the set is going. Start by telling yourself a joke. Remind yourself that you aren't sick or in jail, but playing a game. Concentrate on the basics: Hop, bounce. Get your arm back. Keep your eye on the ball. Turn your shoulders, and hit the ball in front of you. Follow through. Think through each serve before hitting it. Slow down the pace of the match. Concentrate on each point, not the game.

• Backhand problem. Too often, players come in too close on a high bounce. Result: A cramped stroke. Practice by staying far away from the ball, and reaching out wide to the side. The exaggeration will lead to correct balance.

Source: Dennis Van der Meer, tennis coach, writing in *World Tennis*.

• When at the net in tennis, imagine yourself as a goaltender in hockey. Like a goalie, move to cut down on the opponent's angle of attack. Crouch slightly, ready to spring in any direction. Keep your weight forward and be alert for shots that come right at you. Insight:

have an idea where you want to put the ball, then allow your instincts to guide you.

• Blind spot. Tennis players often lose their eyesight very briefly as they follow the flight of the ball into the sun or strong artificial lighting. Cause: A momentary bleaching of the eye's visual purple, a chemical in the cone of the retina. What to do: Take the ball on the bounce and lob back. This gives you four seconds before the ball is returned. That's enough time for your eyesight to return to normal.

• Players who hold the racket with both hands are vulnerable to shots hit directly at them. Why: They must back away from the ball quickly for their two-handed shot to be effective. Result: Much of a two-hander's power is dissipated. Note: This strategy also works when serving. Aim your service directly at the two-handed player.

• Oversized tennis rackets are not a form of cheating. That's the opinion of the USTA, which authorizes their use. Point: Even with a larger racket, the player must develop skill to become outstanding. Contrast: A golf ball recently designed with dimples which stopped it from slicing or hooking was declared illegal. The reason: it allows a hacker to always drive straight and true down the fairway. In tennis, oversized rackets help some players some of the time, but not all players all of the time.

• Tennis warm-up. The fencer's stretch: Place right foot three feet in front of left, with right knee bent and left leg straight. Lean with both hands on the right knee while stretching the left leg as far back as possible. At first, just stretch and maintain balance for as long as possible. Later, add a gentle rocking motion. **Source:** *Lifegain,* by Robert F. Allen, Ph.D., Appleton-Century-Crofts, New York.

• Baseline shots. Hit the tennis ball high over the net. Professionals can skim the tennis net from the baseline, but for most players, doing so is a low-percentage shot. Instead: Hit the ball from the baseline so it crosses the net with several feet to spare. Direction and top spin are both easier this way.

• Tennis players who eat properly are less likely to suffer from muscle fatigue or cramps. Key: Eat enough carbohydrates (in the form of bread, pasta, or other starches) to create glycogen for the muscles. Avoid: Sugar, dextrose, or other very sweet foods. Firm rule: Don't play tennis within two hours after a heavy meal. **Source:** *Tennis.*

Choosing a Tennis Racket

If racket grip is too small, the racket will twist on off-center hits. Too large, racket can't be held firmly enough. Right grip: Hold racket as if you're shaking hands (thumb at about a 45 degree angle to edge of handle). Index finger of other hand should fit snugly into space between fingertips and heel of hand. Thumb and index finger of grip hand should almost touch.

Tennis Ball Care

The average shelf life of a sealed can of pressurized balls is one to two years, depending on the manufacturer and on storage conditions.

To determine if a ball is lively enough to be used, stand next to the net and release the ball from about six feet up. It should bounce nearly level with the top of the net on a hard court, a few inches lower on a soft court.

Professional competition: New balls are put into play after the first seven games and every nine games thereafter. In amateur tournaments, players are usually given a new can of balls at the start of a match. These are used through two sets. If a third is required, another can of fresh balls is provided.

Note: Ball preservers work, but are usually not cost-effective.

Preventing Tennis Elbow

Most important factor in preventing tennis elbow is your swing. While pros usually develop the pain on the inside of the elbow (from their service), recreational players get the condition on the outside of the arm (from the backhand).

Solution: Switch to a two-handed stroke. Also: Be especially careful not to turn the wrist upward as you come through the backhand stroke. And keep the elbow firm at the time of impact. Other preventives:

Racket: Metal rather than wood; flexible rather than rigid; light head rather than heavy; as large a handle as is comfortable, perhaps a 4⅝ -inch grip if you have a big enough hand. Don't string with nylon; choose 16-gauge gut, and avoid tight stringing—52 or 54 pounds will be the right tension for most amateur players.

Balls: Avoid pressureless balls. Beware of heavier balls, particularly the Italian imports. Be careful if you are vacationing in the mountains about using balls bought for sea-level play; they will bounce faster, forcing you to stroke before you've gotten your body ready.

Courts: A problem only if you switch to a faster court from a slow clay surface that you are used to. Makes you prone to taking the strokes late.

Source: *Physicians & Sportsmedicine.*

Better Skiing

• Skiers who tuck their tails forward improve both balance and ankle flex. To tuck, simply pull forward and upward on the perineum (the exact base of the torso, located between the anus and genitals) until the upper-thigh muscles lightly engage. The tucked bottom redistributes and realigns the center of gravity. Also, the ankles will flex naturally and not straighten as they do when the rear sticks out.

• Men generally have broader shoulders and slimmer hips than women. This gives men a higher center of gravity. When skiing, men usually fall forward while women tend to fall backward. Adjustment: Ski boot heels should be raised for women and lowered for men.

Getting into Shape for the Skiing Season

Adopt the standard sit-up exercise with four simple changes: (1) Keep feet on the floor, not hooked under something. (2) Fold your arms across your chest (forcing you to use stomach muscles to lift yourself, rather than pushing with your head). (3) Tuck in your chin. (4) Do not come all the way up to a sitting position (where there's virtually no muscle activity), but only about 8 inches off the floor; hold yourself there; lower back to the floor slowly.

Bargains for Skiers

Ski shops normally run summer sales, lasting until late August. Ski clothes and equipment (some bought specifically for these sales), are discounted 30% to 40% from last winter's prices.

Smart equipment buying:

Swaps: They are organized by ski clubs and local stores to let skiers exchange used equipment. They are especially useful for growing children who need larger sizes each year and whose outgrown equipment and clothes are almost like new.

Consumer ski shows, held in September and October in major cities, feature swaps. Bring your used equipment early, so it can be sold by the end of the show. Expect the sponsoring club or store to charge a commission of 15%.

Before swapping: Learn what equipment will be best for you. Read up on all the equipment in ski magazines. Know what is top of the line and what is ordinary so you can gauge prices.

Boots that fit are the most difficult thing to find. If you find a boot at a swap that nearly fits, go to a good ski shop for a refitting.

Bindings are very important: If you are going to spend money on something new, spend it on bindings. Those five years old or more are totally obsolete. New ones ensure much greater safety.

Join a ski club in your area: They sponsor swaps, offer low prices on some equipment and get special group rates at resorts. A $20 membership may save hundreds of dollars. And they are the center for inexpensive transportation.

Saving on ski trips:

Off-season rates: They're available pre-Christmas, January (when most people are strapped by Christmas bills), and April. You can get more for your money, and the bars, restaurants, and ski lifts are less crowded.

Price breaks are given at some resorts if you begin your vacation on a Monday or Friday morning instead of the weekend. They prefer to avoid overcrowding on weekends. Airlines have less expensive midweek flights, too.

Pick a package at a nonglamourous resort, especially if you're heading for the Rockies. Vail and Aspen packages cost 15% to 50% more than similar ones in other Rocky Mountain resorts (for example Breckinridge). In the less expensive resorts, you can save on ski lessons, entertainment, food, and lift tickets, as well as hotel accommodations.

Source: Otto Tschudi, director of skiing, and Kent Myers, vice president of marketing, Winter Park, Box 36, Winter Park, CO 80482.

Buying Waxless Cross-Country Skis

The new cross-country skis free users from the time-consuming and inexact chore of preparing and waxing them. No matter what the conditions, the skis grip the snow better. Now available:

Pattern-based skis: They have a series of small embossed shapes. Work best in wetter, consolidated snow. Popular brands: Omnitrak, Multistep, Crown.

Free-base skis: Smooth-surfaced. They are quieter, easier to turn with, and waxable, if need be. Free refers to a combination of Teflon and plastics. Freewax combines fiberglass, epoxy, and plastics. These skis work well in packed, dry snow and wetter, transitional snow.

Mohair strips: Best in looser, cold snow and on ice. The nap of the fur stands straight up to grip the snow when the ski is pushed backward and flattens out when the ski is pushed forward for gliding.

Mica skis: Mica particles are added at a slight backward angle to fuse the polyethylene. Work best in looser, colder snows. Extremely durable.

Source: *Ski.*

17

Education

Helping Your Child Plan a Career

While many adults feel uncertain about helping their children with careers, there are ways to offer assistance.

Recommendations:

Recognize that both sons and daughters pass through various career attitudes. Most youngsters spend their childhood believing that they can become anything, from firefighter to the president of the U.S.

During every phase, you must treat your child as a growing person. Don't snuff out the child's interests with your prejudices. Allow exploration and curiosity about all sorts of work.

Promote a sense of worthiness in your offspring. Give them the chance to make choices, even if they seem to be bad ones.

After the age of 17, your child considers a career realistically. Help your child to be practical. But don't stifle experimentation. After all, we spend most of our lives at work. We should find a job we enjoy.

Source: *How to Help Your Child Plan a Career,* by Dean L. Hummel and Carl McDaniels, Acropolis Books, Washington, DC.

How to Get More Out of College

Some students get more out of college than others. They are more assured, speak up in class often, are involved in many campus activities, and establish close relationships with their professors.

Quieter, more diffident students often do well in their studies and enjoy college life generally. But they may be hesitant to join in class discussions and never get to know their professors except on a formal, classroom basis. They are missing an exciting part of their college experience, which could have an influence on other aspects of campus life.

Specific ways to enrich your college years:

Recognize that most college professors choose their profession because they like teaching and working with young people. They are eager to share their knowledge. Respect them, but don't be awed by them.

Don't be afraid to ask questions. Ignorance is no sin. You are in college to learn more.

Use your teachers' conference hours. You will be welcomed. More conference time is unused than used.

Some professors are better teachers than others. Most have spent many years learning the art of scholarship, but very few have much training in the art of teaching. The dull classroom teacher may be a warm, exciting instructor in an informal, one-to-one situation, however.

Good teachers are still learning—they are adult students. Approach them on an adult level by showing that you are taking as much responsibility for your education as they are. The teacher can open intellectual doors for you, but you must walk through.

Establish a personal relationship with at least one or two of your teachers. Building on the interests you have in common can add intellectual spice to your college experience and generate practical benefits when you are looking for a job or applying to graduate school.

College Credits Without Classes or Tuition Costs

Several educational services now give college credits to students who pass examinations rather than take courses. These credits are recognized by 2,100 colleges and universities. They're not the same as mail-order diploma mills.

Result: If you pass the exam, you receive credits exactly as if you had passed a course covering the same material.

What's available:

College-Level Examination Program (CLEP) sponsored by the Educational Testing Service. CLEP offers 50 exams in subjects ranging from business to science and the humanities. For details: CLEP, the College Board, Box 1822, Princeton, NJ 08540 (609-921-9000).

Proficiency Examination Program (PEP), sponsored by the American College Testing Program. Gives exams on business administration subjects. For more information: If you live in New York State, contact College Proficiency-Regents External Degree Examination Program, Cultural Education Center, Albany, NY 12230. Elsewhere: ACT PEP Study Guides, Box 168, Iowa City, IA 52240.

Also available: Advanced placement examinations, for students now in high school. Information: AP Exams, Box 977-IS, Princeton, NJ 08540.

Exam credits offer a shortcut to adults returning to college and they save money.

Caution: A few colleges charge tuition for exam credits. They should be avoided.

Source: *Getting College Course Credits by Examination to Save $$$* by Gene R. Hawes, McGraw-Hill, New York.

Getting Into College

Visit at least 10 colleges before applying. Don't start applying later than the junior year of high school.

Apply to at least 10 colleges.

Don't visit during a weekend or holiday. You'll see empty buildings.

Have the student attend some classes.

Seek out the head of the department in which the student has a special interest to discuss the program.

Have the student write an autobiography. Include background, aims, achievements, and ambitions. It will tell the admissions director what he needs to know about the applicant.

Source: *Financing College Education*, by Kenneth and Irene Kohl, Harper & Row, New York.

'Beating' the Scholastic Aptitude Test

The Scholastic Aptitude Test (SAT) is designed to measure a student's aptitude for college work. It is not an intelligence test, although good students are likely to do better. But with preparation any student can measure up to his full capacity.

Important: The SAT consists of four 30-

minute sections, two verbal and two mathematical. It is critical that the student make efficient use of the allotted time to get as much done as possible.

How to prepare:

Read the instructions for each section in the preparatory booklet supplied by the College Board. They are identical to those on the test itself. Understanding them in advance will give the student more time to concentrate on the actual test questions, rather than on the instructions.

Take the complete SAT test in the preparatory booklet within the obligatory time limit. The score will indicate how much practice the student needs.

Concentrated practice in taking tests can help some students to sharpen their test-taking skills, which will save them time when it counts. Math refresher courses almost always help. Verbal improvement is more difficult.

Where to go for help:

A number of SAT preparation guides provide good advice and sample practice questions. Cram courses can help, too, although not as much as is often claimed. Recommended: Ask for the names and addresses of former students who the service claims benefited from the course.

On the test:

Quickly go through the questions. Answer all those to which the answer is apparent. Use the time that's left to go back and figure out the other questions.

Don't be afraid to guess—if the odds are favorable. All questions are multiple-choice, with four or five possible answers. One point is given for each right answer, and one-third or one-quarter of a point is lost for each wrong answer. Unanswered questions don't count either way. If the student is not sure of the right answer, but can eliminate two or more, the odds are that he'll stand to gain more by guessing.

Above all: Don't panic. Unlike students in the 1960s and 1970s, the present generation is going to college in a buyer's market. Except for some top schools, the admission doors are open wider than ever.

Coaching for Scholastic Aptitude Test

The controversy over the effectiveness of coaching to raise Scholastic Aptitude Test (SAT) scores for college applicants heats up.

Background: The testing service that gives the SAT has always claimed coaching doesn't improve scores significantly. Why: SATs are supposed to measure fundamental scholastic abilities. That is, the potential of the student, rather than past achievement.

Problem: Surveys indicate that coaching can increase SAT scores. Gains of as much as 100 points are reported. Since many colleges rely on SATs in selecting entrants, boosting the numbers is vitally important to students.

Where the situation stands: The testing service now admits that coaching can heighten scores. But, they feel, not by any dramatic amounts. The service's conclusions:

Short-term drilling of fewer than 10 hours has almost no positive effect.

Students who put 20 hours into each subject can raise scores by 12 points in the verbal section and 20 in the math.

After 50 hours of coaching scores might rise by 20 to 30 points. These increases are in addition to the typical 10- to 20-point gains made by students who take the SATs a second time.

A law of diminishing returns sets in after 50 hours.

Question: Are the time and effort of coaching worth it?

The testing service continues to be skeptical. But those who have raised their scores significantly insist that the effort pays off.

How Top Private Colleges Select Their Students

The most selective colleges do not apply the same admissions standards to all applicants. They seek variety and sort their applicants, usually into five categories. This means that applicants don't compete for admission with all the others who have applied, but only with those in their category. Different colleges give varied weight to each category.

Intellectuals. Top academic records are likely to get applicants admitted anywhere. Those who have taken tough courses in high school, graduated at or near the top of the class, and score well on the standardized tests are almost certain to be accepted no matter what other qualities they do or do not have.

Specially talented. Varsity-level athletes predominate in this group. If the athletic department is looking for a fullback, a long-distance runner, or a hurdler, the admissions office is likely to cooperate. Occasionally an exceptionally talented artist, musician, sculptor, or poet will be given preference.

All in the family. Private colleges depend on alumni for financial support and for time and effort spent on behalf of the institution. Family traditions within a school are highly valued. A parent, grandparent, or close relative who has been a loyal and generous supporter of the college gives the applicant an edge. It's still necessary to meet the college's academic standards. But most colleges are generous in judging the applicants from kinfolk of alumni.

Affirmative action. In recent years, most top colleges have placed a strong emphasis on the recruitment of academically competent blacks and other minority-group members. They have considered it an obligation. Students from disadvantaged backgrounds are often judged more on their potential than on their previous academic accomplishments.

All-American boys and girls. This is by far the largest group. It includes all the bright, mannerly, good-hearted kids who are competent in many things, but aren't outstanding in any single area. Because of the large number of applicants in this category, the competition is tough. Note: This group makes up the largest percentage of all those admitted to the top private colleges.

Applicants who are bright, but who don't get into a top school, shouldn't despair. There are many excellent colleges that will accept them and provide a top-notch education.

Also: That kind of education will be just as good as, perhaps better than, the one offered by a school thought to be superior.

Source: *Playing The Private College Admissions Game,* by Richard Moll, Penguin Books, New York.

If the College of Your Choice Turns You Down

If an applicant has not been accepted at a preferred private college, there is little that can be done. Reason: The applicant's admissions folder was carefully reviewed by three or four admissions committee members, who made a decision. But don't give up.

Options:

Review the application and the instructions for filling it out. Was something that could have significantly affected the committee's decision left out? The applicant's special interests? Achievements? Talents or skills? Also: The application process started in the fall, when the senior year of high school was barely under way. What has the applicant done during the last six months? Built a computer? Raised the grade point average? Started playing French horn with the local symphony? All of these are significant additions to the application. Inform the college of them, and ask for a review.

Call the admissions director and ask: Why didn't I get in? Listen carefully for specifics. Example: Your grades were high, but you didn't take enough tough courses. More likely the director will offer general comments, but will give you a clue to the decision, not wanting to get into an argument about specific issues of judgment.

Go to a college that has offered admission. Strategy: Achieve a top academic record during the freshman year. Then: Reapply to the first-choice college as a sophomore transfer. The admissions folder will still be on file. And the continuing interest in the school will get the applicant a first-consideration rating among transfer applicants.

Take a year off. Chances are that the applicant followed all the admissions procedures correctly but has a record that looks exactly like many other applicants' records. Nothing sets it apart. A year working in a public service job, learning new skills in a private-sector job, or traveling and studying may well make the second application more attractive.

Although an application has not been accepted, the person should not feel rejected. Admissions officers in schools where the competition is murderous say that the thousand applications of those under the acceptance cutoff mark look so much like many of those who were accepted that it is impossible to tell them apart. Chance just worked against them.

How to Get into Medical School

Undergraduates who want to go to medical school must know what factors are important in getting in. The 126 medical schools in the U.S. and Puerto Rico admit 16,500 first-year students out of as many as 36,000 applicants. The number of applicants has been declining in recent years, but the competition is still stiff.

Since most students apply to 10 or more schools, a typical medical school is likely to receive 6,000 applications for a class of 180. About 600 applicants are selected for interviews. Here are the bases on which they are chosen.

Grade Point Averge (GPA): An admissions committee's first question is whether an applicant can succeed academically. A student's grade point average is the best measure of academic competence. Many schools compute an overall GPA and a science GPA separately. Both are important.

Medical College Admissions Test: Since no admissions committee can be familiar with all the colleges that applicants come from, the Medical College Admissions Test (MCAT), required by nearly all medical schools, is the equalizer. If an applicant's GPA is a little low, a high MCAT can make the difference, especially if the undergraduate college's recommendations are strong.

Recommendations: Letters from former professors are read very carefully. If they are strongly supportive and specific about the student's competence and character, they can make a significant difference. Before asking for a recommendation, a student should ask whether the professor can give a clearly positive report.

The interview and essay: Medicine is a helping profession that requires commitment and compassion, as well as academic competence. The essay and interview are designed to reveal the kind of human being the applicant is. The admissions committee wants to know whether an applicant has the qualities that will make a good doctor. Qualities: Commitment to the profession, ability to communicate, compassion for people, motivation to complete a demanding course of study. The more tangible evidence an applicant can offer from past activities in sports, social activities, jobs, and home life, the better.

Undergraduate schools: A degree from a top private college may give an applicant a slight edge, but not much. It is most likely to be helpful if an applicant's GPA is a little low. A student's course of study is examined for breadth, as well as for science courses. Doctors don't spend their lives in a laboratory. Thus, a grounding in the humanities and social sciences is important. No matter how high a student's GPA is, if there are too many easy courses on the record, the response will be negative.

Dealing with rejection: If an applicant is not accepted, there is always next year. If your GPA or MCAT scores are too low, spend the next year raising them. If your academic record is fine, but other applicants are given preference, spend the year working in a hospital or other helping profession to prove your commitment to serving people.

More Information: *Medical School Admissions Requirements: U.S.A. and Canada,* Assn. of American Medical Colleges, 1 Dupont Circle NW, Washington, DC 20036, and *Getting into Medical School,* by S.J. Brown, MD, Barron's Educational Services, Inc., Woodbury, NY 11797.

Outstanding Non-Ivy League Colleges

There are many high-quality institutions that are less well known nationally. They welcome students from other parts of the country. Worth looking into:

Bowdoin (Brunswick, ME, 25 miles northeast of Portland). A top-quality liberal arts college for men, now coed. More than half its graduates go to graduate or professional school.

Carleton (Northfield, MN, 40 miles south of Minneapolis/St. Paul). A coed, liberal arts college notable for its outstanding faculty and scholars.

Claremont Men's (Claremont, CA, 35 miles from Los Angeles). A coed liberal arts college. It places special emphasis on economics and political science to prepare students for careers in law, government, and business. Benefits: Cross-registration with five other colleges in the Claremont area.

Colgate (Hamilton, NY, 38 miles southeast of Syracuse). Prestigious liberal-arts college for men, now coed. Traditionally has trained students for business and the professions.

Davidson (Davidson, NC, a small town 20 miles north of Charlotte). One of the most academically-oriented liberal arts colleges in the region, more than half of its graduates go to graduate or professional school. Church-related, two terms of religion are required.

Duke (Durham, NC). One of the top universities in the South. Two-thirds of its graduates go on to graduate or professional school.

Franklin and Marshall (Lancaster, PA, 60 miles west of Philadelphia). For many years a quality liberal arts college for men, now coed. Emphasis: Preparation for law, business, the sciences.

Georgetown (Washington, DC). Founded as a Jesuit college for men, now coed. The School of Foreign Service and College of Arts and Sciences are very high quality. A high proportion of graduates go into business or law. Religious studies are required.

Grinnell (Grinnell, IA, 55 miles east of Des Moines). A small, highly-respected, coed, liberal arts college. More than half of its graduates go into business, law, or medicine.

Hamilton (Clinton, NY, a small town 9 miles from Utica). For many years a small liberal arts college for men, now coed. Traditionally, it has prepared students for careers in law, business, and medicine.

Middlebury (Middlebury, VT, 40 miles south of Burlington). It has a high reputation for programs in languages and literature. Greatest number of students major in the social sciences. There is a strong student interest in sports like skiing and mountain-climbing.

University of North Carolina at Chapel Hill (25 miles northwest of Raleigh). The first state university in the country, its College of Arts and Sciences has a nationwide reputation.

Oberlin (Oberlin, OH, 35 miles southwest of Cleveland). A highly esteemed, coed, liberal arts college, which combines strong academic programs with an eminent conservatory of music.

Pomona (Claremont, CA, 35 miles from Los Angeles). The oldest of the Claremont-area colleges. Coed. One of the most eminent of West Coast colleges. Benefit: Cross-registration with other Claremont colleges.

Rensselaer Polytechnic Institute (Troy, NY). The oldest engineering school in the country. It now admits women to its high-quality student body, but is still predominantly male.

Washington University (St. Louis, MO). A major midwestern institution. It includes five high-quality schools and colleges. It sends 75% of its graduates to graduate and professional schools.

More information: *Guide to American Colleges*, by Cass and Birnbaum, Harper & Row, New York.

Finding Good, Inexpensive Colleges

Today, more families are looking for good low-cost schools. There are still some bargains around.

In general: Tuition and fees are lowest at

public institutions in the Southwest and West. Private schools are less expensive in the South and Southwest. For both public and private institutions, they are highest in the Northeast.

Private colleges: Although they are more expensive than public colleges, they offer more financial aid to a greater number of students. This can cancel out the difference in costs between the private institutions and public colleges.

Best bet: State college and universities. Start with your home state. Reason: All states add a substantial fee to the tuition charges to out-of-state students.

State universities: They usually enjoy more prestige than state colleges. And they are only slightly more expensive.

State colleges: They vary widely in quality, ranging from excellent to marginal. Look closely at faculty, academic programs, and facilities. Some have developed strong programs and facilities in special areas. Other schools were founded to concentrate on particular fields of study.

California. Humboldt University has an unusual School of Natural Resources, offering studies in fisheries, oceanography, forestry, wildlife management, watershed management, and natural resources. California State University in Fresno has one of the best-equipped agricultural plants in the West.

New York. State University of New York (SUNY) College at Purchase is a liberal arts school that focuses on the visual and performing arts. SUNY College at Cortland is highly regarded for its physical education program.

Two-year community colleges: They are designed to provide higher education for a local geographical area and rarely provide residential facilities.

The least expensive way to get a four-year college education: Live at home and attend a local community college for two years while completing basic required courses for a degree. Then transfer to a state college or university for the last two years.

Caution: Check with your state college and university system to make sure that credits earned at the two-year college are accepted by the senior institutions.

Canadian Colleges: Quality Education at Bargain Prices

Canada offers quality education in the humanities, the professions, and in business at a fraction of the cost of U.S. universities. There's also something to be said for the broadening experience of life in another country—even another country as close to the United States as Canada.

Canada has no private universities in the sense we have. All Canadian universities are supported by provincial governments. Private funds are added.

College applications are made the same way as in the U.S. Students accepted by a school in Canada, however, must supply proof of adequate funds for the school year. Students heading for schools in Quebec must also be accepted by the provincial government.

Language: Despite controversy in Canada over language requirements, only three Canadian universities are bilingual (Laurentian University of Sudbury, University of Ottawa, and the College of St. Anne in Church Point, Nova Scotia). The others either teach in English or French, as noted below.

A fact sheet for prospective foreign students, along with other information and a complete listing of the available universities, is obtainable at the Information Division, Association of Universities and Colleges in Canada, 151 Slater Street, Ottawa, Ontario KLP 5N1. For a detailed breakdown of education costs write Information Division, Statistics Canada, Education, Science & Culture Costs, Ottawa, Ontario K1A 0T6.

The following are some of Canada's oldest and best known universities, going roughly from west to east.

British Columbia
U. of British Columbia
Vancouver, B.C.
V6T 1W5 (English)

Alberta
University of Alberta
Edmonton, Alberta
T6G 2E1 (English)

Saskatchewan
University of Regina
Regina, Saskatchewan
S4S OR2 (English)

U. of Saskatchewan
Saskatoon, Sasketchewan
S7N 0WO (English)

Manitoba
University Of Manitoba
Fort Garry Campus
Winnipeg, Manitoba
R 3T 2N2 (English)

Ontario
Laurentian U. of Sudbury
935 Ramsey Lake Road
Sudbury, Ontario
P3E 2C6 (bilingual)

University of Ottawa
Ottawa, Ontario
K1N 6N5 (bilingual)

University of Toronto
Toronto, Ontario
M5S 1A1 (English)

University of Waterloo
200 University Avenue W.
Waterloo, Ontario
N2L 3G1 (English)

U. of Western Ontario
1151 Richmond Street
London, Ontario
N6A 3K7 (English)

Quebec
Universite Laval
Cite Universitaire
Quebec, Quebec
G1K 7P4 (French)

McGill University
Montreal, Quebec
H3C 3G1 (English)

Universite de Montreal
C.P. 6128
Montreal, Quebec
H3T 1J4 (French)

New Brunswick
U. of New Brunswick
Fredericton, N.B.
E3B 5A3 (English)

Nova Scotia
College Sainte-Anne
Church Point, Nova Scotia
BOW 1MO (bilingual)

Nova Scotia Agricultural
Truro, Nova Scotia
B2N 5E3 (English)

Nova Scotia College
  of Art and Design
6152 Coburg Road
Halifax, Nova Scotia
B3J 1N6 (English)

Nova Scotia Tech. Coll.
Halifax, Nova Scotia
B3A 2X4 (English)

Prince Edward Island
University of
  Prince Edward Island
Charlottetown, P.E.I.
C1A 4P3 (English)

Newfoundland
Memorial University
  of Newfoundland
St. John's, Newfoundland
A1C 5S7 (English)

The Best Undergraduate Business Schools

The universities of Pennsylvania and Michigan are the best undergraduate business schools, according to a poll of business school deans and key personnel managers. Criteria: Faculty and academic repute, student body and curriculum quality, finances, performance of graduates. Next best in order: California (Berkeley), Indiana, Texas, Illinois, Ohio State, Virginia, NYU, MIT, Washington, Southern Cal. Missing but accounted for: Big ones such as Harvard, Stanford, Columbia, Chicago and Northwestern, which offer only graduate business programs.

Source: Pollsters J.D. Hunger and T.L. Wheelan, University of Virginia, Charlottesville, VA 22903.

The Best Graduate Business Schools

Chief executive officers of the country's largest companies ranked business schools as sources of talent for their own companies in the following order (the percentage indicates how many chose that school as number one):

1. Harvard (33%)
2. Stanford (18%)
3. Pennsylvania/Wharton (7%)
4. Michigan (5%)
5. Dartmouth/Tuck (5%)
6. Chicago (4%)
7. Texas (4%)
8. Northwestern (3%)
9. MIT/Sloan (3%)
10. Purdue (2%)
11. Columbia (1%)

Stacked deck: A Master of Business Administration from Harvard is the most widely held degree among the participants themselves.

Nearly 60% of those surveyed think MBAs contribute more to management than non-MBAs. But 40% rank MBAs and non-MBAs as making equal contributions. In industrial companies, the split is almost 50-50.

Source: *The Chief Executive, Background and Attitude Profiles*, a report by Arthur Young Executive Resource Consultants, 277 Park Ave., New York 10017.

An MBA by Mail

Syracuse University offers the country's only accredited MBA degree that can be earned by independent study. Problem: Students must appear on the school's upstate New York campus for the first eight days of each trimester for orientation. Solution: A number of students who live a distance from Syracuse coordinate their business travel schedules with enrollment in selective trimesters. About 50 credit hours are needed to complete the program, depending on previous education and job experience.

College Budget Plans

As college costs soar, parents are becoming increasingly receptive to programs that promise to make meeting those costs less painful. But are these plans worth the price?

For example, one company offers a monthly budget plan. It is not a loan. Rather, it is a forced savings plan. You get a book of payment coupons and make monthly payments to the tuition plan. It accumulates your money and then makes direct payment, on your behalf, to your child's college twice a year.

Direct cost: A $25 initial fee, and a 50-cent charge for each payment. A four-year, 48-payment plan would bring the total cost to $49.

Indirect cost: More important is the lost interest on your savings. Under a $5,000 yearly tuition plan, for example, semiannual payments of $2,500 would be made to the school. The average balance over the year in your tuition account would be half that. Assuming a very conservative, simple-interest rate of 6%, without compounding, that sum would earn $75 a year, or $300 over four years.

The total direct and indirect cost of having a fund manage your money would be at least $349. It would be greater if the college cost exceeded $5,000 a year and if the lost interest rate were higher than 6%.

Alternative: Assuming you are paying college bills out of current income rather than from accumulated savings, it would be wiser to be your own tuition fund. Make monthly payments into your savings or money-fund account. There are no fees, and you keep the interest.

Your tax adviser can suggest ways to reduce or eliminate taxes on that interest. One possibility: Put the account in your child's name. Reason: Parents can jointly give tax-free gifts of up to $20,000 to each of their children each year, and to anyone else they may choose.

Insurance: The tuition plan offers group term life insurance to an insurable parent to fund completion of the plan if the parent dies before making final payment. The insurance amount decreases with each monthly payment, and the cost is 50 cents for each $1,000 of initial coverage. Example: A $20,000, four-year plan requires $20,000 of insurance initially, and the four-year cost is $480, at $10 per month.

If educational expenses are not already part of your family's life insurance program, consider cheaper insurance from companies promoting low-cost term plans.

Advantages of Not Declaring a Student as Your Dependent

When a student is independent of parental support, only the student's income is considered in determining financial need and, consequently, the level of financial aid. Parental income is not a factor.

Achieving independent status can be a complicated question because federal and state governments, as well as individual colleges and universities, have different regulations governing their financial-aid programs. All are cautious because some parents who are able to pay for their children's education try to have them declared independent to save money.

Three basic questions are asked in determining qualification for every federal financial-aid program:

Were you declared a dependent on your parent's income tax return last year?

Did you live with your parents for more than six weeks last year?

Did you receive more than $750 from your parents last year?

State and institutional regulations vary from federal requirements.

Other variations:

In some states, more than one year of independence from parental support may be required.

Some colleges and universities take family income into consideration even though the student has achieved independent status under federal and state regulations.

Some universities will not allow a student to acquire independent status after enrolling as a family dependent.

Under new federal regulations, married students are assumed to be independent if they satisfy the three basic requirements for the current year.

Caution: Federal and state regulations are subject to frequent change because of political pressure. Institutional regulations remain more consistent.

Best advice: If the need to obtain independent status during a college career is foreseen, check current college and state regulations before enrollment in the school.

Which Colleges Give the Most Scholarships

The most expensive schools offer the widest array of scholarships. Reason: They are the best endowed colleges in the country.

The richest 20: Harvard, Stanford, Yale, Columbia, Princeton, University of California, Massachusetts Institute of Technology, Rochester Institute of Technology, Chicago, Cornell, New York University, Northwestern, Rice, Washington University (St. Louis), Cal Tech, University of Pennsylvania, Johns Hopkins, Dartmouth, Wellesley, University of Delaware.

Source: *Don't Miss Out,* by Robert Leider, Octameron, Alexandria, VA.

Tax Treatment of Scholarships

Scholarship funds from an educational institution or a fellowship grant are generally not taxable. Among the exempt items: Tuition, matriculation, and other fees; family allowances; room, board, and other living expenses; allowances for travel, research, clerical help, and equipment.

Limitations: Recipient must be a degree candidate, or the exemption is limited to $300 per month. Amounts paid for past, present, or future services, such as teaching, are taxable. Employer-paid scholarships are taxable if the student must return to the employer when he finishes school.

Certain student loan programs erase all or part of an educational loan, if the student performs certain services for a period of time in certain geographical areas. The discharge of such a debt does not result in taxable income to the student.

Financial Aid for Middle-Class College Students

Parents and students faced with the problem of financing a college education often are not aware of the many sources of financial aid available. Nearly everyone, no matter what the family income, can get some aid. Best advice: Start your search for funds early.

Source of information and aid:

College financial-aid officers. They are the best single source of information. Talk with them when visiting a college. Most colleges make some scholarship and loan funds available to students. The colleges also administer funds that come from federal programs.

The Scholarship Search Company. This firm has the largest scholarship information data bank in the country. The application form requests detailed information about the student, which is then matched against the specifications of more than 250,000 scholarships. There are scholarships reserved for an amazing variety of individuals, ranging from golf caddies and newspaper carriers to members of religious sects and ethnic groups. Many of these scholarships go unclaimed because eligible students are not aware of them.

For more information: Contact the Scholarship Search Co., 1775 Broadway, New York 10019.

State scholarship programs. Every state makes some financial aid available to college students. A high school counselor can tell you what agency administers the program in your state. If not, write to your state's education department.

Federal government programs:

Basic educational opportunity grants. They were originally designed to help low-income families. But, in 1978, they were made available to middle-income families as well. The amount of the grant is based on financial need as determined by a government formula.

Guaranteed Student Loan Program. It is designed specifically for middle-income families. No financial need is required. The student secures the loan from a bank or savings and loan association. (Some, but not all, banks participate in the program.) Repayment is guaranteed by the government if the student defaults. The loan is interest-free while the student remains in school. Dependent undergraduate students can borrow $2,500 a year up to a maximum of $12,500. Independent undergraduates can borrow $3,000 a year up to a maximum of $15,000. The interest rate is 9%, payable six months after the student leaves school. Interest rate clause: If Treasury-bill yields drop below 9% for the previous 12 months, the interest rate for subsequent borrowers drops to 8% and remains at that level.

National direct student loans. They are made to students who demonstrate financial need as determined by the college financial-aid officer. The loans are interest-free as long as the student remains enrolled. Repayment at 4% interest begins nine months after a student leaves school. Students have been able to borrow up to $6,000 for juniors and seniors, $3,000 for freshmen and sophomores.

Part-time employment. Most colleges offer financial-aid packages, consisting of scholarship aid, loans, and part-time work. The federal College Work-Study Program funds most of the part-time student jobs on campuses. In addition, individuals and businesses often seek part-time help through the college. The financial-aid officer can tell about the scope of the college's program.

ROTC scholarships. The Army, Navy, Marine Corps, and Air Force maintain Reserve Officers Training Corps programs on several hundred campuses across the U.S. They also offer several thousand four-, three-, and two-year scholarships on a competitive basis to students in ROTC programs. In return, the students agree to serve a stipulated number of years on active duty.

Corporations and unions. These often provide scholarships for the children of employees or members of a union.

The American Legion. The Legion publishes a scholarship handbook called *Need a Lift to Educational Opportunities, Careers, Loans, Scholarships?* It lists a wide variety of scholarship programs. It also has fact sheets on financing possibilities under the Vietnam GI Bill, Junior GI Bill, and Title II of the Social Security Act. For more information: Write to the American Legion, Box 1055, Indianapolis, IN 42606.

Source: Kenneth Kohl, former head, Federal Guaranteed Student Loan Program, and co-author with Irene Kohl, *Financing College Education*, Harper & Row, New York.

Athletic Scholarships for Women

Colleges and universities are required by law to provide proportionately equal scholarships and equivalent opportunities in their athletic programs for women. Since this 1972 act of Congress, women's intercollegiate sports have been booming. Main reason:

Record growth of scholarship funds available.

Programs are divided into three levels of competition by the Association for Intercollegiate Athletics for Women (AIAW). Financial aid at each school is determined by the level of competition in each sport. Colleges in Division 1 may offer 100% of the student-athlete's expenses; Division 2, up to 50%; Division 3, a maximum of 10%.

How to apply: Students seeking scholarship aid should write the athletic directors at their preferred schools in early fall of their senior year. List: Athletic achievements, academic record, reasons for selecting the school and which sports are of interest. The school may request an interview. Best: Student should visit the campus and talk to the athletic director.

Importance of financial need: Varies among schools. Generally, it's less important at the big Division 1 institutions (Ohio State, Cornell, etc.), long famous for substantial men's athletic programs.

Caution: Students should not let sports interest overshadow the primary purposes of college, which are preparation for a career as well as a well-rounded life. Application for an athletic scholarship does not preclude applying for academic aid through the school's admissions office.

More information: The AIAW Directory. It lists the 970 member institutions, sports offered, application regulations, competitive level, financial aid available, and names of each school's athletic director. Write: AIAW, 1202 16 St. NW, Washington, DC 20036.

Establishing Residency For Tuition Benefits

Students who attend a state college outside their home state pay much higher tuition than do residents of that state. In some cases, the difference exceeds $2,000 a year. Moreover, as nonresidents they do not have access to statewide scholarships and student-aid programs.

Equalizer: In 1973, the U.S. Supreme Court ruled that while state colleges and universities can charge higher tuition of nonresidents, those students must be allowed to earn residency status while they are enrolled on a state campus.

The process is strictly regulated. Public institutions, after all, are subsidized by state tax dollars. Substantial tuition income is lost when out-of-state students become entitled to lower rates as residents.

Requirements for residency vary from state to state, but follow similar patterns. All states, for example, require continuous residence for a period of time immediately preceding applications for resident status, usually one year, though a few states demand as little as six months.

Most states require evidence that the student-applicant intends to become a permanent resident. This stipulation is enforced with varying degrees of vigor.

At the University of Wisconsin, for example, an elaborate system of hearings and appeals is set up. When an out-of-state student registers at the university, the presumption is that this has been done for educational purposes rather than for a permanent change of residence. Therefore, when the student applies for residency status, the burden of proof is on the applicant.

Most important: The questions asked to find a pattern of behavior that either sustains or denies the student's application.

Key questions:

Do you file a Wisconsin state income tax return? (The income tax supports the state's higher-education system.)

Are you dependent on your parents for financial support? (In New York, students must be financially independent of parents. In Wisconsin, it's just one of many factors considered in the application, and is not necessarily governing.)

Do you have a record of employment in the state? (Students who seek financial aid of any kind are expected to earn some money through summer and part-time work in Wisconsin.)

Do you have a Wisconsin driver's license or motor vehicle registration?

Have you registered to vote in the state, particularly for local elections?

Bottom line: Residency-status application is a serious step.

Returning to the Classroom

Thousands of self-supporting adults have gone back to school in recent years to complete an education, upgrade job skills, or develop new abilities for a career change. However, many others need help in identifying realistic career goals and in finding appropriate educational and training programs. The sources of information and counseling listed below can help.

National Center for Educational Brokering (NCEB). A clearinghouse of information on education for adults. It is experienced in helping adults to make career decisions, to identify appropriate education programs, and to embark on learning programs. The annual *Directory: Educational and Career Information Services for Adults* identifies brokering programs. A free list of NCEB publications is available on request from NCEB Office for Research and Publishing, 405 Oak St., Syracuse, NY 13203.

Educational Information Centers. They are supported by federal funds and have been set up in nearly every state to provide educational counseling for adults. For locations of the centers in your state and the services they provide, get in touch with the higher-education division of your state department of education. For more information: Write to the Community Service and Continuing Education Branch, U.S. Dept. of Education, 400 Maryland Ave., Washington, DC 20202.

Catalyst: This is a nonprofit organization that works to expand career opportunities for women. Publications of the organization reflect its wide ranging interest in many aspects of women and work in contemporary society. A network of 187 Career Resource Centers offers counseling on careers and educational programs to women across the country. An extensive library is open to the public at the national headquarters. For more information: Contact Catalyst, 14 E. 60 St., New York 10022.

American Council on Education. It publishes three books that could prove to be useful and helpful, although they are primarily for professional use. They are:

Guide to External Degree Programs in the United States.

National Guide to Educational Credit for Training Programs, published annually. It evaluates noncollegiate education programs in government and industry.

Guide to the Evaluation of Educational Experience in the Armed Services, published biannually.

To order any of these books: Write to the American Council on Education, One Dupont Circle, Washington, DC 20036. Or check your local library for these publications.

Educational Opportunities for Older Adults

There is a network of 400 colleges, universities, independent schools, and other educational institutions in the 50 states and Canada that offers low-cost, week-long residential programs for older adults during the summer months. Courses in the U.S. and Canada usually start Sunday evening and end the following Saturday morning. Taught by regular faculty members, the classes usually have 30 to 40 students.

Range: A variety of liberal arts and science subjects, including Genetic Engineering, Introduction to Yoga, the Ancient World, Geology, and so on.

Prerequisite: Age is the only one. Participants must be over 60 or be married to a participant who is over that age. There are no exams, no grades, no required homework. Lack of formal education is no barrier. In general, courses do not presuppose previous knowledge of the subject.

Accommodations: Participants live in a college dormitory, often sharing a room with another student. Single rooms are sometimes available. Most meals are eaten in the college cafeteria with other students. Bathroom facilities are usually shared in typical dorm fashion.

Campus life: Campuses vary widely from small, rural, liberal-arts colleges to large urban universities. Each offers extracurricular activities and free time for participants to explore the campus area on their own.

More information: For the summer catalog, which includes general information on the program and descriptions of all summer programs offered, write to Elderhostel (an international education program for older citizens), 100 Boylston St., Suite 200, Boston, MA 02116.

Financial Aid for Adult Students

Financial aid for education is no longer reserved for the young, the bright, and the poor. Greatly increased amounts of money are becoming available to the thousands of adults who are streaming back to the classroom to upgrade job skills, complete a degree, change careers, or, as with many women, preparing to reenter the work force. Today, one out of every five adults is enrolled in some kind of postsecondary education or training program. One-third of all college students are over the age of 25.

Who is eligible for financial aid? According to a publication of the College Board, *Paying for Your Education: A Guide for Adult Learners*, ''Your chances are good for some aid, even if your income is high . . . .'' But for most programs you do have to show financial need. Most money is available only to students enrolled in degree or certificate programs on at least a part-time basis. It is harder, though not impossible, to find aid for noncredit courses or for less than part-time enrollment.

Sources of aid: The best bet for many adults lies in the many thousands of special aid programs for adults that are designed to help special groups such as workers, women, taxpayers, the elderly, the unemployed, or the handicapped. Most of these programs are not tied to financial need. They are flexible about the kind of courses that may be taken and about less than part-time enrollment. Examples:

Workers. Many employers make generous funds available to employees for education as part of the worker's fringe-benefit package. Programs vary widely in the kind of education covered and the type of financial aid available, but many are very flexible. Only a small fraction of the available funds is used each year.

Women. Many colleges now offer special aid programs for women who want to enter or reenter the work force. A number of organizations such as the Project on the Status and Education of Women, Association of American Colleges, 1818 R St., NW, Washington DC 20009, provide information on national aid programs available to women.

Taxpayers. The federal government allows as an income tax deduction costs incurred for education needed to maintain or improve job skills in the taxpayer's current job. A full-time student with a working spouse and children under age 15 may deduct expenses for babysitting, nursery school, or a day-care program. Many states also provide some tax benefits for education expenditures.

Elderly. Several states allow adults age 60 or older to attend public colleges and universities free of charge or at greatly reduced tuition.

The federal government provides student aid. Policies for awarding aid are more restrictive than most special aid programs in degree of financial need required and kind of study programs covered. But many adults can qualify.

Most colleges and universities have financial-aid programs designed primarily for younger students, but increasingly they are being opened up to adults.

Save money by reducing the time it takes to get a degree and cutting expenses at the same time. Possibilities:

Credit by examination. Many colleges offer up to two years of credit toward a degree for successfully passing examinations such as those of the College Level Examination Program of the College Board and the College Proficiency Examination Program of the New York State Education Department.

Credit for prior learning. Formal courses in the military service or in places of employment are being credited by a growing number of colleges.

Nontraditional degree programs are sponsored by many colleges and universities for both undergraduate and graduate students. They require only limited classroom attendance. Credit can be picked up through examinations and transferring credit from other colleges. They offer flexible time schedules too.

More information: For sources and a guide to organizing a campaign to obtain aid see *Paying for Your Education: A Guide for Adult Learners*, College Board Publications Orders, Box 2815, Princeton, NJ 08541.

Index